PHYSICS, METAPHYSICS, AND GOD

A Perspective on Physics Yielding to Metaphysics

Third Edition

Jack W. Geis

authorHOUSE®

AuthorHouse™
1663 Liberty Drive
Bloomington, IN 47403
www.authorhouse.com
Phone: 1-800-839-8640

© 2010 Jack W. Geis. All rights reserved.

No part of this book may be reproduced, stored in a retrieval system, or transmitted by any means without the written permission of the author.

First published by AuthorHouse 6/22/2010

ISBN: 978-1-4520-4660-0 (sc)
ISBN: 978-1-4520-4659-4 (e)

Printed in the United States of America
Bloomington, Indiana

This book is printed on acid-free paper.

Notes to the Reader

- **FRONT COVER:** (*designed by Mark W. Geis*) the yin yang symbol, according to traditional Chinese cosmology is composed of the *yin* (represented by passivity, darkness, cold, wetness in nature), which combines with the *yang* (represented by activity, light, heat, dryness in nature) to cause or produce all that exists. The author has modified the symbol to show *physics* on one side and *metaphysics* on the other side. In our human experiences when physics and the material world are dominant in our lives, metaphysics (the things of the Spirit) begin to disappear, and God, who is Spirit, becomes largely unknown. On the other hand when we place a greater trust in the things of the Spirit, matter and physical laws become less dominant, and we begin to understand the nature of God and experience the effect of God, who is Mind, in our lives. In contrast to the Chinese symbol, where yin and yang are said to combine to produce all that exists, only the science of metaphysics reveals God and the true nature of reality as wholly spiritual.

- This book has been written especially (but not exclusively!) for those who have some background in the physical sciences, who possibly consider that the foundation for reality lies exclusively with matter and physical law, and doubt the need of a compassionate and intelligent Creator. "…for God is Love." (I John 4:8).

- My PURPOSE: [The following statement is repeated farther along under *INTRODUCTION AND HISTORICAL PERSPECTIVE.*] *My purpose, especially in Part I of this book, is two-fold: first, it is to show how the study of basic quantum mechanics principles and phenomena strongly suggests that consciousness plays a primary role in the shaping of physical reality. Secondly, this conclusion, once reached, hopefully will encourage the reader to consider investigating on his own the limitless possibilities of mankind which exist beyond the constraints of any physical models, including the quantum model.* To this end I have endeavored in Part II of the book to assist the reader in taking a "quantum leap" in thought to explore the concept of a reality – a spiritual reality – based on the universality of Mind or Spirit.[**]

- Please do not be intimidated by equations: most of them are in APPENDICES, and the reader can skip over most of them without losing continuity. The healing experiences recounted in Part II of this book are not presented to support the thesis that scientific prayer is more effectual than material means (medicine, surgery) – although one can argue that it is – but to illustrate that legitimate transformation of the body and of lives can occur through a change in the state of consciousness; and that in some instances these changes appear to violate physical law. It is left

---

[**] Names for God.

to the reader to conclude whether the source of consciousness is to be found in the matter-brain, or in Spirit, God, Mind. I present arguments throughout the book for the thesis that the first and only cause is Mind.

❖ Recently, as this book was going to Press for the Second Edition, a number of newspapers reported on the results of a study supported by the Templeton Foundation that seemed to indicate that intercessory prayer performed by several prayer groups for patients recovering from heart surgery yielded no positive results. I have included a brief discussion on this subject. First, go to page 238 for a discussion about similar past studies, and then go to the ADDENDUM on page 341, **Intercessory Prayer**.

Third Edition : This book has been revised from the Second Edition 2006 printing. Fotios and Carole Dardamanis have performed a thorough and professional editing of the book to correct punctuation, syntax, and typos. I am very appreciative of their help. Nevertheless, I assume full responsibility for any errors that may remain in the book. I have extensively revised the pages about Einstein and Christian Science as a result of new information that has been given me by William Cooper who has done extensive research in this area. Gratitude abounds for the work of the three of them! I have modified and made some corrections to Figure (15-18), Results from Wheeler's game of *Twenty Questions*. Also, I have expanded Part II, Chapter 11, *Final Thoughts*.

I have added in the ADDENDUM at the back of the book additional information on quantum experiments that are on-going and planned, and several additional and inspiring healing experiences accomplished entirely through communion with universal Mind (God) in prayer.

INDEX

There is no index located in the body of this book, but an excellent one can be found at www.Amazon.com. Click on "books"; type author's name (Jack Geis); click on book title ("Physics, Metaphysics and God"); click on "Search inside the book"; type in word to look up, such as "quantum." Amazon will list the pages where the book uses the word.

REVIEWS

(Additional reviews on back cover)

Dr. Barbara Neighbors Deal, Literary Associates, Crescent City, CA

"Jack Geis is a lifelong student of metaphysics, more particularly *Christian Science*. He is also a physicist. From years of in-depth study of spiritual principles and the new physics,

Geis has produced a remarkable document that presents the new physics to the spiritual explorer in a way that is both accessible and fascinating. *Physics, Metaphysics, and God* is a major contribution toward the harmonization of cutting edge physics and spiritual practice. He uncovers the parallels between spiritual healing and wholeness, and the principles of quantum physics. Don't be afraid of the "physics" - Geis offers illustrations, examples, charts and graphs that make the subject come alive even for those like me with little exposure to the new science. "

William C. Gough, Chairman of the Board (Foundation for Mind-Being Research)

"I recommend the book as an impressive overview of the interface between modern physical science and its implications to our spiritual evolution and healing."

Amazon.com reader from Australia

"Mr. Geis...demonstrates absolute respect for the rigors of scientific discipline, coming to valid conclusions in the only way possible...by arguing logically according to pertinent facts. There is no end of people ready to make an assertion, but hardly any are willing or even able to design a crucial experiment. The latter ability is characteristic of critical thinkers such as Mr. Geis."

ACKNOWLEDGEMENTS

I wish to thank the following without whom the writing and publishing of this book would have been impossible: Gust Bambakidis, Ph.D. for review and critique of most of the sections of Part I ; Laurance Doyle, Ph.D. for a complete read of the book, and for graciously responding to my technical questions ; Amit Goswami, Ph.D. for his review of my discussion in Part II, Chapter 1, of his article, "The Idealistic Interpretation of Quantum Mechanics;" Leonard Mandell, Ph.D. for his critique of my discussion in *Part I,* Chapter 15, of his work on non-interfering, delayed-choice experiments; Philip Yam, Staff Writer, Scientific American, for his critique of my discussion in Part I, Chapter 18, of his article, "Bringing Schrodinger's Cat Back to Life;" Edward R. Close, Ph.D. for his valuable comments and ideas regarding certain sections of Part II, Chapter 1; Benard d' Espagnat, Ph.D. for his critical review of my discussion in Part I, Chapter 15, and APPENDIX I-15B of his article, "The Quantum Theory and Reality," (he was especially helpful in clarifying my concept of Einstein's view of quantum mechanics); Dr. Larry Dossey for his encouragement, and Letter of Recommendation; Mary Reed, CSB; Gordon Clarke, CSB; and Jack Hubbell, CSB for their spiritual support of *Part II* ; and especially to Jack Hubbell for his encouragement and efforts to find a suitable publishing house, and for sharing with me several of his experiences with spiritual healing; Steven L. Fair, CS for his review of most of Part II, and his invaluable suggestions for improving the readability of this part of the book; Ellen Blue for reviewing most of the book and making invaluable suggestions for formatting; Barbara Neighbors Deal, Ph.D., Literary Agent for her helpful suggestions and for her effort to interest the publishing community in my book; Dik Bouwmeester, Ph.D. for his review and comments on my discussion in APPENDIX I-15B of his article, "Experimental Quantum Teleportation;" Thomas Gross; Sally Ekkens, CS; and Bob McFall for relating to me their personal spiritual healing experiences; my sons Mark and David, for encouraging me early on to put in writing my thoughts on physics and metaphysics, and for their invaluable assistance in enabling me to traverse the many pitfalls of using a computer; and especially for my wife, Marian who spiritually supported me every step of the way in developing the book, and who had no complaints for all the hours I spent at the computer. In some instances reviewers have not seen recent changes, modifications and additions that I have made to the book. They also might not entirely agree with my final interpretations of physical phenomena or metaphysical statements. Therefore, I, alone assume full responsibility for the degree of correctness of my statements on physics and metaphysics.

RELEVANT QUOTATIONS [∞] [♥]

"The laws of physics themselves may come about as a result of interactions between the universe and its participant-observer. We do not simply observe the laws of nature, there is also a sense in which we create them."
John Archibald Wheeler[Π]

"Although quantum theory is an abstruse and formidable field, its philosophical and theological implications reduce to one shattering effect: the overthrow of matter…For some 200 years… nearly all leading scientists shared these materialistic assumptions [that the foundation of nature is based on solid and impenetrable particles] based on sensory and deterministic logic…The contemporary intellectual, denying God, is in a trap, and he projects his entrapment onto the world in a kind of secular suicide. But the world is not entrapped; man is not finite; the human mind is not bound in material brain."
George Gilder[⊕]

"Strangely enough, we ask for material theories in support of spiritual and eternal truths, when the two are so antagonistic that the material thought must become spiritualized before the spiritual fact is attained… Mind's control over the universe, including man, is no longer an open question, but is demonstrable Science."
Mary Baker Eddy[∇]

"If any other form of treatment were as effective [as prayer], practitioners [of medicine] would be screaming to get hold of it, and would be sued for malpractice it they didn't use it."
Larry Dossey, M.D.[Σ]

"Any model of reality that excludes consciousness is at the very least incomplete. If mankind can begin to grasp the idea that consciousness and not matter is prime, then it will have taken a giant step toward the eventual recognition that ultimate reality is Mind, Spirit, and Mind's spiritual ideas: man and the universe."
Jack W. Geis

[∞] Although Wheeler, Gilder and Dossey (quoted above) believe in varying degrees that consciousness plays a major role in shaping reality, I do not mean to imply that they go as far as I do in asserting the primacy of Mind, God, and the spiritual nature of man and the universe.

[♥] Additional relevant quotations are found later in the book.

[Π] John Archibald Wheeler, PhD, is an American theoretical physicist, and a pioneer in the field of quantum gravity; past professor at *Princeton University*, and then at the *University of Texas* at Austin; first coined the term, "black hole."

[⊕] George Gilder is Founding Editor of *Forbes ASAP;* Fellow International Engineering Consortium; Recipient of White House Award for Entrepreneurial Excellence.

[∇] Mary Baker Eddy is the Discoverer and Founder of Christian Science, and an influential American author, teacher and religious leader noted for her groundbreaking ideas about spirituality and health; the author of the best-selling book, *Science and Health with Key to the Scriptures*.

[Σ] Larry Dossey, M.D., former *Chief of Staff, Medical City,* Dallas Hospital, is a world-renowned author of nine books and numerous articles of the subject of mind in health and the role of spirituality in healthcare.

TABLE OF CONTENTS

Physics, Metaphysics and God

Part I: Physics – The Quantum Universe

- **Introduction and Historical Perspective**.. xiii
  - Purpose for writing the book
  - Book structure
  - Part I Summary
- **Chapter 1: Quantum physics – What is it?**.. 1
- **Chapter 2: The Newtonian universe**.. 5
- **Chapter 3: Quantum world beginnings – Wave/particle duality of light** 6
- **Chapter 4: Quantum world beginnings – Black body radiation**............ 8
- **Chapter 5: Quantum world beginnings – The photoelectric effect** 11
- **Chapter 6: Quantum world beginnings – The Compton effect** 13
- **Chapter 7: Quantum world beginnings – Quantized electron energy states** 14
- **Chapter 8: Particle/wave duality for matter**... 18
- **Chapter 9: The principle of complementarity**... 19
- **Chapter 10: Probability**... 21
  - Child's swing and coasting automobile
- **Chapter 11: The wave equation**.. 26
- **Chapter 12: Particles in potential wells**.. 27
- **Chapter 13: The possibility of finding quantum objects in bound systems**.. 29
- **Chapter 14: The Heisenberg uncertainty principle**................................ 30
- **Chapter 15: Physical and thought experiments in quantum physics** .. 32
  - Double and single-slit experiments
    - Single-slit experiment with cannon balls
    - Double-slit experiment with cannon balls
    - Double-slit experiment with single photon or electron pulses
  - The delayed-choice experiment
  - Non-interfering, delayed-choice, double-slit experiment
  - Wheeler's game of twenty questions
  - The EPR paradox
- **Chapter 16: Virtual particles**.. 54
  - Virtual particles as messenger particles
  - Size or scale- From virtual particles to galaxies
- **Chapter 17: Possible interpretations of quantum phenomena**............. 58
  - Quantum wholeness
  - Non-local, non-causal, objective universe (super-luminal)

- ➤ Conventional Copenhagen interpretation
- ➤ Non-objective, observer-created reality
- ➤ The many-world's interpretation (parallel universes)
- ❖ **Chapter 18: Quantum superposition experiments and experimental results**.. 77
  - ➤ The Squid
  - ➤ Experimental results for non-macroscopic systems
  - ➤ Decoherence histories
  - ➤ How large can Schrodinger's cat become?
  - ➤ Experimental results for macroscopic systems
  - ➤ Macroscopic effects in astronomy – Quantization at super-macroscopic levels?

- ❖ **APPENDIX I-8: Particle-wave duality for matter**............... 87
- ❖ **APPENDIX I-10: Probability**... 90
- ❖ **APPENDIX I-11: The wave equation**................................ 94
- ❖ **APPENDIX I-12: Particles in potential wells**.................... 97
- ❖ **APPENDIX I-13: The possibility of finding quantum objects in bound systems**... 105
- ❖ **APPENDIX I-14: The Heisenberg uncertainty principle**........ 111
- ❖ **APPENDIX I-15a: Physical and thought experiments in quantum physics**.. 118
- ❖ **APPENDIX I-15b: Physical and thought experiments in quantum physics** 140
- ❖ **APPENDIX I-17: The measurement problem**..................... 158

Part II : Metaphysics – The Universe of Spirit............... 160

- ❖ **Introduction:** 162
  - ➤ Physics versus metaphysics: matter versus Spirit: unreality versus reality
- ❖ **Chapter 1: Wave function collapse and the observer**............ 165
  - ➤ Conscious observers versus inanimate observers
- ❖ **Chapter 2: Is consciousness found in the brain and in computers?** 177
  - ➤ The brain
  - ➤ Computers (artificial intelligence)
    - Jumping out
    - "Kangaroo" computers
    - The computer Game of Life
    - Arguments against the computer Game of Life claims for life, intelligence and consciousness based in matter
    - Godel's theorem
  - ➤ Summary
- ❖ **Chapter 3: Experiments in consciousness**............................ 206

- ➢ Leaders in the field of mental phenomena
- ❖ Chapter 4: Paradigm shifts………………………………….. 212
- ❖ Chapter 5: The scientific method…………………………… 214
  - ➢ Metaphysics over physics (potassium cyanide accident)
  - ➢ Evolution of human thought
- ❖ Chapter 6: A mindless, purposeless universe, or an eternal, purposeful universe of Spirit?………………………………….. 218
  - ➢ Bertram Russell
  - ➢ Richard Dawkins
  - ➢ Albert Einstein
- ❖ Chapter 7: Evidence for the existence of God……………… 223
  - ➢ The universe and the observer
  - ➢ Good and evil
- ❖ Chapter 8: The mental realm………………………………… 236
  - ➢ Meaningful coincidences
  - ➢ Spiritual prayer and healing
  - ➢ Resistance to spiritual healing and to spiritual man
  - ➢ Ways that work, and ways that do not work
- ❖ Chapter 9: The nature of reality…………………………….. 277
  - ➢ The sleeping dream
  - ➢ The waking dream
  - ➢ The eye, macroscopic objects and human perception
  - ➢ The waking dream (hypnotic illusions), and face cancer
  - ➢ The difference between matter-healing, mortal mind-healing and divine Mind-healing
  - ➢ Possible explanations for healings
- ❖ Chapter 10: A new paradigm……………………………….. 295
- ❖ Chapter 11: Final thoughts…………………………………… 297
  - ➢ The physical universe of matter particles versus the spiritual universe of ideas
  - ➢ Additional explanations for healing experiences
  - ➢ Quantum theory and reality
  - ➢ Consciousness is primary
  - ➢ Summary
    - ▪ Selected key points in the book
    - ▪ Additional Revolutionary Ideas 314
- ❖ APPENDIX A: Word Definitions……………………………… 319
- ❖ APPENDIX B: Possible means for the creation of what is called the universe………………… 328
- ❖ APPENDIX C: The paradigm of physics: why does what is called the physical universe appear and act the way it does?………………… 332
  - ➢ Complementarity or duplicity
  - ➢ Randomness or chance
  - ➢ Inertia or resistance
  - ➢ The solution

*Introduction to the ADDENDUM ADDENDUM	342
➢ Part I: The Quantum Universe	343
➢ Part Ii: The Universe of Spirit	351,
➢ FINAL, FINAL THOUGHTS and BOOK CONCLUSIONS	362, 365
*Bibliography	367
• About the Author	398

LIST OF FIGURES

Note: All figures have been computer-drawn by the author. No figures or illustrations have been taken directly from any manuscript reference. The reader is encouraged to seek out particular references listed in the Bibliography for more complete descriptions of experiments and experimental apparatus and set-ups.

FIGURE	DESCRIPTION	PAGE
PART I		
1-1	Momentum	2
1-2	Speed, Velocity and Position	3
1-3	Predicting the Future of Elastic Balls	4
3-1	Interference Aspect of Light Waves	7
4-1	Black Body Power Radiation Distribution	9
5-1	Photoelectric Effect of Light Particles (photons)	12
6-1	Dual Nature of Light	13
7-1	Childhood Puzzlements	14
7-2	Classical and Quantum Views of Hydrogen Atom	16
7-3	Linear and Circular Standing Waves	17
8-1	Bohr Model of Hydrogen Atom	88
9-1	Position and Momentum for Free and Localized Particles	20
10-1	Probabilities for Coin and Dice Tosses	90
10-2	Probability of Heads Being Tossed in a Game of Thirty Tosses	91
10-3	Independent Measurement of Momentum and Position Uncertainties	92
10-4	Probability of Locating Child on a Swing	22
10-5	Probability of Locating Car on a Hill	24
11-1	Simple Harmonic Oscillator	95
12-1	Possible Energy Levels for Electron Confined in Infinite Potential Well	97
12-2	Wave Function for Different Quantum Numbers (N) for Electron Confined in a Potential Well	100
12-3	Probability Per Unit Length for Electron Confined in Potential Well	27, 102
12-4	Alpha Particle Wave Function	103
13-1	Radial Probability Density Function for Electron about Hydrogen Atom Nucleus	105
13-2	Collapse of the Wave Function Through Observation Reduces Probability Spread and Localizes the Particle Within the Constraints of the	108

		Uncertainty Principle	
13-3		Simple Pendulum	109
13-4		Position Probability Amplitude and Wave Function for Quantum Mass Pendulum	110
14-1		Heisenberg Uncertainty Principle – Simple Explanation	30, 112
14-2		Particle Diffraction and the Uncertainty Principle	113
14-3		Effect of Decreasing Slit Width (A-D)	116
14-4		Uncertainty Principle Relation	117
15-1		Young's Double-Slit Experiment	33, 119
15-2		Intensity Pattern Contribution Due to Slit Diffraction	121
15-3		Intensity Pattern Contribution Due to Beam Interference	122
15-4		Resultant Intensity Distribution Obtained by Combining Figure (15-2) and Figure (15-3)	123
15-5a		Intensity Distribution as a Function of Increasing Slit Width (D)	124
15-5b		Intensity Distribution as a Function of Increasing Slit Width (D)	125
15-6a		Intensity Distribution as a Function of Decreasing Slit Separation (d)	126
15-6b		Intensity Distribution as a Function of Decreasing Slit Separation (d)	127
15-6c		Intensity Distribution as a Function of Decreasing Slit Separation (d)	128
15-6d		Intensity Distribution as a Function of Decreasing Slit Separation (d)	129
15-7		Cannon Ball Distribution Through Single Slit	34, 130
15-8		Cannon Ball Distribution Through Two Slits	35, 131
15-9		Variance in Intensity Distribution as a Result of a Single Particle Passing Through One or Two Slits	135
15-10		Impossibility of Determining Which Slit a Single Particle Passed Through	136
15-11		The Effect on Intensity Distribution When a Detector is Placed Behind a Slit	137
15-12		Summary of Intensity Distributions for Macroscopic and Sub-atomic Particles	37, 139
15-13		Experimental Set-up for the Delayed-choice Experiment	39
15-14		A Cosmic Delayed-choice Experimental Set-up	41
15-15		Experimental Set-up for the Non-interfering Delayed-choice Experiment	43
15-16		Blocking the Path from Down-converter #1 to	45

	Down-converter #2 in the Non-interfering Delayed-choice Experiment	
15-17	Rules for Wheeler's Game of Twenty Questions	47
15-18	Results from Wheeler's Game of Twenty Questions	48
15-19	Reality Depending Upon Observation	49
15-20	EPR Interpretation of Quantum Events	51, 142
15-21	The Measurement of Proton Spin in the EPR Experiment	144
15-22	Degree of Spin Correlation with Angle Between Detector Axes in the EPR Experiment	146
15-23	Experimental Set-up for Measuring Proton Spin Correlations in the EPR Experiment	150
15-24	Experimental Results Indicate Bell's Inequality is Violated	52, 151
15-25	Experiments in Quantum Teleportation	154
16-1	Transfer of Photon (Virtual Particle) Between Electrons	55
17-1	Predictions of Local Realistic Theories and Quantum Theories	58
17-2	Quantum Wholeness	60
17-3	Hidden Order – Passage of Right Circular Cone Through Two-dimensional Plane	63
17-4	Hidden Order – Passage of Irregularly Shaped Three-dimensional Object Through Two-dimensional Plane	64
17-5	Schrodinger's Cat Thought Experiment	68
17-6	Increased Entropy States	71
17-7	The Many-Worlds Interpretation of the Quantum Universe	75
18-1	Simplified Schematic of Superconducting Quantum Interference Device (SQUID)	77
PART II		
2-1	"Jumping" or Stepping Out	179
2-2	Self-referential Systems	181
2-3	Simple Circuits for Computers	182
2-4	Simple Circuits for Computers	183
2-5	Simple "Computer and Logic "Circuit"	184
3-1	The Effect of Conscious Intent to Influence a Random Distribution of a Positive/Negative Bit Output String	207
4-1	Consciousness and Paradigm Shifts	213
9-1	A Distortion of Reality: The Relation Between Mind, Matter and the Senses	281
11-1	Interpretation of Reality drawn from Experimental Results and Individual Life Experiences	302

PHYSICS, METAPHYSICS AND GOD

INTRODUCTION AND HISTORICAL PERSPECTIVE

"We are in the midst of a revolution; physics are yielding slowly to metaphysics; mortal mind rebels at its own boundaries; weary of matter, it would catch the meaning of Spirit." [1]
Mary Baker Eddy,
Author of *Science and Health with Key to the Scriptures*

The idea for this book began as far back as 1968, when I read an article in *Fortune Magazine,* entitled, "The Shimmery New Image of Matter." [2] This article described a physics that was far different from the conventional view of matter, which states that matter is solid, basically impenetrable, and enduring. The "new physics" has revealed a physical universe that is far less substantial, and that to a great degree, owes its existence to observation.

The Roman philosophical poet and writer, Lucretius, in the first century B.C., who espoused the philosophy of the Epicureans, believed that the only reality was the reality the senses perceived - that the senses were infallible - and things were just the way they appeared. He said,

"The sun must be as large, as hot, as it
Appears to us, no more, no less....
So, since our sense feels the flooding heat
Of sunlight's comforting appearances,
Our apprehensions of that form and size
Must be correct: there's nothing you can add,
Nothing subtract. The same way with the moon-
Whether its light is borrowed or derived
From its own substance, makes no difference-
The moon can be no larger than it seems
To our watching eyes." [3]

Modern man still believes that the evidence he sees with his eyes, assisted by complex optical and sensitive recording devices, is all there is to reality, and that the mind or consciousness plays little, if any, role in shaping or defining the universe.

Physicists generally do not concern themselves with questions concerning the validity of physical phenomena or the "reality" of matter. They are more interested in the practical application of physical theories to the solution of problems and in the development of new technologies based on quantum physics, such as the design of semiconductor circuits for computer chips. To this end, quantum physics has been an unqualified success.

The reader should begin to appreciate and comprehend the role of the observer in the universe - and the implications for an overarching Mind[*] governing all. In early times, man believed he lived on a flat Earth that was located at the center of all that existed. Hell was below, and the heavens and God were above him. The sun, followed by the stars and the known planets miraculously moved across the heavens and disappeared over the western horizon only to reappear over the eastern horizon the following morning. Later in history, Copernicus and others showed that the Earth as well as the planets revolves around the sun. In more modern times Edwin Hubble (1924) discovered that the sun and its companions - planets, minor planets, comets, and assorted debris comprising the *Solar System* - are located near the outer edge of a pinwheel consisting of a massive swarm of stars, (more than 200,000,000,000) [⊗] gas clouds, and dust which we call the *Milky Way*. And this galaxy of stars is but one of many in the universe. In fact, in the known universe there may be as many as a *trillion* galaxies!

As a result of these discoveries, it was believed that mankind lived a somewhat meaningless existence on a small planet orbiting an insignificant yellow dwarf star (our sun). Mankind was reduced, in the minds of some, from central prominence to a mere speck in an unfathomably large cosmos. Indeed, it is thought by some astronomers that our universe is but a tiny bubble in a vast sea of universes!

Also, since the time that man could think and ponder the concept of *infinity*, he was puzzled by a conundrum: How was it possible for the universe to be infinite - or worse still, - if the universe were not infinite, how could there be a boundary or "edge," because if there were an edge, what would lie beyond it? Along came the *Theory of Relativity* developed by Albert Einstein in the early 1900s. Relativists could now explain how a three-dimensional (3D) universe [∇] could be finite in size but be unbounded or have no "edge." The simplest way of understanding this idea is to consider a two-dimensional (2D) surface such as the surface of a sphere. A hypothetical 2D person (having length and width, but no height) would be able to move radially outward from any starting point on the surface, and if she walked long enough, would return to the starting point, having never reached an "edge" of her "universe." Unknown to her, the 2D universe in which she resided was embedded in a higher dimension - the third dimension of length, width, and height. To an observer in the 3D universe, the 2D universe would be seen to curve back or "close" on itself, and would appear as the surface of a sphere.

Astronomers and physicists have conceptualized that our 3D universe may be finite in size, but boundless, provided, they say, there is enough matter to gravitationally cause our universe to be "closed". If this were the case [Ψ] we could conceivably travel radially outward from the Earth for billions of light-years in distance - and eventually come back to our starting point - the Earth! This universe would be a finite universe, but with no boundary. One might conceive of our 3D universe (plus time) as embedded in a higher dimension. In fact, some theorists believe that the fundamental laws of physics

---

[*] God.
[⊗] This number is continually changing as new information is gathered on the size of our galaxy.
[∇] Actually, three spatial dimensions plus one time dimension.
[Ψ] Recent astronomical data indicate the expansion of the universe is actually accelerating.

governing all of nature must be written in mathematical equations that involve many dimensions *

The development of quantum theory, which began in the late 1800s, has pointed us, though subtly, towards finding answers to the questions concerning man's position in the universe and his bafflement about finiteness and infinity. The conclusions of at least some physicists, as previously alluded to, are that mind or consciousness plays a primary if not absolute role in the shaping and/or interpretation of the physical universe.

Many of the ideas presented in this book about the universality of mind may seem bold, but the reader should remember that it has not been many years since the ideas of Einstein as set down in his theories on *Special* and *General Relativity* have seeped into popular consciousness. It has been fewer years than this that the sometimes-bizarre theories of quantum mechanics have become faintly understood by the man on the street. And fewer years still since the world has begun to recognize the role of consciousness or the *observer* in the shaping of the physical universe, and in the interpretation of reality. The next step, I believe, will be the growing awareness that **divine Mind, Spirit** (not the human mind) is the fundamental reality of all.

PURPOSE FOR WRITING THIS BOOK

Many books and articles have been written on the subject of quantum mechanics. A listing of some of the ones used in aiding the writing of this book have been included in the *Bibliography*.

My purpose, especially in Part I of this book, is two-fold: the first purpose is to show how the study of basic quantum mechanics principles and phenomena strongly suggests that *consciousness* plays a primary role in the shaping ▽of physical reality. This conclusion, once reached, hopefully will encourage the inquiring individual to consider investigating on his own the limitless possibilities of mankind which exist *beyond the constraints of any physical models*, including the quantum model. To this end, I have endeavored in Part II of the book to assist the reader in taking a "quantum leap" in thought to explore the concept of a reality – a spiritual reality - based on the universality of Mind or Spirit.**

MIND AS A NAME FOR GOD

---

* However relativists say that a flat four-dimensional space has nothing whatsoever to do with the real physical world of space-time. Although it is convenient to do so, we should not think of our universe of three spatial dimensions (plus time) as actually embedded in a higher fourth dimensional universe (as the two-dimensional surface of a sphere is embedded in the higher third dimension). An ant living on the two dimensional surface of a sphere, lives in a finite universe with no perceivable boundary. That boundary exists in the third dimension; that is, the ant cannot leave the surface of the sphere. But Einstein - and later, Wheeler - have told us that the only natural boundary condition imposed upon our physical universe is that there is no boundary! [4]

▽ "shaping of physical reality": Throughout the book I discuss how collective mortal consciousness creates physical reality. But, strictly speaking, consciousness does not shape or "create" a physical reality. It merely interprets in a very finite, distorted way the universe of Spirit, God, which is the only reality.

** Mind and Spirit, when capitalized are names for God.

Because some Christians believe that Jesus literally was God incarnate, they, unlike some Eastern religions, cannot comprehend that God could be defined as infinite Mind. It was only in 325 AD that the First *Council of Nicaea* voted to include in their doctrinal platform the concept of God as existing in three persons in one (the Trinity): the Father, the Son and the Holy Ghost or Spirit; even though insisting at the same time that God is One in "substance." In discussing this subject, the *Encyclopedia Americana* says that although the doctrine is "beyond the grasp of human reason, it is...not contrary to reason, and may be apprehended (though it may not be comprehended) by the human mind." [5] This somewhat arbitrary decision based on scriptural interpretations has missed the mark, and has contributed to gross misunderstanding of the nature of God and man. The *Bible* clearly declares God as Love, Life, Truth, Father, Spirit, and indirectly refers to Him as unchanging Principle, Mind and Wisdom (all different ways of describing *one* God). The evidence of the physical senses not withstanding, what other kind of standard for God are we willing to accept?

Is your God too small? Describing the First Cause or Principle of all existence or Reality, as Mind, should be self-evident. What can be greater than omnipresent, omnipotent and eternal Mind? How could chaos, indeterminacy, or mindless matter, be the creator of intelligence and awareness? How could the Creator of All be anything less than Mind? All subsequent action throughout all eternity must therefore be the effect of Mind or Spirit, and it is our task to discern the true nature and character of this action or activity. It must be a spiritual nature, because like produces like.

If we can begin to appreciate the above ideas about the concept of God as Mind, then we might begin to understand how infinite Mind cannot be confined to a finite, fleshly body. The *Bible*, itself, states that "God dwelleth not in temples made with hands." [6] We will also better understand the statement in *Genesis* that man is made in the image of God, Spirit, [v] and not in an image of an anthropomorphic God who sometimes dwells in a material form.

Stephen Hawking, quantum physicist and author of *Black Holes and Baby Universes,* [7] has said that he believes that all theories of physics are just mathematical models, and that it is not realistic to assert that they necessarily correspond to reality.

But despite the evidence of the five physical senses, I believe good is *supreme*; good is intelligence, righteous, harmony, order, Law. Good is omnipotent, eternal and ever- present God. Therefore, the evidence supporting the opposite claim that impersonal, indifferent physical laws are supreme, and often result in cruel and chaotic experiences must - in the final analysis - possess no ultimate validity or reality. Philosophers for centuries have been trying to reconcile physical reality with spiritual reality and to rationalize the existence of an omnipotent, omniscient, loving and benevolent creator who creates physical laws and permits what could be described as evil events to occur. It can't be done. Either reality is wholly spiritual and mental or it is entirely material. It can't be both.

CHRIST JESUS

---

[v] Illustrated so clearly by the life and works of Christ Jesus, and to degree in the lives of prophets and apostles, as well.

Being of the Christian faith, I believe in the virgin birth of Jesus, that he was unique among men, the Savior and Way-shower, and that he performed the ""miracles" as related in the Bible; but I do not believe that Jesus was God.[8] He never said that he was. [V] There is a clear distinction between Jesus and the Christ. The Christ is the *Truth* - the holy message from God that the human Jesus lived, taught and exemplified by his healing works; the *Comforter* promised in the *Bible*. This divine nature is the truth about man (every man and woman) and his relationship to God; a truth which unites each one to God as his beloved child, and reveals to us our spiritual sonship with Him. This spiritual sonship describes the true God-like nature of man.

A *paradigm shift* has been evolving for some years. No longer can the physical universe be thought of as purely mechanical in operation, or as entirely predictable and functioning independent of observation. It is becoming increasingly important for each of us to recognize this shift.

The popular books written on the subject of quantum theory are mostly for the nonscientist, and generally omit all but the simplest mathematical equations and formulae. College textbooks, on the other hand, delve into many of the basic equations that describe the sub-atomic world, and give little, if any, discussion and interpretation of the philosophical implications. This book has attempted to go a step further in presenting mathematical and illustrated descriptions of the basic elements of quantum theory, *plus* a review of several current philosophical interpretations. I also present my own thoughts on this fascinating subject, and in addition, include lengthy discussions on a metaphysical or spiritual interpretation of reality (Part II), that I believe exists beyond the physical interpretation.

CHOICE

It seems that in this life we have three choices in regard to how we conceive of the nature of God and reality:

(1) - We can accept the general world belief in a God who knows both good and evil, and who in fact is the creator of evil as well as good. To all appearances He "sits back" and dispassionately watches His laws of physics result in destructive hurricanes, droughts, tornadoes and horrible diseases, all in the name of "Mother Nature." This God, because of His mysterious and capricious ways, will sometimes perform "miracles," but invariably leaves mankind to suffer as the result of its own "free will" or for the "greater good." This concept of God engenders no real love of God, and many would rather accept no God at all than to believe in this kind of creator.

[V] The book of John in the *Bible* [9] says that "the Word was God," and "the Word was made flesh, and dwelt among us." The Word is the Christ, or Truth - the divine idea of God so wonderfully manifested or exemplified in the human Jesus. The *Bible* also records (in the book of John) Jesus as saying that those who believed on him did not actually believe on him, but on the God who sent him. And then he said that those who saw him saw the God who sent him (John 14). Understanding that God is infinite Mind and Love, and not an anthropomorphic being (Infinite Mind cannot be confined in a body), enables us to understand that Jesus must have meant that the faithful saw God manifested or reflected by his (Jesus') spiritual nature. Manifestations such as love, compassion, purity, forgiveness, authority, meekness, power, wisdom and intelligence.

(2) - We can accept the theory of many scientists that creation evolved out of mindless chaos in accordance with quantum mechanical probability laws. That is, creation did not require a God or a divine Purpose. Robert Park of *the American Physical Society* has said, "Its 'not only unscientific, it is antiscientific' to affirm the existence of any force other than laws of physics involved in the creation of the universe." [10] In this view of reality mindless matter evolved mind, and some degree of temporal order was established from initial chaos. This creation is indifferent to the thoughts and feelings of sentient beings. Discord, pain, disease, suffering, death are simply by-products of creation. We are left with no hope of salvation, and morality is no more than a viewpoint held by the majority. But quantum mechanical probability laws must have existed "before" the material creation; and any kind of law requires a mind or minds to conceive it.

(3) - We can begin to consider the somewhat *radical* idea that the first and only Cause is Mind. Ultimate reality - which is spiritual - is not created out of chaos, nor created by finite mind or minds. Infinite Mind is Principle (Law), and this Principle is infinite, omnipotent Love.* Man *must* be created in the image and likeness of God, the only Cause, because God could not create anything unlike Himself. Therefore, what appears to be in contradiction (evil) to this universe of harmony is nothing more then the false evidence (a lie) of the physical senses; this false evidence being the subjective state (or belief) of collective thought$^\oplus$ that mind and identity exist in matter, separate from God. Since reality at the very basic level is mental (Mind), an improved understanding of the nature of God and man restores a lost sense of harmony.

THE AUTHOR'S POSITION

I do practice a specific religion, Christian Science, but I make no attempt to sell the religion or to promote its tenets. Mary Baker Eddy, the *Founder* of the Christian Science religion, early on hoped that all Christian churches of her day would eagerly embrace her ideas about the nature of God and man, but since this did not happen she felt she had to form her own church in order to promote her ideas. What I have done in the book, is to discuss ideas about the nature of reality in which I deeply believe. To do otherwise would be dishonest and a disservice to both science and religion. To this end, I have included numerous quotations from the *Old* and *New Testaments* of the *Bible*, and from the writings of Eddy that are the source of many of my thoughts on various subjects in the manuscript. I believe that no one is excluded from embracing the metaphysical ideas discussed in the manuscript. We all begin with various levels or approximations of absolute truth, and hopefully, by whatever path, we will merge into universal agreement as to the nature of the Creator and of His laws governing the universe. Thus said, I maintain that all physical law, while immensely useful today in advancing technology and the quality of life, must eventually give way to the laws of Spirit, Mind. Then science will be wholly spiritual and spiritual healing will be in accord with merciful spiritual law, and will be practiced by all races and faiths.

---

* Principle, God, establishes and perpetuates laws that result in order, harmony. These laws cause no harm or fear, but they protect and bless man and the universe. Therefore this protecting, nurturing Principle of the universe must be Love. In Part II of this book we will learn more about the nature of God as Mind, Love, and the ultimate myth of matter and matter images that are presented by the senses.

$\oplus$ collective or consensus thought or belief, or world opinions "planted" in consciousness.

Hopefully, all of the arguments that I present for the primacy of Mind, as the Principle and reality of all, are supported by the writings of the *Discoverer* and *Founder* of Christian Science (Mary Baker Eddy), including those found in the textbook of the religion, *Science and Health with Key to the Scriptures.* Quotations from this book, as well as from the *Bible*, are presented mainly throughout Part II of the book, as well as accounts of individual experiences of Christian Scientists who have relied exclusively on the God who is *Mind* and *Love* for spiritual healings.

If the reader is interested in a full explanation of the spiritual science that underlies spiritual healing, and which describes the nature of God and man, he or she should refer to *Science and Health*, which is based solely on the teachings of the *Bible*.

Throughout the book I have taken the liberty of including quotations from notable physicists and scientists in support of my thesis regarding the primacy of consciousness and the mental nature of reality. I do not intentionally mean to misinterpret the meaning behind their statements. However, in most instances, I know, they have not gone as far as I have in asserting the absolute spiritual nature of reality. The reason for this, I believe, is that they are unwilling to deny the absoluteness of physical sense testimony. They either declare that all is matter and physical law, or that in some impossible way matter and spirit work together in defining reality. I accept the reality model as described by Eddy in her book, *Science and Health with Key to the Scripture*, where she affirms that matter is the subjective state of mortal mind [*] and says, "Either Spirit or matter is your model. If you try to have two models, then you practically have none. Like a pendulum in a clock, you will be thrown back and forth, striking the ribs of matter and swinging between the real and unreal." (p. 360)

BOOK STRUCTURE

Prior to the era of so-called modern physics, mind and the material universe were thought to be independent of one another. With the arrival of *Relativity*, and especially *Quantum Mechanics*, some physicists and philosophers were beginning to see a connection between minds (consciousness) and the physical universe. I believe the next step in the evolution of our understanding of the nature of reality is the recognition and understanding that Mind is the *Observer,* and Mind's creation or *ideas* - man and the spiritual universe – is the *Observed.*

The book is divided into two parts.

Part I: Physics -The Quantum Universe describes the basic differences between the quantum interpretation of the subatomic world and the Newtonian or classical concept. It discusses how quantized energy states must be considered in order to explain certain phenomena. The concept of probability, and the role it plays in quantum theory is discussed; as well as the *Heisenberg Uncertainty Principle* - one of the bedrock principles upon which quantum theory is built. Part I looks at certain phenomena of quantum physics that indicate the relationship between the *observer* and the *observed*,

---

[*] mind, or mortal mind(s) (lower case): the universal belief or delusion that consciousness, intelligence, awareness and will-power originate, evolve in, and depend on matter; that infinite Mind (upper case), God, can be subdivided into many minds.

and describes experiments such as the *Delayed- Choice Double-Slit* experiment, the *Non-interfering Delayed- Choice Double-Slit* experiment, the *SQUID* experiments, and the *EPR* thought experiment, including actual laboratory tests that indicate that the universe is non-local in nature. Several interpretations and implications of quantum theory made by respected physicists are discussed, such as the *Copenhagen Interpretation, Quantum Wholeness, Consciousness-Created Reality,* and the *Many-Worlds* views.

Part II: Metaphysics - The Universe of Spirit. The reader is asked to set aside preconceived ideas about reality, and consider in what direction quantum physics may be pointing us, or rather, what interpretation of reality may lie *beyond* quantum physics. Consciousness is seen as playing a primary role in determining what we perceive as reality. Ideas promoted by well-known and respected physicists and other scientists who have had thoughts similar to those held by the author are presented and compared with the author's views.

Physical theories or models for reality, no matter how sophisticated, cannot explain mind or consciousness, cannot explain spirituality or *spiritual healing*, and cannot explain or adequately interpret the First Cause, Mind [*] or God. The current paradigm of reality considers matter as primary and nonphysical consciousness as secondary. This prevents most physicists and philosophers from considering any phenomena of life, which appear to violate our present understanding or concept of law entwined in space-time as invalid, ludicrous, or illusory. Reports of "miraculous " happenings as related in the *Bible*, and in the present age, they dismiss as "paranormal" and *anecdotal*. But no thinking person should dismiss these events without first examining the evidence.

I have by no means attempted to treat such a subject in detail. But if this book instills in the reader a desire to explore further the place of consciousness in the universe – and to consider that beyond and above matter, and what is thought to be human or mortal consciousness, there exists a universal Consciousness or Mind – a spiritual reality - then I will have succeeded in accomplishing my goal.

In Part II I attempt to show that through what is called spiritual prayer or communion with Mind, *spiritual ideas of Mind or God are seen to be the only real and tangible ideas.* In the mental universe, phenomena that are seen as cancer cells and AIDS virus, are certainly not spiritual ideas of Mind. Nor is the idea behind the creation of a torture chamber a spiritual idea. Rather, these notions must be gross inversions of reality.

Throughout Part II I quote from notables such as Eugene Wigner, John Wheeler, Depak Chopra, Larry Dossey, Fred Wolf, Amit Goswami, and Edward R. Close. In varying degrees each believes that consciousness plays a significant role in interpreting, or even shaping reality. Each ascribes to consciousness a mental nature, but not necessarily a *wholly* spiritual nature independent of matter, space-time. The wholly spiritual nature of man is such that it is not necessary for him to manipulate or control

---

[*] The use of the term "mind" (lower case m) refers to our present and limited sense of intelligence as dependent on material structure such as the brain, and as existing entirely separate and independent from Mind (upper case M). That is, it is a belief that intelligence is in matter. Mind refers to the First Cause, Principle, or God, and is understood to be the source of all the intelligence manifested by man and the universe. This Mind is Spirit and is above or beyond the realm of the physical universe. It is Reality.

matter in order to sustain life and awareness. Here is where the above-mentioned individuals and I begin to "part company."

I have structured Part I of this book in such a way that ideas and concepts of physics (especially quantum physics) are constantly being explained and reviewed. This is done because many of these ideas and concepts are radical, and possibly new to the reader.

I have also structured Part II of this book in such a way that ideas and concepts concerning God and man are frequently repeated and explained (almost "ad nauseam") in different ways. This has been done in order to reinforce on the reader's thought the vast differences between orthodox views of God and man, and the views expressed in this book.

As mentioned previously, although this book is primarily written for the reader who has some knowledge of mathematics, and is familiar with equations and formulae displayed in graphic form, I have *minimized* (but not entirely eliminated!)[V] use of equations and complex figures and graphs in the chapters of *Part I*. Instead, I have added APPENDICES for those chapters where I feel the more technical reader would want a more expanded and detailed discussion of the subject. Here, I make more liberal use of equations, figures and graphs.

The APPENDICES for the chapters of Part I are found at the end of Part I.

In each chapter of Part I, I explain – sometimes very briefly - the basic concepts of quantum physics that are discussed in that section, This should enable the reader to grasp these concepts and ideas without the necessity of wading through mathematical relationships and complex figures that will be found in the APPENDICES. Hopefully, the non-technical reader will at least begin to appreciate the illusory nature of physical reality, and the role that the observer (consciousness) plays in the interpretation of reality. In some instances, I have also included a brief *Summary*, which is located at the beginning of that chapter. In the APPENDICES I have included many illustrations, far beyond the norm, in an attempt to show graphically the implications derived from quantum phenomena in regard to consciousness and the interpretation of reality.

There are two APPENDICES for Part II of the Book: A, and B. They are located at the end of Part II.

PART I SUMMARY

Delving deep into material structure, to the quantum level, physicists have discovered there is no direct cause and effect relationship to be seen in quantum events. Individual particle position and momentum must be defined by probabilistic laws. The precise path, for example, of an electron from a source to a target is indeterminate. Single electrons emitted from a source and passing through a small aperture at some pulse rate (say, one pulse per second) will appear at a downstream target plane in an apparent random pattern. We have no definite way of determining the path of the electron to the target - we can

---

[V] Any figure, equation or graph shown in a chapter will be repeated in the APPENDIX for that chapter (if that chapter has an APPENDIX).

only determine its probability of traversing a given path. That is, single quantum events have no direct cause and effect relationship. We know the electron was caused to be emitted by the source, but physics cannot calculate where an individual electron will strike the target.

P.C.W. Davies, the author of *God and the New Physics* [11], points out that "...the very concept of an atom with a definite location and motion is meaningless...What right have we to say that an atom is a *thing* if it isn't located somewhere, or else has no meaningful motion?"

The strict or conventional interpretation [*] of quantum theory (*Copenhagen* or *Niels Bohr Interpretation*) - the view supported by most physicists, even if they do not give much thought to it - is that *there is no deep reality*. The physical world is real, they say, but there is no way we can perceive a higher reality than what the probabilistic world of quantum theory presents to us. A modification of the *Copenhagen Interpretation* states that although matter is real, its dynamic attributes such as position and momentum do not exist until an observation has been made. This has been called an *Observer-Created* reality. An inanimate recording device is considered sufficient to make this measurement or observation. But still, it requires a conscious mind to *choose* how the measurement will be made. By our choosing of the experimental set-up for a *Delayed-Choice Double-Slit* experiment, we can decide whether a photon will exhibit its wave-like or momentum characteristics and pass through both slits, interfere, and contribute to an interference pattern on a downstream plate; or whether the photon passes through only one slit, exhibiting its particle and position attributes.

But according to this interpretation we cannot select where the two-path photon will strike the downstream plate or what path the single photon will take to the slit apparatus. That is, we have no choice on the *value* of the particle attribute, only on the type of attribute (position or momentum). Fred Wolf and John Archibald Wheeler have been associated with these interpretations; and Wheeler has stated that consciousness is required to give the quantum event "meaning" and that this meaning must be communicated to another observer so that it can be "put to use."

What has been called *Consciousness-Created* reality asserts that the world is non-objective, and depends on the mind of the observer. Such notables as Henry Stapp, Eugene Wigner, Jonn Von Neumann, and Amit Goswami have held this view. Physical attributes of particles (positions and momenta) do not exist until seen by a conscious and aware observer.

The conclusions, therefore, resulting from examination of the quantum-mechanical *Double-Slit* experiment, the *Delayed-Choice Double-Slit* experiment and the *Non-Interference Delayed-Choice Double-Slit* experiment, [**] suggest that at the very least the dynamic properties of a particle, such as position (particle-like characteristic), and momentum (wave-like characteristic) exist as potentials. An electron can exist as a wave spread out over vast distances when not observed, [∇] but when looked for, will appear as a

---

[*] See Part I, Chapter 17, for discussion of quantum theory interpretations
[**] See Part I, Chapter 15, for discussion of these experiments.
[∇] Some argue that if a particle such as an electron can seem to be everywhere at once until an observation has been made, then it should be equally plausible that consciousness itself is not confined to space-time; that is, it is non-local.

particle. Most proponents of *Consciousness- Created* reality believe the wave function is physically real, and is collapsed by consciousness. However, not only does *Consciousness-Created* reality decide what *attribute* will be exhibited, *but the theory declares that consciousness can decide what **value** will be seen* (that is, what the position is of the particle as it contacts the downstream plate).

It is also impossible to see how a random quantum activity (i.e., possessing no defined attributes), registered at an inanimate detector, can exchange ignorance for knowledge or information (the wave function has been irreversibly collapsed) that remains hidden until a conscious being eventually arrives on the scene and observes the data.

In the *Non-interference Delayed-Choice Double-Slit* experiment, all that appeared to be necessary for light to exhibit particle-like attributes (without any interference with the light by trying to physically observe the particle with a detector) was the acquiring of potential knowledge about the experimental set-up. If this is true, then the collapsed wave function could not be identified with a quantum process occurring inside an inanimate detector.

In the *EPR* discussions, the results of experiments give stronger indication that the universe is non-local and possibly nonobjective; that is, it does not exist independent of consciousness. *The SQUID* experiments (Part I, Chapter 18) lend justification to the argument that at the very least under certain conditions the dynamic properties of matter (even macroscopic objects $^{\oplus}$) are indeterminate; and this says something about the insubstantiality of matter, itself. The experiments at least suggest that it may be collective consciousness that "collapses" wave functions and affects correlation between the two random proton spin component values in the *EPR* experiments discussed in Part I, Chapter 15.

The experimental results from quantum experiments in general suggest a relationship between matter and mind. The observer who sets up an advanced *EPR*-type experiment can theoretically affect the experimental results instantaneously over great distances. *EPR* and *SQUID*-type experiments should further be verified and refined. At present, the individual observer has little control over the *values* of the observables. But if non-locality is true, then the universe may act like a single whole, with individual manifestations of consciousness unconstrained by matter-brain and space-time, and in tune with universal Mind.

In Part II of the book we examine even stronger arguments for the primacy of consciousness in the interpretation and/or framing of reality. Along with other subjects I discuss experiments that examine the effect of direct conscious intent to control matter objects (*Pear* experiments), and experiences (sometimes called "meaningful coincidences") that involve the effect of human thought on the health of the body (*Spindrift* experiments). I discuss at some length the sometimes-controversial issue of *spiritual healing* * and its relationship with Mind. I discuss explanations for events that

---

$^{\oplus}$ **macroscopic**: objects that are large enough to be observed by the naked eye.

* spiritual : not spiritualism, or having anything to do with seances, ghosts, actions of matter, or psychic phenomena associated with minds; but having to do with reality and being outside of matter; spiritual healing: as opposed to healing by material means or by the human mind.

are sometimes explained as "miracles," but that can be understood to occur - not as the result of chance or of matter manipulation by *mind* - but rather as the result of the human mind or thought yielding or coming into agreement with the divine *Mind* or God.

Part I

Physics – The Quantum Universe

CHAPTER 1

QUANTUM PHYSICS: WHAT IS IT?

Here we begin in *Part I* of this book a rather brief discussion of some of the physical phenomena that are necessary to know if the reader is to understand and appreciate the nature of the universe. Many of the phenomena discussed include the fact that light can be viewed either as a particle (photon) *or* a wave, but never as wave and particle at the same time.

The physics of Isaac Newton (1642-1727) allowed one to examine the universe from a deterministic point of view. It was believed that if one knew, in principle, the momentum and position of every atom in the universe he could predict the position and momentum of every atom for any time in the future. Figure (1-1) defines momentum as the product of the mass and the velocity of an object.

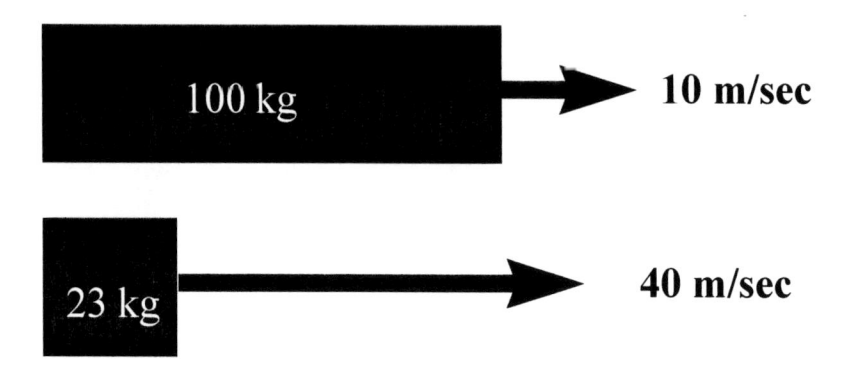

MOMENTUM = MASS X VELOCITY

100X10 = 1000 KG-M/SEC

25X40 - 1000 KG-M/SEC

Figure (I-1): Momentum
(Note to reader: The small mass should be 25 kg, not 23 kg.)

Two moving objects can have the same momentum if the products of their different masses and velocities are equal. Figure (1-2) shows the difference between the speed of a body and its velocity. Speed is a *scalar*, and relates to the motion of a body in any arbitrary direction. Velocity is a vector, and defines the motion of a body in some definite direction. The position of an object is its spatial location in reference to some coordinate system (in this example, two orthogonal axes). If the position and momentum of an object could be known to any degree of accuracy then, in essence, future events (as well as past events!) would be known or predicted. The future would be an open book. Since every thing physical is made of atoms, including the matter that comprises the human brain, some people claimed that free will would no longer be considered possible. If someone robbed a bank, he had no choice in the matter, because the arrangement of atoms in the brain at any given time was preset in the very distant past or at the beginning of the universe. In other words, the interactions of all the particles in the universe, from time "zero" to the present occurred precisely according to physical law – one particle striking another and exchanging momentum – continuing down through the ages. One could then say, " I had no choice in what I did or in what I thought." Nor would the author of this book have any choice in writing the very words you are reading this instant!

Now, let us consider Figure (1-3). A billiard table (with no pockets), constructed of perfectly elastic material, and with two billiard balls with masses, $M_1 and M_2$, with initial

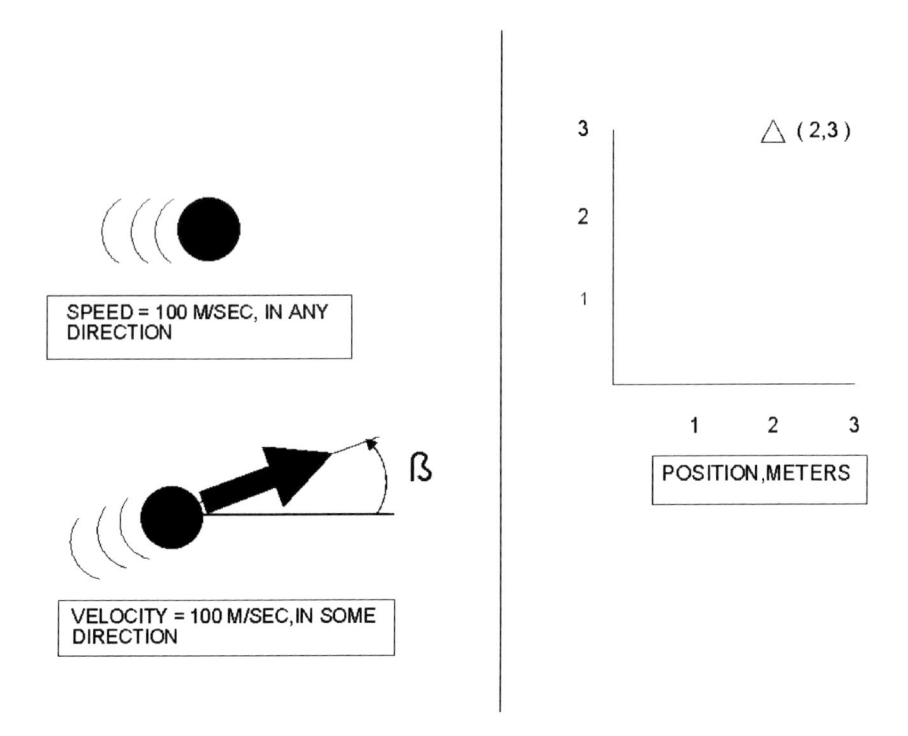

Figure (1-2): Speed, Velocity and Position

velocities, V_1, V_2.* The table has dimensions of A (length) and B (height). The balls are initially located at coordinates $X_1, Y_1, and X_2, Y_2$, respectively.

In theory, it would be possible to predict the future of each ball, even though the balls may strike the walls innumerable times and also strike one another. For the idealized case of elastic walls and balls - zero friction of the balls with the tabletop and with each other - the balls will not slow down. Increase the number of balls without limit, allow the balls to be unconstrained to move in three-dimensional space, and this assemblage might represent matter in the universe; and we may wish to echo the words of Pierre Laplace (1749-1827), who said, "Nothing would be uncertain, and the future, as well as the past, would be present to our eyes."[1] We shall discover that this is not true in the world of subatomic particles.

---

* Because of the assumption of perfect elasticity, an object that strikes a wall will lose no energy, and therefore, will lose no speed due to its interaction with the wall.

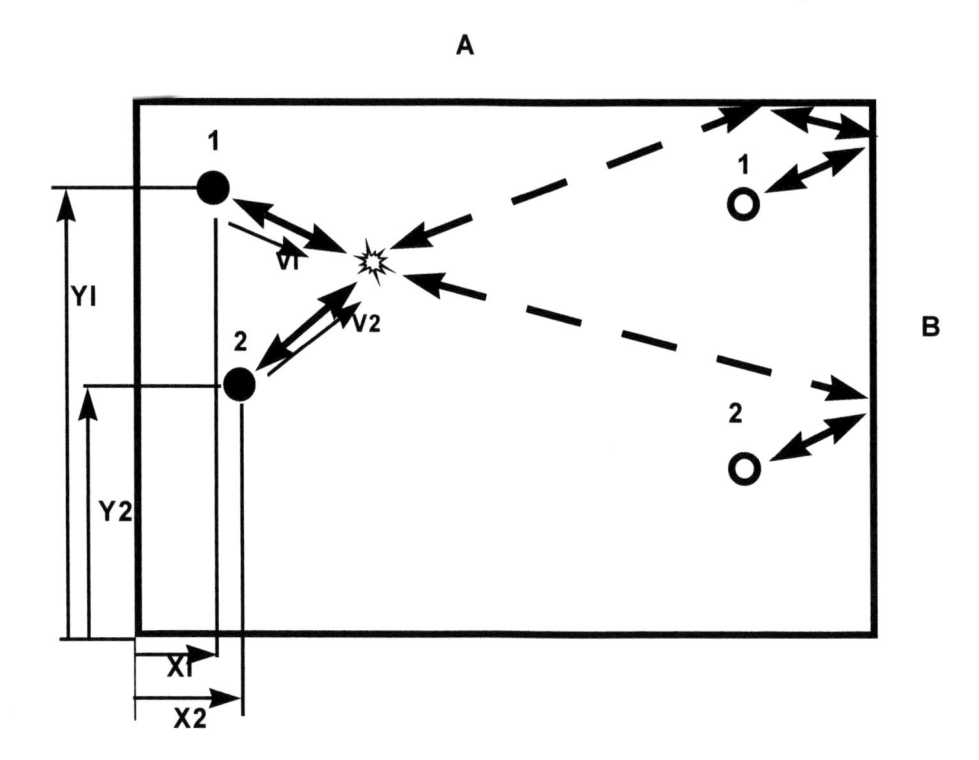

Figure (1-3): Predicting the Future of Elastic Billiard Balls

CHAPTER 2

THE NEWTONIAN UNIVERSE

The state of physics in the late 19th century was such that many physicists believed they knew all there was to know about the fundamental laws of physics. As far back as 1687 Isaac Newton completed his great work, *Principia*, which included the now famous *Three Laws of Motion*, which were believed to govern every particle in the universe. His third law says, that for every action there is an equal and opposite reaction. Newton's laws have been used to compute the paths of rockets as well as planets - as well as the movement of billiard balls. (Later, Albert Einstein challenged the laws of Newtonian mechanics with his *Special Theory of Relativity*.) Newtonian laws say that for every cause (a force) there is an effect (movement or change of momentum). This law caused some people to consider the universe to be similar to a great machine or mechanical clock. This mechanistic interpretation meant that in theory it should be possible to predict future events by observing in extremely minute detail the events of the present. Like a clock, the movements of objects should be as predictable as the movement of gears and hands, and these movements should be continuous in space and time. It was as if *every* particle were set in motion at the beginning of the universe, and that nothing could alter these predetermined interactions and events - nothing could change - nothing could be left to chance. This description of the universe is called "deterministic."

This deterministic theory clearly makes no separation between matter and mind, and has been summed up by Hugh Elliott (1881-1930) when he said, "It seems to the ordinary observer that nothing can be more remotely and widely separated than some so-called 'act of consciousness' and a material object. An act of consciousness or mental process is a thing of which we are immediately and indubitably aware: so much I admit. But that it differs in any sort of way from a material process, that is to say, from the ordinary transformations of matter and energy, is a belief which I very strenuously deny."[1]

CHAPTER 3

QUANTUM WORLD BEGINNINGS - WAVE/PARTICLE DUALITY OF LIGHT

The *Double-Slit* experiment shows that light can sometimes act like waves similar to water waves. If light passes through two openings as shown in Figure (3-1), the waves can interfere with each other and cause crests and troughs in light intensity. If one of the openings is closed, then there is no possibility for two waves to interfere with each other, as only one wave passes through the single opening. If light always acted like a particle, then particles passing through two slits could not interfere with each other and cause alternate light and dark lines.

According to most scientists in the Eighteenth century, all was known about physics, with the possible exception of the laws governing heat and light. It was still generally believed that heat and light consisted of tiny particles or corpuscles. But Thomas Young (1801) performed his now famous *Double-Slit* experiment, and discovered that light could also exhibit the property of waves - one ray of light could be seen to interfere with another ray, even as waves of water on the surface of a pond interact with each other. [1]

The *Double- Slit* experiment consists of a source of light of one wavelength (monochromatic light) that is incident on a surface containing two closely spaced slits, whose widths are on the order of the wavelength of the light. As in the case of water waves, light waves can cause constructive interference, or destructive interference when both slits are open (Figure (3-1), right-hand side). Constructive interference occurs when the crest of one wave exiting slit A lines up with the crest of a another wave exiting slit B. The waves are then said to be *in phase*, and a peak in light intensity is recorded on the photographic screen situated behind the slits at the exact distance where the waves meet. For destructive interference the waves are 180 degrees out of phase; that is, the crest of one wave from slit A lines up with a trough of another wave from slit B, and the light intensity or amplitude is reduced to zero. (The same phenomena would occur if the trough of a wave from slit A lined up with a crest of a wave from slit B.) The result is a series of bright and dark regions running across the plate. At each bright region the light waves are in phase, and at each dark region the waves are out of phase.

The sketch on the left-hand side of the figure represents the case where one of the slits has been closed. The light intensity pattern recorded at the screen is now one simply of light being bent or diffracted through one slit only, as no optical interference can occur. This experiment by Young illustrated that under certain experimental conditions, light could exhibit a wave nature. Particles cannot interfere with each other and cause bright and dark patterns at the screen.

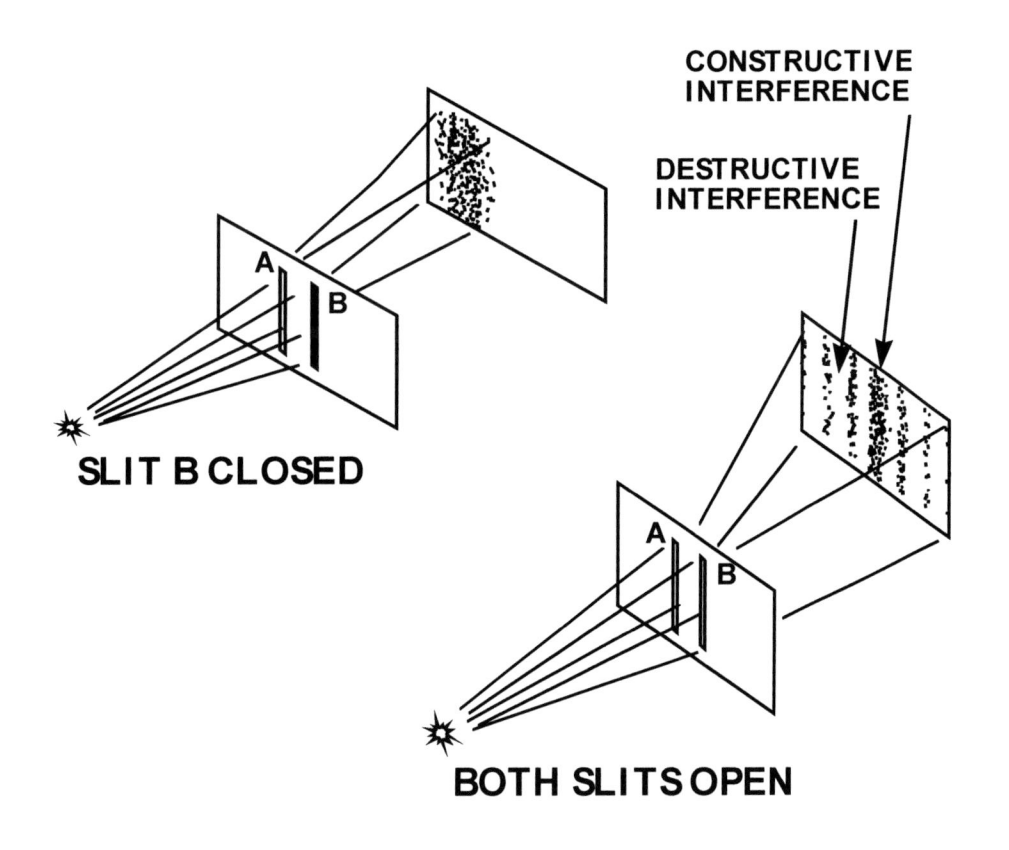

Figure (3-1)

Interference Aspect of Light Waves

CHAPTER 4

QUANTUM WORLD BEGINNINGS - BLACK BODY RADIATION

A "black body" is defined as an idealized object that will absorb radiant energy at all wavelengths and reflect none. It will then re-radiate energy at all wavelengths. It was known in the late nineteenth century that when objects such as pieces of metal are heated to increasingly higher temperatures, their colors change from metallic gray to dull red, to bright red, and then to reddish-white. James Clerk Maxwell (1831-1879), had postulated previously that when bodies were heated they would radiate energy in the form of electromagnetic waves, or light waves, with frequencies corresponding to the frequency of vibration of the individual atoms in the body.[*] Radiation from hotter bodies was thought to consist of electromagnetic waves of higher frequencies. If this theory is carried to its logical conclusion, a very hot object should change color from reddish-white, to blue, and eventually to ultraviolet, as these colors have increasingly shorter wavelengths or higher frequencies.

The question arose as to why this experiment performed under controlled *black-body conditions* should show radiated energy in the manner shown in Figure (4-1). According to theory (Lord Raleigh, 1842-1919), blackbody oscillators (atoms or molecules) should radiate with equal probability at all wavelengths, and the amount of power (energy per unit time) radiated over a small interval of frequencies should be proportional to the frequency raised to the fourth power.[1] Therefore the power radiated should rise dramatically at shorter wavelengths or higher frequencies, as shown by the dotted line in Figure (4-1). This prediction of excessive heat radiation from a black body was called the "violet catastrophe" phenomena. What was actually observed were the solid lines of Figure (4-1). Each of the solid lines represents black body radiation at some temperature, as shown. It can be seen that the amount of power radiated (in the form of light waves of different wavelengths) peaks at a certain wavelength. For a body at a *higher* black body temperature (compare the 1646 degree K and the 1259 degree K curves), the peak in the radiation occurs at a shorter wavelength (note: the wavelength of the radiated light is measured in Angstroms, where one Angstrom $= 10^{-10}$ meters).

In 1899 the German physicist, Max Planck challenged the theory that all frequencies were radiated with equal probability or likelihood. Planck actually suggested that the probability of radiation *decreased* with an *increase* in frequency. He then reasoned in the following fashion: although there are more high frequencies in the electromagnetic spectrum than low frequencies in which to radiate, at some increasingly higher value of frequency the product of the lower probability of radiation at higher frequency, times the amount of radiation at a given frequency interval would peak and

---

[*] The relation between frequency and wavelength is: frequency (cycles/sec) = speed of light (meters/sec) / wavelength (meters).

then begin to decrease. Thus, the curves represented by the solid lines of Figure (4-1) would result.

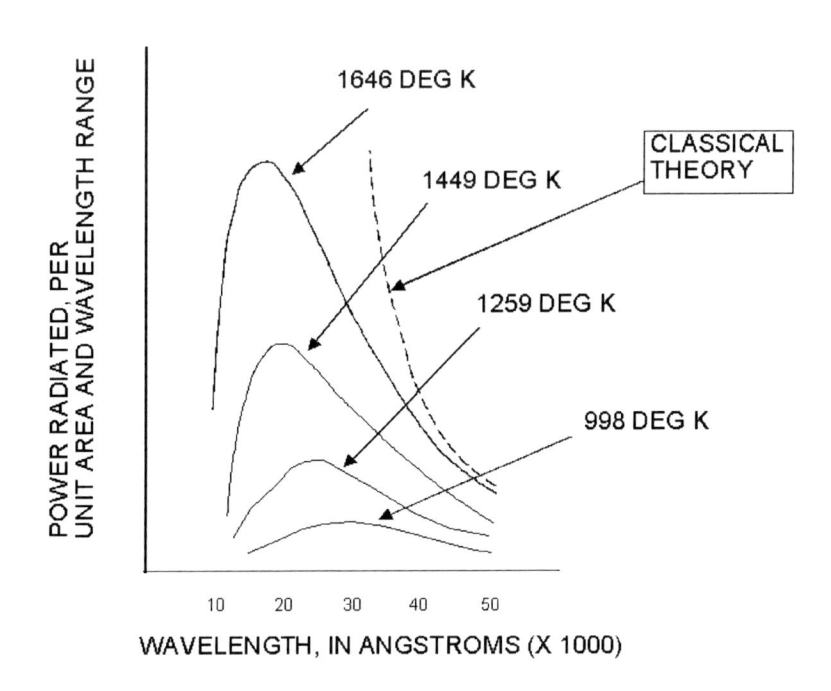

BLACK BODY POWER RADIATION DISTRIBUTION

Figure (4 –1)

The only challenge remaining was to explain what physical phenomena could scientifically explain how the radiation peaked at a certain wavelength or frequency as a function of the temperature.

Planck made what has since been called an intuitive leap in thinking, and proposed that energy was not radiated continuously, but instead was radiated in units of energy called *quanta*. Quanta means *how much* in Latin. A quantum (singular) of anything is considered a whole unit, an undivided whole. Planck proposed that an atom would not radiate energy until a quantum of energy had been accumulated ($E = h\nu$, where h, the constant of proportionality, is *Planck's constant*, and ν represents the frequency in cycles/sec.).

The classical theory of radiation said energy radiated continuously with temperature. Planck suggested that the energy released per atom was proportional to ν. Although an atom could accumulate energy sufficient to radiate a quantum of energy at higher frequencies, the probability was greatest that once a smaller quantum of energy in the form of lower frequency light was accumulated the atom would then radiate. There was less likelihood that the atom would radiate a larger quantum of energy at higher frequencies.

Thus, it was discovered that radiated energy was *quantized*. All electromagnetic radiation from infrared to ultraviolet (and beyond) is a form of light, and the individual quantum of radiation is called a *photon*. Each photon has an energy corresponding to $E = h\nu$. Therefore, the energy in any given monochromatic lightwave can only be in a whole number of quanta. The reason we do not see energy emitted from a heated object as pulses of quanta is that the value of Planck's constant is so small - 6.625×10^{-27} erg-seconds - that the radiation appears to be continuous.* Light was seen to have a particle or corpuscular aspect, as well as a wave-like aspect. Light could still be considered as a wave under certain experimental conditions, and as a particle under a different set of experimental conditions; but in no way could light exhibit both particle and wave-like characteristics simultaneously.

---

* erg: a unit of energy or work; 1 erg equals the work done by a force of 1 dyne acting through a distance of 1 centimeter; where 1 dyne is the force required to cause an acceleration of a 1 gram mass of 1 centimeter/sec per sec.

CHAPTER 5

QUANTUM WORLD BEGINNINGS - THE PHOTOELECTRIC EFFECT

The photoelectric effect is the effect of light irradiation on the free electrons of a conductor such as a metal. A light-irradiated metal will emit electrons. It was discovered that the intensity or brightness of the incident light beam had no effect on the ability of the light to knock electrons out of the metal, nor did it have any effect on the resulting kinetic energy of the electrons (See Figure (5-1), top part). [*] The greater the intensity (closer spacing of lines), the more electrons that would be emitted, provided the incident light had a certain *threshold* of energy. That is, the color or frequency (energy) of the light was the determining factor. (Remember, $E = h\nu$) The threshold energy is the energy of the photon of light required to dislodge an electron; therefore, increasing the light frequency or decreasing the wavelength (or increasing the energy of each photon of light, represented by longer lines), would result in a sudden emission of electrons. As the frequency was increased further, this would not increase the number of electrons, but the emitted electrons would have an increasingly higher kinetic energy. The lower part of the figure shows that incident light photons with higher energy or shorter wavelength, (longer lines) will cause the ejected electrons to leave with higher velocity (higher kinetic energy, represented by longer lines). Albert Einstein explained this effect in 1905, and expanded the results of Planck, concluding that not only was light radiated in quanta of energy (photons), but that it was also absorbed as quanta.

However, strictly speaking, it was later shown by W. E. Lamb and M. O. Scully (See "The photoelectric effect without photons", in *Polarisation, Matiere et Rayonnment*, Presses University de France, 1969[1]) that the conclusions reached by Einstein from his photoelectric experiments were flawed. As a result of experiments they performed, they concluded that the photoelectric effect does not provide proof of the existence of light particles or photons. However, later experiments conducted by Grangier, Roger and Aspect, proved that light can exist as a particle or photon. (See P. Granglier, G. Roger and A. Aspect, "Experimental for a photon anti-correlation effect on a beam splitter," Europhys. Lett, vol. 1, pp, 173-179, 1986 [2]) The discussion of the experimental arrangements to invalidate the conclusion that the photoelectric effect proved the existence of photons, as well as the experimental set-up employed by A. Aspect and his colleagues to verify the existence of light particles, is beyond the scope of this book. The

---

[*] Kinetic energy: energy of motion= 1/2 x particle mass x square of particle velocity

reader is referred to *The Quantum Challenge*, by George Greenstein and Arthur G. Zajonc (Jones and Bartlett Publishers, Sudbury, Massachusetts, 1997 [3]) Suffice it to say, although Einstein's work was somewhat flawed, nevertheless this great scientist was correct in asserting the wave-particle duality of light.

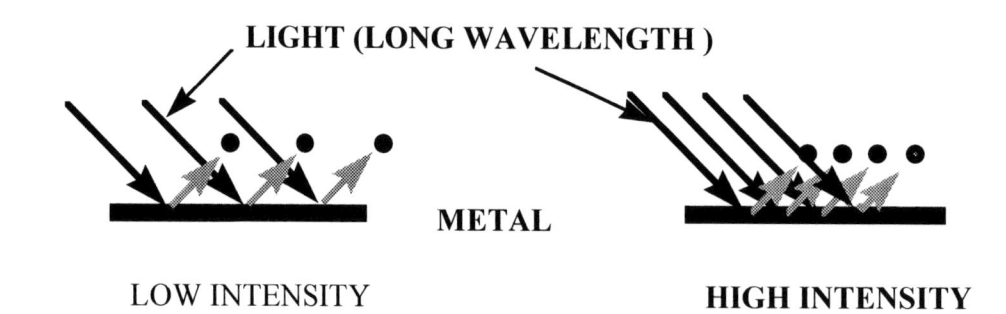

LIGHT (LONG WAVELENGTH)

METAL

LOW INTENSITY   HIGH INTENSITY

LIGHT (SHORT WAVELENGTH)

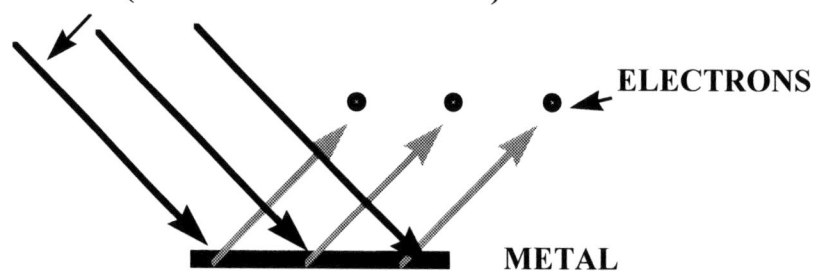

ELECTRONS

METAL

INCREASING NUMBER OF PHOTONS DOES NOT CHANGE THE ENERGY OF EMITTED ELECTRONS. DECREASING THE WAVELENGTH (INCREASING THE ENERGY) INCREASES THE ENERGY OF EMITTED ELECTRONS.

Figure (5–1)

Photoelectric Effect of Light Particles (Photons)

CHAPTER 6

QUANTUM WORLD BEGINNINGS - THE COMPTON EFFECT

In 1922 Arthur C. Compton conducted experiments with X-rays (an energetic form of light). He bombarded crystalline material with X-rays and discovered that when electrons were ejected the incident rays were deflected by the encounter. The decrease in frequency of the deflected X-rays multiplied by *Planck's* constant was equal to the gain in kinetic energy of the ejected electrons. The velocity and direction of the electrons was just as if one billiard ball (an X-ray photon) had struck a second ball (the electron). The wave theory of light could not explain this kind of interaction.

In summary, light was seen to exhibit both wavelike and particle-like characteristics, but never simultaneously or in the same experiment (See Figure 6-1).

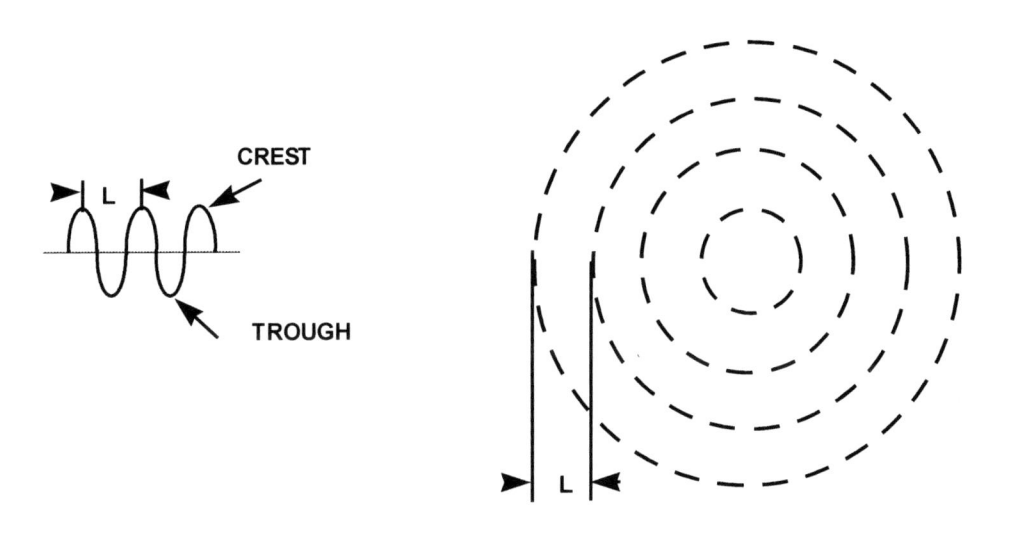

(A) LIGHT CAN ACT LIKE A WAVE ...

(B) OR LIGHT CAN ACT LIKE A PARTICLE

Figure (6–1)

Dual Nature of Light

CHAPTER 7

QUANTUM WORLD BEGINNINGS -
QUANTIZED ELECTRON ENERGY STATES

When I was a child about five or six years of age, two different, but similar phenomena puzzled me: The first puzzle was, "How far could one move a light switch or push a brick before either the light would come on or the brick would fall off a table upon which it rested?" (as illustrated in Figure (7-1A)

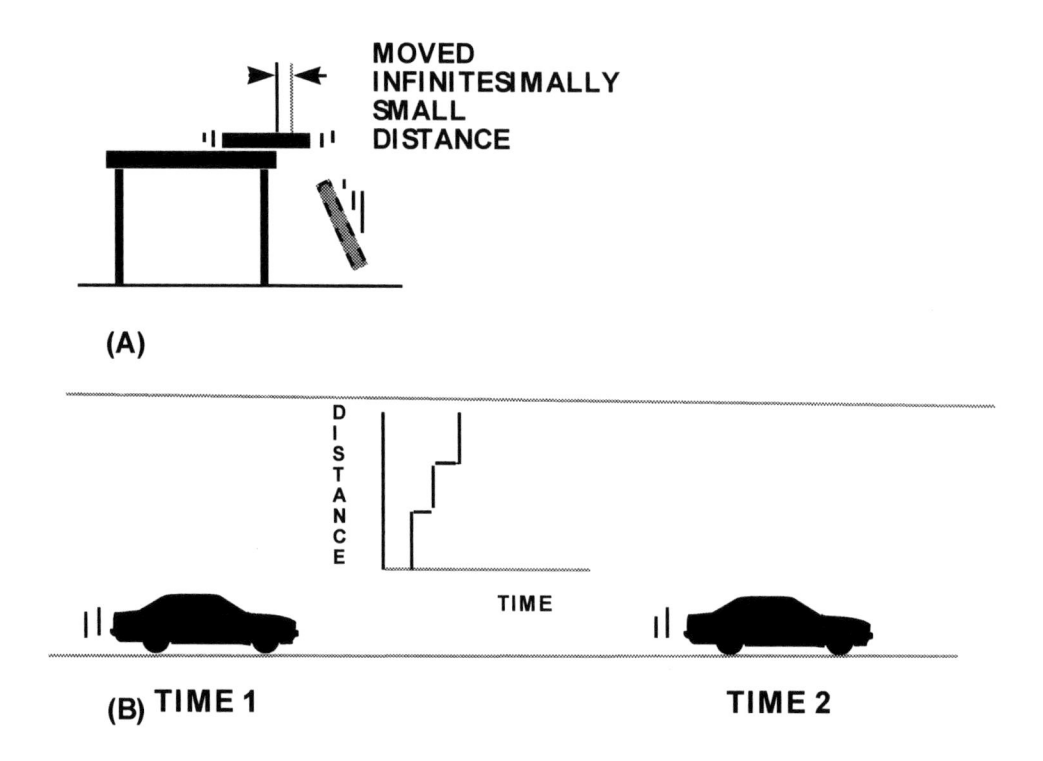

Figure (7–1)

Childhood Puzzlements

I supposed that the movement of either object could -in theory - be made in increasingly smaller increments, and that conceivably one would always have left over a finite distance in which to move the switch before the light came on, or the brick before it teetered on the edge of the table and fell off. Although I did not realize it at the time, I was assuming ideal conditions of infinitely sharp table edges and zero friction.

The second puzzlement was the movement of a car at constant speed down our neighborhood street (Figure (7-1B). I thought that if I looked and thought "fast" [V] enough, the car would be seen as having no motion at all. In some small child's way of thinking, I thought that the car did not move continuously through space as a function of time, but appeared at successive locations down the street (like an infinite sequence of "still" or "now" pictures), as if it were traversing or *jumping* across increments of space instantaneously. I have since discovered that I am not the only person to have thought along these lines, as the quantum physicist, David Bohm, mentions a somewhat similar experience as a child. [1] The Greek thinker, Zeno also discoursed on the difficulty of describing motion as a series of discontinuous or "frozen" views.

I mention these two experiences simply because they show a relationship of thought or a "stream of consciousness" to the perception of reality, which is one of the main themes of this book. Much later in life, I learned that quantum mechanics describes "movement" of electrons in an atom as they absorb energy, as *quantum "jumps,"* (discrete, quantized steps) - the electron jumping instantaneously from a smaller atomic orbit to a larger one.

I have also had, at infrequent times, another interesting experience - an experience unrelated to quantized energy states, but nevertheless interesting because it relates to *mind and perception.* Sometimes when I would glance at my wristwatch, it would seem as if time were standing still, because the second-hand of the watch appeared to be "frozen" in place for what seemed like several seconds. In my experience I - the observer - was stationary with respect to my watch, but time was subjective. We are all familiar with how time 'flies" when we are engaged in an activity which holds our interest, and of how time "drags" when we are doing something uninteresting or are waiting for an unpleasant event to end. But in this case, I had visual confirmation (in my conscious mind) that time was "moving" at a slower rate. If anyone else were measuring time at that moment, they would undoubtedly have registered the passage of time in a normal way, but to my reference frame (my consciousness), I experienced something different. The *Bible* has a statement in *II Peter* that says, ". . .one day is with the Lord as a thousand years, and a thousand years as one day." [2] I believe that our perception of things and events - where we are, and when we are - is in some way a product of *mind.* I mention this experience because I believe that it also has relevance to the general theme of this book: that *mind or consciousness is primary, and not secondary to physical events in space-time.*

Let me now briefly discuss *quantized energy states*. According to classical physical theory for a hydrogen atom (Figure (7-2)), an electron orbiting the nucleus is always accelerating radially inward $((A_n) = v^2 / r)$, and thereby continuously losing energy.[*] As it loses energy by emitting light, it should spiral inward and very quickly strike the nucleus.

[V] "fast enough": that is, if my thinking were somehow accelerated to where one second of car movement could be divided into, say, one thousand intervals of thought (each a millisecond in length); then in one interval of thought the car would be seen to move hardly at all - about four-tenths of an inch, if the car is traveling at twenty-five miles per hour!

[*] Inward acceleration = square of electron orbital velocity / radial distance from center or nucleus of atom.

Since hydrogen atoms are stable, this theory is in error. Around the year 1913, the famous Danish physicist, Niels Bohr (1885-1962), one of the fathers of quantum theory, developed an atomic theory

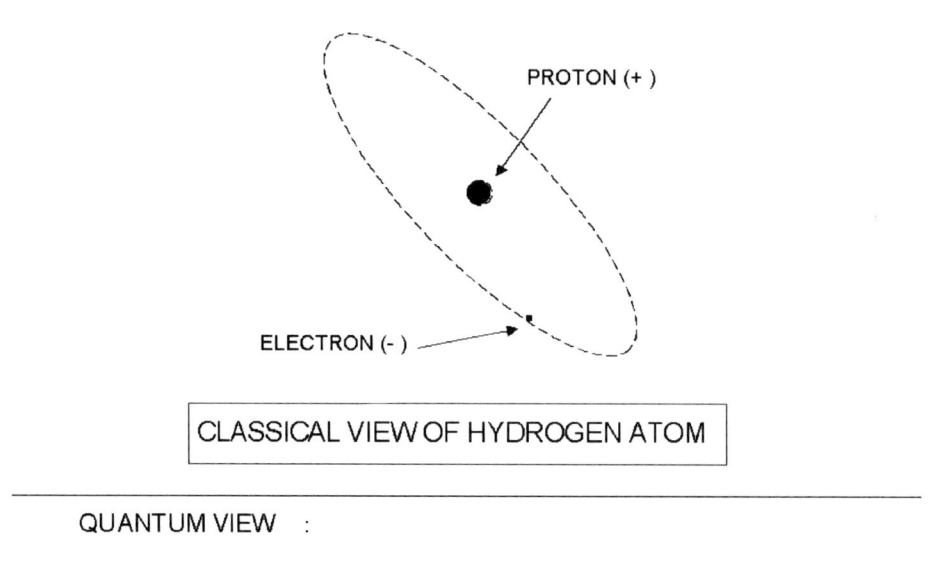

CLASSICAL VIEW OF HYDROGEN ATOM
PROTON (+)
ELECTRON (-)

QUANTUM VIEW :

THE PROPERTIES OF AN ELECTRON OR PROTON HAVE NO EXISTENCE OR REALITY UNTIL WE OBSERVE THEM ...BUT "EXIST" ONLY AS A POTENTIAL

Figure (7–2)

Classical and Quantum Views of Hydrogen Atom

for the hydrogen atom (the simplest of all atoms), which is considered a transition between the classical theory of the proton / electron model and the wave mechanical description of the atom which was later formulated in the 1920's. Bohr began with the classical view of the hydrogen atom (see Figure (7-2)) and incorporated a wave aspect for the electron orbit or energy state.[3] Since hydrogen atoms were observed to be stable (electron remains at constant energy), Bohr proposed that the electron orbit be equated to that of a circular *standing wave* or stationary wave. (To understand this look at Figure (7-3)). Consider a wire or string stretched between two fixed points (top of Figure (7-3)). If the wire is plucked a *transverse wave* will travel along the wire and will destructively interfere with itself unless the length of the wire is an integral multiple of one-half wavelengths. In this case a standing or stationary wave pattern will result. For the case of a standing wave, there are points on the wire (called *nodal points*) that will remain at rest when the wire is vibrating. The wave will oscillate up and down but will not travel along the wire.

Depending on the amount of force applied to the string, the wave pattern will vibrate at different frequencies. As the force increases the frequency increases, and the number of nodal points increases. In principle, this standing wave represents a stable energy state.

N= PRINCIPLE QUANTUM NUMBER, OR NUMBER OF STANDING WAVES

STANDING WAVE - THREE WAVELENGTHS

CIRCULAR STANDING WAVE FOR THREE WAVELENGTHS
N=3 (QUANTUM NUMBER)

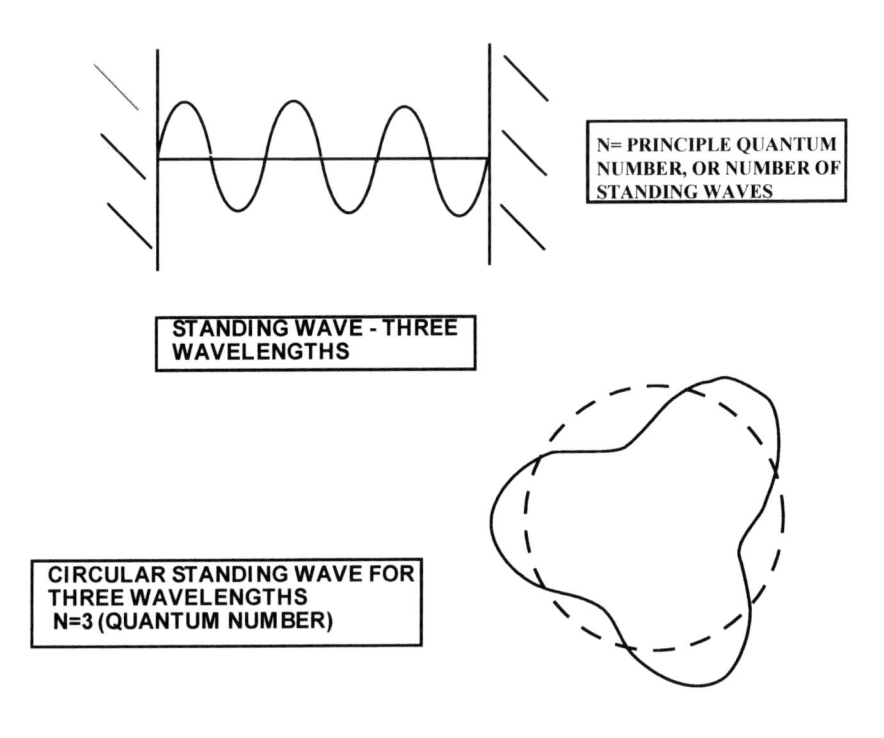

Figure (7–3)

Linear and Circular Standing Waves

That is, the wire can oscillate with a constant energy for an indefinite period of time. Now if the wire is bent to form a circle the standing wave pattern can be maintained if an integral number of whole wavelengths can be fitted into the circumference, as given by:

$$n\lambda = 2\pi r \qquad (7\text{-}1)$$

where n is an integral called the *principle quantum number*, and r is the orbital radius.

A circular standing wave is shown in the bottom of Figure (7-3) for $n = 3$ (number of whole wavelengths). This represents a stable or stationary state for the electron about the atom. As long as the electron is in this state it cannot radiate energy in the form of electromagnetic radiation, and therefore, the electron will not spiral into the nucleus. This Bohr model of the atom, although still describing the electron as a particle, characterizes the possible orbits as a series of *quantized* energy states, because the electron can only occupy discrete energy levels given by the principle quantum number.

CHAPTER 8

PARTICLE / WAVE DUALITY FOR MATTER

A Frenchman by the name of Louis de Broglie proposed that not only did light possess a wave / particle duality, but that one of the basic units of matter itself, that is, the electron should, under certain conditions, exhibit wave-like characteristics. It was seen that by considering the wave aspects of a material particle, it was possible to explain by a new model why an electron would remain in orbit about a proton.[*] If the electron were thought of as a wave, whose wavelength fit into a circular orbit of a given radius r, then that orbit was stable with given angular momentum. Angular momentum is the product of the mass of the electron, the radius of the electron's orbit and the speed or velocity of the electron in its orbit about the proton nucleus, that is, $m \times v \times r$. In order for an electron to change orbits (say, to a lower orbit) it would have to emit a photon or quantum of energy equal to the difference in orbital energies. Thus, the electron could occupy only discrete, quantized energy levels. The wave characteristics of electrons was later verified by irradiating a metal foil with a beam of energetic electrons (150 ev) and observing a diffraction pattern similar to that of *X*-ray light passing through a double slit. These and other experiments confirmed that material particles also could exhibit wave- like characteristics! The wavelength of a *macroscopic* object, such as a gram of some material substance, moving at a speed of 1/10 meter/second, is 6.62×10^{-30} meters![**]

For a more detailed discussion of Particle-Wave Duality of Matter, see APPENDIX I-8 (p. 87) at the end of Part I

---

[*] Remember, according to classical theory, an electron, orbiting the nucleus, is always accelerating radially inwardly, and thereby continuously loses energy. As it loses energy by emitting light, it should spiral inward and very quickly strike the nucleus. Since hydrogen atoms are stable, this theory is in error.

[**] This number is : 0.0000... (25 more zeros !) 662 (an extremely small number.)

CHAPTER 9

THE PRINCIPE OF COMPLENTARITY

We have seen that there are two methods of energy transport: waves and particles. Light behaves as if it were a wave under certain experimental conditions, and as a particle under other conditions. If the wavelength of a lightwave is to be known with infinite precision, the wave must have an infinite extension in space. Similarly, if the frequency is to be known with infinite precision the lightwave must exist over an infinite period of time. The frequency of the wave in question must be compared with the frequency of a wave generated by an oscillator, or standard "clock." Interference of the two waves will produce a *beat*, and the number of beats per second will be equal to the difference in frequencies of the two waves. If the frequencies of the two waves are precisely the same, there will be no beats. But as already stated, the observation of the waves passing by a fixed point would have to be made over an infinite period of time to ascertain that no beats actually occurred, and if the frequency of the wave in question is to be known with absolute accuracy. For a particle which has zero extension in space (an ideal case), it would be impossible to know its wavelength. [1]

Observe Figure (9-1). Δx, and ΔP,[*] represent respectively the *uncertainties* in the position and the momentum. As shown in Figure (9-1a), for a wave of infinite length or extension, we know its momentum accurately; that is, the uncertainty in the value of the momentum is zero: $(\Delta P = 0)$ because we have no uncertainty in measuring its wavelength. We know that the momentum is given by the relationship, $P = h/\lambda$ (where h is *Planck's* constant, and λ is the wavelength). But we have absolutely no information on the location of the particle-nature (photon) of the light, that is, $(\Delta x = \infty)$. The uncertainty in the position is infinite. For a particle of finite extension, its location can be represented by a wave packet of width (Δx) as shown in Figure (9-1b). The wave packet can be represented as a sum of many sine waves [∇] of slightly different wavelengths. Since the packet consists of a range of wavelengths, it cannot have a precisely defined momentum, but has a range of momenta. Thus, we see that one cannot simultaneously apply both a particle *and* a wave description. "By the mutually contradictory characteristics of a particle and a wave, we cannot simultaneously apply a particle description and a wave description - we can and must use one or the other, never both at the same time." [2]

---

[*] These are pronounced "delta x", and "delta momentum."
[∇] sine wave: the periodic oscillations of a wave in which the amplitude of displacement at each point is proportional to the sine of the phase angle of the displacement, that is, it looks like a water wave.

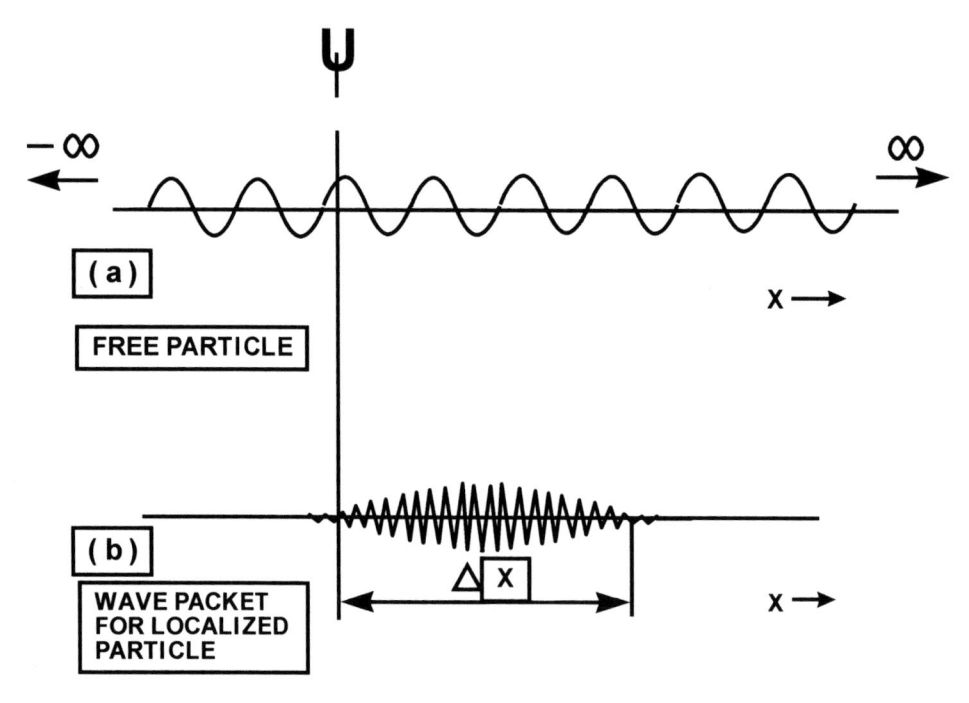

WAVE FUNCTIONS FOR PARTICLES

Figure 9 – 1

Position and Momentum for Free and Localized Particles

CHAPTER TEN

PROBABILITY

SUMMARY

When a coin is tossed into the air, if the coin is evenly balanced, the probability, chance, or odds are that 50 % of the time it will land heads-up and 50 % of the time it will land with the tail-side up. Most of us know from experience that the first ten tosses might yield six heads and four tails, eight tails and two heads, or even ten of either all heads or all tails, but in the long run, a great number of tosses will show the ratio of heads to total tosses - or the ratio of tails to total tosses - approaching nearer and nearer to the value of 0.5. We know that the existence of a head on one side of the coin, and the existence of a tail on the other side is independent of any coin toss. This is so obvious that to question this simple conclusion would be absurd. However, the existence of the *state* of heads-up or tails-up is a *probability*.

With a die, *topside 3* exists as a potential, with a probability of 1/6 for its appearing each time the die is tossed. In theory, if one knew precisely the force vectors, die position, mass, and initial orientation, he or she could predict what side of the die would land topside (the side that lands face-up). This is not so in quantum physics. In quantum physics, position, energy, time and momentum (what are called *observables*) of a particle are seen to have no objective existence until measured or observed by some macroscopic measuring device. Until these properties are measured, they have no more objective existence than a *topside 3,* and have only a potential or probability of existing - this probability being the result of a superposition (for example) of many possible position or momentum states.

See APPENDIX I-10 (p. 90) for a detailed discussion of the probabilities involved in a coin toss. Then return to this chapter.

CHILD'S SWING AND COASTING AUTOMOBILE

SWING

An example of probability or chance is the random observation of a child's swing. (See Figure (10-4)).

Figure (10-4)

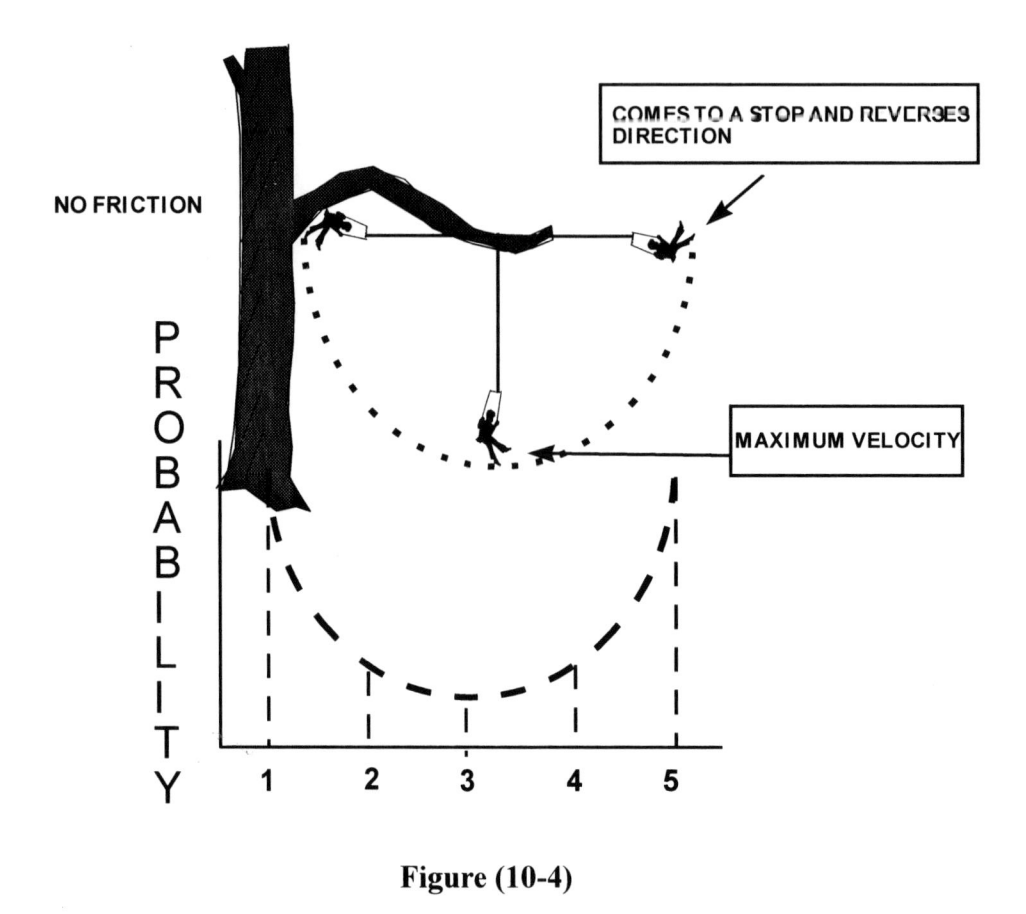

Probability of Locating Child on a Swing
(Note to reader: In some cases where a chapter has an appendix – such as this
one does, Appendix I-10, which begins on p. 90 – the figure sequence
may begin in the appendix and then continue in the main chapter.)

The swing, with a little girl on it has been given a strong push by her father, (perhaps a little too strong!) Since we have assumed the ideal condition of no friction between the rope encircling the tree branch and the branch itself, and negligible air resistance, the swing will continually move sequentially through positions (1), (2), (3), (4), and (5). Then, upon reversing direction, will swing back through all the positions to again return to position (1) with no loss of energy. That is, the swing will accelerate and reach a maximum speed due to gravity at (3), and then decelerate and come to a temporary stop at (5), upon which it will change direction, accelerate in the reverse direction until it again reaches maximum speed at (3), and so on.

The little girl's mother is in the kitchen, and occasionally peers out the window to watch her, as she is a bit concerned that the girl's father has pushed the swing too hard. While washing the dishes she occasionally - or *randomly* with respect to the time on the wall clock - looks out the window. What does she see - or rather - where would she most likely see the child: at the top of the swing path, at the very bottom of the path, or somewhere in between? In a small interval of time (Δt), the likelihood or *probability* of seeing the girl at some small arc region along the swing path [(Δx) = r $\Delta\Theta$] * is a function of how fast the swing is moving at that given interval of time. If the swing is moving slowly at the time interval of observation, then it will spend a longer time in a region where it first was observed. Therefore, the probability is greatest that a random observation will spot the little girl in the region of (1) or (5) because the swing is moving more slowly here. At (3) the swing has the lowest probability of being seen, as it is moving at maximum speed and spends the least amount of time in this region.

We could develop an equation to calculate the velocity of the child along the path swept by the swing. The result (the arc velocity of the swing *tangent* to the arc path) could be in the form of v_t = function (r Θ), and would be called the *wave function*. From this relation a probability curve for the likelihood of finding the girl on the swing could be drawn as a function of a given position (r Θ). This is illustrated in Figure (10-4) below the drawing, and is shown simplistically as a curve similar in shape to the path swept out by the swing.

COASTING AUTOMOBILE

Another example of a probability curve derived from a wave function can be illustrated by an automobile that has been accelerated to a high speed near the bottom of a hill as shown in Figure (10-5). After reaching high speed at (1) the engine is turned off. Again, ignoring friction and air resistance, the car will begin to decelerate and slow down due to gravity, move the slowest at the top of the hill (3), then accelerate to again reach maximum speed at the bottom of the hill (5). Unlike the swing, the car will not coast back up the hill. A random observer of this scene (someone who just happens by and looks at the hill) will most likely observe the car at position (3), and least likely (lowest probability) see the car in the regions of (1) and (2). Although the little girl on the swing, and the automobile are both real, the *state* of the girl/swing and the state of the car at any given point along their respective paths are given by their probability curves which can be calculated by the specific wave functions describing the shapes of the curves.

Referring back to Figure (1-3) we see that if we have precise information about the billiard ball masses, positions, velocities, and the dimensions of the table, we can in theory map out where the individual balls will be after any number of elastic collisions with each

---

* Where r is the length of the rope, and "delta theta" is the incremental angle that the swing has moved.

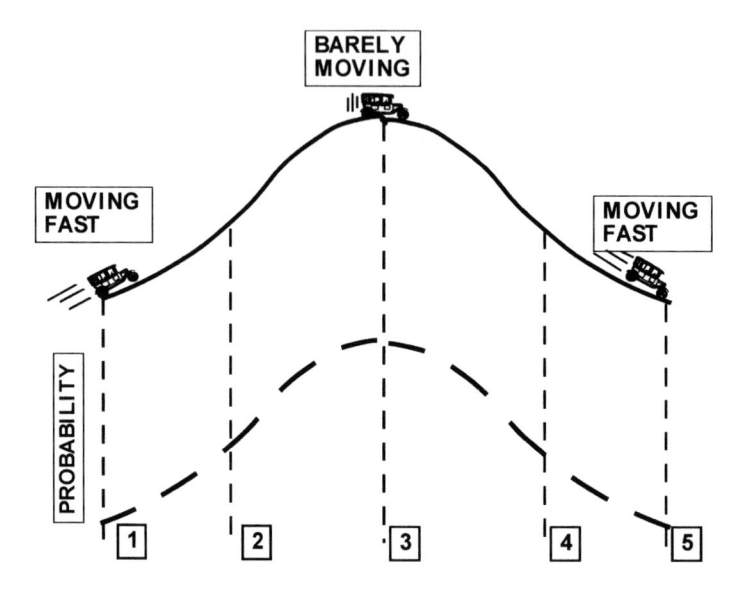

Figure (10-5)

Probability of Locating Car on a Hill

other and with the walls. Using the established laws of physics we could even derive an equation which could be used to predict future positions and velocities of each ball, again assuming no loss of kinetic energy due to friction of the moving balls against the table top, and through collisions. For the examples of the billiard balls, the swing, and the coasting car, we can derive equations of motion that will predict future positions, velocities or momenta $(P = mv)$ * of the individual objects, subject to the accuracy of our initial data. With increasingly accurate data-taking devices, we should obtain more accurate results.

Since we have considered the above objects to be real, the probability of determining the state of an object; that is, the position and the momentum, only come into play for these macroscopic objects where we have set up a situation where random observation in time leads only to a finite probability of observing the position and momentum of each object. Indeed, if we know the initial conditions, and we select any time at random to observe the objects - but know *the time we select* - we can precisely predict future events.

However, quantum mechanics has shown us that at least in the sub-atomic world, not only can we not predict with unlimited precision the state of a particle (simultaneously knowing both position and momentum), but we cannot say that both properties of a particle exist at the same time! The definition of the "real existence" of a particle is that we have knowledge of both position and momentum simultaneously,

---

* momentum = mass times velocity.

because without this information, we cannot locate it, nor know where it will be in the future. *

What is being implied here is that at the very least the *properties* of a subatomic particle (position, momentum) have only a *potential* for existence; and that potential is determined by its given test constraints and conditions.

As the reader moves on further into the book to discussions of quantum probabilities, he should remember that when a particular number comes up from the tossing of a die, we exchange *classical* ignorance for information. But this is not quite like *quantum* ignorance, which lies behind quantum probability. A quantum collapse of a particle wave function exchanges ignorance for information, but here there is a *"sudden change in the rules that influence single events"* (see *Quantum Reality,* By Nick Herbert, p.190-191). [3]

---

* "real existence": this rather philosophical definition of the conditions for particle reality or real existence is not universally accepted in the scientific community.

CHAPTER 11

THE WAVE EQUATION

In the early 1920's a theory of atomic structure was developed that would be entirely separate from the classical theory of the day. A mathematical relationship was formulated that could predict electron energy levels in atoms. Called the *Schrodinger Wave Equation*, it was not *derived* from fundamental principles; rather, it was created to satisfy the de Broglie equation for matter waves, to predict electron energy levels in atoms and the spectra of light emitted or absorbed when an atom transitioned to a different energy state.

See APPENDIX I-11 (p. 94) for a detailed discussion of simple harmonic oscillators and the wave equation.

CHAPTER 12

PARTICLES IN POTENTIAL WELLS

The *Schrodinger Wave Equation* can be used to predict the location of an electron confined in an infinite potential well that would be conceptually similar to a man confined to an infinitely deep pit. No matter how hard he tries to jump out of the pit he simply does not have enough energy to scale the walls. According to classical physics, electrons confined in this manner can be found anywhere inside the well, as shown by the dotted lines in Figure (12-3) below. Figures (12-1) and (12-2) are shown in APPENDIX I-12 (p. 97)

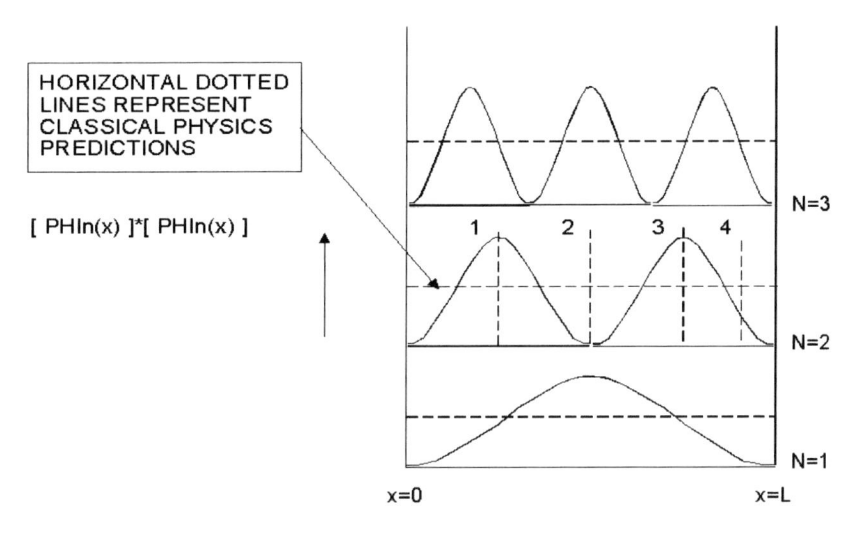

PROBABILITY PER UNIT LENGTH FOR ELECTRON CONFINED IN POTENTIAL WELL

Figure (12-3)

Electron Confined in Infinite Potential Well

For increasingly higher values of electron energies (n =1, 2, 3), the horizontal dotted lines indicate that the electron has equal probability of being found at $x = 0, x = L$, or somewhere in between. But quantum theory, through the use of the *Schrodinger Wave Equation*, predicts that there are different probabilities for finding the electron in the well, and actually some places in the well where it will *never be found!* As shown by the curves of Figure (12-3) (for electron energy level, n =3), the electron has greatest probability of being found at three places, and zero probability of being found at the two troughs of the curve. This is a truly amazing fact when you consider that for an electron to be found at any one of the allowable positions, it somehow has to traverse the region, where according to quantum theory, it can never be found.

Now, let us consider a particle trapped inside a *finite* potential well. An alpha particle is essentially the nucleus of a helium atom. It consists of two protons - positively charged, - and two neutrons, with no charge. Uranium-238 is known to decay to Thorium -234 by emitting alpha particles. But classical physics says that it is impossible for alpha particles to leave the nucleus of Uranium-238 because the energy required to remove the particle is greater than the particle energy. Quantum physics predicts that alpha particle emission can occur by *"tunneling"* through the energy barrier. That is, even though classical physics says the probability of alpha particle emission is zero, quantum theory predicts a finite probability of its occurrence.

See APPENDIX I-12 (p. 97) for a detailed discussion of an Electron in an Infinite Potential Well

CHAPTER 13

THE POSSIBILITY OF FINDING QUANTUM OBJECTS IN BOUND SYSTEMS

According to quantum theory, we can no longer conceive of the electron as occupying a definite point in space and time, but rather as a *cloud of probability*, although the most probable location is at the so-called *Bohr radius*. It would seem, then, that there is no physical law that will predict when a given electron will jump from one energy orbit to another, although for a large assemblage of atoms quantum theory can predict with extreme accuracy energy radiation or radioactive decay. In radioisotope decay an emission of a given photon, for example, may occur within the next second, or it might not occur for the next 1000 years. We have no way of knowing.

Quantum theory states that when an electron in an atom absorbs some quantum of energy, the probability is now greater of finding the electron at a larger radius. The *wave function* of the electron (the solution to the *Schrodinger Wave Equation*) gives us information about the material system under consideration, including the measurable quantities or *observables*, such as, position, momentum and energy. But it is the *square* of the wave function; that is, the *probability amplitude* that gives us the probability of locating the electron at a given position. When we perform an observation, the wave function collapses, and a particle of matter is localized. Once we cease to look for the particle, it again takes on the aspects of a probability wave.

A photon of light from a distant star - or rather, its quantum wave function - reaches us after expanding as a spherical wave front as it traverses the many light years separating the star and the Earth. When the wave front reaches us on Earth, it will be light years in diameter. But the photon - the actual particle - is not localized across this gigantic wave front until you (or I) observe or collapse the wave and localize the particle. Until it has been observed the photon can be thought of as *wave of equi-potential* across the entire surface of the spherical wave front! In like manner, a beam of electrons can be perceived as a quantum wave potential until it is observed via an experiment.

See APPENDIX I-13 (p. 105) for a detailed discussion of Position Probabilities for Electrons and Simple Pendulums

CHAPTER 14

THE HEISENBERG UNCERTAINTY PRINCIPLE

Unlike observing billiard balls, when we observe subatomic particles we inevitably disturb the very particle we wish to observe. We cannot stand behind a glass wall and unobtrusively study a particle. The very act of observation interferes with the object being observed. The *OBSERVER and the OBSERVED* are in some way inextricably connected. Figure (14-1) illustrates the problem. To observe an electron, for example (if science had the technological capability), it must be illuminated with light in order for it to be seen and subsequently photographed. Although light has no rest mass, it does have momentum, and the interaction of the light with the electron will impart momentum to the particle. If we use short wavelength (higher energy) light to observe the electron, we will get a sharp image, but at the expense of imparting a strong kick to the particle. The shorter the wavelength the better the resolution of the particle, but the greater the momentum transferred to the electron, and the resultant uncertainty in the future position of the electron. If we increase the light wavelength (lower energy), the momentum imparted to the electron will be decreased accordingly; but now we do not know the precise position of the particle at the time of measurement, because light with a long wavelength comparable in size to the electron itself will result in poor photographic resolution.

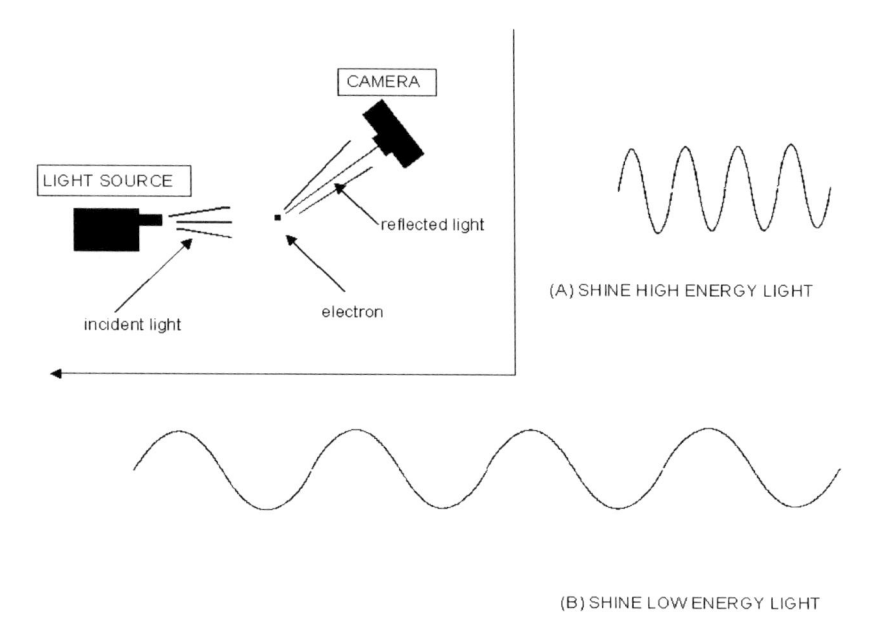

Figure (14-1)

Heisenberg Uncertainty Principle

See APPENDIX I-14 (p. 111) for a detailed discussion of the Heisenberg Uncertainty Principle

CHAPTER 15

PHYSICAL AND THOUGHT EXPERIMENTS IN QUANTUM PHYSICS

The previous chapters discussed at some length the basic ideas of quantum mechanics. It is now time to examine some of the experiments in quantum physics, the results and interpretations of which challenge our sense of credibility of reality.

A – DOUBLE AND SINGLE- SLIT EXPERIMENTS

When two light waves cross each other we get the phenomena of wave interference, and the resultant amplitude and wave intensity will vary from point to point in the region. The change in intensity when two beams of light meet or superimpose is called interference. When two waves are in phase, the crest of one wave matches up with the crest of the other and the intensity is increased. This is constructive interference. Conversely, if the crest of one wave meets up with the trough of the other wave, we see destructive interference.

Let us consider Young's *Double- Slit* experiment, first performed by him in 1801, where the wave nature of light was first revealed. (See Figure (15-1)

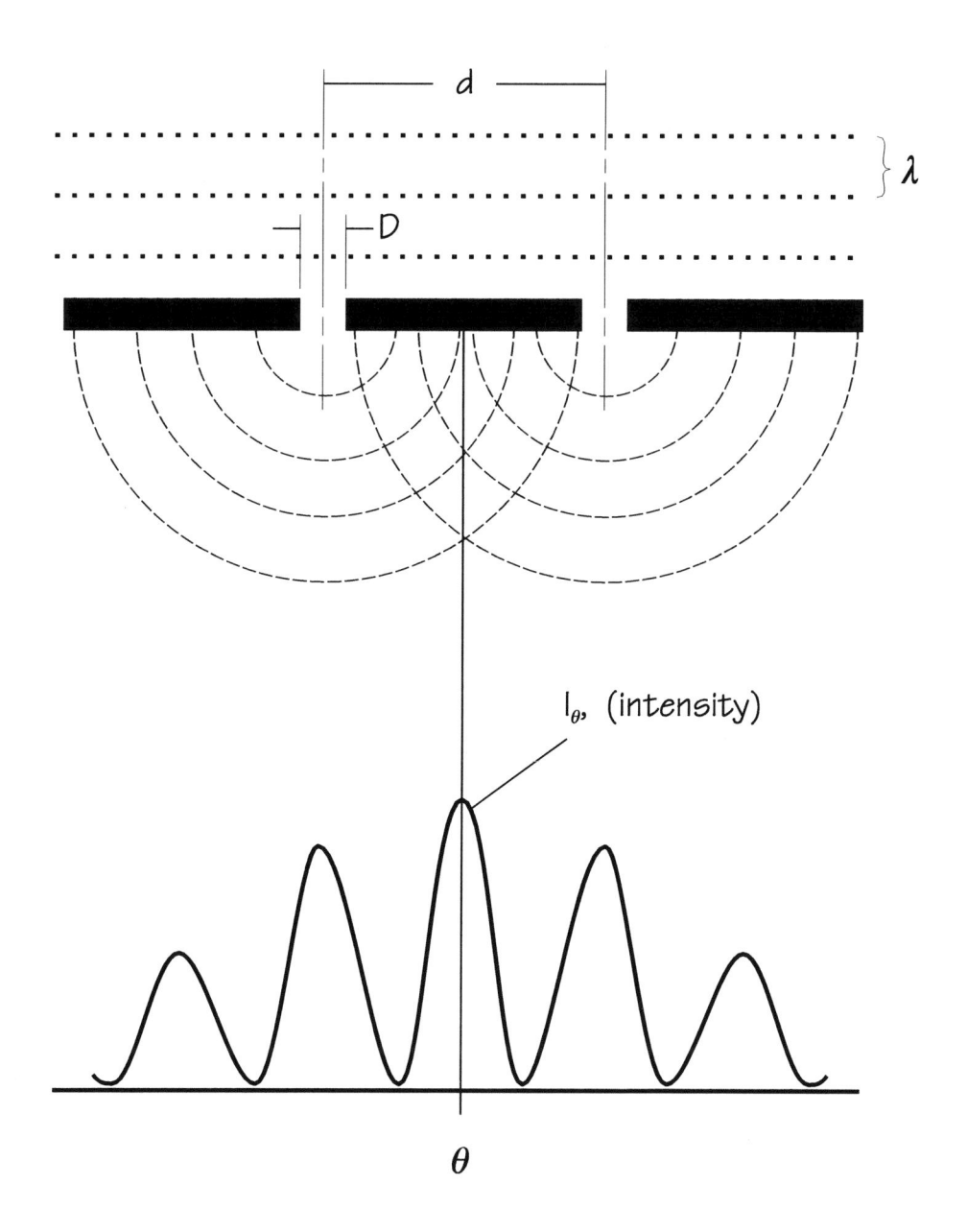

Figure (15-1)
Young's *Double-Slit* Experiment

    We find that the slits will cause the beams to diffract at the slit edges. In addition to this, the dispersed beams will interfere with one another. The resultant intensity pattern is shown in the Figure, and is a combination of slit diffraction and beam interference. The intensity pattern, as measured at the detector, for a beam of light is *not* equal to the sum of the intensity patterns of the individual slits, because there is now an interference term to be considered. We see that in the *Double-Slit* experiment beams of light diffract at both slits, and then interfere with one another further downstream, causing the intensity pattern on the photographic screen as shown in Figure (15-1). We might ask how these intensity patterns compare with patterns we might see in the macroscopic world of bullets and cannon balls for both the single and double slit cases.

SINGLE-SLIT EXPERIMENT WITH CANNON BALLS

Suppose we have a cannon, as shown in Figure (15-7) that fires cannon balls at a single slit that is slightly larger than the diameter of the balls.

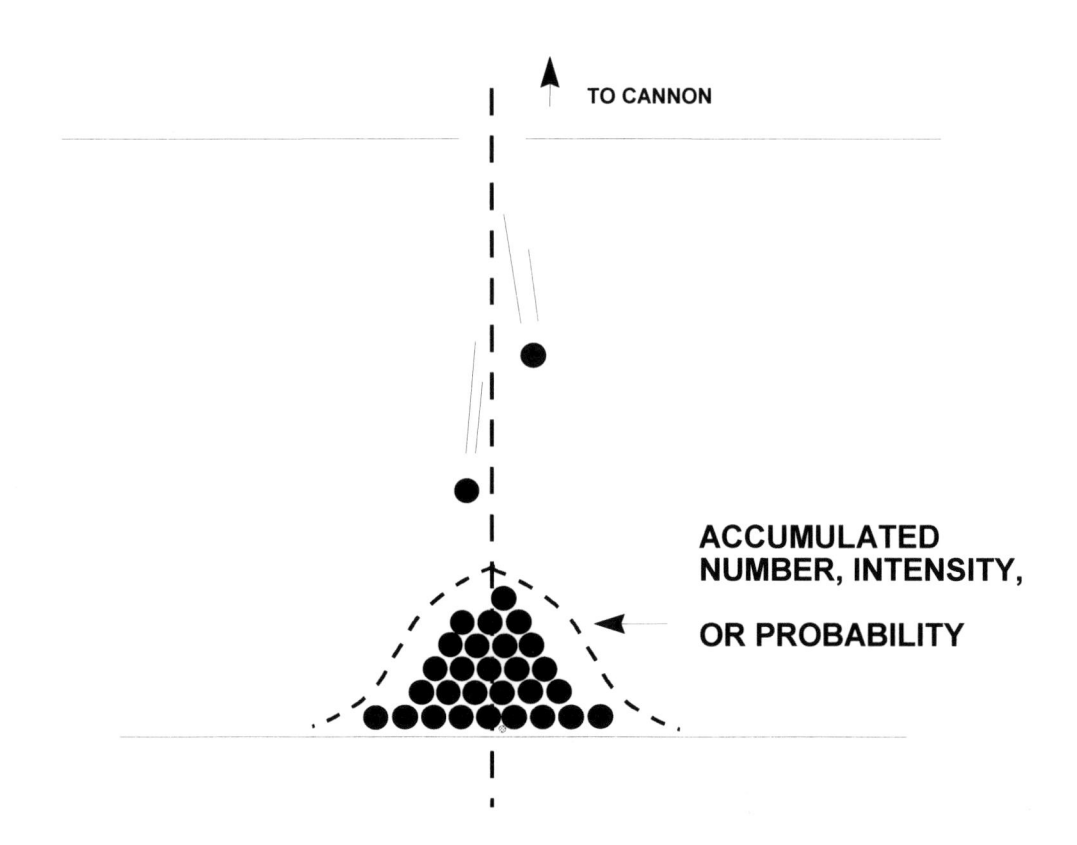

Figure (15-7)
Cannon Ball Distribution through Single- Slit

The cannon is at a great distance from the slits, so the paths of the individual balls are nearly parallel and directed perpendicular to the plane of the slits. In this idealized situation, we assume the balls are rigid and unbreakable, and that the slit edges and the screen placed downstream are hard and will not disintegrate upon impact with the screen. We want to see what kind of distribution we would get if we shot one ball at a time toward the slit. We will assume that each ball "sticks" to the detector screen or to each other upon impact at the screen.

We will soon discover that the distribution arising from the cumulative impacts on the screen would be as shown in the Figure, and would be similar to the diffraction pattern of light waves through a single slit. We notice that each impact is the result of an *integral* unit of mass - that of one cannon ball. The probability is greatest that most of the cannon balls will pass directly through the slit and impact the screen near the slit centerline. However, there is a small probability that some of the balls will graze or strike the slit edges and be diverted or deflected to varying degrees.

DOUBLE-SLIT EXPERIMENT WITH CANNON BALLS

Now let us look at Figure (15-8) for the case of cannon balls fired at *two* slits. One cannon ball at a time is fired toward the centerline of the two slits.

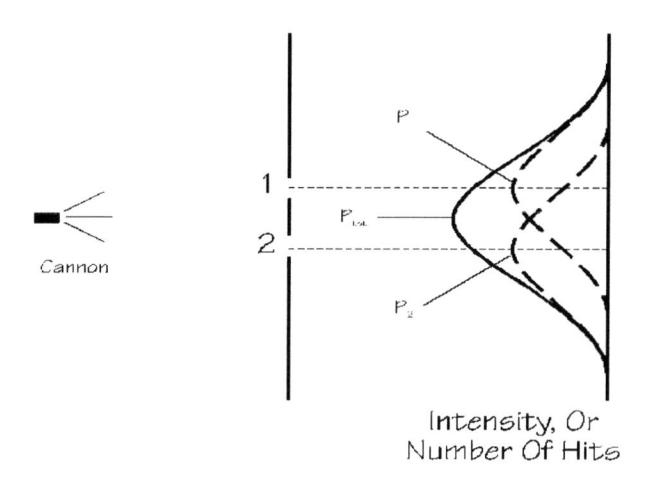

**Figure (15-8)
Cannon Ball Distribution Through Two Slits**

The Figure is greatly exaggerated in that the slit separation is actually much less than the distance between the cannon and the slit plane. The two dotted curves in the figure show the accumulated number of impacts of the balls from each slit as a function of distance x out from the two-slit centerline. These distributions represent the number count, or probability that the balls exiting the upper slit (or the lower slit) will impact the screen at a given distance along the x-axis.

The arithmetic addition of the contribution of individual slit distributions is shown by the solid line, and represents the total probability that the balls exiting both slits will strike at a given point on the screen. This distribution is *not l*ike the double slit intensity distribution for beams of light or particles, Figure (15-1), because large, macroscopic objects such as cannon balls, do not produce a discernible interference pattern because the slit opening is enormous compared to the cannon ball matter wavelength.

DOUBLE-SLIT EXPERIMENT WITH SINGLE PHOTON OR ELECTRON PULSES

Finally, what would we expect if a *single electron* (or single photon) *at a time* were directed toward a double-slit from an electron gun situated a distance in front of the double-slit? As the electron exits the gun and approaches the slits we have no way of knowing which slit it will enter. An electron might go through slit # 1 and impact the photographic screen after undergoing diffraction at the slit. In like manner, another electron at a later time might go through slit # 2. If an electron goes through a slit it will pass through slit #1 50 % of the time and through slit #2 50 % of the time, on the average. Each time an electron hits the photographic screen (a phosphorescent surface), there will be a flash of light of constant intensity or brightness. Because of this constant intensity flash, we are led to believe that an *integral* electron - and not a piece of the electron - strikes the screen each time. The rate of flashing on the screen will vary as a function of x - the distance out from the screen centerline. We observe that the occurrences of flashes appear in a seemingly random manner. We would expect after a period of time to see an intensity build up on the screen that would be similar to that of cannon balls going through the double slit; because, although electrons do have a de Broglie wavelength, it would seem to be impossible for a single electron to go through one slit and interfere with itself. *But the pattern of single point-like flashes that gradually builds up reveals an intensity distribution like that of a beam of electrons or photons passing through both slits and interfering with each other* (See bottom illustration of Figure (15- 12)).

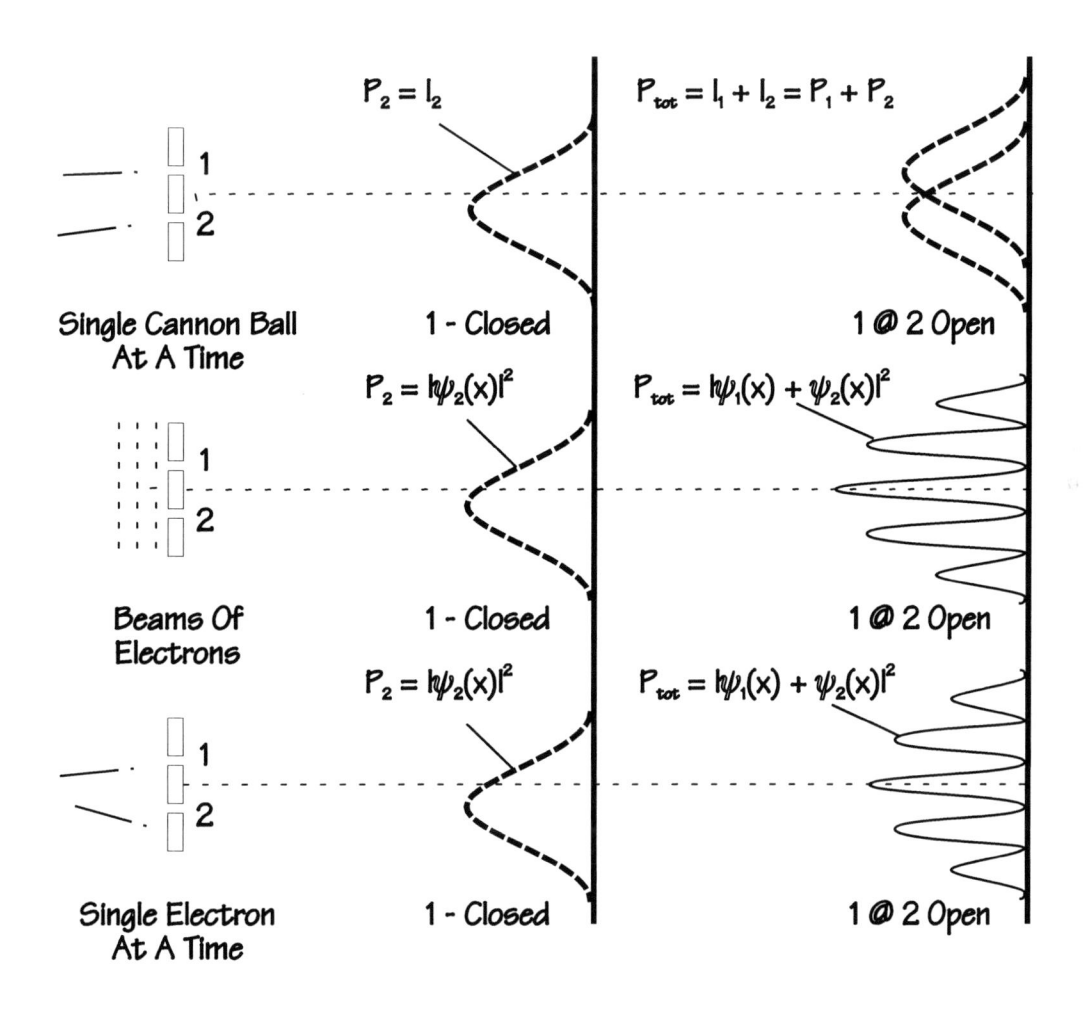

Figure (15-12)
Summary of Intensity Distributions for Macroscopic and Sub-atomic Particles

How can this be? When the single electron strikes the screen we see a tiny, constant intensity flash of light, as if a single particle has impacted. This is definitely a particle impact, but over a period of time other apparently random impacts build up an intensity pattern as if each electron had somehow split in half and passed through both slits, with the two-electron wave components then interfering with each other. The recording (the measurement) of the electron striking the screen shows the electron exhibiting its particle nature.

We might ask the question, "What if the rate of particle impact were only one particle per year?" The particle collisions at the screen would still be distributed in a probabilistic way such that the interference pattern would still appear.

From the results of the experiment, we find an apparent contradiction. Since a single electron at a time was pulsed from the electron gun, only one electron approached the slits and went through either slit #1 or slit #2, and caused a tiny, localized flash of light on the phosphorescent screen, with a constant intensity or brightness, indicating that the impact was caused by a discrete particle, and not a wave. The electron did not somehow split in half, go through both slits and interfere with itself. We should expect the total intensity build - up to be the *sum* of the individual intensities from each slit.

It is impossible to detect which slit an electron goes through without disturbing it and the interference pattern recorded at the screen. If we look for the electron at a given slit, we will know when it goes through that slit. But by "measuring" the position of the electron (observing the electron passing through a given slit), we no longer can predict where the electron will then go. We will have disturbed it and imparted to it a momentum increase that cannot be known precisely. We are either forced to say the electron went through both slits as a wave, but impacted the screen like a particle, or that it somehow "knew" that both slits were open and was "instructed" to distribute in a manner similar to that of an interference pattern. We note here that for macroscopic objects such as cannon balls, detectors and eyes, the matter wavelength is so small that the resolution of an interference pattern is impossible with scientific detectors.

In summary, Figure (5-12) shows the probability or intensity patterns for macroscopic objects and sub-atomic particles in the double slit experiments.

See APPENDIX I-15a (p. 118) for a detailed discussion on *Double and Single- Slit* experiments. Then return to Chapter 15 for other discussions including the *Delayed- Choice* experiment.

B – THE DELAYED-CHOICE EXPERIMENT

One of the world's foremost quantum physicists, John Archibald Wheeler,[*] proposed what he called, the *Delayed-Choice* experiment to determine if indeed there could be some information transferred to the electron as it approached the slit plate. This information as to whether one or both slits were open, could be "used" by the electron in determining which slit or slits to pass through [1].

Let us look closely at Figure (15-13). A single quantum of energy, a photon, in the upper left-hand portion of the figure is directed toward a half-silvered mirror (beam-splitter A) at a pulse rate of, say, one photon/second. The mirror is coated with just enough silver to reflect half of the photons impinging on it, and transmit the other half. If the photon is *transmitted* through beam-splitter A, it will continue on downstream, reflect

---

[*] *University of Texas Center for Theoretical Physics.*

off mirror # 1 and be recorded at photon detector # 1. If the photon is instead *reflected* at beam-splitter A, it will reflect off mirror # 2 and be recorded at photon detector # 2. We can tell which path the photon has taken - path A-1-1, or path A-2-2 - by observing which detector counter responds after the light is pulsed and has traveled a path to the detector. We notice that a single pulse of light (one photon/sec) *never* causes simultaneous detector responses because the photon takes only one path in it's traversal through the apparatus, and is recorded at a constant intensity (Note here that path lengths, A-1-1 and A-2-2 are equal in length).

Now, let us slightly modify the experiment. *After* the light has either been reflected or transmitted at beam-splitter A, we insert a second beam-splitter (B) directly in front of the two detectors as shown in the Figure. This beam-splitter is inserted after the light has been calculated to have been reflected off either mirror # 1 or mirror # 2, *but has not yet reached the detectors.* This second beam-splitter is positioned in time to intercept the incoming light. It is situated such that if light *beams* were coming along both paths, constructive interference would occur on the side of beam-splitter B facing photon detector # 1; while destructive interference would occur at the beam-splitter B-side facing photon detector # 2. The interference would occur because the optical path lengths of the two paths are in phase (one wavelength difference) at the side of the beam splitter facing detector # 1, and 90 degrees out of phase (1/2 wavelength difference) at the side of the beam splitter facing detector # 2. Therefore, there would *always* be a reading at detector # 1, and *never* a reading at detector # 2 (Remember that *destructive* interference cancels the beam intensity). But what we always see with a single quantum or photon pulse of

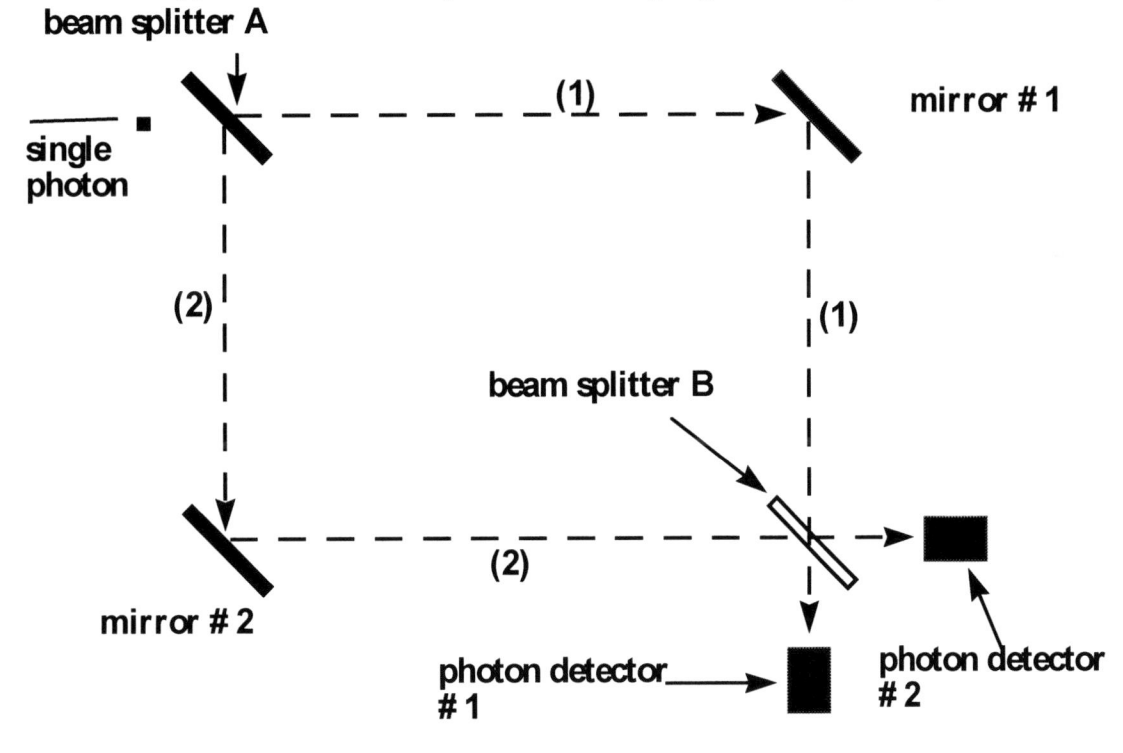

Figure (15-13)

Experimental Set-up for the Delayed-choice Experiment

light (with beam splitter B inserted at the last moment), is a full intensity reading at photon detector # 1, and no reading what-so-ever at photon detector # 2! *It appears that by deciding at the last instant to insert the second beam-splitter, we have decided whether the photon has traveled by one path to the detectors, or has taken both paths - after it has already traveled a specified route!*

John Wheeler said, in speaking about the experimental results, "We now, by moving the mirror [beam-splitter B] in or out, have an unavoidable effect on what we have a right to say about the already past history of the photon; " and "No elementary phenomenon is a phenomenon until it is a registered [observed] phenomenon." [2]

In conclusion, if there is no second beam-splitter in the apparatus, the single quantum of light takes one of two possible paths and registers at either detector # 1 or detector # 2. But, if the second beam-splitter is inserted at the last instant, the photon acts like a wave that has split into two wavelets which travel downstream via two paths and interfere with each other at the second beam-splitter. In the first instance, the light acts like a particle, because we are "looking for it" with detectors. That is, we are trying to localize the particle by determining which path it took. In the second instance, the light exhibits wavelike aspects, because we have decided to allow the light to travel unobserved. We have allowed the light to travel and have the opportunity to interfere before it reaches the detectors.

But how can a photon initially take *one* path, with no second beam-splitter in place, and then take *both* paths when a second beam-splitter has been inserted at the last instant *after* the photon has already begun its travel down *one* path? We conclude that we simply cannot say the photon traveled a given route to the detectors. Physics cannot explain or say with certainty where the next photon or electron will go in the *Double-Slit* experiment; nor, for that matter, when a radioisotope atom will emit a sub-atomic particle. As Wheeler implies, the results of the experiments depend on the "questions we put", or on the experimental conditions we set up, or on the method of measuring we select. We - the observers - play a role in the results we see from experiments with sub atomic particles. Physical reality, it would seem, becomes a matter of observation as well as statistical probabilities.

Consider the implications of the *Delayed -Choice Double-Slit* experimental results: Wheeler proposed examining the light from a distant source in space, such as a *quasar*. A quasar is thought to be a bright nucleus of a galaxy, which perhaps contains a massive black hole at it's center, and which is believed to be responsible for the intense light emanating from a relatively small region of space. Stellar matter is thought to be sucked into the hole, giving off high-energy photons just before it disappears into the hole.

A quasar, designated as *QSO 095 +561*, has been found to be almost directly in line with a nearer galaxy, such as shown in Figure (15-14). The quasar is billions of light years from Earth, while the galaxy is about one-fourth the distance of the quasar from Earth. [3]

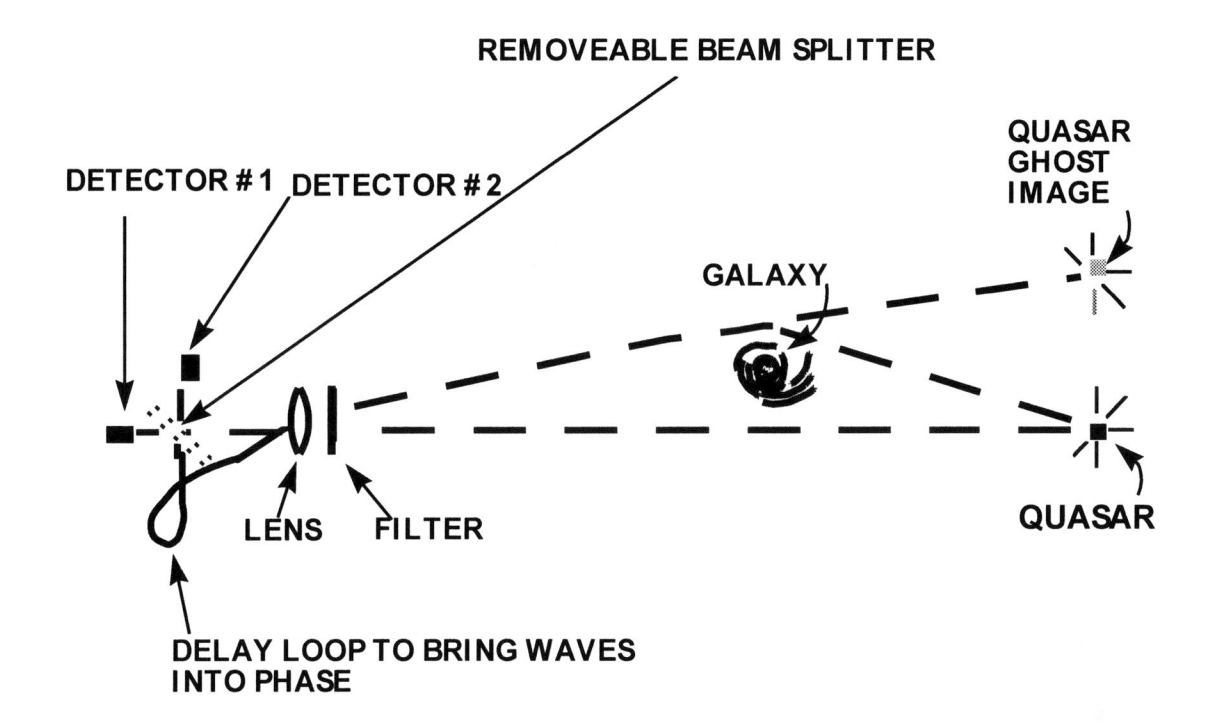

Figure (15-14)

A Cosmic *Delayed-Choice* Experimental Set-up

On the other side of the galaxy away from the quasar is another, but fainter image of a quasar. Evidence indicates that the galaxy is acting like a gigantic gravitational lens and bending the light rays from a single quasar as they pass near the galaxy; some passing around one side, and others passing around the other side. The light rays that have bent the most (see Figure (15-14)) reach the earth at slightly different angles than the rays that are less deflected by the gravitational field, and therefore appear to come from a different region of the sky. Therefore, we see two images of the quasar: a real one, and a *ghost* image.

A *Delayed-Choice* experiment can now be performed over astronomical distances, involving light that began its journey to the earth billions of years ago. By a suitable arrangement of lenses and filters [4] individual light photons received directly from the quasar - and from those bent around the intervening galaxy on the other side from the quasar-Earth direct line-of-sight - can be collected one at a time at individual detectors. The readings of the individual detectors indicate which path each individual photon took from the quasar to the earth. Again, at the last moment a beam-splitter can be placed to intercept the two possible light paths to the detectors. If positioned correctly, we will observe interference effects.

It would appear that a *single photon* starting out from the quasar billions of years ago, and taking only one path past the galaxy, is now seen as taking *two* paths past the galaxy! What we have decided to do with our experimental setup in the *present* - insert the beam splitter at the last instant, or leave it out - has appeared to alter the past history of the photon. We have decided in the *present* whether a photon will take both paths as waves, or one path as a particle. "By deciding which questions our quantum registering equipment shall put in the *present* we have an undeniable choice in what we have the right to say about the *past*"[5] (Wheeler). The conclusions, taken to extreme would seem to say that the existence of the universe, itself, from the *Big Bang* to now, is the "cumulative consequence of billions upon billions of elementary acts of observer - participancy reaching back into the past. . . "[6] (Wheeler).

However, Wheeler has also said (a statement more readily accepted by physicists) that the photon has no definite path or location from quasar to Earth, but exists as a *potential* only - and described by its wave function - until it is registered in an apparatus on Earth.

C – NON-INTERFERING DELAYED-CHOICE DOUBLE-SLIT EXPERIMENT

All the previous *Double-Slit* experimental results reveal that when one attempts to observe an electron or photon by placing a detector in the path of the particle, one indeed finds the particle, but the interference pattern disappears. The pattern was the result of the wave aspects of the particle.

More recently, experimentalists such as Leonard Mandel, of the *University of Rochester*, have devised and performed a *Double-Slit* experiment of a different kind - one that apparently does not involve the intervention of a measuring or detecting device in the path of the photon.[1] The experimental configuration is similar to that illustrated in Figure (15-15).

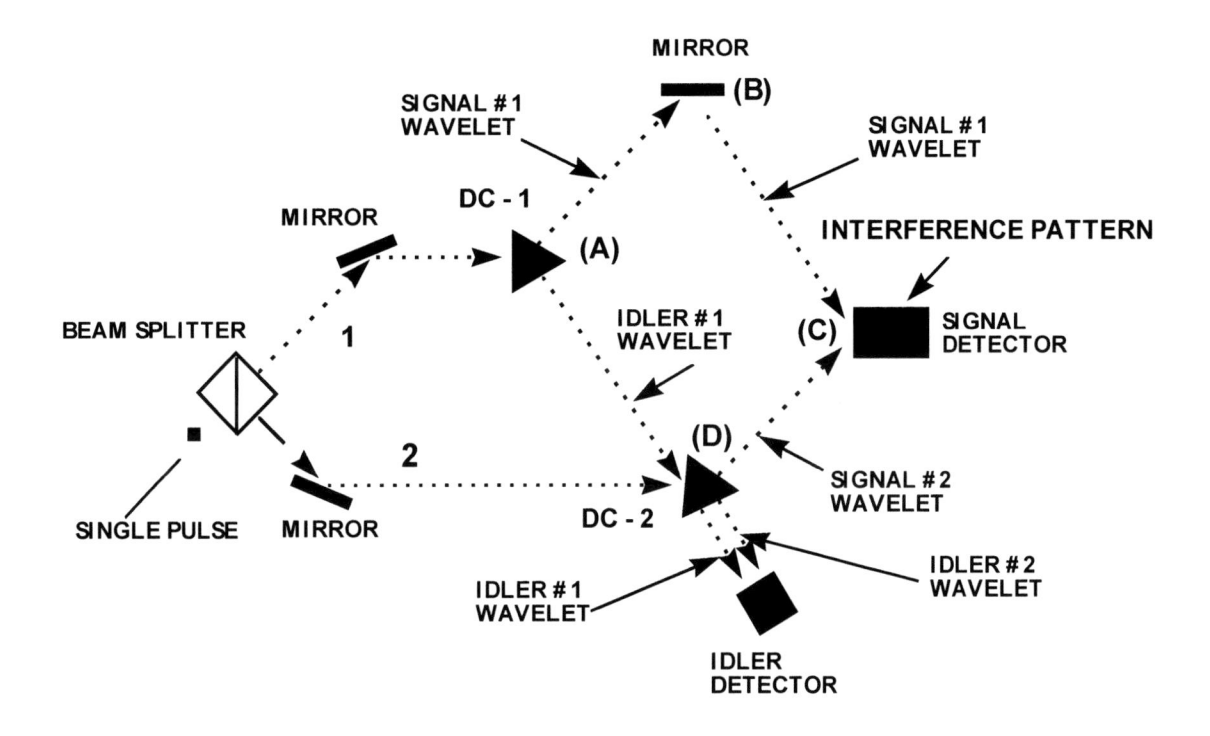

Figure (15-15)

Experimental Set-up for the Non-interfering Delayed-choice Experiment

The experiment and the results are described briefly as follows: Light from a laser is incident on a beam splitter, which, as before, is a mirror half-coated with silver, so that on the average half [*] of the photons will pass through the mirror and travel path # 1, and half will bounce off the surface and travel path # 2. After bouncing off other fully-coated mirrors the photons enter individual *down-converters* - devices that have the capability of "splitting" a single photon into two photons, each of lower frequency, so that the energy of each photon is one-half that of the original photon.[∇] The individual wavelets from each *down-converter* are called *signal* and *idler* wavelets. The idler wavelet from DC-1 (down-converter # 1) is arranged to meet with the idler wavelet from DC-2, and be registered at the idler detector. The two signal wavelets travel downstream to another detector (the *signal detector*) where an interference pattern is observed when the path length for one of the signal wavelets from a down-converter to the signal detector is changed slightly so that the two signal wavelets move in and out of phase with each other. Up to this time we have had no way of knowing which path an individual photon took as it exited the beam splitter at the front end of the experimental apparatus, so we

---

[*] Rather, the photon is put into a state of quantum superposition of two separate states: transmitting through the beam splitter; and reflecting off the beam splitter mirror.

[∇] More simply, as a single photon passes through a down-converter there is a finite probability that it will disappear to be replaced by two photons, in an entangled state (see APPENDIX I-15b for definition), each of lower energy and momentum. But according to conservation laws the total energy and momentum remain constant.

must assume each photon exited the beam splitter and traveled along both paths to the two down-converters as *waves,* and then split up into idler and signal wavelets. We can confirm this because we see an interference pattern caused by two signal wavelets.

Now, at the last instant, before an idler wavelet from DC-1 meets up with an idler wavelet from DC-2, we block the path from DC-1 to DC-2 so that idler wavelet from DC-1 is prevented from mixing with the other idler wavelet (see Figure (15-16)). In the actual experiments performed by the Mandel group, there was no idler detector, only a *signal detector.* Although the illustrations shown in Figures (15-15) and (15-16) show an idler detector, it is only shown to illustrate or explain why the interference pattern disappeared when idler wavelet #1 was blocked.) [2]

At the downstream signal detector we notice an amazing thing: the *interference pattern of the signal photons disappears.* We can compute and compare the arrival time of signal photons to the signal detector with the arrival time of the remaining unblocked idler photons to their detector [3], *and determine which path the light photons took to the signal detector* (Either via path # 1, or path # 2). Simultaneous detection of signal and idler photons indicates that *both* took path #2, and not path #1.

Thus, we have determined the path the light has taken to the signal detector, without interfering with the light on its journey to the detector. Since we no longer observe an interference pattern, we must conclude that each photon entering the beam-splitter took one path to the signal detector (in this example, path # 2). If we would get a recording of light at the signal detector and *no* reading at the idler detector, then we would conclude the photons traveled only path # 1.

Why does the interference pattern disappear when the idler current from DC-1 is blocked? We did not block the path of the light wavelets traveling to the downstream signal detector as we blocked or interfered with the paths in the previous *Double-Slit* experiments. *The answer, according to the experimenters, was that potential knowledge about the particles had changed!* Potential information, rather than actual experimental information was sufficient to destroy coherence. It was not necessary to perform a measurement that will give path information. As Greenstein and Zajonc say in their book, *"The Quantum Challenge,"* (p. 90), *"Information* [about the degree of distinguishability of paths] *alone is sufficient to predict the experimental outcome."* [4] These conclusions bring into question the objective reality of quantum objects states.

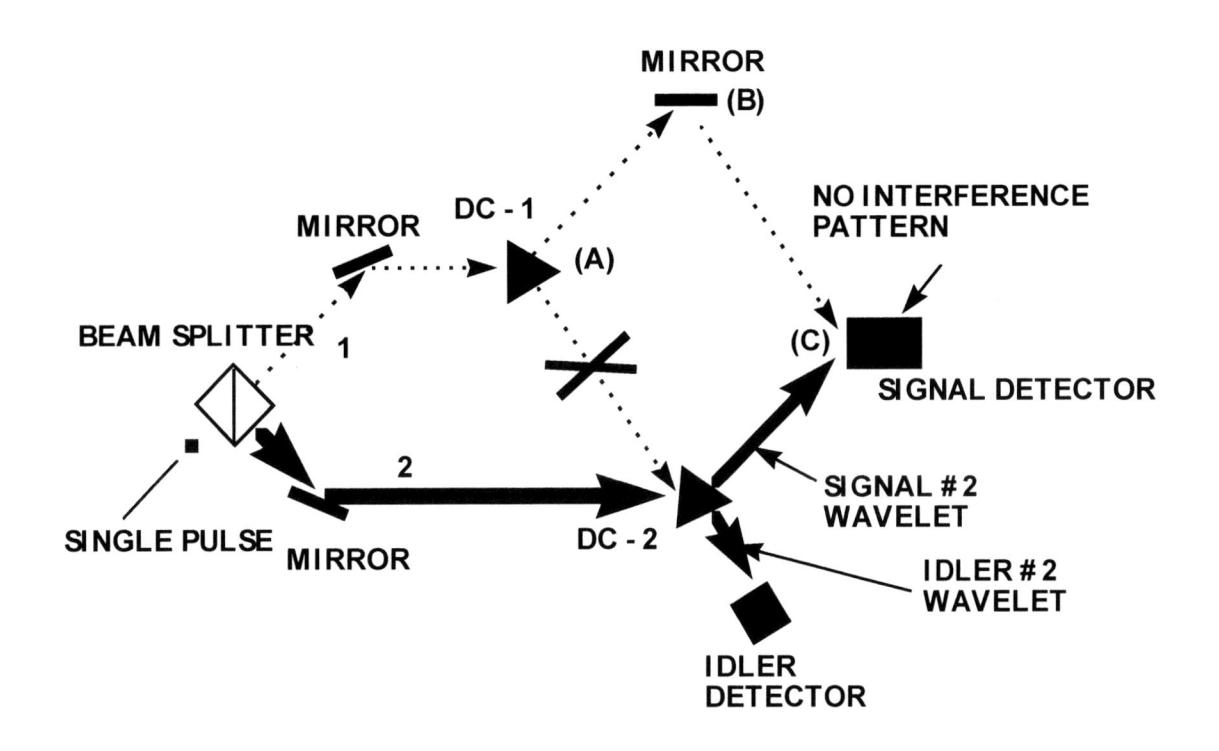

Figure (15-16)

Blocking the Path from Down-converter #1 to Down-converter #2 in the Non-interfering Delayed-choice Experiment

    The light wave function collapsed; that is, knowledge was gained because an observer could at some time examine the experimental setup and results and determine the route individual photons took to the detector. And according to quantum theory this knowledge can only be acquired at the expense of losing information about the momentum of individual particles; therefore, the loss of the wavelike characteristics of the photon and the corresponding disappearance of the interference pattern.[*]

    Thus we realize that when a single particle such as a photon approaches a double-slit or a beam-splitter and exits the device, we have no way of knowing which path the particle took. If we observe an interference pattern, we know that the photon took both paths as a wave. We do not observe the phenomenon occurring for macroscopic objects, such as, cannon balls passing through a double slit apparatus. At the quantum level we observe that the wave function for an unobserved photon is a *coherent superposition* of all possible states determined by the experimental conditions; and this wave function *"collapses"* upon our measurement or observation to a single state of position or momentum as dictated by the constraints of the *Uncertainty Principle*.

---

[*] See also "Multiparticle Interferometry and the Superposition Principle," D.M. Greenberger, M.A. Horne, A. Zeilinger, Physics Today, August, 1993, p. 25: "The wavefunction contains all the information about the system that is potentially available, not just the information at hand." [5]

Each idler and signal pair created at the down converters represents a *quantum system*. Disturbing any part of the system affects the other part of the system.

The experimentalists showed that particle wave functions can be collapsed to reveal particles, but few physicists believed that the reverse could be possible: a collapsed wave function could be restored. But experiments performed by Raymond Y. Chiao of the University of California at Berkeley indicate that it appears to be possible to erase information about the path of a given photon and restore its wavelike characteristics and its interference pattern. [6]

D – WHEELER'S GAME OF TWENTY QUESTIONS

"…every particle, every field of force, even the space-time continuum itself, derives its function, its meaning [*] and its very existence directly or indirectly from apparatus-elicited [∇] answers to yes or no questions."
John Archibald Wheeler [1]

In an effort to explain the role of observer in the interpretation and/or shaping of reality, Professor Wheeler proposed a modification of the game of *Twenty Questions*. [2] The objective of this particular game is to select some item or object. The "questioner," by asking questions that can be answered only with a "yes" or "no" will attempt to guess the identity of the object in twenty questions, or less. The rules for the game are outlined in Figure (15-17), and a sample game is depicted in Figure (15-18).

A person is chosen to be the "questioner" and is asked to leave the room for a short time. In the room are the guests of the party - about twenty or thirty. The people agree to the following rule: Each person will independently think of an object and keep the name of the object to himself. The questioner is then asked to return to the party, where he asks his first question, such as:"Is it bigger than a breadbox?" One person in the room, selected at random before the start of the game, responds to the question with a "yes" answer, because his object in thought is a green car, which is certainly bigger than most breadboxes. The questioner has no knowledge of the special rules of the game, but believes that everyone in the room is thinking of the *same* object. Now since the answer was "yes," according to another special rule, **each person** in the room must check to be sure the object *he* has in thought agrees with the first answer ("yes"). Thus person # 2, who will respond to the second question - and who was thinking of a small black ball (surely smaller than your average breadbox) - changes his object in thought to, say, a black hot air balloon, which is certainly larger than a breadbox. This change in thought must occur for *all* persons who silently answered "no" to the first question.

---

[*] meaning: " the joint product of all the information exchanged between those who communicate - meaning as comparable with that old idea that meaning is agreement" (see Time Today, 1993, by John Archibald Wheeler).

[∇] elicited: to cause, or bring into view.

| RULES OF GAME | **WHEELER'S GAME OF TWENTY QUESTIONS** |

- **PERSON WHO WILL ASK QUESTIONS LEAVES ROOM**

- **REMAINING PEOPLE IN ROOM AGREE TO RULES OF GAME**

- **EACH PERSON INDEPENDENTLY AND SECRETLY THINKS OF AN OBJECT**

- **QUESTIONER ENTERS ROOM AND ASKS FIRST PERSON A "YES" OR "NO" QUESTION**

- **FIRST PERSON RESPONDS ACCORDING TO THE OBJECT HE HAS IN THOUGHT**

- **QUESTIONER ASKS SECOND PERSON A "YES" OR"NO" QUESTION**

- **SECOND PERSON MUST HAVE AN OBJECT IN THOUGHT THAT SATISFIES THE FIRST PERSON'S RESPONSE, AND THEN ANSWERS "YES" OR "NO" TO THE SECOND QUESTION**

- **THE QUESTIONING CONTINUES TO EACH SUCCESSIVE PERSON IN THE ROOM. EACH RESPONDENT MUST ALTER THE OBJECT HE HAS IN THOUGHT SO THAT EACH OF THE PREVIOUS ANSWERS BECOMES THE RIGHT ANSWER FOR HIS OBJECT IN THOUGHT**

- **FINALLY, THE QUESTIONER WILL ASK,"IS THE OBJECT A _____ ?" MOST PROBABLY EVERYONE WILL ANSWER, "YES !"**

Figure (15-17)

Rules for Wheeler's Game of *Twenty Questions*

Question # 2 is now asked, such as, "Is it sometimes found in the sky?" Person # 2 responds this time with the answer "yes." The questioning continues with a different person responding each time. Each respondent must alter the object he holds in thought so that each of the previous announced answers becomes the correct answer for his current object held in his thought.♣ Each person at the party makes the necessary alterations in his own thought, and reveals them to no one.

Finally, after a few more questions, the questioner, feeling he has sufficient knowledge to identify the object - which he erroneously believes everyone originally had in thought - asks, "Is it a cloud?" Most probably everyone in the room will answer in unison "yes!"

Wheeler uses this simple example to indicate that phenomena, at least at the sub-atomic level, are largely dependent on how we, the observers, choose to interact with

---

♣ The response of the person being asked the question is shown in the block outlined in bold.

quantum events.* The observer is more like a participator in determining how the universe appears to mankind.

Questioner →	1	2	3	4	5	6
Question ↓ Bigger than a breadbox?	Green car **Y** / Green car	Black ball **N** / Black hot air balloon	Red pencil **N** / Brown sofa	Brown dog **Y** / Brown dog	Brown house **Y** / Brown house	Yellow plane **Y** / Yellow plane
Found in the sky sometimes?	Green car **N** / Green kite	Black hot air balloon **Y** / Black hot air balloon	Brown sofa **N** / White helicopter	Brown dog **N** / Brown vulture	Brown house **N** / White clouds	Yellow plane **Y** / Yellow plane
Is it white?	Green kite **N** / White kite	Black hot air balloon **N** / White hot air balloon	White helicopter **Y** / White helicopter	Brown vulture **N** / White vulture	White clouds **Y** / White clouds	Yellow plane **N** / White plane
Does it have an engine?	White kite **N** / White kite	White hot air balloon **N** / White hot air balloon	White helicopter **Y** / White sailplane	White vulture **N** / White vulture	White clouds **N** / White clouds	White plane **Y** / White glider
Is it very large and fluffy?	White kite **N** / White clouds	White hot air balloon **N** / White clouds	White sailplane **N** / White clouds	White vulture **N** / White clouds	White clouds **Y** / White clouds	White glider **N** / White clouds
Is it clouds? (All together)	Yes!!	Yes!!	Yes!!	Yes!!	Yes!!	Yes!!

Figure (15-18)

Results from Wheeler's Game of *Twenty Questions*

Before the questioner came into the room and began the game *no word existed*. But the word came into existence by the choice of questions that he asked and by the answers given ("yes" or "no"). In quantum experiments, what we get depends partly on our choice of questions asked. Wheeler has said, "Do we do not better to recognize that what we call existence consists of countably many iron posts of observation between which we fill in by an elaborate papier-mâché construction of imagination and theory?"[4] See the symbolic illustration in Figure (15-19).[5]

---

* Einstein was quoted by Werner Heisenberg in his book, Physics and Beyond, (New York, Harper and Row): "It is the theory which decides how we observe."[3]

48

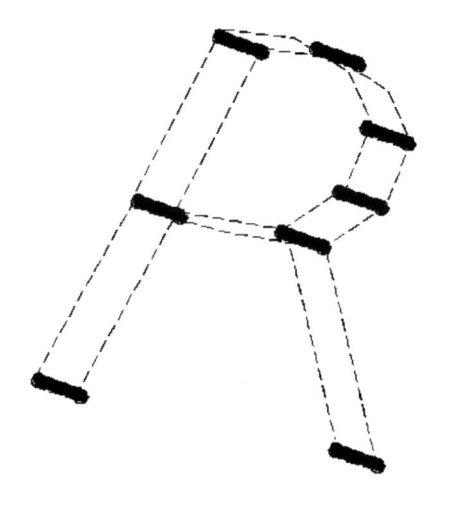

REALITY....IRON POSTS OF OBSERVATION, FILLED IN WITH PAPIER-MACHE CONSTRUCTION OF IMAGINATION AND THEORY?

Figure (15-19)

Reality Depending Upon Observation

E - THE EPR PARADOX [*]

Albert Einstein did not like the implications of quantum theory, even though as we have seen, he was largely involved in the discovery of the fundamental principles governing the theory. Einstein believed that the description of reality as given by the *Copenhagen* interpretation of quantum theory was incomplete. A reasonable definition of reality as stated by Einstein, Nathan Rosen, and Boris Poldolsky in their paper (the *EPR* paper) presented in the *Physical Review*, May 15, 1935, was, "If, without in any way disturbing a system, we can predict with certainty (i.e., with probability equal to unity), the value of a physical quantity, then there exists an element of physical reality corresponding to this physical quantity." [1] The assumption that objects possess a reality independent of observation has been called, "realism".

Although Einstein believed that it was impossible to measure any physical property (such as position), without affecting the measurement of another property (such as momentum), he could not accept the *Copenhagen* interpretation that a particle such as an electron did not simultaneously possess a definite position and momentum, even if these properties could not be measured precisely. Quantum theory denied objective reality to a particle's position or momentum until that physical characteristic had been measured. If the position were measured, one could not attribute any reality to the particle's momentum, and the choice of which physical property was to possess objective reality was left to the observer and not to the particle itself. The accuracy of any measurements made, however, still fell within the constraints of the *Uncertainty Principle*.

But in addition to his objection to the quantum theory denial of objective reality, Einstein had a conviction of the principle of "local causality" - that an object situated a distance from a local object cannot instantaneously influence or affect in any way the local object. That is, no influence can propagate faster than the speed of light. The assumption that no influence can travel faster than the speed of light has been called "local causality," "locality," or "Einstein Locality."

A third assumption for the interpretation of reality is based on the legitimacy of forming conclusions based on a series of experiments that yield consistent results, and has been called "inductive inference." These three assumptions collectively form a basis for "local realistic" interpretations of the world around us. [2]

EPR proposed a thought experiment that was intended to prove that it was possible to predict either the position or the momentum of an object without disturbing it. If this could be accomplished, reality would then be seen to be objective, and a particle would possess physical characteristics independent of observation. But if reality were seen to be objective, and *if* quantum theory was complete, then there should be no way of predicting both of these properties without disturbing the particle; and this could only happen if one assumed non-local effects (faster than light influences) - something which Einstein could not accept. Einstein therefore concluded that quantum theory must be incomplete. [3]

---

[*] Named after Albert Einstein, Nathan Rosen, and Boris Poldolsky.

The argument went as follows. Consider one possible example of the *EPR* thought experiment: A stationary atomic reaction occurs in such a manner that two protons fly away in opposite directions. By the conservation laws, the total momentum of the two particles is conserved. In this example, each particle has the same momentum - equal in magnitude but opposite in direction, so that the net momentum is zero, as shown in Figure (15-20).

proton # 1　　　　　　　　　　　　　　　　　　**proton # 2**

● ◄―――――― ✹ ――――――► ●

(1) - momentum (P) of proton #1 and proton # 2 are equal and opposite in direction.

(2) - Measure P1…We now know P1 = - P2, without disturbing P2.

(3) - Measure the position of proton # 2.

(4) - We now know, at this precise instant, the position and momentum of proton # 2, an act which would be a violation of the *Uncertainty Principle*

Figure (15-20)

EPR **Interpretation of Quantum Mechanics**

According to *EPR*, if one would measure the momentum of proton # 1 after it has traveled downstream some distance, it would seem we would instantaneously know the momentum of proton # 2. Although proton # 1 was disturbed by the measurement it would not matter, because proton # 2 has not been disturbed by the proton # 1 measurement. (Also, since the atomic reaction is symmetrical, both particles will have moved the same distance from the origin of the reaction, so if we instead had measured the distance proton #1 has moved from the reaction, we could deduce the distance of proton #2.) [5]

Now, after we have deduced the momentum of particle #2 without disturbing it, we can measure its position. At that precise moment, we have determined both the position and momentum of particle #2, an act which would violate the *Uncertainty Principle* which was part of the *Copenhagen* interpretation of quantum theory. This theory describes physical reality through wave functions. A wave function can be constructed to describe the state of the two protons including the sum of their momenta. This *total* momentum is considered real, although the individual momenta are indeterminate. [6] As long as both protons remained unobserved their properties, such as, position and momentum are uncertain and are the results of a superposition of all possible states given by the wave function for the proton pair. This means that each proton has some potential for being located in any direction, and can be thought of as being smeared out over a large region of space. According to quantum theory, the correlation between the two particles' positions and momenta immediately after the reaction continues to exist as the particles move away from each other, but once a measurement has been made on one particle, and its momentum has been affected to some unknown degree, this very act of measurement will also affect the momentum of particle # 2, so that the net momentum remains the same (in this instance, zero). This has been called *quantum entanglement,* the result of the creation of a two-proton pair due to the atomic reaction. [7] The created proton pair is called a *singlet state.* In 1964, John Bell of *CERN* (*European Organization for Nuclear Rese*arch) proposed a method for determining whether the two protons had objective reality, or whether they (or their physical attributes) were indeterminate until a measurement had been taken. As a result of Bell's work it can be shown that if quantum theory is correct, then the distant particles will display a different degree of correlation of certain physical quantities. A lesser degree of negative proton-spin correlation with increase in angle between the two distant proton spin detectors would be predicted by quantum theory than by statistically-real particle theory predictions. See Figure (15-24).

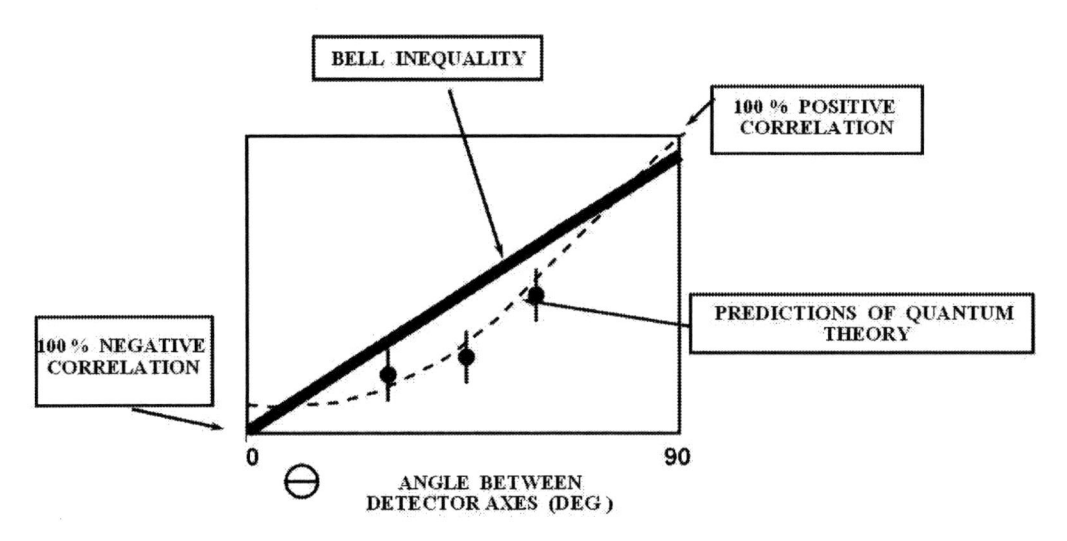

Figure (15-24) Experimental Results Indicate Bell's Inequality is Violated

The degree of proton spin correlation with change in the angle between the widely separated detectors, as predicted by classical (non-quantum) theory is shown by the solid straight line; and that predicted by quantum theory by the curved dotted line. The experimental data indicated by the small dots with vertical error bars follow closely the quantum theory prediction. Experimental results appear to validate the predictions of quantum theory, and the conclusions that the doctrine of Einstein local reality is false; that is, reality is *non-local*. Some physicists also claim that the results indicate that reality is *non-objective*: quantum particle properties have no objective existence unless observed. The observer by changing the orientation of his spin detector at proton #1 brings into existence different spin component values for distant proton #2.

See APPENDIX I-15B (p. 140) for detailed discussion of the *EPR* Paradox, and also Experiments in Quantum Teleportation

CHAPTER 16

VIRTUAL PARTICLES

It has been speculated by some physicists that at the beginning of the universe all of the created particles possessed quantum entanglement in their relation to each other. In fact, John Wheeler believes that the physical universe, itself, arose out of a quantum fluctuation in the geometry of space (For a discussion on theories of creation see Part II, APPENDIX B). Some physicists believe that the vacuum fluctuates, creating quanta out of seeming nothingness. The phrase "seeming nothingness" is used, because physicist Paul Dirac in 1928 theorized that the vacuum of space contained particles and energies undetectable in our universe. It was known that the solution of the relativistic equations for electrons resulted in two sets of solutions - one set that revealed positive energy states for electrons, and another set that revealed *negative energy states.* [1] The electrons that we observe in our world have positive energies, but Dirac believed that there were also negative states in the vacuum, that under normal conditions were occupied by electrons and were unobservable. If one of these electrons were to acquire sufficient energy, it would be possible for it to appear in a positive energy state. What is left behind after the departure of the electron from the negative energy state is a vacancy or "hole." What we will see, however, is the appearing of a positively-charged particle in a positive energy state, having the same mass as a normal negatively-charged electron. This particle, which Dirac predicted, and which was later discovered in 1932, has been designated the "anti – electron," or "positron." These quanta are always created in pairs - for example, an electron and an anti-electron or positron. The positron is similar to the electron (ordinary matter) in all ways except that it possesses a positive electrical charge rather than a negative charge. The *Uncertainty Principle*, expressed in terms of *particle energy and lifetime* (instead of position and momentum), says that if we attempt to determine the energy of a particle over a finite period of time, like the measurements of position and momentum (which are called complementary characteristics), we discover that the degree of uncertainty of the energy of the particle becomes greater as the time interval becomes smaller:

$$\Delta E \Delta t \geq h/2\pi \qquad (16\text{-}1)$$

In fact, if the time interval is zero the range of possible energy values for the particle would be infinite! If we observe, therefore, a sufficiently small region of space over a small interval of time, it is possible that our uncertainty of the energy contained within this region is so great that quanta can appear out of nothingness! However the quanta can exist only with the time constraint given by the *Uncertainty Principle* before they (one electron and one positron) annihilate each other and again disappear from the universe. *For a brief moment, the Conservation of Energy appears to have been violated* (matter cannot be created out of nothing). We can never be certain, though, for over a larger region of space that an equal number of recently-created quanta are being annihilated at the same time that other quanta are being created. These particles created out of the vacuum of space are called "virtual," because they appear real within the uncertainty of measurement and just as quickly disappear.

VIRTUAL PARTICLES AS MESSENGER PARTICLES

Virtual particles play a prominent role in the interpretation of the quantum universe and its operation. The electromagnetic field can also be understood in the quantum sense as a quantized field consisting of a sea of virtual photons, which appear and disappear within the time constraints permitted by the *Uncertainty Principle*. [2] The electrostatic charge of the electron itself is thought to consist of a cloud of virtual photons. When one electron approaches another electron, quantum theory says that a virtual photon (a "messenger particle") is emitted from one electron and transports energy and momentum to the second electron causing what appears as a repulsive force between them as shown in Figure (16-1).

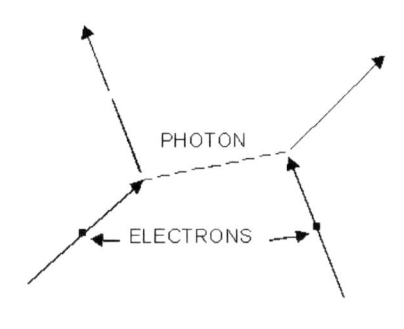

Figure (16-1)

Transfer of Photon (Virtual Particle) Between electrons

Energy is not conserved from the time of photon emission to the time of absorption, but, as mentioned before, this is allowable within the constraints of the *Uncertainty Principle*.

Quantum theory allows for the emitted virtual photon to undergo many transitions of state - it can transform into a virtual electron-positron pair, annihilate, or reconvert back to a virtual photon before it is again absorbed. All these possibilities for virtual particle creation out of the nothingness of space appear to be a fundamental requirement of quantum physics in order to conceptualize a workable model of the universe, but, like all models, it is our best attempt to explain the workings of the universe.

Physicists - and especially mathematicians - have formulated many exotic theories in an attempt to define reality. Various quantum space-time theories have proposed such building blocks upon which to structure reality such as: *twistors, gravitons, superstrings,* and *quantum foam,* but it must be remembered that mathematical concepts are sometimes no more than convenient methods to make some meaning out of physical phenomena, and to connect one theory with another.

Sten Odenwald, a member of the science team for the *Cosmic Background Explorer* satellite, says that the strangeness about the physical vacuum of space (which abounds with virtual particles), is that it may be rooted in the way the human brain works, rather than in the objective aspect of nature. He quotes Einstein as saying, "Space and time are not conditions in which we live, but modes in which we think." [3]

Not all physicists are comfortable, however, with the thought that the very foundation of physics and the interpretation of physical reality is built upon virtual particles and particles such as *neutrinos,* which have little or no mass or physical dimension. Dr. Jovanovic of *Fermi National Laboratory* questions, "But how can a particle without the property of mass be a building block?" [4] *

Surprisingly enough, it appears that when all the contributions to the energy in the universe are summed - the negative energy due to the universe's gravitational potential energy, and the positive energy due to the observed (and unobserved) matter in the universe - the net energy may be zero.[5] Thus the universe may have been created essentially out of nothing!

At the very early stages of the universe (less than 1×10^{-43} sec, called the *Planck time*), the universe was infinitesimally small, less than $1 \times 10^{-35} m$ in diameter. According to the *Uncertainty Principle*, a quantum fluctuation could occur over an extremely small interval of time. Out of this fluctuation, it has been postulated, the quantum universe, containing all the matter and energy was formed. This infant universe then participated in the so-called *inflationary expansion era* which began at about 1×10^{-35} sec and lasted until 1×10^{-32} sec. After this period the universe continued to expand, but at a slower rate to its present state. ∇

But what caused the quantum fluctuation to occur? As with the *Double-Slit* experiment, the quantum wave function (a quantum wave function for the early

---

* It has been discovered recently that neutrinos undergo quantum mechanical oscillations, and in the process change their particle identities and quantum properties. These oscillations may imply that neutrinos have a small (non-zero) mass.

∇ Recently, new, independent evidence from the astronomical community indicates that the expansion of the universe is actually accelerating, rather than slowing down. [6]

universe?) can only collapse to reveal a particle (the quantum universe?) when a *measurement or observation* is made. Who or what made the observation, and was the observer a part of the universe or out of it? Wheeler again offers an explanation through his *Delayed- Choice* experiment, where he says ". . . billions upon billions of elementary acts of observer - participancy. . . " [7] reaching back into the past have brought the universe into being. What we choose to observe in the "now" apparently contributes to our present view of reality. Rather, the universe that we now see may have been formed by our expectations, *the thoughts we entertain*, the questions we ask (see *Twenty Questions* game), and by our methods of observation.

If matter reveals an objective existence only when observed, and if space-time has essentially no meaning without the presence of matter, and if the net energy of the universe is zero, and if particles seem to be created out of nothing, *then what can we say about the substantiality of the physical universe?* Is it in some way a construct of –or a misinterpretation of – collective consciousness, or minds? The famous British astronomer, Sir Arthur Eddington, in an article entitled "The Domain of Physical Science," (from *Essay in Science, Religion and Reality*) said "Not only the laws of nature, but space and time and the material universe itself, are constructions of the human mind."[8] The most profound discovery may be the ". . .discovery and practical proof that substance is exclusively spiritual, not material." [9]

SIZE OR SCALE – FROM VIRTUAL PARTICLES TO GALAXIES

It is interesting to discover the size range of matter, from the subatomic size to the super-macroscopic scale, that is, at the galactic level. Curiously enough, we can create a convenient scale for comparing sizes by shrinking the earth-sun distance from 93,000,000 miles to *one inch.* On this scale, one mile becomes nearly equal to one *light year*, and the nearest star, other than the sun, would be about four miles distant.

In the other direction, the diameter of a hydrogen atom nucleus (a proton) is on the order of $10^{-13} cm$, the diameter of an electron about $10^{-20} cm$; while the diameter of a virtual particle such as a *graviton* * is calculated to be on the order of $10^{-33} cm$. Scaling up: if a graviton were scaled to one cm, an electron would be about 60 million miles in diameter (almost two-thirds the distance from the earth to the sun), and an atomic nucleus would be on the order of 100 *light-years* in diameter! Clearly, space - although overrun with subatomic virtual particles - is "virtually" emptiness.

Recently, particle physicists at the *Fermi National Accelerator Laboratory* announced the possible discovery that quarks, one of the so-called fundamental particles in the makeup of matter may themselves have a substructure. Protons are said to be made of three quarks: two *up* quarks each with two-thirds of a positive electronic charge, and one *down* quark, with one-third of a negative electronic charge. These particles have been given the name, *preons.* [10] In theory, even preons could be made of smaller particles - there may be an infinite chain of ever smaller and smaller particles.

---

* According to theory, the undiscovered graviton is the messenger particle that transmits gravitational force between particles.

CHAPTER 17

POSSIBLE INTERPRETATIONS OF QUANTUM PHENOMENA

Figure (17-1) shows the steps the reader should take in working his or her way from classical determination of reality to possible quantum interpretations.

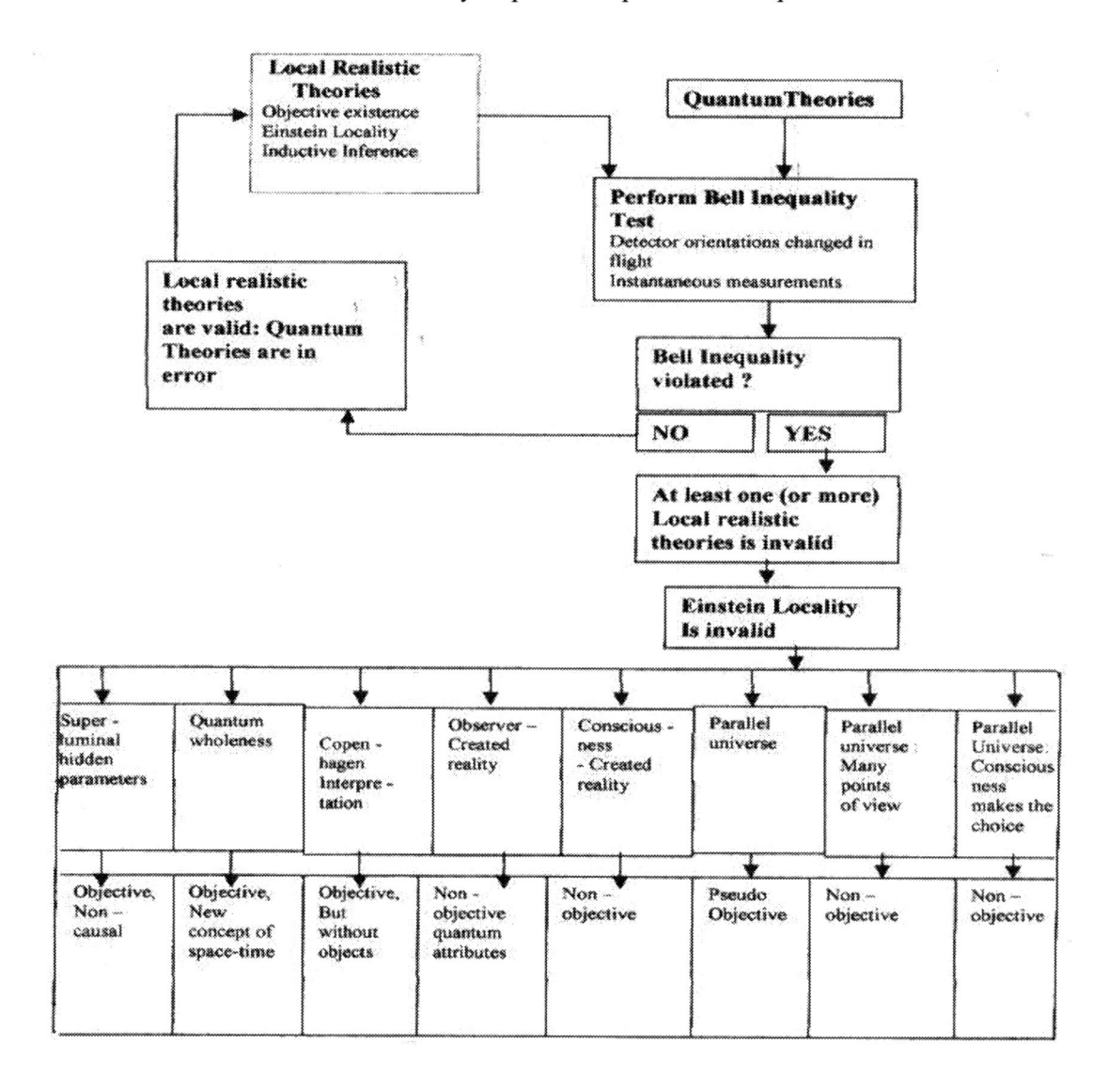

Figure (17-1)

Predictions of Local Realistic Theories and Quantum Theories

Interpretations of reality that hold that the local realistic theories of nature (*Realism* or objective existence, *Einstein Locality*, and *Inductive Inference*) * are valid, are in conflict with quantum mechanics in making certain experimental predictions.(See top of Figure (17-1). The local realistic theories predict that the *Bell Inequality* will be obeyed, while quantum mechanics predicts it will be violated. Experimental evidence as shown in Part I, Chapter 15, indicates that the *Bell Inequality* is indeed violated, and that at least one (or more) of the premises that make up the local realistic theories is invalid. Many physicists believe that the results prove fairly conclusively that reality is *non-local*.

Since Bell's inequality has been violated there have come forth a number of interpretations or models of the universe in an attempt to explain the strange and sometimes bizarre phenomena occurring in the quantum world. In discussing only a few of the quantum theory interpretations (see bottom of Figure (17-1) for eight of those interpretations), we must heed the statement by Bryce De Witt, "Despite its enormous practical success, quantum theory is so contrary to intuition that, even after forty-five years [article written in 1970] the experts themselves still do not agree what to make of it."[1]

The reader is referred to the book by Nick Herbert, entitled, *Quantum Reality*, which discusses in *detail* no less than eight quantum interpretations.[2]

A – QUANTUM WHOLENESS

Some physicists maintain there is a wholeness or relationship between all particles in the universe, since presumably they all were created out of the *Big Bang*, and that the quantum attributes of the two-proton singlet state are the attributes of the *system*, including the experimental set-up, and not simply localized in individual particles. They say there is an undiscovered "hidden order," and that " . . .God does not play dice."[3] And if the code of this order were known, we would perceive the universe operating in an orderly fashion with a natural cause and effect relationship.

Noted quantum physicist, David Bohm, does not believe that the instantaneous correlation between two protons in an *EPR* experiment is due to faster than light signals or message carriers. He believes that what he originally called non-local "hidden variables " are responsible for the correlation, and represent a deeper view of reality - a reality below the quantum, or *explicate* level.[4] Thus, in the *Double-Slit* experiment, at the explicate level it appears that a single electron or photon passed through both open slits simultaneously, but at the *implicate* level (the deeper level of reality below the quantum level) the appearance of two particles represented different aspects of one "unbroken whole."[5]

Bohm illustrated what he meant by quantum wholeness by an illustration.[6] (see Figure (17-2)), which is a modification of a Bohm illustration: Two television cameras (1 and 2) observe *one* fish in a fish tank. The individual orientations of the cameras are such that each camera sees a different view or aspect of the one fish. Observer #1 situated many miles away from the fish tank (picture not drawn to scale) sees a profile of the fish on his television monitor. Observer #2 sees a head-on view, while a third observer (observer #3) sees both profile and head views of the single fish on his *two* television

---

* See Part I, Chapter 15 and APPENDIX I-15B on the *EPR* paradox.

screens hooked up to the cameras of observer #1 and observer #2. Observer #3 believes he is watching two separate fish in the tank, but after observing for some time he sees a pattern or correlation between the movements of fish on the two screens.

In like manner, what two observers see – being situated at great distances from, and on opposite sides of the *EPR* experiment - are similar to what observers #1 and #2 at the fish tank see: unique and seemingly random results of the individual proton- spin component measurements. If fish tank observer #1 would take a television recording of his view of the fish tank and compare them with observer #2's television recording, both might conclude by the different views that there were two fish in the tank. But if they observed long enough they would see a correlation of movements of the "two" fish. Since both observers initially believe there are two fish in the tank, they might be tempted to believe that there has been some faster-than-light message transfer between the "two" fish that causes them to have correlated movements. But there is only one fish in the tank, and what is seen are ". . .two-dimensional projections (or facets) of a three-dimensional reality." [7] In like manner our view of the three-dimensional (spatial) universe would be

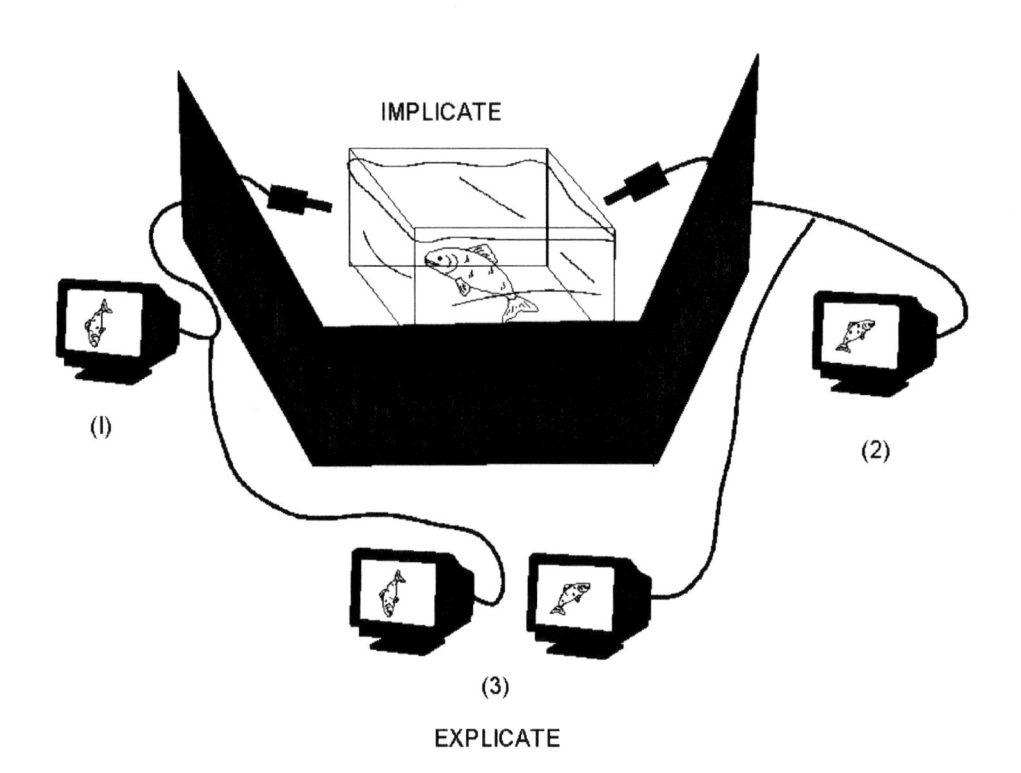

Figure (17-2)

Quantum Wholeness

but a projection of a higher dimensional reality. The two protons in the *EPR* experiment are really a quantum system and are part of an "unbroken wholeness." [8]

The universe, according to the *Quantum Wholeness* theory, therefore, must be considered *non-local* at some level below that of the visible quantum level. For the case of the two electrons in the *Double-Slit* experiment or the two photons in the *EPR* experiment, the two particles do not have separate identities in space and time, but under certain conditions may be seen to go through both slits simultaneously, or to exhibit instantaneously correlated spin characteristics - a projection of a higher-dimensional reality into three-dimensional space.

According to the *Quantum Wholeness* interpretation of *EPR*, there may be in actuality no separation between any objects in what we perceive to be a physical universe comprised of three dimensions in space, and one in time. According to the *Big Bang* theory, it is impossible to have space-time without the presence of matter, but it is matter that distorts space-time - resulting in the phenomenon we call gravity. It is also the distortion of space-time that creates matter. This cyclic reasoning leads to the conclusion that matter and space-time are one and the same thing, [9] and did not Einstein say that matter and energy (of space-time) were equivalent?

Now if quantum wholeness is the way things are, and matter and space-time are essentially one and the same, then our present concept of matter as occupying space, with separation between various objects, and as the foundation or substance of everything, may need to be revised. This conclusion would suggest strongly that the *observer* and the *observed* are not separate in space-time, but that there is some sort of wholeness or interconnectedness between *mind* and the *universe.* Non-separation in space-time strongly implies *mind* as the reality.

As Michael Talbot says in his book, *Beyond the Quantum,* " . . .if every particle of matter interconnects with every other particle, the brain itself must be viewed as infinitely interconnected with the rest of the universe." [10] The universe itself, then, might be thought of as an infinitely dimensional *hologram.* A hologram is a film strip recording of the interference pattern created by irradiating an object with one component of a split beam of light from a laser, and allowing the reflected light to interfere with the other laser beam component at the film strip surface. A *virtual image** of the object can be reconstructed by shining light through the developed film. The film represents the *implicate* order, because all the information about the image (the projected or virtual image in three-dimensional space) is contained or hidden within the interference pattern. The image, itself, is the *explicate* order, and represents what is perceived. As Talbot implies in another book, *The Holographic Universe,*[11] both the wave aspect and the particle aspect of an electron, (for example, in a *Double-Slit* experiment) are contained within the deeper, hidden or implicate order; and one or the other of its characteristics is manifested according to how an observer interacts with the implicate order (opening or closing one of the slits).

An interesting fact about holograms is that every section of a hologram that has been cut into many pieces contains all the necessary information to reproduce the image in its entirety, albeit with less resolution than would be obtained with the full film strip.

We see now, according to this quantum interpretation of reality that if the universe itself can be thought of essentially as an infinitely dimensional hologram, then

---

* An optical image from which light rays appear to diverge, as if the image were real.

there would be little difference between mortal consciousness and matter. Like light shining through a holographic film strip, the pattern of human thought would image forth the three-dimensional or explicate order: the universe, itself. *Matter would be the subjective state of consciousness - an image in mind.*

But the true implicate order - the real, hidden order invisible to human perception may not be the creation of *mind or minds,* but of universal *Mind.* Indeed, there are many differing opinions on this subject. On the one hand, it is thought that human consciousness and matter represent different aspects of a material reality - the one mental and the other physical; while another interpretation has it that the present view of reality is a *mask* for the deeper reality of Mind. [12] Brian Josephson, of *Cambridge University*, and a 1973 *Nobel Prize* winner in physics, says that the implicate order as defined by David Bohm, may require that *God,* or *Mind* be included in any discussion of the structure or foundation of the universe. [13] But is this a universe of matter or of Spirit?

HIDDEN ORDER

Presented here are some further illustrations of hidden order that appear at the explicate level to have no order at all:

(a) - As an example of hidden order or information, consider the string of numbers which appear to be random: 426487092, but which is the sum of two non-random strings: 303030303 and 123456789; where the special rule is that each integer in one string is added to the corresponding integer in the other string, and then displayed:

```
303030303
 123456789
426487092
```

The new string appears to be random until we discover the relation or correlation between the original two strings.

The reverse can also be seen to be true: Two random strings can be seen to be correlated, such as: 43659538732 and 21437316510; because when the second string is simply subtracted from the first string we get: 22222222222.

(b) - A further example of hidden order may be seen and appreciated by taking an example of three-dimensional (3-D) objects, and observing how they would appear to a hypothetical two-dimensional being as the objects passed through his two-dimensional (2-D) universe. The reader is referred to an interesting little book, entitled, *Flatland* [14] for a discussion of two-dimensional universes, and of how a two-dimensional being could perceive or infer the existence of higher dimensions.

To a (2-d) person living in a hypothetical universe of width, length and no height (or constant height), the passage of a (3-D) object through his universe would only be discernible by his perceiving the outline or boundary of a cross-section of the object.[*]

---

[*] The observer in the two-dimensional plane would not actually see the cross-section of the three-dimensional object passing through his two-dimensional universe. But he could perceive the degree of roundness or squareness of the object by moving around the object. Only a three-dimensional observer

This cross-section could vary in size, shape and orientation as a function of time as the object moved through, as shown in Figure (17-3). In this figure, a right circular cone (see inset at upper right corner of figure) is oriented so that the long axis of the cone is

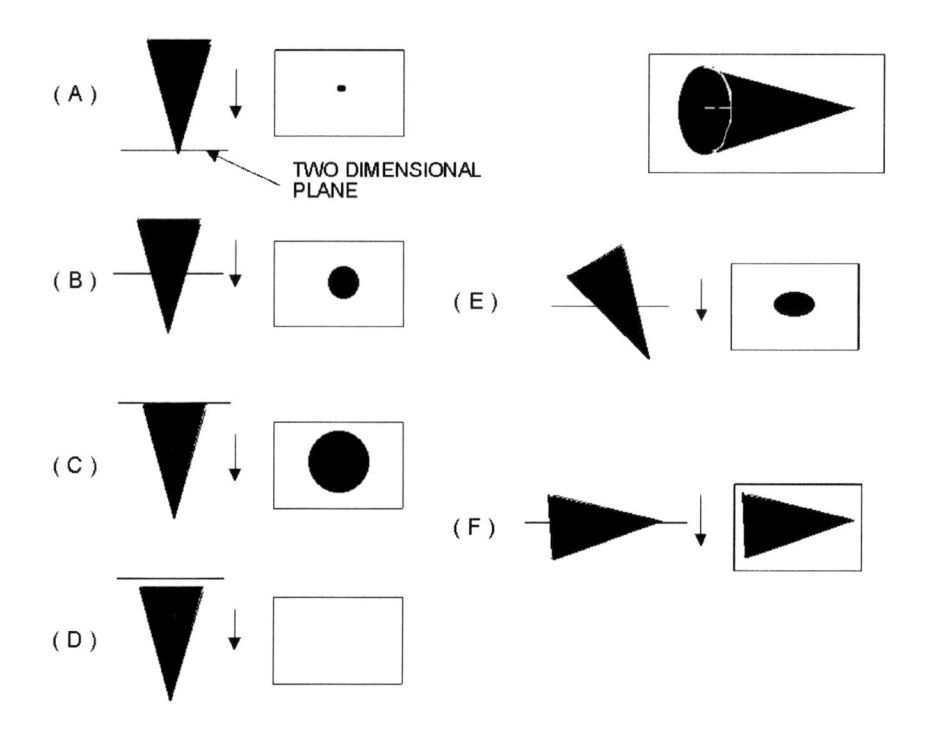

Figure (17-3)

Hidden Order – Passage of Right Circular Cone Through Two-dimensional Plane

perpendicular to a (2-D) plane or universe seen edge-on as a horizontal solid line. If the cone is traversing downward through the plane, the intersection of the cone with the plane will be perceived, first as a tiny dot (Figure (17-3A)), which will grow in size (Figure (17-3 B, C)), and then suddenly disappear (Figure (17-3D)) as the cone exits the plane. Since our hypothetical observer cannot perceive "up" or "down" (he can only perceive length and width in his (2-D) world), it would seem a mystery to him how the object suddenly was perceived as a tiny dot, rapidly grew in size, and then disappear in a wink. But still, the movement or change in size of the object would be somewhat orderly to him.

Note, however, if the cone were tumbling in (3-D) space; as it entered the plane it might be perceived at one instant to be a circle, and at another time to be an ellipse (Figure (17-3E)); and still another moment in time to be a triangle (Figure (17-3F)). The

---

situated above or below the plane could see the cross-sectional shape of the object as it intersected the plane.

movement to the (2-D) observer would now seem to be totally random, but to the (3-D) observer situated outside of the plane, it would seem perfectly predictable according to the laws of physics and geometry governing the movement of the object.

As one final example, consider the passage of the odd- shaped object shown in Figure (17-4).

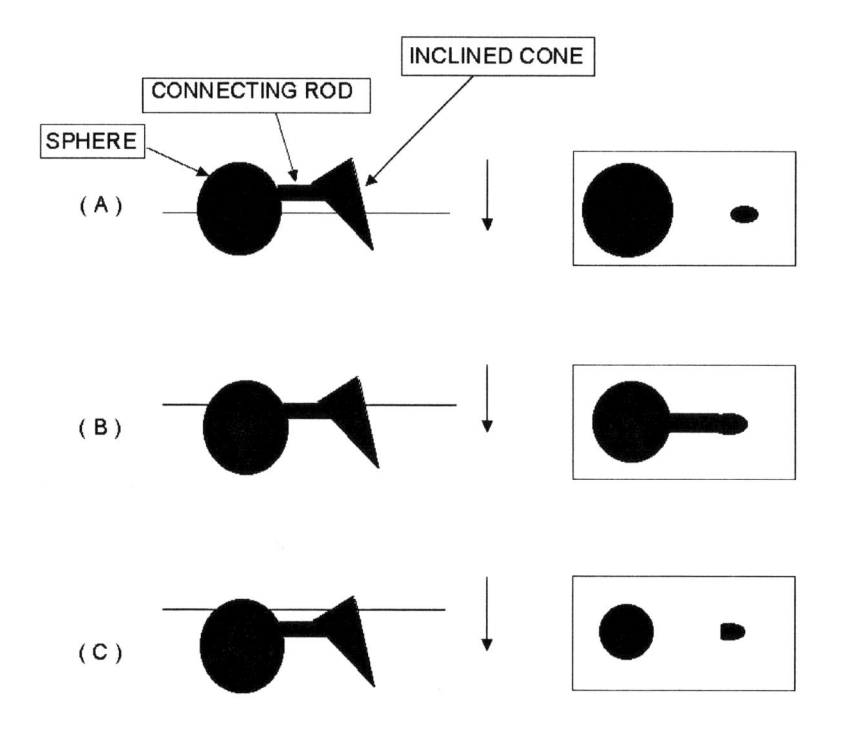

Figure (17-4)

Hidden Order – Passage of Irregularly Shaped Three-dimensional Object Through Two-dimensional Plane

The object resembles somewhat a sphere mounted on a stand with an inclined conical base. As the object passes through the (2-D) plane, a person "living" in the plane first would deduce a circle and an ellipse separated from each other. Part way through the plane the expanding circle would suddenly be connected to the ellipse by a rectangular piece. Near the end of the traversal, (See Figure (17-4C)) one would perceive a circle (by moving around the circle) and only part of the ellipse. There would appear to be no correlation between the changing patterns of the circle, ellipse and the rectangular piece, but as before the (3-D) observer would see a correlation between the images formed in the plane.

The underlying argument to all of this is that if we knew more about the laws governing the quantum particles - if we could perceive the true nature of particles and their relationship with each other - the apparent random, changing and sometimes chaotic nature of the universe would disappear. If we could see beyond the limited three-dimensional (plus one temporal) constraints into the "higher dimensions," we would see a natural order of effect following cause.

The examples just described (three-dimensional objects moving through two-dimensional space) do not necessarily mean to imply that there exists another *dimension* hidden to us that could be used to explain away quantum randomness. To date, quantum entanglement experiments performed in recent years indicate – with a great deal of confidence – that hidden variables are not possible within the structure of quantum mechanics. However, the above illustrations can be useful tools in helping to explain the reasons why some people believe that a quantum wholeness, or quantum entanglement may exist between all objects in the universe. We may yet discover that the "hidden variable" [*] is mind - or many minds collectively holding (consciously, or unconsciously) to a universal belief system which in some as yet unknown way structures our present concept of reality - or rather, clouds our sense of reality. "For now we see through a glass darkly; but then face to face: . . ." [15]

B- NON-LOCAL, NON-CAUSAL OBJECTIVE UNIVERSE (SUPERLUMINAL)

If *Einstein Locality* is violated, and influences can propagate faster than the speed of light, they may be directed by so-called "hidden variables" - forces that as yet are unknown and undetectable by present-day scientific instruments. The world could still be viewed as deterministic with particles retaining objective existence. If hidden variables exist, the *EPR* data taken at the two widely-spaced detector locations may not be random at all, and real, useful data or information may be able to be transferred instantaneously across vast distances. As mentioned before, such propagation of an influence faster than the speed of light is called *superluminal,* and would be in violation of Einstein's *Special Theory of Relativity*, which is founded on theory and experimental data.

The entire formulation of the relativity equations is based on the premise that no influence can travel faster than the speed of light, which is considered a constant of nature. In the *EPR* example, it is not believed by many that any kind of signal is traveling between the two protons at speeds faster than the speed of light, because such occurrences would mean that the *law of causality* would be violated. This would mean that some events in the past would appear to be caused by events in the present! Besides, the influences appear to occur instantaneously, regardless of the distance between the two particles. Recall that measurements taken on the *EPR* experiments indicate that the data accumulated at each detector is random in nature, because we have no way of knowing the orientation of the spin vectors before measurements are made. It is only when the two sets of data are brought together and compared, that we see a correlation. So, any influence, if it occurs at all, cannot apparently transfer any useful message.

C - CONVENTIONAL COPENHAGEN INTERPRETATION

---

[*] But not in the sense that quantum variable theorists use this phrase.

Neils Bohr, Werner Heisneberg, and most physicists of today accept the so-called *Copenhagen Interpretation* of reality. In this theory, electrons exist, but do not possess dynamic attributes (position, momentum) until a measurement has been made. The attributes of an entity such as an electron are related to the type of measurement performed. In other words, the attributes cannot be separated from the apparatus performing the measurement. And these attributes can be changed by changing the measurement apparatus. The properties of the electron are observable only through their interaction with the measurement apparatus. Heisenberg has said, "Atoms are not things." According to Nick Herbert the quantum universe is objective,* but without objects. He also said "An electron's attributes do not belong to the electron itself but are a kind of illusion produced by the electron *plus* the 'entire experimental arrangement' " [16] (emphasis added).

The drawback to this interpretation of reality, says Herbert, is that the macroscopic measuring device is considered to possess a special and definite actuality (a non-quantum entity), while all the other entities made of matter particles are described as "superpositions of possibilities." Otherwise, the measuring device would also become an object of measurement (like all the other entities); then there would be an infinite regression - an endless sequence of measuring devices, measuring each other in turn. Reality, according to this interpretation would consist of a world of material entities described by quantum wave functions, *plus* a world with a physical objectivity (the material measuring device) *not* described by a quantum wave function.

D – NON-OBJECTIVE, OBSERVER-CREATED UNIVERSE

Another possible interpretation of the *EPR* results is that the world is non-objective, and electrons have no dynamic attributes until observed. But in this interpretation, which is a modification of the more conventional *Copenhagen Interpretation*, the observer creates reality, by *freely selecting* the specific attribute he wants to see. John Archibald Wheeler has been a proponent of this interpretation (see the *Delayed-Choice* experiment and the game of *Twenty Questions*). In the *Delayed-Choice* experiment the experimentalist creates not only present quantum entity attributes, but also the attributes they had in the distant past, which according to conventional thinking existed *before* the experiment was conceived or performed. According to this interpretation, the observer can select the *type* of attribute to be seen, but not its *value*. Proponents of this interpretation also believe that the observer does not have to be a conscious being, but could be a measuring or recording system such as a *Polaroid* film strip or a *Geiger* counter. [17]

E - NON-OBJECTIVE, CONSCIOUSNESS-CREATED REALITY

There are some physicists who believe that the particle dynamic attributes (position and momentum) exist only in the mind of the observer, and do not come into

---

* objective: people with the same viewpoint see the same thing.

being until a measurement or macroscopic observation has been made. And that the *final measurement* - the one that really counts - is through the action of *consciousness* (perhaps intelligent, knowing consciousness) in the process of recording or examining data from a quantum event. They say "Consciousness 'creates reality'' by deciding what particular attribute *value* shall materialize." [18] A philosophy that in many ways is similar to the above is called "*monistic idealism."* We shall have occasion to discuss this subject further in a later section.

Proponents of consciousness-created reality include the famous mathematician John von Neumann, Nobel laureate Eugene Wigner and Henry Stapp. In this interpretation, *consciousness lies outside the wave function for physical entities, or rather, cannot be described by any quantum processes*. Von Neumann concluded that the physical world was not objective, but depended on the consciousness of the observer. The measurement *act,* was more important than the measurement apparatus. The difference between *Observer-Created Reality* and *Consciousness-Created Reality*, as explained by Herbert, is that in the consciousness-created interpretation the observer can choose what *value* the entity's attribute will take. And it is a *conscious* observer – not an inanimate measuring device - who decides what kinds off attributes the entity will possess.

SCHRODINGER'S CAT

We shall now examine the famous *Schrodinger's Cat* thought experiment created by the physicist, Eugene Schrodinger. We can ask if quantum effects can be experienced in the *macroscopic* world of trains, planes and automobiles. In 1935, Erwin Schrodinger conceived of a thought experiment where a cat was placed in an opaque box, and the box was closed so no one could observe what was going on inside. Inside the box was a container of radioactive material which was calculated to have a 50% probability of emitting one radioactive particle during a given time period, say, one hour. This is illustrated in Figure (17-5A). The experiment was configured such that if a small amount of radioactive material were emitted, a detector (*Geiger* counter) would trigger a device that would mechanically open a valve on a canister of poisonous gas.* According to the argument behind the thought experiment, if we accept the *Copenhagen Interpretation* of quantum theory, the cat becomes a part of the superposition of quantum wave

---

* For humanitarian purposes, we could substitute for the cat a cockroach. We could call it the *Schrodinger Cockroach Experiment.*

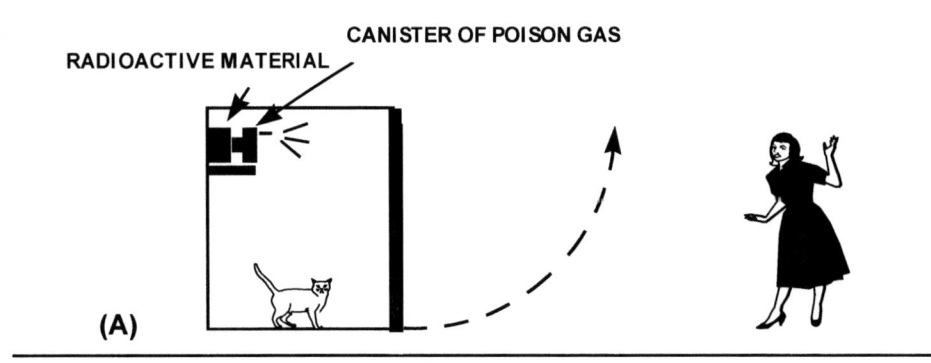

Figure (17-5)

Schrodinger's Cat **Thought Experiment**

functions, similar to that shown in the *Double-Slit* experiment (see Equation (15-6)). The superposition includes the quantum wave function representing the radioisotope particles, the *Geiger* counter *and* the cat. The solution of *Schrodinger's Wave Equation* (a linear equation) [∇] includes one that represents a dead cat, another that represents a live cat, and also solutions that represent a cat that is only 25% alive and 75% dead, 60% alive and 40% dead, and so on. According to the proponents of *Schrodinger's Cat* theory, the cat is both dead and alive, because it is a superposition of dead and alive quantum wave functions, and not until an observer opens the box and peers inside, is the wave function collapsed and a single solution to the wave equation results. *Then*, one sees *either* a dead cat *or* a live cat, and not a mixture. It would therefore appear that not until someone observes - opens the box - does the wave function for *Geiger* counter, radioisotope particles and cat collapse from a function that was multi-valued and representing many different possibilities for the state of the cat, to a single value, representing either a dead or a live cat.

    This comment deserves further examination. In the quantum world (for example, the *Double-Slit* experiment), if we determine the photon's path (or the electron's path) by closing one or the other slit, we will see the result at the downstream detector of the

---

[∇] linear equation: for example, $aX+bY+C=0$, where for the two unknowns X and Y, there are an unlimited number of solutions.

68

arrival of a single integral particle. This is similar to looking inside the room (Figure (17-5A)) and seeing either a live or a dead cat. But if we choose *not* to observe the path (leave both slits open) we will obtain interference: a *superposition of two quantum states*. One state represents the photon going through one slit, and the other represents the photon going through the other slit. The *superposition* of states imply that the single photon somehow went through both slits simultaneously. This is similar to saying that if no one peers into the room, the cat will exist in a superposition of *both* live and dead states. In the macroscopic world in which we live, "we never observe in it anything corresponding to interference between dead and living cats." [19] But recent experiments raise the possibility that macroscopic or near-macroscopic objects can exist for a finite time as a superposition of two states (see Part I, Chapter 18).

Now what if the cat-in-the-box *and* the human observer are *both* inside a closed room, and unseen by another person who is standing outside the closed door leading to the room? This is shown in Figure (17-5B). At the end of the first hour this second observer cannot say whether the cat is dead or alive, even if unseen to him the first observer has opened the box. The container with radioactive material, the canister with the poisonous gas, the cat, and even the first observer, according to the argument, are all included in the superposition of quantum wave functions. It is this *second* observer, who upon opening the door and looking into the room, collapses the wave function. But it is easy to imagine that there could be an unlimited series of observers located in an unlimited number of nested rooms, each larger room enclosing the previous room, in an infinite recursion of events.

It should be noted that the first "observer" might have been a macroscopic inanimate recording device, such as a television camera/recorder. However, some scientists conclude that if the first observer is a conscious, aware being, it is at this point where the wave function irreversibly collapses and reveals some form of objectivity. [*] Einstein was disturbed by this kind of conclusion, and asked at one time "Is the moon really there when no one looks at it?" [20] Does the moon come into being when a mouse looks at it, or does it require an *intelligent* consciousness that is aware of what it is looking at? It has been said by some that the moon exists independent of human observation, but *how* it is perceived depends somewhat on how we in thought create our theories about reality, and about the type of experiments we perform. (See Wheeler's Twenty Questions, Part I, Chapter 15.)

The argument about the correct explanation of *Schrodingers' Cat* thought-experiment from a quantum mechanics viewpoint has never been resolved to everyone's satisfaction, even though it has been many decades since it was first formulated. What concerns physicists and philosophers is that no one can agree as to what constitutes the measurement that reduces or collapses the wave function to a single value. That is, *what constitutes an observation*? Is human consciousness required to collapse the wave function - which originally was a superposition of many states of the cat - to a single state of either a live or a dead cat? Or could possibly a small insect inside the box accomplish the feat? Or, finally, could the collapse be caused by an inanimate and macroscopic-sized recording device, which would bring about an "irreversible act of amplification" resulting

---

[*] It is thought by some scientists and philosophers that the recording made by some inanimate device exists in an ambiguous state until it is observed by an intelligent and knowing consciousness.

in wave function collapse? For that matter, if an inanimate device can bring about the wave function collapse, where is the dividing line between the subatomic or micro world, and the macro world?

** Entropy

Let us leave the cat for a moment and discuss the topic of *entropy* and how it relates to microscopic and macroscopic systems---

> "All the kings horses
> and all the kings men,
> couldn't put Humpty together again. "
> Humpty Dumpty
> (An example of an irreversible act)

Some people maintain that there is a difference between observing an electron in a two-slit experiment and in observing a macroscopic object such as a cat. [21] The argument is that in a macroscopic, closed system, the entropy or the state of disorganization always increases with time; that is, the system becomes more disorganized as time goes by.

Consider the following: The right half of a sealed glass jar, that has a divider plate with a large opening at the top to allow for particles to be transferred from one side to the other, is filled with particles of black pepper. The left half has the same amount of white salt. This represents a condition of low entropy, because the particles are in some degree of organization: all black on one side, and all white on the other side. Now, if the jar is shaken vigorously in many directions for a period of time, there eventually will come a time when there is a fairly uniform distribution of black and white particles on both sides. The system entropy has increased. There is a greater degree of disorganization. If we continue shaking the jar, it is astronomically unlikely (but still possible) that the particles will return to their initial state: black on the left, and white on the right.

If the initial number of particles is drastically reduced to, say, two pepper and two salt particles, as depicted in Figure (17-6), the shaking will result in a variety of possible distributions as shown in the figure, but there is now a measurable and far greater probability that further shaking can return the bottle to its original state of low entropy: all white on the left, and all black on the right. It is left to the reader, if he or she desires, to determine from the different distributions shown in Figure (17-6), the probabilities of returning to the original distribution of all white on the left side and all black on the right side. As the system becomes more complex; that is, more particles in the system, the statistical probability for random distribution (increase in entropy) becomes greater. In fact, for a very large assemblage of particles, such as gas molecules, the process of mixing is considered *irreversible*. Heinz Pagels says in his book *The Cosmic Code*, that the law of entropy increase [the *Second law of Thermodynamics*] is statistical, and is not absolutely certain.[22]

A way of viewing the statistical property of irreversibly increasing entropy is to look at a hand of thirteen playing cards that has been deliberately set up as all spades, and laid out on the table face-up in the sequence beginning with the ace-of-spades and ending with the king-of-spades. If the cards are picked up and again shuffled several times, and then laid out on the table, the distribution will now almost be totally random. Further shuffling will not restore the original sequence, because there are many, many more ways for random distribution to occur than for the single possibility of the numerically-increasing sequence of ace-to-king to occur.

Suppose we zoom in with an imaginary high-power microscope and look at only a few individual particles or molecules of a low-density gas contained within some enclosure, and observe their interactions with each other, and then take a short movie of this scene. Then we ask someone to run the movie. If he or she decided to run the film backwards, we would have no way of knowing if the film were moving forward or backward because the interactions of the particles with each other and with the walls would look the same. There would be insufficient numbers of particles, and insufficient time to observe a *statistical expansion* of the gas according to the irreversible laws. There would be no

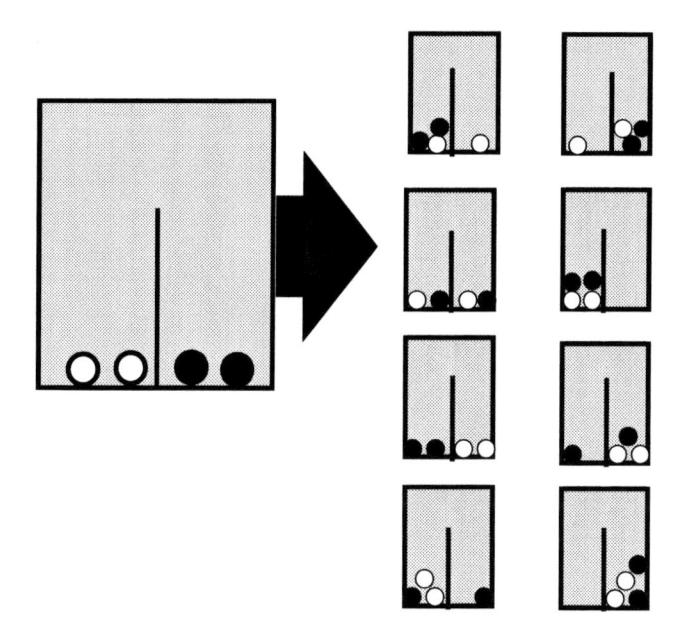

Figure (17-6)

Increased Entropy States

"arrow of time," and the entropy increase would not be observed. As we zoom out, the statistical laws begin to predominate. We begin to lose information about individual particle motion, and now gain information about the average motion of the gas. Macroscopic viewing of average gas motion replaces detailed sub-microscopic viewing of individual molecule motion, and inevitably, entropy increases. The so-called time-reversible scene we observed with a few particles is no longer possible to be observed. [23]

SCHRODINGER'S CAT, REVISITED

Let us now return to the discussion of the cat. According to the view of entropy increase for macroscopic objects, the presence of a television camera recorder in the box, or the cat itself, can be considered as a macroscopic "observer." "An irreversible act of amplification" (from sub-microscopic to macroscopic) has occurred, and "information" has been recorded in some manner, either with the recorder, or by the cat. [24] The result of this information recording is either a dead or alive cat. The process is irreversible, because future observations by conscious humans or unconscious recording machines cannot possibly record the macroscopic volume of gas returning to the canister and the dead cat returning to life.

However, there are always differing opinions! Please read on...

John von Neumann, once expressed the thought that only consciousness could resolve the measurement problem, and, as mentioned earlier, some physicists conclude from this that the manifestation of the universe in which we exist, depends on the *mind of the observer*; [25] Again, the more conventional interpretations of quantum theory claim that the recording of a quantum event by a detector of some kind, such as a *Geiger* counter or a cloud chamber, constitutes an observation. The macroscopic recording device is not considered a part of the quantum wave function, but does collapse the wave function by an "irreversible act of amplification" - that is, a *thermodynamically irreversible process* has occurred. The process is considered irreversible because a recording by a macroscopic object, - a *Geiger* counter or a cat - has been made, and it is unlikely that the astronomically large number of molecules and atoms making up the counter or the cat will move in such a way that the information registered on counter recorder will disappear, or that the dead cat will regain life.[26] But as Nick Herbert points out in his book *Quantum Reality*, it is difficult to understand how a random, irreversible process can exchange uncertainty or ignorance at the quantum level (a quantum wave function containing a multiplicity of potential quantum states) for information at the macroscopic level (a wave function collapses to a single state; and a record is made by an inanimate or non-conscious recording device, *with this information still hidden from a conscious observer*). [27] That is, how can any material object collapse a wave function; how could a material structure gain information or knowledge unless it possessed or shared in some conscious awareness? How can a wave function (a "probability wave") collapse into a particle if the wave function is no more than a mathematical formulation?

See APPENDIX I-17 (p. 158) for a detailed discussion about whether consciousness alone can collapse the wave function, or whether an inanimate observer, such as some kind of recording device, can accomplish that feat. Then return to The *Many-Worlds Interpretation*

F – THE MANY-WORLDS INTERPRETATION (PARALLEL UNIVERSES)

This brings us to a discussion of a bold and radical interpretation of quantum theory: the so-called *Many-Worlds Interpretation (*MW) first formulated by Hugh Everett

III in 1957. I will give an outline of the most basic postulates of the theory. For a more complete discussion I recommend a couple of popular books on the subject: *Parallel Universes* by Fred A. Wolf, [29] and *The Nature of Reality* by Richard Morris. [30]

Everett implied that chance or probability plays no role in quantum theory. For example, according to conventional quantum theory interpretations, the time when a single radioactive atom will decay by emitting a photon or some other particle cannot be determined - it could decay one second from now, one year, or in the next 100,000 years.[31] It is only when we observe a large assemblage of atoms - a container of radioactive gas, for example - that we can predict with extreme accuracy the rate of decay. According to *MW*, there are an *infinite number* of worlds or universes that contain the specific atom. In one world the atom decays in one second; in another *parallel world* the atom decays in 100,000 years, and so on - *each world existing side by side but not connected with any other world.* There are also an infinite number of universes where the decay time for a particular atom is the same as that in another universe, but some other quantum event is different. Each world would be identical to all other worlds except for the decay time for that one atom. *In this theory, the atom decays every instant of time, but each occurrence is in a separate universe.*

Each time a quantum event occurs – such as an atom decaying, an electron "jumping" to a different energy level in an atom, or the encounter of an electron with a screen containing two narrow slits - the universe splits in two, or *bifurcates*. For the *Double-Slit* experiment, the electron goes through the left slit in one universe, *and* travels through the slit on the right in another parallel universe. Moreover, "you," the observer - since your body is also made of atoms - also participates in the splitting, and therefore, "you" exist in each universe observing the atom. But each "you" is unaware of any other "yous" existing in other universes! When we close one slit and observe the electron going through the other slit, this tells us what universe "we" are in. [32] If *MW* is correct, all possible choices exist for the electron, and no element of chance is involved.

Recall the discussion of the *Double-Slit* experiment: one possible conclusion for the phenomena occurring when both slits were open was that a single electron entered the region of the screen containing two slits and passed through both slits as waves, because when a beam of electrons was incident on the screen the resultant pattern on the photographic screen was that of two waves - one from each slit, traveling downstream and interfering with each other. *But what we actually observed for a single electron at a time, was a single impingement on the screen in the shape of a discrete spot. A wave would have registered everywhere on the screen.*

But according to *MW*, as the electron encounters the two-slit screens, *the universe splits in two.* Upon reaching the photographic screen the two universes *again* merge into one.[33] The reason given for the two universes merging into one at the photographic screen, is that this is the only explanation for how a single particle, such as an electron, could go through both slits, interfere with itself (like two waves), and then act like an electron (a discrete particle) at the photographic screen. [34]

Wolf gives an excellent example or metaphor of how *MW* might account for the state of electrons in the vicinity of an atomic nucleus.[35] The following is a brief description of the atom from the standpoint of *MW*. To begin this discussion, recall that quantum theory says that an atom is surrounded by a so-called electron cloud - an infinite number of energy levels - the occupation of any specific energy level by an electron determined by a probability wave function. This degree of uncertainty of the energy of an electron - until it is looked for (with the resultant collapse of the wave function) - permits the electron to exist in a somewhat vague state. It also avoids the problem of a classical atom with electrons occupying precise atomic orbits and energy levels, and radiating energy as they revolve about the atom's nucleus and quickly spiraling in to the center of the atom.

The *Many-Worlds Interpretation* views the electron cloud as consisting of an infinite number of electrons, each with different energy levels, and each occupying a different universe. (See Figure (17-7)). The figure shows an infinite number of filmstrips or viewgraphs placed on top of each other. Each viewgraph represents the position of an electron about an atom, and each viewgraph shows the electron in a separate but parallel universe. Each electron has a defined position, but an undefined energy (these are "position" viewgraphs). If the infinite collection of viewgraphs were placed on top of a lit viewgraph projector, we would have an overlap of an infinite number of universes. We would see an unchanging electron cloud in our particular universe (assuming ideally, that the infinite number of viewgraphs are totally transparent to the light from the viewgraph machine). *Collectively*, these are designated as "energy" viewgraphs, because the cloud is stable and we no longer have any knowledge about electron positions. If instead we had placed only one "position" viewgraph at a time on top of the machine, and then rapidly removed it and replaced it with another one, and so on, the electron would appear in our universe as *jumping instantaneously* from one energy level to the next. Now, if we would selectively choose viewgraphs according to a prescribed set of rules or instructions, and overlap only these on top of the projector - what would we expect to see? We would see a particular cloud pattern representing a particular energy state of the atom, as illustrated in Figure (17-7B). Selecting a different set of viewgraphs can also show other energy states or electron clouds.

Now, lastly, overlap all the infinite sets of energy state viewgraph packages and set them on top of the viewgraph machine, as in Figure (17-7C). According to Wolf, you will not see an overlap of clouds, but an infinite number of parallel universes where each atom has a different but stable energy in each universe, resulting in our seeing a single spot representing the position of the electron. But that spot will move, or "quantum jump" as time moves on.

G - MODIFICATION OF MW INTERPRETATIONS: Many Points of View

Some scientists propose, what is to me, a welcome modification of *MW*. These people do not like the idea, for example, in the *Double-Slit* experiment, when the photon or electron enters the region of the slit that the universe splits in two - where in one universe (where you dwell) the particle goes through the left slit and in another parallel universe (also containing "you") the particle goes through the right slit. Then upon observation the two universes come together at the screen, and we see a flash of light, indicating the striking of the screen by one of the particles. Although we see the result of particles hitting the screen one at a time, it is as if the one particle split into two (one in each parallel universe), and the resultant two particles then exited the two slits and interfered with each other causing a random, but gradual build-up of an interference pattern.

"But how could there be more than one 'you' or 'me'," you ask? Rather, some scientists would propose that there really is only one universe, but that there are "*many points of view*" about the universe, "*. . . all of which are simultaneously associated with one and the same observer.*" [36]

H - MODIFICATION OF MW INTERPRETATIONS: Consciousness Makes the Choice

Still other scientists believe that *consciousness or mind, itself, is the hidden variable,* [37] *and that through our consciousness we make the choice ". . . so that the branch we observed was the only branch that was."* [38] How do we make the choice? And are we - or can we - become aware of our decision-making abilities, and thus have some control over the outcome of phenomena occurring in the universe?

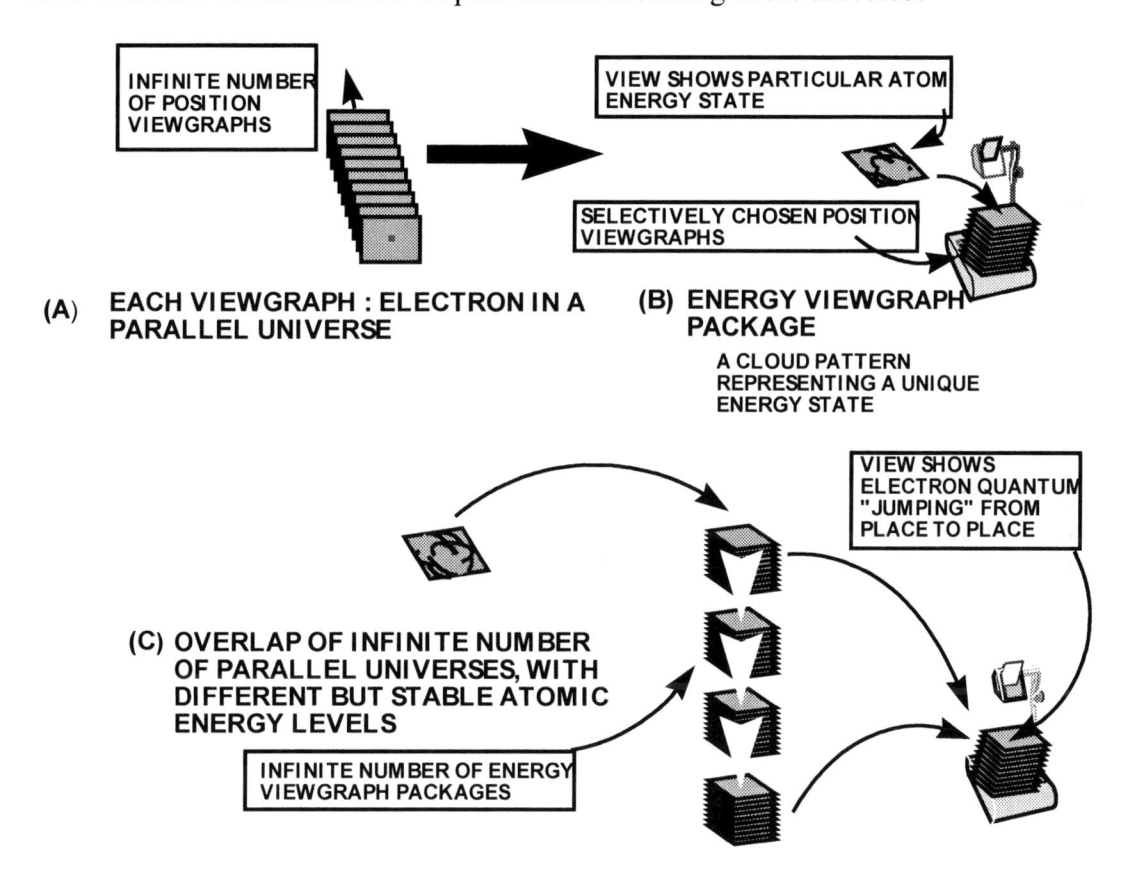

Figure (17-7)

The Many Worlds Interpretation of the Quantum Universe

Our previous discussions about quantum wholeness and holographic consciousness come to mind. The concept of parallel universes, or of different points of view about the one universe, is similar to the theory of holographic images in consciousness, that is, the mind of the observer plays a central role in determining how the universe is perceived. *The observer and the observed are one.* There may not be an infinite number of physical universes - only an infinite number of "mutually exclusive " viewpoints or perceptions, and all these viewpoints *existing simultaneously in consciousness.* [39]

In Fred Wolf's viewpoint, it may be that the unique perception of what we call the universe that we entertain in consciousness determines what the so-called senses perceive externally. And this may be strongly dependent on what we and the rest of the world *mutually agree upon as the present physical paradigm for how the universe is structured, and how it functions.*

Recalling the Wheeler game of *Twenty Questions*: It took the consensus of all of the members of the party to arrive at the same answer. Thus, if would seem that what we see depends to some degree on what is collectively agreed upon as the *paradigm* of physical reality. *What we see depends upon what our senses have "educated" us into accepting as certain physical rules and "facts". Wolf takes a "quantum leap" in reasoning when he says that because of this collective agreement or observations, the past - or the record of the past - can be recreated or restructured provided, . . .enough minds come to agreement."* [40]

Recall in the *Delayed - Choice* experiment our decision, as whether to put in the mirror at the last instant, appeared to alter the past history of the photon. On a larger scale, the collective consciousness or consent of the majority may well shape our perception of the past, present and the future. Although we may have believed that the past has structured the present, it may well be that our conscious or unconscious acceptance of the past is what influences the present.

CHAPTER 18

QUANTUM SUPERPOSITION EXPERIMENTS AND EXPERIMENTAL RESULTS
(See also ADDENDUM, p. 342 for additional results)

Observing a particle, which is in a superposition of several states at the same time, collapses its wave function, and forces the particle into one of the states in the superposition. As a result of the observation some of the particle information content is lost.

THE *SQUID*

In recent years, researchers have been looking into the possibility of constructing so-called "quantum particles," whose dimensions are on the order of macroscopic recording devices such as cats, television recorders and human beings. [1] [2] Scientists at various laboratories have constructed devices called *SQUIDs* (*Super-conducting Quantum Interference Devices*). Figure (18-1) is a simplified sketch of a representative device developed by a *University of Sussex* team of scientists in 1983.

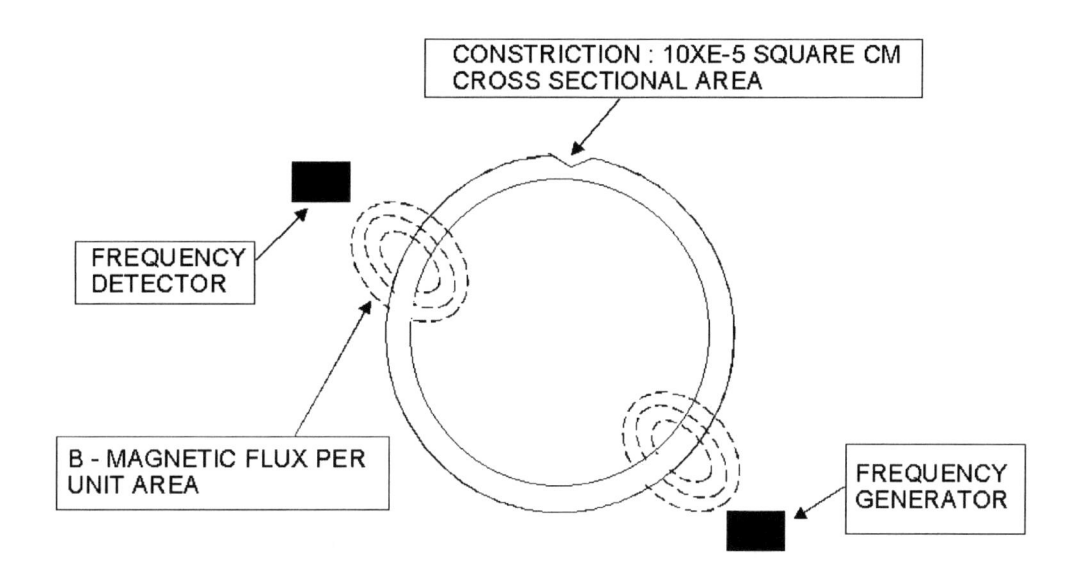

Figure (18-1)

Simplified Schematic of *Super-conducting Quantum Interference Device (SQUID)*

A superconducting ring of material, such as niobium, about one-half centimeter across is designed with a constriction * at one point along the ring, the cross-sectional area of which is about $1\times10^{-15}cm^2$.[3] Since the ring is made of superconducting material, any electrical current generated in the ring will continue indefinitely if the ring temperature is kept close to absolute zero, without the need of an external source of electrical potential such as a battery. (In recent years experiments have been made with superconductors at somewhat higher temperatures).

The circulating current generates a magnetic field, and the product of the component of the field perpendicular to the ring plane and the area of the ring, is called the magnetic flux. The magnetic flux arises from the motion of a huge assemblage of electrons (about 10^{23}), *so the flux, itself can be considered as a macroscopic quantity.* Because of the constriction of the ring the flux can change from one value to another; in fact, there is good evidence that it does not have a definite value but can be represented by a standing wave. This wave, representing the entire assemblage of electrons (essentially a quantum particle whose size is one-half centimeter), can be thought of as a quantum wave for estimating the probabilities of occurrence of the values of the quantum particle flux (the observable). When an external electromagnetic field is applied at one side of the ring (Figure (18-1)), the wave function representing the ring flux (the observable) is changed, and a quantum transition is seen to occur for the entire ring. It should be stressed that the *entire* ring makes the transition simultaneously, not first one side and later the other side.

Later SQUID configurations include those designed by Jonathan Friedman, James Lukens and co-workers at *State University of New York at Stony Brook*, and by Casper ban der Wal, Johan Mooij and co-workers at *Delft University of Technology* in the Netherlands. A current in a super-conducting loop is acted upon by an applied magnetic field. Because of quantum effects, only certain values of magnetic flux (magnetic field per unit area) can pass through a super-conducting loop. If the applied field lies between allowed values, an electric current will flow in the loop creating the correct additional field to bring the total magnetic flux to an allowed value. If the applied flux is midway between two allowed values, the *SQUID* then has equal capacity of producing a clockwise or counterclockwise current. As an article in *Scientific American* [4] says,

"…conditions are most favorable for producing a superposition of these two alternatives." The current values, measured in micro-amperes, traveling around a 140 micron-square loop was truly macroscopic. *All* the electrons flowed "en masse" both ways *simultaneously* around the loop, and they represented the two states of Schrodinger's cats- dead and alive!

As stated by quantum physics, all events are defined by a probability of occurrence, while in *classical* physics an event either happens or it doesn't. It is never

---

* In other designs a thin slice of insulating material (a *Josephson junction*) is used to separate the two ends of the ring from connecting directly with each other.

undefined or uncertain. The state of a macroscopic object, such as an, automobile is usually given by classical physics. It either exists somewhere or it doesn't. [*]

EXPERIMENTAL RESULTS FOR NON-MACROSCOPIC SYSTEMS

BERYLLIUM ATOM

In May, 1996 physicists David Wineland and Chris Monroe at the *National Institute of Standards* in Bolder, Colorado, succeeded in causing a beryllium atom to exist simultaneously in two different states (a "spin-up," and a "spin-down" energy state), until actually measured. They were able to separate both versions of the atom by 80 billionths of a meter, a distance about ten times larger than the original atom. [5] Many quantum physicists would not agree that the particle occupied two locations at the same time. Probably more accurately, the atom, itself, is not actually physically "observed" in two places at once, but according to Wineland, we can say "the well-separated wave packet which describes the different locations of the particle can sense the environment (e.g., a local magnetic field) at these locations simultaneously." [6] Also, Wineland's colleague Chris Monroe, has commented that the fact that an interference pattern was observed is an indication that the atom was not exclusively in one place.

SODIUM ATOM

About a year earlier in 1995, David Pritchard and his MIT colleagues sent a sodium atom through an interferometer, which, like the *Double-Slit* experiment with photons discussed previously, apparently caused the particle to take two paths through the device with the creation downstream of an interference pattern. Then, by directing a laser beam at one of the two paths (an attempt to determine which path the sodium atom took), the interference pattern disappeared; that is, the quantum superposition or coherence disappeared. It would appear that the macroscopic measurement caused the loss of coherence, but as Philip Yam says in his article (*Scientific American*, "Bringing Schrodinger's Cat to Life," June, 1997 [7]), the coherence could be "recovered …by changing the separation between the paths by some quarter multiple of the laser photon's wavelength." That is, the coherence was not really lost. As Pritchard says, "The atom becomes entangled with a larger system."

THE THREE PHOTON STATE

As reported in the March, 2000 issue of *Physics World* (See also, J. W. Pan, *et al. Nature*, 2000), [8] Anton Zeilinger and colleagues at *Vienna*, *Oxford* and *Munich* universities have performed an experiment with a three-photon state. In this experiment, quantum mechanics (non-local theory) gives completely different predictions than local realistic theories for any *single* measurement. That is, past two-photon experiments relied

---

[*] But according to quantum mechanics there is a probability, although astronomically small, that a macroscopic object such as an automobile, can pass through a mountain, rather than traveling over it!!

on a statistical averaging of many measurements. The recent three-photon measurements confirm the predictions of quantum theory: that individual photons in the experiment possess no real,- i.e., no individual or local - properties until these properties are measured.

Recent results of *SQUID*-type efforts on quantum effects in the macroscopic realm have been reported in the technical literature confirming the claim that strong evidence has been obtained which "*suggest that the quantum effect; e.g., quantized energy levels and tunneling* [▽]*, commonly observed in microscopic systems can also be seen in macroscopic variables describing the collective motion of a large number of particles.*" [9]

DECOHERENCE HISTORIES

But there appears to be a disagreement among some physicists as to the nature of the quantum-classical boundary. The supporters of the so-called *Decoherence Histories* interpretation of quantum events believe that quantum phenomenon interpretations for experiments like the *SQUID* should not be forced to include the intervention of a conscious observer to explain experimental results. This explanation [10] for the measurement problem states that decoherence (collapse of the wave function) arises through interaction of the quantum system being measured with the measurement apparatus itself, and the external environment. That is, the collapse of the wave function occurs naturally through the interaction of the particle with the environment.[*] These physicists say that unless extreme precautions are taken during any laboratory experiment, macroscopic objects can never be adequately isolated from their environment – an environment which is constantly fluctuating in an irregular manner. The wave function for a macroscopic object, such as a cat, itself consisting of atoms, will collapse in a very short time due to the movement back and forth of its atoms. The motion of the atoms is the "environment."

How can the system be isolated so that quantum coherence can be maintained? Greenstein and Zajonc *(The Quantum Challenge)* comment on this at length. [11] A brief statement is given below:

The authors say, "A truly macroscopic phenomenon requires that we create a large-scale system that is described by *its own wave function as a whole* and that evolves according *to its own Schrodinger equation.*" If the entire assemblage of atoms within a macroscopic object is to be described by a *single* wave function, then what has been called a "macroscopic variable" must be introduced. Several conditions must be met for the macroscopic variable to be considered a quantum variable. The first condition is that the temperature must be sufficiently low so that thermal motion of the atoms is negligible. The second condition is that the macroscopic variable must be decoupled or insulated from the random motion of the atoms comprising the macroscopic object. (The center of mass of a macroscopic object can be considered a single macroscopic variable.)

[▽] Quantum tunneling: the passage from one state to another of a microscopic system by a path that is classically forbidden.

[*] In quantum interference experiments quantum coherent superposition can be observed only if no information, even in principle, can be obtained about which path the interfering particle has taken.

And the third condition is that the potential energy of the system must be kept very low so that the motion of the macroscopic variable is influenced only by *microscopic* energies.

ENVIRONMENTAL EFFECTS

In December, 1996, Michel Brune, Serge Haroche, Jean-Michel Raimond, and their colleagues at the *Ecole Normale Superieure* in Paris were able to transfer a superimposed state of an atom $^\nabla$ to its resident electromagnetic field, thereby putting the field into a superposition of two different phase or vibrational states. [12] When the team introduced another Ryberg atom to the test cavity, the electromagnetic field transferred the phase information to the atom. By varying the time interval between the injection of the two atoms and also by enlarging the field with the introduction of more photons, the team could observe how the collapse of the E-field superposition varied with time and size.

`The experimental results made it clear to Wojciech Zurek, *Los Alamos National Laboratory*, that the environment, and not consciousness, determined what quantum possibilities become observed in the real world. As Zurek says, "The system decoheres because the system leaks information." [13] Some of the photons in the cavity leak out and reveal the state of the remaining photons. But if the environment in which the experiment is run (a hard vacuum that nevertheless contains cosmic dust and low-energy protons left over from the *Big Bang*) interacts with the experimental system, why does not the interaction occur at times other than during the measurement process?

Not everyone agrees with Zurek's interpretation. Anthony Leggert, *University of Illinois*, observes that in real life, the macroscopic outcomes are definite, but the decoherence model fails to select a particular outcome. [14] But Zurek claims that the environment discards only the unrealistic states while retaining "only those states that can withstand the scrutiny of the environment, and thus might be classical." It is the environment that "selects" the allowed states, and we will not be allowed to predict which state will become real.

In an *EPR* experiment, for example, some proponents of the decoherence model say that calculations of the probabilities of the spin orientations of two protons can be made as a function of what choice has been made for the experimental configuration at one of the detectors. While these calculations will differ from classical calculations, they need no non-local explanations for the experimental results. It is, if we have a mathematical look-up table that gives calculated probabilities for all possible spin orientations as a function of detector configurations. According to this theory, only a certain set of allowed possibilities for wave function collapse exists. But as J. L. Anderson argues in *Physics Today*, "...no one has ever given the rules for obtaining the set of projection operators needed to define the mutually exclusive alternate histories" [15] (for example, two-particle spin orientations that never occur).

$^\nabla$ Rydberg atom: an atom in a high energy state where the outer electron orbit is several thousand times larger than normal.

The reader is encouraged to read these and other articles [16] [17] only if he/she has appreciable technical understanding of physics and of the *SQUID* operation.

Some feel the decoherence model - like some other proposed models - is somewhat ad hoc. It offers an explanation for collapse of the quantum superposition states, but fails to say how the specific results are obtained.

Another interpretation worthy of note is the *GRW* developed by Gian Carlo Ghirardi, (*University of Trieste*), Alberto Rimini, (*University of Pavia*), and Tullio Weber, (*University of Trieste*). The theory briefly says that the wave function of a particle, spreading out over time, can be localized by "something" in the background (or that lurks in space). A macroscopic cat, containing an astronomical number of quantum particles, has a far greater chance of being hit [*] than a single particle does. As Philip Yam reports in his article, "The cat [Schrodinger] never really has a chance to enter any kind of superposition." There is therefore no need for decoherence because the single macroscopic state of the cat "results from spontaneous microscopic collapses." [18]

But Roger Penrose does not believe that environmental decoherence alone can "unsuperpose" Schrodinger's cat. Even though the environment and the state of the cat may become entangled, he says that it does not seem to make any practical difference which reduction method we choose to follow. "But without *some* scheme for reduction...the cat's state would simply remain as a superposition." [19]

HOW LARGE CAN SCHRODINGER'S CAT BECOME?

> "Chemical systems far from equilibrium may ... lead to coherent wave
> behavior... some of the properties of quantum mechanics discovered
> on the microscopic level now appear on the macroscopic scale."
> Prigogine and Stengers
> *Order Out of Chaos*

Quantum experiments performed to date have indicated that the decoherence time becomes infinitesimally small for measurements involving a macroscopic apparatus, but in theory a macroscopic object such as a cat would exist very briefly as a superposition of states. Also, no one is certain how far experiments can go before coherence is lost. But as Serge Haroche points out in a recent article in *Physics Today* that in the quantum experiments performed, "Quantum mechanics predicts a statistical prediction of outcomes over many repetitions of the experiments.....Even when quantum coherence has vanished, we still have ... two possible outcomes. The agency of choice remains mysterious." [20] All of which makes one wonder about what constitutes the real nature of things if sub-atomic particles and near-macroscopic particles (foundational particles for physical reality) have such a blurred existence - an existence which can be subject to measurement choices.

---

[*] for a cat, at least once every 100 picoseconds

The argument continues as to whether it is necessary to collapse the wave function of a macroscopic object - or what is necessary in order to do so. None of the proposed models completely resolves the measurement problem. Zurek admits that the decoherence model does not explain how a conscious mind views an outcome. He says, "Its not clear if you have the right to expect the answer to all questions, *at least until we develop a better understanding of how brain and mind are related.*" [21] (emphasis added.) It is also my conclusion that **no physical model to explain physical phenomena is complete until consciousness is introduced into the appropriate equations.**

Larry Dossey says in his book *Space, Time, and Medicine,* "The interrelation of human consciousness and the observed world is . . . obvious in Bell's theorem; " as he maintains that, ". . .conscious decision making . . . " has determined the outcome of the experiments (experiments related to *EPR*). [22]

As discussed earlier under *EPR*, according to quantum theory the correlation between the two particles' positions and momenta immediately after the reaction continues to exist as the particles move away from each other, but once a measurement has been made on one particle, and its momentum has been affected to some unknown degree, this very act of measurement will also affect the momentum of particle # 2, so that the net momentum remains the same (in this instance, zero). This has been called *quantum entanglement,* the result of the creation of a two-proton pair due to the atomic reaction. [23] The created proton pair is called a *singlet state.*

Now I believe we can safely rule out superluminal transfer of information from one detector station to the other. We also have discovered through experiments like *SQUID* that the *Decoherence Histories* model for wave function collapse (collapse of the wave function by the detector, plus environment "measurement") is inadequate to explain why the value of the magnetic flux observable remains indeterminate.

I maintain that consciousness is *non-local,* and therefore exists independently of space-time. Actually non-locality implies that there is a unity [*] of all things, and that space-time may be no more than a construct of mortal consciousness. The individual intent of the conscious experimenter, or experimenters, determines which physical properties will be measured, and which physical properties will possess objective reality. That is, experimental results suggest that quantum "fuzziness" or indefiniteness can be destroyed only by the *intent* of a conscious observer or observers. Does the conscious observer, that is, the observer who collapses the wave function, have any real choice in determining the *value* of the measured observable, or is the outcome random rather than causal? We will discuss this and more in Part II of the book.

Returning to the *SQUID* experiment discussed several pages back (Figure (18-1)), John Gribbon speculates in his book *In Search of Schrodinger's Cat* [24] that if a sensitive detector were placed at one side of the ring, it could, if designed correctly, measure the change in quantum state (flux) when the ring was excited by the external field at the other side of the ring. If this were shown to be possible it would seemingly violate the relativity constraint that *no information can be transferred faster than the speed of light.* Although the practical aspects of developing such a device to send signals over great distances would seem insurmountable. Still, if this could be achieved on a small scale it

---

[*] By this is meant a unity and spiritual communion with all beings, but still maintaining unique spiritual identities as individual ideas of the universal Mind that is God.

would, along with other wonders of quantum theory, profoundly affect our way of viewing the universe. It should be emphasized, however, that Gribbon's ideas at the time of this writing are not generally accepted by many in the physics community.

EXPERIMENTAL RESULTS FOR MACROSCOPIC SYSTEMS

BEAM OF CARBON-60 MOLECULES

In recent experiments physicists have observed wave-like behavior in a beam of carbon-60 molecules, showing that these molecules can exhibit wave as well as particle properties (See *Nature,* 14 Oct., 1999, "*Wave-Particle Duality of C_{60} Molecules,*" by Markus Arndt, et al). [25] These particles are an order of magnitude larger than any other particles for which quantum interference effects have been seen, but are still about fifteen orders of magnitude below what would be considered as macroscopic particles.

Superconductivity experiments (such as *SQUID*) also claim to demonstrate quantum superposition of objects that possess close to macroscopic numbers of degrees of freedom, but not everyone agrees with the experimental results. Alastair Rae (See *"Waves, Particles and Fullerenes", Nature,* 14 Oct., 1999) [26] says that the C_{60} experimental results are *"quite unambiguous"* (the C_{60} molecule interferes only with itself), and if the experiment could be extended into the truly macroscopic regime, " *the consequences would be profound.*" Markus Arndt and his colleagues expect that experiments similar to their work might be extended to study quantum interference of clusters of larger macromolecules such as virus. J. F. Clauser has calculated that by using newly-developed free-standing vacuum-slit gratings with slit spacings as small as $.03 \mu m$, that de Broglie wave interferometry (recall that $\lambda = h/mv$) with very massive particles (containing some 10^8 nucleons), such as very small rocks or small live viruses, may be realized in the near future (see *Experimental Metaphysics*, by J.F. Clauser, et al, p. 1-11, *Kluwer Academic*, Dordredcht, 1997). [27] He also comments that these kinds of interferometry experiments can levy severe constraints for several theories (decoherence) recently proposed to explain wave-function collapse.

If future experiments being planned at the near-macroscopic, or possibly macroscopic level can maintain the system as isolated from the environment (preventing decoherence or dissipative coupling between the system and the environment), then we may be forced to conclude that the macroscopic world does not possess a definite macroscopic state until it is observed (see *"Quantum Theory: Weird and Wonderful,"* by Tony Leggett, *Physics World*, December, 1999). [28]

TRILLION ATOM ENTANGLEMENT

In an article which appeared in *Nature* ("Atoms Tangle", 27 September, 2001),[29] Brian Julsgaard and associates reported on the successful laboratory entanglement of two clouds of cesium atoms, each considered a macroscopic or system. Each cloud contained about one trillion atoms. The clouds were held in separated jars and placed in a very uniform magnetic field. Quantum entanglement, which lasted for over one-half millisecond, occurred as the result of a laser pulse. A second laser pulse revealed a loose entanglement of the two macroscopic clouds. According to *Nature,* the laser light performed "… a non-local Bell measurement on the collective spin of the samples." One cloud had slightly more atoms in "spin-up" state, while the other cloud had slightly more atoms in the "spin-down" state.

SUPERCONDUCTING FLUX CUBIT

It has been shown that under certain conditions macroscopic-sized solid state devices can behave as single quantum particles. The question then becomes, can a macroscopic object that consists of a superconducting loop with one or more Josephson tunnel junctions exist as a superposition of two macroscopically distinct quantum states? The states would be represented by clockwise and anti-clockwise super currents consisting of "cooper pairs" of electrons (electrons that in some manner are coupled together by an attractive force). (These are considered to be the current carriers in a superconductor.) By a suitable excitation process billions of the pairs in one state – originally all moving or circulating in one direction - can be made to be in a state…" where all pairs move oppositely…and oscillate coherently between these two states." [30] As reported in *Nature*, (21 March, 2003, "Coherent Quantum Dynamics of a Superconducting Flux Qubit."), I. Chiorescu and colleagues report on their experiment that resulted in observations of so-called "Rabi" oscillations in a superconducting magnetic flux "qubit." The qubit in this case is a three –Josephson junction in a superconducting loop threaded by an externally applied magnetic flux measured in webers (a magnetic field measured in webers/square meter, times the projected area in meters).[31] The experimental set-up made it possible to induce hundreds of coherent oscillations in the flux qubit. As John Clarke reports in his article "Flux Qubit Completed the Hat Trick" (*Nature,* 21 March, 2003), a pulse of microwaves of a certain frequency causes the "qubit to oscillate coherently between the two states." [32] And he says that the flux generated in a *SQUID* device (included in the experimental set-up) depends on what state the qubit is in. Clarke also observes that as a result of this experiment and other planned experiments, quantum mechanical tests versus "macroscopic realism" may be in the near future. He believes that it would be "fascinating" to observe *EPR* non-local effects with superconducting circuits.

MACROSCOPIC EFFECTS IN ASTRONOMY – QUANTIZATION AT SUPER-MACROSCOPIC LEVELS?

Recently, two British astronomers completed a survey and study of the "redshift"[*] of over two-hundred spiral galaxies spread across the sky to the edge of the *Local Supercluster*, and out to a distance of about one hundred million light-years. What they discovered after analyzing the data was amazing. The galaxy redshifts fall in clusters or packets, with a recessional velocity difference between packets of *37.5 km/sec.* To date, no one has any satisfactory explanation as to why the redshift appears to be *quantized.* Mike Disney, a galaxy specialist at the *University of Wales at Cardiff*, said if this phenomenon shows up in larger sampling of galaxy redshifts, "Standard cosmology might be turned on its ear." [33]

The jury, however is still out on this subject, as on-going observations by several astronomical observatories so far have failed to substantiate the British observer's claims.

---

[*] A redshift is a change in the spectrum of light received from a galaxy receding from the earth. As a result of the Big Bang, the universe is expanding in every direction, and the light from the galaxy is stretched out to longer - or redder - wavelengths observed from the earth. The greater the distance, the faster the velocity of recession, and the more the light from the galaxy is shifted toward the red end of the spectrum.

APPENDIX I-8

PARTICLE-WAVE DUALITY OF MATTER

Some years after the Bohr model of the atom was developed, a Frenchman by the name of Louis de Broglie, proposed that not only did light possess a wave-particle duality, but that one of the basic units of matter itself; that is, the electron, should under certain conditions, exhibit wave-like characteristics. Based on the work of Einstein, who determined that the energy and momentum of a light quantum (the photon) were $E = h\nu,\, and\, P = h/\lambda$, respectively, de Broglie determined that energy (E) and momentum (P) represent characteristics of the particle aspects of light; while the wave aspects of light are represented by the frequency (ν), and the wavelength (λ). De Broglie reasoned that since no one could decide if light were intrinsically a particle or a wave, then basic particles of matter could also sometimes be thought of as waves.

Bohr had discovered in 1913 that contrary to classical theory, electrons in orbit around hydrogen atoms occupied only those orbits in which the angular momentum and the total electron energy were constant, or quantized [*] de Broglie believed that if the electron, itself - and not simply its orbital characteristics - were considered to be related to the standing wave, then the quantization of the energy states in the atom would correspond to an electron wave equivalent to the wavelength or frequency of the standing wave.

More specifically, the electron angular momentum might be related to the standing wavelength in some manner. Since the wavelength of light in terms of momentum is given by $\lambda = h/P$, de Broglie substituted in the momentum of a matter particle $(P = mv)$ giving the result:

$$\lambda = h/mv \qquad (8\text{-}1)$$

That is, the matter wavelength is *Planck's* constant divided by the particle momentum. When this value is entered into Equation (7-1), and rearranged, we find:

$$mvr = nh/2\lambda = n\hbar, \text{ where } \hbar = h/2\pi \quad \text{(The angular momentum)} \qquad (8\text{-}2)$$

That is, the electron angular momentum (mvr) appeared to be related to the standing wave principal quantum number n, by the product of $n \times h/2\pi$, where h = Planck's constant. The condition, therefore for the existence of stationary electron energy states or orbits, is that the angular momentum of the electron be some multiple of Equation (8-2): $h/2\pi ... h/\pi ... 3h/2\pi ....$ and this was revealed by discovering that the electron matter

---

[*] angular momentum: the momentum characteristics of a rotating object = mass x orbital velocity x radial distance from object to center of rotation.

wavelength was $\lambda = h/mv$. It was shown by physicists that the total energy (kinetic + electrostatic potential) for an electron in an orbit whose angular momentum was characterized by the principle quantum number (where $mvr = n\lambda/2\pi$), could be determined by:

$$E_n = -ke^2/2n^2 r_1 = -E_1/n^2 \tag{8-3}$$

where k is a constant, e is the charge on the electron, r_1 is the radius of the first Bohr orbit - the smallest permitted radius - and $E_1 = -13.58 ev$ is the energy of the electron in this lowest, or *ground* state, and $= -ke^2/2r_1$. The negative sign in front of the energy term means that when energy is added to the atom the electron will "jump" to a new radius, and a smaller value of negative energy. Energy in the form of a photon is released when an electron transitions from a higher energy state ($n = 2$, Figure (8-1)) to a lower energy state ($n = 1$). The photon energy is $hv = E_2 - E_1$.

As the quantum number *n*, approached infinity the electron energy will approach zero; that is, the electron will be at rest with respect to the proton nucleus, and will be located an infinite distance away. The atom is said to be *ionized,* as the electron is no longer bound to the atom. Observe also as n increases in value the difference between adjacent electron levels becomes smaller and approaches zero as n approaches infinity (Figure (8-1).

ELECTRON ORBIT TRANSFER FOR BOHR MODEL OF HYDROGEN ATOM

ENERGY LEVEL DIAGRAM FOR A HYDROGEN ATOM

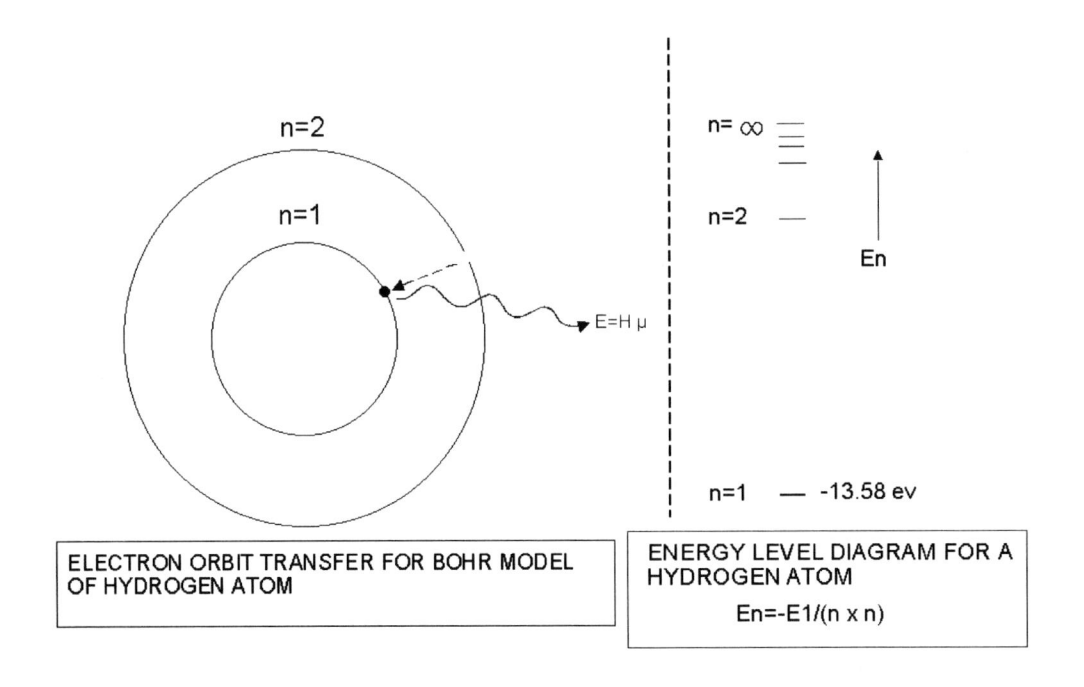

En=-E1/(n x n)

Figure (8–1)

Bohr Model for Hydrogen Atom

It should be noted that according to theory the electron "jumps" instantaneously from one orbit to the next allowed orbit when a quantum of energy in the form of a photon has either been absorbed or emitted. One might naturally ask how a particle of matter could instantaneously cross space, thereby not existing at any time between the two orbits! This challenges our concept of physical reality.

Thus it was seen that by considering the wave aspects of a material particle, it was possible to explain by a new model why an electron would remain in orbit about a proton. If the electron were thought of as a wave, whose wavelength fit into a circular orbit of a given radius, r, then that orbit was stable with given angular momentum and energy. In order for an electron to change orbits (say, to a lower orbit), it would have to emit a photon or quantum of energy equal to the difference in orbital energies. Thus, the electron could occupy only discrete, quantized energy levels.

The wave characteristics of electrons was later verified by irradiating a metal foil with a beam of energetic electrons (150 ev) and observing a diffraction pattern similar to that of *X*-ray light ($\lambda = 1A^0$) passing through a double slit. These and other experiments confirmed that material particles also could exhibit wave-like characteristics. The wavelength of a *macroscopic* object, such as a gram of some material substance, moving at a speed of 1/10 meter/second, is 6.62×10^{-30} meters!

Return to Chapter 9 (p. 19)

APPENDIX I-10

PROBABILITY

COIN TOSS

When a coin is tossed into the air, if it is evenly balanced, the probability, chance, or odds are that 50% of the time it will land heads-up and 50% of the time it will land with the tail- side up; that is, if the coin is tossed a large number of times.

The probability that a head will show is given by:

$$P_h = N_h/N_{tot} \tag{10-1}$$

where N_h, is the number of heads appearing in N_{tot} total tosses; $N_{tot} = N_h + N_t$, and N_t is the number of tails appearing in the same number of tosses. We do not know for certain which side of the coin will appear *up* for any given toss. Most of us know from experience that the first ten tosses might yield six heads and four tails, eight tails and two heads, or even ten of either all heads or all tails, but in the long run, a great number of tosses will show the ratio of heads to total tosses - or the ratio of tails to total tosses - approaching nearer and nearer to the value of 0.5.

Figure (10-1) shows probability examples for the toss of a coin and the rolling of dice in a *YAHTZEE* game.

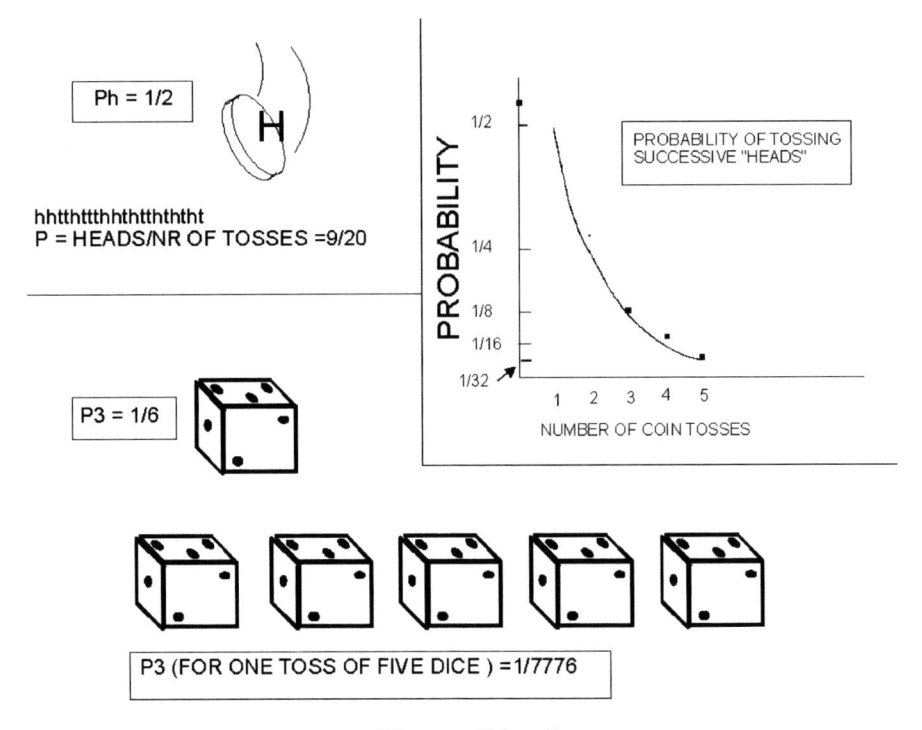

Figure (10 - 1)
Probabilites for Coin and Dice Tosses

For the coin toss, the curve in Figure (10-2) shows a probability-versus-number of coin tosses curve. The curve reveals that the chance of tossing 5 successive heads or 5 successive tails is 1/32; that is, out of 32 series containing 5 coin tosses each, on the average there will be only one series of tosses where either all heads or all tails will turn up. Figure (10-2) shows the probability of heads being tossed in a game of 30 tosses.[1]

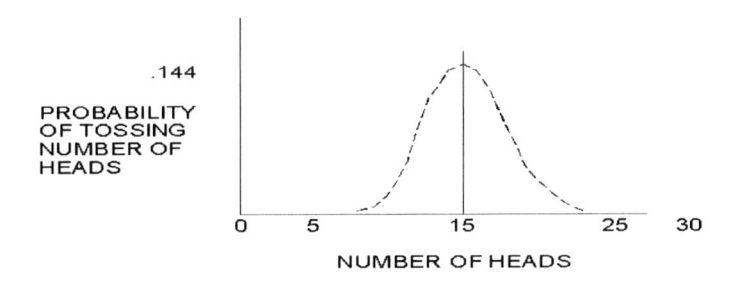

Figure (10-2)

Probabililty of Heads Being Tossed in a Game of Thirty Tossed

As can be seen the greatest probability, [P(k, n) = 0.144], is that 15 heads will be tossed out of 30 tosses, with a lesser probability to either side of 15. We might at first think that the probability of tossing 15 heads out of 30 tosses would be 0.5, (50%), but out of one 100 series of 30 tosses, only about 14-15 series will have exactly 15 heads and 15 tails. The equation for this calculation is given below:

$$P(k,n) = \binom{n}{k} \times \left(\frac{1}{2^n}\right) \tag{10-1}$$

where n = number of tosses ; k = number of heads thrown; and

$$\binom{n}{k} = n! \times \left(\frac{1}{k!}\right) \times \left(\frac{1}{(n-k)!}\right) \tag{10-2}$$

for n = 30, and k = 15 we find that $(n/k) = 154.99(10^6)$;

and $P(k,n) = 154.99(10^6) \times \left(\frac{1}{1073.74(10^6)}\right) = .144$

The probability that *all* heads will be tossed in one series of 30 tosses is $(1/2)^{30} = 9.3 \times 10^{-10}$! The curve shown in Figure (10-2) is called a *bell curve*, and it is like the curves used for determining the momentum or the position of a particle such as an electron [2] (see Figure (10-3)). The bottom curve of this figure reveals that there is a certain probability that a particle will be found near (within Δx) the position X_0. In like manner, the top curve tells us that there is a certain probability that the particle will have

PROBABILITY THAT A PARTICLE WILL HAVE A GIVEN MOMENTUM

ΔP

Po
MOMENTUM

PROBABILITY THAT A PARTICLE WILL HAVE A GIVEN POSITION

ΔX

Xo
POSITION

INDEPENDENT MEASUREMENTS OF MOMENTUM AND POSITION UNCERTAINTIES

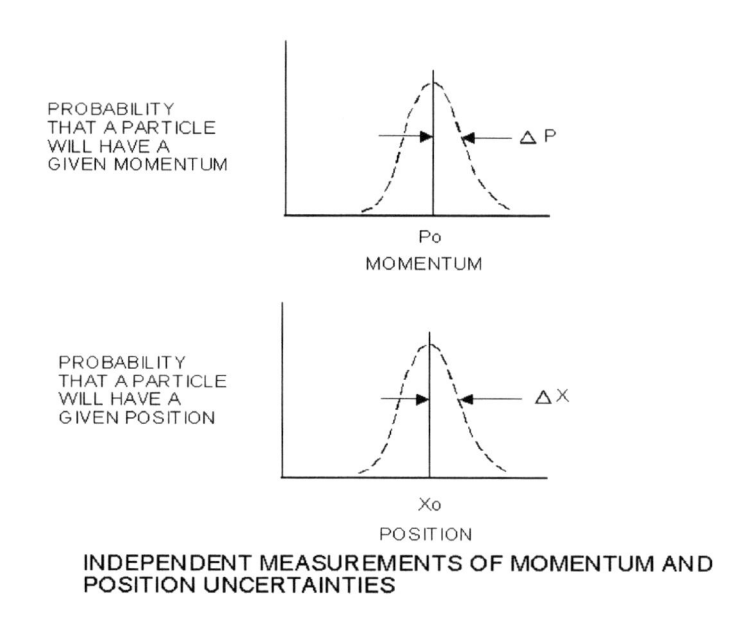

Figure (10-3)

Independent Measurement of Momentum and Position Uncertainties

a velocity or momentum somewhere near (ΔP_0) the value of P_0. We will see later in this book that the simultaneous measurement of position and momentum of a particle involves a greater degree of uncertainty in one or the other measurements than is shown in Figure (10-3). Quantum theory *insists* that the product of $(\Delta x)(\Delta P)$ be at least as large as $h/2\pi$.

From the coin toss we can say that the existence of a head on one side of the coin, and the existence of a tail on the other side is independent of any coin toss. This is so obvious that to question this simple conclusion would be absurd. However, the existence of the *state* of heads-up or tails-up is a *probability*.

With a die, *topside 3* exists as a potential, with a probability of 1/6 for its appearing each time the die is tossed. In theory, if one knew precisely the force vectors, die position, mass, and initial orientation, she could predict what side of the die would land topside. This is not so in quantum physics.

In quantum physics position, energy and momentum (what are called *observables*) of a particle are seen to have no objective existence until measured or observed by some macroscopic measuring device. Until these properties are measured they have no more objective existence than a *topside 3*, and have only a potential or probability of existing - this probability being the result of a superposition of many possible position or momentum states.

Return to Chapter Ten (p. 21)

APPENDIX I-11

THE WAVE EQUATION

In 1925 Werner Heisenberg, a student at the *University of Munich,* began to develop a theory of atomic structure that he hoped would be entirely separate from the classical theory of the day.[1] He believed that his *observables* theory should not include concepts of electrons orbiting atomic nuclei, since these could not be actually observed, but were only inferred. The year before, Louis de Broglie had formulated his theory that electrons had wave characteristics as well as particle properties. Einstein, after hearing of the work of de Broglie, contacted a theoretical physicist in Zurich, Switzerland, by the name of Erwin Schrodinger, and told him of de Broglie's work. Schrodinger, aided by de Broglie's work, was able to develop an equation to predict electron energy levels of the hydrogen atom. It later became clear that the Heisenberg and Schrodinger theories, although different in their mathematical approaches, were essentially equivalent in their results. What Schrodinger actually accomplished was to formulate a *partial differential equation* that could satisfy the de Broglie equation ($P = h/\lambda$) for matter waves, predict electron energy levels in atoms and the spectra of light emitted or absorbed when an atom transitioned to a different energy state.

Schrodinger began by considering that the de Broglie "matter wave" should be similar in form to that of an electromagnetic wave or a light wave. The equation for a light wave is developed from the consideration that any point of a plane monochromatic wave displaces in space and time like a simple harmonic oscillator.

SIMPLE HARMONIC OSCILLATOR

Therefore, let us first take a look at the simple harmonic oscillator. A simple harmonic oscillator is a vibrating system for which the restoring force is directly proportional to the negative of the displacement. In Figure (11-1) a mass, *m*, is shown connected to a fixed point by a spring.

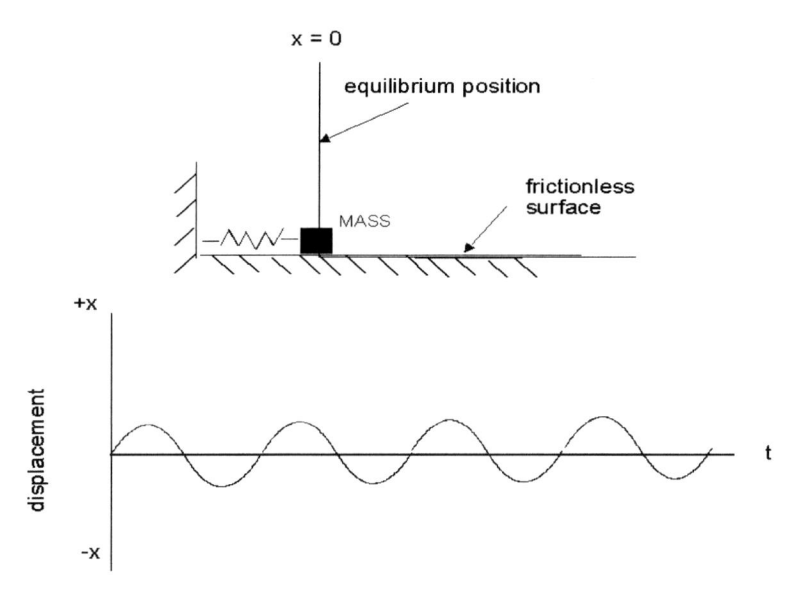

Figure (11-1)

Simple Harmonic Oscillator

When the string is stretched to the right beyond its equilibrium point (the initial position of the mass when no external force has been applied), and then released, the restoring force of the spring will cause it to move to the left past the equilibrium point to a position where the compression of the spring causes a restoring force, which again will cause the mass to move to the right. Ignoring friction, the mass will continue to oscillate indefinitely. The equation for this harmonic motion is shown below:

$$F = m(d^2x/dt^2) = -kx, \ldots or \ldots (d^2x/dt^2) + (k/m)x = 0 \qquad (11\text{-}1)$$

where k is the spring stiffness. We desire a solution to this differential *equation of motion* that is a function of time; that is, $x = x(t)$. General solutions to this type of differential equation are *sinusoidal* (sine or cosine); and a proposed solution of the form $x(t) = (a)\cos(\omega t) + (b)\sin(\omega t)$, will satisfy the above equation provided $\omega^2 = k/m$. The constants a and b are determined by the selected initial conditions: at time $t = 0$, the string has been stretched to its maximum displacement, represented by A. Therefore, $x = A = (a)\cos(\omega 0) + (b)\sin(\omega 0)\ldots$ therefore, $A = a,\ldots$ (since $\cos(0) = 1$, and $\sin(0) = 0$); and since the initial velocity of the mass is zero (We stretched the string, held it, and then released it.), then: $velocity = 0 = dx/dt = -(A)(\omega)\sin(0) + (b)(\omega)\cos(0) = (b)(\omega)..$ Since ω cannot be equal to zero, then $(b) = 0$.

Finally,

$$x(t) = (A)\cos(\omega t). \tag{11-2}$$

To some of you readers this has been rather tedious, but the above equation can be graphed to display the sinusoidal position of the mass with respect to time.

For $\omega t = 0, \pi, 2\pi, 3\pi, etc.$ the displacement of the mass from the equilibrium position $(x=0)$, is maximum $(x=A)$. For $\omega t = \pi/2, 3\pi/2, 5\pi/2,$ the mass is passing through the equilibrium point at maximum velocity.

The motion or displacement of the mass about the equilibrium position as a function of time is shown in Figure (11-1).

For material particles such as electrons, a similar relation applies:

$$\psi(x) = A\sin(kx) + B\cos(kx) \tag{11-3}$$

where *A and B* are constants, and $k = 2\pi/\lambda$. $\psi(x)$ represents the displacement of any point on the so-called matter wave. The term is similar to the electric field strength *E*, for electromagnetic waves such as light. Since the particle of mass *m* under consideration is a "free" particle with no forces acting upon it, the potential energy is constant and it's momentum is fixed.

Since all physical equations must satisfy the *Conservation of Energy*, we have:
Kinetic energy (K) + potential energy (U) = total energy (E): $1/2\,mv^2 + U = E$ (Recall that $P = mv = h/\lambda,,...\hbar = h/2\lambda,...k = 2\pi/\lambda$); therefore,

$$P^2/2m + U = E = (\hbar)^2(k^2)/2m + U; \tag{11-4}$$

What we desire is a differential equation that satisfies both Equations (11-3) and (11-4). The differential equation that does this is:

$$d^2\psi(x)/dx^2 = -(k^2)(\psi(x)) \tag{11-5}$$

Replacing k^2 of (11-4) with $\dfrac{-d^2\psi(x)/dx^2}{\psi(x)}$ from Equation (11-5), we arrive at the time-independent *Schrodinger Wave Equation*:

$$\{-(\hbar)^2/2m\}\{d^2\psi(x)/dx^2\} + (U)(\psi(x)) = (E)(\psi(x)) \tag{11-6}$$

The reader is referred to standard physics textbooks [2] for more detailed discussions and rigorous development of the *Schrodinger Wave Equation*. It should be noted that the *Schrodinger* equation is not *derived* from fundamental principles; rather, it was created to describe physical systems quantitatively at the quantum level.

Return to Chapter 12 (p. 27)

APPENDIX I-12

PARTICLES IN POTENTIAL WELLS

INFINITE POTENTIAL WELL

Let us now use the *Schrodinger Wave Equation* for predicting the location of an electron in a selected case; that is, the electron confined in an infinite potential well. It should be noted here that the *Schrodinger Wave Equation* can be solved analytically only for a limited number of physical cases. For the majority of cases, solutions are accomplished by numerical integration using a computer.

Consider in your imagination, a particle, such as an electron, with mass m, confined to a one-dimensional box of length L, whose walls are perfectly "rigid" or infinitely hard. This is to imply that the "walls" are regions of infinite negative potential energy U (See Figure (12-1).

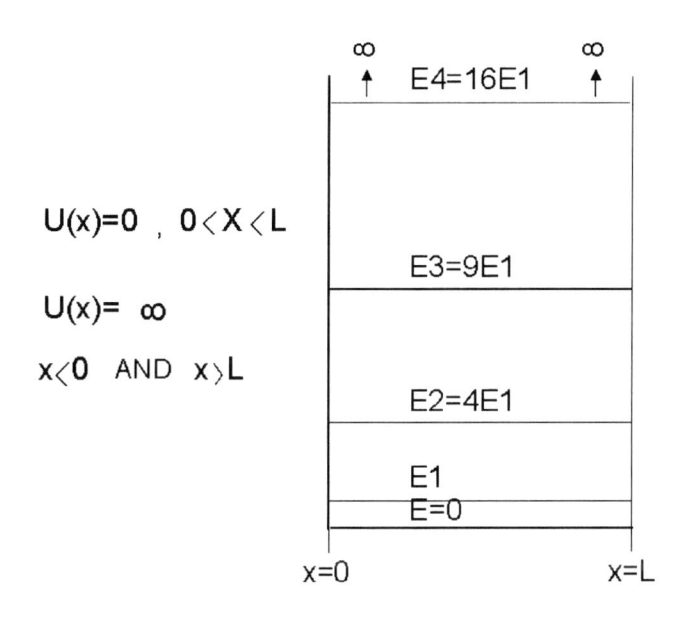

$U(x)=0$, $0<X<L$

$U(x)= \infty$

$x<0$ AND $x>L$

$E_4 = 16E_1$

$E_3 = 9E_1$

$E_2 = 4E_1$

E_1

$E = 0$

POSSIBLE ENERGY LEVELS FOR ELECTRON CONFINED IN INFINITE POTENTIAL WELL

Figure (12-1)

Electron Confined in Infinite Potential Well

We will discover that imposing the boundary conditions of potential energy walls leads to the quantization of allowable electron energy levels. The electron is confined inside this well, and can undergo elastic collisions with the walls; that is, no particle kinetic energy is lost as a result of collision with the walls. Since the electron is free from any external forces, its potential energy is also constant in the region between the walls, and for this example is considered to be equal to zero. Therefore, the particle total energy, E, (potential energy + kinetic energy) is constant.

The solution to the wave equation therefore requires that in the region of $0 \langle x \langle L$ the potential $U(x) = 0.$ [1] Therefore Equation (11-6) of APPENDIX I-11 becomes:

$$d^2\psi(x)/dx^2 = -(2mE/(\hbar)^2)\psi(x) \tag{12-1}$$

A possible solution to the above Equation is:

$$\psi(x) = A\sin kx \tag{12-2}$$

This can be verified by substituting back into the left-hand side of Equation (12-1). This solution can be derived from Equation (11-3) of APPENDIX I-11 by examining the appropriate *boundary conditions* for the problem: we know that at $x = 0, \psi(x) = 0,$ and the electron can never be at or beyond the infinite potential walls. For $\sin 0 = 0$:

$$\psi(x) = 0 = A\sin(0) + B\cos(0) \tag{12-3}$$

therefore $B = 0$, and Equation (11-1) becomes:

$$\psi(x) = A\sin kx \tag{12-4}$$

for $0 \langle x \langle L$

Now, at $x = L, \psi(L) = 0 = A\sin kL.$ If A would have the value of zero, there would be no particle in the well, but since this is not the case, $\sin kL$ must be equal to zero. This will be true for $kL = 0, \pi, 2\pi, 3\pi,...$ or for $k = n\pi/L$, where $n = 1, 2, 3, 4,...$

Finally, the wave function for an electron confined in the region $0 \langle x \langle L$, whose boundaries are of infinite potential is: *

$$\psi(x) = A\sin n\pi x/L \tag{12-5}$$

for $n = 1, 2, 3, 4,...$

Substituting Equations (11-5) and (12-5) into Equation (11-6) we find

---

* This solution of the *Schrodinger* differential equation, with appropriate boundary conditions, is sometimes called the "eigenfunction."

$$k = \sqrt{2mE/(\hbar)^2} = n\pi/L$$

and therefore:

$$E_n = (h/\lambda)^2/2m$$

where $\lambda = 2L/n$ .... therefore *

$$E_n = h^2 n^2/8mL^2 \qquad (12\text{-}6)$$

It can be shown by a normalization procedure [2] that $A = \sqrt{2/L}$, and represents the maximum displacement, or amplitude of the wave.

    Equation (12-6) represents the various energy levels (kinetic energy) possible for an electron trapped in an infinite potential well, and the results are shown in Figure(12-1). The electron is considered to be in a *bound* state; i.e., it is not free to leave the potential well. Figure (12-2) shows the values of the wave function inside the well.

---

* This value given by Equation (12-6) is called the "eigenvalue", and represents - in this illustration - any of discrete, permissible values of energy in the solution of the *Schrodinger Wave Equation*. The "eigenstate" is a state of a quantized dynamic system such as an atom, where one of the variables that defines the energy state has a fixed value.

```
N = 3     PHIn(x)    [~~~]

N = 2     PHIn(x)    [~~]

N = 1     PHIn(x)    [⌒]
                     |←— L —→|
```

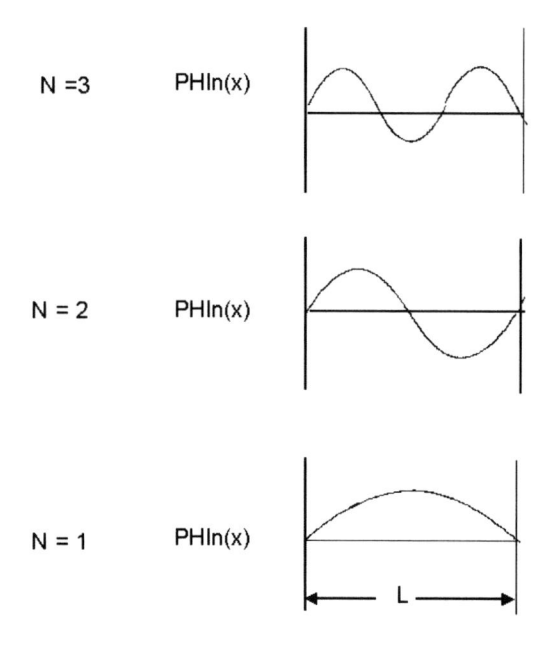

WAVE FUNCTIONS FOR DIFFERENT QUANTUM NUMBERS(N),
FOR ELECTRON CONFINED IN A POTENTIAL WELL

Figure (12-2)

Wave Function for Electron Confined in Infinite Potential Well

WAVE FUNCTION AND PROBABILITY DENSITY

The wave function $\psi(x)$, represents the displacement or amplitude of the electron matter *wave* associated with the particle. The wave function gives us information about the material system under consideration, including the measurable quantities or *observables*, such as position, momentum and energy.

For $n = 2$, the curve looks similar to the curve in Figure (11-1) APPENDIX I-11 for the displacement of the mass/spring harmonic oscillator. The displacement curve for the mass/spring shows both *positive* displacement (to the right of the equilibrium position), and *negative* displacement (to the left of the equilibrium position). Near the point of maximum displacement or amplitude, the mass/spring slows down in speed, comes to a stop, and then accelerates in the other direction. We can declare with a fair degree of certainty that the probability of locating the mass at some arbitrary time would be highest at the maximum displacement points where the mass is moving more slowly. This is also similar to the examples given previously with the girl on the swing and with the coasting automobile.

For the electron in the infinite potential well, the wave function as shown in Figure (12-2) give us an indication, *only*, of the probability of locating its position. The wave function, itself, cannot be measured and does not provide us with a direct indication of the probability of finding an electron at some region in space. However, if the wave function has a value of *zero* (rather than either a positive or negative value), then we know the particle cannot be found in that region of space.

We know from the study of light waves that E^2 - the square of the electric field strength - is proportional to the light intensity. The intensity of a light beam is proportional to the density of photons in a particular region of space. If a particular light wave represented a single photon, then E^2 could be employed to calculate the probability per unit volume that a photon could be found at a specific location. E^2 is similar to the probability of locating a matter particle such as an electron, which has a wave function ψ, at a particular point. Therefore, we must square the wave function in order to find the probability of locating the electron at a given position. The term $|\psi(x)|^2$, is the square of the absolute value of Equation (12-5). Since $\psi(x)$ is usually written as a *complex* function, and includes the imaginary term $i = \sqrt{-1}$, we must include the square of the *absolute value* for any real, physical meaning:

$$|\psi(x)|^2 = A^2 \sin^2 kx = (2/L)\sin^2(n\pi x/L) \tag{12-7}$$

This term $|\psi(x)|^2$, represents the probability per unit length of finding the electron at a given point. It is sometimes called the *probability density* or *probability amplitude*; and the name is more appropriate when the position of the electron is desired in a given volume of space, rather than the more limited case here of linear distance.

Figure (12-3) shows the probability per unit length that an electron in an infinite potential well will be found at a given position, x. Although the square of the wave function gives the probability of finding the electron at a given point - like the tossing of dice - it is an

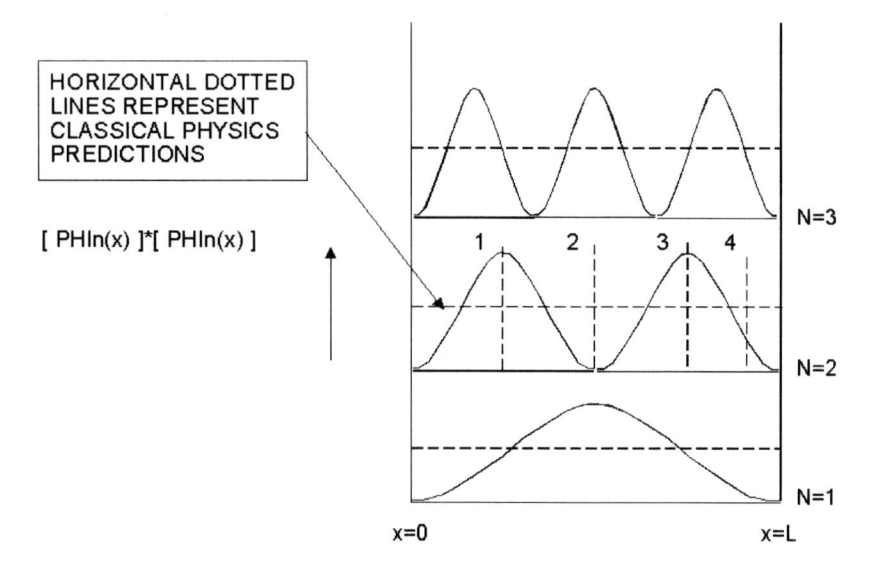

[HORIZONTAL DOTTED LINES REPRESENT CLASSICAL PHYSICS PREDICTIONS]

[PHIn(x)]*[PHIn(x)]

PROBABILITY PER UNIT LENGTH FOR ELECTRON CONFINED IN POTENTIAL WELL

Figure (12-3)

Electron Probability in Infinite Potential Well

average probability for a large number of cases for electrons in this particular potential well.

For $n = 1$, the particle is more likely to be found at the center of the confinement, but according to classical physics the electron will be found equally everywhere between the walls (See the horizontal dotted lines in the Figure). For an electron with greater energy (Equation (12-7), $n = 2$ instead of $n = 1$), the electron will sometimes be found at position #1, but *never* at position #2! It is as if the electron could first be at position #1, and later be observed at position #3, *without traversing the space between the positions!* *

FINITE POTENTIAL WELL-ALPHA PARTICLE DECAY

---

* Recent studies by Valery Nesvizhevsky and colleagues at the Laue-Langevin Institute in Grenoble, France, [3] investigated the motion of very slow-moving ultra-cold neutrons falling from the top of a specially designed detector to the bottom. The neutrons have been isolated from the effects of electromagnetism, and the weak and strong nuclear forces. The studies have indicated that these uncharged particles exist only at certain heights. In the words of Nesvizhevsky, "They do not move continuously, but rather jump from one height to another as quantum theory predicts."

Now let us consider a particle trapped inside a *finite* potential well. An alpha particle is essentially the nucleus of a helium atom. It consists of two protons - positively charged - and two neutrons, with no charge. Uranium-238 is known to decay by alpha particle emission to Thorium-234. This is usually written as: $P_Z^A = (Z-2)P^{A-4} + 2\alpha^4$ where Z is the *atomic number* (the number of protons in the nucleus); A is the *atomic weight* (the number of neutrons and protons) P represents the original or parent nucleus, and D is the nucleus after alpha particle emission. The classical picture of the Uranium nucleus is that of the alpha particle confined inside the nucleus by the so-called *nuclear force*, a very strong attractive force that acts over short distances to prevent the positively-charged protons from mutually repelling each other and flying out of the nucleus. Beyond the nuclear binding force range (approximately 10^{-14} meters), a positively-charged particle would experience the repulsive coulomb force of the protons inside the nucleus.

Figure (12-4) shows the potential well or barrier that a particle such an alpha particle would encounter, as a function of distance from the nucleus.

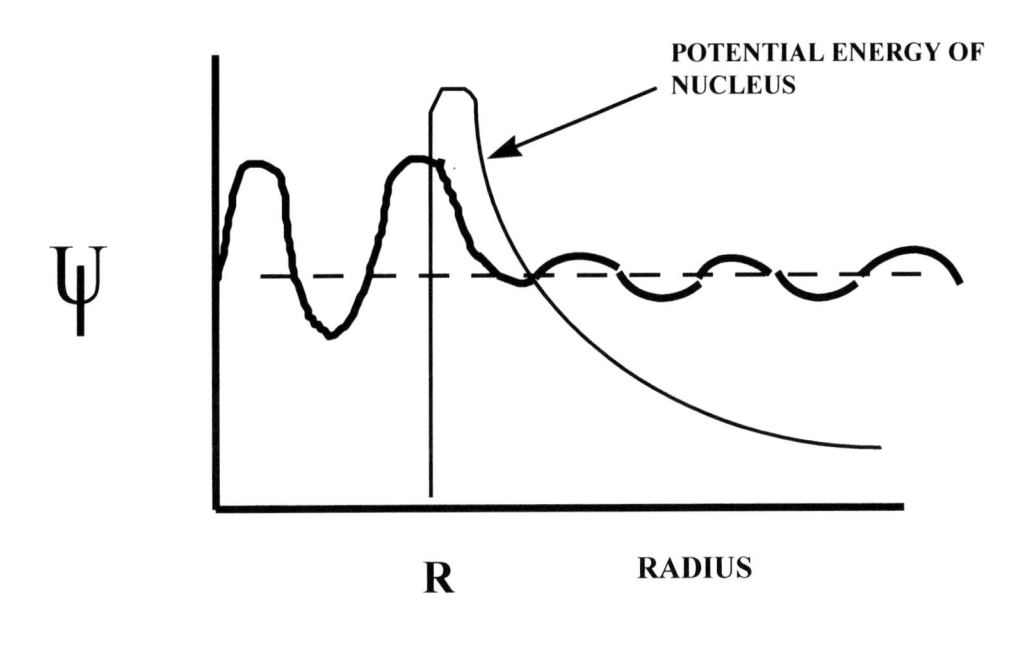

Figure (12-4)

**Alpha Particle Wave Function
(hand-drawn rough sketch)**

According to the classical interpretation, an alpha particle inside the nucleus will continue to oscillate indefinitely between the nuclear "walls" (at the frequency of 10^{20} times per second), as it can not penetrate them. This is because the potential energy just beyond R is greater than the energy of the alpha particle. But we know from experiment that alpha particles are emitted with some energy. Quantum theory to the rescue! Included in the Figure is the wave function for the alpha particle in Uranium-238.

Athough the wave function is severely reduced as it traverses the potential wall, it is again oscillatory outside this barrier, indicating that an alpha particle has "tunneled" through the classically-impenetrable barrier. The *half life* for Uranium-238; that is, the time in which one-half of the original nuclei have decayed,[*] is approximately 10^{17} seconds, so on the average an alpha particle will oscillate about $10^{20} \times 10^{17} = 10^{37}$ times before it escapes through the potential barrier.

Recall the dice-tossing experiment discussed in Part I, Chapter 10. We could not predict when a particular side would land "top-side up." It could occur on the first toss, or not until the 31st, although the probability was that after many tosses, a particular side would appear, on the average, once in every 6 tosses. We see roughly the same phenomena with alpha particle decay.

We can write the *Uncertainty Principle* relationship in another form: $\Delta E \Delta t \geq h/2\pi$. This means that if we know the energy of individual atoms with a great degree of certainty (the value of ΔE being small), then we have a great deal of uncertainty as to *when* alpha particles will tunnel through the energy barrier. An alpha particle could be emitted in 10^{-6} seconds, or in 10^{10} years. We have no way of knowing when an *individual* alpha particle will be emitted; but for a large sampling of Uranium - 238, the average rate of decay is about 10^{17} seconds (about 10^9 years).

Return to Chapter 13 (p. 29)

---

[*] If the half-life of a radioactive material is four seconds, then after four seconds half of the material remains; after eight seconds one quarter of the material remains; after twelve seconds one eighth remains, etc.

APPENDIX I-13

THE POSSIBILITY OF FINDING QUANTUM OBJECTS IN BOUND SYSTEMS

ELECTRON IN A HYDROGEN ATOM

With appropriate boundary conditions the wave function for the ground state, $(n=1)$, of the hydrogen atom electron about its proton nucleus can be determined along with the *radial probability density function*: [1]

$$P_r = (4r^2/r_o^3)e^{-2r/r_o} \tag{13-1}$$

Shown in Figure (13-1) is the plot of P_r versus r/r_0, where r/r_0 is the distance from the center of the atom in units of the classical *Bohr* radius (r_0) for an electron in the ground or lowest energy state.

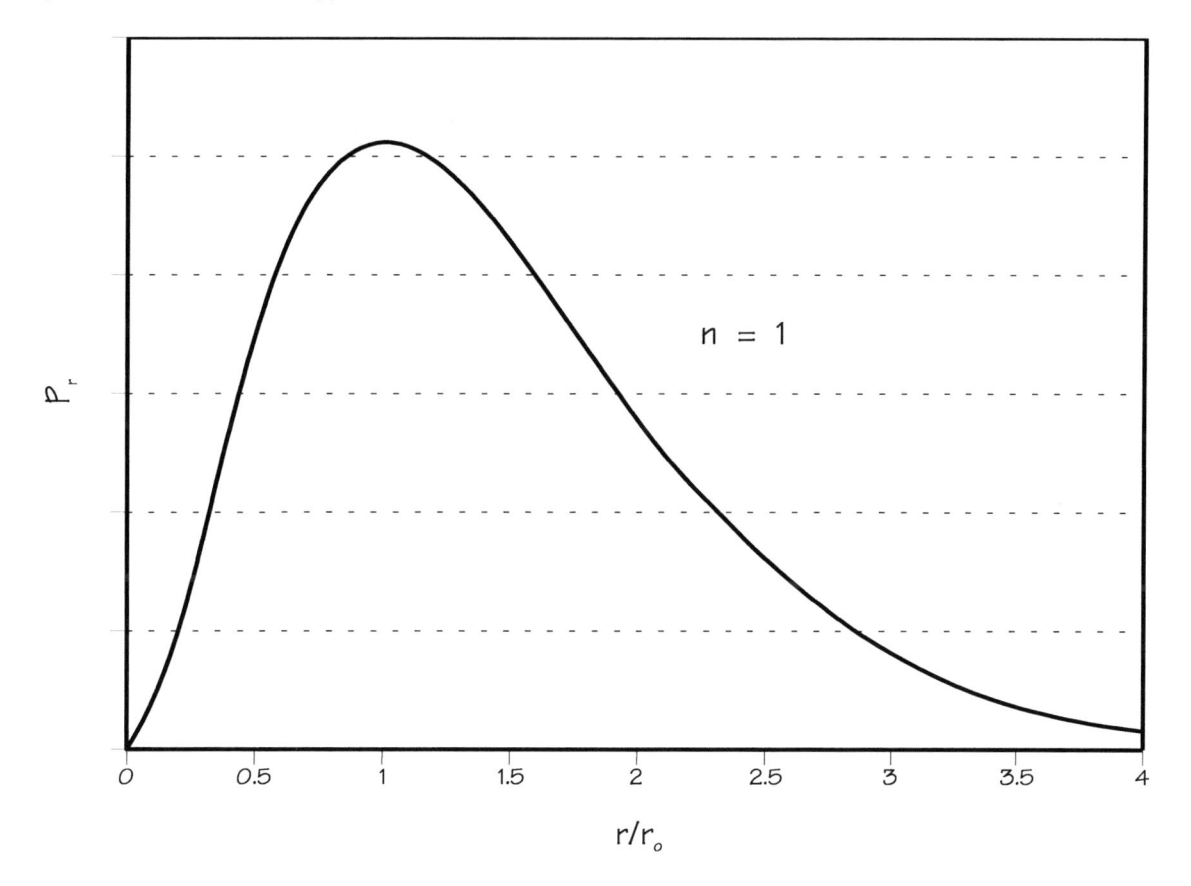

Figure (13-1)
Radial Probability Density Function for Electron about Hydrogen Atom Nucleus

According to quantum theory we can no longer conceive of the electron as occupying a definite point in space and time, but rather as a *cloud of probability*; although the most probable location is at $r/r_0 = 1$, the Bohr radius. It would seem then that there is no physical law that will predict when a given electron will jump from one energy orbit to another. Although for a large assemblage of atoms quantum theory can predict with extreme accuracy energy radiation, or radioactive decay. In radioisotope decay an emission of a given photon, for example, may occur within the next second, or it might not occur for the next 1000 years. We have no way of knowing.

The quantized energy levels for the hydrogen atom are given by:

$$E_n = -13.6/n^2 \text{ e.v.}^* \quad \text{where} \quad n = 1, 2, 3, ... \tag{13-2}$$

The corresponding radius where the electron is most likely to be found is:

$$r_n = 0.529 \times 10^{-10} (n^2) \text{ meters} \tag{13-3}$$

As the atom in the ground state, $(n=1)$, absorbs energy, it will jump to the next energy state, $(n=2)$, when it absorbs a quantum of energy equal to 10.2 ev. That is, the electron makes a quantum jump from a state of -13.6 e.v. to -3.4 e.v.$^\triangledown$, and the atomic size or radius - where the electron is most likely to be found - is increased from .529 to 2.11 angstroms (one Angstrom = 10^{-10} meters). As *n* increases to much larger values, the size of the atom can increase truly astronomically. Going from $n = 100,000$ to $n = 100,001$, means that the most probable location for the electron has increased from a radius of 20 inches to 20.004 inches. The energy absorbed to make this jump is only 27×10^{-14} e.v. It seems incredible to consider a hydrogen atom whose diameter is 40 inches or more, when the diameter of the hydrogen atom in the ground state is slightly over one Angstrom; but there is experimental evidence that such monsters, although unstable, exist.[2] There is no velocity of the electron moving outward from the nucleus. Quantum theory states that when the electron absorbs some quantum of energy, the probability is now greater in finding the electron at a larger radius.

For an n-value of 2.39×10^{13}, the radius of the atom is over three light years – almost out to the distance of the nearest star, the red dwarf *Proxima Centauri*! The energy of an electron with this quantum number is infinitesimally small, about -2.38×10^{-26} e.v. It would take only 2.38×10^{-26} e.v. of additional energy to free the electron from the atom.

---

* e.v.: energy measured in electron volts.

$^\triangledown$ negative energy states in an atom imply that energy must be added to the electron until, at zero energy, the electron is no longer bound to the atom, but is at rest an infinite distance from the nucleus. Additional energy added will impart a kinetic energy to the electron.

$\psi(x)$, is then seen as a mathematical function only. It has no real physical existence - it is a possibility, probability - a wave function that spreads mathematically throughout space-time. It contains the potential for all physical phenomena to be manifested.[3] When we perform an observation, the wave function "collapses" and a particle of matter is localized. Once we cease to look for the particle, it again takes on the aspects of a probability wave. $\psi(x)$, the quantum mechanical wave function or *wave amplitude* is a result whose value depends on how we choose to observe the particle. Under the chosen test conditions, the probability amplitude represents the chance that the particle will be seen in the neighborhood of some point in space and time when we look for it.

A photon of light from a distant star - or rather, its quantum wave function - reaches us after expanding as a spherical wave front as it traverses the many light years separating the star and the Earth. When the wave front reaches us on Earth, it will be light years in diameter. But the photon - the actual particle - is not localized across this gigantic wave front until *you* (or I) observe or collapse the wave and localize the particle. Until it has been observed, the photon can be thought of as *wave of equi-potential* across the entire surface of the spherical wave front. In like manner, a beam of electrons can be perceived as a quantum wave potential until it is observed via an experiment.

Looking once more at Figure (12-3), for the case where $n = 2$, we find there are values of x where the probability of finding the electron in an infinite potential well is zero, and we are forced to again ask the question, "How does the electron go from point # 1 to point # 3 if it cannot pass through point # 2?" This certainly challenges our concept of physical reality. The physical attributes of electrons are seen more as potentials to be brought into existence by *observation* - by the collapse of the wave function.

Figure (13-2) illustrates (approximately) the wave function collapse. The collapse of the wave function occurs instantaneously across all space.[*]

---

[*] Sometimes the phenomena of "wave function collapse" is called "reduction of the state."

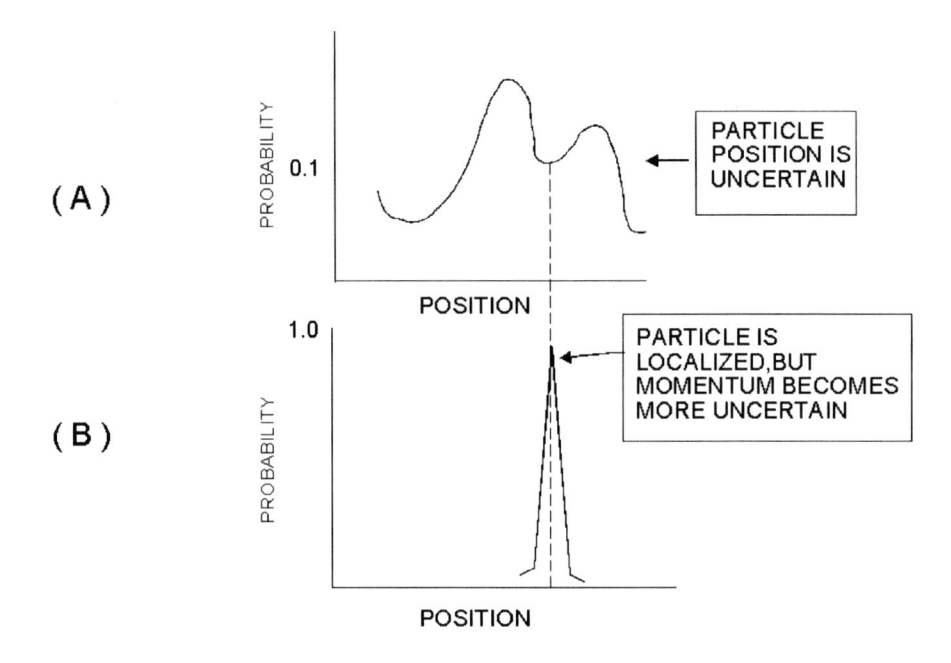

(A) [graph: probability vs position, with two peaks at 0.1, labeled "PARTICLE POSITION IS UNCERTAIN"]

(B) [graph: probability vs position, sharp peak at 1.0, labeled "PARTICLE IS LOCALIZED, BUT MOMENTUM BECOMES MORE UNCERTAIN"]

COLLAPSE OF THE WAVE FUNCTION THROUGH OBSERVATION REDUCES PROBABILITY SPREAD AND LOCALIZES THE PARTICLE WITHIN THE CONSTRAINTS OF THE UNCERTAINTY PRINCIPLE

Figure (13-2)

Wave Function Collapse

The Schrodinger *Wave Equation* can predict with extreme accuracy the average location of a large number of particles, but can only give a probable location for single events; that is, there is no way of knowing where a particular electron with a given energy will be found in the potential well - only that it is more likely to be found at point #3 than at point # 4, and never will be found at point # 2 (Figure 12-3).

A SIMPLE QUANTUM PENDULUM

Now that we know something about wave equations and probability densities, let us again think about the "child on the swing" for just a moment (see Part I, Chapter 10). The child's swing is a macroscopic object, and the probability of locating the swing at any time can be determined from classical dynamics. But what about finding a *quantum mass* on a pendulum? It can be shown that for *small* oscillations, the angular displacement of a *quantum-size mass* suspended on a string is small enough that $\sin\theta \cong \theta$, (see Figure (13-3), and the motion is essentially *harmonic*. [4] *

---

* harmonic motion: a vibrating or oscillatory motion of a mass for which the restoring force is directly proportional to the negative of the displacement, $F = -kx$.

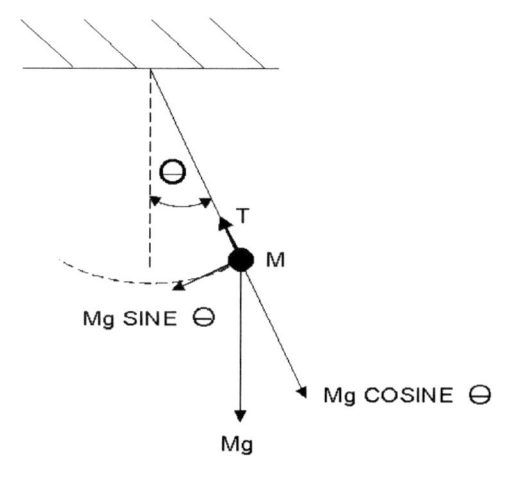

SIMPLE PENDULUM

Figure (13-3)

Simple Pendulum

A wave equation can be derived for a small-oscillation case, and if the mass is of quantum size, a wave function and position probability density can be evaluated as a function of the quantum number, n. The kind of solution we obtain for a small displacement quantum-size oscillating mass is similar to that obtained for the electron in the potential well illustration (See Part I, Chapter 12, Figure (12-3) for $n = 3$). [5] The results are shown in Figure (13-4), (the wave function and the position probability density) for a mass, m, and an

Figure (13-4)

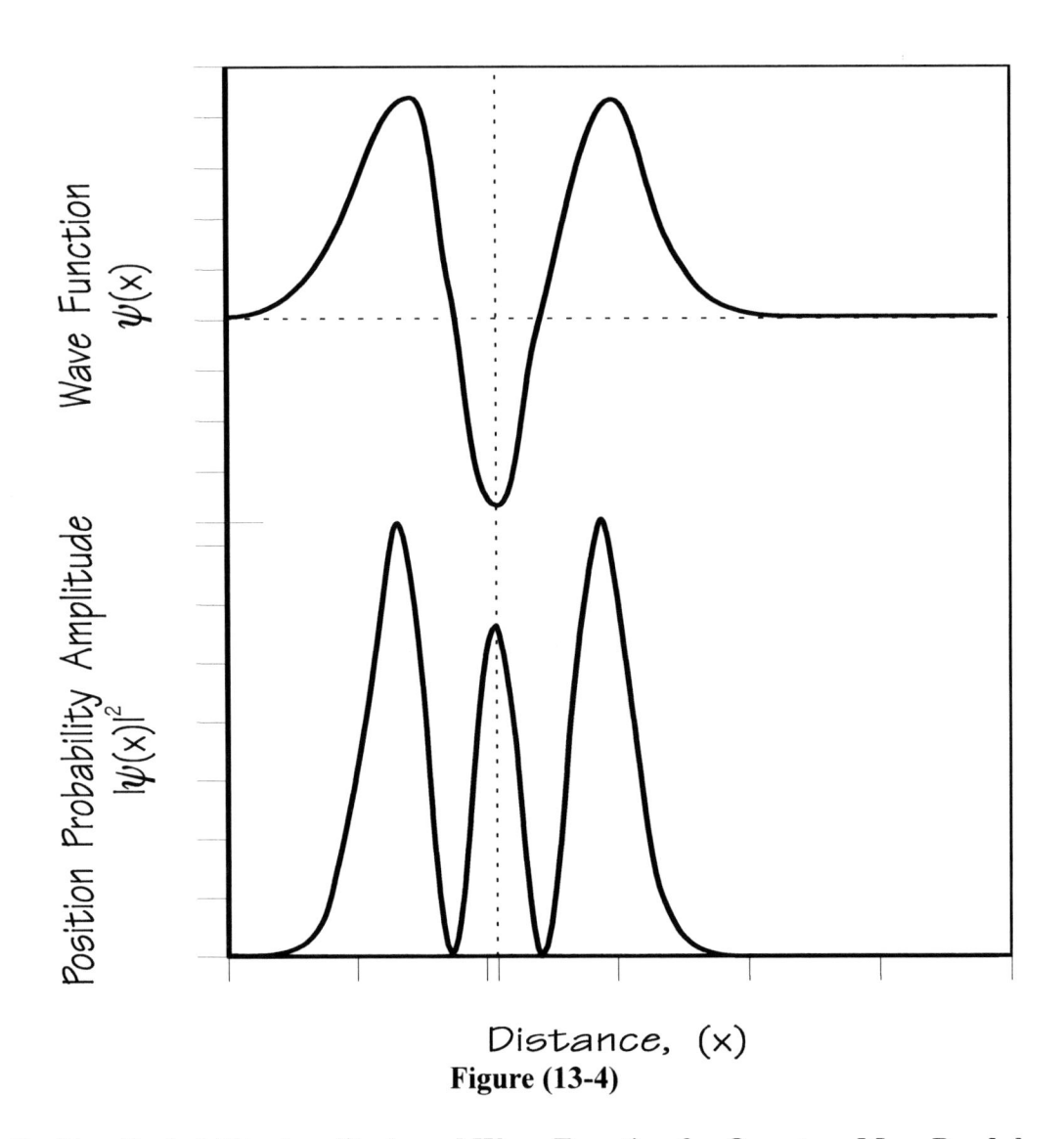

Position Probability Amplitude and Wave Function for Quantum Mass Pendulum

angular displacement θ (for the $n = 2$ energy state). This is a bound state, because the mass is constrained by the string to oscillate back and forth due to the force of gravity. In contrast to what we saw with the child on the swing, the probability curve indicates there are positions that the small mass will never occupy, that is, the probability of its being located at that position is zero ($|\psi(x)|^2 = 0$) (See Figure (13-4)).

As the pendulum system becomes larger - as the mass is increased - the quantum number for the energy state of the larger system also increases; and the position probability begins to look more and more like the probability curve for the girl on the swing (a macroscopic object). The *Correspondence Principle* of quantum physics states that the predictions of quantum theory and classical mechanics should agree as the size of the system under investigation increases. The probability curve for large masses actually shows that there will be increasingly more positions where the mass cannot be, but these positions become so closely spaced that the movement of the mass appears to be uniform.

Return to Chapter 14 (p. 30)

APPENDIX I-14

THE HEISENBERG UNCERTAINTY PRINCIPLE

Unlike observing billiard balls, when we observe subatomic particles we inevitably disturb the very particle we wish to observe. We cannot stand behind a glass wall and unobtrusively study a particle. The very act of observation interferes with the object being observed. The *OBSERVER* and the *OBSERVED* are in some way inextricably connected. Figure (14-1) illustrates the problem: To observe an electron, for example (if science had the technological capability), it must be illuminated with light in order for it to be seen and subsequently photographed. Although light has no rest mass,[*] it does have momentum $(P = h/\lambda)$, and the interaction of the light with the electron will impart momentum to the particle. If we use short wavelength (high-energy) light to observe the electron, we will get a sharp image, but at the expense of imparting a strong kick to the particle. The shorter the wavelength the better the resolution of the particle, but the greater the momentum transferred to the electron, and the resultant uncertainty in the

---

[*] rest mass: according to Relativity, the mass of a particle when measured at rest with respect to the observer. The total or relativistic mass depends on the speed of the particle with respect to the observer. When the speed with respect to the observer is zero, the relativistic mass = the rest mass.

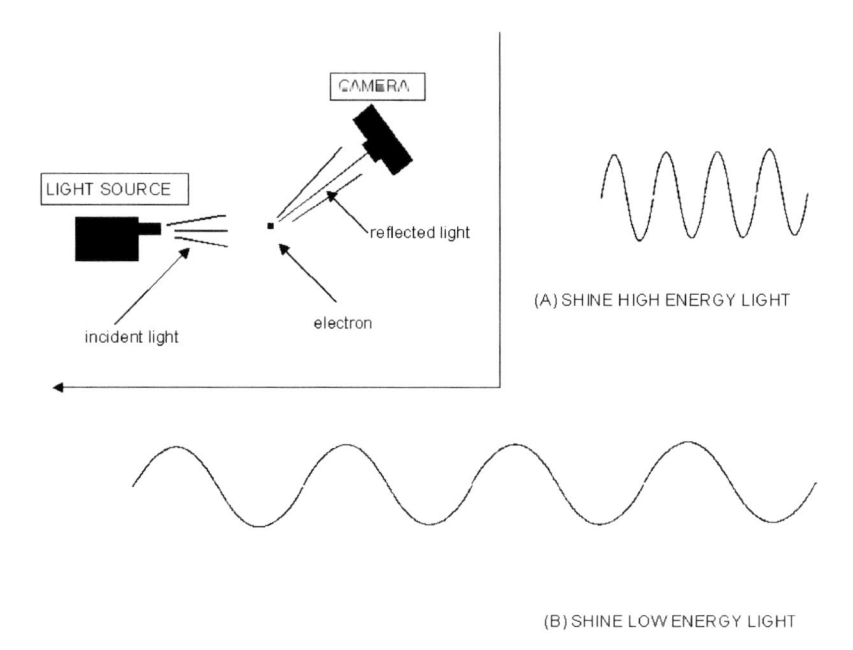

Figure (14-1)

Heisenberg Uncertainty Principle – Simple Explanation

future position of the electron. If we increase the light wavelength (lower energy), the momentum imparted to the electron will be decreased accordingly, but now we do not know the precise position of the particle at the time of measurement, because light with a long wavelength comparable in size to the electron itself will result in poor photographic resolution.

Figure (14-2) illustrates how the uncertainty relation is derived. Werner Heisenberg, in the year 1927, discovered the uncertainty relation. He found there is a fundamental restriction in measuring properties of a photon or an electron, and this restriction is linked with *Planck's* constant *h*. No matter how precise our apparatus's ability to measure, the simultaneous measurement of the position and momentum of a particle cannot be made with an accuracy greater than that shown:

$$\Delta x \Delta P_x \geq \hbar \tag{14-1}$$

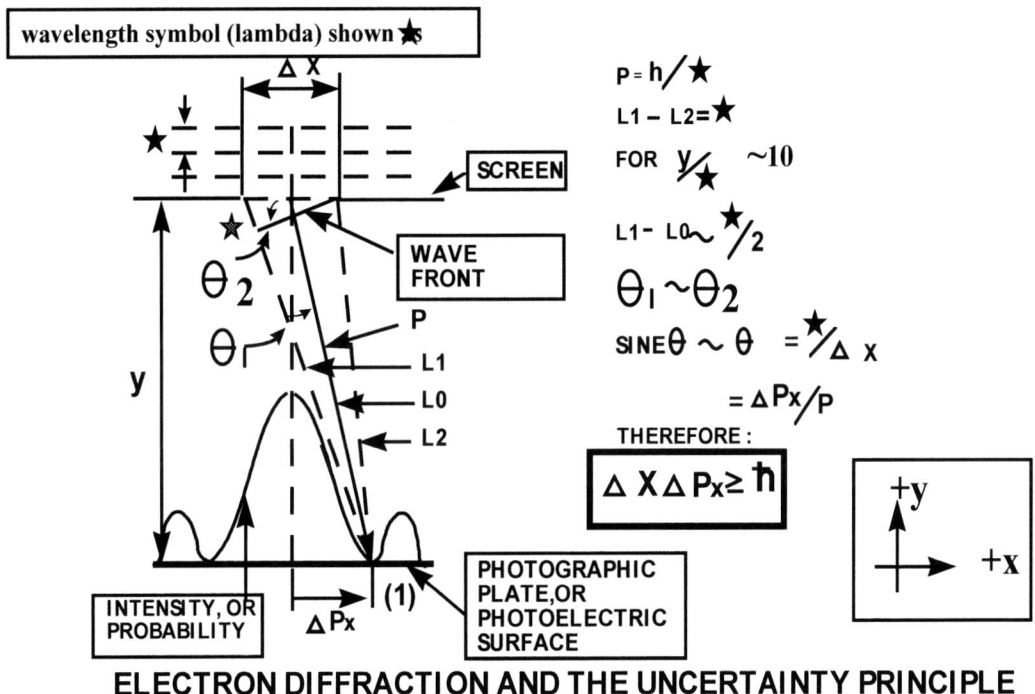

Figure (14-2)
The Uncertainty Principle
(Note: The wavelength symbol in the Figure is shown as a star.)

That is, the uncertainty in the position measurement Δx times the uncertainty in the momentum measurement ΔP_x, (pronounced *delta P*) must always be greater than or equal to $\hbar$ (*Planck's* constant divided by 2π). From this relation we will discover that if we somehow know the momentum of a particle exactly; that is, if the uncertainty of its velocity or momentum were zero - if we could say, in theory the particle is at rest - we would have virtually no idea of where the particle was located. The particle could be practically anywhere in the observable universe!

To understand this relationship better, let us look again at Figure (14-2), which shows the diffraction of electrons through a narrow slit. A monochromatic, low intensity beam of electrons is incident on a screen containing a narrow slit, whose width, Δx (assuming such a narrow slit could be made), is on the order of the wavelength of the electron, $\lambda = h/mv$. The particles are assumed to be moving parallel to the y-axis, that is, with no component of velocity in the x-direction. The electrons, because of their wave characteristics, pass through the slit, are diffracted by interacting with the slit edges and travel downstream where they strike a photographic plate or surface divided into small regions that will respond to electron impingement by emitting photoelectrons, which can then be counted by a *scintillation* counter. (*Diffraction* is caused by the interruption of the
wave fronts by the slit walls, which cause new wavelets to be formed and to bend behind the aperture.[1])

We do not know precisely where individual particles will hit the plate. We wish to determine the positions of the electrons in the x-direction, and their velocity components in the x-direction, simultaneously. We notice under very low electron flow the intensity pattern or number count on the plate increases gradually - impacting electrons causing flashes to appear almost randomly on the surface. The majority of electrons will impact the plate after deviating no more than a small angle θ from the slit axis, but some will hit the screen at larger angles. About three-fourths of the electrons will strike the plate within this angle. As previously stated, we have no way of knowing where a given electron will strike the plate, but only the *probability* that it will strike more frequently at some angles than others.

As an electron first approaches the slit, we have no knowledge of the location of the particle in the $\pm x$ direction at the screen, but its momentum is known precisely, and is directed parallel to the axis of the slit in the $-y$ direction. As the electron goes *through* the slit, our knowledge about its position along the x-axis is improved to where we know its position to within Δx the slit width. Now we certainly have a better idea of the location of the electron, but because of the interaction of the electron wave with the slit edges, the electron has been disturbed, and now has a component of momentum ΔP_x at least as large as indicated in the figure.[*]

We can now appreciate why it is impossible to measure simultaneously the position and the momentum of an electron. A wavelet from the left edge of the slit to the point (1) on the photographic plate will travel one wavelength further than a wavelet from the right edge of the slit. That is, $L_1 - L_2 = \lambda$. For the intensity to be zero at point (1) on the plate, pairs of wavelets must cancel each other out; and this will be accomplished if the relative path difference of the two wavelets differs by $\lambda/2$ (The phase difference will be equal to π).[∇] For large separation of the screen and the photographic plate compared to the slit width ($y/\Delta x \rangle 10$,) the paths $L_1 and L_2$ are nearly parallel; and a wavelet from the left edge of the slit will travel approximately $\lambda/2$ further than a wavelet from a point located halfway between the slit edges. That is, $L_1 - L_0 = \lambda/2$.

These two wavelets will constructively interfere at point (1), and will result in zero intensity. Subsequently, a wavelet originating just to the right of the left slit edge will cancel out a wavelet originating just slightly to the right of the center of the slit. The resultant pairing of wavelets from additional points on the wavefront lead to zero intensity at point (1) on the plate. For large separation distances, the two angles θ_1, θ_2 are nearly equal and so small such that $\theta_1 \cong \theta_2$ and $\sin\theta_1 \cong \sin\theta_2$. Therefore, we find $\theta_1 = \lambda/\Delta x = \Delta P_x/P$ Therefore, $\lambda/\Delta x = \Delta P_x/P$.

(where $P = h/\lambda$ and $h = \Delta x \Delta P$.) Since most, but not all, of the electrons fall within the first intensity minimum, we know that the product of particle position uncertainty (Δx) and momentum uncertainty (ΔP_x) is at *least* equal to h/λ. So we find:

---

[*] We find that we can think of the electron as a particle with a location in space and with a path described by a line or ray, or we can think of the electron as a matter wave with all the diffraction characteristics associated with waves, but we can never think of an electron as possessing both attributes simultaneously.

[∇] An angle measured in radians = 180 degrees/pi. Therefore pi radians = 180 degrees.

$$\Delta x \Delta P_x \geq h \tag{14-2}$$

Heisenberg's detailed calculations showed that at the very best: Equation (14-1) applies.[*]

The square of the wave function for the electrons $|\psi(x)|^2$ is proportional to the probability of finding an electron in the neighborhood of a given point along the x-axis at the plate. As each electron registers on the plate, the intensity pattern or photoelectric count gradually increases. If a monochromatic beam of photons rather than electrons had been incident on the slit, the intensity pattern registered on the photoelectric surface would be proportional to the square of the electric field strength E^2.

The curve for the intensity distribution versus the angle θ shown in Figure (14-2) can be drawn using the following equations:

$$I = A_o^2 \sin^2 \beta / \beta^2, \tag{14-3}$$

where A_0 is a constant for the wave amplitude, and:

$$\beta = (\pi b / \lambda) \sin \theta. \tag{14-4}$$

and where b is the slit width.

These equations have been derived using standard relations for diffraction.[2]

In the experimental setup shown in Figure (14-2), we had an electron wave approaching the slit. Upon exiting the slit each electron - or matter wave - diverged by some small angle from its initial path parallel to the slit axis. As illustrated, as the slit width is made increasingly narrower (Figure (14-3A) through (14-3D)), the electrons or waves will be dispersed even more, and travel further beyond the *geometrical shadow* of the slit, and the probability amplitude or intensity pattern will spread. We now have even less knowledge about the future position of the electron. The particle could be found almost anywhere with equal probability along a wavefront that is spreading outward from the $\pm x$-axis at high speed. If the slit width is widened, our knowledge about the position

---

[*] That is, since there is a higher probability that particles will strike the plate at the center of the intensity pattern (we know that 3/4 of the particles will strike within the angle Θ_1, the uncertainty in the x-component of momentum is not as great as shown, and at the very best, Equation (14-1) applies.

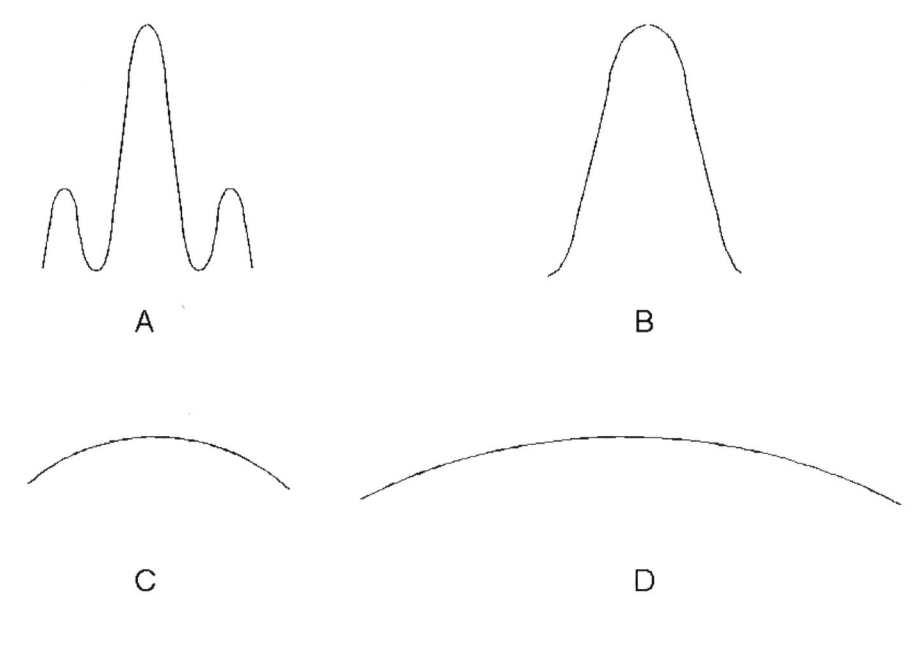

EFFECT OF DECREASING SLIT WIDTH (A - D)

Figure (14-3)

Decreasing Slit Width Effects

of the electron at the slit (Δx) will be less, but because the slit is wider there is less interaction of the electron wave with the slit, and less momentum is imparted to the particle in the x-direction. The accumulated intensity pattern now shows the intensity rings positioned closer together (Figure (14-3A)), and occurring at a smaller angle Θ_1 when compared to the ring spacing for a narrower slit. Now we will have a better knowledge of the momentum of the beam as it exits the slit.

Figure (14-4) shows the uncertainty relation expressed by Equation (14-1). As the uncertainty in particle velocity or momentum is reduced, we have an increasingly higher uncertainty in the position of the particle.

It is satisfying in one respect that the physical world, as it appears to us, is structured on quantum physics principles. In the example of the brick tottering on the edge of the table in Part I, Chapter 7, (Figure (7-1)), we no longer need to fret or "anguish" over precisely what distance the brick (actually, the brick center of mass) could be moved before it would fall to the floor. Because - according to quantum theory - we can not know with unlimited precision the location of any atom within the brick or those that form the table edge without disturbing those very particles (even if that particle is a bound atom). The picture becomes "fuzzy". This is comforting to me from a philosophical point of view, because, like Zeno, I could imagine cutting the distance between the brick center of mass and the table edge in ever-increasingly smaller segments, and thus never arrive at the place where the brick would fall off the table!

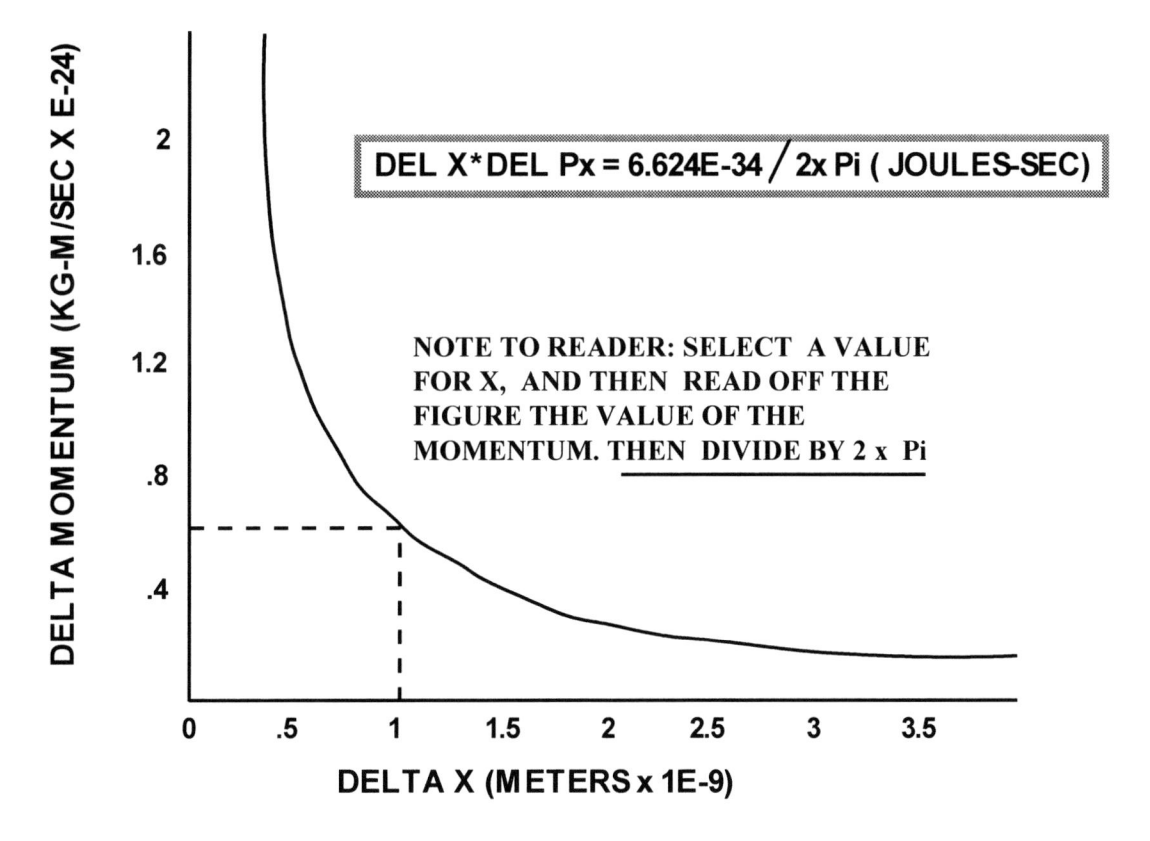

$$\text{DEL } X * \text{DEL } P_x = 6.624\text{E-}34 / 2 \times \pi \text{ (JOULES-SEC)}$$

NOTE TO READER: SELECT A VALUE FOR X, AND THEN READ OFF THE FIGURE THE VALUE OF THE MOMENTUM. THEN DIVIDE BY 2 x Pi

UNCERTAINTY PRINCIPLE RELATION

Figure (14-4)

The Uncertainty Principle

Return to Chapter 15 (p. 32)

APPENDIX I-15A

PHYSICAL AND THOUGHT EXPERIMENTS IN QUANTUM PHYSICS

When two light waves cross each other we get the phenomena of wave interference, and the resultant amplitude and wave intensity will vary from point to point in the region. The change in intensity when two beams of light meet or superimpose is called interference. When two waves are in phase, the crest of one wave matches up with the crest of the other and the intensity is increased. This is constructive interference. Conversely, if the crest of one wave meets up with the trough of the other wave, we see destructive interference.

Let us consider Young's *Double-Slit* experiment, first performed by him in 1801, and where the wave nature of light was first revealed: Observe Figure (15-1).

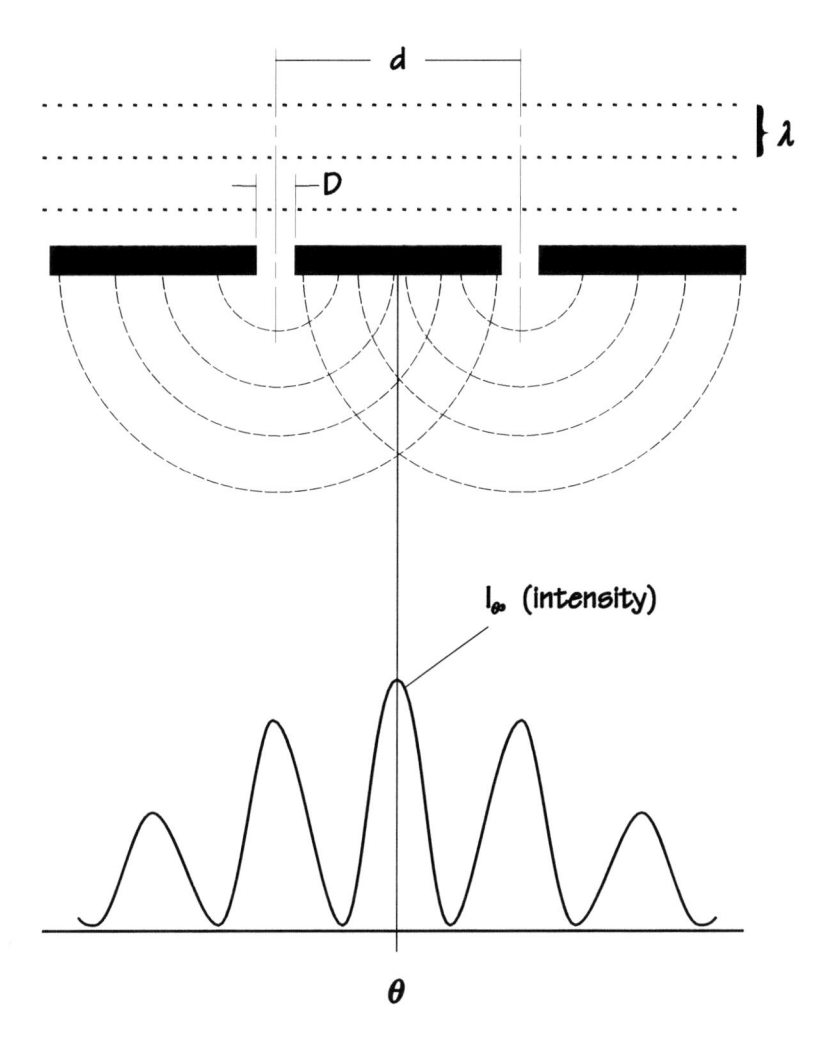

Figure (15-1)

Young's *Double-Slit* Experiment

The slit spacing is d and slit widths are both D. The light wavelength is considered to be of the order of the slit width or less. We find that the slits will cause the beams to diffract at the slit edges. In addition to this, the dispersed beams will interfere with one another. The resultant intensity pattern is shown in the Figure, and is a combination of slit diffraction and beam interference. The intensity pattern, as measured at the detector for a beam of light, is not equal to the sum of the intensity patterns of the individual slits, because there is now an interference term to be considered. The intensity pattern as a function of the angle, θ as measured out from an axis perpendicular to the plane containing the slits is shown in the figure, and is given by: [1]

$$I_\theta = I_o \left[\sin(\beta/2)/(\beta/2)\right]^2 \left[\cos(\delta/2)\right] \tag{15-1}$$

where,

$$\beta/2 = (\pi D/\lambda)\sin\theta \tag{15-2}$$

and,

$$\delta/2 = (\pi d/\lambda)\sin\theta \tag{15-3}$$

The term inside the first bracket of Equation (15-1) represents the result of the effect of diffraction of the waves at the slit, and is identical with Equation (14-3) of APPENDIX I-14 used in the discussion of the *Uncertainty Principle* relations. Notice that Equation (15-2) is identical with Equation (14-4) of APPENDIX I-14. The term inside the second bracket of Equation (15-1) represents the effect of the interference of the waves, whose wavelengths are λ and whose separation is d.

Figure (15-2) shows the intensity pattern contribution due to the *diffraction* at the slits, while Figure (5-3) shows the intensity pattern caused by the *interference* of the beams exiting the two slits. Figure (15-4) shows the resultant intensity obtained by combining the two curves.

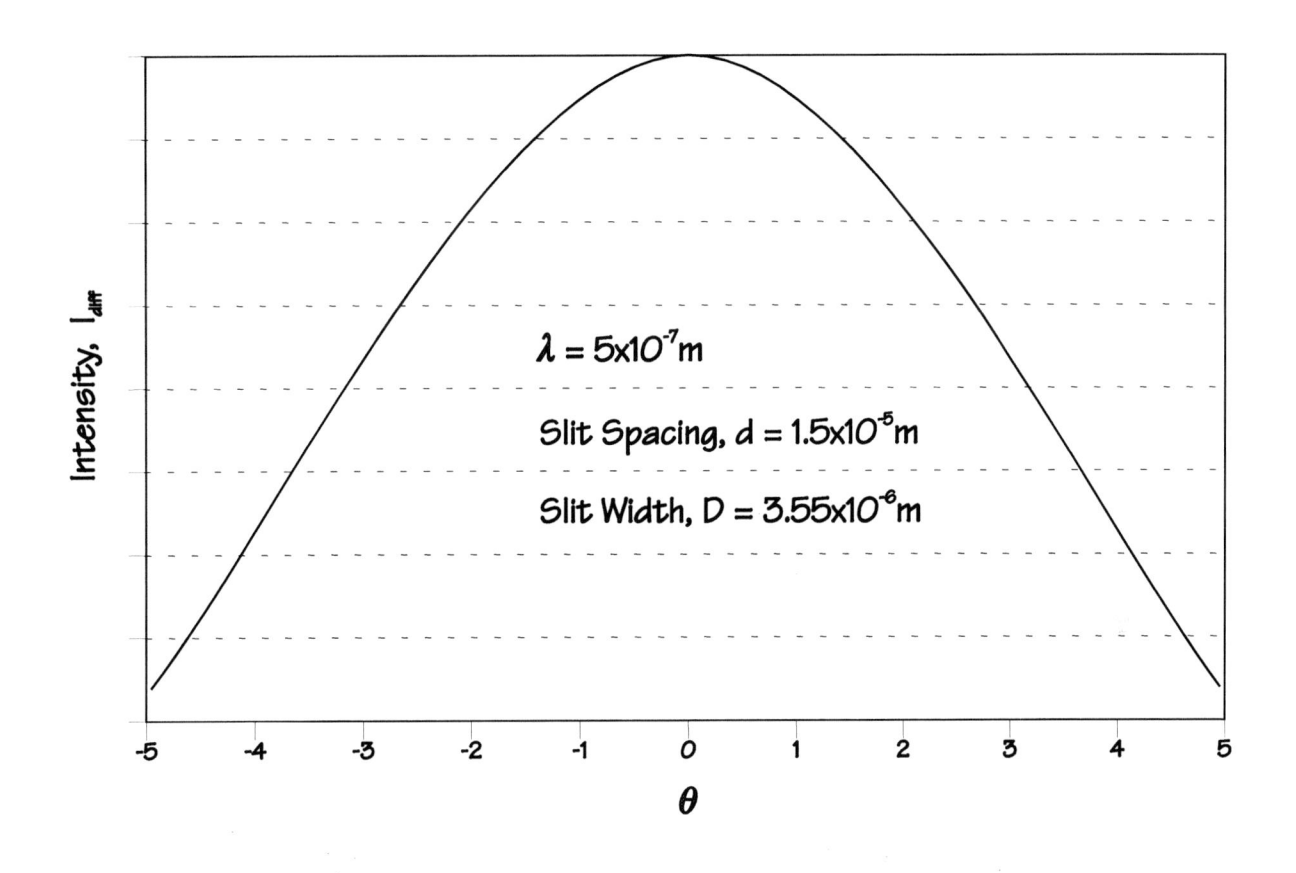

Figure (15-2)

Intensity Pattern Contribution Due to Slit Diffraction

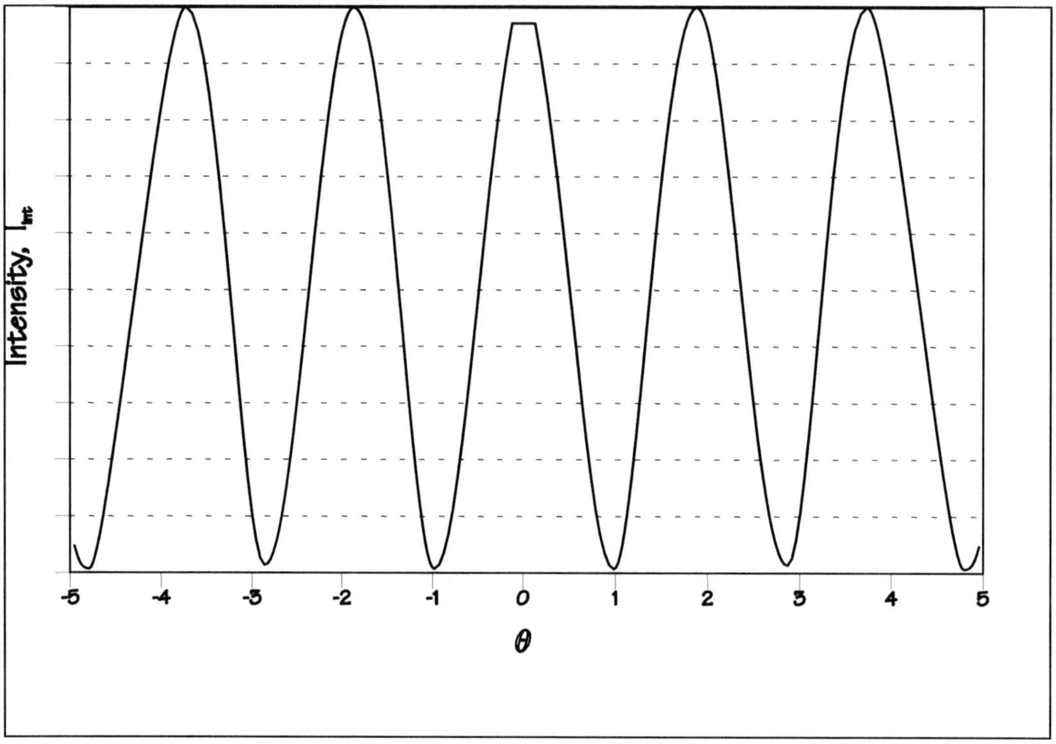

$\lambda = 5x10^{-7}m$

Data for Figure (15-3): $d = 1.5x10^{-5}m$

$D = 3.55x10^{10^{-6}}m$

(Note: Central peak is slightly cut off)

Figure (15-3)

Intensity Pattern Contribution Due to Beam Interference

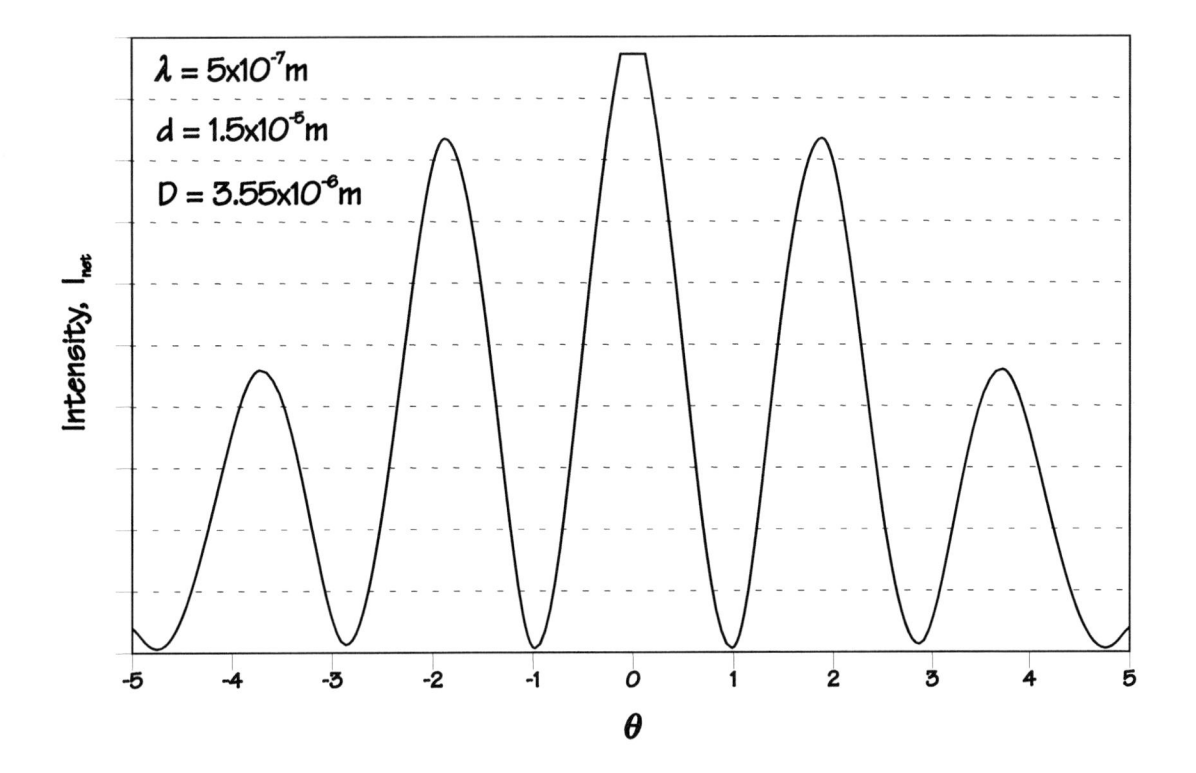

[Graph showing intensity distribution with parameters:
$\lambda = 5 \times 10^{-7}$ m
$d = 1.5 \times 10^{-5}$ m
$D = 3.55 \times 10^{-6}$ m
Y-axis: Intensity, I_{net}
X-axis: θ, ranging from -5 to 5]

(Note: Central peak is slightly cut off)

Figure (15-4)
Resultant Intensity Distribution Obtained by Combining
Figure(15-2) and Figure (15-3)

As the slit widths D get wider the diffraction pattern disperses less, but there is no change to the interference pattern. This effect is illustrated in Figure (15-5a, b). Although the slit spacings are wider than the spacings in the previous figures, it is the change in *slit widths* from $D = 1x10^{-5}$ to $D = 2.5x10^{-5}$ m that cause the overall intensity distribution to change. Holding the slit widths constant and changing *slit spacing* reveals the following, as illustrated in Figure (15-6a,b,c,d): As the spacing or separation d is made smaller the interference pattern rings become more widely spaced with angle until at the condition where the slit spacing is zero (only one slit), it disappears altogether.

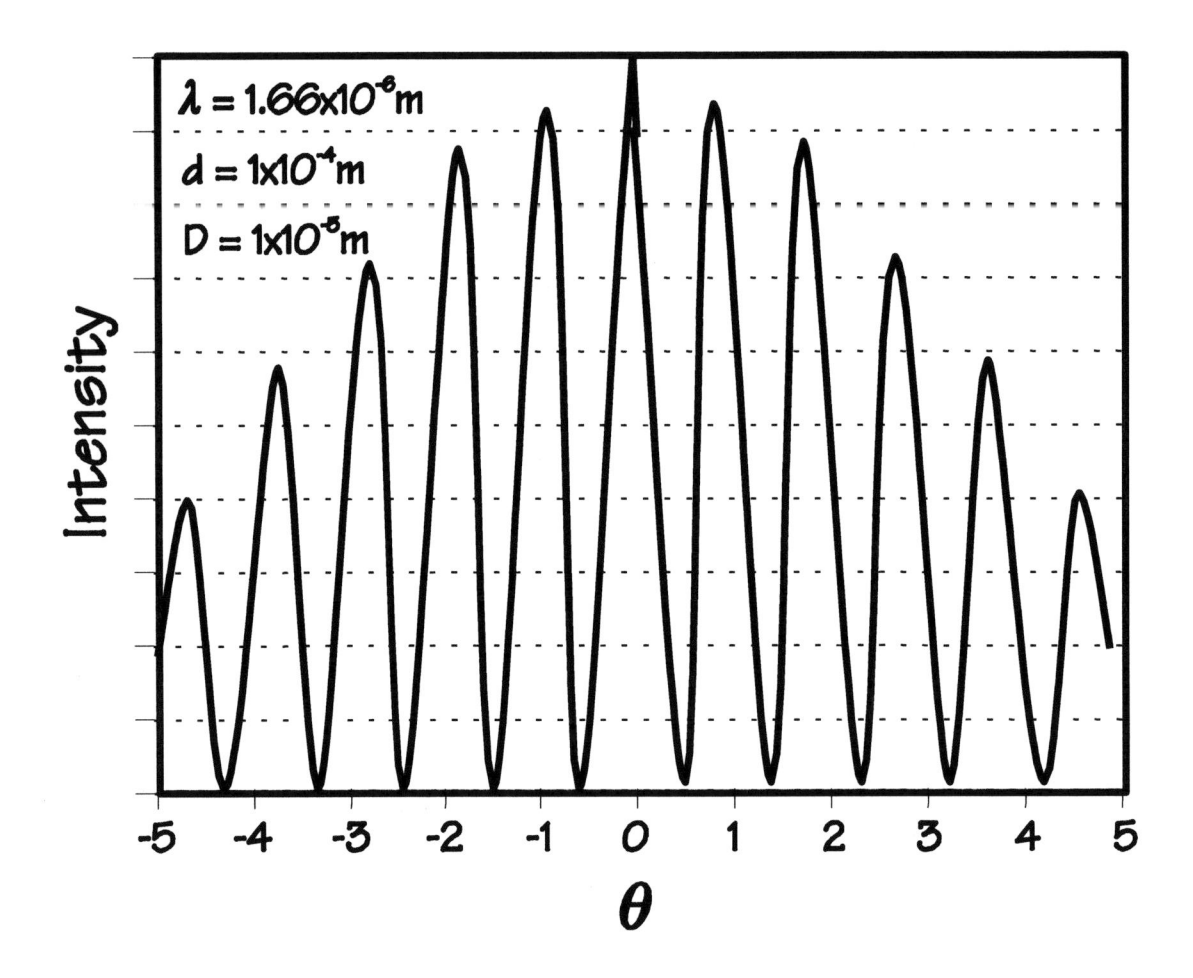

Figure (15-5a)

Intensity Distribution as a Function of Increasing Slit Width (D)

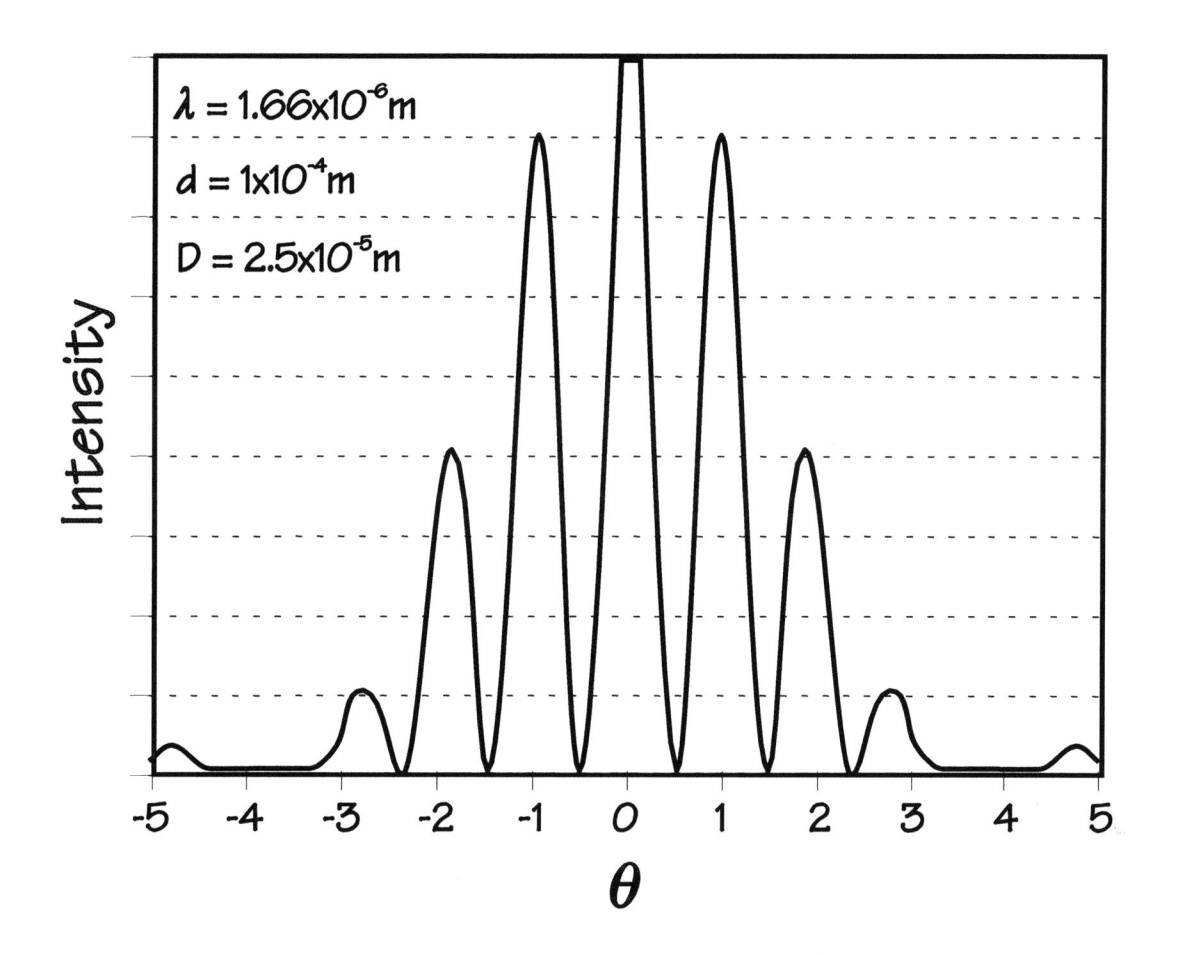

Figure (15-5b)

Intensity Distribution as a Function of Increasing Slit Width (D)

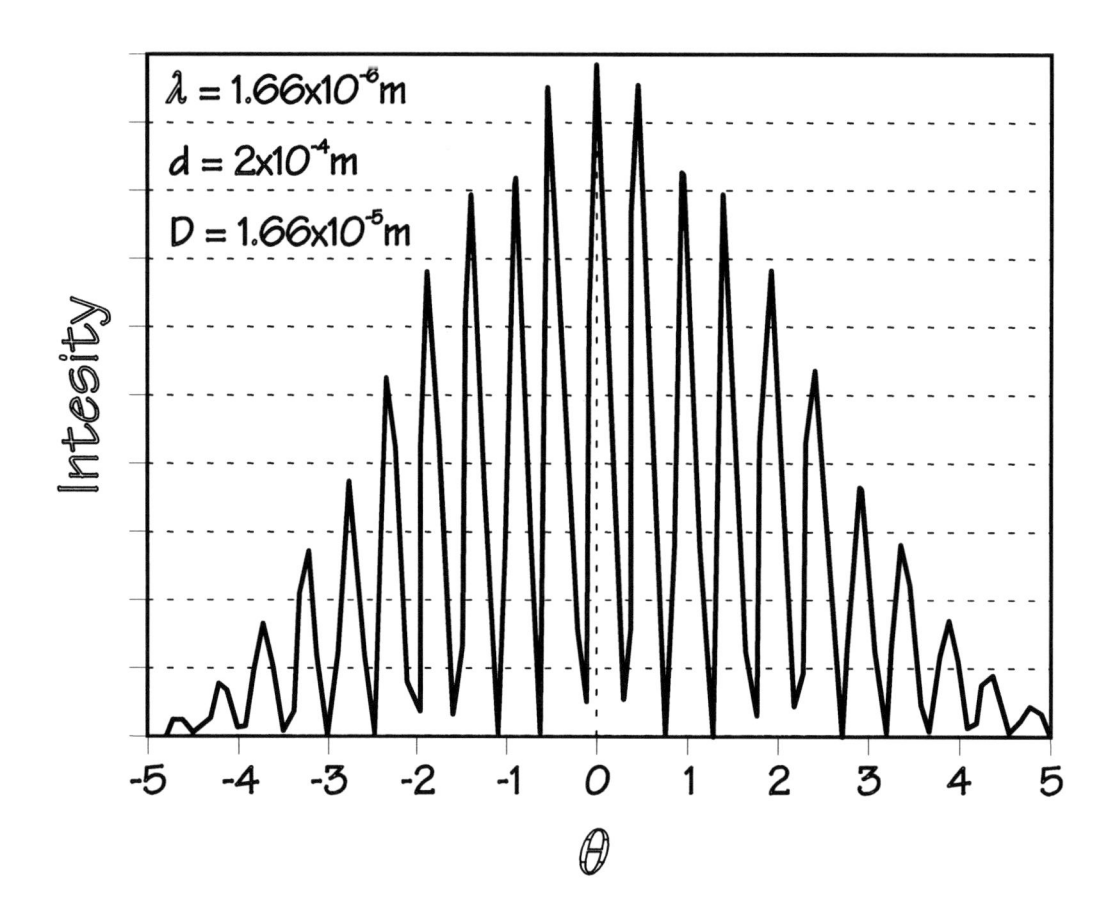

Figure (15-6a)

Intensity Distribution as a Function of Decreasing Slit Separation (d)

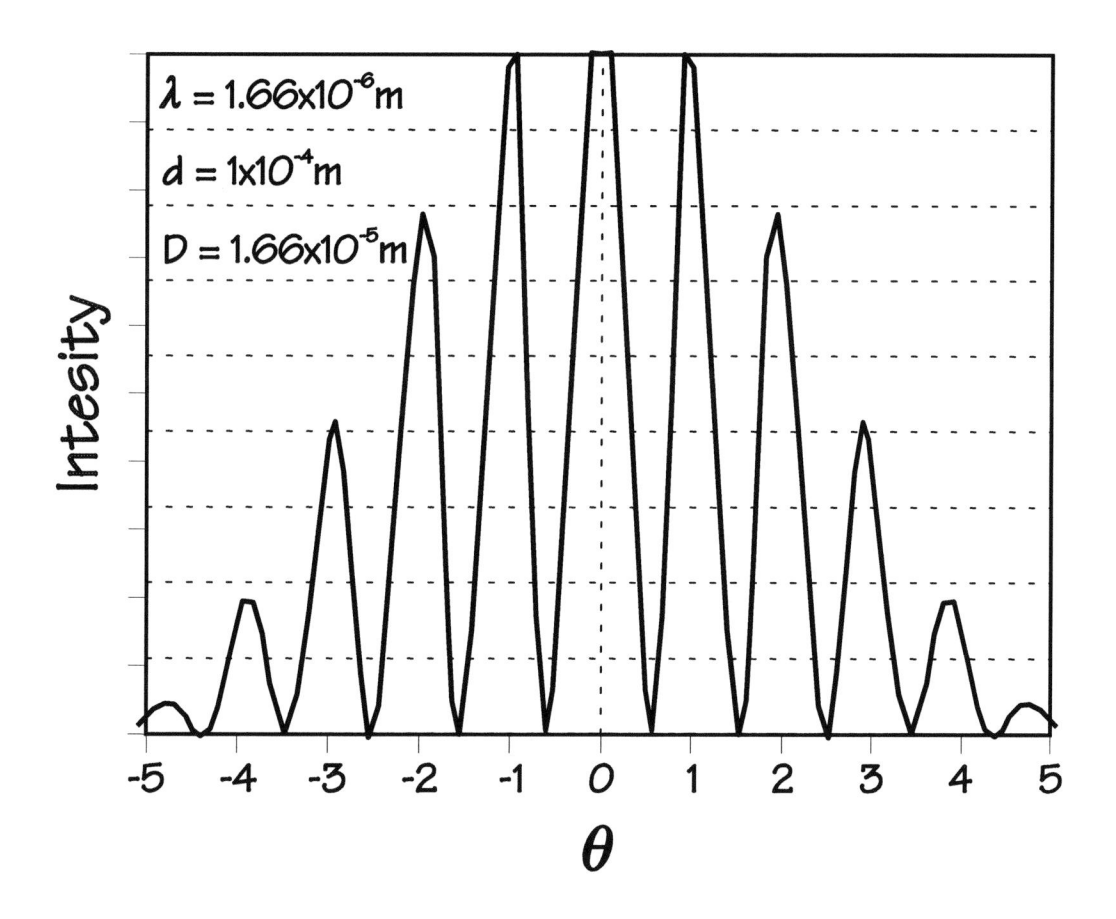

$\lambda = 1.66 \times 10^{-6}$ m
$d = 1 \times 10^{-4}$ m
$D = 1.66 \times 10^{-5}$ m

(Note: Central peak is slightly cut off)

Figure (15-6b)

Intensity Distribution as a Function of Decreasing Slit Separation (d)

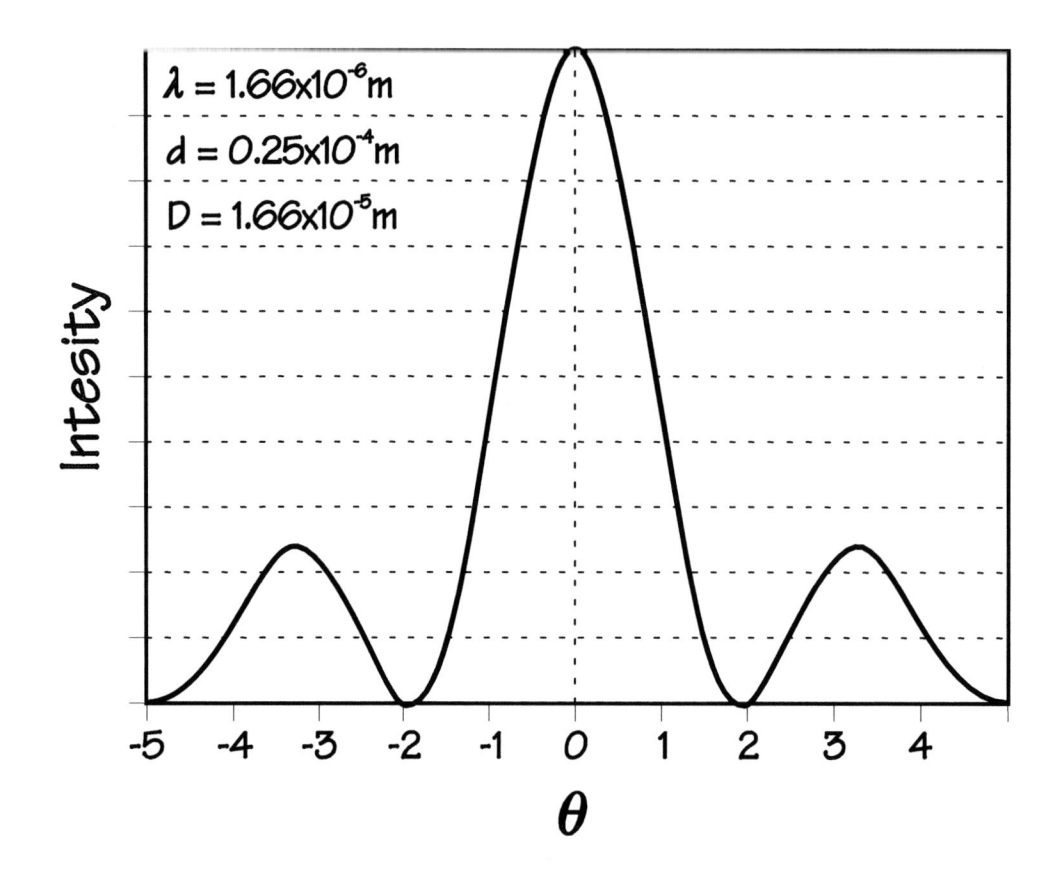

Figure (15-6c)

**Intensity Distribution as a Function of
Decreasing Slit Separation (d)**

$\lambda = 1.66 \times 10^{-6}$ m
$d = 0.0$ m
$D = 1.66 \times 10^{-5}$ m

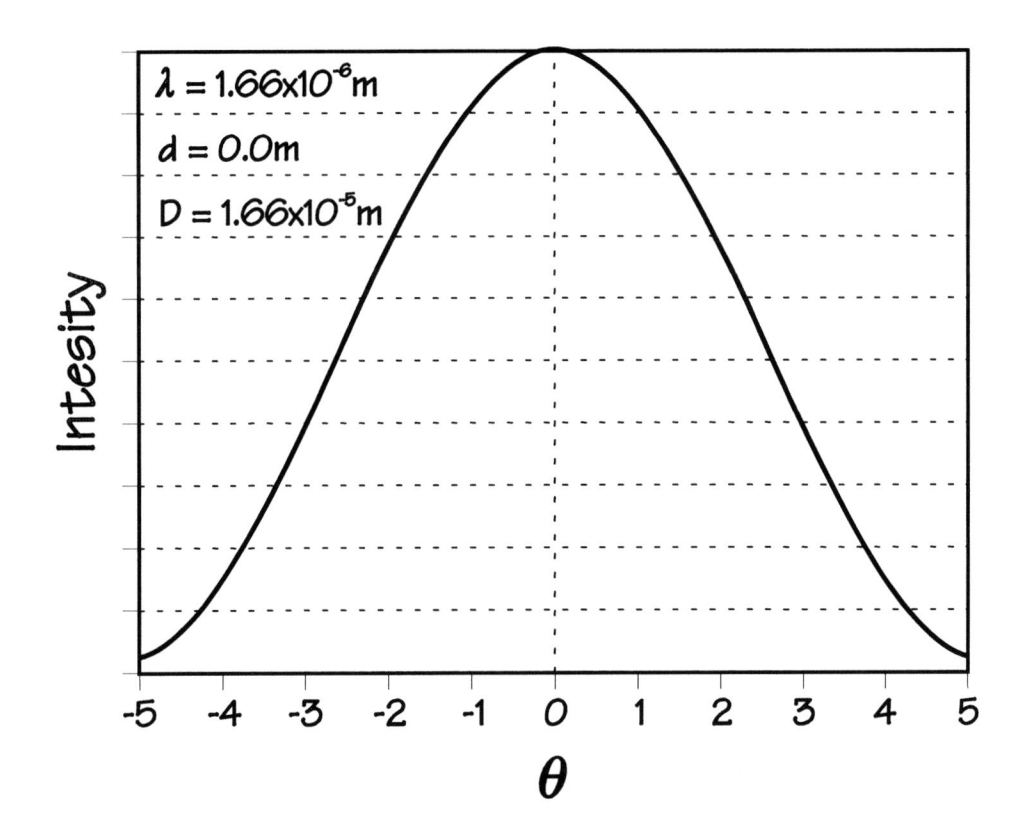

Figure (15-6d)

**Intensity Distribution as a Function of
Decreasing Slit Separation (d)**

We have seen that in the *Double-Slit* experiment, beams of light diffract at both slits and then interfere with one another further downstream, causing the intensity pattern on the photographic screen as shown in Figure (15-1). We might ask how this intensity pattern compares with patterns we might see in the macroscopic world of bullets and cannon balls for both the single and double slit cases.

SINGLE-SLIT EXPERIMENT WITH CANNON BALLS

Suppose we have a cannon as shown in Figure (15-7), that fires cannon balls at a single slit that is slightly larger than the diameter of the balls. The cannon is at a great distance from the slits, so the paths of the individual balls are nearly parallel and directed perpendicular to the plane of the slits. In this idealized situation, we assume the balls are rigid and

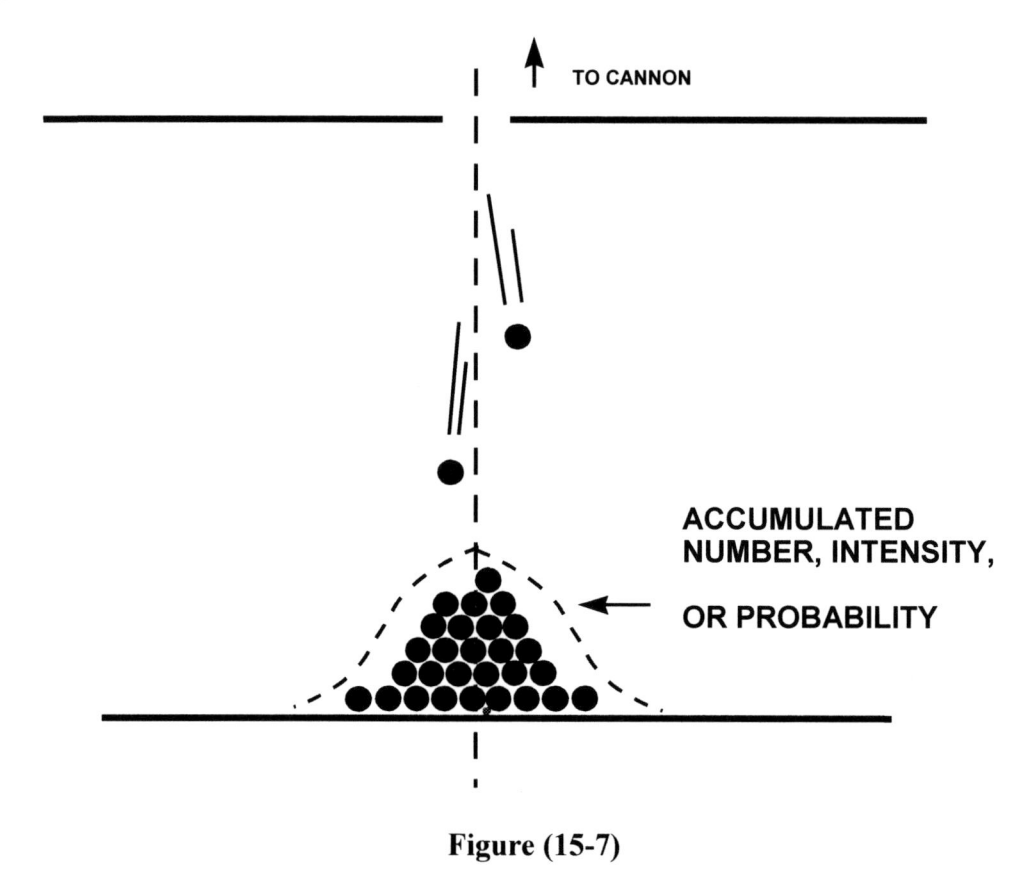

Figure (15-7)

Cannon Ball Distribution Through Single-Slit

unbreakable, and that the slit edges and the screen placed downstream are hard and will not disintegrate upon impact with the screen. We want to see what kind of distribution we would get if we shot one ball at a time toward the slit. We will assume that each ball "sticks" to the detector screen or to each other upon impact at the screen.

We will soon discover that the distribution arising from the cumulative impacts on the screen would be as shown in the Figure, and would be similar to the diffraction pattern of light waves through a single slit. The particle count, or intensity pattern, is represented by $|\psi(x)|^2$ which is proportional to the probability of finding a cannon ball along the x-axis as a function of angle θ. The equation for the probability amplitude is similar to the optical diffraction relation of Equation (14-3) of APPENDIX I-14, and with the appropriate boundary conditions, could be calculated.

We notice that each impact is the result of an *integral* unit of mass or energy - that of one cannon ball. The probability is greatest that most of the cannon balls will pass directly through the slit and impact the screen near the slit centerline. However, there is a lesser probability that some of the balls will graze or strike the slit edges and be diverted or deflected to varying degrees.

DOUBLE-SLIT EXPERIMENT WITH CANNON BALLS

Now let us look at Figure (15-8) for the case of cannon balls fired at *two* slits.

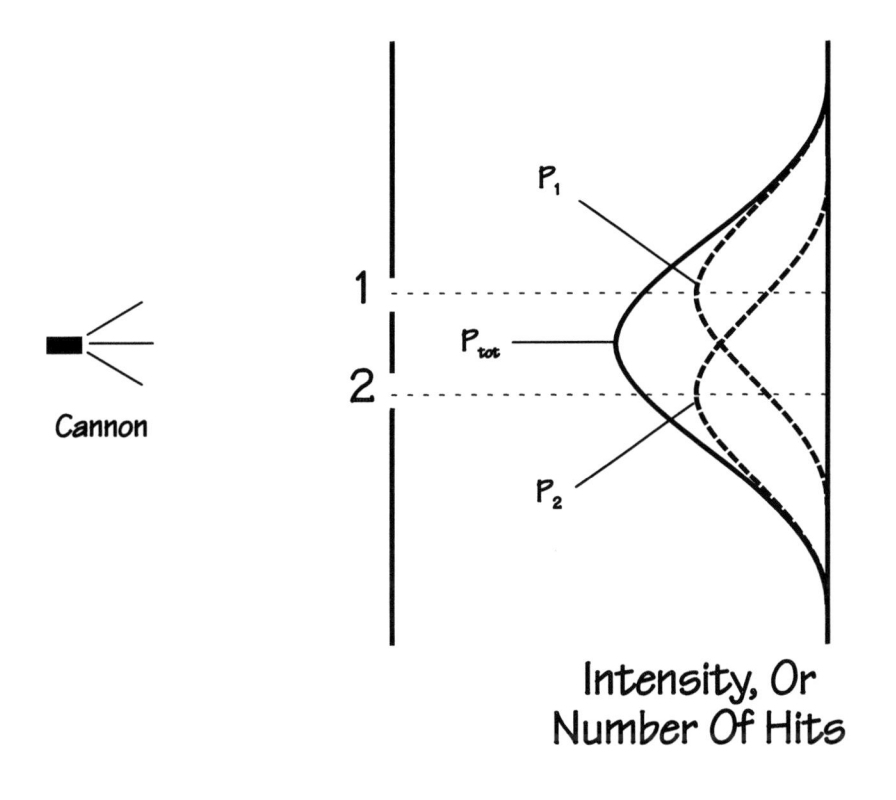

Figure (15-8)

Cannon Ball Distribution Through Two Slits

One cannon ball at a time is fired toward the centerline of the two slits. The Figure is greatly exaggerated in that the slit separation shown is much less than the distance between the cannon and the slit plane. The two dotted curves in the figure show the accumulated number of impacts of the balls from each slit as a function of distance x out from the two-slit centerline. These curves are labeled P_1 and P_2. These distributions represent the *number count* or *probability* that the balls exiting the upper slit or the lower slit, respectively, will impact the screen at a given distance along the x-axis.

The arithmetic addition of the contribution of individual slit distributions is shown by the solid line, and represents the total probability that the balls exiting the two slits will strike at a given point on the screen. This distribution is *not* like the double slit intensity distribution for beams of light or particles, because large, macroscopic objects such as cannon balls - although they do possess a de Broglie wavelength $\lambda = h/mv$ - do not produce a discernible interference pattern because the slit opening is enormous compared to the wavelength.[*] The probability distribution is the sum of the distributions of slit #1 and slit #2, and is given by:

$$P_{tot} = P_1 + P_2 \tag{15-4}$$

DOUBLE-SLIT EXPERIMENT WITH ELECTRON BEAM

Let us now consider the double slit experiment with electrons. The flux of electrons incident on the slits is so high that we do not see individual flashes on the screen or photographic plate, but observe a recorded intensity or brightness distribution that is similar to that of light waves passing through two slits as shown previously in Figure(15-1). Because of the wave nature of these particles and the size and spacing of the slits, [∇]electrons that have exited from both slits simultaneously will interfere with each other and cause the intensity distribution as shown. The distribution is *not* like that of the cannon balls[(2)], but is:

$$I_{tot} = I_1 + I_2 + 2\sqrt{I_1 I_2}\cos\delta \tag{15-5}$$

where δ is the *phase angle* between the two matter waves, the terms, I_1 and I_2 representing the intensities of light at the photographic plate due to slit #1 and slit #2, respectively (If we were considering water waves passing through two narrow openings, I would represent the square of the wave amplitude). The term $2\sqrt{I_1 I_2}\cos\delta$ represents the *interference* term. This expression could have been written as:

---

[*] The wavelength for a 1-kg object moving at 1000 m/sec is 10^{-37} m !
[∇] Comparable to the electron wavelength, in theory, because we could not fabricate an experiment designed of this nature with such small slit sizes.

$$P_{tot} = |\psi_1(x) + \psi_2(x)|^2 = |\psi_1(x)|^2 + |\psi_2(x)|^2 + 2|\psi_1(x)||\psi_2(x)|\cos\delta \qquad (15\text{-}6)$$

where $\psi_1(x), \psi_2(x)$, are the wave functions for the electrons. The vertical line brackets indicate absolute values; where $P_1 = |\psi_1(x)|^2, ... P_2 = |\psi_2(x)|^2$, the probability that the electrons going through slit # 1 will strike the screen, and the probability that electrons going through slit # 2 will strike the screen, respectively, *when one side or the other is closed.* P_{tot} represents the probability that electrons will strike the screen as a function of distance along the x-axis, for the case where *both slits are open* (Note: $P_{tot} \neq P_1 + P_2$). This is due to the presence of the interference term shown in the form of $2|\psi_1(x)||\psi_2(x)|$.

Equation (15-6) can also be written as:

$P_{tot} = |\psi|^2 = \psi^*\psi$, where $\psi = \psi_1 + \psi_2$, and where * denotes the complex conjugate. At each point in space $|\psi|^2$ gives the probability of finding the particle there.

Now, let us consider the following: What would we expect to see if our source emitted a *single* electron at a time at a *single* slit? We would observe a gradual build up of an intensity pattern similar to the diffraction pattern as shown in Figure (15-7) for cannon balls.

DOUBLE-SLIT EXPERIMENT WITH SINGLE PHOTON OR ELECTRON PULSES

Finally, what would we expect if a *single electron* (or single photon) *at a time* were directed toward a *double-slit* from an electron gun situated a distance in front of the double slit? As the electron exits the gun and approaches the slits we have no way of knowing which slit it will enter. An electron might go through slit # 1 and impact the photographic screen, after undergoing diffraction at the slit. In like manner, another electron at a later time might go through slit # 2. If an electron goes through a slit, it will pass through slit #1, 50% of the time and through slit #2, 50% of the time on the average. Each time an electron hits the photographic screen (a phosphorescent surface), there will be a flash of light of constant intensity or brightness. Because of this constant intensity flash, we are led to believe that an *integral* electron - and not a piece of the electron - strikes the screen each time. The rate of flashing on the screen will vary as a function of x, the distance out from the screen centerline. We observe that the occurrences of flashes appear in a seemingly random manner. We would expect after a period of time to see an intensity build up on the screen that would be similar to that of cannon balls going through the double slit, because, although electrons do have a de Broglie wavelength, it would seem to be impossible for a single electron to go through one slit and interfere with itself. *But the pattern of single point-like flashes that gradually build up reveal an intensity distribution like that of a beam of electrons or photons passing through both slits and interfering with each other!* How can this be!? When the single electron strikes the screen, we see a tiny, constant intensity flash of light as if a single particle has impacted. This is definitely a particle impact, but over a period of time other apparently random impacts build up an intensity pattern as if each electron had split in half and passed through both slits, with the two-electron wave components then interfering with each other.

We might ask the question, "What if the particle rate were reduced to one particle per minute, one particle per hour, or one particle per year?" The particle distribution at the screen would still distribute in a probabilistic way such that the interference pattern would appear.

From the results of the experiment we find an apparent contradiction. Since a single electron at a time was pulsed from the electron gun, only one electron approached the slits and went through either slit #1 or slit #2, and caused a tiny, localized flash of light on the phosphorescent screen, with a constant intensity or brightness, indicating that the impact was caused by a discrete particle, and not a wave. The electron did not somehow split in half, go through both slits and interfere with itself. We should expect the total intensity build-up to be the sum of the individual intensities from each slit:

$$I_{tot} = I_1 + I_2 \tag{15-7}$$

But this does not appear to be the case, for we find:

$$I_{tot} = I_1 + I_2 + 2\sqrt{I_1 I_2} \cos\delta \tag{15-8}$$

This is identical to Equation (15-5). We find, then that the probability of an electron striking at a given position is proportional to the accumulated intensity at that position, and can be written as:

$$P_{tot} \cong I_{tot} \cong |\psi_1(x) + \psi_2(x)|^2 \text{ (Same as Equation (15-6))} \tag{15-9}$$

From the total intensity pattern, it would appear that the electron somehow divided in two and passed through both slits simultaneously - the wave-like characteristics of each electron interfering with another electron's wave-like characteristic and causing constructive and destructive interference at the screen.

We also note a curious thing: *With only one slit open, the total intensity distribution reveals there are places on the screen that will be hit by electrons that will not be impacted when both screens are open.* This is illustrated in Figure (15-9).

Which slit did the electron go through? Perhaps, if we tried to localize the electron, that is, if we tried to determine which slit the electron went through, we might understand better how the screen pattern was created. Since an interference pattern is observed, this means that simply observing where an electron impacts the screen, does not give any information about which slit the electron went through, as seen in Figure (15-10). A single electron could pass through slit #1 and strike the screen at point a, or at point b, or it could pass through slit #2 and also strike the screen at *a* or *b*.

In an effort to pinpoint which slit the electron has gone through, we place small detector coils (loops of wire), as shown in Figure (15-11) in front of the entrances to the two slits to detect the magnetic field of the moving electron as it passes through the coil.[3] If each time we see a constant flash of light on the screen, we simultaneously observe a detector reading at one of the coils, we then know that the electron has passed through the slit in front of that coil, and subsequently impacted the screen. However, we see that *the very act of observation* - the "detection" of the electron by the coil as the result of the interaction of the electron's magnetic field with the coil - has caused a momentum change to the electron. The electron may no longer hit the screen at the same place as where it would hit if it had not been observed and disturbed. Thus, the interference pattern will be destroyed. The accumulated intensity pattern now becomes that of the summation of two

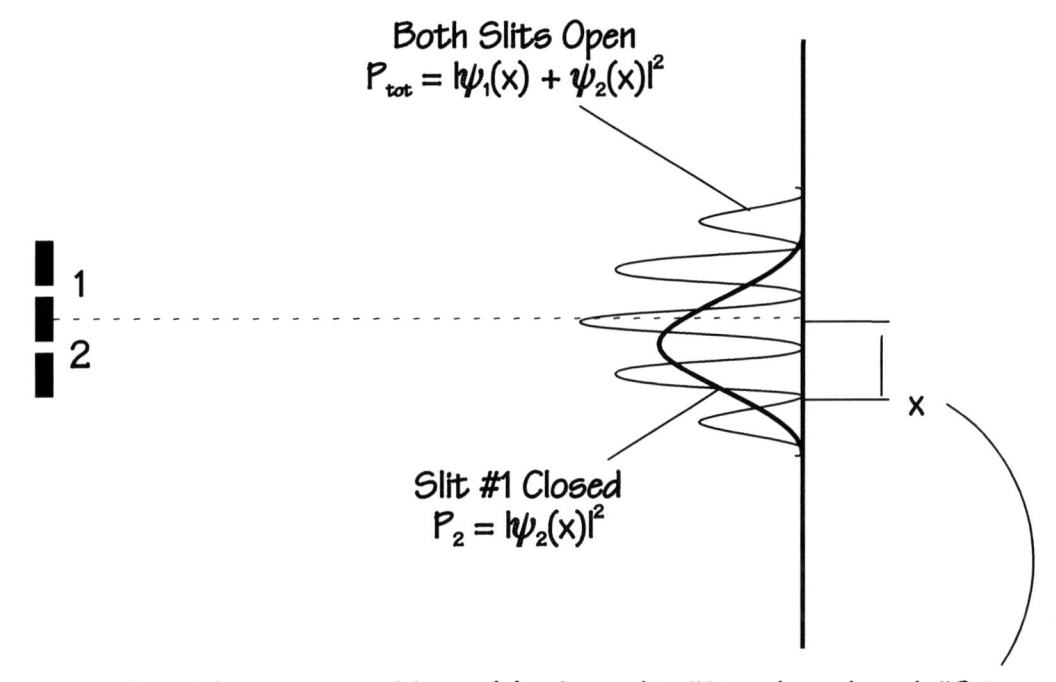

Both Slits Open
$P_{tot} = |\psi_1(x) + \psi_2(x)|^2$

Slit #1 Closed
$P_2 = |\psi_2(x)|^2$

Particle registered here (x) when slit #1 is closed and #2 is open, but not registered when both slits are open !

Figure (15-9)

Variance in Intensity Distribution as a Result of a Single Particle at a Time Passing Through One or Two Slits

diffraction patterns one would see if each electron went through a screen containing a single slit, was diffracted and hit the screen without interference occurring - the same intensity pattern caused by cannon balls exiting both slits, and as shown previously in Figure (15-8).

By trying to localize the electron, that is, by making the uncertainty in the position, Δx smaller so we can try to determine which slit the electron passed through, we no longer see the interference pattern, which is the result of the wave nature of electrons. If we use a larger diameter coil to reduce the interaction of the electron with the coil, then we find ourselves losing our knowledge about the position of the electron; for if the loop diameter becomes so large that the error in position measurement is larger than the slit separation, we will once again not know which slit the electron went through. The interference pattern will then reappear.

By observing the electron we disturb it. We change its momentum by some unknown value ΔP, and the resultant intensity or probability distribution is broader and ed. It

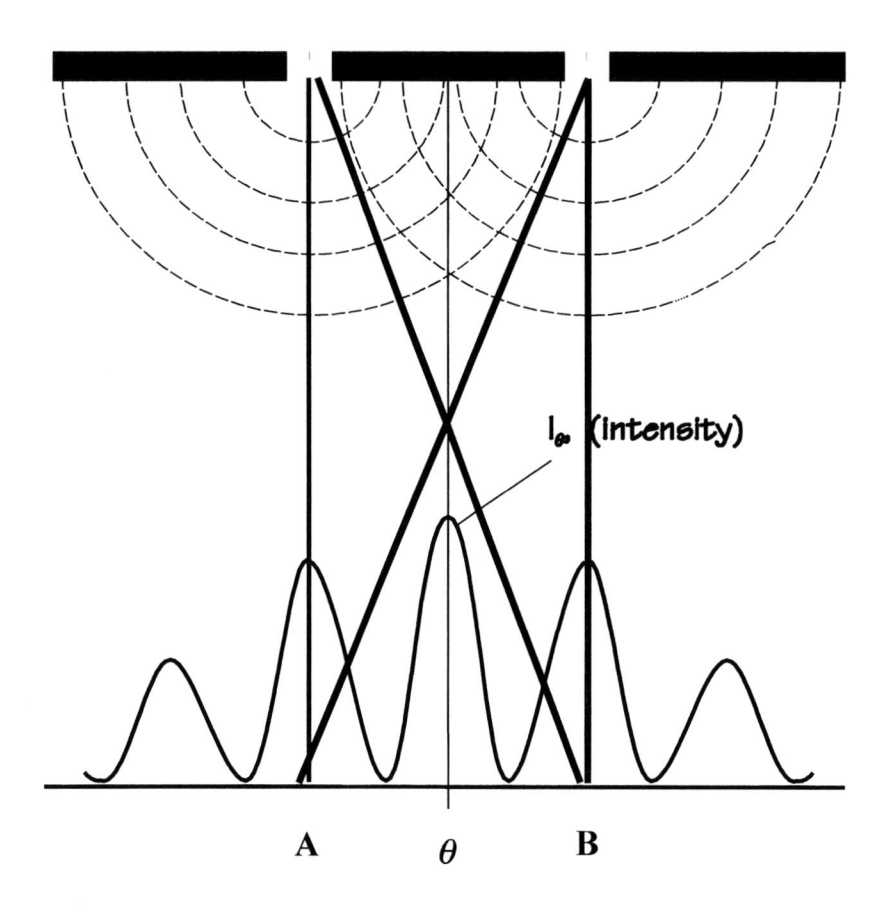

Figure (15-10)

Impossibility of Determining Which Slit a Single Particle Passed Through

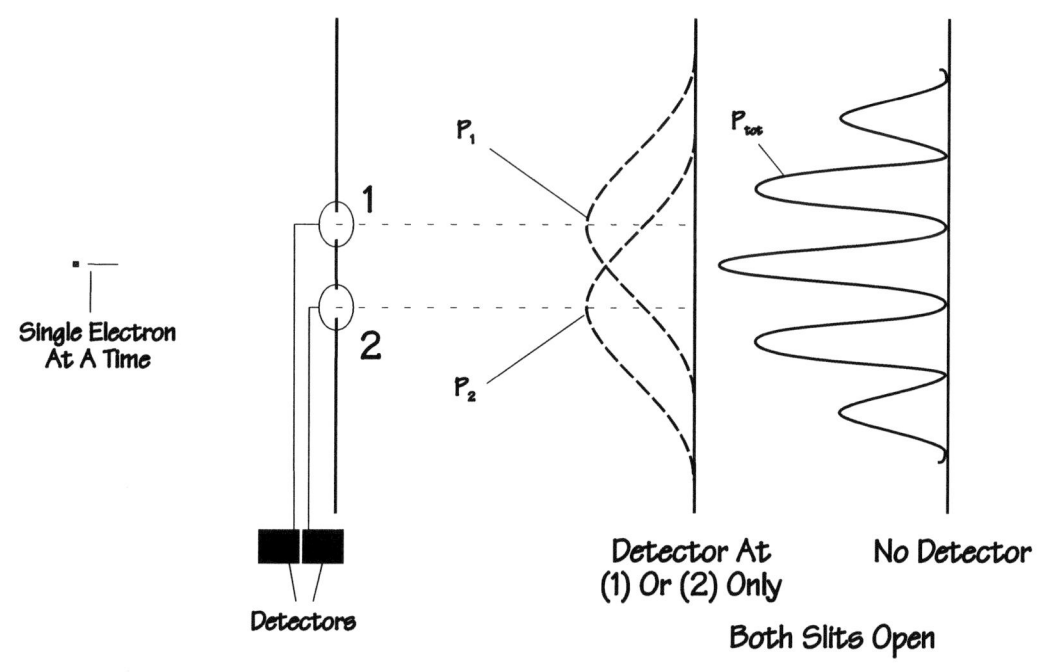

Figure (15-11)

The Effect on Intensity Distribution When a Detector is Placed Behind a Slit

should be noted that closing one slit would give the same results as trying to detect which slit the individual electron went through with a coil detector.

Other attempts have been made to try to determine simultaneously the position and momentum of an electron. One method is to allow the slit plate itself to move freely up and down upon interaction with electrons entering and leaving the slits. [4] It would seem that with this approach we would simultaneously know both the position of an electron going through one slit and the momentum imparted by the electron to the slit plate. From knowing the original momentum of the plate and the final momentum after interaction, we could in principle calculate the momentum of the electron. But in order to determine accurately the momentum of the plate we must know its initial location (and, thus, also the position of the slits), and this we cannot know precisely due to the constraints of the *Uncertainty Principle*. Therefore, if we do not know precisely where the slits are, the location of the interference pattern at the screen will be uncertain and the pattern will be destroyed.

In summary, it is impossible to detect which slit an electron goes through without disturbing it and the interference pattern recorded at the screen. If we look for the electron, we find it and know what slit it went through. That is, if we measure the position of the electron (observe the electron passing through a given slit), we no longer can predict where the electron will go, because we have disturbed it and imparted to it a momentum increase that cannot be known precisely. The pattern on the screen will be that due to electron diffraction only. If we move the screen further downstream of the slits, the probability distribution pattern will continue to spread like a wave, and the electron will essentially be smeared over a wider region. If we do not attempt to measure the position of the electron - we don't search for the electron at either slit - we do not disturb the electron and the momentum uncertainty is minimized, and the particle is deflected very little.

The first *maxima* of the interference pattern is the most probable place the electron will be found after passing through the slit plate, and is shown on the curve on the right-hand side of Figure (15-10).

We are either forced to say the electron went through both slits as a wave, but impacted the screen like a particle, or that it somehow "knew" that both slits were open and was "instructed" to distribute in a manner similar to that of an interference pattern. We note here that for macroscopic objects such as cannon balls, detectors and eyes, the matter wavelength is so small that the resolution of an interference pattern is impossible with scientific detectors.

We conclude that what we are seeing with the single particle in the *Double-Slit* experiment, is what has been called "quantum superposition." The particle is in state #1 when it goes through slit #1, and in state #2 when it goes through slit # 2, and has a 50% probability of going through either slit if no observation is made. (See Figure (15-12), single electron at a time.)[*] Therefore, the particle has *non-zero* probability for being in two states at the same time: a quantum *superposition of states* (state #1 + state #2). Without observation, we can say, in essence, that the particle has gone through both slits, interferes with itself because of the superposition of states, and then impacts on the screen in accordance with interference laws. [5]

Figure (15-12) shows the probability or intensity patterns for macroscopic objects and sub-atomic particles in the *Double Slit* experiments.

---

[*] Recall that Wheeler has said that the particle has no definite location or path from source to detector, but exists as a potential, only, and described by its wave function, util it is registered by a detector.

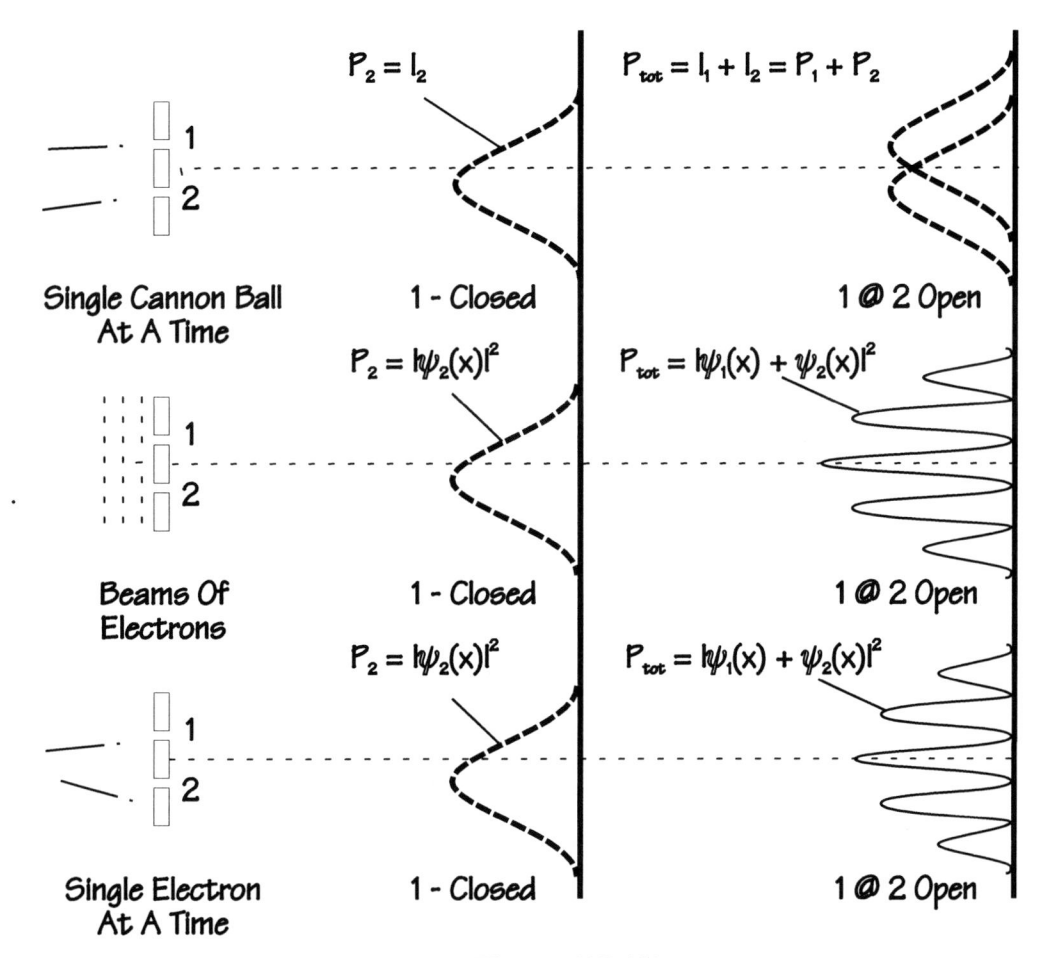

Figure (15-12)

Summary of Intensity Distributions for Macroscopic

and Sub-atomic Particles

Return to Chapter 15B (p. 38) The *Delayed-Choice* Experiment

APPENDIX I-15B

PHYSICAL AND THOUGHT EXPERIMENTS IN QUANTUM PHYSICS

E - THE *EPR* PARADOX

OBJECTIVE REALITY OR REALISM

Albert Einstein did not like the implications of quantum theory, even though as we have seen, he was largely involved in the discovery of the fundamental principles governing the theory. Einstein believed that the description of reality as given by the *Copenhagen* interpretation of quantum theory was incomplete. A reasonable definition of reality as stated by Einstein, Nathan Rosen, and Boris Poldolsky* in their paper (the *EPR* paper) presented in the *Physical Review*, May 15, 1935, was: "If, without in any way disturbing a system, we can predict with certainty (i.e. with probability equal to unity), the value of a physical quantity, then there exists an element of physical reality corresponding to this physical quantity."[1] The assumption that objects possess a reality independent of observation has been called "realism."

Although Einstein believed that it was impossible to measure any physical property (such as position), without affecting the measurement of another property (such as momentum), he could not accept the *Copenhagen* interpretation that a particle such as an electron did not simultaneously posses a definite position and momentum, even if these properties could not be measured precisely. Quantum theory denied objective reality to a particle's position and momentum until that physical characteristic had been measured. If the position were measured, one could not attribute any reality to the particle's momentum; and the choice of which physical property was to possess objective reality was left to the observer and not to the particle itself. The accuracy of any measurements made, however, still fell within the constraints of the *Uncertainty Principle*.

LOCAL CAUSALITY

But in addition to his objection to the quantum theory denial of objective reality, Einstein had a conviction of the principle of "local causality" - that an object situated a distance from a local object cannot instantaneously influence or affect in any way the local object. That is, no influence can propagate faster than the speed of light. The assumption that no influence can travel faster than the speed of light has been called "local causality," "locality," or "Einstein Locality."

---

* Referred to in this book as *EPR*

INDUCTIVE INFERENCE

A third assumption for the interpretation of reality is based on the legitimacy of forming conclusions based on a series of experiments that yield consistent results, and has been called, "inductive inference."

These three assumptions collectively form a basis for "local realistic" interpretations of the world about us.[2] The serious reader is referred to Bernard d' Espagnat's excellent article in *Scientific American* (November, 1979), entitled, "The Quantum Theory and Reality," for a more complete and comprehensive discussion on *EPR*

EPR THOUGHT EXPERIMENT

EPR proposed a thought experiment that was intended to prove that it was possible to predict either the position or the momentum of an object without disturbing it. If this could be accomplished, reality would then be seen to be objective, and a particle would possess physical characteristics independent of observation. But if reality were seen to be objective, and *if* quantum theory was complete, then there should be no way of predicting both of these properties without disturbing the particle, and this could only happen if one assumed non-local effects (faster than light influences) - something which Einstein could not accept. Einstein therefore concluded that quantum theory must be incomplete.[3]

The argument went as follows: Consider one possible example of the *EPR* thought experiment. A stationary atomic reaction occurs in such a manner that two protons fly away in opposite directions. Greenstein and Zajonic (*The Quantum Challenge,* p.110) [4] describe one way of producing polarized particles that move in opposite directions with their spins pointing in opposite directions, prepare an atom of positronium - an electron and a positron that are bound together, and that are in a state of zero orbital angular momentum. When the positron is "ionized" the required pair is produced.

By the conservation laws, the total momentum of the two particles is conserved. In this example, each particle has the same momentum - equal in magnitude but opposite in direction - so that the net momentum is zero, as shown in Figure (15-20). According to *EPR*, if one would measure the momentum of proton #1 after it has traveled downstream some distance, it would seem we would instantaneously know the momentum of proton #2. Although proton #1 was disturbed by the measurement it would not matter, because proton #2 has not been disturbed by the proton #1 measurement. (Also, since the atomic reaction is symmetrical, both particles will have moved the same distance from the origin of the reaction, so if we instead had measured the distance proton #1 has moved from the reaction, we could deduce the distance of proton #2. [5])

Now, after we have deduced the momentum of particle #2 without disturbing it, we can measure its position. At that precise moment we have determined both the position and momentum of particle #2, an act which would violate the *Uncertainty Principle* which was part of the *Copenhagen* interpretation of quantum theory.

Quantum theory describes physical reality through wave functions. A wave function can be constructed to describe the state of the two protons including the sum of their momenta. This *total* momentum is considered real, although the individual momenta are indeterminate. [6] As long as both protons remained unobserved their properties, such as, position and momentum are uncertain and are the results of a superposition of all possible states given by the wave function for the proton pair. This means that each proton has some potential for being located in any direction, and can be thought of as being smeared out over a large region of space. According to quantum theory, the correlation between the two particles' positions and momenta (P) immediately after the reaction continues to exist as the particles move away from each other, but once a measurement has been made on one particle, and its momentum has been affected to some unknown degree, this very act of measurement will also affect the momentum of particle # 2, so that the net momentum remains the same (in this instance, zero). This has been called *quantum entanglement*, the result of the creation of a two-proton pair due to the atomic reaction. [7] The created proton pair is called a *singlet state*. [v]

proton # 1   **proton # 2**

● ◄——————— ✺ ———————► ●

(1) - momentum (P) of proton #1 and proton # 2 are equal and opposite in direction.

(2) - Measure P1…We now know P1 = - P2, without disturbing P2.

(3) - Measure the position of proton # 2.

(4) - We now know, at this precise instant, the position and momentum of proton # 2; an act which would be a violation of the *Uncertainty Principle*

Figure (15-20)

***EPR* Interpretation of Quantum Events**

---

[v] Quantum entanglement can be thought of as a superposition of the quantum states of two or more particles, considered as one system.

A modification to the thought experiment can be made.[8] In this experiment, *proton spin* is to be measured.* Proton spin in some ways can be thought of as somewhat similar to the angular momentum of a ball that is spinning about an axis through its center. By convention, if we would view from equatorial orbit the earth, and observe the earth rotating from west to east, we would indicate this angular rotation by an arrow (a vector) pointing northward as shown in Figure (15-21). This is called *spin-up*. For a particle spinning in the opposite direction from east to west, the arrow would be in the southerly direction. This is *spin-down*.

In general, the entangled state for two particles with opposite spin is:

$$\psi = \frac{1}{\sqrt{2}}\left[(\uparrow)_1(\downarrow)_2 + (\downarrow)_1(\uparrow)_2\right], \qquad (15\text{-}10)$$

where the subscript 1 refers to the first particle, and the subscript 2 refers to the second particle. The up arrow is for particle spin-up, and the down arrow is for particle spin-down. Note that an entangled state cannot be represented as the *product* of $\psi_1\psi_2$.

Quantum theory says that the spin orientation of individual protons are indeterminate as they move away from each other, but that the net spin is zero. However, classical physics states that at the time of creation of the two free protons, each proton has a definite spin orientation, even if unknown. Based on the three criteria for reality as stated earlier, we might expect that if we would measure the spin of proton # 1, then by the law of the conservation of angular momentum, the spin of proton # 2 should be of equal magnitude with the vector for the momentum pointing in the opposite direction, as shown in Figure (15-21).

---

* The spin of a particle can be measured by *a Stern-Gerlach analyzer*, which measures the component of spin along the analyzer's axis. The *exact* configuration is not shown in Figure (15-21).

[Figure showing EPR experiment setup with two protons, spin detectors, and axis diagrams]

THE SPIN OF EACH PROTON CAN BE BROKEN INTO THREE COMPONENTS ALONG THREE AXES (A,B,C).

FOR THE TWO-PROTON SYSTEM, IF YOU MEASURE A SPIN COMPONENT OF EACH PROTON ALONG THE SAME AXIS, (AA,BB, OR CC)YOU ALWAYS GET A STRICT NEGATIVE CORRRELATION:A+A-,A-A+, OR B+B-,B-B+, OR C+C-.

(CONSERVATION OF ENERGY)

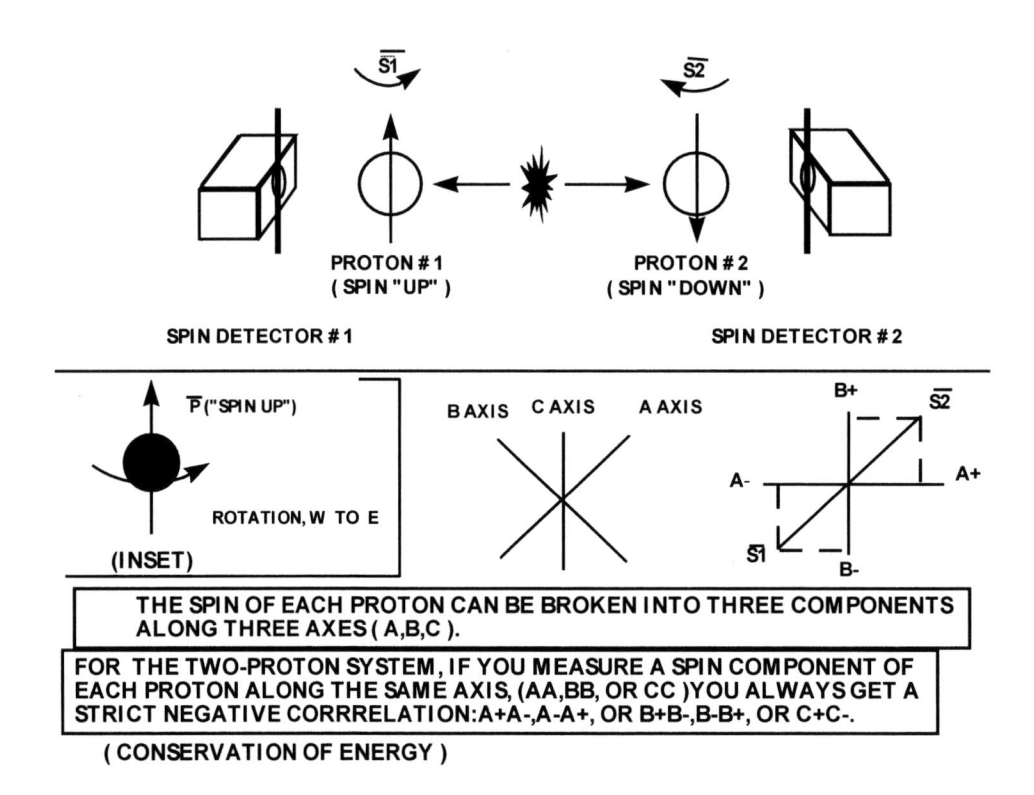

Figure (15-21)

The Measure of Proton Spin in the *EPR* Experiment

For realism to be the order, and for parallel spin-detector axes, for the two-particle case, we would find a strict *negative* correlation of the proton spins.

For a measurement of the spin of proton # 1 as shown by the vector $\vec{S}_1$ we would expect to measure the spin of proton # 2 as equal in magnitude but opposite in direction; that is, $\vec{S}_2 = -\vec{S}_1$. *EPR* proponents would set out to prove that measurement of the spin of each proton would be the measurement of real properties [9], and that one can infer the spin orientation of proton # 2 if he has first measured the spin of proton # 1, *provided* the axes of the spin detectors are *parallel* to each other.

So from all this we have learned little information, because the spin orientations of the two protons at their creation are always equal, and their angular momentum vectors always point in opposite directions. It is as if two *identical* twin children each morning select a hat to wear to school. Regardless of what color hat Birt wears, Bill always decides to wear the opposite color. If Birt wears a red hat, Bill will wear a white hat, and vise-versa. The children walk (one child heading west, and the other heading east) to different schools located at the opposite sides of the small village. *You* - wait outside Birt's school. You can never predict what color hat the child walking toward you will be wearing, but once you see the color of the hat, you can telephone your friend located outside the school at the other end of town and tell him or her what the color of the other child's hat will be. The children *no longer interact* in any way, yet the color of their hats are always correlated. The message of this story (according to F. David Pear, author of

"Einstein's Moon") is that it is possible for distant, classical and local objects (the two children) to be correlated "without needing to interact in any way or sending any cross-checking signals to each other." Both *EPR* and quantum theory predict the same correlation.
****

Before we go further it is necessary to introduce the concept of *spin components*. Initially, we do not know the orientation of the proton spin vectors, but we can set up detectors to measure the spin, or rather, the spin components of each proton. The projection of the proton's intrinsic *angular momentum* onto an axis (such as a detector axis) is called the *spin component* along that axis. [10] According to the theory of proton spin, no matter what the orientation of a detector axis to the spin vector, the spin component along that detector axis can be found to have only one of two values: designated as A^+ for a proton spin whose component lies along the $a+$ axis, and A^- for a spin whose component lies along the $a-$ axis. (We know that for macroscopic objects like spinning cannon balls, the angular momentum component can vary from P to zero.) Figure (15-21) shows spins $\vec{S}_1$ and $\vec{S}_2$ and their projections along axes *A and B* (The *C* axis projections are not shown.). The axes do not have to be oriented in any particular way. For the two-proton system, if the spin component of each proton is measured along the same axis (for parallel detector axes), we will *always* get a strict negative correlation. That is, for spin components measured along three arbitrary axes $A, B, and C$, the only possible spin component values are: $A^+A^-, A^-A^+, B^+B^-, B^-B^+, and C^+C^-, C^-C^+$. However, the sequence of the measurements would be random. In summary, for measurement of spin components along the same axes, if we measure A^+ for one proton, we will measure A^- for the other proton.

The problem is that it is impossible to measure simultaneously the values of the three spin components, that when added vectorally, make up the total spin of a particular proton. And if we try to measure one component at a time, we - in our measuring - affect the value of the other two components.
****

So... if the spin orientations of the two protons at their creation are always equal, and their angular momentum vectors always point in opposite directions, then how can we determine if the particles have, or have not objective reality?

In 1964, John Bell [*] of *CERN* (*European Organization for Nuclear Rese*arch) proposed a method for determining whether the two protons had objective reality (such as the children), or whether they or their physical attributes were indeterminate until a measurement.[⊕] had been taken. (The colors of the children's hats were classically determinate.) Bell proposed modifying the *EPR* experiment to introduce a *relative orientation of the two spin detectors*. He was able to show mathematically that as the spin detectors were rotated with respect to each other, the degree of negative correlation

---

[*] See J. Bell, "On the Einstein-Podolsky-Rosen Paradox," Physics, vol. 1, pp. 195-200 (1964)[11], and "On the Problem of Hidden Variables in Quantum Mechanics," Rev. Mod. Phys., vol. 38, pp. 447-442 (1966)[12]

[⊕] A measurement that changes the status of the quantum world from a world of quantum waves or possibilities to a world of actual particles.

decreased. That is, if the angle between the two detectors is allowed to be some angle other than zero, and to vary from zero to 180 degrees, we will no longer see a strict negative correlation of the spin components. Quantum theory can calculate the exact degree of spin component correlation as a function of angle for the two protons. The correlation is given by: [13]

$$C_{quantum} = -\cos\theta \quad ^\nabla \qquad (15\text{-}11)$$

Classical mechanics cannot predict mathematically the exact degree of spin correlation with angle, but for statistically large samplings, and random measurements of unknown spin components, Bell derived a probabilistic relationship for real particles (particles that have objective existence, independent of observation) that limits the degree of correlation possible as a function of detector angular separation. He discovered that although there is a strict *negative* correlation when the two detector axes are parallel, and a strict *positive* correlation when the axes are oriented at 180 degrees with respect to each other, and no correlation when the angle is 90 degrees. There is less negative correlation (or greater positive correlation) as the angle between the detector axes increases from zero to 180 degrees. This relation is illustrated in Figure (15-22).

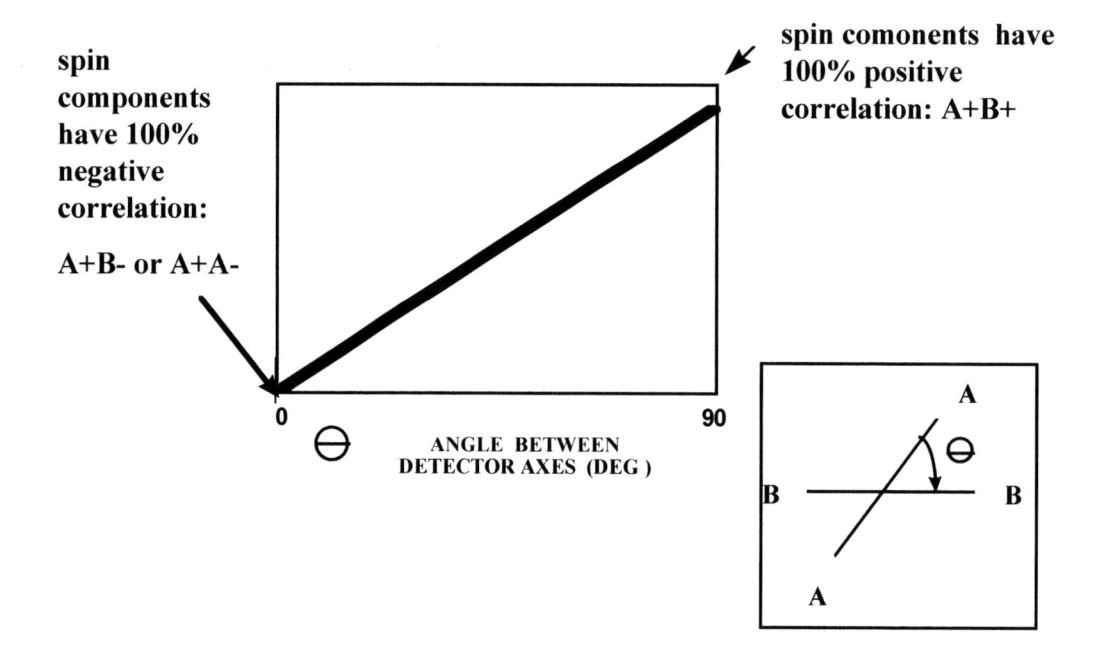

Figure (15-22)
Degree of Spin Correlation with Angle Between Detector Axes in the *EPR* Experiment

---

$^\nabla$ The reader is referred to "Multiparticle Interferometry and the Superposition Principle" (D. M. Greenberger, M. A. Horne, A. Zeilinger, in Physics Today, August, 1993) for this determination. [14]

As shown, when the two detector axes are parallel ($\theta = 0$ degrees), the spin components have 100% negative correlation, i.e., $A^+B^-...or...A^+A^-$.

Quantum theory, on the other hand, predicts that the degree of negative correlation with increase in angle should decrease *more slowly* than the limit for real particles as predicted by Bell. Bell showed that the difference in degrees of correlation for real, objective particles should be greatest in the range of 30 - 60 degrees.

According to *EPR*, each proton possesses a reality that is independent of the reality of the other proton - or of the detectors - and its properties are defined moment-by-moment, by unknown or *local hidden variables* or parameters.[*] We do not know the exact form of these hidden variables, but Bell determined a probabilistic limit on the degree of interaction of the protons with each detector as a function of angle, and on the subsequent degree of correlation of spin components.

For *classical*, real particles, rotating the detector axis for proton # 1 will cause a different probability of registering A^+ (spin-up) or A^- (spin down) independent of the orientation of the detector at proton # 2. The spin-up / spin-down probabilities for proton # 1 are independent of the orientation of the detector at proton #2. This is not true for quantum theory: *how the spin detector is oriented at proton #1 affects the measurement of proton # 2 spin components at its detector.* Therefore, the equation for determining the degree of spin correlation for real particles should be the result of two different probabilities: one at detector #1, and the other at detector #2. We see, therefore, the degree of correlation for real particles cannot be derived from Equation 15-11, because the $\cos\theta$ term cannot be broken up into two parts.[15]

** Can Local Reality Postulate a Mathematical Relationship That Will Give the Same Results as Equation (15-11)?

If the quantum relation for predicting the degree of proton spin correlation cannot be used by the local reality (*EPR*) proponents, could there be another local hidden variable relationship that would give the same results as predicted by quantum theory? Bell, again, was able to show that for a series of detector orientations - axes *AandB*, axes *AandC*, and axes *BandC* - that no local hidden variable relation could be found that would give the same degree of correlation as that shown by Equation (15-11).[∇][16]

The now-famous statistical relationship derived by Bell [17] is (for objective, local reality):

Number $[A^+B^+] \leq$ number $[A^+C^+]$ + number $[B^+C^+]$ (15-12)

The reader is referred to Reference (17) for a more complete discussion of the above relation, which is known as the *Bell Inequality*.

---

[*] Proponents of *EPR*, holding that reality is local, believed that correlation between separated particles arose because local hidden variables or "instruction tables" found in nature in some way would instruct the particles in such a manner that their behavior would be correlated

[∇] That is, no local hidden variable can account for all the phenomena predicted by quantum theory.

If the first letter inside each of the above brackets is the axis for detector #2, and the second letter is the axis for detector #1, then this inequality says that the number of A^+B^+ proton pairs measured can never be greater - statistically, for large number of samplings - than the sum of the A^+C^+ and the B^+C^+ pairs.

As a result of Bell's work, it can be shown that if quantum theory is correct, then the distant particles will display a different degree of spin correlation - less negative (or more positive) correlation with increase in angle then would be predicted for statistically -real particles. Bell predicted the following inequality would hold if quantum theory were shown to be correct (for non-local reality):

Number $[A^+B^+] \geq$ number $[A^+C^+] +$ number $[B^+C^+]$ (15-13)

--- Bounds on local and non-local correlations

If we assume local reality, it is possible to determine a total correlation between two experiments; one experiment with one degree of detector orientation, and a second experiment with a different degree of orientation. The total correlation for the two orientations can be expressed in terms of the individual results (see *Einstein's Moon*, F. David Peat). [18] Bell showed that the bounds of the correlation for the two experiments (local reality) was:

$$-2 \leq F_{local-reality} \leq +2$$ (15-14)

Quantum theory for the two-detector orientation experiment predicts a different result which depends on the orientation of *both* detectors, and is given by [19]:

$$F_{quantum-theory} = 2\sqrt{2} = 2.83$$ (15-15)

This is the value for detector orientation angles of 45°, but other values are possible for different detector orientations. As Peat points out, the formula for quantum mechanical cases has to be calculated for each particular values of the orientation angles, and is rather complicated. Peat concludes, "…the quantum world is more highly correlated than any world that depends on a local reality or locally operating hidden variables." [20]

** Experimental Procedures

The experimental set-up is shown in Figure (15-23), where a series of measurements (set # I) are to be made on a proton pair. Initially, detector # 1 and detector # 2 B and A axes, respectively, are oriented at zero degrees with respect to each other. After many series of measurements have been made and recorded on many proton pairs, *the angle between the axes is increased by a nominal amount, and another series of measurements and recordings are made. This process is continued until the final series of

---

* It should be noted that only one spin component is measured on any given proton.

measurements are made at an angle of 90 degrees. Then the set # II series is made with detector axes C and A, and finally set # III with axes C and B.

However, questions still remained in the minds of some physicists, even after the experiments that had been made showed that *Bell's Inequality had been violated.* "Could it be possible," they asked, "though highly unlikely, that the result of the correlation experiment at detector #1 would somehow be transferred to the second detector and cause that detector to register spin component data that more closely correlated with the data taken at detector #1?"

Alain Aspect, working at the *Institute of Theoretical Physics* near Paris, France, in the early 1980's performed a series of experiments where the time interval between measurements at the two detectors was less than the time required for a signal traveling at the speed of light to travel the distance.[21] The time interval was:

$$\Delta t \leq d/c \qquad (15\text{-}16)$$

where d is the distance between detectors, and $c = 3 \times 10^8 \ m/sec$, the speed of light.

In addition, in one of his series of experiments, aspect changed the orientations of the detectors while the particles (in this case, photons) were in flight, thus precluding any possibility of information about the detector arrangement influencing the results. *Bell's Inequality was still violated* (Equation (15-12)), and the results were in agreement with quantum theory predictions given by Equation (15-11) and (15-13).

In Figure (15-24) [v] we observe that the experimental data (small circles with vertical lines or data bars), does not follow the Bell's statistical inequality curve, (solid, straight line), but is in remarkable agreement with the predictions of quantum theory (dotted, curved line). (Note: Error bars are shown in *approximate* positions.)

---

[v] A. Aspect, J. Dalibard, G. Roger, "Experimental Test of Bell's Inequalilties," Phys. Rev. Lett., vol. 49, pp. 91-94 (1982).[22]

	B - AXIS		A - AXIS
I			
II	C - AXIS		A - AXIS
III	C - AXIS		B - AXIS
	1		2

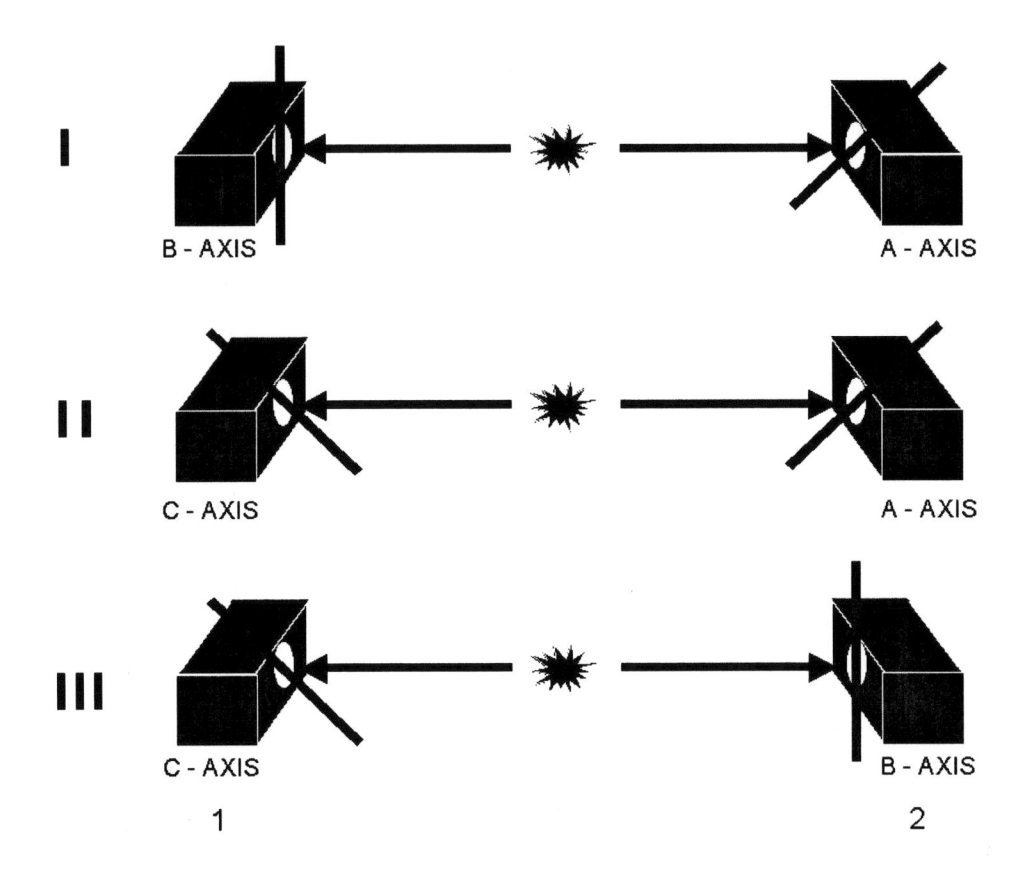

Figure (15-23)

Experimental Set-up for Measuring Proton Spin Correlations in the *EPR* Experiment

** Non-Local Hidden Variables

Thus, it appears that the doctrine of local reality is false, and the particle properties have no objective existence unless observed. But wait! What about the transfer of information by some means *faster* than the speed of light? The transfer of information faster than the speed of light is called *superluminal*. In Einstein's Relativity work, he allowed for the possibility of particles that could travel faster than the speed of light. In fact, they never travel *slower* than light. These hypothetical particles have been given the name *tachaens*. Few physicists want to adopt the theory of tachaens into the interpretation of quantum events because the theory would lead to violation of the principle of causality, which in some instances could result in absurd happenings, such as, an electric light illuminating a room *before* someone flips the switch to "on."

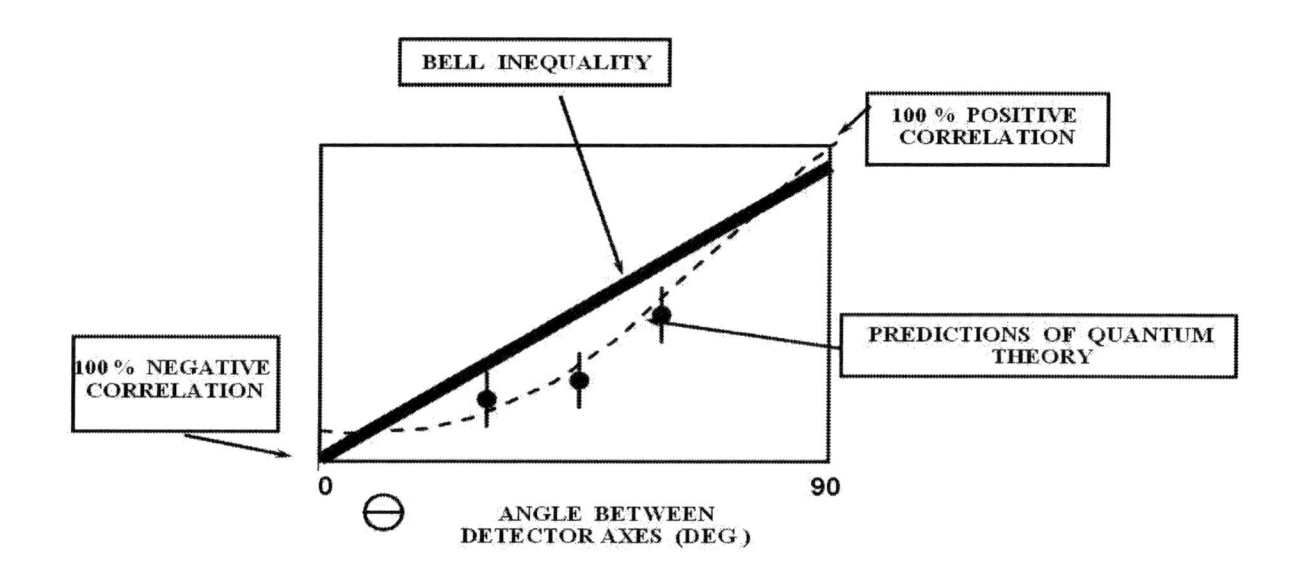

Figure (15-24)
Experimental Results Indicate *Bell's Inequality* is Violated *

** Summary

Bell Inequality: Number $[A^+B^+] \leq$ number $[A^+C^+]+$ number $[B^+C^+]$

Quantum Theory Prediction:

$$\text{Number } [A^+B^+] \geq \text{ number } [A^+C^+] + \text{ number } [B^+C^+]$$

So in effect the results of the EPR experiments are similar to your tossing a coin into the air, and catching it just before it hits the ground. Only at that instant would you learn the state of the coin lying in your hand: say, "heads up." At that same instant your friend miles away catches his or her coin in mid-air and discovers it is "tails up", always the opposite of your coin (see Chapter 10, Probability, for discussion of die "topside 3" potential (1/6) conversion to "topside 3" actuality).

---

* See Berdnard Espagnat article in *Scientific American*, November, 1979, "The Quantum Theory and Reality."

It is interesting to note that for the *Bell Inequality* experiments, all correlation data accumulated are random in nature. The experimenter at detector #1 cannot control the outcome of a measurement made by an experimenter located at detector #2, even though under certain orientations of the two detectors (see Figure (15-24)) there is a definite correlation between the two measurements. That is, if one looked at the data taken at detector # 1 or detector # 2, each set of data would be entirely random because of the random nature of the individual proton spin vectors. It is only when *both* sets of data are compared that we notice a correlation. So, in the strictest sense, the Relativity restriction that says no useful information or signal can travel faster than the speed of light, has not been violated.

There is now sufficient additional information accumulated in recent years [23] [24] from numerous experiments to support the conclusion that quantum theory is complete - and Equation (15-11), and the inequality given by Equation (15-13) are satisfied. The doctrine of local reality is false. *And some physicists also believe that particles have no objective existence until they are observed: reality is non-objective.* The observer, by changing the orientation of his spin detector at proton #1, brings into existence different spin component values for distant proton #2. The reader should also refer to "Quantum Theory: Weird and Wonderful," by Tony Leggett, *Physics World*, December, 1999 [25] : Experiments performed over the last decade or so have convinced some physicists that "...nature cannot be described by any objective local theory." Also, "The experimental tests of Bell's inequalities...go so far as to change the very way we should think of physical existence at its most fundamental level." (*The Quantum Challenge*, p.- 144) [26] *

Not all physicists agree with the above statements. Although it appears that so-called *local* hidden variable theories will never be able to account for the entire range of quantum phenomena, this does not – according to Greenstein and Zajonc (*The Quantum Challenge*, pp. 144-145) [28] – rule out some *non-local* theories that attribute *objective* properties to the quantum world.

In 1992 David Bohm introduced a quantum potential Q, to go along with the usual potential, V for a quantum particle:

$$Q = -\frac{h^2}{2m}\frac{\Delta^2 R}{R} \qquad (15-17)$$

where Q is obtained from the Schrodinger equation in polar form. [29]

Bohr believed that he could explain all the features of quantum mechanics by this term. In the *Double-Slit* experiment, in regions around the slit, this quantum potential changes rapidly, resulting in a force that "guides the particle into the interference maxima and away from the minima." [30] This approach, although non-local, maintains the classical picture of particles with clearly defined positions and velocities, and that move along known paths through space. Some physicists believe Bohm's approach to describing quantum phenomena, but acknowledge that it requires the addition of a new

---

* J.S .Bell has said, "It remains a logical possibility that it is the act of consciousness which is ultimately responsible for the reduction of the wave packet;" but he hoped that physics would eventually describe a more objective theory of nature.[27]

quantum potential (Q) that differs at the very fundamental level from traditional physics potentials. The approach appears somewhat ad-hoc.

Recently, Karl Hess and Walter Philipp at the *University of Illinois* (Urbana) have shown mathematically that "the introduction of time-like correlated random parameters" allow for the construction of a model which supports the quantum theory prediction for results obtained for spin pair correlation. If, as they say, hidden variables are time-correlated, then *EPR* results can be explained without resorting to "spooky action at a distance." An article in *Nature* [31], "Exorcising Einstein's Spooks," gives an analogy: the hands of clocks in New York and London circulate periodically, but do not influence each other. But the times on the clocks, although not the same, are correlated. The writer of the article hastens to add that the results do not necessarily mean that hidden variables exist, only that they cannot be completely ruled out.

F- EXPERIMENTS IN QUANTUM TELEPORTATION

The *EPR* experiments discussed earlier indicated that reality, at least at the quantum level is non-local, and that quantum particles possess no definite dynamic attributes until an observation has been made. In the *EPR* experiments, two particles created from some quantum event possess the property of quantum entanglement;[*] and the observed characteristics of each particle depend on the measured characteristics of the other. If one particle is observed to have a horizontal component of polarization (for photons), the other particle will have the orthogonal characteristic of vertical polarization.

Recently, basic experiments in quantum particle teleportation [**] have been made by a team of scientists at the *Institute fur Experimentalphysik, Universitat Innsbruck,Technikerstr,* Austria, and published in *Nature*, vol. 390, 11 December, 1997. [∇] The title of the article is, "Experimental Quantum Teleportation."(see Dik Bouwmeester, et al, "Experimental Quantum Teleportation," *Nature*, vol 390, 11 Dec., 1997). [1] A brief description of the theory behind quantum teleportation is given below.

We know that a single photon can be polarized in the general superposition of two states: (using the symbol notation appearing in the *Nature* article) horizontally polarized, $|\leftrightarrow\rangle,$ *and* vertically polarized, $|\updownarrow\rangle.$, such that the state of the photon is given by:

$$|\psi\rangle = \alpha|\leftrightarrow\rangle + \beta|\updownarrow\rangle \qquad (15\text{-}18)$$

where α and β are complex numbers, such that $|\alpha|^2 + |\beta|^2 = 1.$

---

[*] Quantum entanglement: the result of the creation of a two-photon pair due to the stationary atomic reaction. The created photon pair is called a singlet state. As long as the particles are unobserved, they remain entangled no matter how far they are separated, and their properties remain indefinite and are a superposition of all possible states. As soon as one particle is measured and put into a definite state the other particle is instantaneously put into a definite state.

[**] Quantum teleportation: the transmission and subsequent reconstruction over arbitrary distances of the state of a quantum system; the transfer of the quantum *state* of one particle onto another particle. It is possible to transfer the state of one particle onto another particle only if no information is acquired about this state during the transformation.

[∇] Dik Bouwmeester, Jian-Wel Pan, Klaus Mattle, Manfred Eibl, Harald Weinfurter, and Anton Zeilinger.

If a photon in the above state goes through a beam-splitter – a device that will reflect (for example) horizontally-polarized photons with a probability of $|\alpha|^2$, and transmit vertically-polarized photons with a probability of $|\beta|^2$ – we find that it is impossible to perform this measurement on $|\psi\rangle$ to obtain all the needed information to reconstruct the state $|\psi\rangle$.

Now, Let us look at Figure (15-25) for a brief explanation of the experiment and the theory behind it.

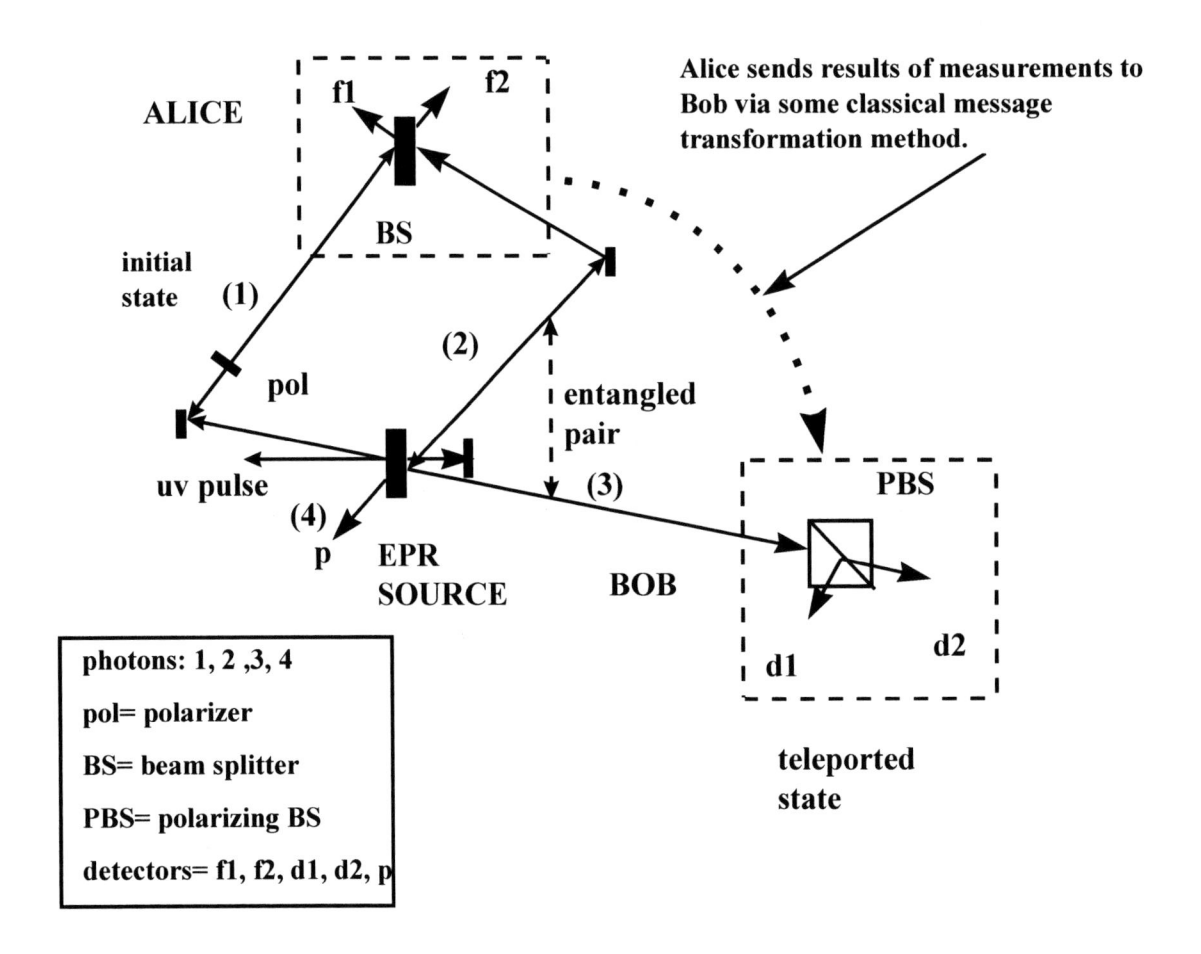

Figure 15-25

Experiments in Quantum Teleportation

A pulse of ultra-violet radiation passes through a non-linear crystal (*EPR* source),[*] and entangled photons #2 and #3 are emitted. The entangled photons #2 and #3 are identified by:

$$|\psi^-\rangle_{23} = \frac{1}{\sqrt{2}}\left[|\leftrightarrow\rangle_2|\updownarrow\rangle_3 - |\updownarrow\rangle_2|\leftrightarrow\rangle_3\right] \qquad (15\text{-}19)$$

It should be noted that the entangled state contains no information about the individual particles, but does indicate that the entangled particles will be in opposite, or *orthogonal* states, (horizontally-polarized, and vertically-polarized). But according to quantum theory, as soon as a measurement of one of the photons projects it into one state (say horizontally-polarized), the state of the other photon will be instantaneously determined to be vertically-polarized, and vise-versa.

After retroflection back through the crystal, the pulse creates another pair of photons: one of which will be prepared in the initial state of photon #1 to be teleported, and one (#4), which will be a trigger indicating that a photon (#1) to be teleported is under way.

The initial state of photon #1 is:

$$|\psi\rangle_1 = \alpha|\leftrightarrow\rangle_1 + \beta|\updownarrow\rangle_1 \qquad (15\text{-}20)$$

Suppose Alice wants to teleport a photon in this initial state to Bob who could be located at a great distance from her. She takes one entangled photon (#2) and Bob takes the other (#3). She superposes photon #1 and entangled photon #2 at a beam-splitter and looks for correlation between the two photons. The data is taken at detectors f_1 and f_2. Her objective was to perform a specific measurement on photons #1 and #2 which will project them into an entangled state given by:

$$|\psi^-\rangle_{12} = \frac{1}{\sqrt{2}}\left[|\leftrightarrow\rangle_1|\updownarrow\rangle_2 - |\updownarrow\rangle_1|\leftrightarrow\rangle_2\right] \text{ *} \qquad (15\text{-}21)$$

Bob receives the other photon (#3) that was entangled with photon #2. Alice now has to transfer the results of her correlation measurements of entangled photons, #1 and #2, via some *classical* transformation method (less than or equal to the speed of light), to Bob.

Now quantum theory says that once photons #1 and #2 are projected into the state, $|\psi^-\rangle_{12}$, photon #3 is instantaneously projected into the initial state of photon #1. To

---

[*] Incoming ultra-violet photon decays in to two photons, (#2) and (#3).

[*] It has been pointed out by the experimenters that this state "is only one of four possible maximally entangled states into which any state of two particles can be decomposed" (The negative sign in $|\psi^-\rangle_{12}$ indicates that this state differs from the other three states by the fact that there is a sign change upon interchanging particle #1 and particle #2). Because of the four possible states, teleportation is achieved.

see why this is true, remember that photons #1 and #2 must be in opposite states. Also, since photons #2 and #3 had been initially prepared in state $\left|\psi^-\right\rangle_{23}$, their states are also orthogonal to each other. For example:

photon #1	photon #2	photon #3
	vertical polarization	horizontal polarization
↕........	........↕ ↕........	........↕
Therefore photon #1 must have horizontal polarization		

Therefore photon #3 must be in the same state as photon #1 was initially, where the state of photon #1 was:

$$\left|\psi\right\rangle_1 = \alpha\left|\leftrightarrow\right\rangle_1 + \beta\left|\updownarrow\right\rangle_1 \tag{15-22}$$

and photon #3 state is:

$$\left|\psi\right\rangle_3 = \alpha\left|\leftrightarrow\right\rangle_3 + \beta\left|\updownarrow\right\rangle_3 \tag{15-23}$$

Bob studies the data received classically from Alice which shows that Alice obtained a correlation or coincidence count in detectors f_1 and f_2, identifying the state $\left|\psi^-\right\rangle_{12}$. By the argument given above he now knows that his photon (#3) is now in the initial state of photon #1, and he can verify this by his own polarization measurements at d_1 and d_2. Photon #1 has lost its identity through entanglement with photon #2. Therefore the state of photon #1 at Alice's station has been destroyed by the teleportion process. Since no information has been gained in this process by either photons #1 or #3, and since photon #1 is no longer available in its original state, photon #3 is *not a clone or copy*, but is the result of *teleportation.* [*]

If, in the far future, it were found possible to transfer the state of atoms comprising a macroscopic object (an assemblage of quantum particles), then presumably the quantum states of the atoms of the brain could also be teleported. But by its own physical laws underlying the mechanism of teleportation, modern physics has itself declared that consciousness and memory cannot be teleported. This is so, because teleportation cannot transfer information. Consciousness and the memories that are

---

[*] Not all researchers agree with this conclusion.

located there, represent *information,* and therefore, cannot be teleported. Also, I believe, consciousness is not dependent upon the complex arrangement of atoms in the brain.

In actual fact consciousness – which is non-local - cannot be acted upon - influenced - by quantum mechanical laws. Information itself is not conscious awareness. A collection of the volumes of the *Encyclopedia Britannica* that resides on your bookshelf contains no conscious awareness.

We hear many knowledgeable people assert that consciousness *emerges* (intelligence out of non-intelligence) when the number of neurons in a brain is drastically increased; that consciousness therefore is caused by the material brain. And the proof of that, they say, is that if a hammer is banged on the top of the head, consciousness is reduced, and may be entirely eliminated.

But…Christians, take note!

It was shown by Christ Jesus in his resurrection from the dead and his subsequent ascension beyond the physical senses, that consciousness does not depend on material structure, and space-time (his instantaneous transfer across the Sea of Galilee.) [2] And consciousness is not a quantum phenomenon. Today, some individuals are performing so-called "instantaneous" healings that would appear to violate the laws of physics. More on this in Part II of the book.

Return to Chapter 16 (p. 54)

APPENDIX I-17

THE MEASUREMENT PROBLEM

Let us consider further the argument about whether it is consciousness alone that can collapse the wave function, or whether an inanimate observer, such as some kind of recording device, can accomplish that collapse.

Consider an object that has only two states Ψ_1 and Ψ_2. The first state could be that of a light that is "*on*," while the second state could be that of the light that is "*off*." (I have closely followed the measurement problem example given by Eugene P. Wigner, prominent quantum physicist, in his book, *Symmetries and Reflections*). [28] The state of the object before observation is:

$$\text{State} = \alpha\Psi_1 + \beta\Psi_2, \tag{17-1}$$

where $[\alpha]^2$ is the probability that the light source is in state Ψ_1 (light "on"); and $[\beta]^2$ is the probability that the light source will be in state Ψ_2 (light "off"). Now if an observer, without your knowledge, watches the light source to determine if the light is "on" or "off," according to quantum theory the wave function after the interaction of the observer with the object is:

$$\text{State} = \alpha(\Psi_1 \times X_1) + \beta(\Psi_2 \times X_2) \tag{17-2}$$

where X_1 is the state or wave function of the observer who would respond to the question, "Did you see the light 'on'?" with a "Yes." X_2 is the state of the observer who would respond to the question, "Did you see the light 'on'?" with a "No." X_1 and X_2 would also be the states of an inanimate recording device that either registered that the light was "on" or "off," respectively.

After the observer interacts with the light source, the state of the observer after interaction would be $\Psi_1 \times X_1 ... ([\alpha]^2 = 1)$ if the state of the light is Ψ_1 (light "on"); and $\Psi_2 \times X_2 ... ([\beta]^2 = 1)$ *if* the state of the light is Ψ_2 (light "off").

Now if you believe that consciousness is part of the wave function that describes *object + observer*, it is because you believe that consciousness or mind is material, and essentially constructed of atoms and molecules; that is, the *brain*. Therefore, the observer or an inanimate recording machine should both be in the quantum state as given in Equation (17-2).

But if you had asked the observer how he or she felt about the state of the light source *before* you asked the above question, he or she would have replied that he or she had already decided in his or her own mind whether the light was "on" or "off" before you asked the question. Therefore, we would have to conclude that the wave function of the conscious observer immediately after interaction with the light source was indeed either $\Psi_1 \times X_1,$ or $\Psi_2 \times X_2, ... ([\alpha]^2, or [\beta]^2 = 1)$.

To repeat, if instead of the conscious observer, we had used some sort of macroscopic recording device, such as a photographic plate, then we would expect the wave function of *object + observer* to be that given by Equation (17-2): $\alpha(\Psi_1 \times X_1) + \beta(\Psi_2 \times X_2)$. We would certainly not expect a conscious observer to be in this state because she either saw the light "on" or "off," and, in fact, said so when you later asked her. There is a contradiction here because there are two descriptions of the wave function of *object + observer*. As Wigner says, "It follows that the being with a consciousness must have a different role in quantum mechanics than the inanimate measuring device..."

This latter argument receives support from the *Non-Interfering, Delayed-Choice* experiments conducted by Mandel and associates at the *University of Rochester* and discussed in Part I, Chapter 15, of this book. The *potential knowledge* of the path of a photon, with no actual physical interference occurring between the detection devices and the particle path, is sufficient to collapse the wave function. If this truly is the case, then an irreversible act of an *inanimate* device is not required. Physicists, who believe that consciousness plays the predominant role in the collapse of the wave function, say that a measurement is only accomplished when it is seen (and comprehended?) by a conscious observer. Presumably, this could either be an on-the-spot observation, or a somewhat later observation of a filmstrip or a video recording.

Return to Part I, Chapter 17 F (p. 72) – The *Many-Worlds Interpretation*

Part II

Metaphysics – The Universe of Spirit

"Not only the laws of nature, but space and time and the material universe itself, are constructions of the human mind." [1]
Sir Arthur Eddington

"The material universe cannot be the thing that always existed because matter had a beginning...This means that whatever existed is non-material. The only non-material reality seems to be mind." [2]
Robert M. Augros and George N. Stanciu

"If the statistical predictions of quantum theory are true, an objective universe is incompatible with the law of local causes." *[3]
H. P. Stapp

"The recognition that physical objects and spiritual values have a very similar kind of reality has contributed in some measure to my mental peace...The principle argument [against materialism] is that thought processes and consciousness are the primary concepts, that our knowledge of the external world is the content of our consciousness, therefore, cannot be denied." [4]
Eugene P. Wigner

"Resurrection is not resuscitation. . . . To say that Jesus was ' raised from the dead' does not mean that he returned to haunt Jerusalem or Galilee as a terrifying, though familiar, ghost, but that he entered upon a new mode of existing, a new relation to God, a new and different way of interacting with the world." [5]
Brian Josephson

"Strangely enough, we ask for material theories in support of spiritual and eternal truths, when the two are so antagonistic that the material thought must become spiritualized before the spiritual fact is attained." [6]
"Mind's control over the universe, including man, is no longer an open question, but is demonstrable Science."∇ [7]
Mary Baker Eddy

"Science without religion is lame, religion without science is blind." [8]
Albert Einstein

---

* objective universe - One that exists apart from consciousness.
Law of Local Causes - No influence can travel faster than the speed of light. The statistical predictions have been shown to be true. Therefore Stapp maintains that the universe is non-local and non-objective.
∇ Mind's control: God's control.

"...the kingdom of God is within you." [09]

"Verily, verily, I say unto you, He that believeth on me, the works that I do shall he do also; and greater works than these shall he do; because I go unto my Father." [10]

Christ Jesus

"...I would simply ask, you of orthodox belief, you who pursue disinterested truth, you who - whether you know it or not - are molding the very face of the future with your scientific knowledge, you who - may I say so? - bow to physics as if it were a religion itself, to you I ask: what does it mean that the founders of your modern science, the theorists and researchers who pioneered the very concepts you now worship implicitly, the very scientists [*] presented in this volume [*Quantum Questions*] what does it mean that they were, *every one of them, mystics*?" ∇ [11]

Ken Wilbur

"Although quantum theory is an abstruse and formidable field, its philosophical and theological implications reduce to one shattering effect: the overthrow of matter...For some 200 years... nearly all leading scientists shared these materialistic assumptions [that the foundation of nature is based on solid and impenetrable particles] based on sensory and deterministic logic...The contemporary intellectual, denying God, is in a trap, and he projects his entrapment onto the world in a kind of secular suicide. But the world is not entrapped; man is not finite; the human mind is not bound in material brain." ⊕ [12]

George Gilder

"Willis Hannon, Roger Sperry, and others have speculated that Western society is on the verge of a 'second Copernican revolution,' in which the dominant attitudes will evolve into a belief in consciousness as the primary 'stuff of the universe.' In this context, consciousness, or mind, is defined as the primary force from which all matter and energy derive...For empiricists, the individual brain is the basis for consciousness. Under the new model, no such limit exists." [13]

Charles Leighton

---

[*] Heisenberg, Schrodinger, Einstein, DeBroglie, Jeans, Planck, Pauli, Eddington.

∇ Mysticism: the belief that the direct knowledge of God, or ultimate reality, is attainable through intuition or insight, in a way different from sense testimony.

⊕ Those who scoff at this statement would say that when the brain dies, consciousness ceases to exist. But the matter-brain is only a manifestation of finite mortal thought. Christ Jesus showed that life and consciousness exist independent of matter.

INTRODUCTION

WORD DEFINITIONS

A few definitions of key words are given in **Part II, APPENDIX A**, located in the back of the book (p. 318). These definitions are given in order for me to convey certain ideas based on either a material, or on a metaphysical or spiritual perspective. In addition, I make, in some cases, additional comments about the usage of a specific word. *The list of the words is given below.* I would hope the Reader – as he or she begins reading Part II - will turn to Appendix A when a question comes up as to the precise meaning of a word. In many instances, the definitions are somewhat radical, and I hope that you will withhold your final opinion of them until you have completed Part II of this book.

WORD
Chaos
Evil
Healing (Faith healing; Spiritual healing)[⊗]
Idea (Material; Spiritual)
Man
Matter
Metaphysics
Mind (Mortal **m**ind; God, divine **M**ind)
Prayer
Sin
Spiritual
Spiritual sense
Reality

PHYSICS VERSUS METAPHYSICS / MATTER VERSUS SPIRIT / UNREALITY VERSUS REALITY

There is more, far more, to reality than physical phenomena governed by physical law. As the above quotation of Albert Einstein implies, religion and science must work together to discover fundamental truths. They must eventually come together in

---

[⊗] In Part II of this book, I present a number of testimonies or experiences of people who have been healed through prayer alone- some of the healings being nearly instantaneous, and thought to be impossible by the medical community. These kinds of experiences present strong evidence that reality is mental and spiritual, but I do not want to give the reader the impression that at present all prayers result in complete healings. More growth in understanding the nature of God and man is needed before mankind can demonstrate more fully and consistently the truths of God and the genuine power of Scientific prayer.

explaining life and reality. Many physical scientists cannot accept orthodox religious beliefs that, as they see it, are largely emotional, and based on faith with little or no scientific law or evidence to support them. They do not believe in a compassionate Creator - and certainly not one who would miraculously set-aside physical laws and correct mistakes that He supposedly made at the beginning of creation. On the other hand, most religious faiths cannot accept the view held by many scientists that there is no God - no compassionate and loving Father who cares for his creation.

Physical science, which claims to interpret and explain reality, has no room for Spirit and spiritual laws. But science *should not* ignore the spiritual components of life, and religion *should* be scientific, or else one or both disciplines are to some degree, in error.

It is consciousness that is the link between science and religion because it is consciousness that is the prime observer in the way we perceive law and reality, and it is consciousness that is the "conduit" for mankind's connection with the Divine. In Part II of this book, I hope to persuade the reader to consider strongly the possibility that the true law or Principle of the universe is the law of Love, the law of Mind.

We see that physical science has held largely to the paradigm of the primacy of matter with its physical laws and defining forces, while religion, in general has emphasized the role of God or Spirit in creating and vitalizing life. Many people, however, hold to some belief that man is some kind of mixture of matter and spirit. This latter belief is reflected in the statement of Wigner (See quotation, Part II, page160), but is in contrast to that of Mary Baker Eddy $^{\oplus}$ (See quotation, Part II, page160), the Discoverer and Founder of *Christian Science*. She believed that the universe and man are entirely spiritual, and are ideas of the universal Mind or God, who, as the *Bible* declares, is also Spirit, Love and Truth. Eddy did not believe that God performed what are called "miracles," but that the miracles reported in the *Bible* were the result of man coming into agreement with *spiritual* law. $^{\nabla}$

Some physicists believe that it is improper to mention physics and consciousness in the same breath, because they believe that consciousness is simply the result of the evolution of increasingly organized and complex matter. They assert that consciousness has little or no influence on the structure and activity of the physical universe, and that theories including Quantum Mechanics and General Relativity are sufficient to explain reality, and even consciousness itself. They believe that spiritual thoughts entertained in consciousness such as love, joy, peace, honesty, courage, etc., possess no real substance, influence or actual reality. Many do not accept this conclusion, and therefore, we are left with a choice from one of the following conclusions:

(a) - Love, joy, peace, honesty, courage, etc., are illusions of the mind.

(b) - There are really *two* sets of laws: (1) quantum mechanics/ relativity for the physical universe; and (2) metaphysical laws for the mental and spiritual universe.

$^{\oplus}$ Mary Baker Eddy: a spiritual thinker and healer, the Founder of the Christian Science religion, and the author of *Science and Health with Key to the Scriptures*.

$^{\nabla}$ Christ Jesus said that he had not come to destroy the law, but to fulfill it. Yet, he certainly violated - or rendered null and void - what we call "physical law," in his utilization of spiritual law. Mortal thought - through finite physical sense testimony and reasoning - has perverted spiritual laws into a perverse and distorted sense of what is termed material law.

(c) - The higher law, or the law that *supersedes* physical law, is the Law of Spirit, Mind, Love, God in which individual identity is under the control of, and is the manifestation or reflection of, the Divine. ⊕

If (a) is correct, life is meaningless. If (b) is correct, we are left with two *First Causes*, which in many ways would war with each other, for they are diametrically opposed. Physical laws, as can be observed, do not point to a compassionate and understanding Creator since physical laws appear to operate with indifference to the needs of mankind.

If (c) is correct, we would do well to devote more time and effort to learning more about this law of Spirit.

THE AUTHOR'S HOPE

I hope that Part I of this book on quantum theory and related phenomena has at least brought to the reader, for his or her thoughtful consideration, the claim that basic matter particles and physical laws are not all that there is to reality, and that the evidence based on physical measurements and observations do not define absolute reality. Quantum physics has **pointed the way** toward a new paradigm based on the primacy of consciousness, and hopefully, to the possible future recognition that Spirit and Spirit's laws supersede physical laws in the macroscopic as well as the sub-atomic realm.

Quantum physics has shown us that conscious observers are participants in defining what we perceive as reality. What remains controversial is whether a macroscopic inanimate recording or measuring device can be called an *"observer;"* or does an observer have to be a conscious, intelligent being. And does this conscious observer actually perceive reality, or is the reality which is perceived one that is an illusion, a view which depends in large measure upon individual and collective unconscious faith in matter-based law? And finally, if this present concept of reality is in error, is there a higher, permanent reality of Mind, Spirit that can be apprehended or made known in *practical* ways? There is, therefore, need of further unbiased and unemotional investigation of the place of consciousness in the defining of reality. Because if consciousness is found to be outside of space-time and independent of physical law, then mind (or rather, Mind), not matter, is primary.

I hope that you, the reader - especially if you consider yourself a rational scientifically-minded person - will have little objection to the above statements, references from the *Bible*, or discussion of religious doctrines and accounts of Christ Jesus that I will use to carry the argument of the primacy of Mind over matter. If you are willing to explore some ideas, that at first may seem radical, then I urge you to read on.

⊕ Disasters, such as hurricanes, tornadoes, earthquakes, droughts and flood, even the kind caused by the possible impact of asteroids or comets, exhibit either a mindless cause, or an indifferent and cruel universal mind without moral principles. A mindless cause is absurd, but an indifferent and cruel universal mind lacking high moral principles would surely be a myth - a senseless cause!

CHAPTER 1

WAVE FUNCTION COLLAPSE AND THE OBSERVER

"Because of the infinite regression of cause and effect, the whole universe may owe its 'real' existence to the fact that it is observed by intelligent beings."
John Gribben [1]

The assertion by some physicists (see Part I, Chapter 17), philosophers, and religions that reality may be non-objective (a reality that does not exist apart from consciousness), does not destroy science nor throw life into chaos. What needs to be done is to elevate science to a new level: that of a mental nature – and still further to a *spiritual* level. Collective mortal thought, grounded in the belief that the physical senses reveal reality, abides by what seems to its senses to be immutable physical laws.

If collective thought or consciousness could at will, and at any time, affect what are perceived as physical laws by a change in state of collective consciousness ⊕ – and it could do this *only* if it truly understood the mental nature of what is called physical "reality" - there would indeed be madness. To date, individual thought has been shown to have only a weak effect on physical objects that are seen to be external to the body and mind.(see Part II, Chapter 3). But as mankind realizes more of the mental nature of reality, it will begin to look *beyond physical sense perception*, and no longer concern itself with trying to change or "improve matter." Rather, it will begin to apprehend the changeless nature of spiritual reality.

CONSCIOUS OBSERVERS VERSUS INANIMATE OBSERVERS

Much has been said in Part I of this book (especially Chapter 15) about the collapse of quantum wave functions as if they were real entities. These wave functions are said to define the properties of real particles which exist independently of conscious observers, instead of being mathematical constructs describing non-objective particles whose physical existence depends on observation by sentient beings.

The following are brief comments by several noted physicists, philosophers, and mathematicians in regard to their impression of the role of mind or consciousness in the shaping and interpreting of reality. Taking quotations of others out of context is always somewhat risky. I assume full responsibility if I have in any way misinterpreted any of the quoted statements. I recommend that the reader consult the references cited along with the quotations in order to gain a broader and clearer interpretation of the quoted statements.

⊕ I use the term, "collective consciousness" throughout the book to describe the non-local, unitive effect of the conscious (and unconscious) thoughts of sentient human beings on what they perceive to be the state of the physical universe. The effect of collective spiritual consciousness that is in tune with Spirit, God, is something else! As recorded in the Bible, Stephen was killed by stoning. No one was there to help him in prayer.[2] Paul was stoned and left for dead, but almost certainly, the disciples with him joined him in prayer, and he rose up. [3] Prayer (communion with God) reveals that all of mankind have a unity with God, Mind.

In many instances, I have also added my own observations and conclusions.

NICK HERBERT

Nick Herbert says in his book, *Quantum Reality*, "The wave function collapse is *not an actual physical event*, but represents the change that occurs in our *knowledge* when we become *aware* of the result of a measurement." [4]

RENE DESCARTES

Rene Descartes (1596-1650), was a French mathematician, philosopher and physiologist. He was the first to present a systematic account of the mind/body relationship. Descartes claimed mind to be separate from matter. About his so-called *dualistic* theory of mind and matter, he said that the human being consists of two distinct, separate kinds of things: the body, and the soul or mind; and that this mind, while not located in the brain, or even anywhere in space, is coupled to the body through the brain, and uses the five senses to gather information. [5] The mind was thought to be mental while the body and the brain were material.

JOHN ECCLES

John Eccles is a distinguished neuro-scientist and *Nobel Prize* winner in medicine. He has said, "I maintain that the human mystery is incredibly demeaned by scientific reductionism, with its claim in promissory materialism [*] to account eventually for all the spiritual world in terms of patterns of neuronal activity. This belief must be classed as a superstition." [∇] [6] We see Sir John Eccles declaring mind and matter to be separate, but believing that the mind can by *will* or selected thought or intent, control the actions of the body. Eccles says, "It will be objected that the essence of the hypothesis is that mind produces changes in the matter-energy system of the brain and hence must be itself in that system . . . but this deduction is merely based on the present hypothesis of physics."[7]

The experiments described in *Margins of Reality* [8] (to be discussed In Part II, Chapter 3) also appear to substantiate the claim that thought can act independently of space and time, as if it were not constrained by matter or a matter brain.

Can matter explain mind? Does the wave function developed by the *Schrodinger Wave Equation* - which is a *deterministic* relation for the precise prediction of an assemblage of sub-microscopic events, but which can only give a probability for the state of individual events - also describe consciousness? That is, is the state of a conscious observer described by the probability amplitude of the matter wave function?

---

[*] promissory materialism: the belief that certain problems will be resolved when scientists have a more complete understanding of the brain.

[∇] Unfortunately, Eccles then goes on to assert that we are *both* spiritual and material.

JOHN ARCHIBALD WHEELER

"The analysis of the physical world, pursued to sufficient depth [crystals to molecules, to atoms, to quarks, and so on..., will lead back in some now hidden way to man himself, to conscious mind, tied unexpectedly through the very acts of observation and participation to partnership in the foundation of the universe." (J. A. Wheeler, "The Universe as Home for Man") [9]

John Archibald Wheeler, physicist, is the first American involved in the theoretical development of the atomic bomb, and he also originated a novel approach to the *Unified Field Theory*. He believes that the state of a conscious observer can not be described by the probability amplitude of the matter wave function. He had said that the wave function, ". . . tells nothing, and can tell nothing, about the 'state of consciousness' of an observer. The consciousness of the observer is outside the wave function." [10] In an interview with P.C.W. Davies and J.R. Brown [11] made about nine years after the above reference, Wheeler implied that a quantum phenomenon when registered, for example, on a photographic screen, has no *meaning* until it is registered in *consciousness.* He said that if the inanimate recording device is destroyed before anyone has a chance to look at the picture, that " . . .nothing has been accomplished by that picture in the establishment of meaning, although certainly the elementary quantum phenomenon itself has indeed been brought to a close." Wheeler believes the quantum phenomenon has actually occurred, in contrast to some physicists such as Eugene P. Wigner, who believes that the phenomenon itself never occurs *until* it enters consciousness or mind. In other words, Wheeler is of the opinion that consciousness is required to give the quantum event "meaning" in the world. And this "meaning" must be communicated to the observer so that the event can be "put to use". [12] *

He indicates that, although there is a difference between inanimate observers and conscious observers, the understanding and interpretation of the role of consciousness in the measurement and interpretation of quantum events is a difficult problem, indeed. He continues by saying that until any phenomenon can be assumed to be in the realm of reality and not like a dream, that phenomenon must be confirmed by other people.

Recall the game of *Twenty Questions* (see Part I, Chapter 15). The game illustrates that the bringing of a sense of reality to something depends in part on the collective agreement of a "community of communicators" [14] to establish meaning. It took a collection of minds to agree on the same object before that object was revealed as the "chosen" object. The great mystery would seem to remain as to who or what did the initial observing and communicating at the inception of the *Big Bang* in order to establish meaning. Wheeler asks rhetorically whether the galaxies in the early universe were as real *then* without *meaningful* observations, as they are *now*. The physical universe and the laws that we observe may in some way be brought about through the collective "agreement" of many minds. ∇

---

* "meaning: the joint product of all the evidence that is available to those who communicate. "Meaning," according to Wheeler, includes communication between conscious beings, asking questions and distinguishing between answers. [13]

∇ Some physicists believe the evidence for the existence of God is to be found in the theories underlying the so-called *Anthropic Principle*, which is defined briefly as follows: Many of the fundamental physical

In an article titled, "Does the Universe Exist if We're Not Looking?"[15] Tim Folger reports on an interview with John Wheeler. He reports that Wheeler has implied that human observation in some way contributes to the creation of physical reality, and that the physical universe exists as a *quantum potential* until it interacts with *inanimate* as well as with conscious beings. Suppose, for example, a billion years ago particles (such as high energy particles released by radioactive radium) interacted with *unconscious, inanimate* mica atoms, transforming what *might happen* (a potential), into what did *happen* (disrupted atoms in the mica). The disrupted atoms, reports Folger, now become a part of reality through an "irreversible act of amplification." Consciousness was not involved at the time of arrival of the high energy particles to make it a phenomenon. But Wheeler says if the mountain which contained the mica somehow dissolved and disappeared due to some catastrophic event millions of years ago, "the potential phenomena would never have been ' put to use' to make 'meaning'."

ANDREI LINDE

But physicist Andrei Linde of *Stanford University* (one of the authors of *Inflationary Cosmology*) has a slightly different conclusion from Wheeler. Linde believes that consciousness, *alone,* is responsible for bringing the physical universe into reality – not like Wheeler, who claims that consciousness is only needed to give the universe *meaning.* Linde says, "You can say that the universe is there only when there is an observer [a conscious observer] who can say, 'Yes, I see the universe there'…The moment you say that the universe exists without any observers [consciousness], I cannot make any sense out of that. **I cannot imagine a consistent theory of everything that ignores consciousness**. (Emphasis added) A recording device cannot play the role of an observer, because who will read what is written on this recording device?…It's not enough for the information to be stored somewhere, completely inaccessible to anybody…In the absence of observers [conscious observers] our universe is dead." [16]

These comments made by Linde suggest strongly that what we call the physical universe is mental, and is a product of collective minds.

FRED WOLF

Noted physicist Fred Wolf, believes that the interaction between two subatomic particles establishes a correlation between them - for example, their relative positions and moments - and that the deterministic quantum mechanical equations predict accurately future relations of this quantum system. But he believes that the act of *observation by a conscious mind* destroys this correlation to the point that if we know the momentum of a particle precisely, then its position could be virtually anywhere (*Uncertainty Principle*). Wolf says, "Thus it is that mind and matter cannot be truly separated." [17] He is of the opinion that matter interacts with matter to build the universe, while mind tears down the

---

constants in the universe are precisely right for life and intelligence to evolve. An extremely small change in the value of any of these constants, and life could not exist. Therefore, as the argument goes, it would require a divine Planner to set the constants to permit life to evolve in matter.

material structure and recreates a new one. "Mind (lower case) is the creator;" and the observer has a choice in what he observes by " . . . setting up his instruments and measuring devices so that they will produce a value corresponding to his expectation. . . The data of our senses repeat and appear to our minds as lawful and causally meaningful [18] ...Thus, mind and matter are included in the quantum wave function - and quantum physics can be used to understand the mind's basic functions such as . . .intuition, feeling, sensation, and thought." [19]

EUGENE WIGNER

A noted physicist in Einstein's time, Eugene P. Wigner, does not believe that quantum mechanics can explain consciousness. He says, ". . .if one wishes to be entirely constant, one can reconcile the probabilistic nature of the measurement or observation process with quantum mechanics only by admitting that the equations of the latter do not describe the behavior of living beings, of beings with consciousness." [20]

Since the mind can influence the matter-body by will or intent, then the mind is not probabilistic like material particles, and cannot be described by a wave function. (Emphasis added)

According to one interpretation of the *Schrodinger's Cat* example (See Part I, Chapter 17, Figure (17-5)), the canister of gas, radioactive material and the cat are described as a *quantum system*, and possess a probability of existence given by $\Psi(x,t)$. *Until* the system is "observed" - that is, the woman in Figure (17-5a) standing next to the room containing the cat and apparatus, opens the door and peers inside - they exist as potentials or possibilities: In this case, closed canister / live cat, *and* open canister / dead cat.

What about the woman standing next to the room which contains the cat and apparatus, as shown in Figure (17-5A)? Does she also exist as a potential until the man shown in the next illustration (Figure (17-5B) opens the door to the larger room (which contains the cat in the smaller room, and the woman standing outside), and peers inside? Wigner believes that the recording by a mechanical recording device does not collapse the *wave function*. It requires the observation of a conscious being to do this.

Physicists disagree as to the nature of the wave function. Some believe that is simply a mathematical description of the possibilities of locating a particle at a particular location, and that consciousness, although having a physical origin cannot collapse the wave function through observation. Others believe that it is a real, physical entity. Consciousness - which they also believe has a physical origin - is then seen as collapsing this function during observation. Recall in Part I, Chapter 17 (*Schrödinger's Cat, Revisited*), it was stated that the collapse of the wave function exchanges uncertainty or *ignorance* of the state of an object (quantum wave function containing a multiplicity of potential states) for *information* (wave function collapsed to a single state), with that information still hidden from a conscious observer. But it is difficult to see how an inanimate recording device (the "observer"), by interacting with an object, can obtain "knowledge" or information. Information or "knowledge" is meaningless (as Wheeler seems to imply), until a conscious observer, observes - and *comprehends*.

The "collapse" of the wave function will be mentioned several other times throughout the remainder of this book, but it is the author's opinion that the wave function for a particle or particles represents - or is the outcome of - the collective, unitive consciousness' present "knowledge" or perception of reality. It represents the possibilities of an *idea* (an electron or collection of electrons), - with no physical collapse of the wave function required. It exists in the *mental* realm of consciousness - a consciousness which cannot be explained by quantum mechanics.

Wigner points out that energy levels in a cubic centimeter of a gas (a macroscopic system) are so close that the presence of a particle such as an electron a fair distance away (meters) can cause a transition between states. [21] All particles in the universe, he says, interact with each other over a sufficient length of time, so that no system of particles can truly be "isolated" from other particles. Since the deterministic quantum mechanical laws only apply to *isolated* systems, we must conclude that the *entire* universe is a quantum wave function or *state vector*. And Wigner says that since we are considering the entire universe, it must also include the person doing the observing.

How did the *Big Bang* happen if matter has no objective existence until an observation occurs, and if the observer is part of the universe? How could the universe come into being? Unless the observer was "outside" the physical universe he could never observe the state of the universe through the collapse of the wave function. Wigner therefore concludes that since it is not possible for the observer to be outside the universe (isolated), a quantum wave function cannot be applied to macroscopic objects.

AMIT GOSWAMI

Amit Goswami is currently a *Senior Resident Researcher* at the *Institute of Noetic Sciences*. He believes in *Monistic Idealism* (*MI*). *Webster* defines this as "a system of philosophical idealism, emphasizing the primacy of the One (as the Absolute or Nature), rather than of the many." As some physicists see it, this philosophy states that reality is structured on *consciousness* and not the other way around. In fact, consciousness is seen as the only, ultimate reality. In the *Schrodinger's Cat* illustration the cat can be represented by a coherent superposition of multifaceted quantum waves that describe potentials or possibilities (50% probability for a live cat, and 50% probability for a dead cat), and according to Amit Goswami [22] exists as a "formless, albeit highly-mathematical idea(s)" in a "transcendent domain," until an observation or measurement is made, at which time the wave function collapses to a single facet or *eigenstate* of the particular observable being measured. The "transcendent domain" is a domain outside of space-time, and therefore, beyond perception. This is the domain of *consciousness*.

The result of the observation is the appearance of either a live or a dead cat. If the observation or measurement is made first by a material, macroscopic and inanimate recording device, and later by a television camera set up to automatically record the event, then the wave function remains un-collapsed, and cat and recording remain in a state of limbo.

According to *MI*, only consciousness can complete the measurement process and collapse the wave function. The *Copenhagen Interpretation* of quantum theory states that quantum systems cannot be separated from the macroscopic measuring device, but because consciousness is outside of space-time - and therefore is non-local - the conscious being performing the observation can, in effect, jump *out* of the "material order of reality" and complete the measurement.

Goswami implies that although the cat exists* in the transcendent domain of human consciousness, it is not that we mentally exercise some physical force or will to shut the valve on the bottle of poisonous gas, or bring the cat back to life after the gas has been released. He says we bring either the dead cat or the live cat into our experience by "choosing and recognizing the result of choice," [23] and the results of this choosing are manifested in what we perceive. And it is *collective* consciousness that does this, a collective consciousness that possessed the attributes of *awareness*.

Consider *EPR* experiments (Part I, Chapter 15) with correlated protons that have been allowed to separate. When an observation is made on one proton of the pair, Goswami and many other physicists agree that not only is its wave function collapsed, but the wave function of the other proton also collapses, apparently instantly. Because the protons are space-like separated, that is, phenomena occur in less time than the time it would take for a message to travel at the speed of light from proton #1 to proton #2, the event is non-local. The universe itself is said to be *non-local*. Non-local consciousness (not located in space-time, and not described by a quantum wave function) is said to be the *observer* that collapses the wave functions of the entangled protons and causes the violation of *Bell's Inequality*.

It is my opinion that correlated quantum statistical results have arisen long *after* past collective, unitive non-local consciousness based on matter-based thinking (APPENDIX C, p. 330) has painstakingly "agreed" as to how quantum mechanical statistical laws - laws that currently form the foundation of the physical paradigm describing reality - should be formulated or perceived.[∇] Amir Aczel, has commented in his book, *Entanglement*, that it is amazing that one of the properties of quantum systems (entanglement), and its associated weirdness would *first* be found mathematically, and that this strengthens our belief in the "transcendent [⊕] power of mathematics." He says that *after* this discovery many physicists used "clever and ingenious" methods to verify that entanglement actually occurs. [24] (Emphasis added)

Why is it that there appears to be a paradox, for example, in the *Double-Slit* experiment, where a single electron or proton appears to go through both slits and interfere with itself? Goswami says the results of the experiment show that as we look for a particle at a specific slit, we collapse the wave function that had described the particle as having equal potentials for going through both slits. Unless we observe, the "undisturbed wave sustains the quantum dichotomy," as a sort of formless potential or possibility, and we observe a gradual build-up of an interference pattern on the screen.

---

* Many of the Christian faith who have witnessed the death of a loved one, still maintain their faith in the Biblical promise of life after death. But, in fact, some Christians subconsciously and paradoxically believe that in some other way that person is also simultaneously dead and buried in a grave! In a crude way this reminds one of the quantum interpretation of the *Schrodinger's Cat* experiment that postulates equal possibilities for the existence of both live and dead cats until an observation has been made. But, as I point out later in the book, God – who is Life, itself – could not create a being with the capacity to be both dead and alive.

∇ The world's conscious and unconscious acceptance of these so-called laws essentially place a mask over spiritual law, thereby hiding the true nature of reality.

⊕ transcendent: beyond our knowledge and experience; being above what we call human existence, and apart from the universe.

In the *Parallel Universe* or *Many Worlds* interpretation (see Part I, Chapter 17), there is no collapse of the wave function through observation or through the measurement process. Both live and dead cats in the *Schrodinger's Cat* paradox exist, but in parallel universes. There is one of us in each universe able to observe: (a) -a dead cat in universe #1, and (b) - a live cat in universe #2.

I personally cannot accept the theory that individual consciousness or awareness can be split into an infinite number of conscious entities, with each one residing in a separate physical universe.

In the strict interpretation of *Many Worlds*, we could also envision parallel, but totally separate universes, where in one universe *you* recover from a serious illness, while in another universe *you* - and possibly thousands or millions of people besides you - suffer miserably from the same disease with no hope of recovery. If we accept that somehow your individual being can exist simultaneously in many real physical universes, then pity the "you" in the universe where there is never any hope of cure, regardless of efforts made to effect a cure! There is certainly no concerned creator there in *Many Worlds*! These "stacked" universes are not much different from the old *Newtonian* universe, wherein philosophers believed that the world was deterministic and utterly fore-ordained, and in theory predictable if one knew with great precision the positions and momenta of all particles.

Perhaps it is true that what we perceive through our "colored lenses" of thought are objects and symbols that have been colored and distorted by the collective world's unconscious acceptance of the present paradigm of materiality. Within this belief system are the claims that this limited framework for reality is all that exists.

In Part II, Chapter 8 the subject of *synchronicity* is discussed. Examples of synchronicity are given indicating that individuals can experience "meaningful coincidences" that transcend space-time. That is, the experiences originate in consciousness and are non-local. Goswami believes that these kinds of experiences are not unlike what is occurring in the Aspect *EPR* experiments (Part I, Chapter 15). Like some synchronicity experiences, meaningful information occurs when both observers in the experiments come together, compare seemingly random data and discover a correlation. Goswami concludes, "Our non-local unitive consciousness collapses the wave function of a quantum object when we observe it, but we are unaware of the non-locality * of the collapse or of making the choice." [25]

HENRY STAPP

Noted physicist, Henry Stapp wrote a book entitled, *Mind, Matter and Quantum Mechanics.* The reviewer of his book commented that Stapp believes that the state of the

---

* There are some physicists who say that, although *Bell's Inequality* has been violated, non-locality does not come into play in any interpretation of *EPR*. The data accumulated at the two space-like detectors is random, but correlation is observed only after the two sets of data are brought together (over a time period that precludes space-like separation) and examined by at least one of the conscious human experimenters. It is only after this examination occurs, they say, that the experimental results - violation of *Bell's Inequality* - take on any physical meaning. This explanation, it would seem to me, ignores the memories of the human experimenters who observed the data at the space-like separated detectors, and then who later verified their results when they met to observe the correlated results.

entire universe can be represented by a wave function which is a compendium of all the wave functions that all of our minds individually can cause to collapse by observation. He says, "all that exists is ...subjective knowledge, therefore the universe is not about matter, it is about subjective experience...Each knower's act of knowledge (each individual increment of knowledge) results in a new state of the [material] universe. One person's increment of knowledge changes the state of the entire [material] universe, and, of course, it changes it for everybody else" (My comments in brackets}. [26]

I believe collective thought cannot actually change the state of reality, which is wholly spiritual, but only the *perception* of the state of reality (that which masquerades as the physical universe) as perceived by the five senses. And in the majority of incidences *individual* thought must have only a negligible effect in the macroscopic world, which it believes exists external to consciousness.

Mary Baker Eddy said "… creation consists of the unfolding of spiritual ideas and their identities, which are embraced in the infinite Mind and forever reflected. These ideas range from the infinitesimal to infinity, and the highest ideas are the sons and daughters of God." [27] Spiritual thoughts (ideas of Mind), when entertained in consciousness have the potential for moving "mountains"! [28]

As to the maintaining of individual identity Eddy said, "The loss of man's identity through the understanding which Science confers is impossible; and the notion of such a possibility is more absurd than to conclude that individual musical notes are lost in the origin of harmony." [29] And this identity is not to be found in matter: "Every material belief hints the existence of spiritual reality; and if mortals are instructed in spiritual things, it will be seen that material belief, in all its manifestations, * reversed, will be found the type and representative of verities priceless, eternal, and just at hand." [30]

HENRY SWIFT

Henry Swift, Editor of "Science Within Consciousness" believes that non-local consciousness is the agent for the collapse of the single wave function representing both particles in the *EPR* experiment. He has said that correlation exists in the experiment because each experimenter's brain is correlated non-locally with each other, especially if they have been meditating or feeling each other's presence. In the spirit of Dick Jahn and others (see Part II, Chapter 3, Experiments in Consciousness) it may be possible for specific "meditation" to produce final results in an *EPR*-type experiment that are predicted by both observers. As Swift says, this would be a "propagation of influence without local signals" (a type of super-luminal transfer of a message, without the expenditure of energy.) [31]

EDWARD R. CLOSE

Dr. Edward Close, Ph.D. (Physics) had commented about *Double-Slit* experimental results in his book, *Transcendental Physics.* [32] In the *Delayed-Choice*

---

* From atoms to galaxies.

Double-Slit experiment, a single photon at a time is released from a source. Close says that as soon as the photon is released from the source "the wave of all possible photon states exists at the source, slits, and the receptors, simultaneously." A conscious observer then makes a choice in having one slit open or in having both slits open, but acts on this choice *after* the first photon passes the slits. If both slits are opened after subsequent single photons pass the slits, the observer will see a gradual build-up of an interference pattern due to photons impacting on the downstream photographic plate. From the photon's point of view, says Close, the lateral dimensions of everything that passes must be zero, and time will be stopped. Because of special relativistic effects (photon moves at velocity, c.) there will be no space around the photon. The space along the line from source to receptor has collapsed to a point. From the point of view of the relativistic photon in its reference frame, it is everywhere at once – simultaneously at the source and the receptor. [33] The interference pattern builds up because "the timeline that we create by separating the individual photon releases does not exist from the photon's perspective." From the point of view of the photons in the reference system (which is moving at the speed of light relative to the slits), one photon passes through each of the double slits and interferes with the other, thereby helping create an interference pattern on the photographic plate.

Close has said that what we perceive as reality is built up by "the conscious thoughts and beliefs of all sentient beings and is constantly confirmed and maintained by the feedback of continuing observation." Past and present realities therefore change as collective (or consensus) beliefs of participating observers change. But beyond consensus belief (what Close calls "secondary consciousness", exists what he calls "primary consciousness." [34]

I believe that we may call this primary consciousness (which by its very nature is non-material), *God*. The so-called secondary consciousness, which judges reality by the evidence of the five senses, is a mask or misperceptions of the nature of God, Spirit, Mind.

Again, mortals do not really create a physical reality; they only change their perception of "primary, spiritual reality", which is changeless. "Spirit and its formations are the only realities of being." (Eddy) [35] "The non-local and non-objective aspects of reality anticipated by Bell's theorem and verified by the Aspect experiment are indicators of the involvement of consciousness." (Close) [36] In the *EPR* experiments the two created particles are "entangled" (Entanglement is the superposition of a state of a system consisting of two or more subsystems or particles.) The two particles are not separate entities. Until an observation or measurement is made the two-particle system exists only as a set of possibilities. The measurement of a property of one particle instantly affects the results of the measurement of the property of the second particle.

One can conclude that reality is non-local and probably non-objective. In the *EPR* experiments a conscious being *selects* what kind of measurement will be made on particle #1, and thereby influences to some degree the dynamic characteristics of particle #2- a particle that has no such characteristics until a measurement is made. (In essence, the particles are in a non-objective state until a measurement is made. It is interesting to note
* that for the *Bell Inequality* experiments, all correlation data accumulated are random in

---

* These following statements, as well as several others throughout the book, are repeated for emphasis.

nature. The experimenter at detector #1 cannot control the outcome of a measurement made by an experimenter located at detector #2, even though under certain orientations of the two detectors there is a definite correlation between the two measurements. That is, if one looked at the data taken at detector # 1 or detector # 2, each set of data would be entirely random because of the random nature of the individual proton spin vectors. It is only when *both* sets of data are compared that we notice a correlation. So, in the strictest sense, the Relativity restriction that says no useful information or signal can travel faster than the speed of light, has not been violated. However, Amir Aczel notes in his book, *Entanglement*, that some physicists (including John Bell) still believe the "spirit of relativity theory" is violated because "something infinitely fast, travels" between the two entangled particles. [37]

It is impossible to simultaneously know precisely both position and the momentum of a quantum particle, and it is impossible to determine the path of the particle from source to the measurement apparatus. Therefore it cannot be said the particle has any definite path until an observation establishes a path. In the *Double-Slit* experiment, a quantum particle has different (but not necessarily equal) probabilities of being in two different places at the same time until a measurement collapses the wave function and reveals the particle in one place or the other. There is no physical mechanism or force for wave collapse.

Many physicists would say that all that is required to cause the wave function of an object to collapse is to have the object interact with a camera, a photographic plate or simply the environment of the experiment. But the macroscopic measuring device is also made of quantum particles. And according to the *Copenhagen Interpretation* of quantum mechanics quantum particles "are not localized objects separate from the apparatus used to detect them." The particles are not separate from the detector, or from any subsequent macroscopic detectors, only their observable effects.[38] The quantum wave function, described by the *Schrodinger Wave Equation*, now describes both particle *and* inanimate detector. And this system gives us no knowledge or information about any object in the universe, unless consciousness observes.

The implication is enormous: *no event occurs (has any meaning) without the involvement of consciousness.* The receptor that ends the chain of measurement is non-quantum, non-material, non-local consciousness, which is separate from any physical detector, and avoids the contradiction of infinite regression. The non-locality of the universe is the result of consciousness. There is a unity of consciousness among all things, and consciousness is universal.

Amir Aczel points out that a number of discoveries in physics have been made, more or less simultaneously, by more than one person working independently from each other. [39] Close observes that some experimental results become easier to obtain as more scientists and physicists become convinced of the theories that purport to explain the results. [40] And proponents of *Social Constructivism* believe that reality is not something to be discovered, because it has no preexistence prior to our social invention of it. That is, "We invent the properties of the world rather than discover them." [41]

In summary, I want to again emphasize that it is my opinion that correlated quantum statistical results arise *after* past collective consciousness has "agreed" as to how quantum mechanical statistical laws - laws that currently form the foundation of the physical paradigm describing reality - should be formulated. However, the reader should know that I maintain that all of what is called "physical law and physical reality are "masks", illusions or beliefs of collective mortal thought that would hide and misinterpret the changeless reality of Spirit and spiritual laws.

CHAPTER 2

IS CONSCIOUSNESS FOUND IN THE BRAIN AND IN COMPUTERS?

"I can't believe that!" said Alice.
"Can't you?" the Queen said in a pitying tone. "Try again: draw a long breath, and shut your eyes."
Alice laughed. "There's no use trying," she said: one *can't* believe impossible things."
"I daresay you haven't had much practice," said the Queen. "When I was your age, I always did it for half-hour a day. Why sometimes I've believed as many as six impossible things before breakfast."

Lewis Carroll [1]

THE BRAIN

RENE DESCARTES

In the mid-1600's (1649) Rene Descartes, a French philosopher stated that there was a distinct separation between mind and matter, and the mind could in no direct way act upon matter. (The reader is referred back to Part II, Chapter 1, Consciousness Observers Versus Inanimate Observers, for similar Descartes comments.) It was the *matter-brain,* not the mind, that could act on matter; that is, matter acting on matter. This so-called *Cartesian* theory is now being challenged by people working in several disciplines besides physics. In the book *Nobel Prize Conversations,* Dr. Robert Sperry, *1981 Nobel Laureate in Physiology / Medicine,* states, "Mind controls matter, is superior to brain in its capacity to will, intend, command and direct." [2]

JOHN ECCLES

Sir John Eccles, 1963 *Nobel Laureate in Physiology / Medicine*, describes a series of experiments involving brain reactions caused by the *intention* or desire of a subject to perform a muscular action. [3] The popular view is that the human brain is essentially like a computer, and is a self-regulating system needing no external input from a mind. Experiments with different human subjects revealed that thought or mental intention, will, or desire, to move the arm or lift the hand to the face, which involves a complex series of muscular actions, is sufficient to selectively initiate the burst of discharges of the brain's nerve cells (supplementary motor area [SMA] near the top of the brain) that send signals to the muscles. In other words, the non-material mind has acted in a "discriminating fashion" on the material nerve cells, directing them through *intent, alone* to discharge in a pattern required to activate certain muscles. [4] □ *

ROBERT SPERRY

Robert Sperry is a noted psycho-biologist and expert in brain research. Sperry speaks of a person whose arm had been amputated and who still experienced pain in the *phantom* limb as if it were still attached to his body, although the amputation had occurred several months before. He says there is a ". . .unique pattern of cerebral excitation that produces pain instead of something else" [7] [such as pleasure].

Think of what this appears to imply: it was not the severance of the arm which produced the pain, and certainly not the absence of the arm that caused pain to originate in the wrist and hands. It was the *thought* of the person - the fear, anxiety, the remembrance of the incident that perpetuated the sensation of pain - just as it was the acceptance of the paradigm of physics in the first place that established the belief that there is sensation in matter. The opposite thought of a sense of well-being, and some appreciation of a sense of reality that exists beyond the ken of the five senses, might go a long way toward alleviating or eliminating entirely the sense of pain, and restoring peace.

As Sperry says, "In the brain model. . .the causal potency of an idea, becomes just as real as that of a molecule, a cell, or a nerve impulse. Ideas cause ideas and help evolve new ideas." [8]

But we need to ask the question, "Where does the mental phenomenon of mind originate? Sperry and Eccles differ as to the origin: the former believing that mind originates in the brain, and the latter holding that mind derives from an "*elsewhere*", which at present is not clearly discerned.[9]

BRIAN JOSEPHSON

Dr Brian Josephson is the 1973 *Nobel Laureate in Physics*. He has pondered the question as to whether it is necessary to relate or link mind - that which appears to control the formation and activity of matter - with a universal God or Mind. He states, ". . .if we want to put God or Mind in science, then the primary feature of Mind, the one which is most closely connected with the science we've got, is intelligence." [10]

And, "Intelligence manifests itself by making certain unlikely situations appear."[11] Intelligence can be seen at work in the design of a watch ▽ or the artistry and form of an oil painting. The appearance of these objects in the universe can not be

---

□ For additional information on the subject, see: The Emperor's New Mind by Roger Penrose [5]; and "Voluntary Finger Movements in Man: Cerebral Potentials and Theory." Deeke, I., et al [6]

* Matter nerves are not the source of pain; we can experience the same pain in our dreams without nerves coming into play. Pain is a mental phenomenon. Some researchers, though, believe that pain can be genetically regulated, but if pain can be eliminated through prayer, there would be no need for gene alteration. Might not the structure of DNA be an effect rather than a cause?

▽ Richard Dawkins' strictly materialistic philosophy as described in *The Blind Watchmaker*, not withstanding.

explained by looking deeply, in a reductionistic way, into matter to determine the laws governing the random motion of sub-atomic particles.

COMPUTERS (ARTIFICIAL INTELLIGENCE)

JUMPING OUT

** Douglas Hofstadter

Douglas Hofstadter is a professor of *Cognitive Science and Computer Science* at *Indiana University*. In his book, *Godel, Escher, and Bach,* Hofstadter discusses the impossibility of a computer ever jumping or stepping out of itself; that is, getting entirely out of dependence on its program and the constraints imposed by the program, so that it can truly be able to perform increasingly complex and logical tasks independently of human input. [12] He does this by showing a photograph of a wood engraving created by M.C. Escher, called *Dragon.* (1952). A less exotic illustration created by me is shown in Figure (2-1).

"JUMPING" OR STEPPING OUT

Figure(2-1)

In this simple two-dimensional drawing, a two-dimensional kangaroo is trying very hard to convince himself and us that he can "jump" out of his two-dimensional world, by jumping through a piece of paper containing a large slit or opening. This, of course, would only be possible if the kangaroo were actually three-dimensional to begin with, but no matter how the scene is drawn, it is still a two-dimensional scene. Hofstadter seems to imply that neither a two-dimensional being nor a three-dimensional human being can ever jump out of its own physical limits, see itself or himself, or be capable of performing increasingly complicated tasks without limits. He believes the computer and the human brain are essentially the same and that we may see computer intelligence some day rival human intelligence and claim the right to be *"alive"* and aware of itself as much as any human being.

** Edward Harrison

In his book *Masks of the Universe*, Edward Harrison points out that if a painter sets out to portray everything inside his studio, the painting should include the painter at his easel painting the entire studio, but the painting on the easel in the painting should include the painter painting the entire studio, and this painting should include . . . and so on - an *infinite regression* of paintings. He says "If we claim that a universe is a complete and faithful representation [of everything that exists], then it must include the cosmologist [you, me] conceiving and thinking about that universe. This also entails an infinite regress: the universe contains the cosmologist conceiving the universe that contains the cosmologist conceiving the universe that contains. . .and so on indefinitely. Unless the mind that conceives and studies the universe is *excluded,* we lapse into infinite regress" [13] (emphasis added).

A graphic example of recursiveness or self-referential systems is represented by a television camera hooked to a television monitor, and pointed directly at the screen. Figure (2-2) illustrates the example, which is an adaptation of the illustration in the book, *Godel, Escher and Bach* by Douglas Hofstadter. [14] The screen shows a picture of what the camera is looking at (the screen itself), which shows a picture of what the camera is looking at (the screen itself), which shows a ..... Similar to the example of the painter painting a complete picture of everything in the room, a complete picture of the television system would include the sensor the television monitor uses to "see" itself. This could be accomplished by a suitable positioning of several mirrors so that the camera would include in its view, the view of itself as well as the backside of the monitor. But the entire system of television camera and mirrors is insufficient to see the backside of the mirrors, which were included to see the camera and the monitor backside. It would never be possible for any *physical* system, including the human brain and computer, to jump out or step outside of itself, because the substance or being of the particular system derives its existence from the framework of matter in four-dimensional space-time (three spatial dimensions).

"KANGAROO" COMPUTERS

A simple computer must respond under the constraints of the hardware design and construction. Even if the circuits are constructed at the quantum level where some degree of uncertainty may result in its response to questions asked of it, it would seem that it can never get outside of its own material boundaries and truly think and be aware of itself and its surroundings.

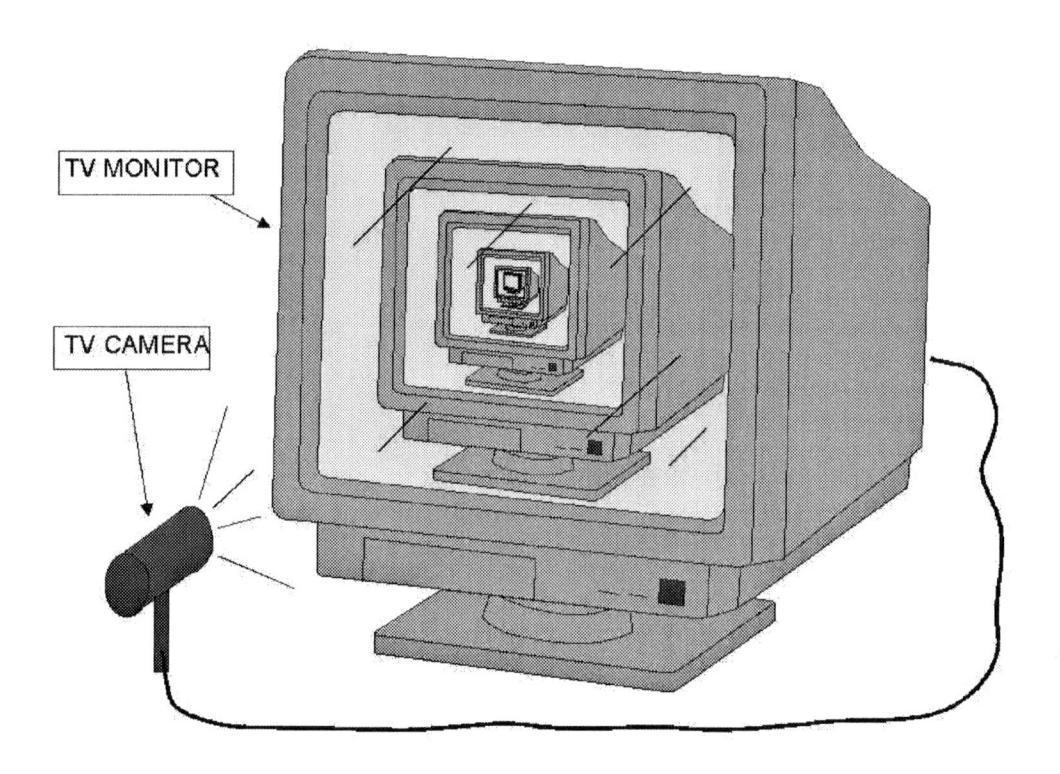

Figure (2-2)

Self-referential Systems

Suppose a simple computer, which has been wired to display a light in response to questions asked with a "yes, and to display no light in response to questions answered with a "no", is asked the following question: "Is your light off?" It cannot answer the question because it cannot get "outside of its own circuits. [15]

In *theory*, it would be possible to construct a computer out of bricks of clay, with springs and with tubes containing water to convey information from one part of the system to the other, instead of relying on electrical or chemically-generated currents to carry the messages - for there is nothing magical about electricity.

Let us now think a little bit about the basic theory and logic behind computers. Observe Figure (2-3) which shows three of the simplest kinds of computer logic circuits: the AND, OR and the NOT circuits. [16] Modern-day computers do not use mechanical switches to transfer electrical current from one part of the circuit to another. Input data is now fed into the computer by a string of + (current on) and - (current off) charges. We can begin to understand how a computer processes information by looking at the next several illustrations.

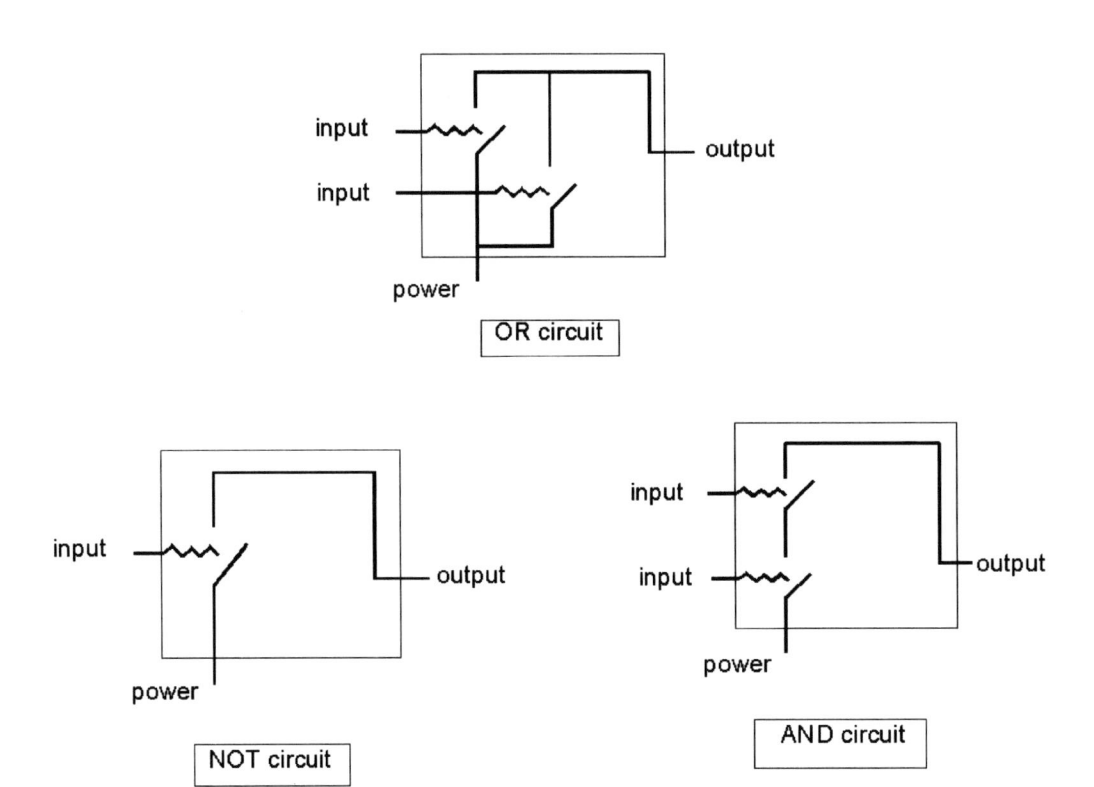

SIMPLE CIRCUITS FOR COMPUTERS

Figure (2-3)

    The OR circuit takes two pieces of information and presents one piece of output information. As can be seen, the output part of the circuit passes current if only one of the solenoid switches, which are connected in parallel, is closed. In the case of the AND circuit, both switches must be closed for current passage. The NOT circuit has the unique property of passing no current to the output contact when the input contact sends current to the switch; because contrary to the previous two circuits, the switch is normally closed until it receives a current pulse.

    Figure (2-4) shows a simple logic circuit employing two NOT and three AND circuits to solve the following simplistic "truth" problem: Suppose your son has a car to drive only on Tuesdays, Wednesdays and Sundays of each week, and your daughter has another car on Mondays, Tuesdays, Wednesdays, Fridays and Sundays of each week. (Why the father favors the daughter is not clear!) For some reason, you would like to determine by computer logic what days of the week both have a car; what days only the son has a car, and what days neither offspring has a car. To the left of the input contact are black and white squares that represent current flowing to the input contact on the days one of the offspring has a car.

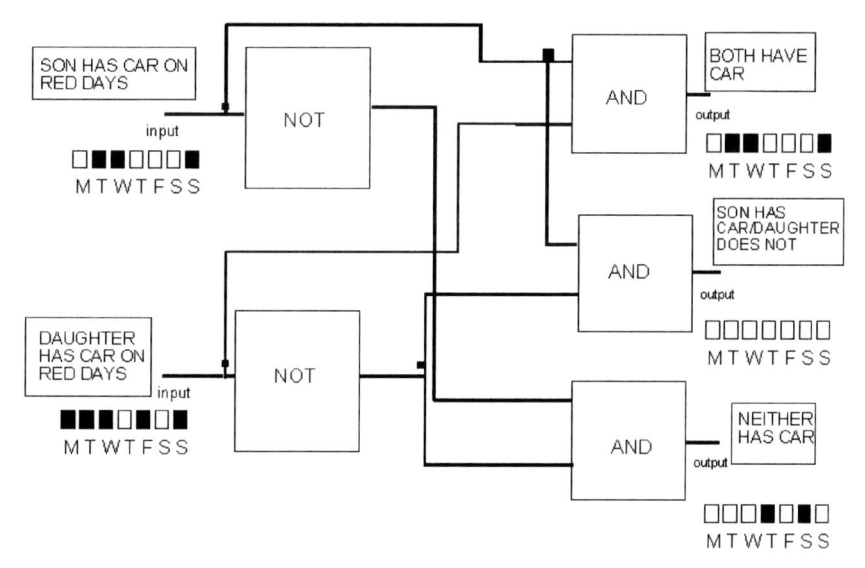

SIMPLE CIRCUITS FOR COMPUTERS

Figure (2-4)

The logic circuit will give the answers to the three questions, and the answers are shown to the right of the appropriate output contact. The answers could appear as a light shining for the day in question, the light being activated by current reaching the output contact.

Now Figure (2-5) attempts to show how a computer of this simplicity (or essentially vastly complex) could be designed using basically dumb, but *trained kangaroos,* hopping-paths, water valves or gates, water and water buckets. The input data is "entered", not with electrical charges, but with white and black-colored flags. This circuit, as before, still has two NOT and three AND circuits, but *trained kangaroos take the place of the electrical current.* As shown, the input data consists of a series of white or black flags, one for each day of the week. The top seven flags indicate when the son has possession of a car: white indicating that he has a car, and black indicating the days he does not have a car. The lower series of flags convey similar information about the daughter. The rules are that trained *black* kangaroos respond to *white* flag instructions by taking each white flag in series (one at a time) and hopping down their particular path to a water tank where they jump up and down to open a water gate or valve.

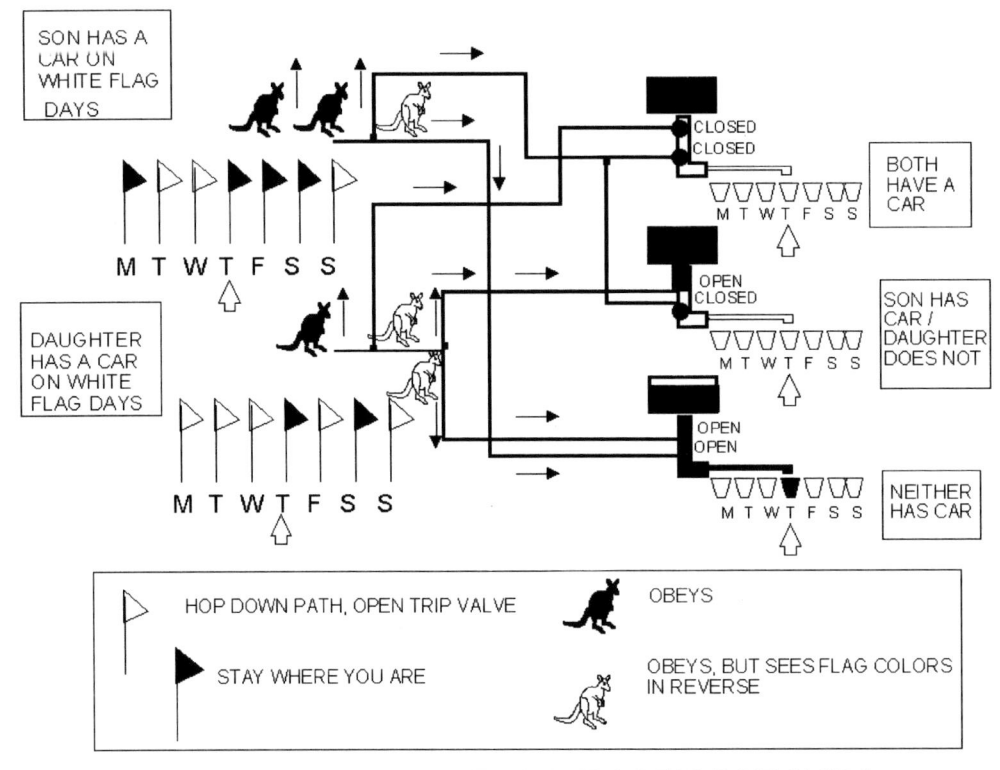

SIMPLE " COMPUTER ", AND LOGIC " CIRCUIT "

**Figure (2-5)
Results for Thursday**

The *black* kangaroos respond to *black* flags by not moving. On the other hand, *white* kangaroos respond in reverse order to the flag instructions, and therefore, respond to *black* flags and hop down their individual paths and open a water valve. They remain stationary if they see a *white* flag. If two valves in series have been opened, water will flow, filling a bucket that has been positioned near the tank for a particular day. The illustration is shown for *Thursday*, and the answers to our previously- asked questions are shown at right. Only one bucket has been filled for Thursday, which indicates that for Thursday neither person had a car.

It would be possible to build an advanced computer with kangaroos, flags and water buckets that could perform the same degree of complex and logical functions as today's computers, but the computer would be monstrously large and would take possibly centuries to yield some answers. Still, it would have every right to be considered a "thinking machine" [*] as much as any super-fast computer run by electricity. But is it

---

[*] The purpose of the kangaroo / water bucket example is simply to show that there is nothing magical about computers operated by electrical currents and voltages. Mind, intelligent awareness, is more than material logic circuits, no matter how complex they may be. Mind and awareness are not products of matter.

really a thinking, conscious machine? No matter how much you try, kangaroos cannot learn much more than to obey simple instructions, and they certainly do not comprehend why they are performing certain feats. If you had a million kangaroos, there would be no more cumulative intelligence than that possessed by one kangaroo. The entire circuit of kangaroos, water buckets, flags and hopping paths does not constitute a higher intelligence and awareness.

In 1980 [*] John R. Searle formulated an argument or a thought experiment that he claimed would discount the claim by many researchers working in the field of cognitive science that machines could be built that could manifest true intelligence and possess real consciousness; that is, *Artificial Intelligence* or *AI* machines. [∇]

The argument goes as follows: You are in a sealed room that contains two slots in the wall. The one slot is for you to receive any number of Chinese characters. However, you have absolutely no knowledge of Chinese, and cannot recognize any of the characters as words. You have a very large "rulebook" which gives you instructions in English on how to construct other Chinese characters from those that were given to you. After you have constructed new characters according to the rulebook instructions, you send them out of the room through the second slot.

You might, through the Chinese characters sent to you, be asked the question, "Do you understand Chinese?" You may follow the rules and form characters that give a meaningful answer such as "yes, I certainly do" even though you in fact have no idea what is going on because you do not know Chinese! Searle likens this scenario to a computer with a program (the rulebook) that simulates a human being who understands Chinese. But the important point in all this is that given any rulebook, *you* would never understand Chinese – never understand the meanings of the characters that you constructed. According to Seale a machine has been constructed which can never manifest intelligence and consciousness.

There are many scientists for and against the *Chinese Room* argument, and the issue is definitely not settled. [(17)]

See web-site,www.helsinki.fi/hum/kognitiotiede/searle.html, for an article entitled, "John R. Searle's Chinese Room." An imaginary conversation is presented between Searle and a C.S. ("Cognitive Scientist").

THE COMPUTER GAME OF LIFE

Computer games, such as one called *Life*, [⊕] have been developed from a simple modification of the game of "checkers." To manually play the game, place about 32 checkers, more or less, on a checkerboard in any arrangement that you desire. You could place them randomly if you like. Now, formulate rules for a game. They might be as follows:

---

[*] I was not aware of the *Chinese Room* argument thought experiment until years after I wrote the above paragraphs on "kangaroo" computers.
[∇] *"Strong AI"* machines are ones that act intelligently and possess real, conscious minds; *"Weak AI"* machines are defined as those that appear to act intelligently, but in actuality only mimic conscious minds.
[⊕] The specific rules for the *Life* game given below were developed by John Conway in 1970.

- The state of a checkerboard remains the same (either occupied or unoccupied by a checker) if exactly two of any of neighboring squares (including diagonal neighbors) have checkers on them.
- If a square is occupied with a checker, and has three adjacent occupied squares, it remains occupied.
- For all other cases, the square becomes or remains unoccupied.
- After the rules have been applied, apply the rule again and again.

Each time the rule is applied the pattern on the checker board changes slightly, and new patterns appear.* The *Life* game can be put on a computer and expanded greatly in size and speed, which results in vastly more complex patterns and movement of the checkers, which are now represented by individual screen pixels. An amazing variety of *Life* forms can be created through this iterative or recursive process of applying the rules over and over again. Some forms keep their shape and "move" across the screen as each sequence of commands is implemented. Upon collision, other forms can be created. Some forms even reproduce or replicate themselves, and others destroy forms that come near them. Because of the deterministic or clockwork nature of the game ▽ it has been called *"cellular automata,"* the cells in this case being the computer screen pixels.

The movement, creation and destruction of the shapes remind some of the activity of biological organisms because they simulate or mimic the activity of life forms.

Paul Davies discusses how John Conway has reasoned that in an infinite *Life* universe containing randomly-distributed dots, that after a long period of time, self-reproducing forms will be created just by chance. Conway suggests that "It's probable, given a large enough *Life* space, initially in a random state, that after a long time, intelligent [conscious], self-replicating animals will emerge and populate some parts of the space."[19] Davies considers whether a computer can actually be built in the *Life* universe; that is, can logic circuits (AND, OR, and NOT operations) be constructed. Computers are made up of many circuits of this kind, which permit a computer to take in an input-bit string of encoded instructions written in binary form consisting of a string of ones and zeros. The computer creates an output-bit string of information, again written in binary form. A "one" is encoded if current passes through a circuit, and a "zero" if no current is passed.

According to Conway suitable logic circuits can indeed be built, so that any physical system that *acts like a computer* can be simulated or mimicked by the *Life* system. Stephen Wolfram [20] has said that "Cellular automata that are capable of universal computation can mimic the behavior of any possible computer...*since any physical process can be represented as a computational process,* they can mimic the action of any possible physical system as well." [21] (Emphasis added)

In the 1930's Alan Turing and John von Neumann began to develop the formal logic for the modern computer of today. In a seminal paper, "Can Machines Think?", they said that sophisticated computers could simulate the responses of a human being to questions

---

* For an extensive description and discussion of this subject, see The Mind of God . [18]

▽ Results occurring consistently according to the fixed rules of the game.

asked it so effectively that no one could tell whether the answers given to the questions were given by a human mind or a computer. If the computer were in a different room from the questioner, and the responses were printed out, then the human questioner would be tempted to believe that the responder (the computer, or computer simulation) was conscious.

If cellular automata or computer simulations can simulate or mimic all physical forms, including living forms that manifest intelligence and consciousness, then how are we to distinguish these simulations from what we call the real world? And what is the real world? Some think that the physical world - the universe itself - is a gigantic cellular automaton! [22] If this is true, then you and I are no more than robots responding to some cosmic rules or input-bit string commands. Life, consciousness and activity would be pre-programmed, and love, joy and all other feelings would be nothing more than illusions. Life would be purposeless. Even though it would appear that we are free thinkers, in truth, we would be acting out a gigantic play. As Shakespeare put it "All the world's a stage, and all the men and women merely players." [23]

ARGUMENTS AGAINST THE COMPUTER GAME OF LIFE CLAIMS FOR LIFE, INTELLIGENCE AND CONSCIOUSNESS BASED IN MATTER

In summary, *The Game of Life* asserts the following:

- "It's probable, given a large enough *Life* space, initially in a random state, that after a long time, intelligent [conscious], self-replicating animals will emerge and populate some parts of the space." (quotation repeated from *The Computer Game of Life*, above).
- "Cellular automata that are capable of universal computation can mimic the behavior of any possible computer...since any physical process can be represented as a computational process, they can mimic the action of any possible physical system as well." (quotation repeated from *The Computer Game of Life*, above).
- ". . . a 'mind' finds its existence through the embodiment of a sufficiently complex algorithm, as this algorithm is acted out by some objects in the physical world." (quotation repeated from *The Computer Game of Life*, above.)
- Mind can evolve from matter.

The author's response to the above assertions about the generic term for matter-based minds ("cellular automata") are given below:

** (1) – Matter-based Systems (Including AI) Only Mimic Life, Intelligence and Consciousness

Rather then acknowledging that all physical systems, including biological systems, can be explained as the product of *Life* games or cellular automata, I believe they actually suggest a diametrically opposite conclusion. As seen by the example of the kangaroo-operated computer, and by the simple game of *Life* played manually with checkers - with no electrically operated circuits - computers, or computer software possess no intrinsic life or conscious awareness. *They only mimic it*. Trying to evolve non-material or "infinite dimensional" consciousness and ideas from matter that is embedded in a four-dimensional space-time manifold, is like the two-dimensional kangaroo trying to escape from his two-dimensional paper world into some three-dimensional world. It can't be done. The complex assemblage and activity of pixels on a computer screen, and the atoms and molecules that comprise the human *DNA* and the human brain only ape life and intelligence. But they point to a significant conclusion: *Like the game of Life, the claim for conscious awareness originating in, or reposing in, the brain is an illusion.* The claim for life and intelligence in matter is an illusion, and the game of *Life* makes this more apparent than ever.

--- DNA: the Secret of Life, or the Creation of Collective Minds?

"There is no chance, no destiny, no fate, that can circumvent or hinder
or control the firm resolve of a determined soul."
(Ella Wheeler Wilcox) [24]

A *DNA* molecule in human cells consists of two strands that twist around in the form of a double helix. The sides of the helix are made of sugar and phosphate molecules. The connections between the two strands, which resemble the rungs of a ladder, consist of nitrogen-containing chemicals, and are called *bases*. Four different bases - adenine, thiamin, cytosine and guanine - are arranged in particular order called the *DNA* sequence. The sequence specifies the exact genetic instructions needed to create a specific organism with its unique characteristics.

But as impressive and significant as they are in determining the characteristics and functioning of living organisms such as human beings, the complex *DNA* molecule, when reduced to its basic components, consist of your basic protons, neutrons and electrons. Reduced even further the proton and the neutron are seen to be made up of quarks. From a *reductionistic* standpoint, no life or consciousness can be seen at this level.

From a *holistic* viewpoint, we see what appear to be life and consciousness arising from ever-complex matter. Paul Davies has said that the secret of life is not to be found in the fundamental particles, such as atoms, but in their appropriate and complex arrangement.[25] But it is impossible to create life out of non-life particles no matter how much effort is made to do so. Rather, some philosophers would postulate that *somehow* a *life force* (from Spirit, God?) * is introduced into matter as the result of the increasing complex arrangement of lifeless particles.

But in some respects today's scientists are following in the footsteps of the Roman philosophical poet and writer, Lucretius, of the first century B. C. who espoused the philosophy of the Epicureans: that the only reality was the reality the senses perceived-that the senses were infallible-and things were just the way they appeared (see Part I, Introduction and Historical Perspective). We see life and intelligence manifested in

---

* It is widely believed that the human body has a "soul," a life force and identity constrained in matter and space-time that continues on for man (but not for other life forms) after the death of the physical body; whereas God, alone, is eternal Life - and this Life or Soul is manifested (reflected) by the spiritual universe, including man.

material objects and we assume that not only do they have their origin there, but, in fact, depend upon the material body for continued existence.

In speaking of *DNA*, Deepak Chopra (*Quantum Healing*) believes that some transformation in our experience happens that turns non-material thoughts into molecules * inside the body (brain). [26] And if one molecule, why not many and vastly more complex molecules chains like the *DNA* that are in every cell of the body?

In his book, *Healing Words, the Power of Prayer and the Practice of Medicine*, Larry Dossey comments on experiments involving consciousness and its apparent influence on the growth of bacteria and other microorganisms. He says "If genetic mutations can be influenced by the conscious efforts of others, as in one of the studies, [as mentioned in his book] then genes cannot be the absolute controllers they are represented to be. Biology, in other words, *is not destiny*" (Emphasis added). [27] Repeating what was said a few pages back: might not the structure of *DNA* be an *effect* rather than a *cause*?

Going one giant step beyond the above observations and conclusions: if thought or consciousness – as claimed by Dossey - is prime in the creation of the molecular chains which define the structure and function of the body, then is it really necessary for thought to create DNA at all in order to manifest life, consciousness and form? ᵛ

Mary Baker Eddy has said that matter is the subjective state of (mortal) mind. [28] And, as mentioned earlier, since the mind can influence the matter-body by will or intent, then the mind is not probabilistic like material particles, and cannot be described by a wave function. What is being implied here is that reality exists first at the mental or non-material level. It is not the *DNA* comprising our genes that is responsible for the transfer of hereditary characteristics: it is mind. The *Biblical* writer of *Ezekiel* had a remarkable spiritual insight to this, when he wrote "What mean ye, that ye use this proverb concerning the land of Israel, saying the fathers have eaten sour grapes, and the children's teeth are set on edge? As I live, saith the Lord God, ye shall not have occasion any more to use this proverb in Israel." [29] And Eddy said that: "The elements and functions of the physical body and of the physical world will change as mortal mind changes its beliefs."[30] That is, if collective thought (non-local, unitive) ⊕ believes that physical law and material structure are necessary to define and maintain life and intelligence, then the effect of thought influenced by this paradigm will be the creation of *DNA* molecular chains to carry out this belief. Part II, Chapter 9, Figure (9-1), further along in the book,

---

* In this case, a non-material thought (notice: not a physical force in space-time) configures a neuro-peptide molecule out of the hydrogen, carbon and oxygen atoms in the glucose that is used by the body as fuel.

ᵛ In the future, if cloning of a human being becomes possible, in no way will a cloned individual have the same consciousness or identity as the original person, because identity or individual consciousness does not depend on the structure of the brain.

⊕ Collective thought: The author cannot speak for Goswami (Part II, Chapter 1) and others as to their precise meaning when they say that collective consciousness - through observation – collapses the wave function of objects. Goswami said that material objects are brought into our experience by the way we choose and the way we recognize the results of our choice. My interpretation is that this observation is – at the grass roots – entirely mental, and is performed continuously by non-local, universal and collective minds. The result of this mental observation is dependent on what the majority of minds currently believe (choose) is the accepted physical paradigm describing reality. And the results of this belief (a mask over reality) are reinforced by the physical senses (recognition).

illustrates this. The correlation between certain *DNA* structures - as well as the correlation of conditions and activities in the brain - with some bodily functions or dysfunction in the body as claimed by Antonio R. Damasio in *Scientific American*, (December, 1999) [31] is "not indicative of a cause-effect relationship"(see "A Genetic Basis for Intelligence?" *Christian Science Sentinel*, January 3, 2000). [32] The brain and bodily functions, as well as *DNA*, are *all* constructs of collective mortal thought. As stated in the above article (*CS Sentinel*) the brain is the primary manifestation of the collective belief that intelligence is in matter. In like manner, the human eye is the outcome of collective belief that vision or observation depends upon material structure.

Leaving the DNA discussion for a minute, please recall the *EPR* experiments, the results at least suggest the possibility that it may be consciousness that "collapses" wave functions and affects correlation between the two random proton spin component values, as described in Part I, Chapter 15, of this book. The experimental results from these kinds of quantum experiments, in general, suggest a relationship between matter and non-local mind: the *observed* and the *observer*. Because it is non-local mind that consciously and intentionally changes the orientation of the spin detector at proton #1, thereby bringing into existence different spin component values for distant proton #2. Perhaps if the observer understood more of the non-locality of mind, and the relationship between matter and mind, he/she could in theory affect the *degree of data correlation* instantaneously, and over great distances. Perhaps even exercise some control over the *random* nature of the experiment. This would be in violation of Einstein's *Theory of Relativity,* which says that no message or influence can travel faster than the speed of light. But now we are dealing with what I believe is, at the very fundamental level, the *wholly mental nature of reality.*

In a similar manner, may not the structure and activity of body's *DNA* and brain, which are offshoots of mortal consciousness – and not the other way around – be simply a correlation with, or a reflection of mortal thought models for physical reality? [*]
What mortal thought incorrectly believes about the nature of reality, mortal thought to a great extent sees and experiences.

Our understanding of the mental nature of reality, and especially of its spiritual nature is in its infancy. [∇] At this period of time, we appear to need the body, and to need a healthy one. And at this period of human development we appear to be characterized to a great extent by our genetic makeup, but individual experiences indicate that even at this period we do not have to be servants or slaves to hereditary claims. For example, many of today's diseases are believed to be hereditary in nature and passed down from generation to generation, but the following experience hints of the unlimited possibilities of good for mankind as it learns to pray scientifically.

--- Predestination, Hereditary Asthma, and the Nature of God

---

[*] But as consciousness begins to understand a little more of the primacy and control of Mind (not mind) it will be filled with thoughts and ideas of this universal Mind. Then, the apparent physical evidence of any correlation between consciousness and brain activity should begin to fade away.
[∇] See the definition of idea (mental vs. spiritual), Part I, Introduction and Historical Perspective.

"The determination to hold Spirit in the grasp of matter is the persecutor of Truth and Love."
Mary Baker Eddy [33]

--- Predestination

John Calvin (1509-1564) was a French theologian and reformer. Colonial New England Puritanism was based largely on the Calvinistic doctrine of *Predestination* - that God has *fore-ordained* that certain of His children were to be saved and would be destined, along with the angels, for eternal life; while others were damned and destined to spend eternity suffering in hell. This doctrine is no longer accepted by most major religious organizations, because they have come to believe that a God of love and forgiveness would not levy such a doctrine on innocent new-borns.

But what about the law of heredity? Is this not a law of predestination that some people will be born with hereditary diseases and disabilities, and that others will have a predilection for negative behavior because of their genetic makeup? And are we slaves to this cruel so-called law of God, or to indifferent laws of physics?

--- Hereditary Asthma

A younger son of a woman, who in the past had been plagued with asthma, again came down with an attack. Asthma had been hereditary in their family for generations. [34] But about six months earlier the mother had begun to take up a serious study to understand God and His laws of Spirit. She called an experienced spiritual healer to help her. She began to realize to a degree that Spirit and its manifestation (man and the universe) cannot be held subject to material laws, no matter how determined the secular world was in believing in the dominance of physical law. Genetic patterns – whether for "good" hereditary characteristics (long life, strong bones, etc.) or for "bad" hereditary characteristics (malformations, diseases, etc.) – were seen as essentially mental rather than material conditions. In three days the child was healed. There was one brief reccurrence later on, but none after that. The healing has been permanent.

--- The Nature of God

A friend related an experience that at one time she was very ill with a stomach problem, which was often accompanied with severe pain. Her prayers had failed to heal her, until one day she reviewed how she had been praying. She said that while she had been praying, in the back of her mind she had been hoping that if she could just get through the year, everything would be "OK". That year had been a particularly trying one for her, with many problems that needed to be resolved. She felt that if she could put that year behind her, and through the passage of time, possibly be healed, then she could begin to experience more harmony in her life and less frustration. It was then that she realized that she had been *insulting* God! She began to realize that God never forsakes, never delays good, and never sets up mankind (through *DNA)* for future pain and suffering. In a few days, her stomach problem disappeared.

** (2) – Consciousness Not a Computational Process

As computer input-bit strings and output strings increase in length, more information can be stored and retrieved, but this does not lead to some kind of spontaneous appearance of conscious awareness. Perhaps over 99% of what we label as our "thinking" can be encoded in logical programming. But the sense of beauty, the thoughts of love, joy, humor, wisdom in deference of human logic, compassion, forgiveness, gentleness, kindness, *conscious awareness*, cannot be represented as a "computational process."

** (3) – Mental Manifestation versus Artificial Construction

You may ask, "Why is the creation of organic life and consciousness that has its beginnings in a physical body with a physical brain * any different than the fabrication of an inorganic computer in a laboratory?" Some day artificial intelligence devices may eventually be structured very similar to that of the human brain. The present belief or paradigm regarding reality is that man has a separate mind from God, and that this mind resides in, and depends upon a matter-brain for life and expression. Therefore the conclusion resulting from this belief is that intelligence, life and awareness somehow evolve out of matter. And, if an artificial device is properly constructed, it should also manifest the above mentioned characteristics of the human brain.

My argument against the above claims is that the source of all awareness is in Mind, which is eternal and omni-present Consciousness, and which has always existed even "before" the *Big Bang*, and certainly before artificial intelligence devices. Therefore, what is called "man" - as a compound *spiritual idea* of this Mind - has always existed, has always manifested or reflected Consciousness; although mortal thought or belief has perverted this concept as having a temporal origin and a specific structure in matter, and with a mind in matter.

The human brain is a mental creation of this thought and is in a fundamental way different than a computer engineer's physical creation of any kind of computer. It would be like the difference between the mental ideas of an artist and his external artistic creation painted on a canvas. But – and here is the important part – ***neither an advanced AI device nor the human brain originate or contain consciousness.*** The fundamental structure of both matter-brain and so-called artificial devices or computers is atoms, but the *thoughts* of the mother form the embryo of another mind, and unconsciously shape it, observes Eddy. [35] This shows the ***continuity of consciousness*** from mother to embryo, a universal and eternal consciousness *outside of, and independent of* material structure called brain or *AI*. Mortal thought creates the physical body and brain, and then would endow (in belief only) this pair with something they could never possess: life and consciousness. But there is no continuity of consciousness from man to *AI*. In truth, spiritual man *reflects the consciousness of Soul*, God. Infinite Mind could never be confined in a finite material brain or *AI* machine. Infinite Soul can never be sub-divided

---

* The embryo may be removed from the body and nurtured in a laboratory environment.

into finite souls and minds. Man does not have a soul residing in a body. Neither matter-brain nor matter-*AI* can reflect Spirit, Mind, the only source of consciousness.

If the mother's thoughts are influenced by the Divine, then there will be greater signs of the Divine in her worldly experiences, but in some way our individual earthly presence is linked to our own *consent* to mortality. We consent to the belief of death, and we consent to the belief of birth in matter, space-time. That is, we *consent* to this belief of birth *before* the mortal body and brain is manifested. The virgin "birth" of Jesus, which occurred without the need of human intervention and the union of sperm and egg, illustrates that man is the eternal offspring of Mind, and does not accrete intelligence and life from matter. Intelligence and life exist before material creation and do not evolve as cells are accreted one by one to form a material body and brain.

In a statement remarkably similar (but with somewhat different reasoning) to that of Wheeler [*] (Part II, Chapter 15), Eddy replies to a rhetorical question as to how a *belief* can "affect a result which precedes the development of that belief," by declaring that there are no mortal beings because being is immortal, like God, and is inseparable from God. [37]

At this very moment, we are defining our past, the origin of the belief that life, substance and intelligence have existence in matter. (The reader is referred to APPENDIX B for further discussions on how the physical universe may have been created.)

The intelligent ideas of Mind that flood the waiting consciousness of spiritual man are not communicated through matter-brain, or indirectly through artificial neural networks. The rapidly developing science of neural networks (*ANN*s: *Artificial Neural Networks*) and *fuzzy logic* [∇] may lead to advanced computers that even more closely simulate human logic, creativity and reasoning, but this advancement in itself does not lead to conscious awareness.[⊕] All the lives and intelligences that supposedly have evolved in brain structures, and in increasingly complex computers, cease to exist once these structures have been disorganized or destroyed. But man, the spiritual idea of Mind, as exemplified by Christ Jesus in the raising of Lazarus from the dead, and by his own resurrection exists now and forever.

--- *ANN*s

Artificial neural networks (*ANN*s) are computers that attempt to simulate the functions of the human brain by mimicking the structure of the interconnected nerve cells (neurons [∞]) of the brain. Individual nodes, which are analogous to neurons, are located in layers of the network. (For a more complete discussion of the subject, the reader is

---

[*] "By deciding which questions our quantum registering equipment shall put in the present we have an undeniable choice in what we have the right to say about the past." (Wheeler) [36]

[∇] Fuzzy logic: the theory that states the questions about most phenomena in the real world cannot be answered with a 100% "yes" or a 100% "no," but fall somewhere in between. (The apple is not all red, or all not-red, but somewhere in between; that is, the apple in varying degrees is both red and not-red).

[⊕] For an interesting discussion on fuzzy logic see *Fuzzy Thinking/The New Science of Fuzzy Logic*.

[∞] Neurons: nerve cells with special processing. Neurons are connected to other neurons by long fibers or axions. At the end of each neuron are shorter, tree-like structures called dendrites. The junction between a dendrite and an axion is called a synapse (connection weight).

referred to the Internet address: http:/www.imagination-engines.com [39] and to the *New Scientist* article, "The Creativity Machine." [40] A user feeds in data to an input layer, and an output layer yields the result. Between the input layer and the output layer are two or more so-called "hidden layers." Each node (in the "off" mode) receives signals from nodes located in the previous layer, adds them, and compares this cumulative value with an internally stored threshold value. If the threshold value is exceeded, the node (in the "on" mode) fires a signal to nodes in the next layer. Information is processed from the *ANN* and generated as a series of "off" and "on" states, represented by a "0" for the "off" state, and a "1" for the "on" state.

The information stored within the network takes the form of connection strengths or "weights" between nodes, and the programmer can change this result by adjusting or multiplying individual nodal signals before they are sent out to other nodes.

But according to those working in the field, artificial neural networks can be *trained*, something which is impossible to do with conventional computers. For example, the programmer might input in digitized form, data to represent a specific type of automobile, and then modify the strength of the signals in the network
until the output shows the "on- off" pattern that corresponds to the specific car design. The network now begins to associate certain combinations of nodal patterns with a given car design. It can now pick out certain features needed to identify automobiles to the point where it can classify different models which it has never seen. And this has been accomplished without the need of extensive input of what is called "if-then" rules.

Stephen Thaler, one of the pioneers of advanced *ANN*s, has developed a computer program, which he believes is capable of independent, creative invention similar to that of the human brain. He calls this his *Creativity Machine*. [41] He trained a network and observed what happened when the inputs were held constant while connections were turned off at random. Rather than "dying" or disintegrating, the system produced a continuously changing stream of recognizable or familiar outputs. The same kind of response happened if he simply changed some of the connection weights. Apparently the network "perceived" the internal state changes as caused by input changes, and "guessed" as to what should be a reasonable output. Later, Thaler discovered that by simply introducing noise (random inputs) into the network's internal workings he could get the same response; that is, response to non-existent inputs.[*] Thaler called these phenomena the "virtual input" effect.

With the *Creativity Machine,* it is believed that "…no intelligent information is presented to a neural network in the form of inputs. Instead the network uses internal disruptions or random signals [noise], applied to neurons or connection weights to generate useful information." [42]

--- Caution Urged

Not all artificial intelligence researchers who are aware of his work are as enthusiastic as Steve Thaler when it comes to claiming that *ANN*s have creativity capacities and will eventually be able to think the way humans do. Jordan Pollack at

---

[*] It is hard to believe that random noise (chaos) can be the spark that generates genuine creativity and be the source for free will.

Brandeis University, Mass., says that for *ANNs* to be truly creative they must be able to distinguish "good" results from "bad" results. In Bob Holmes' *New Scientist* article he says that Thaler, it would seem, "imposes all the creativity from outside by training the filtering network to his own standards." Pollack asks the question, "Is that creativity or is that trainable, mechanical filtering * based on the person who selected the network?" [43] In any case, most agree that at present there is no universally accepted definition of creativity.

Proponents of *ANN* believe that "...artificial creativity and consciousness do not spontaneously arise as hardware and software become more complex and extensive." [44] But it is admitted by some that to truly simulate human consciousness would require hundreds of billions of neurons connected in some kind of *complex tangle*, and this process would be the most difficult task on the path to obtaining artificial consciousness.

--- Impassable gulf

I am in the camp that believes that there is an impossible gulf between Spirit and matter - between Mind and matter. Creativity, consciousness, and self-awareness do not originate through the collective action of neurons. It is my conviction that it would be impossible for a principle or law of nature or reality to exist without an Intelligence to first conceive and formulate it. Mind, not chaos, must be the First Cause. We must not put the cart before the horse. And Mind must have existed before what mankind perceives as matter. Therefore it would not have depended upon matter for its existence and expression.

Some people believe that the sensation of being – the feeling of unique identity - is no more than "simply a complex activation pattern of diverse association within the brain's cavity." [45] To these people consciousness is nothing more than essentially a response to chaotic stimuli. Higher feelings of love, compassion, tenderness and beauty are essentially meaningless.

I do not believe that brains or *ANN* systems are the source of intelligence and awareness. Mind is distinct from brain, and does not require matter in the form of neurons or something else in order to be expressed. If consciousness is indeed *non-local*, how could it be confined in brain or in an *ANN*? Why, indeed, would it need a complex structure of neurons in order for intelligence and consciousness to be manifested?!

No physicist, biologist, philosopher, or *AI* specialist has satisfactorily answered the question, "How does consciousness and self-awareness or evolve from matter?" Perhaps the answer to the question is: "They do not."

"Are thoughts divine or human?" Mary Baker Eddy asks. [46] In the degree that thoughts are based on the false paradigm that life and substance are in matter, and conclusions about reality are reached - based largely on the evidence of the physical senses – to that degree, they do not manifest any real level of intelligence, wisdom and creativity. Why? Because these *finite* thoughts – however grand they may seem to be - are based on untruths and illusions, and eventually ** lead to failure, chaos, and death.

---

* Filtering neural network: programmer introduces a set of examples (for the car design) and indicates which design is considered "good" and which is considered "bad."
** Including the so-called universal entropy increases, leading to the end of all life and activity in the physical universe.

Mind's (upper case) ideas to man are orderly, intelligent, creative, *infinite*, useful and harmonious. *Spiritual man* is therefore not governed by chance, uncertainty, or internal chaos. But because mortal minds believe in the paradigm of physics - which embraces in it the phenomena of chaos, uncertainty – are we surprised that our view of what we call the external world (including the structure of the brain) is largely chaotic and chancy? Should not the structure and activity of brains mirror what collective minds believe in? As previously mentioned, matter is the collective state of mortal minds (mortal beliefs). (For further discussions on this subject the reader is referred to Part I, APPENDIX C.)

As mankind gradually over a period of many years begins to understand and appreciate its eternal unity with Mind, we should expect to see greater intellect and more genuine creativity manifested by individuals, irrespective of the size of their brains. Also, more effectual and consistent spiritual healing works should be accomplished, Eddy spoke of this [47], and Christ Jesus, two thousand years ago, prophesized this when he said: "Verily, verily, I say unto you, He that believeth on me, the works that I do shall he do also; and greater works than these shall he do; because I go unto my Father" [48] ▽

** (4) – Distinguishing Between AI and True Consciousness

It is possible to distinguish between the "consciousness" of cellular automata and *ANN*s, and true consciousness, because these devices do not possess awareness, and cannot bring about what are called spiritual healings through prayerful, conscious communion with God or Mind. ⊕ (Spirituality and spiritual healing will be discussed in some detail in subsequent chapters, especially in *Part II*, Chapter 8).

In order to explain this more fully, let us consider the ability of a sophisticated computer to understand the meaning of words. Suppose you were to ask a computer the meaning of the word "humor." The computer could check all its dictionary databases for definitions of the word "humor." Based on its research it could develop a broad guideline for what makes people laugh. It could then analyze and correlate all relevant passages in a book known for its humorous stories and produce a list of sentences that were considered humorous. It might even create a sentence of its own that would be considered humorous. However, the computer would accomplish this task without any actual comprehension or awareness of what it was doing. Selmer Bringsjord, director of the *Minds and Machines Laboratory* and program at *Rensselaer Polytechnic Institute*, Troy, New York, says, "Future robots [and computers] may exhibit much of the behavior of persons, but none of the robots [computers] will ever be a person… If some of the claims for spiritual reality are true, *it short-circuits the whole thing* [*that robots/computers can be conscious*]" [49] (emphasis added). What Bringsjord implied in his statement was that if people by nature are non-physical entities (having a soul), then it would be impossible to

---

▽ "Because I go unto my Father." The author believes Jesus was saying, "Because I have demonstrated to you my (and your) unity with Mind."

⊕ Some have said the difference between *AI* devices and man is that *AI* devices do not possess a "soul." The author agrees with *Christian Science* that declares that anything material cannot reflect Soul, which is Spirit, God… that as we give up concepts based on the evidence of the five senses, exchanging them for thoughts of the divine consciousness, we will have demonstrations of spiritual healing.

build a machine person, an *AI* "on your own." [50] The same would be true if man, who is *spiritual*, *reflects* Soul.

If conscious beings can bias the random distribution of ones and zeros generated from some kind of random number generator experiments (see forth-coming Chapter 3), then we might want to test an advanced *ANN* machine to see if it can accomplish similar results. **If advanced *AI* devices cannot bias the distribution of a random series of ones and zeros, or affect the physical well-being through conscious intent, or through "prayer," ▽then we must conclude that these devices manifest no real consciousness.** Then we can say that non-living, non-conscious *AI* machines cannot affect the external world, as consciousness can. And since quantum physics has shown us that the material "observer" cannot be separated from the material system being observed, can we not conclude that, in some way, it is non-material, conscious observation - not inanimate recording devices - that "collapses" the wave function in quantum experiments?

Spiritual healing comes about through communion with Mind. It is not the mere repetition of beautiful sounding words or phrases found, for example, in the *Bible*. We can intellectualize about the phrase in the *Bible* that God is Love, but the deep meaning and inspiration comes from God, by-passing, if you will, the computer circuitry and even the fleshly brain with its infinite density of blindness to spiritual ideas and truths. In fact, if we mainly repeat *Biblical* passages like a mantra, but with no understanding or feeling, we will accomplish healing on a par with a computer, that is, *zero*. But when our thoughts are in communion with universal infinite Mind, then the ideas we receive become our ideas.

A computer need not be "conscious" in order to perform computational processes or to parrot beautiful words, but the words, without the divine influence, understanding and inspiration behind them, cannot affect a *change* in consciousness and bring healing. Recall the discussion about the collapse of the wave function of an object (Part II, Chapter 1): The argument was made that "observation" by a macroscopic inanimate detector cannot exchange ignorance for knowledge – it requires a conscious observer to do this. In similar fashion a computer cannot comprehend the deep meaning of its own programs.

--- Conscious Union with Mind

"The evidence is overwhelming that mind behaves in a non-local way…if mind is non-local, there is one mind, or Universal Mind, which is identical to what the West has regarded as the Soul." (Larry Dossey) [51] Computers and mobile robots will continue to make giant strides in mimicking human intelligence and action. But we should also expect - as mankind learn more about the nature of God and man – that it will exhibit a far greater degree of insight, creativity, and intelligence without the aid of computers.

As previously mentioned, the subject of healings and spiritual prayer will be addressed further along in the book in some detail (see Part II, Chapter 8), but one

---

▽ At this period *AI* or *ANN* devices are not advanced or sophisticated, and humanity has not consistently acquired and demonstrated the *science and soul* of spiritual healing for such a practical comparison to be made.

example will be given here to illustrate the difference between matter-based mind and infinite, non-local divine Mind that is God:

A man was participating in a military parachute training exercise. The parachutes that were being used by the men had no ripcords. [52] They were to open automatically. The man was the last parachutist to go outside of his plane. Because of strong, gusting winds, he found himself only three to four feet away from the previous jumper. As this jumper's parachute opened the man fell feet first through the rigging lines and out through the other side. The result was that his parachute never opened, but just bunched into a great glob of canvas, which collapsed the other man's parachute. They were both falling to earth almost in a free fall. This accident occurred at about 800 feet above the ground.

The man, who had been pondering the meaning of the *Ninety-first Psalm* several weeks before the training started, later related that immediately after the accident occurred he saw in his mind what he termed "a sort of slide show of ideas - of dwelling in the secret place of the most High and of divine protection." He recalled the *Biblical* statement he had been pondering weeks before: "He shall send His angels to bear thee up lest thou dash thy foot against a stone." [53] He said spiritual concepts came to him in rapid succession – ideas from the *Ninety-first Psalm*. He felt himself completely giving over the situation to God.

Both men hit the ground at an estimated speed of about 70 miles per hour.[*] The man heard later from the ambulance crew on the ground that he hit the ground, bounced about 10 feet into the air before he landed sprawled out. The man got up and immediately walked away. Both he and the other parachutist were unhurt. The ambulance crew could not believe what they had witnessed and shook their heads in disbelief.

Laws of physics would dictate that the human body can only survive a certain level of impact due to the force of gravity, but – as the man related – "God revealed these so-called laws to be null and void. Superceded by divine law, they were powerless to affect us." Also, this law – the law of *universal* or *infinite* Mind – understood and affirmed by the one man, protected *both* men. [54] [∇]

** (5) – Breaking Universal Life Rules

Christ Jesus communicated with Mind. He, and many people since his time, broke the so-called universal *life* rules described as physical law by his remarkable demonstrations over physical limitations. These "laws" were set aside, and life and health were restored to the individual seeking help. .

** (6) – Non-local Consciousness

---

[*] With a little bit of canvas providing some braking effect, the speed of 70mph represents a fall from a building of approximately 12 floors in height!

[∇] It should also be obvious that the human mind was not a factor in protecting the two men from injury or death.

Consciousness is non-local. Although this fact is only faintly understood today, it is demonstrated in varying degrees by spiritual healings. It was shown by Christ Jesus in his demonstration of dominion over space-time by his near-instantaneous transfer across the *Sea of Galilee*. This was accomplished by conscious communion or union with infinite, ever-present, (non-local) Mind. This was also demonstrated by his resurrection from death. Today, spiritual healings have occurred where the prayer of one person has affected the state of consciousness and well-being of another individual located sometimes a great distance from the person doing the praying. This could only be accomplished if, at the very fundamental level of things, reality is mental.

** (7) – Complex Circuitry and Ideas

The "rules" of the so-called universal game of *Life*: who created them? Was it God, or was it somehow the result of - as Wheeler suggests, "... billions upon billions of elementary acts of observer-participancy reaching far back into the past..." [55] which somehow defined the *Big bang*, itself? "We do not simply observe the laws of nature, there is also a sense in which we create them." [56] The current perception of laws is founded on the basic premise that the physical world as seen through the senses is all there is to reality. By our universal collective expectations, our matter-based thinking, we arrive painstakingly at certain conclusions about reality and the laws that govern the universe, but these are but shadows of the true, spiritual laws of Mind.

The circuit of the computer – the "hardware," like that of the human brain, is similar to that of an electronic blackboard, where initial input data can be calculated and processed in accordance with the given "software" or program instructions. Data can be displayed from intermediate steps and will not be lost or forgotten as might happen with a human brain. Simple as well as complex ideas can be manifested and shown visually on a television monitor in a pattern recognizable to the human mind. But the intelligent ideas are not *in* the computer circuitry.

It cannot be said that thousands or millions of kangaroos could be used in a complex computer circuit, and that the sum total of kangaroos, brick paths, water tanks, buckets and valves constitute a higher order of intelligence or comprehension. Indeed, the kangaroos could have been replaced by just about anything, dead or alive, by some ingenious inventor, and still the system would manifest no intrinsic intelligence. And we should not say that billions upon billions of atoms, themselves consisting of basic subatomic particles, can be arranged even over a period of billions of years in complex circuitry in a brain or in an *ANN* to somehow evolve life, intelligence and awareness. For, contrary to some semi-popular opinions today, there is no conscious molecule. In order for a growing, complex pattern of matter to evolve consciousness, one would have to assume that individual sub-atomic particles possessed rudimentary consciousness. It would be as if Mind, the First Cause, could be subdivided into an astronomical number of matter particles, with each possessing a tiny bit of mind. This is the doctrine that declares that the universe as a whole - the summation of all the forces and particles, i.e., the doctrine of *pantheism* - is God.*

While in some instances, the whole may be greater than the sum of its parts, the addition or summation of *nothing*, is still *nothing*, as illustrated in the equation below:

$$\sum_n \alpha_n = 0 \tag{2-1}$$

where $n = 1,2,3...\infty$

represents the intrinsic life, intelligence or awareness of each subatomic particle, atom or molecule that collectively make up the brain. This term has a value of *zero*, so the summation of an *infinite* number of zeros is itself equal to *zero*. There is nothing magical about this. Intelligence, life and awareness are not *in* matter, and no matter how hard we try, we cannot create a theory of evolution that evolves these qualities out of matter.

Again, mind or intelligence is not *in* the computer algorithm circuit, nor on the page of the written program, nor can it appear spontaneously through various associations within the computer network. Running the computer program does not create the solution to a complex problem - *but the answer already exists as an idea.*

Some proponents of *Artificial Intelligence* (*AI*) believe that ". . . a 'mind' finds its existence through the embodiment of a sufficiently complex algorithm, as this algorithm is acted out by some objects in the physical world."[57] Some people in *AI* believe that it is *information* or information processing which somehow holds the key to evolving artificial intelligence. But all the complex organic or inorganic circuits, with storage capacity to retain and recall almost unlimited information and knowledge, cannot bridge the gap between mindless matter particles, and consciousness or life. Mere information, if thrown in the face of blind, dense matter, cannot yield life and consciousness. Non-intelligence cannot produce intelligence. Information without awareness is useless. Awareness without comprehension or understanding can accomplish nothing. As Roger Penrose comments in his book, *The Emperor's New Mind*, ". . . ideas are things, that, as far as we know, need conscious minds for their manifestations."[58] Selmer Bringsjord, of the *Minds and Machines* Laboratory at *Rensselaer Polytechnic Institute*, Troy, New York, has said that he believes that the "inner life" of any advanced computer will *be* "as empty as a rock's."[59]

It is interesting to speculate what would happen to one's consciousness if each one of the brain's one-hundred billion or so neurons were surgically replaced one by one with microchips, until the entire brain were made of computer-like hardware. Or suppose we replaced each neuron with a radio transceiver that "talked" with a computer that was running neuron simulations. Could we say that consciousness was transferred into a series of numbers in a computer? Would *we* still be conscious, and reside inside the computer, and have the same behavior and memories as before?

If we believe that any physical process (such as the activity of the brain) can be expressed as a computational process, then we should consider the following thought

---

* Some physicists hold to the view that consciousness emerges at a critical level of complexity, and does not depend on the "consciousness" of individual atoms. The threshold for this is not evident, and there would appear to be no good reason for increased complexity of matter to evolve awareness.

experiment envisioned by Jaron Lanier.[60] Let us suppose that we have an advanced super sensor that can measure over some period of time all the motions and instant positions of all the asteroids * that exist in a truly gigantic swarm somewhere out in space. Since we are imagining this, we can make the swarm as large as we desire, up to a certain finite size. Now, by using a sophisticated sensor we can record all the asteroid positions and motions as a set of numbers, and list these numbers as a computer program. We can then start searching through all the number of computers that could exist up to a certain very large size until we find one that treats the asteroids' positions and motions as a program that is exactly equivalent to the positions and motions of the neurons in a brain as it changes with time. If the sampling of computers is sufficiently large, this will in theory be possible. According to Jaron Lanier, we now have "a physical system whose internal actions [for a brief moment] perform the computation of your mind." ∇

Can we now conclude that the created computer program manifests consciousness for a finite period of time? Has consciousness evolved randomly out of the swarm of asteroids? I believe we can say with some assurance that a swarm of asteroids does not possess consciousness, nor does any computer program derived from its individual asteroid positions and motions. As with an exceedingly large and complex assemblage of kangaroos and water buckets, or with a computer made of clay bricks, springs, and tubes, it is impossible for consciousness to evolve. *We must, therefore, conclude that even the human brain is not the seat of consciousness, but that consciousness is entirely mental, and somehow exists independently of matter structures.*

David Chalmers [61] speculates that one could fabricate a visual cortex with silicon chips rather than with neurons. Then both visual cortices (the one with silicon chips, and the other with neurons), could be connected to the brain via a two-position switch. When the switch is in one mode you would experience what the artificial cortex is conveying to you, say a red sky. When the switch is in the other mode you would experience what your natural cortex was conveying to you: a blue sky. Your experience would constantly change from red to blue as the switches are rapidly activated in turn. Chalmers concludes that systems with the same organization (say, an artificial computer with silicon chips, and a human brain where neurons have been replaced with silicon chips) will have the same conscious experience. That is, a synthetic or artificial brain would have the same conscious experience as a human brain that has been reorganized (at least the visual cortex) to have the same organization as the artificial brain. But in this illustration the visual cortex is acting like a sensor for the brain. And, of course, this also assumes the artificial computer (*AI*) is conscious.

There appears to be little difference in the above example and in the example of a person fitted with sunglasses that could be electrically changed from a red glass to a clear glass, unbeknownst to the wearer. The wearer would have different conscious experiences as the color of the sunglasses was changed from red to clear, and back again,

---

* Asteroids have been chosen because they have gravitational fields, and therefore, can interact with each other.

∇ Jaron Lanier coined the term, "Virtual Reality"' in the early 1980's and developed the first glove device for virtual world interaction.

but if informed of the nature of the sensors (sunglasses) providing the information, he would immediately become aware that the red experience was false; that is, an illusion.

The premises for the above argument of similar experiences of an artificial brain and a human one are:

(a) - although consciousness is subjective, awareness is objective; and

(b) - consciousness arises from the matter-brain.

But human consciousness and awareness, I believe, are *both* subjective in the mental realm of human experiences. We could say that awareness (of our surroundings), is objective, because it depends on the physical senses (sensors) which are supposed to be objective and function relatively independently of consciousness. However, this is also a false assumption. There is an interconnection between mind and the senses, as discussed in Part II, Chapter 9, and illustrated in Figure (9-1). In the example of the sunglasses, the wearer would still not perceive a clear view (not red) even if he knew he had on red glasses, but in this mental universe, to a great extent whatever collective thought believes in, collective thought experiences, until this belief is changed, either to another belief, or is improved by Mind.

The same kind of question might be posed in a diametrically opposite way. What if, one by one, each neuron were destroyed or somehow disconnected until the entire brain was rendered non-functional; that is, the brain was dead. Would we still have a consciousness? That is, does life and consciousness arise from and depend upon the matter-brain, and can it continue after the death of the body and the brain? The materialistic, reductionistic response would be an emphatic "Yes!" to the first question, and an equally emphatic "No!" to the second question. But some physical healings brought about by apparently physics-defying spiritual means alone, that have occurred in the present should cause us to think deeply about the validity of the claims of the resurrection of Lazarus (four days in the grave) and Christ Jesus (three days in the tomb) from the claims of death. *If these events actually occurred, they would be ultimate proofs that consciousness and life do not depend upon any kind of brain function, whether that brain is made of organic matter, or consists of microchips.* Unfortunately, I know of no present-day examples of the resurrection of the dead after being buried in a grave, for we cannot prove what we at present so poorly understand about the nature of God and man. We do have the promise of Christ Jesus, "If a man keep my saying, he shall never see death." [62]

Eddy said to one of her students, [63] "There is only one Mind, but there seems to be two, one is a reflection* of the other. The *divine Mind is the One* and the other is only the human sense of the divine." Mankind is the effect of a Cause, Mind. It is not the source of Mind. Since God is Spirit, man must be spiritual. Brain, being matter, cannot reflect Mind, nor can it be the source or repository of mind.

GODEL'S THEORM

Princeton mathematician, Kurt Godel around the year 1931, proved to astonished mathematicians that "mathematical statements exist for which no systematic procedure could determine whether they are either true or false." [64] *Godel's Theorem*, sometimes

---

* Reflection: an effect produced by an influence or cause, the reflection manifesting the characteristics of the cause

called the *Incompleteness Theorem*, arises from paradoxes that surround the subject of self-reference. For example, consider the sentence: "This sentence is false." It is a self-referential sentence because it refers back to itself. And it is paradoxical because:

- If you agree that what the sentence says is true, then it must be false.
- If you agree that what the sentence says is false, then it is true.
- And so on, and so on - an infinite regress.

Noted quantum physicist, David Bohm, says that *Godel's Theorem* suggests that neither the theories of physics or doctrines of mysticism (the belief that the direct knowledge of God, or ultimate reality, is attainable through intuition or insight, in a way different from sense testimony) can be absolutely proved. He says "*Godel's Theorem* alone would suggest that for every assumption we are aware of, there must be countless others not known to us. Some of these may be false, some true." [65] Most physicists and philosophers would agree that like the self-referential sentence given above, mortal man can never get out of himself, out of the physical universe and know ultimate truth. Hofstadter, the author of *Godel, Escher and Bach* says, "No matter how a program twists and turns [like the kangaroo] to get out of itself, it is still following the rules inherent in itself. It is no more possible for it to escape than for a human being to decide voluntarily not to obey the laws of physics. Physics is an overriding system, from which there can be no escape." [66]

The above view would seem to represent essentially the present paradigm of physics, which ultimately points to matter and physical laws as superior to mind. And why not, if brain/mind is the result of complex organizations of matter; that is, the mind cannot rise above itself to some higher level - it cannot get outside of itself.

In the book, *The New Story of Science*, R.M. Augros and G.N. Stanciu comment, "If thinking and willing are activities of the brain, then there in no reason to suppose these activities can continue after the brain is destroyed." But later on in their book they conclude "The actions of the mind . . .transcend the mechanisms of physics and chemistry." [67] And Deepak Chopra says, "I believe the reason nobody can find the soul or the spirit inside the brain or the body is because it is not there. We are looking in the wrong place. We are not in the body, the body is in us; we are not in the mind, the mind is in us; we are not in the world, the world is in us." [68] *

The key, I believe, to the argument as to whether man can escape from his material selfhood, is that *no escape is necessary. Mind is not in matter*, neither in the brain nor in the computer. But, contrary to Chopra, mind (or rather, Mind) cannot be confined *in* man. It is outside of matter; and you and I are in reality the individualized images or manifestations of this Mind, this infinite, eternal and only true Consciousness, and therefore, dwell outside of matter and space-time.[∇]

Absolute truth cannot be obtained by matter-based brains or *ANN*s. Spiritual man, the image or *reflection* of Mind, is capable of understanding ultimate Truth, but this will

---

[*] Again, at the risk of undue repetition - neither Augros/Stanciu nor Chopra distinguish between mind and non-spiritual ideas, and Mind and spiritual ideas as I have attempted to do.

[∇] As mentioned earlier in this chapter, matter is the subjective state of mortal consciousness (See ref. 28). Eddy said, "The dreamer and the dream are one, for neither is true nor real."[69] It is not that man is dreaming that he is a mortal locked up in a material universe, unable to get "outside," but it is the **belief** that he is dreaming that he is a mortal (with a mortal consciousness) living in a material universe.

not occur in the realm of matter, space-time. The human mind can only refer back to what its senses perceive, and is locked in the perception of existing in space-time. Mind's ideas go from universal Mind to man, and examples of this phenomenon will be illustrated later on in the book (especially in Chapter 8).

SUMMARY

- In the "beginning" Mind was first and only. There was no need in this mental universe for matter. Therefore, *at the very ground of being*, man - the idea of Mind - requires no material brain for comprehension or expression, despite much evidence to the contrary. This great fact flies in the face of the testimony of the physical senses, and is only dimly comprehended at this period.
- The human mind (a limited sense of Mind) is not probabilistic in nature, because the mind can influence matter by will or intent. Therefore, it would appear that consciousness cannot be described by a wave function. It would also appear that it is mind that "collapses" the wave function for physical objects. If the observer that collapses the wave function is mind, or collective minds, then reality is mental.
- The universe is non-local; therefore, it would be reasonable to conclude that consciousness is also non-local, and independent of the physical constraints of a matter-brain or an *ANN*.
- In the "beginning" - according to quantum mechanics - the emergence of the nascent physical universe, including space-time, itself, required an observer. Was that observer, collective, unitive, non-material mind, and existing outside of space-time?
- There is a unity of consciousness, even on the material plane of things. The thoughts of the mother -not *DNA* or an *ANN* construction - result in the formation of the embryo of another mind. ⊕
- Dr. David Darling, *Astrobiologist* and author of the book, *The Extraterrestrial Encyclopedia: An Alphabetical Reference to All Life in the Universe,* has said, "The freeing of the mind from its organic shackles will be the most spectacular leap in the evolution of consciousness as a whole." [71] Dr. Laurance Doyle, an *Astrophysicist* who works at the *SETI Institute* (*Search for Extraterrestrial Intelligence*) agrees with the opinion of the "spectacular leap," but he believes that any version of organic mind (presumably including so-called non-organic artificial intelligence devices), is a misconception of mind. As an illustration of this point, (quoted in the *Christian Science Sentinel,* July 1, 2002) [72] he said, " [It's] like saying 'The unlimiting of time from a watch will be a great breakthrough.' Time was never in a clock." He also observed that time is no more than the repetition of matter. And mind or consciousness was never *in* a brain. In our present conception of reality we might liken the brain to a finite *substrate or display* upon which we *apparently* witness the affect of intelligent thoughts emanating from a consciousness confined within a brain.

⊕ Bruce Lipton, a scientist and *Cellular Biologist* at *Stanford University*, disagrees with the widely-accepted belief that people are born with a fixed set of genes that determine their present and future lives. He has said, "Our perceptions turn on our genes and turn off our genes, and our perceptions can rewrite our genes." [70]

Doyle has said that we must give up the premise that the senses are first [that they report absolute reality], and put intelligence first.

- *Spiritual healings* present strong visible [∇] evidence for the superiority of Mind over matter (See Part II, Chapter 8, for examples of spiritual healings). The examples of Christ Jesus, as well as present-day examples, indicate the reality of Spirit and the power and *Principle* of Love.[*]

[∇] Visible evidence: to the one who has been healed of some serious disease, it is the inward evidence of the presence of God that eventually is seen outwardly.

[*] Mind, Spirit, Principle, Love are different names for God. (See definition of God, Part II, Introduction)

CHAPTER 3

EXPERIMENTS IN CONSCIOUSNESS

LEADERS IN THE FIELD OF MENTAL PHENOMENA

In Part I of this book we have looked at quantum phenomena and the sometimes controversial relationship between the quantum world and consciousness. In this chapter we investigate, briefly some of the experiments whose objectives are to determine the direct effect of human conscious on the external world.

ROBERT JAHN AND BRENDA DUNNE

In 1987, Robert G. Jahn and Brenda J. Dunne jointly completed the writing of a book, *Margins of Reality* that discussed the results of efforts of the *Princeton Engineering Anomalies Research* (*PEAR*) program to investigate the effect of consciousness on physical objects. Other experiments determined the ability of consciousness to perceive and interpret remote occurrences and scenes not directly experienced by a conscious observer. [1] The results of the experiments, which were performed under carefully controlled conditions, have shown that there is indeed evidence for the influence of consciousness on modifying previously random-occurring events, not only at the sub-microscopic level, but also at the macroscopic level. In a series of experiments, random-event generators (*REG*) were employed. A *REG* is a device that uses micro-electric circuitry to sample a random source noise pattern, and then displays the results as positive bits if the noise signal is greater than the mean value at the time of sampling, and as negative bits if the signal is less than the mean value. [2] Data accumulated over a period of time is called a *trial*. A single trial may contain as many as 2000 bits. A *series* is defined as a block of data consisting of anywhere from 2500 to 5000 trials for a given set of experimental conditions. As the authors say, "The primary goal of the *REG* studies is to explore correlation of statistical biases in the output count distributions with pre-stated intentions of the operator." [3]

Each test is performed by having the operator or individual make a deliberate conscious decision to try to influence the random distribution of the positive/negative bit output string, by deciding before the experiment is begun whether he or she wants to influence the distribution to obtain an excess either of positive or of negative results. If the intention is to achieve higher than chance results, the plotted curve from the data is labeled Pk+, while data taken with the intent of achieving lower than chance results is labeled Pk-. Data taken under the same conditions but with no conscious intent to influence the results is labeled BL (baseline). Figure (3-1) shows the kind of results typically achieved by a series of experiments (this is representative data only, and has not been taken from the John/Dunne book).

Although some experiments (with some operators) did not yield results that were different from statistically random data, the cumulative data of thousands of experiments revealed a significant effect of consciousness on the external world. The authors state that the total volume of experimental data taken with different operators over a period of eight years, shows "clear evidence of a legitimate scientific anomaly." [4] They conclude "... the classical paradigm separating physical process from the conscious and subconscious desires of the human psyche must admit some pragmatic and philosophical problem." [5]

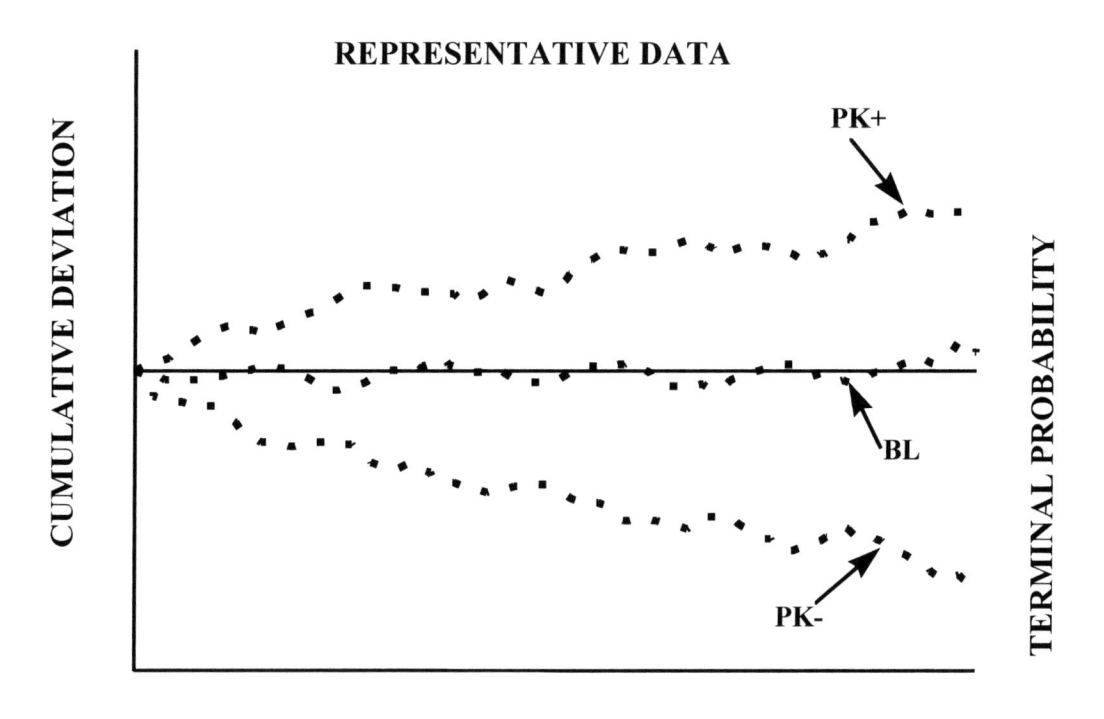

REPRESENTATIVE DATA

(Figure: plot with CUMULATIVE DEVIATION on left y-axis, TERMINAL PROBABILITY on right y-axis, NUMBER OF EXPERIMENTAL SERIES on x-axis, showing three curves labeled PK+, BL, and PK−)

Figure (3-1)

The Effect of Conscious Intent to Influence a Random Distribution of a Positive/Negative Bit Output String

Jahn and Dunne also make a startling statement in regard to the impact of consciousness in the physical world: ". . .attempts have been made to ascribe to consciousness an *entropy-reducing* capability that allows it to exert an ordering influence on otherwise random physical processes, thereby reversing their normal thermodynamic tendency toward minimum information and maximum chaos." They believe that some of their data agrees with the above statement. [6]

As related by Larry Dossey in his *Space, Time and Medicine* book "Jahn. . .has demonstrated that a subject watching an optical interference pattern on a Fabry - Perot interferometer can change the spacing of two parallel images." [7] ∇

MAY, UTTS AND SPOTTISWOODE

∇ No further *PEAR* studies along this line have been made due to the extreme sensitivity of the experiment to ambient influences.

More recently, a statistical test [8] has been developed to determine the existence or nonexistence of psycho kinesis (*PK*). * The test has been applied to data from random number- generator experiments. The operator, in a manner similar to the experiments just discussed, mentally tries to influence a randomly-generated bit string to contain more *ones* than *zeros*. A large database now exists from the experiments that show that experimental results correlate with the operator's intentions. However, the statistical analysis indicated that the operator had simply *selected at the right time* a bit string that had more *ones* than *zeros*, rather than actually influencing the random noise generator output. The conclusion was that the operator *actually used psi*, but it was to select the bit strings that had excessive *ones*, rather than to influence matter.

But, as discussed in an article on the test results, written by Jean Burns, [9] a Ph.D. physicist doing research in the area, two important points must be considered:

(1) - Not all *PK* experiments were set up in which the operator had a bit string available in which to choose. This would seem to imply that removing any possibility of a choosing component of the test might give different *PK* statistical results.

(2) - The statement that the experimental results indicate in a general way that consciousness cannot influence matter; that is, we do not have "free will," fails to consider the fact that consciousness (with deliberate intent) selectively initiates the burst of discharges in the nerve cells of the brain which in turn control the muscles of your fingers, for example. This mental control of matter involves no physical force as far as can be ascertained.

And a*s* most physicists agree, a dynamic force does not accomplish the collapse of the wave function of a subatomic particle. All of which leads me to conclude that if a mental thought or intent that can move molecules or an assemblage of molecules in the body without the use of physical force, then how substantial or real are these molecules themselves? We should at least consider the claim that if the wave function for particles is no more than a mathematical formulation of conscious mind (representing many quantum states), the particles themselves are no more than ideas in consciousness, externalized.

PALLIKARI

In another instance Fotini Pallikari, a physicist from the *University of Athens, Greece*, analyzed data from a group of German psychologists who experimented to see if operators could influence random "noise" from a semi-conductor diode. The random positive and negative pulses were fed into a computer as a series of ones and zeros. Operators were then asked to mentally "influence" the statistical distribution of millions of bits. The results showed that the operators had no influence on the average, but were able *to* "weekly sustain the 'direction' of any naturally occurring localized deviations from chance, such as a run of ones and zeros." [10]

We may ask why the data in some *PSI* experiments is not more positive - less marginal - in showing the effects of consciousness in perceiving and affecting the

---

* psycho kinesis: the alteration of motion of an object external to the body, by the influence of the human mind.

physical world, although some operators have shown consistently higher capabilities than others to affect physical objects. A possible explanation for the sometimes less than definitive results may be due to the *state* of thought of the experimenter. We at this time know so little about how the *state* of thought: fear, ignorance uncertainty, happiness, expectancy, calmness, and our pre-conditioned biases and beliefs may mask reality.

Even so, if the goal is simply to control matter with the human will, with no other objective than to show the influence of consciousness on the external world, then the results may at times be disappointing.

SPINDRIFT

The *Spindrift* experiments, on the other hand, involved experiments conducted by people whose primary - but not exclusive - objective, was to improve or invigorate the state of a living organism. An organization called *Spindrift* has for several years, investigated the efficacy of "prayer" on the health and vitality of biological systems, such as, sprouting seeds. The statistical data from the scientifically-organized and directed studies indicated that seeds "treated" with prayer were healthier and grew taller, and rye seeds deliberately soaked in salt water to cause them stress, actually became healthier under the "prayer" treatment. [11] What the studies apparently revealed is that thought or human consciousness can influence matter, even if the "treatment" was performed at a significant distance from the test specimens.

BENOR

In addition to the *Spindrift* work, there have been numerous other studies on the effect of "prayer" or the "...intentional influence of one or more people upon another living system without utilizing known physical means of intervention." This is a definition of healing through prayer or conscious intent as defined by Daniel J. Benor, *M.D.* in his survey of studies on spiritual healing.[12]

It should be emphasized that the terms "spiritual" healing and "prayer" in this instance, are broad definitions that encompass phenomena that range from mind-body, mental control or manipulation of matter, to the yielding of the human will to the divine Will (either by a blind faith or by some degree of spiritual enlightenment). Larry Dossey, in his book *Healing Words/ The Power of Prayer and the Practice of Medicine*[13] reports extensively on the results of the Benor survey, and these will not be repeated here. But he did report that out of the 131 controlled "trials" or studies on the non-local as well as local effects of prayer - on such living objects as enzymes, fungi, bacteria, plants and animals including humans - that 56 showed significant statistical results. The likelihood of the positive results due to chance alone was less than 1 in 100. In 21 other studies, the results due to chance alone were 2-5 parts in 100.

The significance of these results were discounted by the *National Research Council,* a government group that evaluates studies in certain science areas, but Dossey argues strongly that in some instances faulty assumptions as to the nature of prayer or meditation, and a glaring omission of a large data base (about 40 published reports) may have contributed to the indifferent conclusions. *

But the objective of prayer that has a right to truly be called *spiritual*, is not to *change matter,* but rather to bring thought in to accord with the Will of God, whereby one recognizes spiritual reality as the *ever-presence* of harmony and order. Rather than being the solution to physical and mental disorders, the action of the human will is, in the long run, not conducive to lasting harmony and happiness.

Prayer, I feel, is not the manipulating of matter, or begging or imploring God to "do something;" for the All-knowing does not have to be instructed in what *we* think needs to be done. Prayer is not a *process* of the human mind, but it is the yielding of thought to God. Then we embrace the thoughts of God, and these divine thoughts become our thoughts. ** By this yielding, we demonstrate our unity with Mind.

BOUCHARD AND DOSSEY

Larry Dossey, in an article, entitled, "Lessons From Twins: of Nature, Nurture, and Consciousness,"[19] reports on studies made on identical twins who were separated from birth, and raised by different parents. Later on in life, after each twin learned for the first time he or she had a twin brother or sister, they made arrangements to meet. The coming together of each member of a twin set revealed a truly remarkable similarity in their physical characteristics, their likes and dislikes, peculiarities, and lifestyles. Studies have been made by Psychologist Thomas Bouchard, Jr., *University of Minnesota*, of a number of twins in an effort to determine why these similarities occurred. One of Bouchard's case studies' remarkable subjects were middle-aged twins Bridget and Dorothy who had been separated when very young and raised apart in different environments.[20] As described by Dossey, when they first met each had "…seven rings and two bracelets on one wrist, and a watch and a bracelet on the other. Bridget had named her son Richard *Andrew, and Dorothy had named hers Andrew Richard."* Bridget's daughter had been named Catherine Louise, and Dorothy had named her daughter Karen Louise. This especially impressed Bouchard because choosing a name is a joint decision between husband and wife, thus lessening the chance that the similarity in the names was merely a coincidence.

---

* In one instance, the conclusions of a highly respected NRC-commissioned world expert (Robert Rosenthal of *Harvard University*) in evaluating highly controversial research claims (in this case, parapsychology results), were rejected by the committee chairman, even though Rosenthal considered the data as being of high quality.[14] As Dossey says, scientific debates should be rigorous, but also, unbiased. The conclusions are significant because they suggest strongly the primacy of non-local consciousness in the universe. Analysis indicates that the "effects [experimental results] are not a function of experimental quality…" and "…the application rate is as good as that found in exemplary experiments in psychology and physics."[15]

** "For I know the thoughts that I think toward you, saith the Lord, thoughts of peace, and not of evil, to give you an expected end."[16] This appears to be in contrast to the Biblical statement,[17] "For my thoughts are not your thoughts, saith the Lord." But here the writer is comparing God's thoughts to the thoughts attributed to fleshly, mortal man. Further along in the *Bible*, we have the statement that through spiritual discernment, "…we have the mind of Christ."[18]

Other twin cases are mentioned in the Dossey article, but Dossey asks the question as to whether the similarities were due to nature (*DNA*) or nurture (environmental) factors, or to possibly some other factor such as "the non-local nature of the human mind."

Dossey comments that if consciousness is indeed non-local, then it is not confined in space-time; it is infinite. "In this case there are no absolute boundaries between individual minds, and we are not separate from each other but are ultimately 'one in consciousness" - what our ancestors called *Universal Mind*." [21] (Emphasis added)

Dossey reports David Chalmers, a mathematician and cognitive scientist at *UC Santa Cruz,* as believing that "consciousness is fundamental in the universe, perhaps on a par with matter and energy, and that *it is not derived from, nor reducible to, anything else."* [22] [23] (Emphasis added)

CHAPTER 4

PARADIGM SHIFTS

Let us consider for the moment the definition and the nature of *paradigms,* and how they have influenced science. A "paradigm," as used by Thomas Kuhn in his book *The Structure of Scientific Revelations*, [1] is essentially a foundation of thought or baseline from which a model of the universe is conceived and constructed. Around this baseline, "data of experiment and observation are organized." [2] A *paradigm shift* occurs when, as the result of preliminary data or new postulates, the present paradigm begins to look a little shaky. It sometimes takes many years for a new paradigm in some field such as art, biology, or physics to become accepted by the general public.

A paradigm way of seeing can be likened to the wearing of a pair of spectacles containing colored lenses. If Mark has on a pair of glasses with red lenses, he will see a red kangaroo when he looks into Farmer Smith's pasture; while Tina will view the same kangaroo as green because she has donned spectacles with green lenses. David, on the other hand, has on a pair of spectacles that distorts his view to the point where he is not even sure he is seeing a kangaroo, but perhaps a bear! (Figure (4-1))

Who is seeing reality? Both Mark and Tina, if they are unaware that their lenses are colored, will be convinced that what they are viewing is reality. David may be uncertain as to the accuracy of what he perceives. *I,* on the other hand, have elected not to wear glasses of any kind, and therefore, I know that I am not being disillusioned, and that the kangaroo has always been white. But am *I* right? We can envision an imaginary world where *everyone* has been born with blue-tinted contacts and with the lenses configured so that the images seen with the eye are somewhat distorted - a world where everyone is ignorant of the presence of the lenses. We would all accept that our perceptions of the world were natural, because we would have known no other perception. If some wise person told us that our view of the universe was incorrect, we would probably laugh at him - until after being told that we were wearing contacts over our eyes, and being instructed on how to remove them - did remove them. Then we would discover the world as it has *always* been.

Can the five physical senses we employ to perceive and interpret reality be like the lenses, colored and distorted by our preconceived premises and rigid ideas about what reality should be? Wheeler, in commenting about the coming new revolution in physics that will dwarf all present revolutions, said that "...when it comes, we will say to each other, ' Oh how beautiful and simple it is! How could we ever have missed it so long!' " [3]

The paradigm in physics in the early years of the twentieth century was a universe constructed with clockwork simplicity and regularity. For every cause there was an effect; and in theory it would be possible to predict the future position and momentum of every atomic particle.

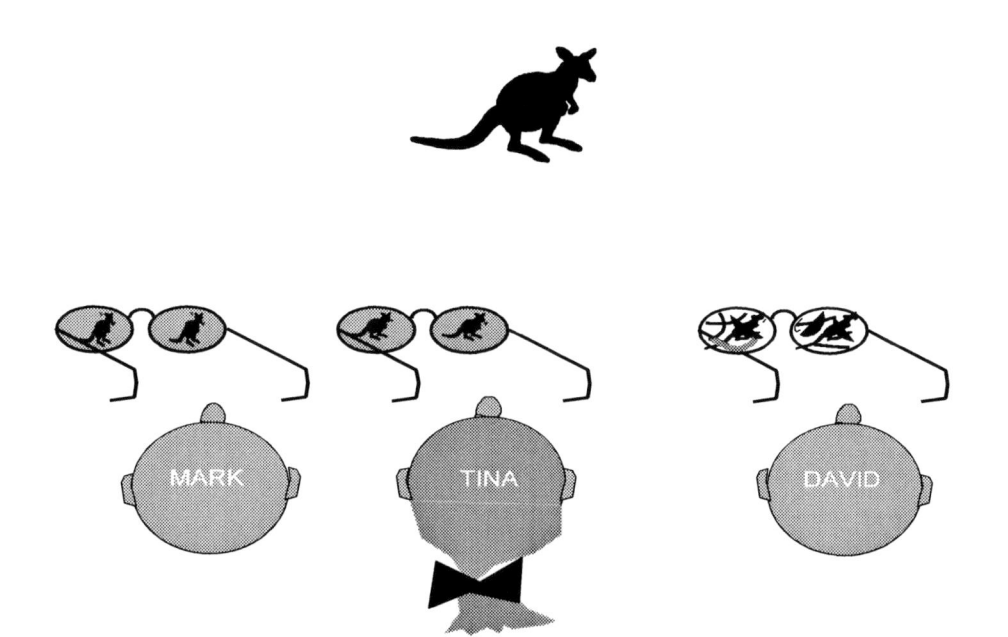

Figure (4-1)

Every event in the future would be predictable - the universe would be *"deterministic."* *

But questions began popping up in the physics arena about the interpretation of some physical phenomena, such as the dual nature of light, the "*violet catastrophe*" in blackbody radiation analyses, and the decay of electrons in atomic orbits as predicted by classical physics, but not observed experimentally.

As an example of how paradigms color reality, consider the following experience in chemistry: Near the end of the eighteenth century, the meteorologist John Dalton, developed a chemical theory of compounds based on the law of chemistry that said that atoms could only combine in some simple, fixed whole-number ratio, or multiples of this ratio. This ratio, which was based on the atomic weights of atoms, was 2:1 for oxygen / copper in copper oxide. [4] However, experimentalists such as the Frenchman Proust, measured the ratio as 1.47:1. Since he was known for his accuracy in experimental measurements, and was considered a fine experimentalist, the chemists of that day could not in general accept Dalton's theory. Even after there was general acceptance of the theory it took almost another generation before experimental data agreed with the theory! As Kuhn says, *"The data themselves had changed."* [5]

---

* determinism: all occurrences in nature take place in accordance with natural law.

CHAPTER 5

THE SCIENTIFIC METHOD

Alfred North Whitehead, in his book, *Science and the Modern World* [1] said the following in regard to the essence of the *scientific method* for the formulation and verification of physical models for reality: "Search for measurable elements among your phenomena, and then search for relations between these measures of physical quantities."

Science is always concerned with *quantitative* measurements that aid in validating theoretical models proposed for the interpretation of reality. But how can science, based primarily on the measurements of physical quantities alone, deal with what can be called, nonphysical or qualitative values of the state of consciousness, such as, hate, fear, uncertainty, lust, intent, desire, love, joy, meekness, honesty, faith, courage, knowledge, wisdom, purity or *spirituality of thought?* These values exist in the realm of consciousness, and cannot be measured with physical instruments. Fritjof Capra, the author of the best-selling book *The Turning Point* [2] said, "Science, in my view, need not be restricted to measurements and quantitative analyses." He went on to say that knowledge should be the result of systematic observation, and that it must be expressed in terms of "self- consistent and approximate models."

Although quantum theory is concerned with physical models or paradigms for reality, and in measurements to validate these models, it is now recognized by some that the consciousness of the observer plays - as Capra says - a crucial role in the observation process, and that therefore, reality - at least at the quantum level - can no longer be considered objective. And it is the kind or *state* of collective, unitive consciousness that has a bearing on which model of reality will be "validated." Quantum theory cannot measure qualities or states of consciousness.

What are the self-consistent models, and how are they validated? To the materialist, they are physical models described by physical laws and imbedded in space-time. These laws are laws of limitation, and result in a universe where hate, fear, uncertainty, lack, chaos, destruction and death are natural outcomes. To the spiritually-based thinker, the self-consistent models are based on the laws of Mind, Spirit, Love. These models include spiritual man and a spiritual universe, which evidence forth the spiritual qualities of love, joy, meekness, harmony, abundance, etc. To the spiritual healer, spiritual laws are validated through a degree of restoration of health and harmony that occur through prayer alone.

METAPHYSICS OVER PHYSICS (POTASSIUM CYANIDE ACCIDENT)

In 1955, a professor of chemistry at a college in Illinois publicly related an incident that involved an accident that occurred to him while preparing potassium cyanide in order to carry out the *Wohler Synthesis* of urea [3] (The reader is referred to this reference for a more complete and accurate account of the experience).

As he was melting potassium cyanide in an iron dish over a powerful burner, he inadvertently picked up the hot end of the stirring rod. His hand was severely burned; the wound, which extended across his right palm, was deep and exposed his tendons. As he later related, there appeared to be "several masses of white crystals in the fluids and burned tissues" which had been dislodged from the rod into the wound. He washed his hand in water and wrapped it in a towel, and went on with his work.

But during this experience he prayed. He said he soon became calm, and "conscious of the presence of infinite Life, God, overruling the picture of accident and possible death." Within three days there was scarcely a scar, and in less than a week all effects had disappeared.

Later, in discussing the incident with an expert on cyanide poisoning, the expert said that ordinarily, an experience such as this would prove fatal in a few minutes. It should be noted that the professor had a *BS* degree from the *Massachusetts Institute of Technology*, an *MS* degree from the *California Institute of Technology*, and a *Ph.D.* from the *University of Illinois*, and was the author of numerous papers on electrodeposition and a contributor to technical publications.

After the professor had made public his experience, he was severely criticized by a consulting chemical engineer, who had implied that the experience was fraudulent. He felt that the professor had done the profession of chemistry a disservice by making public statements about the experience, which, if true, violated well-established physical laws. The professor replied to the critic in a letter. An abbreviated version of his argument is given below.

He said essentially there were five possible explanations for his survival:

(1) - The material was not potassium cyanide, or an old sample might have been completely hydrolyzed to the carbonate. But this could not be true because the urea was obtained easily.

(2) - Because of shock, pain, etc., the professor mistakenly imagined crystals in the wound. But the end of the stirring rod which had been grasped had been heavily coated with crystals, and it would have been virtually impossible that some were not dislodged and entered the wound. And as the professor mentioned he quickly became calm as the result of his immediate prayers.

(3) - The amount of the potassium cyanide absorbed was below the lethal level. But this level is so low that such an occurrence was highly improbable. In fact, symptoms that might result from a smaller absorption level were unobserved.

(4) - The cyanide was washed out before it was absorbed in the wound. Under the circumstances described (a deep, open wound), a safety expert's opinion was that this was impossible. A workman in the plant where he was employed had been exposed to a relatively dilute solution on the lower portions of his body, had been immediately removed from the solution, clothes removed and thoroughly washed down with water until his death ten minutes later. There had been no break in his skin.

(5) - Cyanide was absorbed in the wound, but was rendered ineffective by a higher law of Life, Mind. A higher view of reality was seen.

The professor concluded in his letter that "The existence of a higher law, which can save life and relieve suffering in even the most hopeless circumstances, is so important that I am constrained to bring my experience to public notice. I cannot see that this will be any disservice to my profession; rather, the contrary."

This, of course, gives one no license to foolishly and deliberately inject herself with a poisonous solution. By doing so, one is essentially saying "Here is something I truly believe is harmful and the result of a physical law, but I am going to show everyone that there is a *second law*, existing along with the *first law*, that can counteract the *first law.*" That approach would probably lead to failure, and in an instance like the above, would lead to death. We usually cannot successfully serve two "masters." Christ Jesus said, [4] "No man can serve two masters: for either he will hate the one, and love the other; or else he will hold to the one an despise the other. Ye cannot serve God and mammon" - ["or whatever is trusted in"]. *

"Whatever is trusted in" - God, Spirit and spiritual laws, or matter and material laws and remedies? This experience, which might be looked upon by some critics as an anecdotal experience - although it is not unique in the annals of spiritual healing - points out the difficulty of controlled tests to determine the degree of success of prayer. In a controlled experiment, such as the *Wohler Synthesis* of urea, the scientist sets up experimental conditions, and observes and measures the results to see if they agree with new or established physical theory. A conscientious spiritual healer would not think of setting up controlled experiments to, in effect, observe the effect of prayer on the manipulation of material objects or altering the state of the body, *for this is not the purpose of prayer.*

EVOLUTION OF HUMAN THOUGHT

In this book we have differentiated between mind or mortal mind(s) (lower case), and Mind (upper case), the former being an erroneous belief that life, consciousness and intelligence evolve from or originate in matter; the latter being Reality, itself: the ground, substance, foundation or Principle of all.

In exploring the realm of thought, we discover that human *belief* goes from one thesis or paradigm to another :

(a) - Matter superior over mind;

(b) - Mortal mind(s) controlling matter;

(c) - Mortal minds interpreting a higher, mental view of reality - a mixture of matter and Spirit;

(d) - Mind as All, and Only.

We also discover that the healing of body and soul evolves in a similar manner to the four phases listed above:

(1) - Chemical and mechanical means;

(2) - Mental methods of reconstruction in concert with (a) above;

(3) - Mankind's belief that mortal consciousness and Mind can work together – which is inefficient and counter-productive – in bringing about lasting healing and harmony;

---

* Interpretation in brackets from *The Amplified Bible*, Expanded Edition, Zondervan *Bible* Publishers, Grand Rapids, Michigan, 1987.[5]

(4) - Recognition that divine Mind is *All* (i.e., no material mind at all), and that Mind's formations - man and the universe - need no correction or manipulation of matter, and that mankind only needs a clearer recognition of this grand fact or reality.

In (d) and (4) we begin to recognize that the universal belief of finite mind (or minds) in matter *somehow separated from Mind or Love* [*] is the cause of all discord in the world, and of the apparently cool indifference that we see in the physical laws governing the universe. This false assumption results in feedback from the senses that verify our assumptions (See Figure (9-1).) Through the human mind's acceptance of the paradigm of life, substance and intelligence in matter, arise thoughts of fear, uncertainty, hate, and finiteness. The eye perceives what the mind believes.

Studies involving fake drugs (placebos) have shown that the belief in their effectiveness creates a powerful effect on the physical state of the body. [6] But as human consciousness takes on more of the divine, the scene changes for the better. In speaking of this translation of thought, which appears in consciousness by degrees, Eddy said, "In the third degree mortal mind disappears, and man as God's image appears." [7]

It is difficult to mix material things with spiritual things, because they are diametrically opposite in nature. An old English proverb says, "You can't make a silk purse out of a sow's ear." Neither can we make "evil" good and "spiritualize" matter. If thought has been grounded in the material world and accepts without question that the laws of nature are indifferent to the hopes and aspirations of consciousness, and that consciousness is the slave to matter-based laws, then spiritual reality fades into uncertainty, or into merely a fanciful and insubstantial dream. But if we come to appreciate that there are spiritual laws that can be applied practically in our lives through actually living these laws of Love, then material models of reality and their accompanying laws will seem less dictatorial. They will become more of a servant to humanity. Eventually this new understanding of the omni-presence of Mind will lead us entirely away from materiality to Spirit and spirituality.

---

[*] In examining many of the so-called spectacular and sometimes quick healings accomplished by the person needing the healing (the patient) and/or by the healer working with the patient - some of which have been described in following sections of this book - it is highly significant that most involve one or more of the following:

(1) - a measure of understanding of matter's innate nothingness and the allness of God, good;

(2) - persistence, along with gratitude and thankfulness for present blessings, regardless of sense testimony to the contrary - a hungering for truth beyond what can be found with the physical senses;

(3) - a letting go of an obsession with the body and fear of its physical state or condition, along with an increased and sometimes almost overpowering sense of the presence of Love in one's life;

(4) - a forgetting of one's own personal state of health while loving and praying for someone else.

CHAPTER 6

A MINDLESS, PURPOSELESS UNIVERSE, OR AN ETERNAL, PURPOSEFUL UNIVERSE OF SPIRIT?

"The fool hath said in his heart, There is no God."
(Psalms)[1]

BERTRAND RUSSELL

Bertrand Russell, the famous philosopher in the early 1900's was quoted as saying, "That man is the product of causes which had no provision of the end they were achieving; that his origins, his growth, his hopes and fears, his loves and beliefs are but the outcome of accidental collocations of atoms. . .that all the labors of the ages, all the devotion. . .all the noonday brightness of human genius are destined to extinction." And later on: "Only within the scaffolding of these truths, only on the firm foundation of unyielding despair, can the soul's habitation henceforth be safely built." [2]

This pessimistic view is certainly seen at the sub-microscopic level, although Russell was referring to the universe itself. Nevertheless, at the minute level of examination, nothing of any real significance appears to be happening. At this level we cannot even detect that a piece of fruit will ripen on the vine and decay.[3] All action is seen as random and purposeless.

In Daniel Cowan's book *Mind Underlies Space-time,* he comments that "The more closely matter is examined from within its own premise that finiteness is fundamental, the more complex and contradictory it becomes." [4] Thus we may come to understand that the application of quantum theory to explain physical phenomena and give *meaning* and *purpose* to life, bears its own seed of self-destruction; for the very foundation of physical reality may be seen to be on shaky ground.

In this connection, Dr. Jovanovic of *Fermi National Laboratories,* asks the question, "How can a particle without the properties of mass [the neutrino] * be a building block?" [5] And at a conference on particle physics, Andrei Linde of *CERN* (*Center for European Nuclear Research)* said that he could conceive of a universe composed entirely of mind. [6]

RICHARD DAWKINS

The pessimistic thoughts of Bertrand Russell about life and reality have been to a large degree echoed by Richard Dawkins, the author of *The Blind Watchmaker*, and more recently, *River Out of Eden: A Darwinian View of Life*. In an article published in

---

* At this writing the neutrino is thought to have a very small discernible mass. (about 0.1 MeV; the electron has a mass of 0.5 MeV, which is $9.1 x 10^{-31}$ kg.)

Scientific American (November, 1995) entitled "God's Utility Function," Dawkins says that in this world the total amount of suffering among all creatures [♦] including man, is " ...beyond all decent contemplation". He concludes that "The universe that we observe has precisely the properties we should expect if there is, at the bottom, no design, no purpose, no evil and no good, nothing but pitiless indifference." [7] Dawkins, like Russell before him is correct, if, indeed, all there is, is a mindless universe of matter-energy.

RELIGION CAN SURVIVE

But if religion is to survive, and people are to believe in a God or a First Cause that has *practical* meaning in their lives, they must be ready to describe that primal Cause as infinite, eternal, omnipotent *good*. They must not attribute physical laws to God nor ascribe to Him the creation of matter. Why? Because it is the operation of indifferent physical laws of matter that in the long run is responsible for all "evil," limitations and disasters in our lives. They must acknowledge that man and the universe are wholly spiritual, and can be only discerned through our mental, spiritual capacities (spiritual "senses") to understand God and the nature of reality.

I believe that the reality perceived by Russell and Dawkins, (the reality perceived by the physical senses) is not the reality perceived, demonstrated and lived by Christ Jesus. Many people who subscribe to a God-less universe have thoughts that tend toward *cynicism*. In regard to spiritual things, this kind of thinking can result in a contemptuous and mocking disbelief of any idea that flies in the face of physical sense testimony. It is a lost faith in the goodness of God and of creation itself. Even what you might feel is the most convincing example of spiritual healing indicating the presence of the invisible[*] God or Spirit, falls on deaf ears; for they can always find another, more "plausible" answer (for them, at least), one which does not tax their comfortable belief system. Christ Jesus spoke of these kinds of people when he said; "... they seeing see not; and hearing they hear not, neither do they understand." And he said the only way they could understand would be "with their heart..." [9]

ALBERT EINSTEIN AND CHRISTIAN SCIENCE

It has been known by more than a few people that Albert Einstein, a Jew by birth, possessed more than a passing interest in Christian Science. There have been many reports from church members of seeing Einstein (not infrequently) at church *Wednesday Testimony* meetings, Sunday church services, and Reading Rooms at two churches in *New York City* (*Eighth Church, Fifth Church*), *Princeton, New Jersey*, and *Pasadena, California.* Some church members could point out the seat in Fifth Church near Grand Central Station in New York where Einstein usually sat during Wednesday services during the period of 1952-1953.(As told by Marcyne Johnson, Tucson, Arizona.) [10]

[♦] An example: there are some insects that paralyze their "victims" (other insects), providing live meals for their young ! But surely this is a gross misperception of the reality of infinite Love!

[*] A very young girl wrote to God, "Dear God, are you really invisible, or is this just a trick?!" [8]

A number of people have sent letters and affidavits testifying to direct and indirect experiences concerning Einstein and *Christian Science* to Robert Hough, author of the unpublished booklet "Professor Albert Einstein on Religion, Math and Life in General."

More recently W. S. Cooper [Π] has completed a far more extensive, accurate and complete study entitled, "On Einstein's interest in the metaphysics of Mary Baker Eddy." (School of Information, University of California, Berkeley, CA, 2008) In the introduction to his study, he says, "There is credible evidence, including testimony of eyewitnesses still living [2001], that Albert Einstein had a special interest in the metaphysical system of Mary Baker, the founder of the Christian Science movement. He is reported to have attended Christian Science churches, studied in the denominational reading rooms, complimented Eddy's writings, and defended her against criticism in private. The objections raised by Einstein against traditional religious doctrines are largely inapplicable to Eddy's metaphysics." [11]

Unfortunately, because of recent new information, the Hough statements in the unpublished booklet, made ***specifically*** in regard to Einstein's purported relationship with Nancy Kiefer's father, Dr. William Frederick Underwood, can no longer be considered to be verified by oral or written testimony of witnesses other than Kiefer. I have, therefore, removed these statements from this Third Edition; and highly recommend the reading of Cooper's paper. The following statements and comments regarding Einstein's connections with Christian Science are given below.

- Mary Spaulding, the wife of the famous violinist Alfred Spaulding had a conversation with Einstein in a *New York Reading Room* at Madison Ave. near Third, where he said - after making complimentary remarks about " *Science and Health* - "to think that a woman knew this over eighty years ago." [∇] Einstein was also reported being seen at the Central Park South Reading Room in the 1954 time period. [12]

- Virginia Bailey of Floral Park, N.Y., saw Einstein at a Christian Science church Reading Room, and also at a Wednesday evening testimonial service in Princeton, New Jersey. His comment to her at the Reading Room was: "See this pipe? ... If it wasn't for this pipe, I would join your church." And at the Wednesday service: (told to her by a church member who heard it), "You people do not know what you have." (Bailey letter to Robert Hough, March 12, 2001 [13]

- Robert Peel ("Spiritual Healing in a Scientific Age" (San Francisco: Harper and Row, 1987, pp.28, 201 n.16 ; and also noted in William Cooper's paper), that he – Robert Peel - heard directly from George Nay (a German-speaking editor and Christian Science lecturer, a conversation between Nay and Einstein where Dr. Einstein said, "Do you people realize what a wonderful thing you have?" Cooper says the conversation was witnessed by George Millar, London England, April 28, 1954. [14]

[Π] W.S. Cooper is Professor Emeritus, SIMS, University of California, Berkeley, CA, 94720

[∇] There can be no absolute assurance that all the quotations attributed to Einstein are exact word-for-word.

- Cooper's sources indicate that Einstein made repeated visits to Christian Science reading rooms in the New York area and in Princeton. Apparently he was one of the most frequent visitors at the Princeton reading room, often spending more than an hour in reading "Science and Health" (S&H). His generous remarks about S&H were recorded as follows: "One day as he was leaving the Reading Room, he stopped at the librarian's desk, and said: 'If everyone realized what is in that book (meaning "Science and Health") you would not have room enough anywhere to accommodate the people who would be clamoring for it.'"
(*Reminiscences of Elizabeth Earl Jones* as quoted in "The Healer: the Healing Work of Mary Baker Eddy, p. 189") [15]
- Paul Stark Seeley, a Christian Science Teacher and lecturer, said that a close friend of his and his wife's made an appointment with Einstein near the end of the war. She asked him what he thought of "Science and Health," and he immediately replied, "Blessed art thou!" (Mentioned during Mr. Seeley's lecture, "Spiritual Forces Bring Mankind's Liberation," public lecture printed in the Christian Science Monitor, October, 20, 1965; also noted in Cooper paper). [16]
- Harold W. Stewart of Alamada, California, has stated in a letter to Robert Hough (August 10, 2001) that his mother saw several visits Einstein made to the Christian Science church in Pasadena, California, probably during the time period of 1930-1933. [17]
- Pat Archer of Boynton Beach, Florida, in a letter to Robert Hough (April 15, 2002), said that her mother told her that Einstein, while occasionally attending Sunday services at Eighth Church of Christ, Scientist, New York, told her, that if he had had "Science and Health" in his formative years, he would be five hundred years in advance of his present stage (1950's). [18]

Einstein never joined the *Christian Science* church, jokingly admitting, if it were not for smoking his pipe, he would join the church! (Quoted from Virginia Bailey letter.) As far as can be known, he continued until his death in 1955 working in the physics realm, looking for an ultimate solution for determining the basic physical laws of nature.

Because of Einstein we should no longer think that we live in a universe of absolute linear time. ("…one day is with the lord as a thousand years, and a thousand years as one day." [19] Larry Dossey believes the biographical data on Einstein that relates to his personal views on life and death were greatly influenced by the ideas embraced in his *Special Theory of Relativity* which he developed in 1905. When a very close personal friend (Michele Besso) died in 1955, Einstein wrote a letter to his surviving son in which he said, that although Besso had preceded him in bidding farewell to this present world, that "This signifies nothing. For us believing physicists the distinction between past, present, and future is only an illusion, even if a stubborn one."[20] As Dossey says, "Einstein's personal spiritual and philosophical transformations that flowed from his remarkable insight are possibilities for us all." [21]

Dossey asks why the ideas of *Relativity* influenced Einstein's thoughts about space-time and death, when these same ideas have had little impact on most physicists of this day who work with them.[*] Einstein was describing the physical world as he understood it, based on *Relativity*. Mary Baker Eddy described reality from a spiritual standpoint when she said, "One moment of divine consciousness, or the spiritual understanding of Life and Love, is a foretaste of eternity. This exalted view, obtained and retained when the Science of being is understood, would bridge over with life discerned spiritually the interval of death, and man would be found in the full consciousness of his immortality and eternal harmony, where sin, sickness, and death are unknown." [23] And who also said "Life is without beginning and without end. Eternity, not time, expresses the thought of Life, and time is no part of eternity. One ceases in proportion as the other is recognized." [24]

Many years after Eddy,[v] John Archibald Wheeler, in commenting on the implications of the *Uncertainty Principle,* said that this principle of physics deprives us from predicting or giving meaning to the classical description of space evolving in time. He concluded that we cannot view nature in which any event in the past, present or future occupies a preordained position in what we call "space-time." That is, "There is no space-time, there is no time, there is no before, there is no after. The question of what happens 'next' is without meaning." [25]

Wheeler was speaking about quantum and general relativity effects that are the foundational stones for the structure of the physical universe. Eddy was referring to the experiencing of a higher, more spiritual nature of reality, whereby the physical universe, including the aging of the body were no more than an illusion of the physical senses, which themselves were a product of a false belief about the nature of reality.

---

[*] Kurt Godel, a brilliant mathematical logician and philosopher, undoubtedly influenced by conversations with Einstein, attempted to show that the passage of time is an illusion; that the past, present and future events in the physical universe are different regions of a single vast space-time. That is, time does not flow, said Godel. It simply exists in its entirety, stretched out, like space (see "A remark on the relationship between Relativity theory and Idealistic Philosophy" in Paul Schilpp's book, *Albert Einstein: Philosopher and Scientist*, vol. II, Harper and Row, 1959, pp. 557-562). [22]

[v] Eddy's book, *Science and Health*, was first published in 1875.

CHAPTER 7

EVIDENCE FOR THE EXISTENCE OF GOD

"All the world's a stage..."
Shakespeare

THE UNIVERSE AND THE OBSERVER

Was there a creator, and did He have a purpose in what He created? Does consciousness have a central place in this creation? And does the physical universe have any objective existence independent of consciousness? What purpose is the universe if there is no one to observe it?* Shakespeare said, "All the world's a stage, and all the men and women merely players." [1] Who or what is doing the watching or the observing?

At about the same time period, Johannes Kepler (the discoverer of the laws of planetary motion), upon his learning of Galileo's discovery of four of the moons of Jupiter, and his (Kepler's) conviction that Jupiter was inhabited, commented: "For whose sake [are the moons] ...if there are no people on Jupiter to behold this wonderful varied display with their own eyes?" [2] Ervin Schrodinger, in his book *Mind and Matter*, said, "...without man the universe would be a drama played before empty stalls." [3] John Wheeler paraphrases R. H. Dicke in an article entitled, "Genesis and Observership": "What possible sense could it make to speak of 'the universe' unless there were someone around to be aware of it?" [4] Fred Alan Wolf says in *Parallel Universes*, "...without an observer, there is no such thing as a universe - for if there were, who would be there to know it was a universe?" [5] And in *The Emperor's New Mind, Roger* Penrose exclaims, "Material reality according to classical theory, let alone in the quantum theory..., is a much more nebulous thing than one had thought. Its quantification - and even whether it is there or not - depends upon distinctly subtle issues and cannot be ascertained merely locally!" [6]

One of the fathers of quantum theory, Erwin Schrodinger, said "The observer is never entirely replaced by instruments: for if he were, he could obviously obtain no knowledge whatsoever... The most careful record, when not inspected, tells us nothing." [7] We cannot suppose that mechanical recording devices can act upon gathered information and make independent "decisions." We cannot believe that these decisions could result in actions that were *outside* of probabilistic laws, and that these actions could be made independent of consciousness.

Consider a rocky, airless planet orbiting a neutron star located in some outer regions of our galaxy. Now expand this idea to consider the entire universe containing similar inanimate objects; that is, inhospitable to any life forms. Without consciousness to perceive and to comprehend, the universe is meaningless. Consciousness does not evolve

---

* The latest estimate places the number of *observable* galaxies at three hundred billion!

out of *matter over eons of years.* Consciousness is first, consciousness is prime, and a universe without consciousness cannot exist.

GOOD AND EVIL

GOOD AND ITS ALLNESS

Philosophers have been debating for centuries the reality of good and evil. Sometimes the argument goes as follows:

(1) - If God exists… then He must be omnipotent and infinite good.
(2) - If God exists…but is powerless to prevent evil, then He is not omnipotent.
(3) - If God exists…and is omnipotent so that He could prevent evil, but does not, then He is not infinite good.
(4) - Evil does exist. *
(5) - Therefore God does not exist.

The *Bible* shows clearly that the record and words of Christ Jesus indicate that he firmly held to # 1. He declared his unbroken relationship with God who is Love. He *knew* God existed and he proved that Love is a practical and omnipotent power by his compassionate acts of healing. Therefore, if presented with the five-step logic shown above, I believe he would have undoubtedly concluded that statement # 4 is *incorrect*, even though it would be a denial of the evidence of the physical senses, and he would also know that statement # 5 was an incorrect conclusion.

His statements bear this out. "Having eyes, see ye not?" he asked them. [8] He declared that what the world personalized as the "devil" was nothing but a "… murderer from the beginning, and abode not in the truth, because there is no truth in him. When he speaketh a lie, he speaketh of his own: for he is a liar, and the father of it." [9]

The definition of *evil* in part is given as follows: "the fact of suffering or wickedness…the totality of undesirable, harmful, wicked acts, experiences… marked by bad moral qualities… something that is injurious to moral or physical happiness or welfare: misfortune, calamity, disaster…a necessary means of recognizing the good…a cosmic force producing evil actions or states." [10] Evil doesn't "just happen", and the cause of all evil must lie in the claim by the physical sciences that the world is grounded in matter, alias, energy, and in the physical laws required to explain the state of matter particles.

The effects of matter and physical laws embedded in space-time are seen in limitations and discords of all kinds. We either have too little matter (poverty, drought), too much matter (floods, abnormal growths), or the wrong kind, quality, or state of matter (diseases, tornadoes, decay and death). Since matter and physical laws are the roots of what is called "evil", it would then appear logical that we could replace statement # 4 in the above logic statement with the following:

---

* It is amazing that in this age millions believe in the reality of a deity (the Devil, or evil) who is equal, or near-equal in power with God, and whose sole purpose is to cause chaos, inflict diseases, and tempt mankind to act in sinful ways.

(4) - Matter and physical laws exist.

Again, the arguments given above for denying the validity of statement #4 are the same. I agree with the *Christian Science* doctrine that holds that Christ Jesus did not ascribe absolute reality to matter and material laws and forces. He proved this by instantaneous physical healings and physics-defying experiences: walking on water, the raising of Lazarus from death, and by his own resurrection.

** Free Will

As to the capability of mankind to have "free will" in choosing between good and evil, there are people who point to the indeterminacy of quantum mechanics to show that man is not a robot or puppet to the inevitability of material circumstances or the Will of God. They say he has the freedom to make a choice and suffer the consequences or reap the benefits of his own choosing. [*] There is, I believe, a two-sided answer to the question as to whether man has free will or not:

- "No," because as an image or God he is not free to do or be anything that God is not causing him to do or be. If each human being had the ability to go against the Will of omnipotent Mind, then there would be truly many minds or gods (breaking the First Commandment). God would not be the supreme *Cause* or Principle of existence, and chaos [∇] would surely be the order of the day.
- And "Yes," because as he apprehends the nature of God and of his unity with this Mind, he begins to understand the *limitless* possibilities he has as *spiritual idea* or image of God. The apostle Paul said, "Let this mind be in you which was also in Christ Jesus." [(12)] That is, the mind (rather, *Mind*) that Jesus manifested is *our* Mind – is God Himself. And to obey the Will of God gives us *unlimited possibilities* of doing good, expressing creativity and accomplishing great tasks. Believing that mortal minds have free will often results in the loss of our ability to express freedom, wisdom, health, joy, because we have shut out the ideas of Mind. Rather than being a slave or puppet, we begin – if ever so gradually – to discover we have dominion over the cold claims of materiality. I do not believe that infinite good needs to "experiment" with sin or evil.

---

[*] People who believe that mankind have free will to choose between good and evil, miss the point: in order for mankind to be tempted by evil, the all-loving God would have had to create it. If this all-knowing Mind knew man would sin if given the opportunity, what would be the point of the "Experiment?" The all-knowing Mind does not need to experiment with man and evil. Evil, therefore, is a supposition in the minds of mortals, and is not identified with spiritual man.

[∇] Does the reader ever wonder how a universe which supposedly begins in chaos and lawlessness, and without the need of Mind as First Cause, can somehow evolve consciousness, and the higher qualities of Mind, such as love, compassion, wisdom? But such is the theory of evolution: that somehow life and consciousness can rise above its source. The writer of Isaiah had the proper question when he asked rhetorically, "…shall the thing framed [such as man] say of him that framed it [the Creator], He hath no understanding [intelligence"] ? [(11)] What stops us in our tracks from appreciating and accepting the statement that Mind, Spirit, is - and must be - the first and only Cause, is the evidence of the five senses, along with the ancillary evidence for the substantiality of matter derived from physical measurement and detection instruments.

EVIL AND ITS NOTHINGNESS

I feel it would be *blasphemous* to believe that God is the cause of all discord, evil, or that He must share control of the universe with another power and cause, whether it be the "Devil," or whether it be blind physical laws such as relativistic or quantum laws. It would be a sin to believe that God is less than infinite, ever-present and omnipotent good.

Mary Baker Eddy's concept of reality was indeed radical, for it did not include "evil." She insisted that an all-knowing, all-loving, all-wise, all-powerful God (the *First Cause,* or Principle, *Love,* itself!) could not create what she called "evil" or "error.

As Robert Peel says in his book, *Mary Baker Eddy, The Years of Trial,* she believed that "...God could not create a man [even] *capable* of error; therefore a sinful mortal was not God's man gone wrong, but a lie about man, and the lie was to be systematically rejected as ontologically unreal." * Eddy knew her views about God and man would "stand philosophy on its head;" [13] but it was based on her conviction that if God was *good* as the *Bible* stated, then in His perfect spiritual universe of good, evil was a logical impossibility, and thus could be proved to be so by spiritual healings approximating those of Christ Jesus. Since it appeared to the senses that all discord had its source in a matter-based concept of reality, she declared matter itself - in the final analysis - to be unreal, to possess no intelligence, truth, substance nor life.[14] Thus said, it was inappropriate to simply *ignore* what claimed to be evil, as in "see no evil, hear no evil, speak no evil." Mankind was not to close its eyes to evil, but *first* to open them to face these claims, and *then* to realize the nothingness of these assertions, and their inability to harm.[15] **

In summary, I believe that if we can ascribe to sin, evil, disease, disorder and death a reality and substantiality (original logic statement #4), then God does not, can not exist (original statement #5).

---

* I find it difficult to believe the *Biblical* interpretation made by some theologians that man is a sinner, not because of what he does, but because of what he is. When the *Bible* speaks of man as a sinner, it is speaking about the so-called Adam-man. This is not the man of God's creating, but only a belief or myth (the Genesis story is an allegory) about man arising from the "dust of the ground." This myth is "supported" by the evidence of the physical senses, which report back to mind what that mind believes. To believe that man is a sinner because of what he is, is depressing. You might be making great sacrifices in caring for a sick friend. You might even catch the disease of your sick friend and suffer horribly. Your acts of good would have been admirable, even heroic, but you would still be considered a sinner. The doing of good, at the very least, should not be rewarded by punishment. Good is a manifestation of love that has its source in Love, God. Doing good deeds alone does not make us eligible for the kingdom of heaven. The manifestation of good reveals, in some degree, that we exist now in the kingdom of heaven. The gift of God is eternal life, but in order to come into agreement with this gift, to become aware of, and to acknowledge its presence, we must do more than utter, "Yea, Lord, I believe."! As Christ Jesus said, we must follow him in doing the Will of God.

** The apparent existence of evil and sin is an illusion of the physical senses, educated as they are as to the existence of life and intelligence in matter. It is not an absolute, but a relative view of reality. The sun appears to move across the sky from east to west, but scientific man knows better. The sun does not revolve about the earth; the earth's rotation on its axis creates the illusion of the movement of the sun across the sky.

But love, life, good, mercy, joy *are* real, and something infinitely more than the result of chemical and physiological actions in the matter- brain and body. Therefore, despite the evidence of the senses the above-mentioned discords are unreal, unsubstantial. *At the very ground of being* – mankind are free, untouched by these discordant beliefs.

But it is not enough to repeat the words of great people like Christ Jesus and mouth glorious statements about the omnipotence of infinite good, if - individually - *we* are unprepared to prove what *we* say by the lives we live and the practical examples we show as the result of spiritual prayer. The examples of physical healing and other experiences that are described later on in this book, certainly lend argument, if not conclusive proof, to the claim for the omnipotence of God, good, and - in the final analysis - the absolute unreality of evil and matter.

It would seem to most of us as if the reality we daily walk around in is a mixture of chaos and order, cruelty and gentleness, indifference and compassion, hatred and love, disease and abundant life. However, there are times when through deep and consecrated prayer, insight and inspiration, and a sense of importunity to see righteousness in our lives, we are figuratively "lifted" out of this state of consciousness to receive and accept the pure thoughts of Mind. We see and appreciate a little more of the order, harmony, gentleness, compassion, love and abundant life that are the *ironposts* of reality. This is called "healing". All too often however, we find ourselves slipping back into the old ways of thinking.

But here is an important point: *our sense of reality has been altered.* For a moment we have glimpsed a higher view of reality. Perhaps a physical healing has occurred, a personal relationship has been improved, or a needed place of employment has been found. We are conscious of this event, even though every thing else in our lives has stayed relatively the same.

Although many of us appear to have these experiences on a somewhat infrequent basis, this was not so with Christ Jesus. He was so attuned to the Father that life and reality were seen as outside matter, outside space-time, and unconstrained by quantum probabilities and uncertainties. This enabled him to rise from the tomb and "ascend" beyond or above the ken of the five senses.

Eddy said, "The Science of Mind, as well as the material universe, shows that nothing which is material is in perpetual harmony. Matter is manifest mortal mind, and it exists only to material sense. Real sensation is not material; it is, and must be, mental: and Mind is not mortal, it is immortal." [16] She further stated, "Self-renunciation of all that constitutes a so-called material man, and the acknowledgment and achievement of his spiritual identity as a child of God, is Science that opens the very flood-gates of heaven; whence good flows into every avenue of being, cleansing mortals of all uncleanness, destroying all suffering, and demonstrating the true image and likeness. There is no other way under heaven whereby we can be saved, and man be clothed with might, majesty, and immortality." [17]

Many people, after hearing about, or experiencing a horrendous act by an individual, are apt to come to the conclusion that some people are "pure evil". But this conclusion dishonors God, who is infinite, omnipotent, omniscient Love! You may find it incredible that in the final analysis, mankind should deny even the awareness *or conception of evil, discord and lack (much less their apparent reality in the world), but this is, I believe, the only rational explanation of how Christ Jesus multiplied the loaves and fishes, raised Lazarus from the grave, and cast out sin.

Almost all religious organizations, except *Christian Science*, believe in the reality of evil; ▽and *if* evil exists then it must have a cause. As suggested in the discussion of the five logic statements presented a few pages back, if a *First or only Cause* (God) exists, then this Cause must be omnipotent, ever present and eternal. The human heart shouts that this prime cause must be good, itself; the *Bible* telling us that this First Cause or Principle of all that exists is Light: "...God is Light, and in Him is no darkness at all." (18) *Light* signifies Truth, wisdom, understanding, perception, Mind, idea, order and harmony; while *darkness* symbolizes evil, ignorance, falsehood, chaos, uncertainty, disorder, disease and death. In fact, Light and Love are synonymous.

QUANTUM PHYSICS AND GOD

Do the theories behind quantum physics prove or disprove the existence of God? I believe that they neither prove nor disprove the existence of a First Cause or God.ᵠ **What they do, however, is *point the way* - so to speak - to the recognition of the primacy of *non-local consciousness, and the illusion of matter*.**⊕ Quantum theories are employed to predict the activity and state of matter. Physical theories cannot explain God who is Spirit. But the results of quantum theories and experiments lead us to give consideration to the claim that matter and physical force depend on mind for their manifestation, and that the ultimate and final observer of the *physical* universe is mind; that is, *collective mind observing itself, seeing its own thoughts.* But surely, the First Cause is not represented by the consciousness of many mortal minds in conflict with one another, of hateful, fearful minds, and of minds that can only conceive of a finite physical universe!

It has been said by some that matter itself, was created, not to *repress*, but to *express* or show forth God. Presumably, then, this Creator also finds the time and sport to "express" Himself in acts of violence. This activity - resulting in chaos and destruction (earthquakes, floods, etc.) - gives little or no indication of a Cause that *cares* for its creation. Indeed, we may as well say that the *First Cause* is chaos.

The discerning and thinking individual, however, yearns for something more. As a human parent cares for his / her child, we would expect that the Creator of All is also

---

* As to the argument made by some philosophers that evil must exist along with good so we can make a comparison and choose the good, it is not necessary to eat a piece of a rotten apple in order to appreciate a fresh and delicious fruit.

▽ Many Christians refer to "evil" as 'Satan' or the "Devil : evil personified.

ᵠ **Neither does quantum physics "prove" *Christian Science* and its claim for the absolute spiritual nature of reality**. But quantum physics illustrates the effect of an "enlightened" consciousness on the illusory belief of life and substance in matter, thereby helping mankind to consider the mental nature of reality and spiritual causation. (19)

⊕ If quantum physics is eventually modified or superceded by another theory, this will probably not invalidate experimental data that point to a primary role for consciousness in defining and interpreting reality. Indeed, some new theories already consider consciousness as a unique and significant participant in defining reality.

mindful of his offspring, cares for them, and evidences forth His love. But we will not find this by delving deeper into matter. Indeed, God is shown forth or expressed, first in *spiritual ideas*, which require no material particles for expression, because these ideas are made apparent in thought or consciousness.

BIBLICAL MIRACLES

Biblical "miracles" as well as similar experiences occurring in this age, in my opinion, offer the strongest arguments for the immortality of spiritual man, and the primacy of Mind as Reality. Extraordinary claims, such as the one stated above, demand a high level of proof. At this period the art and science of spiritual healing is in its infancy. We hear of, read about, and even experience spiritual healings, but the most dramatic ones – those that clearly defy physical law – are not so frequent. But genuine spiritual healings challenge the claim that substance is matter; they hint of the actual existence of a spiritual universe. What new discovery could be more profound and exciting than this!?

The teachings and the life of Christ Jesus certainly illustrate a central point that the "soul" or the substance and being of man is not trapped in a material body, and that the universe, including man is governed, in the final analysis, by spiritual laws, not by physical laws. Jesus showed by the sacrifice of his mortal body - and his subsequent resurrection and ascension - man's eternal unity and oneness with Love and Life. He revealed mankind's wholeness and sinless nature as a spiritual image of Mind. And he demonstrated this great truth for all to comprehend, and follow (eventually) in his footsteps. By his resurrection and ascension he proved that, unlike the two-dimensional kangaroo trying to escape to a higher dimension, spiritual man is already free of the constraints of matter. God is the *Sou*l of man, but this is never found *in* matter.

Eddy, in discussing this point with students of her religion, pointed out that they should "emerge gently" from the erroneous assumption that life and intelligence are resident in matter, and that this emergence would occur as the result of spiritual growth in understanding of the spiritual nature of man. Of course, no single experience - or even a collection of experiences - can be absolute proof in this age for the validity of the above statements about God and man.

What have been *erroneously* called "miracles" in the *Bible* are, in most instances, the fulfillment of the laws of Spirit, and are never a violation of these laws

When it comes to the interpretation of miracles, we are tempted to apply *Occam's Razor*: accept the simplest solution for the occurrence of a certain phenomenon with the minimum of assumptions, and reject convoluted and fantastic explanations. For example:

- It was simply a result of chance that the one who had prayed deeply in the morning for that day's recognition of the presence of God, was uninjured in a serious accident later in the day.
- It was highly circumstantial in some of the healings related further along in this book that just the right kind of physical transformations were happening to bring about "spontaneous healing" of the body.
- The physical examinations of the state of the body's health were in error.

But these kinds of explanations are - at least in some instances - the easy way out. We can "rest easy" if we simply ignore the ever-increasing database on genuine spiritual healing. But is incumbent upon those who claim that spiritual healing is a real and normal process, to continue to live such a *holy* life as demanded by Christ Jesus (and other great religious thinkers), that they approximate in this age his healing works on a more consistent and convincing basis. The evidence for the existence of God must first begin with a right apprehension of the nature of God and of his universe. We cannot begin with the paradigm of life, substance and intelligence as existing in matter, and which is based on the testimony of the physical senses. If we do, then what we will arrive at will be models of reality that do not require God (no cause at all), and result in conclusions that life and awareness evolve from matter - from the *Big Bang* itself. *Something arising out of nothing.* * Order arising out of chaos. Non- intelligent matter, with no intelligent Cause or Law, arising from the *Big Bang* and somehow evolving into form, intelligence and life.

Many people believe that reality consists both of the physical world and things of the spirit; but it would be impossible for a universe consisting of both matter and spirit to exist because they are diametrically opposite in nature. The illustration below shows that we have a choice as to which type of reality to believe in:

---

* The Big Bang presumably was created literally out of nothing, because before that moment there was no matter, no space-time!

DIFFERENT CONCEPTS OF REALITY

Physical Universe	Spiritual Universe
THE EVOLUTION OF THE PHYSICAL UNIVERSE	THE "EVOLUTION" OF THE SPIRITUAL UNIVERSE
NOTHINGNESS ⇓ CHAOS AND BIG BANG ⇓ EVOLVING ORDER FROM FOUR BASIC FORCES ⇓ EVOLVING INTELLIGENCE AND LIFE FROM INANIMATE MATTER ⇓ DISORDER AND DEATH ⇓ ???	THE ALLNESS AND *NOWNESS* (timelessness) OF MIND AND TRUTH, AND THE SPIRITUAL UNIVERSE INCLUDING SPIRITUAL MAN ⇓ THE ETERNAL REVELATION AND UNFOLDMENT OF SPIRITUAL IDEAS

EITHER ONE OF THE ABOVE CONCEPTS OF REALITY IS REAL, BUT NOT BOTH, BECAUSE THEY ARE DIAMETRICLLY OPPOSITE IN NATURE. ONE IS REAL, AND THE OTHER IS AN ILLUSION.

But the physical senses cannot know God, who is Spirit, or observe His spiritual universe. "Spiritual living and blessedness are the only evidences, by which we can recognize true existence and feel the unspeakable peace which comes from an all-absorbing spiritual love." [20]

God must be the exact opposite of the *Old Testament* description of an anthropomorphic being knowing both good and evil.[*] Human logic cannot successfully include God and His universe in physical models of reality. But our innate spiritual capacity - our *spiritual senses* - enable us to begin to understand God. When the nature of God is even faintly understood or *felt in the human heart*, then even the physical scene begins to take on the hue of the divine.

What is called spiritual healing or regeneration occurs, sometimes in what appears to be as a flagrant violation of physical law, but most times they are seen as simple expressions of God's love and care for us.

The appreciation that the law of Spirit, Mind, is *always* seen as a law of harmony, enables one to dismiss the silly notion that the law of God is also responsible for disasters

---

[*] Since infinite Spirit is not an anthropomorphic being, the *Biblical* description of man as made in the image and likeness of God must refer to man as wholly spiritual in nature.

and catastrophic diseases. [**] This concept of law that leads to pain and chaos are not laws of God, but are gross distortions of real, spiritual law.

CATASTROPHES (FLOOD, EARTHQUAKE, AND BUILDING COLLAPSE), THALIDOMIDE, SELF-FLAGELLATION . . . AND LOVE!

Not long ago I saw in a newspaper a photograph of a statue of Jesus that had survived the ravages of flood waters from a swollen river, while a score of people drowned and hundreds of millions of dollars were lost in houses and businesses that were severely damaged or totally destroyed by the water. The newspaper article seemed to imply that the presence of the statue of Jesus, left unscathed by the flood and mud from the river, indicated some sort of a minor miracle had occurred, and that God was still showing His presence. But where was God for the thousands of people whose lives were ruined by the flood? Instead of looking for the face of the Virgin Mary on the side of a silo, or the image of Jesus in the clouds as a sign of a miracle, should we not rather look for and acknowledge the presence of the *practical* Truth (God) in individual and collective consciousness that enables one to experience the practical, restorative and healing power of God?

We read in the newspaper of the day about major catastrophes such as the collapse of a building due to an earthquake or to terrorists. We discover that many of the building's occupants, including small children, died, some after suffering in great pain. Sometime later, perhaps, it is announced that a survivor has been found under the wreckage, and the media joyously proclaims *"a miracle!"* Ministers ask their parishioners not to question the wisdom and actions of God in allowing some people to live and others to die.

But where was God for the hundreds or thousands of people who died in the collapse of the building? Although the human spirit sometimes rises to great heights in times of disaster, and many examples of selfless love and concern are shown to the victims, the burning question still remains: *Did God cause - or permit - the flood and earthquake to occur?* In the case of the earthquake, were the lives of small, innocent children less worthy than the life of one of the people who survived - a man whose past record known to his neighbors may have been one of dishonesty, cruelty, and indifference? Did the children's parents have a higher sense of love and righteousness than God who *is* Love? Did God have some mysterious plan that we are not privy to? Are certain individuals destined to suffer [*] for some unknown "greater good?" [▽] Was God

---

[**] The plagues of Egypt, as related in the *Bible* have been attributed by some writers in *Old Testament* times to the wrath of God, whom they believed to be very vengeful as well as righteous. In *New Testament* times we find Christ Jesus and one of his disciples (John) as describing the Creator or Father of All as Love, and therefore, not the author of cruel, destructive forces.

[*] It is not comforting to me to believe that some of us are destined to suffer for the "greater good." And how would we know, when we are praying (or employing medical or surgical methods) for the restoration of health of someone (perhaps a child) that our prayers and other efforts may not be in vain, because - unknown to us - God has decided that this particular individual should suffer and be sacrificed for the "greater good?"

[▽] Although Jesus acknowledged the Will of God, it is unthinkable that perfect God, the all-mighty, all-knowing, would find it necessary to improve upon His creation, and to sacrifice anyone in the process. Jesus knew that his and all of mankind's identities are eternally in God. He gave up his temporal life in

actually helpless before the tragedy, or do we chalk up the whole event to god-less occurrences whose foundations are in quantum mechanical probability laws, or some later to-be-discovered law?

Millions of people were enraged at the acts of a few men who several years ago blew up the federal building in Oklahoma City, killing hundreds, and of a group of individuals who destroyed the two *World Trade Center* towers on September 11, 2001, killing thousands, and who also destroyed part of the *Pentagon* building, killing hundreds. They may question why God did not intervene and stop the carnage, but how many were enraged at the God whom they believed caused the giant tornado in Oklahoma City in 1999? Or the God they believed either permitted or caused the earthquake in Haiti in 2010 that resulted in over 100,000 lives lost? These latter two incidents many attribute to an "act of God'" which they believe is clearly out of their hands. Some may be enraged, but many will come to the conclusion that the only "god" is mindless physical law. Some even go so far as to believe that the Haitian earthquake was the work of the devil, or even worse – a form of divine punishment meted out to the Haitians to placate an angry God because of their collective "evil" ways.

Few things show more clearly the need to reexamine our concept of God than the belief held by many that a compassionate creator creates foundational laws for medicines, and then endows man with the ability to discover methods of healing through the creation of drugs, than the following: The drug thalidomide was developed over thirty-five years ago, and was sold as a sleeping pill and as a morning sickness cure. [21] But it was discovered to be responsible for causing at least 12,000 babies to be born with birth defects, such as malformed and missing limbs, defective organs and deformities of the face. The drug was banned around the world in 1962, but the *FDA* at one time was considering permitting it to be sold in the United States. The reason? Thalidomide, they explained, has been shown to have unique and beneficial effects on patients who have immune-related diseases such as *AIDS* and leprosy; although it is acknowledged that in addition to the above effects on babies, thalidomide can severely damage nerve cells causing painful and incurable disabilities. *FDA Deputy Commissioner*, Mary Pendergast said, "Thalidomide has the capacity to cure, as well as damage."

Is this our concept of a compassionate and wise creator - a God who offends our sensibilities; one who causes or permits good people to suffer; one who inspires mankind to conceive and implement new methods to sustain and improve bodily health, such as the eating of dirt, drinking of its own urine, and the employment of maggots to cleanse wounds? This apparently is some of the latest recommendations coming from a few in the medical community! [22]

The above four incidents should challenge our concept of God. If we continue to believe in the old concept of a God who metes out both good and evil [*] then this belief

---

matter in order to show that reality is in Spirit and that life is eternal. He showed that his identity could never be extinguished, and that a knowledge of the presence of Love overcomes hate, and even the belief of sin and death.

[*] We hear, not infrequently, about an individual thanking God for allowing him to score the winning basket in an important game, as if his team alone was worthy of God's blessings, and saying something like, "we were hoping and praying that we would win the game. It was truly a miraculous shot. It was divine intervention that caused the ball to go into the basket."

will continue to demean the creator. It would - if it could - bring infinite Love down to finiteness; and the message of the Law of Love Jesus brought to mankind would in many ways seem to be meaningless. But the message of James is that, "the wisdom that is from above is first pure, then peaceable, gentle, and easy to be intreated, full of mercy and good fruits, without *partiality*, and *without hypocrisy.*" [23] (emphasis added) There is - *there must be* - a law of Love, a law of Mind, that can restore harmony - and even *perpetuate* it!

Surely our concept of goodness and mercifulness is no greater than that of God's. We know that Christ Jesus stilled the storm, provided food in the wilderness and restored a lost sense of health through his understanding of the divine law of Love, and we know that he instructed his disciples and all mankind to follow him in healing the sick, and even in the raising of the dead.

Eddy, I believe, gave the world the best answer to the above questions about God and disasters: "It is our ignorance of God, the divine Principle, which produces apparent discord, and the right understanding of Him restores harmony." [24] This statement is not to imply that mankind has created a reality of disasters – only a *belief* of evil. We all must grow in our understanding of God. We must acknowledge more of the presence of the Love that is God, and put into practice our love for all mankind, knowing that His/Her laws of Spirit must eventually be seen in greater clarity. Then, evil, disease, disasters, hate, chaos – the apparent results of our ignorance of the true nature of God and of spiritual law as *wholly* good - will begin to diminish.

This higher concept of God as infinite, omnipresent and omnipotent Love, containing no element of evil or chaos, does not rob Christianity of the Christ and its impact on humanity, but rather it enhances it. Jesus showed by his teachings and marvelous acts that we *all* have a unity or oneness with God. Nor does this concept of the reality of Spirit require that mankind at this period dispense entirely with physical law. The translation of all living things and objects in the universe back into Spirit will come gradually and the amount it takes will depend on the tenacity of the belief in matter;s reality.

Self-flagellation⊕ : I believe it is important to at least make a few observations about *self-flagellation*, because, I believe, it points to (along with the belief of a God who punishes his children with so-called natural disasters and hopeless diseases), a gross misunderstanding of the nature of God, and of mankind's relation to Him as loved children. Beating the body to attain a "state of grace" is in apparent conflict with the Biblical statement that our bodies are temples of Spirit, and something to be glorified instead of beaten. ♥

The universe as we discern it through our finite senses is more than chaos, indifference, cruelty and uncertainty. No acts of self-inflicted punishment are demanded of anyone in order to placate an angry God. In a multitude of ways, reality is manifested

---

⊕ **self-flagellation: extreme criticism of oneself; self-inflicted punishment to one's body in a belief that this act will obtain divine grace.**

♥ "What? know ye not that your body is the temple of the Holy Ghost which is in you, which ye have of God, and ye are not your own?

For ye are bought with a price: therefore glorify God in your body, and in your spirit, which are God's." (I Cor. 6:19, 20)

as beauty, order, grandeur and purpose that transcends the material and points to the realm of Spirit, Mind, and unselfed *Love.*

Love: James G. McMurtry, a former *Professor* of Greek, Philosophy, and *Biblical* literature, and who later became a *Presbyterian* minister, published a pamphlet, called "My Own Interpretation of the *Twenty Third Psalm* (1959). [24] He had lived for many weeks with shepherds of Greece and Palestine. One day while with one shepherd and his sheep, professor Mc Murtry saw an old ewe that daily fed only a short distance from the shepherd, and would come many times during the day to have him pat her head and talk his "shepherd-talk" to her. McMurtry asked the shepherd if he would please turn around and not look at the ewe. To his great surprise the shepherd agreed to do this! The ewe did not know what to make of this, and began to walk around to his side. The shepherd turned away even more, and the ewe again moved around even more in an attempt to get nearer to him so it could be patted on the head. Finally, the shepherd said (translation), "I am not able…. I can't treat my sheep like that for such a man as you." McMurtry said that this experience revealed to him the spiritual message of one part of the *Twenty Third Psalm* ("He restoreth My Soul") : The shepherd (the Father) never turns away from his sheep (each of us) [⊗] – and the "utter dependence on the part of the sheep (each of us) wrought results as would beautify human life beyond comprehension if carried out in the realm of our spiritual life." Our Shepherd is divine Love, and our complete trust and obedience to His Will results in safety, protection, and in beautiful blessings!

[⊗] Although many sheep eventually enter a slaughter house, the higher, spiritual message of this part of the *Twenty Third Psalm* remains.

CHAPTER 8

THE MENTAL REALM

"To see what is in front of one's nose requires a constant struggle."
George Orwell, 1946

MEANINGFUL COINCIDENCES

CARL JUNG

Carl Jung (1875-1961) was a Swiss psychiatrist and one of the founding fathers of modern depth psychology. He was interested in the subject of "meaningful coincidences," or *synchronicity*. Synchronicity, as defined by Carl Jung, is "psychically conditioned relativity of space and time," or ". . . coincidences. . . connected so meaningfully that their ' chance ' concurrence would be incredible;" (that is, "meaningful coincidences").[1] Jung cites a particularly interesting example of "meaningful coincidences" or synchronicity: He says that the astronomer Flammarion, in his book *The Unknown* [2] tells of the story of Monsieur de Fortgibu. It seems that a M. Deschamp, as a boy in Orleans, France, was given a piece of plum pudding by Fortgibu. About ten years later, while in a restaurant in Paris, he asked for a piece of plum pudding, but it turned out the pudding already had been ordered by Fortgibu. Quite a few years later Deschamps was attending a party, and was offered a piece of plum pudding as a special treat. While he was eating the pudding he said ". . . the only thing lacking was M. de Fortgibu."[3] Suddenly, in walked a very old man - M, de Fortgibu - who had somehow got the wrong address, and had come across the party by mistake!

THE RED BALLOON

I would like to relate a personal experience. Recently, during the time I was revising this manuscript prior to publication, I was preparing to give a talk on astronomy to a class of seventh grade inner-city students. I had thought at the last moment to show visually the relative size of the sun, which is classified as a yellow *dwarf* star, with super-giant stars such as red *Betelgeuse* and *Antares*. I thought I could use a blown-up red balloon for the super-giant stars, and a small seed to represent the sun, but there were no available balloons, red or otherwise to be found in my office. Since I needed to be in the classroom in about forty-five minutes, I dismissed the matter, got into my car and began the drive to the school. As I stopped for a red light at a busy intersection, I looked out the right side of the front windshield and saw.....*a red balloon bouncing across the highway!* It passed behind my car, and as I looked in the rear mirror I saw it bounce and float across the highway only to descend and disappear behind a culvert. After the light changed to green, I passed through the intersection, found a place to turn the car around, and drove back the way I had come to park along the roadside. Dodging the traffic, I ran across the highway and scrambled down a creek bed embankment to the place where the balloon had become wedged precariously between a rock and a small ledge in the middle of the creek. Kneeling down, I quickly snatched the balloon from its watery resting-place, and upon returning to my car, proceeded along the highway to the school. The red balloon was successfully used as I had planned.

If we accept the easy explanation that the appearance of the red balloon at precisely the right time and nearly the right place was due to no more than pure chance, then we can safely and conveniently conclude that reality was described naturally by the laws of physics, probability, and structured in space-time. That is, someone lost his balloon, and I just happened by at the right place and at the right time to see it. But this simple experience was, to me, an illustration of our connectedness or unity with a universal, omnipresent Mind - a Mind of infinite ideas. [*] The useful idea that appeared to my consciousness as a red balloon was not due to chance, nor was it a miraculous occurrence. The entire experience, I believe, was in accordance with a higher law which defines an *implicate* order beyond the ken of the physical senses and transcending the material universe. That we do not experience these phenomena more frequently is due to ignorance of these possibilities, and our lack of awareness of them when they do occur.

THE FIRING SQUAD [▽]

Another example of what may be called "meaningful coincidences" is the story of a man who was living during the time of a civil war in Angola [(4)] Rebels of the *UNITA* were attacking the city in which he lived. As he and his family attempted to leave the country in order to find refuge, the rebels caught them. The seven men along with him were forced to leave their wives and children, and were to be taken to a field where all those who were taken prisoner were to be put to death!

The man prayed. Essentially he prayed to understand that in the realm of one Mind, Spirit, there were no rebels on one side and they on the other, but that there was only one side - the side of Love. Therefore, evil, in the form of hate [⊕] revenge, etc., could occupy no space from which to influence his present experience.

The soldiers of the execution squad were ordered to shoot the eight men, and although the triggers of the guns were pulled repeatedly over a period of fifteen minutes, no bullets left the guns. One of the rebels said to them (Portuguese), "Deus esta com vosco," which means, "God is with you." They then let the men go and informed their headquarters that they were innocent.

---

[*] See the definition of Idea in APPENDIX A. Under the definition of idea (s). I describe two kinds of ideas in the mental realm: the first definition refers to finite and limited thoughts or beliefs of mortals; while the second definition refers to unlimited ideas originating in God, and which lead to spiritual healing and regeneration.

[▽] This example of meaningful coincidence could just as well be put under the next heading: Spiritual Prayer and Healing

[⊕] To say that mortals - who are often wicked and evil in their ways, are the result of God's creation, or that they can be molded to reflect more of the divine goodness of God - is misleading. But to look beyond the physical senses as Christ Jesus did, and see in place of mortal man, the true, spiritual identity and nature of man - that is healing! And these very acts of Jesus resulted in instantaneous transformations of soul and body.

SPIRITUAL PRAYER AND HEALING

> "When from the lips of Truth one mighty breath
> Shall, like a whirlwind, scatter in its breeze
> The whole dark pile of human mockeries;
> Then shall the reign of Mind commence on earth,
> And starting fresh, as from a second birth,
> Man in the sunshine of the world's new spring,
> Shall walk transparent like some holy thing." [5]

It has been said in the past that any scholar who writes seriously on the subject of spiritual healing runs the risk of "academic suicide;" the reason being that many of these kinds of healing – especially the so-called instantaneous ones - occur in single events and without the presence of doctors or physicians to verify the result. These kinds of experiences are generally labeled as "anecdotal." But tell that to the individual who has experienced the healing!

Some, but not all of the examples of spiritual healing presented in this chapter and beyond have occurred in the presence of the medical community, and/or have been verified by some kind of medical examination prior to, and after the healing.

If there is a God or Principle of All, then to Him, it would seem, must be attributed the source of all evil, disease and death. We read in the *Bible* that Christ Jesus, who said that he came from the Father, destroyed all kinds of diseases and sins, but he is recorded as saying that he had not come to destroy, but to fulfill the laws of God. Jesus declared his unity with God. Can we believe, then, that sin, disease, death have their origin in God? Can we believe that the material laws underlying all diseases constitute the foundation for reality? Jesus must have come to fulfill a law of Spirit, and by this law he nullified laws of matter.[6]

A headline article in the daily newspaper *USA Today* (December 21.1993), entitled "The Healing Power of Prayer," reports that more than one hundred thirty studies done over the past thirty years have revealed that ". . .prayer works overwhelmingly,
yet ". . .it has been marginalized and shoved aside." [7] The article pointed out that the evidence is "staggering" for the effects of prayer on peoples' lives and health, and that prayer had been shown to "work at a distance."

I have included in the *Bibliography* several publications (Part II, Chapter 8 (8-13)) that refer to present-day remarkable experiences that are similar to those experienced by people in *Biblical* times. Each publication approaches the subject from a different standpoint or baseline of thought, but there is at least a beginning convergence of thought about the effectiveness of prayer in solving problems and changing human experiences. Some people believe that mental activity or thought can have a pronounced influence on the body, and also on objects that appear to be external to consciousness - this thought acting independently of space and time.

Many devout people believe that asking God to heal or perform a miracle is all that is required, and that He will then grant the request according to his mysterious and incomprehensible grand plan, and to the degree of faith of the individual making the request. In so doing, He temporarily sets aside His physical laws, and effects a healing. But the result of prayer of this kind is merely the effect of the human mind to bring about a physical change in the body.

A 1988 article in the *Southern Medical Journal* reported on a rigorously controlled study which looked at the effect of prayer on the recovery of patients in a coronary care unit. Individuals of different religious denominations living in different cities made prayer or meditation on behalf of several hundred patients. *The patients themselves were unaware of the prayers.* It was discovered that patients (half of total), who were prayed for, suffered fewer medical complaints than patients who received no support of prayer. **[Note: See recent comments in ADDENDUM]**

[14] After the study's positive results of the effectiveness of prayer, Dr. William P. Wilson of *Duke University Medical Center* commented that the report on the study results is "likely to arouse strong prejudice in some readers who believe that religion is not worthy of scientific consideration." But he also said that "...we in medicine who claim a holistic approach to diagnosing and treating the whole man should throw away our deterministic prejudices, expand our knowledge, and enlarge our therapeutic armamentarium. We need not only change in the way we think, but also do more research on the role of religion in healing." [15]

More recently, 800 doctors, scholars, chaplains, nurses and clinicians convened in Boston, Massachusetts, to attend a course titled *Spirituality and Healing in Medicine.*[16] * The course was conducted under the auspices of the *Harvard Medical School.* In what was called an unusual departure for medical audiences, time was provided for discussions and presentations on healing traditions of faiths including *Islam, Roman Catholicism, Christian Science, Seventh Day Adventist,* and *Hinduism.* Dr. Herbert Benson, MD of the *Harvard Medical School*, in his address to attendees commented that the question of how far spiritual healing can go - how spiritual matters can lead to healing - keeps coming up. He believed that the model for spiritual healing was that shown by the *Christian Science* church; and ***it is this model that I will be referring to again and again in Part II of the book.*** Such a statement made by a prestigious medical school would have been unthinkable ten years ago.

Included in the healing experiences was the testimony of an Hispanic *Pentecostalist*, who had been declared mentally retarded at the age of two, and had suffered in his teen years from a medically diagnosed condition that left him deaf and blind. He was healed through prayer alone.

After the meeting, Steven Kosslyn, a *Harvard* neurologist and professor of psychology, said that "No one could sit through all those panels on healing and think this is nothing, that there is no relation between spirituality and healing." [17]

A spokesperson for the *Christian Science* church told the conference attendees that the concept of *Mind* is synonymous with *God,* and is the only scientific basis for true spiritual healing. One of the signs that healing is "truly spiritual," and not simply the result of blind faith or the manipulation of the human mind whereby one material belief is exchanged for another, is whether the individual healed has had - to a degree - some transformation of human character and improvement of moral values.

---

* Yearly follow-up meetings have been held since 1997.

For healing to be on a solid, scientific foundation, and to be accomplished on a consistent basis, it must rest on a Principle or *Law*: *Mind* - and not on a brain-centered mind, or mind-body basis, or else it will be sporadic and often ineffectual. Eddy early in her life concluded that disease, as well as reality itself, was mental, [*] and that "... mind does the healing..." but she desired to "... learn *which* mind, whether the human or the mind of Christ." [19] [∇]

From 1900 to 1988, over 53,000 healing experiences[⊕] have been published in the *Christian Science* church weekly and monthly periodicals, the *Christian Science Sentinel* and the *Christian Science Journal,* respectively. The list of healings accomplished by prayer is by no means confined to cases that had "unsubstantiated diagnoses" or that could be labeled as *psychosomatic*.[21] From 1969 -1988, the total number of healings in the two periodicals exceeded 10,000, and of these, 2337 involved healings of medically diagnosed conditions. Many of the cases included patients who were diagnosed by specialists, who had more than one physician, who were examined by X-rays, and who received follow-up examinations (623 case healings).

In addition, all published testimonies of healing must be verified in writing by those who can vouch for the integrity of the testifier, or know of the healing. Three written verifications or vouchers are required.

A partial list of *diagnosed* conditions healed include: malignancy or cancer (at least 27, including bone cancer, lymph, skin, liver, breast, intestinal, and uterus cancers), polio (16), tumor (42), tuberculosis (68), pneumonia (38, seven of double pneumonia, two with collapsed lung), heart disorders (at least 88), kidney disorders (23, two of Bright's disease), childbirth complications (71, including uremic poisoning, four still births), meningitis (9), appendicitis (24, eight acute), scarlet fever (16), rheumatic fever (16), pernicious anemia (13), rheumatoid or degenerative arthritis (12), broken bones (203), cataract (11), gangrene (2), glaucoma (3), epilepsy (13), blindness (7), other vision deficiencies (48, including astigmatism and nearsightedness), leukemia (3), multiple sclerosis (6), diabetes (12), goiter (13), curvature of the spine (8), crossed eyes (3), and cleft palate (1).

---

[*] Eddy at one time administered very dilute solutions of common table salt dissolved in water to a patient in the last stages of typhoid fever.[18] This was given at intervals of three hours until the patient was cured. Through these and other experiments Eddy arrived at the conclusions that,
- (a) - either faith in the drug or Mind is the healer;
- (b) - the drug, itself, has no healing power, and
- (c) - that in the mental universe it was not the belief of disease that caused disease, but that it was the belief of disease that was the disease.

[∇] "It may seem a tremendous leap from recognizing the effect of the human mind on the body to a realization that 'Mind is All '" (Nathan A. Talbot "The mind, the body, and God's allness," *Christian Science Journal*, Jan., 1997). [20]

[⊕] That these experiences have not been more generally acknowledged as legitimate is probably due to:
- (a) - intransigent disbelief in, and ignorance or fear of, new and radical ideas and concepts that challenge and defy present and comfortable physical paradigms and physical sense testimony;
- (b) - absence of strict laboratory controls (which are impractical), when examining and
- (c) evaluating spiritual healing claims; and
- (d) - the long-held belief in the Western world that we live primarily in a mechanical age, and must know how things happen before we can even begin to believe that they do.

The reader may also be interested in reading about the experience of two parents who adopted a child at birth who had been born with multiple handicaps, such as, unformed vocal cords, a blood condition that prevented normal blood coagulation, a serious bone condition, a damaged heart, and cerebral palsy. The medical prediction was that the child would not live beyond six months. As the parents later related in an interview and in a sworn affidavit, each of the physical conditions was entirely healed over a period of years through "prayer, love, and hard work." It was a remarkable experience of courage, trust in God, and persistence (See reference (11), p.54-63).

Spiritual healing is actually *remembering how we are* - how, as the *Bible* tells us (first chapter of *Genesis*) we have been made in the image of God, Spirit. [22]

As mentioned above, the case history of physical healings and solutions to seemingly insurmountable problems through the exclusive reliance on what can be termed *scientific* prayer or metaphysical "treatment" has to some extent been documented. In some instances, extensive physical examinations and X-rays have been made, which have verified the "incurability" or "hopelessness" of a physical condition, prior to the praying by either the person needing restoration or by a church-approved practitioner,[*] who may effect a healing over great distances. Included are affidavits by those experiencing and witnessing the healings.[∇] The objective of this particular faith (*Christian Science*) is the complete demonstration over material laws and conditions through obedience to God's Law of Spirit. This, of course, is the idealized goal at this period in time, and any defender of this faith must in all humbleness admit that there is a long way to go before mankind realizes complete dominion over materiality. "We must be able to stand before we can walk or run," they would say.

Not all of these experiences are so convincing that skeptics would agree that they have occurred as described, but some quite remarkable experiences indicate that something besides the action of physical law is at work.[⊕]

The followers of this faith are convinced that true, permanent, spiritual healing is the result of the action of *Mind* revealing to human consciousness the presence and reality of harmony, which, they believe, is entirely mental and spiritual.

Spiritual prayer, as understood and practiced by adherents of *Christian Science* is not a pleading [Δ] with God, but an affirmation of the presence of good even if it is not seen. It is gratitude and thanksgiving. Prayer is not performed to change something going on in matter or to improve material conditions. Reality, which is wholly spiritual, needs no changing. What prayer *does* do is bring into human perception some aspect of the

---

[*] A member of the First Church of Christ, Scientist (Christian Science), and one who has been qualified by the church to engage in full-time the practice of Christian healing in the manner of Christ Jesus. Because of all mankind's inherent unity with God, a Practitioner can mentally help a patient to lift his consciousness so that he may acknowledge the healing presence of Love. This phenomenon can be explained as follows: You and a friend are inside a large, darkened room. But your friend (the Practitioner) can see more clearly than you, and has knowledge of the location of the light switch. She turns on the switch, dispelling the darkness so you can also see and apprehend more clearly the objects in the room (or, the eternal harmony of being.)

[∇] See especially *Spiritual Healing in a Scientific Age*, Robert Peel, Harper and Row Publishers, 1987 [23]

[⊕] Even if most people were somehow convinced that astronauts had never walked on the moon, those who actually had would know the facts!

[Δ] As Eddy said, "The beneficial effect) of such prayer for the sick [asking or pleading with God] is on the human mind, making it act more powerfully on the body through a blind faith in God." [24]

permanent, changeless spiritual reality [*] that is harmony, beauty, order, and which is the outcome of the pouring forth of Love. Human thought is touched by this new insight. In place of the finite, changeable and uncertain, we catch a glimpse of *spiritual being*, and the thought of the body, including the *resultant* condition of the body - is improved.

Effectual prayer can begin with a humble reaching out to God to see what beautiful, pure and grand things He has for us to discover about ourselves today. It does *not* begin with the old concept of sinning man, but begins with the premise of a universe of Spirit or Mind, and good that cannot go awry. By this beginning, the one who is praying (or is being prayed for) begins to recognize man's true heritage, and the *belief* that man or mankind could - or would want to act out sin - disappears.

Eddy said, "When the evidence before the material senses yielded to spiritual sense, the apostle [Paul] declared that nothing could alienate him from God, from the sweet sense and presence of Life and Truth." [25] Not that the physical evidence of disease *first* disappeared, and *then* the apostle made his declaration, but that the evidence assumed less importance as his spiritual sense or spiritual view of things increased. *Then* the apostle made his declaration, that despite the material evidence, he could not be separated from God. The result of this kind of spiritual insight would be the eventual appearance to the physical senses of health restored.

As to the mixing of what is called "*spiritual metaphysics*" with medical methods for the healing of the body, Robert Peel, the author of *Spiritual Healing in a Scientific Age,* said, "Beautiful results may sometimes follow from cooperation with a doctor who himself believes deeply in Christian prayer, but a central ambiguity remains a permanent weakness in such an undertaking. Pragmatically the two approaches may work; logically they represent incompatible theories of cause and effect." [26] Material medicines depend largely on the power of human faith and belief in their efficacy.

It should be mentioned here (as well as in the Notes to the Reader in the beginning of the book) that the compilation of healing experiences such as those listed above, as well as the recounting of healing experiences throughout the rest of this book, are in no way an attempt to verify the efficacy, or degree of success of prayer, or to compare this method with medical practices. Spiritual healing has been practiced throughout the world with varying degrees of success, and sometimes with failure. But the *success or failure of spiritual healing is not the issue here*.[∇] The examples of successful spiritual healing described in this book have been selected in an attempt to show the effect of human consciousness yielding to the divine Consciousness or God. The recognition of man's inseparability or unity with God reveals life as spiritual and eternal.

---

[*] According to this view, harmony, beauty, order, activity, are the realities, but they never originate in matter, nor do they depend upon matter or matter laws. Thus, spiritual healing does not make "sick" matter into healthy or "well" matter. It has nothing to do with matter at all.

[∇] But it is interesting to note that Larry Dossey, M.D., former *Chief of Staff,* Medical City Dallas Hospital, and noted author of popular books exploring the relationship between physics, medicine, and prayer (such as *Space, Time and Medicine,* New Science Library, 1982), believes that prayer is a vital ingredient in any healing process. He has said (See also Notable Quotations in the beginning of the book): that the power of the mind exercised in the form of prayer, is so effectual that he can see a day "…when doctors who didn't recommend prayer for their very sick patients could be sued for malpractice…I think prayer is communion with the universe or the one mind." [27]

SPIRITUAL LEADERS AND HEALERS OF THE PAST [*]

** Christ Jesus

The *Biblical* record of Jesus is impressive, including healings of lameness, deafness, blindness, insanity, lack (loaves and fishes), death, and many more. Jesus' healing of the man blind from his birth [28] resulted in a dramatic change in evidence. We might say, that the "observer" was *spiritual sense*; that is, Christ Jesus' capacity to discern great truths that enabled him to see things in a new and different way. It was as if the material record of a blind man was false, as if it had never happened. This experience of blindness in the past had no real history because it doesn't exist in the kingdom of God - the realm of Mind where you and I and all mankind exist as spiritual ideas. For the blind man, it was like being awakened from a dreamlike state of consciousness.

Recall the stories of Jesus' raising of Lazarus and of Jairus' daughter [29] where he said death was akin to sleep. But also recall the typical reactions to Jesus' healing efforts, which are echoed by many today: "They laughed him to scorn, *knowing* that she [Jairus' daughter] was dead." [30] (emphasis added)

The new paradigm of reality that begins with consciousness rather than with matter would fit well with unexplained phenomena, such as, the so-called miracles of *Biblical* times as well as those that have occurred in the present. Science and religion eventually must come together, as both are seeking fundamental truths. But compromises need to be made. Religion must be based less on blind, unthinking faith, and science must consider as primary, an intelligent Cause that is not cold, indifferent, or unconscious.

What was Jesus showing us by his life and actions? I believe that Mary Baker Eddy thought it was proper to discuss the possibility that Jesus was trying to show us by his words and his examples some simple, yet profound truths about the first Cause, which she described as *Love*.

And what did the acknowledgement of great truths (such as: God is Love) do for Jesus? It enabled him to:
- Overcome sin (the *belief* of life and sensation in matter);
- Overcome hate and other sins (from those who wanted to kill him);
- Overcome disease (for those who came to him for healing);
- Overcome physical limitations of space and time (stilling of the storm, instantaneous transfer across a sea, the discovery of a coin in a fish's mouth):
- Overcome death...(for those who thought they had died, and in his own resurrection and ascension);

In other words, demonstrating that the *Principle* of the universe of Spirit - the only universe in which we live - is *Love*. And as Eddy said, "...Principle is Love, and Love is Mind..." [31]

The remarkable experiences of Jesus simply can no longer be brushed aside or ignored because they do not fit in our current paradigm of fixed physical laws. I do not

---

[*] Although there have been other spiritual leaders and healers of the past, I have singled out Christ Jesus and Mary Baker Eddy for mention in this book because I believe these two have most clearly discerned the true nature of God and man.

believe that Jesus altered wave functions in his resurrection of Lazarus, but he brought to Lazarus' consciousness a beginning awareness, that as part of God's creation he was at that very moment an image of eternal Spirit or Life itself. Jesus' own resurrection from death is the ultimate demonstration that man's life is not in matter, and is wholly spiritual.

A statement from "Nobel Prize Conversations" speaks of the resurrection of Jesus: "Resurrection is not resuscitation . . . To say that Jesus was ' raised from the dead' does not mean that he returned to haunt Jerusalem or Galilee as a terrifying, though familiar, ghost, but that he entered upon a new mode of existing, a new relation to God, a new and different way of interacting with the world." [32]

The acts of Jesus, such as the restoration of life to Lazarus would violate the *Second Law of Thermodynamics* [*]- the law of entropy. Two *Biblical* statements come to mind that seem to say that a new understanding of reality, of a universe outside of disorder and decay is required: The first one is:

(1) - "Enter ye in at the strait gate: for wide is the gate, and broad is the way, that leadeth to destruction, and many there be which go in thereat: because strait is the gate, and narrow is the way, which leadeth unto life, and few there be that find it." The second is:

(2) - "It is of the Lord's mercy and loving-kindness, that we are not consumed, because His [tender] compassions fail not. *They are new every morning.*"[33] (emphasis added)

The first statement speaks of the narrow way to heaven or spiritual reality, and the broad way to chaos and destruction. The broad way is the way of *entropy* (See Part I, Chapter 17, discussion of entropy), the law of the physical world that says that eventually the universe will reach a state of total degradation of matter and energy, a state of inert uniformity. The second statement speaks of the promise that in the universe of Spirit, Life is eternal and vital. This present reality can be apprehended in the degree that we understand - and live - God's laws of order and harmony.

** *Mary Baker Eddy*

Mark Twain, who lived during Mary Baker Eddy's time had a double-minded attitude in regard to the religion she preached, and to the woman herself, but he somewhat ruefully admitted that if she were to be judged by her achievements, that it was thirteen hundred years [**] since the world had produced anyone who could even approach her stature. [34]

Sir John Templeton, founder of the prestigious *Templeton Foundation* [▽] was quoted as saying the following about Eddy and her book, *Science and Health with Key to*

---

[*] Recently (2002), the *Second Law of Thermodynamics* (a statistical law) has been violated in experiments on small macroscopic systems for short periods of time (fractions of a second).

[**] Thirteen hundred years, referring to Muhammad and his founding of the Islamic religion.

[▽] The *John Templeton Foundation* was established in 1987 by renowned international investor, Sir John Templeton, to encourage a fresh appreciation of the critical importance - for all peoples and cultures - of the moral and spiritual dimensions of life. Through its programs, the Foundation seeks to encourage the world to catch the vision of the tremendous possibilities for spiritual progress in an open and humble approach to life.

the Scriptures: "I [want] to say to the world that progress in spiritual information is vastly more beneficial than in physics or chemistry or anything else. One of the great advances was made a century-and-a-half ago when Mary Baker Eddy published her book [*Science and Health*]. If the [*Templeton*] prizes had been available at that time, in all likelihood she would have been a prizewinner, because she did something totally original in [the field of] religion...Mrs. Eddy was one of the first to have a larger concept of God." [35]

A larger, more practical concept of God was certainly needed for Eddy to bring about radical spiritual healings, such as a few of those described below.

--- Cancer of Jugular Vein

After one of many instances in her life that firmed up her conviction of the false record of matter-based reality, the absolute unreality of evil and the absolute allness of Spirit or good, Mrs. Eddy declared, "When I have most clearly seen and most sensibly felt that the infinite recognizes no disease, this has not separated me from God, but has so bound me to Him as to enable me instantaneously[*] to heal a cancer which had eaten its way to the jugular vein." [36] A man had come to Mrs. Eddy with the cancerous condition. Eddy related that the cancer had eaten away the flesh of the neck so that the jugular vein was exposed "...so that it stood out like a cord." [37] It had looked so horrible that she had turned away from it. But she knew that God knew nothing of such a disease. When she again looked, the man had been perfectly healed.

--- Cancer of the Chest

In another instance a woman had visited Eddy for spiritual treatment for a cancerous condition located in her chest a little above her breasts. In one treatment the pain had stopped and the cancer had immediately begun to heal, *so* that in a very short time there was no longer any trace of the cancer. Years later the woman returned to Eddy's house with a desire to see her and thank her for what had been to her a miracle. With tears of gratitude she said, "I wanted to see the woman that performed such a miracle once more and thank her."[38]

--- Cancer of the Face

Around the year 1885 Mary Baker Eddy and a woman friend had been looking at rugs in a Boston rug emporium. The two of them could not help notice that the man who waited on them had a partially bandaged face. As told by William Turner and related by Yvonne Cache Von Fettweis and Warneck in their book (See, *Mary Baker Eddy / Christian Healer*, by Yvonne Cache Von Fettweis and Robert Townsend Warneck, *Christian Science Publishing Society,* Boston, Mass., 1998) [39], Eddy soon lost all interest in looking for rugs and suggested to her companion that they should leave and return on another day.

---

[*] It is gratifying when a healing by prayer occurs quickly, but healings that take some time can still be explained by consciousness gradually yielding to an improved sense of reality. The body manifests outwardly what the mind believes or knows.

Two or three days later, Eddy's friend returned to the shop only to discover that the salesman no longer had a bandage on his face. In a very earnest manner the man asked the woman who might be the lady who had been with her on the first visit to the store. In a reverent and awe-struck voice he said, "I can't explain it, but that lady had something to do with a very wonderful thing which has happened to me." He then said to her that not long after the two women had left the store his face, which had been scarred, began rapidly to heal. Looking at his face, the woman saw that it was perfectly clear. The affliction had been cancer.

Eddy at one time, in response to a question as to what was the best way - through prayer - to bring about an instantaneous healing, replied as follows: "It is to love, to be love and to live love. There is nothing but Love. Love is the secret of all healing, the love which forgets self and dwells in the secret place, in the realm of the real." She said this was not merely human love, but Love, itself. (As recalled by Clara Barton and quoted by Irving L. Thomlinson in his book, *Twelve Years with Mary Baker Eddy*, p-91.) [40]

In the above experience, it was the pure love of Love itself silently understood and felt by Eddy that was the communicator of ideas to the man who believed he had cancer. So we see that spiritually- inspired thought - communication without words - was the avenue to healing, a communication that would be impossible via a human brain or an artificial intelligence device.

Many of the healings accomplished by Mary Baker Eddy were, for the most part, nothing short of phenomenal; although critics will say that there is no more substantial record of them than that of the healings recorded in the *New Testament* of the *Bible*. [41] But in many instances the account of people who had actually been healed, those who also witnessed the healings and the continuing practice of spiritual healing today lend credence to her record.

---Healings by Eddy's Students

In the 1880's Eddy taught classes of students in the art and science of spiritual healing, emphasizing the fact that the student must declare as Jesus: "I can of mine own self do nothing…The Father that dwelleth in me, he doeth the works." [42] Sometimes after several days of instruction in class, she would ask each student to go out and heal someone before returning to class the next day (see *A Century of Christian Science Healing*, p. 8).[43] With rare exception each of them did (fifteen out of sixteen after one class). One man reported that he returned to his lodging house and told his landlady he had no idea where to find a sick person, whereupon she replied, "You can heal me: for I am totally deaf in one ear." With *great joy* he returned to his room to pray. As the book recounts: "Instantly the woman felt a report like a pistol shot in the ear and ran up after him, calling, ' I am healed.'"

PRESENT-DAY HEALING EXPERIENCES

** Cancer of the Abdomen

A striking example of an apparent violation of physical law is related by Robert A. Peel in his book *Spiritual Healing in a Scientific Age*. He tells of an experience of a woman in the early 1950's who had a cancer of the abdomen at a very advanced stage (For a more complete account of the experience, see *New Concepts of Healing* by A. Graham Ikin, New York: *Association Press*, 1956, pp 104-108). [44] But the woman had an absolute faith that her prayers to God would be answered, and she would be healed.[*] After a time elapse of about two years, with little or no change in her physical condition, the woman went to bed around midnight, still with the "radiant certainty" that the healing would come. She dreamed of the crucifixion of Jesus, and seeing in her dream the cross with the body of Jesus nailed to it, being lowered into the ground prepared for it, she in anguish raised her hand to help ease his suffering. At that moment she awoke, and realized her abdomen was completely flat. The doctor who had been attending to her needs was called to verify her condition. No water, blood, or material mass was in evidence that might have indicated that a physical change had occurred abruptly. As Peel says, the disappearance of the thirty-eight and one-half pound cancer that night, if it had been transferred into equivalent energy as required by the laws of physics, would have been sufficient to destroy the entire town in which she lived!

The Kansas City Star recounted this incident for many years after on the anniversary of its occurrence. But Peel makes a profound statement for physicists and scientists to ponder: " … but there is no evidence that any of those involved in it went on afterwards to conduct a passionate search for answers to such questions as: 'What did the disappearance of that thirty-eight and a half pounds show about the nature of matter? If God could choose to bring about such a healing, why did he permit the disease to develop in the first place? What kind of law may be involved in such a healing? How does this relate to faith in medical means? How does it relate to Jesus' announcement of the kingdom of God within? What are the implications of such a healing for our very concept of reality?' " [45]

Peel goes on to say that the tendency today is to dismiss occurrences like this as mere "anecdotal evidence," and therefore, not worthy of credibility. [46] But incidences similar to this have occurred on a non-infrequent basis since the time of Christ (Refer back to References (8-13, Chapter 8)). We cannot afford to dismiss these phenomena simply because they do not fit in to our present paradigm of reality.

** Tumor in Uterus

The following is an account of a similar experience of an African *Christian Science Practitioner* and his wife that occurred when he and his wife were political refugees in Zaire. [47] His wife had developed severe complications after the birth of their second daughter. A tumor had been diagnosed in the uterus, and the doctors had insisted that an immediate operation be called for. A team of three doctors and a gynecologist invited the man to view the tumor on the screen of the scanner. It was clearly visible. They told him that it was urgent that his wife be evacuated by helicopter to the nearest university hospital located in Lausanne. The gynecologist knew that the man and his wife were accustomed to relying on prayer for any emergency. She told the man that the situation was very serious and his wife should be operated on immediately, but that she

---

[*] She had engaged the help of a small prayer group in St. Louis, led by Dr. Rebecca Beard, a physician who was also interested in faith healing.

would request that the operation be delayed for twenty-four hours, but no more. She said, "In that way we can pray the psalms." (As they were political refugees, they depended on the authorities for everything concerning health care).

The man told his wife, "What the doctors say [about the tumor] is of little importance. I know one thing, there is only God. And this God, who is good itself, is here, now, omnipresent, and I will not accept anything else but good." He then returned home to give additional time to deep prayerful communion with God.

He found in the *Bible* the statement, "Every plant that my father has not planted will be uprooted." [48] He began to understand that the tumor could not maintain itself as a presence, a reality, because it had not been "planted" there by God. He later related that his "thought was so filled with the totality of good and God's oneness that I did not even question the outcome of the situation." The next day, to everyone's surprise, there was no evidence of a tumor - the scanner showed not a trace. Together the man and his wife knew that what was originally seen as a tumor - a piece of abnormal matter - was simply "a ball of illusion, which only existed in mortal thought, not in reality."

An important point to consider in reviewing the above healing of a tumor is the following: Physicists say that some kind of observation - either by an inanimate or conscious observer - is required to collapse the wave function and reveal a matter particle or collection of matter particles. But how reliable were the observations and the resultant physical evidence if inspired, uplifted thought, in communion with God, results in the overnight disappearance of the offending masses?

Almost all religious organizations believe that one should pray to God for inspiration and guidance. The prayers of Jesus were not made to implore God to change a discordant situation or diseased condition. God does not need to "reach down" to us and cause "miracles;" that is, to violate His own laws. *"Miracle"* means "to wonder;" and our only need is to reach out to the Mind that is Love - not to change *reality,* but to recognize and understand to some degree the Reality which is above or outside the material condition. That spiritual healing is more "anecdotal" than consistently demonstrated today, does not disprove its scientific basis. Its occurrence will be more frequent and more consistent when each individual practices what he or she professes to know about God.

** Concern for Daughter's Safety

Because of a strong desire to do something for her country a young woman volunteered to serve as a *Vista* volunteer (the *Domestic Peace Corps*). [49] Part of her training included living with another single woman in a distant and poor part of the country in a house that had no running water, no inside plumbing and no telephone. This was also an area of strong racial tension. She was the only one of her race living in the area. One evening, after living in the area for about five weeks, the volunteer returned from a community meeting and walked up to the porch of the empty house. At that moment a carload of young men drove up. The woman calmly walked into the house and was able to latch the screen door before the men got up on the porch. The men knew the other woman who lived there was not at home and that there was no telephone. The nearest house was blocks away. Although the young men taunted her, jiggled the screen door, and made strong and crude overtures to her, she continued to stand just inside the screen door and silently pray. She looked at the young men and spoke out loud to them, all the while silently affirming that each had the God-given capacity for good, although he may not be aware of it. In about twenty or thirty minutes they left, only to return again in an hour, this time banging on the windows. Finally, they left for good. The young woman humbly thanked God for His great love and protection.   Several points stand out about this experience:

> (a) - Although initially fearful, the woman denied the evidence of the human senses that literally shouted that evil men were going to perform evil acts. Instead she affirmed the presence and power of God, and his creation of good, alone. On the surface this would seem to be absurd to affirm that goodness was at that present moment being manifested by each of the men. But she believed that in the realm of Mind or Truth, good alone is manifested, and that this is the only reality of being.
>
> (b) - Upon returning home three months later, the woman was asked by her mother if she had been in any danger. The mother said that she had keenly felt the urgency to pray for her daughter's safety and her well being. The two of them compared notes and it was discovered that the mother had felt this need to pray on the very evening that the young men had been on the porch.
>
> (c) - The prayers of the mother at the precise time of need were more than simple chance. It was a "meaningful coincidence." Space (space-time) was seen to be no obstacle to communication. The prayers of the mother (separated from her daughter by over six hundred miles), as well as the prayers of the daughter were effectual. In the realm of Mind, there is neither separation nor isolation of one person from another - or from God.

The above experience is an illustration of the non-local and unified effect[*] of inspired thoughts in communion with God.

** The Pilot in the Jungle

Although Carl Jung (see Part I, Chapter 8, first page) says that Flammarion connected meaningful series of coincidences with the subject of telepathy - minds communicating independent of space and time - the following story goes beyond the concept of communication between individuals:

Another friend related to me [v] an experience of a buddy he knew from his college days. During *World War II* the man was a pilot of a twin-engine C-46. [(50)] On one occasion, he was flying some British soldiers over the *Hump*, the rugged foothills of the *Himalayan Mountains*, on their way back to *India*. Suddenly, one engine caught on fire and failed. Through heroic efforts they managed to put out the fire, but the pilot was unable to feather the propeller. Because of engine failure and the heavy load, the plane began to lose altitude. At the time, they were flying over dense and rugged mountain jungle. It appeared that the plane would crash and all hands on board would perish, but the pilot was a deeply religious man, and he knew it was time to pray. He told everyone to be quiet. The crew was familiar with this request, because on every flight the pilot would let the copilot begin the flight while he pushed his seat back and prayed. They had

---
[*] See non-locality experiments, Part I, Chapter 15).
[v] A few years ago I talked directly with the pilot.

learned to put their trust in these prayers. The pilot had prayed before each flight in just about every one of the 500 or so missions he had flown, and the plane with crew had earned the nickname, the *Bad Penny* because they were always turning up.

The pilot's method of prayer was to lift up his consciousness to commune more deeply with God as universal Mind, and Life that would meet the needs of all the men in the plane. As part of his prayer at this time of severe crises and imminent danger of death, the pilot prayed thus: "I really know that God is infinite Intelligence, and He can do anything. I can do nothing. He wants me to use [or manifest] intelligence, and not kill the passengers. God has always been with me." [51] In praying in this manner the pilot began to feel a oneness with God. He felt a sense of certainty that because God is Intelligence, He could reveal Himself as a divine or spiritual Law that would restore a temporary loss of peace, order and harmony.

The plane was now brushing the treetops. Then - at the last instant - straight ahead, he saw a narrow dirt landing strip in a jungle clearing.[*] He was able to lower his landing gear just in time. He made no correction in his plane's orientation, and came in dead center. He said that he was so overcome with this wonderful experience that for awhile he could not get out of his seat.

Several days later the Colonel of the outfit flew in with a maintenance crew to repair the airplane. He remarked that what had happened was certainly a miracle. When he asked the pilot how he found the dirt runway out of the thousands of square miles of dense jungle, the pilot replied, "I didn't find it; it found me!" The pilot said that this experience changed his entire life, and he later wrote a small book about the experience, and about other remarkable experiences he had during the war. [▽]

Was this incident just the result of "pure chance" - a finite possibility that out of thousands of square miles of jungle and rugged terrain there would appear a runway precisely at the right place and time for the safe landing to be made?

My friend - the one, first related this story to me, and who devotes his life to helping others through prayer - said that if cases like the above *World War II* incident were rare, he might be convinced that what happened was the result of mere coincidence, but he said that he was familiar with many similar experiences in his own life, as well as the lives of other people. He said, "What we physically sense as our human experience is but the objectification of our human consciousness. The world you look out upon is the world of your own thought. " [52]

Did not the runway in the jungle represent an *idea,* at first limited, distant and unseen to the pilot, but when understood as representing a refuge from fatality and a passageway to safety, was then observed or experienced as part of the pilot's external experience? Eddy said that creation "consists of the unfolding of spiritual ideas and their identities, which are embraced in the infinite Mind and forever reflected." [53] That is, the spiritual ideas of safety, security, protection, innocence that came to the man were unfolded in the pilot and the passengers' human experience as the immediate presence of a runway.

---

[*] It was later learned that the Japanese had bulldozed the landing strip for their reconnaissance aircraft, but had to abandon it due to the area being taken over by the Allies.

[▽] The book, *Dear Son*, was written for his son, but was never published.

We will again approach the discussion of the pilot and the runway later on in the book, at which time this experience will be compared with other phenomena that have occurred, which defy conventional explanations.

** The Lost Cat

These simple, but profound truths are seen in the experience of a close friend. [54] He had been praying off and on to help his neighbor find her lost cat, but without success. One night several days later, late in the evening, he decided it was time to give a more consecrated period of prayer to the situation than he had before given. After a few minutes (as he later recounted) he felt greatly inspired and knew with absolute conviction that he, as well as everyone else, *including the cat*, were at that moment in the kingdom of God, safe and secure. This inspirational moment lasted for about twenty seconds. Immediately after that the telephone rang. The cat's owner reported that her pet had been found, safe, with no ill effects. A chance coincidence that the prayer and the finding of the cat occurred at about the same time? Is it not possible that the cat may had been found *before* my friend's moment of inspired prayer? These questions though, become meaningless when we begin to realize that existence is *now*. The appearance of ideas (either simple or complex) is not a creation of matter objects in time or space-time, but is an unfolding or realization of great and eternal truths that exist yesterday, now and forever.

** The Water in the Desert

When Jesus "multiplied" the loaves and fishes in order to feed the multitude, the later recounting of the event could have been "magnified" out of proportion, or the story could simply be an allegory to illustrate some truth he wanted to teach, but there are parallels in this present age.

For example, a man was in a party of three on a geological expedition in Utah. [55] They journeyed into a remote desert area, but could only carry enough water for three days. They had expected to find water in the region, but after two days of fruitless searching they concluded they would have to return to civilization the next morning. The man asked himself if the *Biblical* stories of Jesus and the loaves and fishes, and of Moses striking a rock and receiving water were actual experiences, or were they no more than myths or allegories. He reasoned that if they were demonstrations of divine Law, then that Law would be available today. When he finished this prayer, he was at peace, and went to bed.

The next morning he decided to make one last trek through a narrow canyon near the camp site in search of water, but he saw nothing but rocks and sand, and no signs of any kind of vegetation. As he sat down to remember his prayer of the previous day, his eyes fell upon a tiny patch of green moss about the size of his thumbnail growing in a crevice in the canyon wall. He struck the moss with his pick and it became moist. He then struck it several times more and water gushed out - enough water to meet the needs of the team!

Instead of believing that out of thousands of acres of sand and rock, he was lucky enough to find a water source, he was convinced that "...there is a definite relation between our human consciousness and what we physically sense as experience." [56] He felt that prayer does not change reality; *it simple reveals it.*

** Four Tuberculosis Cases

"Thou shalt not be afraid for the terror by night; nor for the arrow that flieth by day; nor for the pestilence that walketh in darkness; nor for the destruction that wasteth at noonday. Because thou hast made the Lord, which is my refuge, even the most High, thy habitation; There shall no evil befall thee, neither shall any plague come nigh thy dwelling. For he shall give his angels charge over thee, to keep thee in all thy ways."
(Psalms 91: 5-11)

How many today actually believe the above wonderful statement found in the book of *Psalms*? The world in general lives in constant fear that the next plague or contagious disease lies on the horizon of human thought, waiting to physically appear and cause untold destruction. The fear is also that medical science may not have an immediate solution, or perhaps no solution at all. But the *Bible* statement is telling us that God's *angels* - His thoughts, entertained in consciousness - will protect us from evil.

--- Case #1

That a new kind of reality has and is being seen is illustrated in the case of a man who had been medically diagnosed as having tuberculosis in its final stages, and was given only six weeks to live.[57] X-rays had indicated a large cavity in one lung. He was introduced by someone to the healing method of *Christian Science*, and began to earnestly pour over the *Scriptures* and the writings of Eddy, including *Science and Health*. For about six weeks there was no appreciable change, and X-rays taken every week confirmed this. Then one morning while he was contemplating his relationship with God, he caught (as he later related) a glimpse of the fact that a perfect cause, divine Spirit, would not, *could not*, create an imperfect man in the image of Spirit, and therefore, there could be no vacuum or cavity in omnipresent Spirit, nor in Spirit's manifestation. He felt "...a great surge of God's love..." and "he *knew* he was healed."

The next morning he was due for his weekly examination and X-ray, but he told the doctors, "You won't find anything wrong; I've been healed." X-rays confirmed his declaration. As the man was packing to leave the sanitarium the doctor in charge came in and commented there was no possible explanation from a medical standpoint for the healing they had witnessed, and added it must have been somehow connected with the man's prayerful efforts. He asked the question, "Where did the molecules come from that filled the cavity in the lung?"

Although it is a legitimate question, how the "creation" of molecules [*] occurred was not the issue. In the reality of Spirit, matter is non-existent. But in our finite

---

[*] See Chopra and Eccles discussions on the relation of thought to matter: Part II, Chapter 2 ("The Game of Life"). Also, see discussions on multiple-personality disorders in reference (58): A woman who had a split personality, had diabetes when one personality was in control and exhibited no symptoms of the disease when one of her non-diabetic personalities was dominant. Molecular changes in her body had to occur, apparently as the result of a change of consciousness, that is, a change of belief. However to the Christian

apprehension of this grand reality, the spiritual idea of substance that most nearly represented mankind's appreciation and recognition of health, was the symbol of healthy lungs.

But it is important for the reader to understand what is meant in the above illustration about the "symbol" of healthy lungs. Eddy, in recognizing the mental state of reality, said that faith in the combined effects of time and medicine could lessen fear and change a belief of disease to a belief of health. She said, "It is as necessary for a health-illusion, as for an illusion of sickness,$^\nabla$ to be instructed out of itself into the understanding of what constitutes health; for a change in either a health-belief or a belief in sickness affects the physical condition." [59] A friend told me that as thought improves - as it becomes more spiritualized, more in tune with Spirit, Mind - then the human concept of body improves also, like the play-toy, *Slinky*, which obediently follows itself down a staircase as the result of a child's desire and the initial force she imparts to it with her hand.

Just as an electron possesses no intrinsic position or momentum until it is observed, in a similar fashion the mortal body - an objective state of consciousness - manifests what the mind, or minds, believes in; that is, either health or disease. Health in the body is not a sign of grace; nor a healthy physical body more acceptable to God than a sick body, since man's true nature is spiritual and in the image of God. Sinners often possess healthy and robust bodies. Nor should disease be considered as a "noble" state of being. Disease, suffering and disorder are not to be ignored - absolutely not! As consciousness learns more of the deeper things of Spirit, old ways of thinking about life, health, disease and death in matter are replaced to some degree with a spiritual and fresh sense of Life. The goal of mankind is not to improve upon the belief of life in matter, but to exchange this belief for some understanding that health and harmony have their source in Spirit, are eternal, changeless, and do not require material "symbols" for their expression.

--- Case #2

Mental, spiritual healing can be practiced in a scientific and systematic manner, and is not simply a result of a number of bizarre, low-probability, unexplained and favorable physiological reactions somehow coming together at just the right time. This is indicated by the following experience: The doctor (mentioned above) told the man who had been healed, that another patient in the sanitarium had only a few more days to live, but that someone had recently given him, also, a copy of the same book, *Science and Health*. The doctor asked the man if he would speak to the patient about his recent experience, and offer him encouragement. The man did so, and two months later this patient also was released, healed entirely through his studying and pondering the message in the book.

Scientist, healing is not thought working on matter or in creating matter molecules. It is the revelation of the reality of Spirit, harmony, appearing to consciousness.

$^\nabla$ The placebo effect (health illusion), and the nocebo effect (the opposite of a placebo: a mental catalyst that causes a person to be worse off). It is well known that a health belief, or a belief in sickness can be affected by suggestion, and by strong emotional feelings - an hypnotic effect, sometimes self-induced.

--- Cases #3 and # 4

Although the probability of recovery from acute tuberculosis is extremely rare without medical intervention, what is the likelihood of recovery of *two more* cases at another hospital, both occurring at nearly the same time and under the *same* conditions (specific, spiritual prayer)? A very similar "low probability" experience occurred with two other people - a young man and woman who were tuberculosis patients in a tuberculosis sanitarium in Switzerland. [60] The man had been declared terminally ill, but was restored to complete health by the same method of prayer as mentioned above. A required medical examination by medical authorities verified his healing. He later told the young woman about the experience, and subsequently she too was restored to health by prayer alone. The two later were married.

If reality is truly mental, and matter is the phenomenon of mind rather than the other way around, then why cannot you or I more readily manipulate material objects at will? Why can't we simply will away disease? Why are many of the results of the Jahn experiments (see Part II, Chapter 3) so marginal? That is, why don't we see more of these kinds of phenomena than we do – and on a larger scale?

The reason, I believe, is that attempting to accomplish global effects through the collective thoughts or beliefs of many minds - minds which consciously or unconsciously accept the paradigm that matter and material laws enforce are prime – is fraught with dissatisfaction and failure. Working within the dream of life and substance in matter, learning to control matter with human will, of what lasting benefit will it be to the human race exchanging one finite belief for another?

It is only when human consciousness figuratively steps "outside" of the dream belief or illusion of life, intelligence, and substance in matter, and acknowledges the primacy of Spirit and Mind (not mind) that spiritual healings and true progress can occur. This is a major claim of *Christian Science*.

Spiritual healing is generally not amenable to controlled laboratory tests because we are dealing with thought or consciousness. For consistent healing to occur, it will require a more thorough understanding of the nature of spiritual reality and its laws. And it will require less belief in and reliance on the physical paradigm. "That these wonders [spiritual healing] are not more commonly repeated to-day, arises not so much from lack of desire as from lack of spiritual growth. [Mary Baker Eddy, *Science and Health with Key to the Scriptures*, p. 243:13-15]

As Eddy says in her book, *Science and Health with Key to the Scriptures*, "The universal belief in physics weighs against the high and mighty truths of Christian metaphysics." [61] She continues by saying that the percentage of power on the side of these truths must "mightily outweigh the power of popular belief in order to heal a single case of disease." It is also true – if reality is mental – that if one wants to conduct a study to determine the beneficial effect of prayer on the body, his own thought should be receptive to the possibility of healing through prayer. *A negative attitude prior to and during a research study on the power of prayer might negatively affect the results.*

The effectual practice of spiritual healing must also include the *spirit* as well as the *letter*. Eddy explained that the vital part, the "heart and soul" of genuine Christian healing, was Love, and that without this, the letter or scientific law underlying healing was, as she said, "pulseless, cold, inanimate." [62]

And how do you measure or weigh the degree and quality of trust, humility, purity, obedience, which is at the heart of every genuine healing or regeneration? That is, the capacity to effect what can be termed "extraordinary" healings is *inversely* proportional to the amount of mental concentration or will-power exercised, but is *directly* proportional to humble yielding of thought to the divine Will. Most importantly, the healer must herself /himself live a life of selfless love. An arrogance, or blind *faith* in the power of God to heal is generally insufficient in many cases to bring about genuine healing. This is clearly illustrated in the *Biblical* story of Elisha and Naaman. [63] The *great Syrian general*, in his arrogance and pride, expected the prophet Elisha simply to call upon the name of God and strike his hand over him, and his leprosy would disappear. Instead, Elisha asked him to wash in the river Jordon seven times, and "thou shalt be clean." It was not until he was humbly obedient to this command that he was healed.

** Man with Cataracts

In more recent times we see the same need to live spiritual law and not simply speak it. A man who had been medically diagnosed with an eye condition that an ophthalmologist had said would eventually result in blindness unless medical aid or surgery was sought, prayed to know what he needed to do in order to be healed without resort to material methods. [64] * He came upon this passage in the book of *Micah (Bible)*: "What doth the Lord require of thee, but to do justly, and to love mercy and to walk humbly with thy God?" [66] Recalling his past behavior that included moments of irritation, impatience and intolerance, he realized that he must put on the *"new man."* The previous mental states of thought were like a closed door to his acceptance of the law of spiritual causation. As he continued to pray, and exercise (over a period of time) the godly attributes of patience, tolerance, compassion and *unconditional love*, he noticed a decided improvement in his vision until he was completely healed.

** Woman with Cataracts

The conventional view of physical law (Newtonian, or quantum) cannot explain these kinds of transformations. This is further illustrated by the healing of a woman with a similar eye condition (cataracts), who had been told that the only thing that could save her sight was an operation. [67] Although she had done much praying about the condition, her eyesight had deteriorated to the point where everything appeared as somewhat formless blobs of color. But she was convinced of the love of God for her; and one day

---

*

A line-of-duty injury retired a police officer from the *New York Police Department* and left him a cripple for over twelve years.[65] After three years of the finest medical treatment he was advised that fractures to his feet had left him a permanent cripple. Although eventually he was able to walk sufficiently to obtain new work, he was in constant pain, and was ready to take his life rather than put up with the daily suffering. Through the loving insistence of his wife, he began a sincere effort to learn more about the nature of God, and of His tender love for all His children. Frustration was replaced with an "overwhelming sense of peace," and his daily prayerful study became a source of joy. He was entirely healed.

she set about recalling all the past instances in her life where she had been "helped and blessed by God." She later related that at the end of about two hours of this mental exercise in gratitude, she became so conscious of Love's care for her "that nothing else mattered." The testimony of the physical senses did not matter. About an hour later, upon looking out of her window she became aware that she could see clearly - the cataracts had "melted away" - and this was later verified by the optometrist.

Clearly this experience, and others like it, illustrates the effect of thought on the body. The question that needs to be answered is: Was this experience the result of human consciousness or thought, or was it the result of the *divine* consciousness? Human thought can affect the body, but it tends to exchange one belief (the belief that physical law can cause a specific disease or malfunction) for another (the belief that "wellness" can be achieved in matter). This latter state of consciousness still believes that physical law is primary, and it is still filled with fear that in the future some worse calamity may occur. Human thought would likely have concentrated on the physical body and its problem, and on how it could be improved. But in the above experience it is fairly evident that the woman had more than a blind faith in some Deity or in some humanly mental process. Her thoughts of gratitude – of *God's* thoughts welling up inside her – enabled her to feel her unity with God, who is perfect Being. She lost her fear, and was healed.

** Girl with Brain Tumor

Some of the healings previously related included those that were considered medically incurable, or at least not treatable unless surgery was performed. This was true for the case of an eleven-year old girl whose father was a neurophysiology researcher at a university. [68] She had been diagnosed in 1987 as having a tumor in the tissue surrounding her brain, and a *CAT* scan, an angiogram, and a magnetic resonance image (*MRI*) had confirmed this. The parents had been informed that the condition was only partially accessible to surgery and that radiation treatment would have to be initiated after the surgery.

The mother had a strong trust in the power of prayer as understood in *Christian Science*, and the husband had a basic faith in the healing power of "nature," so it was agreed they would hold off the surgery for three months. Prayer was begun, and the daughter was freed from *immediate* symptoms of discomfort.

As the mother later related, the little girl had a wonderful summer that included swimming, riding, and sewing. At the end of the three months, the girl received another *MRI* scan. The doctors were amazed at the result of this new examination, and asked where the daughter had received radiation or had surgery since the last time that they had seen her. The doctors then said there was no sign of growth, and that the absence of the growth was inexplicable.

** Broken Bones

Included in the list of published healings (1969-1988) [*] were cases of broken bones:

- --Broken Wrist

One involved "...a broken wrist, where one X-ray confirmed the break, and a second X-ray several hours later showed no break." [69] A woman had fallen heavily on one wrist. The pain had continued overnight and by the morning the hand was very swollen. X-rays taken at a local hospital indicated the wrist had been broken. The woman was asked to wait in a large room until her name was called. During this time, which turned out to be several hours, the woman prayed, shutting out as best as she could the noises around her, and remembering Christ Jesus' instructions: "When thou prayest, enter into thy closet [a spiritualized state of conscious union with God], and when thou hast shut thy door [the act of refusing the entrance of physical sense testimony into consciousness], pray to thy Father [Spirit, Mind] which is in secret [unknown to the physical senses]; and thy Father which seeth in secret shall reward thee openly [with a visible blessing]. [70] (Note: the comments in the brackets are my own interpretation of the statement from *Matthew* 6: 6).

In her prayer she affirmed that in the realm of Spirit there was no reality other than that of "good, God and His reflection [man]." When a second set of X-rays were taken, no break was found. By the following day all evidence of swelling and discoloration had disappeared. [v]

--- Cracked Vertebrae

Another experience involved cracked vertebrae. A young man was injured while riding his motorcycle. [73] X-rays taken at a nearby hospital showed three compound-fractured vertebrae. The father of the young man agreed with the hospital that he should be transferred to an orthopedic facility. However, the mother and the grandmother were deeply and intensely involved in prayer for the boy. The *Biblical* verses from *Isaiah* (41:10), strengthened them and calmed their fears: "Fear thou not; for I am with thee: be not dismayed; for I am thy God: I will strengthen thee; yea, I will help thee; yea, I will uphold thee with the right hand of my righteousness." [74] They believed that, " Bones

---

[*] Refer back to the list, Part II, Chapter 8.

[v] Other documented instances can be cited of broken bones that had been set by a physician, and later discovered after removal of the cast to have been set improperly, but healed entirely through prayer. The doctor in each case, said the only solution to the improperly set bone was to have the bone re-broken and reset! (See, The Truth that heals, Radio program # 76R, 1972; [71] and *Christian Science Journal*, February, 1998, p. 17-18 [72]). When reality is seen as mental rather than physical, it should not seem so surprising that an adjustment or change in the state of consciousness (through the power and presence of God), and the removal of fear, human willfulness, lust, anger, etc., would have a positive effect on the body.

have only the substance of thought which forms them." [75] And with fear dissipated, the healing would come about.

The next day two doctors at the orthopedic hospital showed the family the X-rays they had taken that indicated that the three vertebrae had, at one time, been crushed, but were now mended. The astonished doctors could not believe that the accident had occurred just the night before. They remarked that the bones were "healed over" as if they had been damaged months ago. One doctor commented that only a miracle of God could have accomplished such a quick and perfect healing of the bones.

--- Shattered Nose #1

Two other experiences were of severely shattered noses. [76] While attending a fraternal organization ceremony, a man was struck on the bridge of his nose by the elbow of an associate standing next to him, when the associate excitedly jumped. A physician who had been summoned urged that the man be rushed to a hospital as he felt that the nose was too badly shattered to be cared for at the ceremony. At the hospital emergency room, X-rays were taken. They revealed that the man's nose was so badly shattered that none of its original form could be distinguished.

During this time, the man had been praying, and after the X-ray had been taken, the attending nurse left to find a physician who would attend to him. The man had the opportunity to step out to a telephone a speak to a *Christian Science Practitioner*, who among other things, said that the man should remember that God was closer to him than his nose, and that there was no separation in the *"oneness and allness of His being."* Also, that the law [the law of Love] that man comes under does not include anything that can be shattered or broken.

The hospital then requested that a *second set* of X-rays be taken. After these had been taken, there was a period of waiting, so the man decided to go and wash up. Upon looking in the mirror, he noticed that his nose was perfectly straight, and that there was absolutely no sense of pain or discomfort. There was no discoloration or sign of blood. He felt that his nose was completely healed. He found one of the nurses who had been looking for a doctor and told her to stop trying to locate one. He later said that the nurse was so stunned when she looked at his nose and saw it completely healed that she did not speak. He thanked her and left, permanently healed.

--- Shattered Nose #2

A woman ran into a heavy glass door, breaking her nose, which was verified by a company- required medical diagnosis (X-ray). [77] In this instance, as with the above cases of broken bones, prayer to God was initiated. About twenty minutes later, the woman felt a movement in her nose, and asked the doctor if he would take another X-ray. The second X-ray showed no sign that the nose had ever been broken. The surprised doctor said that he had heard of these kinds of healings occurring as the result of prayer, but he had never witnessed one until now.

--- Broken Joint in Toe

I have a personal acquaintance [*] with a young girl who at the age of twelve years had a quick healing of a broken toe. She had jumped out of a tree into a trampoline (not a wise idea), and had felt immediate pain in her toe. She ignored it and continued playing with a friend. Two days later she awakened with a sharp pain in her toe, which by now had turned - as she later described it - black and purple. Her parents took her to a hospital where an X-ray revealed that a joint in her toe had been broken. A cast was installed and the young girl and the parents were told that she would have to wear the cast for nine weeks. The girl called a *Christian Science Practitioner* to help her in prayer.[∇] Some of the thoughts that came to the girl as the result of prayer were: "I was one of His [God's] beloved children ... God is all power ... He is supreme and infinite ... He is all goodness ... There is no room for error [an accident] of any sort."

She contemplated these and other simple, but profound truths, and began to feel at peace. She felt that she had an unbroken relationship with the God who is Life. She also prayed to restore harmony and heal a broken relationship with a friend. Throughout the first day of wearing the cast, she kept hearing an insistent voice speaking to her, (a mental sound) "Take off the cast!" She and the *Practitioner* continued to pray, and on the second day of wearing the cast she and her father removed the fiberglass cast. After the cast had been removed she ran and jumped around in perfect freedom shouting, "I'm free, I'm free!" And, indeed, she was. The next morning when she awakened there were no black, purple or blue marks on her toe. The young girl is grateful for the quick healing[⊕], but especially grateful that she can continue to learn more about the great *Bible*-based truths that set her free. [78]

-- - Broken Neck

A recent account of the healing of a broken body part [79] was the quick healing of the broken neck of a young girl. She had fallen off a bed, forcefully landing on her neck. She had heard a loud cracking sound as she hit the floor, and she screamed in pain. She could not move, but family members came to her aid. Her grandmother and mother remained at the foot of her bed from the morning, when the accident occurred, to the

---

[*] In addition to having personal knowledge of this experience, I have written and/or verbal communications or information regarding the following healing experiences described in this book: "Concern for Daughter's Safety," "The Pilot in the Jungle," " The Lost Cat", "The Water in the Desert," "Four Tuberculosis Cases", "The Lost Key and Eye Problems", " HIV/AIDS Cases Healed" (tested positive for HIV).

[∇] I am withholding the name of the girl. The girl's parents were not interested in Christian Science, but had permitted her to attend a *Christian Science* Sunday School.

[⊕] This experience occurred during the summer of 1999. Many adults, especially those steeped in medical theory, would have been fearful and reluctant to place such absolute reliance on, and trust in God! Her parents were not interested in spiritual healing, but this young girl had an unusual thirst for spiritual things, as evidenced by her own desire to attend church on her own (Sunday School classes), and by her clear spiritual insights shared at special church meetings. (The author does not recommend that any young person remove a cast from any part of their bodies without the consent of their parents.)

evening, praying for her in a way that acknowledged the immediate presence and healing power of God. They had agreed with the father that if the girl were not healed by the time he got home from work, she would be taken to the hospital. Just before the father arrived home the girl felt a sudden movement in her neck. She then felt a sense of peace and calm, and went about playing on the porch with some friends. Upon arriving home, the father still insisted that the child be X-rayed by an X-ray specialist. This was done, and later that evening the doctor reported that the neck, in fact, had been broken, and that the girl should have died on impact with the floor. The neck, he said, was mending perfectly - in fact beyond the skill of medical science.

Several important observations stand out to the author in regard to this experience:

- The calm, steadfast, and *persistent* prayerful effort on the part of the mother and grandmother;
- The recognition that in this instance medical science would not have accomplished the complete healing as effectively as spiritual prayer. We can say, with some degree of confidence, that the immediate reaching out in prayer to - as the family described it - the God who is Life, Truth, and Love, was what saved this girl from death.
- The elimination of fear was an essential element to complete and rapid healing. And fear is mental - an undesirable state of consciousness. But it was consciousness that entertained the healing presence of God, Life, that made all the difference in what kind of reality would be acknowledged and experienced by the family.

** Dental Surgery

A similar example to the broken bone cases given above, illustrates the superiority of *spiritual observation* over that of material records: A dentist had scheduled oral surgery for a woman after an examination and X-rays had indicated the need. The surgery was to take place at a hospital in two hours. The woman had decided, however, that the condition could be healed through prayer. Again, as with the healing of the woman with advanced cataracts, she decided that she could express gratitude for the spiritual nature or unseen reality of everything that came into her experience in that two hours before her appointment for surgery. What she did, how she prayed, was later related to another person [80] who gave the following account:

"As she drove, she saw in the other automobiles on the road symbols of mobility, agility, usefulness, and comfort. Safety, control, order, and harmony were qualities indicated in the traffic lanes marked out by white and yellow lines. The traffic lights and stop signs spoke to her of obedience, perfection, alertness, and honesty. Originality, beauty, color, design, substantiality and inspiration came to thought when she looked at the buildings and houses along the way. Trees that gave shade and homes for animals evidenced supply, provision, loveliness, purification of the atmosphere." She continued in this manner of observation, including and embracing in love everyone with whom she met at the hospital on her way to the surgery. When she got to the room the surgeon did a "double take" after he examined the tooth and the new X-rays. He examined them several times and told her she did not need the operation, as there was nothing wrong with the tooth.

We should ask the question, "What happened to the evidence provided by the X-ray recorder in this case and in other instances similar to this one?" What or *who* was the observer for the first X-ray? *Was not a wave function irreversibly collapsed during the first observation?* * We have the record of Christ Jesus as saying, "For this cause came I into the world, that I should *bear witness unto the truth*"[81] (emphasis added). Then he healed all manners of diseases, even death, itself. He observed (bore witness), but gave little credibility to the physical evidence or history of discord and chaos. If X-rays or other sophisticated diagnostic tools had been available, I doubt that he would have had need of them. The truth that Jesus spoke of bearing witness to, I believe, is the message or information (a collection of coherent ideas) about man and the universe. It is not a wave function, and it revealed to Jesus and to those with whom he met, a new reality that included spiritual wholeness.

** Terminal Cancer

A man announced to a person engaged full time in the practice of spiritual healing that the finest clinics in the state had agreed that his mother would die of a malignancy within two weeks. [82] The disease had spread over her entire body and nothing further could be done for her. He described to the healer in minute and graphic detail the medical diagnosis and evidence (repeated *observation*). When the healer visited the woman the nurses in attendance showed him the evidence of the disease. No further medicine or medical treatment was being administered because they said nothing more could be done. It was - as seen by the hospital staff - a picture of incurability and hopelessness.

Prayer was taken up immediately, and within one week the patient reported that all evidence of the cancer had vanished. The woman's son had been a close friend of the Governor of the state, and had made personal arrangements for her examination by several highly reputable clinics. All the diagnoses had been the same: the woman would not live.

Instances like the above are sometimes grouped together under the broad description of "spontaneous remission;" and the response of some critics to spiritual healing is that they believe that in most instances health is restored through this process. They say that spontaneous remission is simply a natural explanation to account for the body's own recuperative powers. But these kinds of healings are almost certainly a result of the *change of state* of the patient's consciousness. In the above case, the patient was receptive to the spiritually uplifted thought of the healer who in turn was in conscious spiritual union with Love.∇ Spontaneous remission as described by the medical profession, is tantamount to saying, "We don't know why health was restored."

** Multiple Sclerosis

---

* Assuming that a complex and open system (the patient and the X-ray) could be described by a wave function.

∇ The healer later commented that he wished his state of thought was always so spiritually uplifted that quick healings, such as the one described above, would be the norm. The thought of any spiritual healer should be so pure that he/she will be a transparency for Mind.

Spontaneous remission is seen to be virtually meaningless in the following example of an Australian man in the late 1980's who had multiple sclerosis, and who had helplessly watched his condition steadily degenerate over a period of two and one-half years. His condition was such that he was completely paralyzed, practically blind, and was unable to speak or feed himself. In addition, one leg was shorter than the other. [83] Immediately after prayer was begun his condition stabilized, and after several weeks began to improve gradually but steadily. After eight months he was again walking. He canceled his pension, which he had been receiving for invalidism.

Clearly, just thinking "good thoughts" did not bring about the healings described above, and although the faith that a patient might have in the healer (if a healer had been asked to support the patient in prayer) might have some effect - just as the faith one might have for her doctor - that alone is insufficient to bring about most of the above-listed healings.

Mind, beyond quantum mechanical-described physical law, *unconstrained by distance of the healer from the patient*, is a possible explanation for the healing works accomplished today as well as those recounted in the *Bible*. Mary Baker Eddy, in speaking of the unreliability or uncertainty of physical sense testimony, said, "Jesus of Nazareth was the most scientific man that ever trod the globe. He plunged beneath the material surface of things and found the spiritual cause." [84] That is, he discovered the spiritual reality and substance of harmony in place of discord - a discord which today we would explain as a natural result of physical law, including quantum uncertainty.

** Contagious Disease

Prayer has also protected people from highly contagious diseases, where laws of probability would predict almost certain infection or even death. An example: [85] A ten-year-old boy began to act abnormally as if he had been drugged, but this was not the case. His parents immediately began praying for him. Although the symptom disappeared, he developed coughing spells. Suddenly, one night his condition worsened and it was obvious he needed immediate help. His parents knew from previous experiences that "God is...a very present help in trouble." [86] With deep humility and confidence they continued to pray to gain a fuller understanding of their son's well being as established by God. The divine thought that came to the mother was that "The kingdom of God is within him" (see Luke 17:21 for a similar statement [87]). This realization, she said, was the turning point, and immediately there was dramatic improvement in her son's condition. They continued to pray over the next few days until full health was restored.

Later, the family learned that a friend of their son's had been ill and had been cared for in a children's hospital, but had died from diphtheria. They realized their son had the same symptoms. The *Center for Disease Control* in Atlanta, Georgia, asked that anyone who had been in contact with the suspected disease be examined. Their son was found to be free of any trace of the disease.

** Law Student

Some years ago a young man was attending law school at the *University of California*[88] Just after he had finished his second year a friend suggested that he take the bar exam. The man laughed at his friend, because the third year of law school was the most difficult with thousands of cases to be studied, and with the heaviest course load. Nevertheless, he asked the Dean of the law school about taking the bar after only two years in law school. The man laughed at him and said it simply couldn't be done, and that no one had ever accomplished this kind of feat. Then, in discussing his plan with someone else, the person responded by saying to him, "When you are going to school, all you are doing is pulling aside the curtain of limitation to reveal what is already there." That is, it is not a limited matter-brain that is vainly going to try and gather up sufficient knowledge and comprehension in an extremely finite time period (about two weeks!) so that third year exams and the bar exam could be passed. It is Mind revealing itself to a waiting consciousness.

He learned the third year in only two weeks (no innate photographic memory capability was involved), took all the third year required tests and received straight A's, and passed the bar exam. He later related that this was the first time this had ever happened in the history of the *University of California*, and it was not because he was considered especially bright. There were a number of people in the class who were brighter. But, for a period, he had caught a "...glimpse of the infinity of...supply" [Mind's ideas]. [89] *

** Severed Fingers

Three examples of severed fingers restored by spiritual prayer are given in references (90),(91),(92). Reference (90) is related below.

A little boy about five years of age had the middle finger of his left hand severed just above the second joint. Physical law, as related to the physiological phenomena of the body, would say that the loss of the finger was permanent, unless the severed finger could somehow be surgically sewn back on the boy's hand. But in the early 1950's when the accident occurred, the success of such a procedure would have been problematical.

Two things were in favor of the finger being restored by natural growth:

- The child-like faith and innocence of the young boy, (innocence of the finality of effects caused by the laws of physics);
- The spiritual prayers, including those of family members, that were brought to bear on the situation.

Mary Baker Eddy recognized that in the animal kingdom, if the claw of an unthinking lobster is lost, a new one will be grown, so why not the limb of an intelligent human being? What was needed was a change in consciousness, an acknowledgment that the law

---

* Can we see how there may be something else to think with and generate ideas besides the human mind or matter-brain, or even an artificial neural network? The law student did not believe that he had inherited a specific DNA makeup that resulted in his being born with a matter-brain that possessed a superior intellect and memory (see Part II, Chapter 2, Is Consciousness Found in the Brain, and in Computers?). And can we also see that a humble acknowledgment of the presence of Mind brings ideas to consciousness that in many instances cannot be conceived nor understood by a matter-based sense of mind?

of Spirit, Mind would restore to human consciousness, that which seemed to be lost, and that consciousness would again experience a sense of wholeness, completeness.

It was interesting that during the month that the healing was occurring, the child did not suffer pain. During this period flesh, bone, joint, nail grew again until the finger was completely restored.

** Prayer in an Emergency

More than a dozen years ago a man's feet were caught under the rear wheels of a large farm-type tractor as it suddenly moved forward. The tractor was about ten feet in length, and had rear tires about six and one half feet in diameter. As the tractor rolled over his torso and also over the side of his face, he lost consciousness.[93] When he regained consciousness he began to pray, affirming that God is "a very present help in trouble." [94] He was taken to a hospital, where tests and scans were initiated, but no medication was given. His wife was notified that he had been taken to the emergency room at a trauma hospital in San Jose, California, and that there was little hope for his survival. She called a *Christian Science Practitioner* to pray along with them.

It was an extreme situation. Upon her arrival at the hospital, the wife learned that many X-rays had already been taken that indicated **at least 33 bones had been broken**. The man's chest had been flattened and she could see that part of the right side of his face had been sheared off, revealing the bone. No medication had been given and no surgery had been performed because the hospital at that time felt that they should leave her husband still until they had a better idea what they should do.

But as prayer continued, the results were becoming visible to the wife and the nursing staff. On an occasion, when she had not been at her husband's bedside for some time, the wife, upon returning, noticed her husband's face had already begun to heal - and this without surgery. In three days he had brand-new pink skin without any scars.

At one time a nurse kept going to the man's chart, leaving the room, and then coming back to look at him, and again looking at his charts. She asked the wife, "Will you tell me what's going on here? His chart does not explain to me how his body is transforming before our very eyes." She asked the wife if she knew what was going on. The wife responded by saying that specific prayer for her husband was based on the fact that God had created the man, and that, "nothing could change what God has created."

Prayer was transforming the human scene - all of the bodily functions were being restored to normalcy. A second set of X-rays indicated that all the bones had set on their own. The man was released from the hospital in sixteen days and was back at work in six months. During the experience the doctors said, "We know you are praying; keep it up." And a doctor's comment to the couple when they left the hospital was, *"You're going to get a bill, but I didn't do one thing."* When the couple got back home they discovered that the experience was front-page news.

Clearly, something extraordinary happened in each of the above experiences. The effect of a change in consciousness through prayer was experienced. It was a dawning recognition that there is a law higher than physical law, and a more effectual force to change lives then even the largely unrecognized capabilities of the human mind to *will* physical transformations.

RESISTANCE TO SPIRITUAL HEALING AND TO SPIRITUAL MAN

> "Earthly minds, like mud walls, resist the strongest batteries;
> and though, perhaps, sometimes the force of a clear argument
> may make some impression,
> yet they nevertheless stand firm, keep out the enemy, truth,
> that would captivate or disturb them."
> John Locke

> "Ye shall know the truth, and the truth shall make you free."
> Christ Jesus

SPIRITUAL HEALING RESISTANCE

The minute examination of and theorizing about discordant physical conditions, is to me, roughly similar to the quantum problems associated with the interference or interaction of the observer in the *Double-Slit* experiment: "You get what you look for." That is, the mental environment of disbelief in things spiritual, blind acceptance of matter's substantiality and the control of physical law, are not conducive to successful healing. It is recorded that even Christ Jesus accomplished little healing work in his hometown of Nazareth because of their "unbelief."

** Christ Jesus and the Palsied Man

Humankind's resistance to spiritual healing was also evidenced in Christ Jesus' healing of the palsied man. [95] The Pharisees, with their entrenched views of vulnerable life and substance as existing in matter, questioned among themselves as to Jesus' ability to restore health to the palsied man. At first the man was not healed by Jesus' efforts. But Jesus perceived their thoughts, their doubts and disbeliefs. He held his ground and refused to back down. The physical evidence of disease did not impress him, and subsequently he restored the man immediately to health.

When Jesus healed the man whose right hand was withered [96] it was reported that "...they were filled with madness; and communed with one another what they might do to Jesus."

Another example of the resistance of the human mind to spiritual events was the experience of Christ Jesus' disciples when their master walked over the waves. They (especially Peter) became *fearful*! Jesus had taught them about spiritual things; but here they were, afraid if they acknowledged the power and reality of spiritual forces and laws, that they would be forced to give up their relatively safe and comfortable lives that were firmly grounded in matter.

** Surgeon and Cancer Patient

In 1962, a medical practitioner (Dr. William S. Reed) established the *Christian Medical Foundation*. The purpose of the foundation is "to acquaint the medical profession with the truth of the uninvestigated field of spiritual healing." By 1996 there were approximately five thousand doctors as well as about five thousand nurses, clergy and lay people who desired to see Christian prayer as an important component of medical care.

As a young *Episcopalian*, and later as a surgeon, Dr. Reed came to believe that cases considered medically "hopeless" were in large part due to the patient's thought, and to the fact that the spiritual component or factor of the patient was being ignored. [97] On one occasion he visited a friend who was suffering with cancer. He believed that her mother and others in the house were not particularly happy about his presence because they did not want him to say anything "religious" to her. As he sat beside the agitated woman as she lay in her bed, he became convinced God could heal her. Because she was so agitated and had so little peace, he asked if he could play her violin: he played *Amazing Grace*. In his own words he later related, "And then I sang it to her. Then I loved her and embraced her" (The woman then prayed). "I saw peace, just like a great wave of God's love, come into her." [98] He later took her out into the fresh air.

But, sadly, in many cases similar to the above there are obstructions. At a later time when she again became agitated, she was taken to a hospital where she was administered large doses of medicine to render her unconscious. Apparently, those around her had become fearful and pessimistic about her recovery and did not want to instill a false sense of hope in her. She eventually died of the cancer.

RESISTANCE TO MAN AS WHOLLY SPIRITUAL

Why is it that so many genuine healings accomplished solely by prayer are considered irrelevant? One would think that the report, for example, of the effect of prayer in causing the instantaneous disappearance of the continual pain of a severe migraine headache, would be sufficient in opening the eyes of the medical community, but apparently this is not so. The author believes that R. A. Johnson's comment is appropriate: "To the human thought buried in material theories, spiritual healing seems an anomaly, totally separated from reality." [99] Systems based on the supremacy of matter resist mightily whatever challenges that premise. Resistance to accepting the spiritual nature of man is largely due to the material evidence that is amassed to show that man is material and a slave to his body.

For example, happiness and joy, according to many psychologists appear to be determined largely by genes. According to some scientists working in the field of psychology the brain may be "wired" to a "mood level" that - although it may change periodically due to external influences such as a death in the family, winning the lottery, etc. - nevertheless maintains on the average a fairly constant level. As reported in the *New York Times*, "With time, the grouchy tend to become as cranky as before [before the external influence], and the lighthearted cheery again." [100] Dorothy Nelkin, a sociologist, has commented, "Beyond the curious notion that every quality has a gene, there is a resigned attitude to much of the reporting: our fate is in our genes." [101]

Not everyone agrees with Dr. David T. Lykken, a behavioral geneticist at the *University of Minnesota*, who published the result of his studies on human behavior in identical twins, in the May 1996 issue of *Psychological Science*. [102] Lykken estimates that 50% of a person's sense of well being - which would include a sense of happiness and joy - is dependent upon his genetic make-up; while others say that no one really knows at this time, because there is insufficient statistical data. It could be 25% or even 75%.

But true and lasting joy, as *Christian Scientists* see it, is God-centered. "In thy Presence is fullness of Joy", [103] is a *Biblical* statement worthy of note. It is only when human consciousness observes and examines man in the context of being strictly matter-based that we are forced to draw conclusions that joy and happiness are a by-product of the arrangement, proximity and energy levels of atoms. [*]

It has been proven over and over again that joy and gratitude (see healing examples in this book, for example) can be present even when some horrible external influence (serious disease, destruction of home by tornado, etc.) is also present. *Joy is one of the components of the healing process.* It is not a *Pollyanna*, "Be happy, everything is OK." attitude, but a state of consciousness that is Mind-centered, rather than brain-centered.

** Permanently Crippled Boy

An experience that illustrates this Law of Love was the healing of a young boy who had become crippled in all his joints and was in great pain. [104] He had been hospitalized for tests, and later his parents had been told there was no cure for his disability. The damage to his body would be permanent and the condition would worsen. It was at this point that *both* parents decided to turn to God in prayer. The child was entirely healed through prayer alone, but two comments that appeared in the written testimony of the experience were highly significant:

(1) - The parents began to understand that "...God is in the blessing business. He does not, cannot, curse." [∇] And the comment of the mother about the experience:

(2) - "The evidence of the disease was no longer as impressive to me [physical observation] as God's great love. I expected to see our son healed."

Jesus came preaching the law of Love, and of Love's infinite capacity to meet all emergencies perceived by mankind. He showed us by his resurrection that the kingdom of heaven is intact and with us, now. [**] He revealed a *present* reality of Spirit that is immediately apprehensible. But he also explained that if we don't seem to apprehend this reality in its fullness, that it is never too late to discover it. The last *enemy* that shall be overcome is death, the *Bible* says, and death is the human fear that life and intelligence can somehow be separated from God and are dependent upon matter for their existence.

** Fibroid Tumor

---

[*] True joy has a spiritual origin, and is a cause rather than a response.

[∇] See I John 4:16, "And we have known and believed the love that God hath to us. God is love; and he that dwelleth in love dwelleth in God, and God in him." [105] (Contrast this to physical law.)

[**] The full text is, "The kingdom of God cometh not with observation: Neither shall they say, Lo here! or lo there! for, behold, the kingdom of God is within you. [106]

Another example which illustrates the Law of Love, the effectiveness of true gratitude and the true nature of spiritual healing, is the experience of a person that occurred about a century ago, and which is recorded in Eddy's work, *Science and Health, with Key to the Scriptures*. (107) Afflicted for eighteen years with a fibrous tumor weighing about fifty pounds, and the last eleven years with continuous hemorrhaging, she began to read the book after receiving it from a lady at the boarding place where she was staying. Upon reading the book, she made the following comments:

"The revelation was marvelous and brought a great spiritual awakening. This awakened sense never left me, and one day when walking alone it came to me very suddenly that I was healed, and I walked faster declaring every step that I was healed. When I reached my boarding place, I found my hostess and told her I was healed. She looked the picture of amazement. The tumor began to disappear at once, the hemorrhage ceased, and perfect strength was manifest."

The important thing about this healing experience was that the healing was not the removal of the tumor from the body, but the change in consciousness – what has been called "*spiritualization* of thought' - that enabled the testifier to glimpse somewhat a spiritual reality existing beyond the false testimony of the physical senses. The manifestation of the healing was the return to normalcy of the body.

Another important point was the testifier's response to the landlady, who was the "picture of amazement." The testifier does *not* say: "Here was a great spiritual awakening and I knew I was healed. I told my landlady, 'I am healed.' The landlady, who was the picture of amazement, said, 'What do you mean you are healed? You still have the tumor, don't you?' I said, 'Well, yes.' So you are not healed, are you?' 'No, I guess I'm not.' " (108) The testifier was healed when his consciousness accepted ideas or truths of God, and refused to listen to the resistance or disbelief of human minds that would deny the spiritual nature of man.

** Fatal Internal Growth

Here is a third example that illustrates the Law and *power* of Love to overcome human resistance brought upon by the evidence of the physical senses. This experience illustrated dramatically the effect of a change of state of thought brought upon by prayer and obedience. It involves the experience of a woman in the 1930's who had been diagnosed with a large internal growth, and which had been pronounced incurable and ultimately fatal, by physicians. She had been told she had anywhere from one year to one year and a half to live. (109) After moving to a new city she and her husband became acquainted with a couple who seemed always to be joyous even in trying situations. From their example the woman and her husband began to learn how to turn to God in prayer.

At this time in her experience with the internal growth, the woman became totally blind and paralyzed. But she and her husband had engaged the services of a spiritual healer (a *Christian Science Practitioner*), and one evening during a physical crisis he came to her home. The woman had lapsed into semi-consciousness and was having great difficulty in breathing. The healer sat at her beside and spoke to her about her inseparable relationship to God. During this time the woman awoke from the semiconscious state and came to understand that there was no benefit in learning about God if that knowledge was inaccurate.

Just before he left, the healer asked the woman to hold to the thought that "There is no power apart from God." She resolved to be obedient to this command. When a pain would sweep over her, she would think that pain must be a power apart from God. Then she would remember to be obedient and declare that "There is no power apart from God;" even though at that time she didn't understand the statement. When she tried to move and couldn't, and when she tried to see and couldn't, she at first thought that paralysis and blindness were powers apart from God. But she kept repeating slowly and with a real effort to understand that there was only one power and that was God.

Finally, it came to her consciousness with great clarity and force that, "either there wasn't any God, or He must be All-power. He must be the only power and presence that exists or He wouldn't be God." This thought dawned on her with radiance and beauty. She knew with unshakable knowledge that pain, blindness, and paralysis have no power or existence, no matter what physical evidence was in front of her. God had never made them; and this was a great truth to her about God.

In a very short time she experienced a sudden and severe pain, and the entire growth passed from her body. Instantly she could again see and move freely. In a few days she was walking outside. Two years later she permitted a doctor to examine her, and he reported there was no trace of the disease. He acknowledged that it was prayer, alone, that caused the healing to occur.

For the woman, there had been a sudden influx of new ideas about the nature of reality, about the relationship between God and man. Her experience was akin to what Christ Jesus had said - that he had come into the world "that they which see not might see; and that they which see might be made blind."[110] In other words, he had come into the world to give sight to those who were literally and figuratively blind, and to show to those who thought they were seeing reality through the physical senses, that they were blind to spiritual reality.

Now, honest reader, picture yourself - as a pragmatic, hard-nosed, no-nonsense realist and materialist, perhaps - What do *you* think about the sudden transformation of the woman's body from one of near-death to one of health? *What if this had been your experience?* Do you have doubts about the accuracy of her account of her experience? Do you think it is impossible for established physical laws - quantum or otherwise - to be violated, and that there is a rational explanation for her healing? Do you think that a transformation in the state of her consciousness [*] had nothing at all to do with the nearly instantaneous healing results? Many would agree with you, and would dismiss all of the healings described in this book as anecdotal and of no meaningful consequence. This would be unfortunate because it would tend to suppress an honest investigation of spiritual healings, and claims regarding their validity.

---

[*] A mere change in the state of consciousness from one limited belief to another limited belief does not cause healing. Jesus said that we should "know the truth," and that this knowing would free us from all ills. It is Truth (God), entertained and known in consciousness that frees one from belief in sickness. The ideas of Truth - not human belief - establish harmony.

Two more examples illustrate the presence of an all-seeing, all-knowing Mind to overcome resistance to a lost sense of harmony:

** The Lost Keys and Eye Problems

A young woman and her family had been visiting the *Grand Canyon* at Christmastime. [111] On this particular morning the sky was a clear blue with brilliant sunshine reflecting off several feet of newly fallen snow. The woman had been having severe problems with her eyes being overly sensitive to light. The glare from the snow was so great that she could not open her eyes, and even if she had she would not have been able to seen anything. Her mother had been leading her around an ancient Indian site and reading to her the inscriptions on the various markers.

Presently, a member of another family who had been touring the site came up to them and excitedly told them that they had lost the car keys to their rental car, and asked for help in finding them. They had searched the snow-covered paths to no avail.

All that morning the young woman had been turning her thought to God in prayer, so it was now natural for her to turn wordlessly to Mind. Immediately she *knew* where the keys were! Although she could barely open her eyes she walked several feet off the path to a snowdrift, and reached down into the unbroken snow. But she did not find the keys. Then she again turned to God almost wordlessly asking if she heard or perceived the spiritual guidance correctly. The thought from Mind was so clear that she should continue to reach straight down into the snow, *until* she felt the keys. She reached down beyond the reach of her arm, and this time grasped the keys. During this entire time she had been unable to see a thing. She later related that the experience was the result of *grace* [no human sight or human intuition involved]: "the divine influence ever present in human consciousness." Later that same day she was permanently healed of the eye problem.

--- Partial Blindness

This woman at another time of her life suddenly experienced large portions of her vision in one eye blocked out by black regions. [112] An ophthalmologist told her the condition was permanent - not treatable by medicines, and that surgery offered little hope of restoring her sight. This condition was also completely healed through prayer.

Recall the example of the two-dimensional man viewing the passage of a three-dimensional object - such as a sphere or cube - through his universe (see Part I, Chapter 17). He would have an extremely limited perception of the object and would not appreciate the full grandeur of its form and beauty. In a crude sort of way, the reality we perceive in matter is but a finite or crude perception of the ever-present, infinite-dimensional universe of Spirit and its spiritual ideas; ideas which are never lost or damaged, and which exist in the realm of Mind..

** Incurable Eye Problems

Finally, two more examples are presented that illustrate the effects of overcoming the world's resistance to acceptance of spiritual law of vision. The examples describe the complete healing of severe and incurable eye problems:

--- Astigmatism and Myopia

A woman had astigmatism and myopia so bad she could not see clearly beyond 8 to 10 inches from her face. [113] She also had what is called "tunnel vision" - the inability to see anything in focus other than straight ahead. She began a sincere and consecrated effort to understand the nature of God and of her relationship to Him. After some time she began to drop a sense of a mortal selfhood and adopt a more spiritual sense of her relation to God as His idea, made in His image. She prayed that she might be a clearer transparency for "God's nature and qualities to shine through."

It was not too long before the "tunnel vision" disappeared, as well as the astigmatism, but the myopia continued. Then one day the woman entertained a profound `thought. She later related that the thought that came to her was "*that when I would become conscious of seeing only good, I could then become conscious of only good seeing.*" More than a play on words, or a *Pollyanna* approach to life, this angel message from God resulted in a gradual but distinct improvement in vision. The woman began observing (mentally) in a spiritual manner, and in so doing magnified, or brought to bear to some degree in her experience the realities of the spiritual universe (see "Dental Surgery" experience, Part II, chapter Eight). About two years later she had to get her driver's license renewed, and she passed with flying colors, reading the smallest print on the eye chart. The healing was permanent.

--- Blindness

An aerosol can containing fluid used to repair rusty musical instruments exploded in the face of a professor of singing. [114] The pain was intense, and the woman was unable to see. As she was on college property at the time it was insisted that an eye specialist examine her. In fact, two different specialists examined her at different times, both of whom stated that nothing could be done to save the sight of either eye. They said that the iris and pupil in each eye were irreparably damaged. She was urged to undergo rehabilitation at a center for the blind, but she declined to do this. However, she continued to pray to understand that true sight is included in spiritual understanding (of her relationship to God), and that her real being was always at the "standpoint of perfection" and needed no rehabilitation. Bold words for a blind woman…or an absurd misplaced faith?

However, as the result of persistent prayer [*] to overcome negative traits such as human will, pride, and self-justification - traits that would "blind" her to apprehending her true, permanent and spiritual nature - she was again able to travel and fulfill concert engagements. *But she remained totally blind.* As she persisted in prayer she finally could say that she "truly felt enveloped in God's love" despite the physical evidence. Within six months she was entirely healed, to the point where she no longer required glasses she had previously used for reading and television viewing.

---

[*] Including study and research of the *Bible* and *Science and Health with Key to the Scriptures.*

These experiences, such as the last two (above), are not a daily occurrence, but this does not in any way negate their validity or lessen their significance. Healings of this kind, and especially very quick healings - a few of which have been described in the preceding pages - will not occur regularly on a day-to-day basis until individuals and humanity, itself, come closer to living the life that Christ Jesus lived.

WAYS THAT WORK, AND WAYS THAT DO NOT WORK

WAYS THAT DO NOT WORK

Quite a number of years ago I developed a pain in one tooth. I was very anxious about this, but still largely ignored it as best as I could. A few weeks later the tooth became extremely painful, even when I did not bite down. This was during *Christmas* holidays and I had trouble finding a dentist to examine the tooth. I began to get somewhat panicky. I had half-heartedly tried to pray about the problem, but I spent most of the time in anxiety.

Finally, I found a dentist who would look at the tooth. I recall that he performed five different diagnostic procedures, including the taking of X-rays. He concluded that there was nothing wrong with the tooth, and recommended that I make an appointment with a pain clinic to try to find out why I was experiencing pain. I declined.
I went home, now doubly anxious, and fearful. Six days later I found another dentist who examined my tooth and took X-rays. He said that the tooth was abscessed and that he wanted to do a root canal. This was done. Apparently in six days the evidence went from a normal tooth to an abscessed tooth! I believe that the *nocebo effect* was in operation; that is, extreme fear caused the tooth abscess, or at the very least, greatly accelerated the process.

WAYS THAT WORK

** Abscessed Tooth

A number of years ago a woman was having a great deal of discomfort with a tooth.[115] During routine cleaning and examination, including X-rays, the dentist told the woman that she had an abscessed tooth. He said that the nerve had died, and that the only cure for the condition was through root canal surgery. When she declined the surgery he made dire predictions as to her future health.

Through prayer, and listening, the words of Christ Jesus came to her: "...cleanse the lepers, raise the dead,."[116] She had always believed that "cleanse the lepers" meant getting rid of any kind of sinful thoughts (a cleansing of consciousness), and that this kind of thinking was necessary in order to "raise the dead." Although she was not literally raising the dead, she realized the importance of purifying her consciousness by watching what she was thinking and saying. Before speaking she would ask herself, "Is there any self-justification or self-righteousness in the motive or statement?" She came to see how often what she thought or said was based on defending or glorifying self - truly a need for purification of thought! She later related that initially this was very difficult, but that eventually it was very rewarding. God was "truly raising the dead in spirit right in me!" Eventually, she never gave the tooth another thought, and two years later made an appointment for routine dental maintenance. She told the dentist that she had had an abscess but that it was not bothering her.* The dentist disagreed, saying that the X-ray he had just taken indicated there was no abscess.

The major difference between the author's experience years ago, and the more recent experience of the woman was her elimination of fear through *persistent* prayer and in her obedience and unwavering trust in God $^\nabla$

** Solution to terrorist activity

A woman boarded a bus in New York City. Standing in the rear of the bus was a thoroughly intoxicated man who was yelling obscenities. The man moved toward the front of the bus to where the woman was sitting, shouting vulgar insults to each person. Initially the woman found it hard to pray because she felt a sense of outrage and repulsion. But silently, she began to realize that she could not be mesmerized into believing that God could create such a man who could disrupt harmony and her sense of peace. She declared the man that God created to be – in truth – an image of God, of Love. Therefore, she must love this image, but *not* the image of a discordant man.

Because of the great import of this experience for handling terrorist activities of any kind, I quote directly from the article describing the experience: "Prayer: A Solution to Personal and Political Terrorism," a public lecture given by Jack Hubbell, a *Christian Science Teacher* and *Practitioner*:[117] "She became so absorbed in prayer that she didn't realize the man was looking at her. He said, 'But here sits a lady. Anyone can see...she's a lady.' He sat down across the aisle from her and was quiet. At no time did the woman speak directly to the man. Later, when she arose to get off the bus, he too stood, took off his hat, put it over his heart, and quietly said, *'God bless you, lady. Thank you for what you've done for me today'* " (emphasis added).

Now, as Hubbell says, the woman was not responsible for the actions of the man. He alone was responsible for his acts. But each of us is responsible for what we accept in our consciousness as true about another person. Hubbell concludes, "...wouldn't the same principle of prayer apply to a terrorist or an enemy anywhere in the world, no matter how far away they are?"

HIV/AIDS CASES HEALED

I, II - A man and his daughter from the country of Rwanda were freed of HIV.[118] His wife had died of the disease, and both he and his daughter were predicted by the medical profession to die in the near future. But the man became acquainted with the book, *Science and Health with Key to the Scriptures* by Mary Baker Eddy. He began to read the book, as he later said, "*greedily.*" He also called a healer (a *Christian Science Practitioner* and *Teacher*) to pray with them. Together, they contemplated the thought that God made him and his daughter "moral and good," and that His/Her children could

---

* Although not specifically stated, this must have been a different dentist than the one who had first diagnosed the abscess.
$^\nabla$ I believe I have since made some progress in this direction, having recently been healed of a severe back problem through prayer alone

not lack or be deficient in anything, including immunity from all discord. They were also learning that God is *unconditional* Love; therefore, it could be possible for them to be totally free from fear because Love would not harm any of His children. When they returned to the doctor to determine the state of their diseases, he diagnosed that neither the man nor his daughter had HIV. The doctor was very surprised, as the test was done three times, and all the results were "negative."

The *Practitioner* has on record documentation of the existence of *HIV* in the father and daughter and verification of the states of health after the healings. I am also personally acquainted with the *Practitioner.*

III - A man, who had been diagnosed with *Kaposi's sarcoma* (a form of cancer that is often seen in advanced aids patients) came to a *Christian Science Practitioner* - not to be healed (he knew death was near) - but to get a better self image. [119] His past life had been tragic and very sad. Somewhere in the past he had become *HIV*-positive, and then developed *AIDS*. Over a period of weeks the man and the *Practitioner* talked and prayed about his spiritual growth, about being "hid with Christ in God," and how his life in God was so different and so much more than the life he had several years ago. After a period of time he became symptom-free. This healing experience occurred around (1992).

IV - A practitioner was asked to pray for a child with *AIDs*.[120] She talked with the girl about the fact that the child had a right to experience his spiritual inheritance from God.". After a matter of months the child became symptom-free; and this healing occurred around 1998.

ALZHEIMER'S DISEASE REVERSED

In the late 1980's a woman began experiencing peculiar memory losses, and was given a diagnosis of early senile dementia by a memory research group.[121] She also began experiencing a number of other ailments including arthritis, borderline diabetes and hypothyroidism. When medical treatment would reduce the symptoms of one disease, another would spring up. Eventually she was diagnosed with Alzheimer's disease, and tests revealed a blood factor associated with some cases of Alzheimer's. Also, her family history gave legitimate concerns for genetic transmission of the disease.

When the drug Tacrin was observed to be ineffective (1996), she feared the worst: a precipitous, irretrievable decline into dementia.

But through a set of circumstances she was introduced to *Christian Science*, and subsequently to the healing practice of *Christian Science Practitioners* (January,1998). One *Practitioner*, in talking with her, urged her to "Lean on God." For about a month she prayed as well as she could, and by late February used up the last of her medication. She again visited the *Practitioner,* aware that there had been no sudden mental decline after she stopped taking the medication. The *Practitioner* asked her if she would like for her to pray for her. The woman said Yes." Together, the woman and the practitioner prayed silently for a number of minutes. The practitioner then smiled and said as the woman left, "Let me hear how you are doing. Results are guaranteed." [∇] There had been no laying on of hands, but only "peaceful conversation and silent prayer."

The woman felt happier than she had ever been, and felt - regardless of the condition of the body – a sense of God as truly Love, and that Love, good, was everything she could want Him to be.

The reader may think that the woman gained from this moment of prayer no real understanding about the nature of God, and of man as being spiritual rather than material. But this is not true as shown by her remarks that she sensed that God was "truly Love" (and not merely a loving God). It is also true that she felt the *spirit* of Love – a spirit that in some degree had given up trust in matter, and also the fear of it.

Several weeks later she attended her regular Alzheimer's support group meeting. Because of her unusual alertness manifested at the meeting, the doctors requested she be reevaluated. The results of the test scores showed that the woman scored better then the average twenty-seven year old person. The doctor who administered the test said that he had never before reversed a diagnosis of Alzheimer's disease. Today the woman remains free of Alzheimer's. [123]

PROGRESS IN OVERCOMING THE "LAST ENEMY" [124]

(1) - Christ Jesus brought Lazarus back from death even after he had been dead for four days. [125] He, himself, overcame death through what has been called the *Resurrection*. Through his *Ascension*, where he disappeared from human sight, he demonstrated eternal life independent of matter. No one in this present age has ascended; that is, demonstrated life in Spirit to such a degree that he/she has not gone through a death experience. Never the less, some, like Lazarus, have temporarily thwarted a death experience.

(2) - In the year 1905, Calvin Frye - Mrs. Eddy's private secretary, was found slumped in a chair. [126] George Kinter, who along with Julia Bartlett [*] saw Frye in the chair, later related the following: "Mr. Frye had passed on – he had no pulse, he was stone cold – and rigid." Mrs Eddy was then summoned. She immediately began to pray for him, speaking out loud to him, telling him to rouse himself from the *belief* in death, and to declare that "Life is as deathless as God Himself for God is Life." After about an hour of this kind of prayerful affirmation of eternal life, Frye began to stir, saying, ""Don't call me back. Let me go. I am so tired." But Eddy persisted in prayer, and in another half hour Frye was completely recovered. The next day he was back doing his normal work.

[∇] "If the Scientist [student or *Practitioner* of *Christian Science*] reaches his patient through divine Love, the healing work will be accomplished at one visit, and the disease will vanish into its native nothingness like dew before the morning sunshine" (Eddy). [122]

[*] These two were workers in Eddy's household during this period of time. They assisted her in her work of founding the Christian Science movement.

OBSERVATION

Part I of this book speaks at length about the recording and observation of physical data, and the effect of the *observer* on the measurement process. In a number of present-day physical healings described above, the healing eventually came about as the person - after persistent prayer - literally forgot about or dropped any concern about the physical condition that needed healing. It was as if the initial "observation;" that is, continual mental contemplation of, and fear about the condition (and perhaps a physical examination) lasting possibly over a long period of time, prevented the recognition of a better sense of health and well-being.

But in the realm of Spirit there are no limits! Jesus walked on the water, and crossed a lake instantly. A pilot, during *World War Two* found a landing strip in mountainous terrain. (See experience related elsewhere in this chapter.) In commenting on Jesus' experience as related in the book of John in the *Bible,* the authors of a reference book on the *Bible* are quoted as saying the following: "The Lord annihilated distance, abolished time. * I [one of the authors] see it as another miracle, a harbinger of that life in another dimension which awaits us when our days on earth are done." [127]

---

* Jesus walked on the water. Gravity is thought of as a supreme, all-powerful universal force, yet Jesus walked over the waves in obedience to a higher, more powerful law of universal Mind.

CHAPTER 9

THE NATURE OF REALITY

THE SLEEPING DREAM

Recently, during the period I was drafting this manuscript, I had a dream. A vivid dream in *color*, which according to people who research these things is a somewhat rare phenomenon. I was flying in a military airplane that had no less than 36 piston-driven propellers (definitely a dream)! We were flying *inside* what must have been a huge cave whose entrance (or exit) was located very high up (about thirty thousand feet) on the side of a canyon wall. As we exited the cave, I suddenly exclaimed, *"Oh!"* as I saw for the first time the scene outside the cave. The view was absolutely spectacular, and incredibly beautiful and magnificent in grandeur and immensity. Stretching away from me and curving in a graceful arc was the top of the canyon walls, aglow in a rich, reddish brown. The entire scene was rich in many colors and I observed it in minute detail. It has only been on rare occasions that I have recalled a dream in color, *and with such clarity.* I do not believe that I have ever witnessed a more splendid scene in my so-called waking life; yet all that I experienced was *mental* - It all occurred in thought or consciousness. Shortly after this view, I awakened. I asked myself how the human mind could conjure up such a scene, with no external data inputted by the physical senses; that is, the eyes. And how was it possible for me to view this scene - which I had never seen before - with such clarity and sharpness of focus? Since then, on a number of occasions, I will *awaken* in the dark morning hours - *and with my eyes still closed* – see some image, such as a green and white striped box with black letters on one side. I will see the object hanging in space in perfect detail – as perfect as if my eyes had been open.

Richard Feynman, the famous theoretical physicist mentions in his book, *Surely you're Joking, Mr. Feynman!* (p-51) [1] that he was curious about how in some of his dreams he could see images in perfect detail (such as seeing each hair on someone's head) with his eyes closed. He decided that when you are awake with your eyes open, there must be an "interpretation department" of consciousness that takes the series of nerve discharges in the brain and tells you what you should be seeing. In the case of dreaming this department is still working, but is determining the "random junk" entering the brain as a clear and detailed image.

Nevertheless, these experiences show that what we see depends on how we interpret reality. If we can interpret random electrical impulses (eyes closed) as some physical object, when there is none, this proves to me that "educated" thought is the "interpreter". It does not require electromagnetic irradiation or electrical impulses from the brain in order to see. We do not see what is called "external reality" with our eyes closed because we have been educated to believe that we need organized matter in order to see.

When I am not in bed dreaming, or with my eyes closed, I require a strong prescription in my eyeglasses at this time of my life in order to see things in focus. But this is merely a false belief about sight. It is not the eye that sees. Seeing is a mental phenomenon.

THE WAKING DREAM *

The senses do not report reality. A rapidly changing pattern of colored dots of varying light intensity and hue appears on the screen of your television, and reproduces in marvelous detail the moving image of, for example, a baseball game. Video conferences are now routinely held between companies located at great distances from each other. Here, a person located in Tipp City, Ohio sees on a large screen the image in "real time"[∇] of a person in Cincinnati, and interacts with the image, speaking to it as if he and the image were in the same room. We may even forget for a moment that all that we are perceiving are tiny dots on the screen, spaced so closely together that they form a distinct image to the eye. When sophisticated holographic images become a reality, the illusion of thinking we are directly seeing and hearing a person will be almost complete.

THE EYE, MACROSCOPIC OBJECTS AND HUMAN PERCEPTION

We have discovered that the detection of sub-atomic particles depends in some measure on the state of consciousness and intent of the *observer*.[⊕] But what about the so-called direct perception of macroscopic, inanimate material objects, such as a house?

Light is incident on the material object, and is reflected onto the eye's retina. That is, an inanimate matter-particle (a photon) becomes a messenger to convey information or data about the matter-house to the matter-eye. Then electrical pulses (matter-electrons) become messenger particles that travel up the matter-optic nerve to convey information about the image formed on the retina of the matter-eye to the matter-brain. But the brain, being made of matter like the eye, cannot see matter. This chain of "information transfer" must break down at this point, because it is here that the unconscious matter-brain[**] must somehow convey information to non-quantum, non-material mind. But this would appear to be *impossible*, because there is no physical force that causes the transfer of information from matter (material) to mind (mental).

It would be possible for matter to transfer information or knowledge to mind only if matter and mind are one and the same. That is, *unless matter and mind are different*

---

[*] In discussing the relationship between reality, dreams and illusions - which cover the next few pages - it is important for the reader to appreciate, if not agree with, the author's deep metaphysical position, based on the teachings of *Christian Science*, that - at the highest level - man has not fallen out of the grace of God, nor is he dreaming he is a mortal. Rather, what must be addressed in any discussion of reality is the **belief** that man is dreaming he is a mortal and that he has fallen out of the grace of God!

[∇] Close to "real time". It takes about one quarter of a millisecond for a television image to be sent about 50 miles, traveling at the speed of light.

[⊕] Many physicists would object. They would say that all that is required to cause the wave function of an object to collapse is to have the object interact with a camera, a photographic plate or simply the environment of the experiment. But we have no knowledge of any object in the universe without consciousness. The implication is enormous: no event occurs (has any meaning) without the involvement of consciousness.

[**] I maintain that there is no conscious matter, therefore no conscious matter-brain.

mental states of consciousness. Not states of matter described by a wave function, but mental states of human consciousness. "An image of mortal thought reflected on the retina is all that the eye beholds." [2] Therefore the measurement chain in matter ends with mind, and the eye\mind loop (See Figure (9-1) is a creation of this mind or of collective consciousness.

Recall in Part I of this book we discovered that at the quantum level we are dealing with effects without knowable direct physical causes. Sub-atomic matter particles are described as having potential or probability for existence ("being and becoming"). Does not the potential for what is called (or what is perceived as) physical existence "exist" as an idea in the non-material or mental realm of mind? The record of the material sensor (atom, Geiger counter, eye), is the *self-testimony of mind or minds*. And what determines what the mind will see? The mind, itself – not electrical impulses - interprets what it will see.

In the sleeping dream we see our thoughts, sometimes as clearly as when we are awake (see "The Sleeping Dream "on the first page of this Chapter). Who is to say that in what can be called the "waking dream" that we are not also *seeing* our thoughts, and *feeling* our thoughts? [5] And the outcome of this thinking depends greatly upon whether the thoughts are fearful, hateful, or loving and peaceful.

We do not say that matter feels pleasure or pain, or that matter can think; it is the human mind that does this. Neither should we say that the eye, being matter, sees. It is the human mind that believes it sees matter.

Thus, we can appreciate that the eye/mind is actually a *closed loop system* as shown in Figure (9-1). Since *matter is the subjective state of mortal mind*, it is this collective thought that is "perceiving through its own self-organized apparatus [the eye and optic nerve] its own creation or misperception of reality." [6] And Eddy said that this so-called mind "sends its dispatches over its body, but this so-called mind is both the service and the messenger of this telegraphy." [7]

As illustrated in the Figure, the senses – *alias*, mortal mind(s) - deceive. "Garbage in (thoughts entering consciousness such as fear, ignorance, hate, greed, etc) leads to garbage out" (the external world manifested as evil deeds, disease, death, chaos[V]). *Reality is seen to be mental.* The external material world as reported by the senses does not exist. ⊕ Our senses interpret reality based on the mind's acceptance of the present reality paradigm. Wolf has said, "...we have come to agree with each other just what those senses are supposed to sense." [8]

SPIRITUAL SENSE

But if the senses do not accurately report reality, would not this leave us in a hopeless situation of not knowing what is real and what is not? Would we never know the true laws governing man and the universe, and the nature of man? The answer is that we have *spiritual senses*: "a constant and conscious capacity to understand God..." it is

---

[V] By no means is everything perceived with the so-called physical senses "ugly" and "evil!" But in the degree that they manifest finiteness, limitation and inharmony, they fall short of reflecting the Divine.

⊕ But before mankind can demonstrate the total unreality of matter, it must first learn to *subjugate* it, and this can be best accomplished through spiritual healings and lives lived in the progressive demonstration of spiritual reality.

the discernment of things that are "good and eternal" (Eddy, *Science and Health*, pp.209, 269). [9] [10]

** Blind Girl

A man knew a little girl who had a condition of extreme mental dullness and who could not see because of – according to medical science – an optical difficulty that rendered her eyes useless. (See Noel D. Bryan Jones, "I See!", *Christian Science Journal*, December, 1946.) [11] After being in the care of *Christian Scientists* for a few years who prayed for restoration of her sight, she presented an entirely different picture. "She was bright, charming, unusually intelligent, could see perfectly even at a distance, and was accomplished at drawing, painting, and fine work. But at that time her eyes were in the same condition as when I [the author] had previously seen her, showing no signs of performing their natural functions. *She was literally seeing without the use of her eyes*"* (emphasis added). When the author of the article inquired a few months later, he learned that the eyes were functioning more and more naturally. The author said, "It had been proved that the physical organs performed their natural function because of what the child spiritually saw concerning true vision." That is, man sees spiritually without the uses of material eyes. It is only mortal thought that believes that damaged material eyes need to be repaired in order for vision to be restored.

---Child-like Thought

At first, I hesitated about including the above healing experience because I was anticipating a strong negative reaction to the claim that someone could see with useless eyes; that is, that it would be possible to see without material eyes.$^\nabla$ But I have little doubt the healing occurred as related. Christ Jesus once said to doubters, "Having eyes, see ye not…" [12] implying that their lack of understanding of the nature of God and His reflection, man, prevented them from seeing, experiencing and acknowledging the divine power and spiritual reality. It should also be apparent to the reader that child-like receptivity to spiritual truths - not faith grounded in materiality and material laws - contributed greatly to the healing.

The above anecdotal experience of literally seeing without eyes illustrates that it is the change in the state of consciousness, not the change in the state of a material body,

---

* The author of the article, Noel D. Bryan-Jones was a lecturer, examiner and member of the *Council of the British Optical Association* after qualifying for the *Fellowship of the British Optical Association*, and before he became a *Christian Scientist*. (He later became a *Christian Science Practitioner* in 1957). He could therefore verify that the girl's eyes were useless before prayer was taken up. The article was later published in pamphlet form.

$^\nabla$ The Catholic church recently canonized Padre Pio, who in 1947 reportedly healed a blind girl who was born without pupils. Doctors had declared that nothing could be done about her blindness. The girl's grandmother, a woman of great faith, took the girl to Padre Pio for help. He touched her eyes and blessed them. In a very short time she could see clearly. Eye specialists examined her eyes , but even though she still had no pupils, she continued to see. [13]

that results in healing and a restoration of harmonious action. If a change in the state of consciousness occurs as the result of thought becoming more in unity with the divine Mind or Soul, then this would be enough for harmony to be seen and experienced. But the human mind eventually desires to see a subsequent change in matter. Therefore, in line with humanity's acceptance of the laws of matter, mortal thought eventually brings the body into accord with what is considered to be the normal condition for harmony to be demonstrated; that is, the eyes were restored to normal functioning.

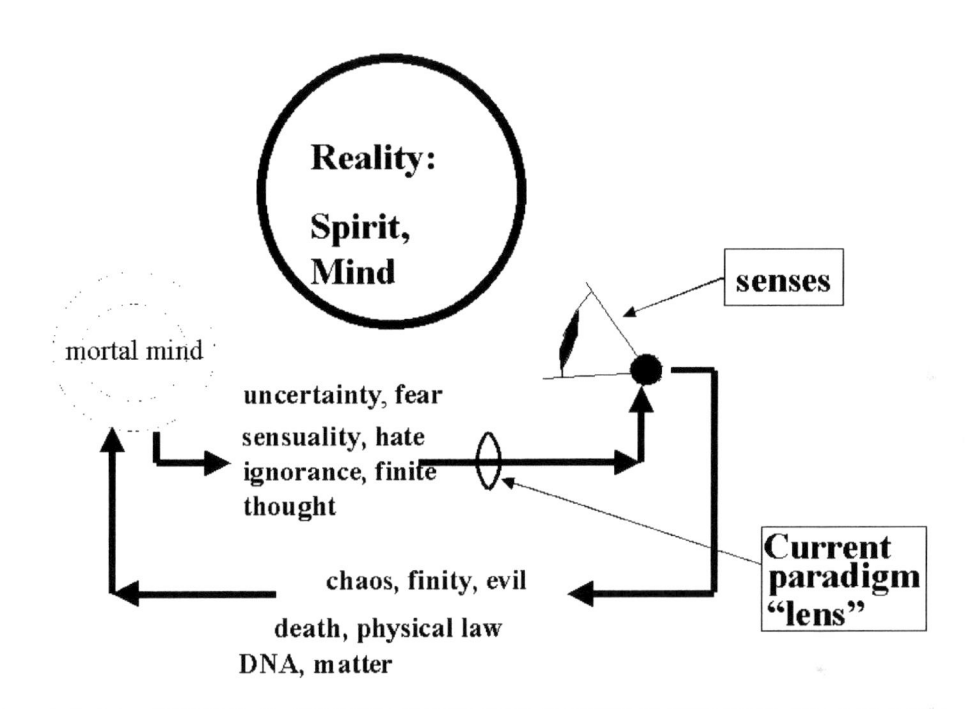

A distortion of reality: "Mortal mind sees what it believes as certainly as it believes what it sees." (M. B.E., "Science and Health with Key to the Scriptures")

Figure (9-1)

A Distortion of Reality: The Relation Between Mind, Matter and the Senses

VIRTUAL REALITY

"An image of mortal thought, reflected on the retina, is all that the eye beholds." [14]

Mary Baker Eddy

It is now possible with sophisticated computers and imaging technology to fit a subject with specially designed headgear which incorporate goggles. Through the electronically-operated goggles, images are projected onto the retina of the subject. The images may be what a pilot would see if he were flying an airplane. If the pilot turns his head to the right he will look out of the airplane window and see the right wing. If he turns 180 degrees in his seat he will see the back of the plane. If he operates controls next to his hand he can move the plane up or down, and the view out of the cockpit window - his visual scene - will show the landscape decreasing in size as the airplane elevation increases. He can fly past mountains and look back at them as they pass by. At present the images projected onto the eye, having been stored as bits in a computer, have only moderate resolution and are flat. But future technological advancements, including three-dimensional imaging, could make the scene take on a greater sense of reality.

Let your imagination run wild and suppose that we have been secretly fitted at childbirth with highly sophisticated contact lenses instead of goggles. The lenses are connected via microcircuits to an advanced nano-computer which has been surgically installed inside the head, and in which is stored a program to display a set of real time images a person might see as he moved through his day, walking and performing daily functions. Upon command of the subject - turning of the head or movement of the arms or legs - the visual scene of the subject would change accordingly. Imagine further that two other senses, hearing, and the nerves governing the physical sensations of touch were also connected in some way to the computer. This may seem far-fetched in the early years of the Twenty-first century, but it may be possible to accomplish this in the next 25 to 50 years. If such a thing were possible the subject could be strapped to a chair, and by the movement of his head, fingers, and by the slight movement of arms and legs (actually muscle contractions), he would receive a sensory feedback (visual, auditory and sensation) from the computer that would give him the illusion (a virtual reality!) that he was walking through a room, climbing stairs, piloting an airplane, while all the time he was strapped in a chair! *

Who is to say with absolute confidence that our mortal experience - or at least the *foundation* of our mortal experience; that is, - what we experience through the five senses - is not "programmed" by collective mortal consciousness? Not by a surgically-installed computer, but by our unconscious or ignorant acceptance of the world's created paradigm for reality. Our individual experiences, occurring within the constraints of the universally-agreed-to physical paradigm, would be in accord with our individual desires and intents. May not our human experiences be a little like virtual reality experiences?

What a horrible thought, you say! But much of our human existence is filled with experiences we cannot attribute to a compassionate and wise Creator. Christ Jesus, himself said, "Having eyes, see ye not?" [15] implying that it is not the eyes, but consciousness that must be changed in order to perceive reality. And Eddy has said that it is our spiritual senses (spiritual capacity to understand God or Reality) that "lifts human consciousness into eternal Truth." [16]

---

* In like manner it conceivably might be possible to physically "stretch" each of the brain's five senses (the body being located in Dayton, Ohio) by connecting them directly to long circuits (miles in length), such that at the end of each circuit the sensors of seeing, hearing, touching, etc, would be located fifty miles distant inside a very small box in Cincinnati. There would be no real purpose in doing this, but it further illustrates the illusion of a conscious being whose body is physically located in one place (Dayton) while his consciousness appears to be somewhere else (in a very small box in Cincinnati).

Our *"salvation"* then, would be the recognition that reality is not accurately discerned by the five senses, but must be perceived through our individual spiritual and innate capacities to understand and live in accordance with spiritual truths and laws, and to receive the tangible ideas of Mind.* In the degree that we do this, spiritual reality becomes more substantial and real than the reality of the physical senses. And our human experience should eventually come into agreement with our spiritual insight, and manifest more harmony and order.

THE WAKING DREAM (HYPNOTIC ILLUSIONS), AND FACE CANCER

The following incident gives further proof of the illusions of the physical senses; that is, the human mind: A man had a very good friend who was an expert hypnotist. The hypnotist had told the man several times that some day he would hypnotize him; and each time the man would good-naturedly scoff at this idea. [17] One day the two men were having dinner at a local restaurant. The man ordered lamb chops. When the waitress brought his dinner to the table, the man looked at his plate and said, "Just a minute, Miss. You've made a mistake in my order. I ordered lamb chops, not watermelon." The waitress said, "What watermelon?" He replied that he was referring to the slab of watermelon resting on his plate, and held it up for her to see. She asked the man if he were trying to "put her on." He said that he was not trying to do that, but he knew that he had ordered lamb chops, but here, resting on his plate, was the red watermelon instead.

The waitress and the man continued to disagree about what was resting on the plate, until the man noticed out of the corner of his eye that his friend, the hypnotist, was smirking. At that moment he realized he had been hypnotized! After this realization dawned upon his consciousness, he again looked at his plate - the illusion or *spell* had been broken - and this time he saw the lamb chops. He apologized to the waitress rather shamefaced.

FACE CANCER

Later in the day, the man went with his mother to visit an aunt who had a cancer of the face so severe that she felt she could no longer be seen in public. He had shared the experience about the watermelon before they went to visit the aunt. As they walked into her room, he caught a glimpse of her face all covered with the growth, and he turned to

---

* Spiritual laws and the *Correspondence Principle*: The *Correspondence Principle* of physics says that any new theory must reduce to a corresponding, well-established classical theory when the new theory is used in the domain of the less general classical theory. We cannot say the same about what are called spiritual law. Spiritual laws cannot be reduced to physical laws, and cannot explain physical phenomena. Nor can the reverse be said to be true, because these laws are diametrically opposite in nature. Spiritual laws are the laws of Mind and exist "outside" or beyond the realm of matter and space-time. Physical "laws" can, and are, subject to change. There is hardly a fundamental physical law that has not been modified or changed during the last 150-200 years. Some interpreters of reality believe that material laws, matter, and mortal thought represent different levels of human belief (the observed and the observer, respectively), and therefore, in the final analysis, are not elements of a permanent reality. They believe that any definition of law and reality must include mind.

his mother, and said, almost with a chuckle, "Why Auntie has watermelon all over her face!" He could see clearly, that like the watermelon, the cancer was nothing more than a *hypnotic illusion* - it was not reality. The man and his mother discussed the watermelon story and his revelation about the "nothingness" of the cancer with his aunt. Together, they began to understand the hypnotic illusion of the physical senses - the illusion that is the feedback of the human mind and which has been graphically illustrated in Figure (9-1).

The next morning the niece who was taking care of the aunt called - so excited that she could hardly speak. She said, "The most wonderful thing has happened! That entire cancerous growth just fell off Auntie's face this morning, and she is WELL!"

Now it should be becoming apparent that we cannot always rely upon the senses for assessment of our well-being. In the experience given above, the man, as well as his mother and his aunt, eventually recognized that although they appeared to be standing knee-deep in the solidity of materiality and experiencing its effects, in actuality there existed a reality transcending the senses.

In regard to hypnotic states, William James, a philosopher and the first distinguished American psychologist, said, "Some subjects seem almost as obedient to suggestion in the waking state as in sleep, or even more so, according to certain observers." He said further, "Suggestions come to us every moment of our lives, and to the extent that we accept them uncritically, unconsciously, passively, or without logical grounds, we are being mesmerized or hypnotized in our waking state. Suggestions may be audible or inaudible, personal or impersonal, random or purposeful, and have immediate or delayed effects." [18] Could it not be possible - especially if the prime aspect of reality is mental - that the suggestions about health and disease that come to us daily through the media of television, radio, the printed word, personal conversations with neighbors, might define in a general but broad way our future state of health? The paradigm that describes physical reality is reinforced by collective thought to the point, which if we are not careful, may dictate – as Hubbell relates - whether we will have failing eyesight in later years, weakened bones, or even gray hair!

PLACEBOS

Now suppose the woman had been given a placebo * (an injection of water, or a sugar tablet) and had been told that this was a new wonder drug that would heal her. Or perhaps a so-called "miracle worker" had said to her that he could heal her by performing some kind of holy ritual or by the repeating of magic words over her. She may have been healed of her cancer as the direct result of her change in her state of thought, and this would be to some degree an indication of the primacy of consciousness over material

---

* Placebos, of various kinds have had remarkable affects on the body, such as: increasing the growth of hair on balding men; helping asthmatic people increase their lung function by one-third; relieving pain and swelling of patients with sore, worn knees as effectively as patients who had undergone surgery with the same objective (see *New York Times*, October 13, 1998, article by Sandra Blakeslee).[19] It is believed by the majority that the chemicals in powerful drugs act with the chemicals in the body to effect changes. But placebos can also change the make-up of the body even when these fake drugs have no medicinal value. It is the patient's and/or doctor's faith in the power of drugs to act on the body to causes changes, not chemicals. Which should give us pause: how much credence can we ascribe to physical laws devoid of consciousness?

laws. Larry Dossey (*Healing and Modern Physics*) has said, "Many researchers are intimidated by the placebo response, because they believe thoughts and beliefs are an insufficient cause to trigger significant clinical changes. Those who demand material causes also turn a blind eye to nonlocal manifestations of consciousness, such as the effects of distant healing intentions and intercessory prayer, because these aren't the right kinds of causes." [20]

In his book, *The Holographic Universe,* Michael Talbot relates the rapid healing of a man who had lymph node cancer in its last stages by the use what was later to be discovered to be a placebo. [21] After being given a new drug that both doctor and patient were led to believe would be effective against the cancer, * the patient experienced a rapid and complete remission, was released from the hospital, and led a healthy life for the next two months. Then several articles began to appear in the news declaring the drug to be ineffectual against cancer. The man, reading about this, had a quick relapse and was back in the hospital with the original disease. The doctor then decided - unknown to the patient - to administer a placebo (a water tablet) to the patient, and he told the man he was giving him a far more powerful version of the drug. Again, all evidence of the cancer disappeared, and the man was again free until *The American Medical Society* announced that they had conclusively determined the drug to be completely ineffectual against cancer. He, again, developed the cancer and died within two days.

A serious, fatal disease comes, goes, comes, goes, and comes again, eventually causing death. What clearer evidence can we find for the effect of a person's mental state on his body?

The above illustration of lymph node cancer being healed through the use of placebos $^\nabla$ is very interesting and informative; but the recurrence of the cancer is another example of the effect of a *nocebo* - in this case, extreme fear - and indicates the effect of a change of state of non-material consciousness on what is perceived as the external, material world.

It also brings into question the advisability of the news media in describing in minute detail the description and symptoms of the latest disease. Ostensibly, the motive is to alert the populace to the dangers of the disease so that preventive measures can be taken. But this action fails to take into account the negative and often disastrous effects of fear that can be manifested in the body.

Anyone who has read or perused medical journals, publications, and popular magazines on the subject of the body and disease cannot help being almost overwhelmed with the almost unlimited varieties of dangerous and horrible diseases in the world. $^\oplus$ As if God (as some believe) could not be satisfied with trying mankind with only a single disease! $^\infty$ Scientists and doctors work diligently with good motives to advance the state-of-the-art of medical diagnostic tools and surgical techniques, and to develop sophisticated techniques for altering the *DNA* in the cells of the body with the hope of the

---

* However, the doctor felt the patient was too far gone for the drug to help him.
$^\nabla$ Actually two placebos: the ineffectual drug, and later the water tablet.
$^\oplus$ We are almost forced to conclude that living is dangerous to your health!
$^\infty$ And why if - as many believe - a loving and compassionate God gave man the insight, intelligence and persistence to create powerful drugs to heal diseases, are there so many dangerous and often lethal side effects resulting from their usage?

alleviation of pain and restoration of health to the body. But is this the answer? Infectious diseases, which were at one time thought to be eradicated, are returning more aggressively. New, and more robust strains of viruses that caused diseases in the past, are coming to the forefront. These new viruses are resistant to today's powerful drugs, where in the past they were not. What is causing this increased resistance? The answer may be *mental observations* - observations by individual and collective minds, which by conscious and unconscious observations strengthen the reality of disease. By accepting the paradigm that reality is in matter and is defined by indifferent, if not cruel physical laws, the world awaits in ignorance and latent fear for the next round of evil to manifest itself.

The man who had the lymph node cancer, in his fearful extremity, believed that a new drug (actually a placebo) would heal him. His belief was so strong that it *temporarily* overcame the collective universal belief in cancer, and his mind (not the placebo) literally transformed his body to one of better health.

GENUINE SPIRITUAL HEALING NOT A PLACEBO EFFECT

If the woman with the face cancer had been healed by a placebo or by words mouthed by a so-called miracle worker, the positive effects may have lasted only until the woman again became fearful she might develop some new disease, because her basic beliefs of the uncertainties of life and health in matter would have remained unchanged. But what actually occurred was that the woman had perceptibly put less faith in material medicines or in her own ability to change her state of consciousness, and instead had yielded her consciousness to accept the ideas or *truths* originating from God who *is* Truth. In a placebo healing the patient *believes* and perpetuates a *lie* about the source of life and health restoration. In a spiritual healing the patient undergoes a change <u>in the state of consciousness</u> whereby mortal thought embraces in some way, and in some degree, an idea or *understanding* of *Truth* and of man's relationship to Him. Thought thus educated in Truth begins to drop a little of the mortal for the divine.

Some in the medical community believe that spiritual healing; that is, healing by prayer, is no more than the effect of a placebo; in this case, the convincing of a patient - albeit without medicines - that physical changes for the better can be effected through prayer. The patient is made to believe, for example, that thinking "good thoughts" such as: "I am happy; This medicine will make me well; I am not sick; I love God, even though He does send evil!" will restore his health.

In some cases this may be true, but how do you explain the healing through prayer alone of a patient who is a very small child, and who knows nothing about placebos, or for that matter, that he was being prayed for?[*] For example, consider the case of a baby boy born with clubfeet. Shortly after birth he was put into a plaster cast

---

[*] Prayer has been known to heal adults who have not audibly requested help through prayer (see Chapter 8 healing of a cancer of the face). It has also healed those who were initially opposed to the fact that the healer believed in God! In both kinds of incidences, it was not a changed belief of the patient where the patient says, "I believe I am sick; now I believe I am well." But at some level of consciousness; that is, at some level of receptivity, it was an increased appreciation of, and a beginning understanding of, a new concept of God as Life and good.

that was changed as he grew. After eleven months the cast was removed, and it was discovered that the condition of clubfeet had not changed. The doctor recommended surgery but could not guarantee positive results. At this time the family decided to rely wholly on prayer for the treatment of the child. Soon after this the infant began to pull himself up onto chairs, and attempted to walk. In about four months' time from the removal of the cast the child was walking. The healing was complete and permanent.[22]

THE DIFFERENCE BETWEEN MATTER-HEALING, MORTAL MIND-HEALING AND DIVINE MIND- HEALING

The table below is my attempt to describe the differences between (A): healing through matter-based drugs and surgery; (B): healing through the action of the human mind [*]; and (C): healing through human consciousness yielding to the Divine.

A – matter-based	B – mind-based	C – Mind-based
Matter is dominant. Human consciousness evolves from matter, is under complete control of matter laws, lives, suffers and is eventually extinguished in strict accordance with material laws. Although of great benefit to millions, matter-based methods of restoring a lost sense of harmony have their limits (including often dangerous and sometimes lethal side effects); because without the presence of certain chemicals in the body, a specific *DNA* structure, the body will become sick and die. Also, laws of chance and probability assure that human consciousness will eventually expire.	Matter and mind are more or less on equal footing, at least with respect to the state of health of the body. The human mind can affect the health of the material body somewhat by working within the constraints of the laws of physics, but the body eventually dies. Human mind-based (mind-body) methods of restoring a lost sense of harmony have their limits, because they are based on limited and false thoughts. *How can we tell the difference between so-called mind thoughts and Mind thoughts? What are mind thoughts?* **mind thoughts** Thoughts entertained in human consciousness often include a mixture of thoughts, such as: hope, trust; but also ignorance (a	The one Mind is all and only, and the *Soul* of man. Matter is naught. A beginning knowledge of the infinitude of Love and Mind is required. Spiritual methods of restoring a lost sense of harmony have no limits; because this kind of prayer reveals reality as wholly spiritual, complete, and always at hand. And this fact can, and must, be increasingly demonstrated. It would be hard to understand that misperceptions and falsehoods believed by the human mind would be the foundation for true healing. The ability to fully demonstrate spiritual healing in all aspects of one's life (including overcoming death) is, at this period, limited, and varies from individual to

---

[*] More often than not this method is combined with matter- based approaches.

	false belief in the power of drugs, of a fake drug such as a placebo, or in the control of one mind over another such as hypnotism, auto suggestion), fear, doubt, sensuality, hate, jealously, envy, revenge, frustration, impatience, etc.	individual. At this period, mankind can only demonstrate what it currently understands about the nature of reality. How can we tell the difference between so-called mind thoughts and Mind thoughts? What are Mind thoughts? ***Mind thoughts*** Thoughts entertained in consciousness (after deep and persistent prayer include limitless thoughts such as: love, trust, gentleness, spiritual understanding, patience, honesty, compassion, purity, courage, wisdom, meekness, holiness. These are thoughts of Truth, God.[23]

At this period the proponents of *A* are just beginning to consider the legitimacy of *B*, which hints of a strong mind-body connection, and which obliquely suggests that the principle cause underlying consciousness is not brain-centered, and is non-local. And if consciousness is truly non-local, then it does not need a matter body to sustain its existence or maintain a sense of health, although collective world consciousness certainly believes it does! But the action of the mind on the body to restore health - through a host of biological mechanisms that can turn a thought into an agent of change in body chemicals, tissues and organs – *is an illusion*.[24] It is the effect of a changed belief: from one of sickness to one of health.

Also, the fact that disease is an illusion was so magnificently demonstrated by Christ Jesus. Christ Jesus exemplified his unity with God, by his own resurrection from the dream or illusion of death, and by his final ascension above all materiality. Life and consciousness were shown to exist independently of the body, and never actually requiring material organs and tissues for sustenance.

Then why is it that when a patient learns that he has been administered a placebo in an effort to heal his body of some disease, the beneficial effects of his consciousness on his body sometimes disappear? It is only when human consciousness begins to put its trust in something besides matter-based remedies, and begins to yield to the divine Consciousness or Mind, that the proponents of *B* will begin to appreciate and understand the primacy, the universality, of *one* Mind, God. True and permanent healing across the broad spectrum of human experience will become more frequent, and health will be seen as a quality of Spirit, God.

POSSIBLE EXPLANATIONS FOR HEALINGS

Think about some of healings and experiences of Christ Jesus, as well as healings of his disciples as recorded in the *Bible*: the loaves and the fishes, the raising of Lazarus from the grave, the healings of the deaf and blind, the appearance of the coin in the fish's mouth, etc.; and present-day healings accomplished through prayer. Possible explanations for the claimed healings are:

1 - (a) *Biblical times* - They never happened, or the experiences were witnessed by overzealous and possibly overly emotional, nonobjective and nonscientific observers, and recorded at a later time by someone not actually at the scene.

If we refuse to even consider that the record of Christ Jesus, is for the most part authentic, then we must be prepared to minimize the importance and relevance of much of what he said, and discard one of the central elements of Christianity: spiritual healing, salvation and regeneration through prayerful communion with God.

(b) *Present-day* - The diseases were diagnosed incorrectly.

2 - The experiences were the result of some yet-to-be discovered physical laws that in some instances appear to violate space-time and energy conservation constraints. Or perhaps they were a result of a quantum-type law that permits extremely rare or low probability occurrences.

3 - In the cases of incurable or life-threatening diseases being healed, it was the result of spontaneous remission; that is, the body's unknown and innate capacity to restore itself.

4 - God reached "down", violated or set aside his material laws, and healed and restored order. He caused a "miracle" to occur.

5 - The physical healings were the result of the human mind (either conscious, or unconscious) acting upon matter to direct physical actions which would restore muscles, heal and regenerate diseased tissue, destroy harmful viruses and bacteria.

6 - The experiences were the result of a change in the state of consciousness through the perception of an existing, omnipresent spiritual reality - a communion with Mind, the result of which brings to bear in human experience the *substance* of Spirit. (That is, the fleshly body and all things material, are not the real, everlasting substance, but are poor shadows of the substance of Spirit.)

COMMENTS ON EXPLANATIONS

Biblical times - Explanation #1 is plausible, but present-day experiences such as those already discussed in this book, and those referred to in other references, lend credibility to the authenticity and accuracy of *Biblical* experiences.

Present-day - Explanation #1 is probably correct for some cases. Diagnoses can be in error, but again, the sheer volume of healings by prayer lends credibility to the claims for spiritual healing as occurring through the operation of non-material law.

If explanation #2 is correct, this would be a revelation in itself, for it would necessitate a radical or wholesale revision of physical laws, and perhaps eventually lead to recognition that fundamental laws are non-material. The volume of physical healings that have occurred through non-material means alone, would preclude the conclusion that laws are totally structured in matter, or space-time.

If #3 is correct, it would be difficult to explain how the mechanism of the body, could suddenly reverse the onset of a disease or restore life after the required body chemicals and nutriments were exhausted. This explanation would also ignore healing at a distance.

If explanation #4 is correct, then we have a God (First Cause) who is not omnipotent, and who is the cause of the downfall of His own creation through disasters, disorders and diseases. We have a capricious God, who the *Bible* declares is all-power and Love, itself, but who finds pleasure in "experimenting" with humankind to make it "better".

Explanation #5 may be correct for some physical healings where strong emotion or blind faith in God (or in a placebo) is sufficient to change the state of human consciousness and bring about physical changes in the body - similar to a hypnotic or dream-like state of consciousness where one perception of a diseased body may be replaced by a perception of a somewhat healthier body.

Explanation #6 is a possible and reasonable explanation for experiences involving the restoration of the body, as well as experiences such as the *loaves and fishes* and the *pilot in the jungle* instance. For it is here that consciousness is "at one" with the First Cause. We may feel astounded at this explanation of what may be called "meaningful coincidences," "miracles" or "blessed events;" because they strongly point to a *mental and spiritual* universe: a manifestation or idea of universal Mind.

** Phenomenon Unexplained by Physics: the Pilot in the Jungle

Now, let us see how explanation #6 can be applied more specifically to the *pilot in the jungle* scenario as shown below:
- Pilot flies over jungle; engine is failing.
- The plane is losing altitude. The pilot prays a prayer of importunity.
- At the last minute the pilot sees a runway and lands safely.

--- Conclusions (from Pilot in the Jungle)

The results of some quantum physics experiments described in *Part I* of this book (*EPR, SQUID*) have given strong indication that reality - at least at the sub-atomic level, and possibly at the macroscopic level - is *non-local*; that is, objects in the universe are not separated by space and time (or, rather, space-time).

As a practicing *Christian Scientist* the pilot already believed this to be true, for he accepted reality as spiritual. However, unlike the results of *EPR* which involved occurrences in a physical universe, the pilot's communion with Mind occurred in the mental realm of Spirit, where God's messages and revelations to his idea, spiritual man, are informative, clear, and timeless. [*]

---

[*] Recall that the non-locality experiences that occurred in the *EPR* cases involved no transfer of useful information. [25]

Through deep and heart-felt prayer to God the pilot knew that he could never be separated in space or in time from God and His ideas or thoughts. He had the absolute conviction that Mind would reveal to him a spiritual *idea* of safety, security, home. Everyone in the airplane saw this idea as a runway in the jungle. If no runway had actually been constructed in the jungle in the past, then some other idea of Mind would have presented itself to human consciousness to save the plane - perhaps the idea of ceaseless, harmonious activity and power - and the failed engine may have re-started! ▽

After discussing this experience with the former pilot, my thought was drawn to the *Biblical* parallel of the experience of Jesus and his disciples on the stormy Sea of Galilee. Jesus had approached the fearful disciples in the ship by walking across the water to them. The *Bible* records his saying,"It is I; be not afraid." Whereupon, "they willingly received him into the ship: and *immediately* ⊕ the ship was at the land wither they went." [26] We see from this experience that Mind does not create an urgent need for a runway (the failed engine) and then provide an answer (no more than God creating a disease and then providing a solution). But in the infinitude of Mind, there is always an answer to meet the human need! There is always a sequence of events to bring about a restoration of order and harmony. ∝

Someone may ask about this experience, "If the pilot really believed that God's laws of order, harmony and mercy are always in operation, why did the engine fail in the first place?" The *Bible* gives many examples of spiritually-minded people who had severe challenges to overcome: the three Hebrew children in the fiery furnace, Daniel in the Lion's den, Peter in prison, and the disciples in the boat on the stormy sea. Each of us has to master in his consciousness the collective belief in a power other than God, whether it appears in the form of tyranny, hate, or in physical laws of chance. In the case of the *Biblical* characters, as well as the pilot, some degree of dominion over materiality was demonstrated. In the case of Christ Jesus and the *Crucifixion*, complete dominion over hate and the belief of any substance or life in matter, space-time was demonstrated through his *Ascension* (spiritualization of thought).

In regard to instantaneous healings - such as where one X-ray revealed a broken bone, and a second X-ray taken a few minutes later revealed no broken bone: these kinds of experiences indicate that a new, higher view of reality was glimpsed. The material record (first X-ray) was essentially seen to be bogus; that is, the accident was as if it had never happened. Which in truth, in the realm of Spirit, it never did.

Physical and medical theories cannot explain extremely rapid healings of broken or crushed bones through prayer alone. Evidence or records from the "past" in the form of

---

▽ An example of the restoration of an object that exists external to the body, see an account of the restoration of a cracked artificial tooth presented at the end of this Chapter.

⊕ The boat was approximately three and one-half miles from shore.

∝ At one time the author thought the explanation for the pilot-in-the-jungle experience was that through prayer, the pilot entered into a parallel, mental universe. In the universe he existed in before prayer, there was no runway, but in the universe he existed in after prayer, a runway had been built years ago. This example, however, is fraught with madness; for we would have to believe every time someone prayed everyone's consciousness would contain new memories and experiences that were not there before. Example: There would have to be people in the second universe who built the runway, but who in the first universe had a different life history, which did not include the building of a runway in the wilderness!

X-rays showed damaged bones in several of the experiences discussed in this book. But new evidence (after prayer) suggests that the past evidence was no longer valid.

If an observer or a recording device had been stationed next to the broken bone, and a constant, intense observation and/or recording made, it is possible that the healing of the bone might have been delayed. Even Christ Jesus on some occasions removed doubters before healing difficult cases, as in the raising of Jairus' daughter from the dead. [27] I believe he recognized the possible adverse influence of doubtful or incredulous thought on the state of the little girl.

The children of Israel thousands of years ago were in desperate need of a new and better perception of reality. They complained to Moses that they would have been better off in Egypt then wandering for years in the wilderness without enough food to sustain them. It was recorded in the *Bible* that God made himself known to Moses as an idea in thought: "I will rain bread from heaven for you." [28] Then the manna appeared. It was as if Mind were saying, "Open your eyes - and observe!"

What the "new physics" has done is to involuntarily support the claim for a new concept of reality by showing that the methods of physics lead us, "...not to a concrete reality, but to a shadow world of symbols, beneath which those methods are unadapted for penetrating" (A. Eddington [29]). As Ken Wilber puts it, the outstanding accomplishments of modern physics are not in the development of the theory of relativity, or even of quantum mechanics, but rather, "It is the general recognition that *we are not yet in contact with ultimate reality.*" [30]

Wheeler has said, "The laws of physics themselves may come about as a result of interactions between the universe and its participant-observer. We do not simply observe the laws of nature, there is also a sense in which we create them." [31] Wheeler, although believing - I am certain, in the reality of a physical universe - still believes that reality is a "participatory" phenomenon, and to some extent depends on the kinds of questions we ask, or rather, how we set up and perform experiments. (Recall the *Twenty Questions* discussion.) But in an even more radical statement [*] he has said, "I do take 100 percent seriously the idea that the world is a figment of the imagination." [32]

Figment of imagination, or not, most people would be hard pressed to proclaim the reign of consciousness over matter, and still deny the reality and substantiality of matter as perceived through the material senses, especially when they are confronted with pain and disease in their lives. But this is what true spiritual healing requires.

**Cracked Tooth Restored

> "Beholding the infinite tasks of truth, we pause, -- wait on God.
> Then we push onward, until boundless thought walks enraptured,
> and conception unconfined is winged to reach the divine glory." [33]

A woman was in pain because an *artificial* tooth had cracked when she had bitten into a hard bread roll. [34] A week later, while still in pain, she visited a dentist and had him X-ray the tooth. The X-ray revealed a vertical crack in the tooth that ran below the

---

[*] John Horgan, in his article in the 16 July, 1990 *New York Times* believes that Wheeler did not mean to be taken seriously.

gum line. The tooth was now loose and there were signs that infection had set in. The dentist recommended that the woman see an endodontist for treatment. But when the endodontist examined and X-rayed the tooth he said that the difficulty was beyond his expertise, and predicted that she would lose the artificial tooth and probably several more. He suggested she see an oral surgeon.

At this point the woman decided it was time to begin praying! The weeks passed by as the woman prayed to gain a better understanding of her relation to the Creator as an image or idea of God. The main challenge that presented itself to her was the following: She knew a lobster could grow a new claw because the claw that had been lost was a real and living part of its body; but her cracked tooth was not a real tooth, but only artificial. As she continued in prayer she began to realize that she was being tricked into believing that one form of matter was more "real" than another form of matter because she was believing that one form had life and the other did not. She realized that "...*there is no life in matter and that matter is not real at all.*"

Months passed while the woman continued to pray whenever it came to her to do so. Eventually she realized that she no longer had pain in her mouth.. At that time she felt she needed her teeth cleaned and made an appointment with a dentist in the city where she had recently moved. It was required that all new patients have a full-mouth X-ray taken. A week later at the appointment the dentist examined her teeth and told her they all looked fine. Then, after the X-rays were developed the dentist looked at them and said that everything was fine. The woman also looked closely at the X-ray of the artificial tooth and saw that there was no longer a crack in it. It was perfect. The infection had long disappeared and the tooth was no longer loose.

Three different X-rays made by different dental establishments: the first two showing the cracked artificial tooth, and the last one taken after the woman had prayed for many months and finally no longer felt pain or experienced a cracked and loose tooth.

I believe the above healing is particularly significant because it clearly does not fit in with the so-called "mind-body" * theories in regard to the health and maintenance of the body.[∇] The artificial tooth (no life!) would appear to exist external to the mind-body

---

* In speaking about mind-body phenomena, Christ Jesus understood the relation of human thought to the body; that is, the mental nature of reality, including diseases when he said, "How can one enter into a strong man's house [mortal mind or thought] and spoil his goods, except he first bind the strong man? and then he will spoil his house." [35] But his understanding of the mental nature of things did not prompt him to attempt healing through this false sense of mind. Rather, he acknowledged God as the source for healing. He declared: "The Father that dwelleth in me, he doeth the works" [36] [37]

[∇] Larry Dossey, M.D., in his best-selling book, *Reinventing Medicine – Beyond Mind-Body to a New Era of Healing*, speaks of three Eras in medicine:

    Era I – mechanical or strictly material methods of healing:

    Era II – mind-body approaches which include the effect of one's own thought upon his/her own body;

    Era III – non-local or "Eternity Medicine" which includes the effect of one's own thoughts on another's physical condition. Presumably this would also include the effect of one's own thoughts on the condition or state of objects supposed to be external to one's thoughts. But beyond this – and what I have been trying to convey to the reader – is the so-called "Trans Era" methods of healing most successfully practiced by Christ Jesus (see *Christian Science Journal*, "The Rebirth of Medicine," June, 2000). [38] In this approach it is recognized that prayer brings thought into line with universal Mind and God's eternal law of love and harmony is seen as the eternal and present reality.

if the mind is considered to be localized within the body. The experience also suggests that reality is mental.

Nevertheless, the artificial tooth restoration involved neither a "happy coincidence" nor a "mind-body" experience. It should be clear that mind is non-local. In this experience the human concept aligned itself more with the divine idea, and the mechanism, or mental processes of the human mind *gave place* to the divine Mind. [39] It was not mind, but *Mind* that brought to human consciousness a small glimpse of what the *Bible* calls the "*Kingdom of God*" or *the* "*Kingdom of Heaven,*" which is not located at some far-off place or future time, but exists *now*. Here man exists as wholly spiritual and perfect.

CHAPTER 10

A NEW PARADIGM

"We know mind plays a big role in our own lives. It's likely, in fact,
that mind has a big role in the way the whole universe functions.
If you like you call it God. It all makes sense."
Freeman Dyson
Physicist and 2000 winner of the *Templeton Prize for Progress in Religion* [1]

Humanity is ready to take another quantum jump or paradigm shift. The paradigm shift that is occurring in this age is the gradual acceptance that increased knowledge of the structure of matter and the functioning of physical laws will not bring us closer to understanding reality. The day will come, I believe, when reality will be seen as wholly spiritual, that matter will be seen as northing more than an illusion, and that our *spiritual senses* - our innate capacity to understand and perceive - will reveal that beyond the evidence of the physical senses, lays a reality of Spirit, Mind.

It has been thought by some that quantum uncertainty is caused by unknown, random influences which contribute to the dance of individual particles when we attempt to measure or observe them but no one has ever discovered any ". . .motive power to cause the zig -zagging." [2] We observe the effects of physical forces - beneath which at the subatomic level lie the laws of quantum mechanics - in the chaotic action of earthquakes, floods, tornadoes - even in star eruptions called *supernovae* that might pose a hazard to human life. These phenomena, as perceived and interpreted by finite, ignorant senses, cannot be the result of universal Mind, for it would be the destruction of Mind's own creation. Might these phenomena in some way be the signs of the activity of the *collective beliefs* of many minds, that when viewed at the quantum level, cause quantum randomness or "zig-zagging." The universe as seen through the spiritual senses manifests harmony, but collective human belief misinterprets nature; and thereby witnesses a mixture of harmony, destruction and discord.

It is difficult to understand how some physicists and biologists find it hard to accept the possibility of a universal Mind as First Cause, but rather accept that the laws of the universe are formed spontaneously out of chaos, and that mind evolves from mindless matter. Part of this reasoning must be due to the resistance of the human mind to any new idea that threatens and challenges its conventional view of the world.

What I recognize as an emerging paradigm is what has been called by Augros and Stanciu in *New Story of Science*, as the "*new story*" - a view that there is more to reality than materialism. But in fact, as we pursue the issue more deeply we will discover that *Spirit and spiritual things or ideas are all that really matter.* A spiritual idealism, if you will, but an idealism that is far different than that conceived by George Berkeley (1685-1753), an Anglo-Irish Anglican bishop who believed that with the exception of spiritual things, material things existed to the degree they were perceived by the senses. [3] * The *New Encyclopedia Britannica* reports in a treatise he published in 1710 that "he brought all objects of sense, including tangibles, within the mind; he rejected material substance, material causes, and abstract general ideas; he affirmed spiritual substance. . . ". [5] Yet he still believed in the mixing of matter theories with spiritual theories when he espoused the medicinal values or healing properties of tar-water [!]; and stated that we undergo, "a gradual evolution of ascent. . . from the world of sense to. . . the mind, her acts and faculties, and thence, to the supernatural and God, the three in one." [6]

---

* In the spiritual, idealistic viewpoint of reality as presented in this book, the material universe is seen as a misinterpretation, a dream of collective minds, an unreality. But this is not to imply, as some would conclude, that we live in a mad world created by the senses. What it does imply, is that the present sense of reality as perceived by the mind/senses is severely limited - a mixture of beauty, order, disease, chaos, and death. Eddy said of the universe of the senses, "I love your promise; and shall know, some time, the spiritual reality and substance of form, light, and color, of what I now through you discern dimly; and knowing this, I shall be satisfied." [4]

CHAPTER 11

FINAL THOUGHTS

"The compounded minerals or aggregated substances composing the earth, the relations which constituent masses hold to each other, the magnitudes, distances, and revolutions of the celestial bodies, are of no real importance, when we remember that they all must give place to the spiritual fact by the translation of man and the universe back into Spirit. In proportion as this is done, man and the universe will be found harmonious and eternal."
Mary Baker Eddy
Science and Health, with Key to the Scriptures

THE PHYSICAL UNIVERSE OF MATTER PARTICLES VS THE SPIRITUAL UNIVERSE OF IDEAS

The reader should now think back to the discussions of probability in Part I, Chapter 10. In the tossing of a die, "topside 3" (the face with three dots is face-up) existed as only a potential along with five other potentials (topside 1, topside 2, etc), until the die was tossed and one side appeared. We may want to speculate that the *state* of *topside face* existed as a superposition of six different configurations until the tossing of the die and a subsequent observation (collapse of a wave function?) has been made. The average probability for topside 3 to appear is one sixth, but we have no way of predicting on any given toss when topside 3 will appear. Topside 3 could appear for six consecutive tosses, or not appear for ten consecutive tosses. So it is with the state of submicroscopic particles in quantum experiments.

But experiments by Jahn and others have indicated that the will or intent of the experimenter (the conscious observer) can modify previously random-occurring events, not only at the sub-microscopic level, but also at the macroscopic level. (see Part II, Chapter 3.) That is, if the experiment was properly set up and precisely controlled, in theory, the experimenter could "will" the occurrence of heads more often than tails, or topside 3 more often than one time out of six.

Goswami implies that a material object exists in the transcendent domain of human consciousness - as a coherent superposition of multifaceted quantum waves that describe potentials or possibilities until an observation or measurement is made, at which time the wave function collapses to a single facet or *eigenstate* (see Part II, Chapter 1). We bring a specific state of the object into our experience by "choosing and recognizing the result of choice." This observation is – *at the grass roots – entirely mental*, and is performed continuously by non-local, universal and collective consciousness, which possess the attributes of *awareness*. The result of this mental observation is dependent on what the majority of minds currently believe is the accepted physical paradigm describing reality.

The method of choosing and recognizing the results of choice is as follows: As Wheeler implied, we do more than simply observe the laws of nature; there is also a sense in which we create or choose them. What we interpret as reality – at least at the quantum level – depends on our choice of the measurement device as well as our choice of the questions asked. But as Ilya Prigogone (a *Nobel Prize* winner for his work on the thermodynamics of non-equilibrium systems) and Isabelle Stengers say in their book, *Order Out of Chaos*, the result of a measurement "does not give us access to given reality." We must, they say, drop the classical notion of objective reality because an "objective description" is the "complete description *of the system as it is*, independent of the choice of how it is observed... The reality studied by physics is ... a mental construct."[1]

The current perception of laws is founded on the basic premise that the physical world as seen through the senses is all there is to reality. But through our universal collective expectations, our matter-based thinking, we arrive painstakingly at certain conclusions about what we call physical reality.

Even so, the manipulation of matter, of things that appear in the mental universe, should not be our major goal, because even this objective has its limits. Why? Because we are doing no more than working within the *dream or myth* that matter and the material universe constitute reality. These dreams or misperceptions of finite, collective minds are but shadows of the true, spiritual, and unchanging universe of Mind.

ADDITIONAL EXPLANATIONS FOR HEALING EXPERIENCES

Now, dear reader, pause with me for a moment to consider the following: What do you think actually happened in some of the remarkable experiences related in Part II of this book? Possible answers could be:

- The broken wrist and the severely shattered nose were mended completely by some unknown accelerated mechanism in the minutes between the taking of the first X-ray and the second X-ray. The eyes were cleared of cataracts by the release of some dissolving chemical in the space of two hours. The cavity in the lungs was somehow filled with new molecules overnight. A change in the state of human consciousness generated a sense of optimism and hope, which reduced fear, anxiety and depression, which are believed to produce toxic chemicals that adversely affect the body's immune and cardiovascular systems. A sense of well-being affected the immune system and aided the mind / body's capacity for self-healing, and for restoring a healthy equilibrium to the physical body

OR

- The evidence of the physical senses was seen to be unreliable. The evidence depends on the state of thought. What is seen and recorded depends on whether thought is filled with its own beliefs (or collective beliefs) of fear, materiality, limitation, or whether it is in communion with Mind.

Most religious faiths around the world, if they truly believe in the healings and remarkable experiences as recorded in the *Bible* or other religious works, and of healings that have occurred in the present age, believe that *somehow* physical processes occur in the body until it is once again made whole. Somehow, Jesus miraculously caused the tissues and muscles of Lazarus' body to be restored and the brain to be reactivated after decay had set in (Lazarus had lain in the grave four days before Jesus arrived on the scene). In other words, Christ Jesus caused a dead man to live again.

Rather, I am in agreement with Eddy that *Lazarus had never died in the first place* ("...that I may awake him out of sleep"). [2] Because as illustrated by the kangaroo / water pail computer, there really is no consciousness or life in material structures. Consciousness cannot be extinguished with the destruction of the body. Life is a synonym for God, as surely as is Mind and Spirit; and our conscious unity with Life can never be severed.

Experiences like the *pilot in the jungle* look for all the world like pure chance; that is, the pilot and plane were at the right place at the right time and in precise orientation with respect to the runway to affect a safe landing. The sensible mind rebels at the thought that a new perception of reality was experienced. But an instantaneous healing of a cancer, for example, openly challenges our sense of credulity; for it is apparent that the laws of physics as we know them have been violated.

Although it is true, to a great degree, that in the present paradigm of physics based on quantum mechanics, the *observer and the observed are inseparable: mind and the universe* - we must look beyond physical observation or sense testimony if we are to discover reality.

In examining experiences, such as, the *pilot in the jungle, the water in the desert*, and others, the following statements have special significance:

♦ "While we look not at the things which are seen, but at the things which are not seen: for the things which are seen are temporal; but the things which are not seen are eternal." [3]
♦ We must look deep into realism instead of accepting only the outward sense of things...The spiritual reality is the scientific fact in all things." [4]

QUANTUM THEORY AND REALITY

"How come the Quantum?"[5]

John Archibald Wheeler

It is my opinion that quantum physical phenomena are not the bedrock of reality. The vibratory nature of the wave function is purported to carry all the information about matter objects, but it is Mind outside of a materiality that is the source of all true knowledge. John Wheeler, in asking what central concept undergirds quantum actions, believed that when we discover this central concept we will say, "Oh how simple, how beautiful! How could it have been otherwise? How could we have been so stupid so long"? [6]

No one has satisfactorily explained how a macroscopic, inanimate mechanical recording device can interact with a quantum particle - which is characterized by a wave function representing a superposition of state possibilities - and cause only one possibility to become physically real. On the other hand, if reality is *mental,* and things in the mental universe are first represented as *ideas,* then when these ideas become entertained in consciousness (collective, unitive) they become manifested in our human experience as physical objects. It is not that this collective consciousness creates you and me - far from it! We exist as ideas in the realm of Mind. What collective consciousness does is create the belief that we are structured in matter in certain limited ways, and that we manifest a finite, temporal existence in accordance with certain physical laws.

The "origin" of the physical universe - in what has been called the *Big Bang*, the evolution of the physical universe, including electrons, galaxies and human beings – that is, *the way simple and complex ideas are perceived* - is the result of finite and limited, non-local and collective, unitive consciousness.

I suspect that if a different view of reality had been conceptualized, a different set of physical laws might have been formulated based on a different mathematical model - perhaps a model that did not involve statistical results arising from the collapse of some kind of *Schrodinger Wave* equation.* However, probability would almost certainly play a part in any formulation of physical law and the phenomena resulting from these laws, because mortal thought, by its very nature, is uncertain, not being based on Truth (God). The subject of why the universe appears and acts the way it does is examined in greater detail in Part II, APPENDIX C, which can be found after Part II, Chapter 12.

Recall Wheeler's comment - along with his illustration of the role of the observer in the framing of reality (game of *Twenty Questions*) - that there is a sense in which we create the laws of physics. Sir Arthur Eddington, the famous British astronomer and physicist, made a comment [7] about the nature of reality and the nature of discovery: "I am not much impressed by the neutrino theory [a fundamental subatomic particle that was predicted would eventually be discovered]. I do not believe in neutrinos... dare I say that experimental physicists will not have sufficient ingenuity to *make* neutrinos?" [8] We might believe that what Eddington was saying was 'tongue in cheek", but Dr. John Gribbon, a *Cambridge* astrophysicist, thinks Eddington's comments should possibly be taken at face value. As mentioned previously in this book, Gribbon questions if it is possible "that the nucleus, the positron, and the neutrino did not exist until experimenters discovered the right sort of chisel with which to reveal their form?" [9]

Would these above comments imply that in a different part of the universe there might be different kinds of particles and different kinds of laws according to how collective, unitive thought in that region of space conceived of reality? That is a difficult question to answer. Astrophysicists and astronomers base their theories and observations of the universe by assuming that the physical laws in the local universe apply throughout the entire universe. Without this assumption it would be difficult to define models of the early universe and to predict future events including the evolution of stars and galaxies. If consciousness is *unitive*, collective; that is, *non-local*, then it is probable that if intelligent beings exist in distant galaxies, they would necessarily be governed generally - if not specifically - by the same laws of physics.

---

* Some physics ascribe to the so-called *Weak Anthropic Principle* which states that the universe is the way it is - with the given values of physical constants - because it is the only one out of a near-infinite number of created universes where life could evolve and be sustained, and where consciousness could observe.

CONSCIOUSNESS IS PRIMARY

"The freeing of the mind from its organic shackles will be the most spectacular leap in the evolution of consciousness as a whole."
David Darling, "Equations of Eternity" * [10]

Figure (11-1) is a capsule summary of what I believe the experiments in quantum theory and in consciousness (including the experiences with spiritual healing) are telling us about reality. Throughout this book I have attempted to cite experiences and experiments in the following areas listed below, which point - to a greater or lesser degree - to the primacy of consciousness, and the illusion of matter:

(1) - Quantum theory experiments including:
   (a) - *Delayed-Choice Double-Slit* experiments
   (b) - *Non-interference, Delayed-Choice* experiments
   (c) - *EPR* experiments
(2) - *Squid*-type experiments
(3) - The work of various groups in the area of parapsychology.
(4) - Examples of "meaningful coincidences"
(5) - The mind-body experiences and the effect on living organizations
(6) - Spiritual prayer

---

* David Darling, the author of more than forty books, has a degree in Physics from *Sheffield University* and a Ph.D. in Astronomy from the *University of Manchester*.

Double-Slit	Delayed-Choice Double-Slit	Non-interference Delayed Choice Double-Slit	EPR
dynamical properties of matter exist as potential, only	"history" of sub-atomic matter dynamical properties determined by experiment/conscious observer	potential observer knowledge sufficient to collapse wave function	universe is non-local, non-objective, and does not exist independent of consciousness
Wheeler	Goswami	Wolf	Wigner
observer is any macroscopic recording device. Later... wave function collapsed by "meaningful" collective conscious observers.	consciousness is primary	consciousness and matter are interconnected. Quantum events split into parallel universes with "you" in each universe	Final observer is consciousness. consciousness cannot be included in quantum wave function
SQUID	PEAR	**Spindrift**	Metaphysics
non-locality at macroscopic level	mind controlling matter, independent of space/time	mind controlling matter, independent of space/time	Mind/Mind's ideas are reality. Collective consciousness fabricates finite sense of reality based on belief of matter/space/time as reality. Hints of permanent spiritual reality are seen as consciousness yields to Mind.

Figure (11-1)

Interpretations of Reality Drawn from Experimental Results and Individual Life Experiences
(The Double-slit experiments, EPR experiments and SQUID experiments all involve
The concept of quantum entanglement.) ⌀

All but the last one in the above Figure (Metaphysics, spiritual prayer) are in some way the result of unitive, collective *human* consciousness, which begins with the paradigm that the foundation of reality is matter-based and structured in physical law (for what could be more obvious than the evidence of the senses?) This paradigm includes the belief that life, substance and intelligence derive from increasingly complex forms of matter.

It is only by the denial of the absolute validity of the senses, and the yielding of consciousness to the universal and infinite Mind in what is called *spiritual prayer,* that this mental reality of Spirit will begin to be seen and appreciated. And then we begin to

---

⌀ Quantum entanglement: *For example in EPR* - the result of the creation of a two-photon pair due to the stationary atomic reaction. The created photon pair is called a singlet state. As long as the particles are unobserved, they remain entangled no matter how far they are separated; and their properties remain indefinite and are a *superposition of all possible states*. As soon as one particle is measured and put into a definite state the other particle is instantaneously put into a definite state.

discover that we *can* think and comprehend with something besides the human brain. And in proportion as this is done on a daily, hourly basis by mankind, laws of matter or manipulations of collective mortal minds will influence us less and less. We will begin to discover that we really are *individual* spiritual ideas of Mind.

PERSISTENCE AND COURAGE REQUIRED

Spiritual prayer, which begins with a humble listening and yielding to the Creator of all, ("I can of mine own self do nothing, Christ Jesus [11]) will reveal new, innovative and fresh ideas about ourselves and about the world in which we live.

That this yielding to the Infinite sometimes takes great effort, and often great courage and persistence, there is no denying. That failures sometime occur, or the results we earnestly hope for are sometimes delayed, there is also no denying.

All sickness is caused by the broad definition of sin as given in the Introduction of Part II; that is, the erroneous belief that life, substance and intelligence exist in matter separate from God. But some disease is linked with the more obvious types of sin such as greed, hatred, dishonesty, murder.

A sick person is not loved less by God than a healthy person, but it is now being acknowledged that a person who commits evil acts can voluntarily shut himself from acknowledging and feeling the presence of Love. And in this way he experiences suffering, and also is required to come under the human laws of punishment. Even so, no one "deserves" to be sick or to suffer, but the patient needs to be awakened to his true, spiritual and sinless nature. Then healing will occur.

As surely as the laws governing electricity were in existence in the period when people were using candles and kerosene oil, just as surely were the scientific laws of Mind available to heal and save multitudes before the time of Christ Jesus. What was missing was a conscious awareness and a measure of understanding of the true nature of God. *

But in the sight of God there are no failures, and no one is unworthy. God never condemns spiritual man. There is no need or justification for horrible guilt feelings if we believe that prayer has failed to heal ourselves or someone else. Divine Love, God, rejoices in each one of His children, and maintains the perfection of His creation eternally. In referring to what is required of us, Christ Jesus said, "If a man keep my saying he shall never see death." [13] And, "Ye shall know the truth, and the truth shall make you free."[14] If spiritual healing is legitimate, it must be based upon a science. When a doctor fails to heal a patient, he usually does not consider himself at fault (lawsuits not withstanding!), but he acknowledges that he and the entire medical

---

* We do not always know why in some instances obviously sincere prayer fails to bring about a desired healing, but Eddy gives us a clue: "If we pray to God as a corporeal person, this will prevent us from relinquishing the human doubts and fears which attend such a belief, and so we cannot grasp the wonders wrought by infinite, incorporeal Love, to whom all things are possible." [12] Another reason as to why prayer may fail, is that we may be unconsciously accepting the world belief that we have been born into sin (The direct opposite of Genesis, chapter 1), and are guilty because we are miserable sinners, and unworthy to be saved.)

profession need to learn more about the science governing physical healing. The *Bible* gives us recipes for life, and they are detailed in the *Ten Commandments*, the *Beatitudes*, and the *Lord's Prayer*. That is, we must "know the truth" about God and man, and then practice that truth in daily living. Truth (God) alone does the healing and not the human mind. Spiritual living ("Blessed are the pure in heart, for they shall see God.") [15] is our ticket to spiritual healing.

We tend, though, to cling to comfortable, familiar ways of thinking, and believe what the senses claim for the reality and substantiality of discord, chaos, evil. Eddy, at one time, commented that the present stage of progress in her church's practice of spiritual healing and living presented, "two opposite aspects, - a full-orbed promise, and a gaunt want." [16] She went on to say that the need of the times (and the need of today as well) was, "not of the letter, but the spirit." Implying that the science (the *letter*) underlying the healing efforts was fairly well understood, but its practice (the *spirit*) required more love and humility on the part of the healer. Spirit-based thoughts - love, compassion, trust, purity, honesty, wisdom, etc., - are ideas of Mind. But the laws behind spiritual healing, she said, must be accepted at this time by induction: the whole is admitted because a part has been proved; and that part points toward, or shows forth the entire Principle. Genuine Truth comes to man in this age - not accompanied with bells, trumpets and whistles, not generally with the moving of mountains - but as a "still small voice" that transforms consciousness and lifts it up to God. [17]

When mankind begins to appreciate its unity and oneness or inseparability with the First Cause, Mind, then it will remember that every good spiritual idea or thought is reality - and has the power of infinite, omnipotent Mind behind it. Individually, we will see *ourselves* as compound ideas or images of Mind - having no minds of our own, but reflecting Mind in an infinity of ways. We will come to see that Reality excludes the belief of sin and death, and is completely orderly and harmonious - the effect of Love or Mind. When will this recognition come? We have barely scratched the surface of this new and profound science of Mind, which promises to shatter the myth of materiality, but the healing experiences of this age are the signposts that point to Heaven.

** Babe, and New Ideas

In the Hollywood film, *Babe* [18], the narrator speaks about some of the impossible ideas that farmer Hoggit has about his pet pig, *Babe* and his ability to accomplish amazing feats: "Farmer Hoggit knew that little ideas that tickled and nagged and refused to go away, should never be ignored." For in them lie the seeds of destiny." A story comes to mind about several students at an agricultural college. The story metaphorically illustrates the power of new ideas. The students had drilled a hole in a steel ball and had then placed some seeds inside the hole. After providing some nutriments and water they sealed the hole with a steel plug, making certain the seal was tight by placing the plugged ball in a vise and exerting pressure. They left the ball in a safe place, and upon returning some time later, they discovered the germinating seeds had shattered the ball! * Such is

---

* Although I cannot vouch for the complete authenticity of this story, I do know that asparagus seeded in a garden that had later been covered with a layer of blacktop, had been able to germinate and penetrate the surface!

the power of new ideas (seeds) that are entertained and pondered (germinated) in consciousness. They work against the straight-jacket of materialism (the walls of the steel ball) and shatter its long-held myths.

SUMMARY

And now, patient reader, we come to the end of this story. Throughout this book I have endeavored to present evidence for the non-materiality (spiritual nature) of the universe, the primacy of consciousness, and the absolute allness of infinite Mind or God. Beyond physical theories of the universe lies the first and only cause: infinite and eternal Mind. In this mental and spiritual universe, man is seen to be the image of the universal Mind, and he forever remains in this eternal unity or oneness with God. Because of this relationship with Mind, there is absolutely no need for the evolution of complex material structures (brain and *ANN*s) in order for intelligence and awareness to exist.

We cannot establish without some uncertainty God's existence and the presence of spiritual law through human reason and logic alone, or even by present-day examples of what has been called spiritual healing. But the mighty works of Christ Jesus, his dominion over matter and space-time, point strongly to the existence of something greater than the human Jesus. In meekness he acknowledged an absolute power beyond physical power and beyond himself ("I can of mine own self do nothing"). [19] [V] By the acknowledgment of this great truth, Jesus actually showed forth power and dominion. He recognized his absolute inseparability or oneness with Mind ("I and my Father are one") [20], and in so doing brought to the world a new view of reality - of order and harmony. He gave us by word and example the means to realize this *Kingdom of Heaven on Earth.* He clearly showed that harmony is the law of God who is Love, and that as we feel this love, to that degree we are experiencing reality.

Eddy continued to promulgate in this age the concept of a universal law of Love. In stark contrast to the ideas of conventional physics, and in diametrical opposition to the concept of a cold and uncaring universe consisting only of matter and cruel or indifferent forces, she made the following declaration: "Beauty is a thing of life which dwells forever in the eternal Mind and reflects the charms of His goodness in expression, form, outline, and color. It is Love which paints the petal with myriad hues, glances in the warm sunbeam, arches the cloud with the bow of beauty, blazons the night with starry gems, and covers earth with loveliness." [21]

Can we see, then, that all must eventually come to discover that Love, Mind, has to be *the* Law? And can we also see that formulations of physical laws described as Newtonian, Relativity, Quantum, and Chaos (recently) - although immensely useful in this present age - must eventually give way to reveal the Law of Love on *all* fronts? They *must*, because the Law of Love is the only law that does not lead to uncertainty and

---

[V] Many proponents of "mind-body" philosophy believe that our awakening to the role of the human mind in the interpretation and defining of the material universe is the final answer to what governs reality. But to declare that all true reality is the product of mind, or collective ignorant, fearful minds, leaves out the Creator or Principle of All: Mind. If reality is left in the hands of minds, which mind will be in control, yours, or mine?

chaos. Paul certainly had it right when he proclaimed, "Love is the fulfilling of the law."[22]

At this period of history, we catch only a hint of what will surely be revealed about reality and we are reminded of what the poet R. Browning said, "On the earth the broken arcs; in the heaven, a perfect round." [23] Breaking free of the self-imposed material bonds characterized by our present paradigms of reality, we ascend in thought out of ignorance, and begin to discern more clearly what has always been - the ***universal realm of Mind and Love: the realm of Spirit.*** The place of Mind may yet be seen as the over-arching Principle of reality, and we may yet echo the words of I Corinthians, "At present we are men looking at puzzling reflections in a mirror. The time will come when we shall see reality whole and face to face!" [24]

SELECTED KEY POINTS[∝]

The comments and quotations cited below (some of which have not been quoted in the book), have been selected to summarize what I believe are the important conclusions that can be reached after reading the book.

Physics

(1) - Experiments performed over the last decade or so have convinced some physicists that "...nature cannot be described by any objective local theory"(Tony Leggett, *Physics World*, December, 1999).

(2) - "The experimental tests of Bell's inequalities...go so far as to change the very way we should think of physical existence at its most fundamental level" (*The Quantum Challenge*, p.144).

Physics and Consciousness

(1) – Amit Goswami implies that although the cat (The *Schrodinger Cat*) exists in the transcendent domain of human consciousness, it is not that we mentally exercise some physical force or will to shut the valve on the bottle of poisonous gas, or bring the cat back to life after the gas had been released. He says we bring either the dead cat or the live cat into our experience by "choosing and recognizing the result of choice"; and the results of this choosing are manifested in what we perceive. And it is *collective* consciousness that does this - a collective consciousness that possessed the attributes of *awareness* (Amit Goswami, *"*The Idealistic Interpretation of Quantum Mechanics", *Physics Essays*).

(2)– Edward R. Close has said that what we perceive as reality is built up by, "the conscious thoughts and beliefs of all sentient beings and is constantly confirmed and maintained by the feedback of continuing observation." Past and present reality therefore change as collective (or consensus) beliefs of participating observers change. But beyond

---

[∝] From SELECTED KEY POINTS through ADDITIONAL REVOLUTIONARY IDEAS the references for various comments in the text are given along side the text, and are not additionally included in the Bibliography.

consensus belief (what Close calls "secondary consciousness"), exists what he calls "primary consciousness"(God). "The nonlocal and nonobjective aspects of reality anticipated by Bell's theorem and verified by the Aspect experiment are indicators of the involvement of consciousness" (Edward R. Close, *Transcendental Physics*.)

(3) - Because matter has no consciousness it cannot manifest any kind of activity on its own, and Spirit, Mind, never created an opposite of itself. The laws of physics appear the way they do because of the way mankind has first perceived and formulated – with the aid of the evidence of the five senses - ideas about reality. Uncertainty has always been a part of the human sense of things. Probability would almost certainly play a part in any formulation of physical law and the phenomena resulting from these laws, because mortal thought, by its very nature, is uncertain, not being based on Truth (God). Since the manifestation of physical reality is a function of illusive, collective consciousness, it would follow that at the very fundamental level of things the physical quantities of sub atomic particles would be indeterminate or illusory, a subjective state of material consciousness. Because we believe in *dualism*, such as the presence of good *and* evil; in *chance,* such as the possibility of the occurrence of various types of evil and disasters; and *inertia,* such as resistance to change for the better; *is there any wonder that the laws governing ponderous matter - and which appear to govern our lives - are based on uncertainty, chance, and that they can cause disease, chaos, lack and death?*

(4) - Correlated quantum statistical results have arisen long *after* past collective consciousness has "agreed" as to how quantum mechanical statistical laws - laws that currently form the foundation of the physical paradigm describing reality - should be constructed or formulated. Amir Aczel, has commented in his book, *Entanglement*, that
"It is amazing that one of the properties of quantum systems [entanglement], and its associated weirdness would *first* be found mathematically, and this strengthens our belief in the "transcendent power of mathematics." He says that *after* this discovery many physicists used "clever and ingenious" methods to verify that entanglement actually occurs. (emphasis added). Many discoveries in the physical and astronomical worlds have been made by two or more individuals working independently of each another. (emphasis added).

(5) - According to the *Copenhagen Interpretation* of quantum mechanics, quantum particles "are not localized objects separate from the apparatus used to detect them." The particles are not separate from the detector, or from any subsequent macroscopic detectors, only their observable effects are. The quantum wave function, described by the *Schrodinger Wave* equation *now* describes both particle *and* inanimate detector. And this system gives us no knowledge or information about any object in the universe, unless consciousness observes. The implication is enormous: *no event occurs* (i.e., *has any meaning*) *without the involvement of consciousness.* The receptor that ends the chain of measurement is non-quantum, non-material, non-local consciousness, which is separate from any physical detector, and avoids the contradiction of infinite regression (Edward R. Close, *Transcendental Physics*).

(6) - Light is incident on a material object, and is reflected onto the eye's retina. That is, an inanimate matter-particle (a photon) becomes a messenger to convey information or data about the matter-house to the matter-eye. Then electrical pulses (matter-electrons) become messenger particles that travel up the matter-optic nerve to convey information about the image formed on the retina of the matter-eye to the matter-

brain. But the brain, being made of matter like the eye, cannot see matter. This chain of "information transfer" must break down at this point, because it is here that the unconscious matter-brain must somehow convey information to non-quantum, non-material mind. But this would appear to be *impossible*, because there is no physical force that causes the transfer of information from matter (physical) to mind (mental). It would be possible for matter to transfer information or knowledge to mind only if matter and mind are one and the same. That is, *unless matter and mind are different **mental states** of human consciousness, not states of matter described by a wave function.* "An image of mortal thought reflected on the retina is all that the eye beholds" (Mary Baker Eddy, *Science and Health with Key to the Scriptures*, p. 479). Therefore the measurement chain in matter ends with mind, and the eye/mind loop is a creation of this mind or of collective consciousness.

(7) - A slightly different perspective from Paragraph (5) above is given here by Edward R. Close: "The *Copenhagen Interpretation* of quantum theory says that sub-atomic particles, including photons have no localized existence until measured by some kind of measuring device, receptor or observer. We may believe that the *final* receptor or observer of these particles is a physical structure, (a brain), itself made of elementary particles, and which must therefore absorb the energy of the incoming particles in discrete units of energy called quanta. We may assert that the observed image – and consciousness itself – are also made of matter and quantized energy. Therefore, the elementary particles that comprise consciousness must have no local form until they are recorded or registered by a prior receptor, and that prior receptor, being made of matter, must have also had a prior receptor, and that prior receptor must have had a prior receptor, and so on and so on." Close comments that the quest for the final receptor becomes an infinite regression in space and time, which in itself is finite. This logical contradiction leads one to conclude that "consciousness is something beyond matter and energy" (Edward R. Close; "Can Matter be Explained in Terms of Consciousness?" in *Science Within Consciousness*).

(8) – "The physical universe expresses the conscious and unconscious thoughts of mortals. Physical force and mortal mind are one" (Mary Baker Eddy, *Science and Health with Key to the Scriptures*, p. 484).

(9) – "What you see, hear, feel, is a mode of consciousness; and can have no other reality than the sense you entertain of it" (Mary Baker Eddy, *Unity of Good*, p. 8).

(10) – "There is a definite relation between our human consciousness and what we physically sense as experience. Prayer does not change reality…it reveals it. Divine truth frees you from limitation" (Jack Hubbell/CSB, "Divine Truth Frees You From Limitation").

(11) - John Wheeler believes that "Observership" is the "ultimate underpinning of the laws of physics. We do not simply observe the laws of nature, there is also a sense in which we create them." Wheeler has said, "Do we do not better to recognize that what we call existence consists of countably many iron posts of observation between which we fill in by an elaborate papier-mâché construction of imagination and theory?" (John Archibald Wheeler, "Genesis and Observership", in *Foundational Problems in Theoretical Physics*).

(12) - Wheeler asks, rhetorically, if the galaxies in the early universe were as real *then* without *meaningful* observations as they are *now*. The physical universe and the laws that we observe may in some way be brought about through the collective "agreement" of many minds (John Archibald Wheeler, "Bits, Quanta, Meaning", in *Problems in Theoretical Physics*).

(13) - Fred Alan Wolf, in his book, *Taking the Quantum Leap*, says the following about what Eugene Wigner, a Nobel prize winner in physics, believes about reality: "[Wigner]...believes that our consciousness alters the world itself because it alters how we appraise the future. That is, we experience the world the way we do because we choose to experience it that way."

(14) - Noted physicist, Henry Stapp, wrote a book entitled, *Mind, Matter and Quantum Mechanics.* The reviewer of his book commented that Stapp believes that the state of the entire universe can be represented by a wave function which is a compendium of all the wave functions that all of our minds individually can cause to collapse by observation. He says, "all that exists is …subjective knowledge, therefore the universe is not about matter, it is about subjective experience…Each knower's act of knowledge (each individual increment of knowledge) results in a new state of the [material] universe. One person's increment of knowledge changes the state of the entire [material] universe, and, of course, it changes it for everybody else" (my comments in brackets}.

(15) - Dr. David Darling, noted physicist, astronomer and author, has said, "We are on the verge of an explosion of mind…the freeing of the mind from its organic shackles will be the most spectacular leap in the evolution of consciousness as a whole" (*Christian Science Sentinel Radio Program*, "Today's Explorers in Physics and Metaphysics: What Are They Discovering?").

(16) - As most physicists agree, *a dynamic force does not accomplish the collapse of the wave function of a subatomic particle*. If a mental thought or intent can move molecules or an assemblage of molecules in the body, or even external to the body, (as demonstrated in the Jahn experiments), without the use of physical force, then how substantial or real are these molecules themselves? We should at least consider that since the wave function for particles is no more than a mathematical formulation of conscious mind, the particles themselves are no more than ideas in consciousness, externalized. Consciousness, then, is the primary reality.

(17) - Larry Dossey says in his book, *Space, Time, and Medicine,* "The interrelation of human consciousness and the observed world is . . . obvious in Bell's theorem. "; as he maintains that, ". . .conscious decision making . . . " has determined the outcome of the experiments (such as experiments related to *EPR*).

(18) - Jahn and Dunne make a startling statement in regard to the impact of consciousness in the physical world: ". . .attempts have been made to ascribe to consciousness an entropy-reducing capability that allows it to exert an ordering influence on otherwise random physical processes, thereby reversing their normal thermodynamic tendency toward minimum information and maximum chaos." They believe that some of their data agrees with the above statement. As related by Larry Dossey in his *"Space, Time and Medicine,"* "Jahn … has demonstrated that a subject watching an optical interference pattern on a Fabry-Perot interferometer can change the spacing of two parallel images."

(19) - In regard to experiments involving consciousness and its apparent influence on the growth of bacteria and other microorganisms: If genetic mutations can be influenced by conscious beings, then genes cannot be the absolute controllers of the human body. "Biology... is not destiny"(Dossey). Might not the structure of *DNA* be an *effect* rather than a *cause*?

Artificial Intelligence and Mind (Consciousness)

(1) - It is possible to distinguish between the "consciousness" of cellular automata and *ANN*s, and true consciousness, because these devices cannot bring about what are called spiritual healings through prayerful, conscious communion with God or Mind. Selmer Bringsjord, director of the *Minds and Machines Laboratory* and program at *Rensselaer Polytechnic Institute*, Troy, New York, says, "Future robots [and computers] may exhibit much of the behavior of persons, but none of the robots [computers] will ever be a person... If some of the claims for spiritual reality are true, it short-circuits the whole thing [that robots/computers can be conscious]."

(2) - If advanced *AI* devices cannot bias the distribution of a random series of ones and zeros, or affect the physical well being through conscious intent, or through "prayer," then we must conclude that these devices manifest no real consciousness.

(3) - As Roger Penrose comments in his book *The Emperor's New Mind*, "...ideas are things, that, as far as we know, need conscious minds for their manifestations." [58] Selmer Bringsjord, of the *Minds and Machines* Laboratory at *Rensselaer Polytechnic Institute*, Troy, New York, has said that he believes that the "inner life" of any advanced computer will *be* "as empty as a rock's."

Metaphysics and Spiritual Healing

(1) – "The elements and functions of the physical body and of the physical world will change as mortal mind changes its beliefs" (Mary Baker Eddy, *Science and Health with Key to the Scriptures*, p.124).

(2) – "The material atom is an outlined falsity of consciousness, which can gather additional evidence of consciousness and life only as it add lie to lie" (Mary Baker Eddy, *Unity of Good*, p.35).

(3) – "Spirit and its formations are the only realities of being. Matter disappears under the microscope of Spirit" (Mary Baker Eddy, *Science and Health with Key to the Scriptures*, p. 264).

(4) – "The visible universe and material man are the poor counterfeits of the invisible universe and spiritual man. Eternal things (verities) are God's thoughts as they exist in the spiritual realm of the real. Temporal things are the thoughts of mortals, and are unreal, being the opposite of the real or the spiritual and eternal" (Mary Baker Eddy, *Science and Health with Key to the Scriptures*, p. 337).

(5) –" Science shows that what is termed *matter* is but the subjective state of what is termed by the author *mortal mind* (Mary Baker Eddy, *Science and Health with Key to the Scriptures*, p.114).

(6) – "Every material belief hints the existence of spiritual reality; and if mortals are instructed in spiritual things, it will be seen that material belief, in all its

manifestations, reversed, will be found the type and representative of verities priceless, eternal, and just at hand" (Mary Baker Eddy, *Miscellaneous Writings*, p. 60).

(7) - Eddy says: "The fading forms of matter, the mortal body and material earth, are the fleeting concepts of the human mind. They have their day before the permanent facts and their perfection in Spirit appear. The crude creations of mortal thought must finally give place to the glorious forms which we sometimes behold in the camera of divine Mind, when the mental picture is spiritual and eternal. Mortals must look beyond fading, finite forms, if they would gain the true sense of things. Where shall the gaze rest but in the unsearchable realm of Mind? (*Science and Health with Key to the Scriptures*, pp. 263-264).

(8) - Extraordinary claims of healing demand a high level of proof. At this period, the art and science of spiritual healing is in its infancy. We hear of, read about, and even experience spiritual healings, but the most dramatic ones – those that clearly defy physical law – are not so frequent. But genuine spiritual healings challenge the claim that substance is matter; they hint of the actual existence of a spiritual universe. What new discovery could be more profound and exciting than this?

(9) - Spiritual healings - the result of communion with universal Mind - present strong visible evidence for the superiority of Mind over matter, space-time, and physical laws/forces. The examples of Christ Jesus and of those of today indicate a reality of Spirit, Mind, and the power and principle of Love. Spiritual healings trumpet to the world this great fact: the allness of God, Love, and the absolute nothingness of evil. But I have also indicated that great trials, tribulations, and failures will be a part of life's scenario until mankind drops its concept of a finite, mysterious and often capricious God, denies the senses as absolute interpreters of truth, and through the exercise of his spiritual capacity to think and reason, begins to understand more clearly the true nature of God and man.

(10) -Larry Dossey, M.D., former *Chief of Staff, Medical City Dallas Hospital*, and noted author of popular books exploring the relationship between physics, medicine, and prayer (such as *Space, Time and Medicine, New Science Library*, 1982), believes that prayer is a vital ingredient in any healing process. He has said: that the power of the mind exercised in the form of prayer, is so effectual that he can see a day "…when doctors who didn't recommend prayer for their very sick patients could be sued for malpractice…I think prayer is communion with the universe or the one mind."

(11) - Suppose you have an ugly and painful lump or growth on your hand. The lump represents discord and inharmony. We know from experience that spiritual prayer can make the lump disappear, sometimes almost instantaneously; [∅] as Mary Baker Eddy has said that matter is the subjective state of mortal consciousness. In this kind of healing the laws of physics appear to be violated. But the hand, although appearing to the limited physical senses as material, does not disappear through prayer (prayer: a change in the state of thought whereby a person comes into communion with universal Mind or God and yields to His will). What disappears, in the words of Ralph Wagers (A *Christian Science Practitioner and Teacher* of the mid-Twentieth Century, "…is that which would limit or restrict or pervert or distort or destroy [the hand]." The hand - *in the highest sense*

[∅] "almost instantaneously", showing that healing is not a process. (i.e., a process of restoring a damaged matter-body), but an awakening to spiritual reality. When Peter and John healed the lame man, he arose immediately, "walking, and leaping, and praising God." (See the Bible, Acts 3:8)

- it is a spiritual idea of "Primary Consciousness" (God). The hand manifests or reflects attributes of God such as: dexterity, usefulness, love and compassion (holding the hand of a loved one), creativity (painting, playing the piano), etc.

God and Reality

(1) - *Is your God too small?* Describing the First Cause or Principle of all existence or Reality as *Mind*, should be self-evident. What can be greater than omnipresent, omnipotent and eternal Mind? In the "beginning," Mind was first and only. There was no need in this mental universe for matter. Therefore, *at the very ground of being*, man - the idea of Mind - requires no material brain for comprehension or expression, despite much evidence to the contrary. This great fact is only dimly comprehended at this period.

(2) - Do the theories behind quantum physics prove or disprove the existence of God? I believe that they neither prove nor disprove the existence of a First Cause or God. What they do, however, is ***point the way*** - so to speak - to the recognition of the primacy of non-local consciousness, and the illusion of matter. Quantum theories are employed to predict the activity and state of matter. Physical theories cannot explain God who is Spirit. But the results of quantum theories and experiments lead us to give consideration to the claim that matter and physical force depend on mind for their manifestation, and that the ultimate and final observer of the physical universe is mind; that is, collective mind observing itself, seeing its own thoughts.

(3) - The physical universe as we know it was created by some kind of inflationary process, possibly as described by Andrei Linde. But Linde admits that explaining the initial conditions - where and when reality began – "still remains the most intractable problem of modern cosmology." Linde concludes by stating that if certain physical models of creation are correct, then physical laws by themselves cannot explain all the properties of the universe in which we appear to inhabit. He asks the question, that if we are to acquire a complete knowledge of our universe, should we not also investigate deeply, "our own nature, perhaps even including the nature of our consciousness?" He ends by saying that, this conclusion would be one of the most unexpected that might come out of the theory of inflationary cosmology (Andrei Linde, "The Self-reproducing Universe", *Scientific American,* Nov., 1994).

(4) - "We know mind plays a big role in our own lives. It's likely, in fact, that mind has a big role in the way the whole universe functions. If you like you call it God. It all makes sense" (Freeman Dyson Physicist and 2000 winner of the *Templeton Prize for Progress in Religion*)

(5) – "The compounded minerals or aggregated substances composing the earth, the relations which constituent masses hold to each other, the magnitudes, distances, and revolutions of the celestial bodies, are of no real importance, when we remember that they all must give place to the spiritual fact by the translation of man and the universe back into Spirit. In proportion as this is done, man and the universe will be found harmonious and eternal" (Mary Baker Eddy, *Science and Health, with Key to the Scriptures*, p. 209).

(6) – "It is well to know, dear reader, that our material, mortal history is but the record of dreams, and not of man's real existence, and the dream has no place in the Science of being" (Mary Baker Eddy, *Retrospection and Introspection*, p. 21).

(7) - The famous British astronomer, Sir Arthur Eddington, in an article entitled, "The Domain of Physical Science," (from *Essay in Science, Religion and Reality*), said, "Not only the laws of nature, but space and time and the material Universe itself, are constructions of the human mind." The most profound discovery may be the "…discovery and practical proof that substance is exclusively spiritual, not material."

ADDITIONAL REVOLUTIONARY IDEAS

Additional Revolutionary Thoughts and Ideas garnered since The Second Edition that in Some Way Relate to the Primacy of Consciousness

Many of the following comments and observations made in this section of the book strongly point to the primacy of consciousness over matter and space-time. But, as has been mentioned previously, the strongest evidence for consciousness, life and intelligence to exist independently of matter/space-time is the many 'instantaneous' healings that appear to defy physical law; and examples given here of the effects of human consciousness in the physical world$^\nabla$ - although highly significant – only point to the reality of universal Mind (divine Consciousness) and Spirit.

(1)"The laws of physics themselves may come about as a result of interactions between the universe and its participant-observer. We do not simply observe the laws of nature; there is also a sense in which we create them."
J.A.Wheeler, "Delayed-Choice Experiment and the Bohr – Einstein Dialog," paper presented at the *American Philosophical Society*, London, (June 5, 1980), preparation for publication assisted by the *University of Texas, Center for Theoretical Physics*, and by *National Science Foundation* Grant PHY78 – 26592.

(2) "I believe that consciousness and its contents are all that exists. Space-time, matter and fields never were the fundamental denizens of the universe but have always been, from their beginning, among the humbler contents of consciousness, dependent on it for their very being." Donald Hoffman, *Cognitive Scientist, UC, Irvine; Author,* "Visual Intelligence"

(3)"Although quantum theory is an abstruse and formidable field, its philosophical and theological implications reduce to one shattering effect: the overthrow of matter…For some 200 years… nearly all leading scientists shared these materialistic assumptions [that the foundation of nature is based on solid and impenetrable particles] based on sensory and deterministic logic…The contemporary intellectual, denying God, is in a trap, and he projects his entrapment onto the world in a kind of secular suicide. But the world is not entrapped; man is not finite; the human mind is not bound in material brain."
George Gilder; Founding Editor or *Forbes ASAP;* Fellow International Engineering Consortium; Recipient of White House Award for Entrepreneurial Excellence

---

$^\nabla$ The reality of Spirit does not include matter.

(4) "Willis Hannon, Roger Sperry, and others have speculated that Western society is on the verge of a 'second Copernican revolution,' in which the dominant attitudes will evolve into a belief in consciousness as the primary 'stuff of the universe.' In this context, consciousness, or mind, is defined as the primary force from which all matter and energy derive…For empiricists, the individual brain is the basis for consciousness. Under the new model, no such limit exists."
Charles Leighton "A Change of Heart", *American Journal of Nursing*, (October, 1998).

(5) The following is from the book, Irreducible Mind.
> Irreducible Mind (2007)
> Edward Kelly, Emily Kelly
> Research and Assistant Professors
> Department of Psychiatric Medicine
> University of Virginia

(a) "After studying phenomena such as I have covered [in *Irreducible Mind*], Myers was confident that 'thought and consciousness' would emerge as a fundamental aspect of the universe, and 'not, as the materialists hold them, a mere epiphenomenon, an accidental and transitory accompaniment of more permanent energies, a light that flashes out from the furnace door, but does none of the work.'"

(b) "Like many of the experiences [placebos, near death, hypnotism, meditation, ESP, quantum measurement] discussed in this book, such cases would suggest that in some conditions, consciousness may be enhanced, not destroyed, when constraints normally supplied by the brain are sufficiently loosened."

(c) Irreducible Mind has a bottom line: Either our current understanding of the material world is woefully incomplete because we still don't know how to explain *mental powers in purely physical terms, or else there is far more to reality than just* the material world."
(Quoted on back cover of book), Richard Shwedar
William Clark Reavis Distinguished Service Professor
Department of Comparative Human Development, University of Chicago

(6) "It is argued that the main reason why quantum theory is relevant to consciousness is that the theory cannot be completely defined without introducing some features of consciousness."
Euan Squires, University of Durham Dept. of Mathematics, Durham, UK.

(7) "We have been led to believe that our genes determine the character of our lives, yet new research surprisingly reveals that it is the character of our lives that controls our genes. Rather than being victims of our heredity, we are actually masters of our genome…The reality is this – we require no drugs for healing; true healing only calls for a change of consciousness."
Bruce Lipton, Ph.D, Cellular Biologist, An international authority in bridging science and spirit.

Lipton has also said that one should watch his thoughts, and that you can change your life as fast as you can change your beliefs; and you can do this instantaneously ... Love is the maximum nourishment for growth ... if you love you will see good things come to you ... if you fear, you see the results of your fear, and this becomes your reality ... "we are not in our bodies; we are in the environment ... Identity exists outside the body."

(8) "When the province of physical theory was extended to encompass microscopic phenomena through the creation of quantum mechanics, the concept of consciousness came to the fore again. It was not possible to formulate the laws of quantum mechanics in a fully consistent way without reference to the consciousness."
Eugene Wigner, Physics Nobel Laureate

(9) "The encounter of physics with consciousness has troubled physicists since the inception of the theory eight decades ago. Many, no doubt most, physicists dismiss the creation of reality by observation as having little significance beyond the limited domain of the physics of microscopic entities. Others argue that Nature is telling us something, and we should listen. Our own feelings accord with quantum theory Erwin Schrodinger's: 'The urge to find a way out of this impasse ought not to be dampened by the fear of incurring the wise rationalist's mockery'"
Bruce Rosenblum and Fred Kuttner, "Quantum Enigma," Dept. of Physics University of California at Santa Cruz

(10) Kelly, Kelly, Crabtree, et al, *Irreducible Mind—Toward a Psychology for the 21st Century*, have a chapter on hypnotism and the physiological effects which result from the power of suggestion; they also talk about voodoo or hex death, saying it is found not just in folk societies but also in Western cultures: "The belief that one is going to die may be generated, not by a witch doctor's curse, but by ... a doctor's pronouncement of a hopeless condition (Milton, 1973), or some other suggestion accepted by the patient." (p. 125; see also pp. 124-127.)
"The hypothesis that consciousness is the product of brain processes, or that mind is merely the subjective concomitant of neurological events, has been and remains the almost universal assumption in neuroscience and psychology. Investigations of certain extraordinary circumstances, however, reveal phenomena that call into question this assumption. (p. 367). By the year 2000 our discussions had advanced to the point where we believed we could demonstrate, empirically, that the materialistic consensus which undergirds practically all of current mainstream psychology, neuroscience, and philosophy of mind is fundamentally flawed. (p. xiii). In a nutshell, we are arguing for abandonment of the current materialistic synthesis, and for the restoration of causally efficacious conscious mental life to its proper place at the center of our science." (p. xiv)

(11). In response to Jack Geis' comments on his book, "Entangled Minds," Dean Radin said: "After giving a talk this past summer a woman handed me a copy of the book 'Science and Health.' I agree that there do seem to be some striking parallels between what Mary Baker Eddy (and many others) have written from religious and mystical perspectives, and what science is slowing catching up to. It is interesting to see how these

traditionally separate realms of knowledge are slowly converging (and not without much gnashing of teeth on both sides), and it makes me wonder what science and religion will look like a century from now."
Dean Radin, Ph.d in Educational Psychology; researcher and author in the field of parapsychology; Senior Scientist at the Institute of Noetic Sciences.

(12) (In response to Jack Geis comments on his writings, Amit Goswami said: "I agree with you. Quantum physics thinking is validating much of Christian Science including Christian Science ideas of healing..."
Amit Goswami, Ph.D; Quantum Physicist, *"The Self-Aware Universe,"* Member of the University of Oregon Institute for Theoretical Physics.

(13 From "Physics, Metaphysics and God", pp-: "It would appear that a *single photon* starting out from the quasar billions of years ago, and taking only one path past the galaxy, is now seen as taking *two* paths past the galaxy! What we have decided to do with our experimental setup in the *present* - insert the beam splitter at the last instant, or leave it out - has appeared to alter the past history of the photon. We have decided in the *present* whether a photon will take both paths as waves, or one path as a particle. 'By deciding which questions our quantum registering equipment shall put in the *present* we have an undeniable choice in what we have the right to say about the *past'* (John Archibald Wheeler). The conclusions, taken to extreme would seem to say that the existence of the universe, itself, from the *Big Bang* to now, is the 'cumulative consequence of billions upon billions of elementary acts of observer - participancy reaching back into the past...') (John Archibald Wheeler).

However, Wheeler has also said (a statement more readily accepted by physicists) that the photon has no definite path or location from quasar to Earth, but exists as a *potential* only - and described by its wave function - until it is registered in an apparatus on Earth.

John Archibald Wheeler, "Delayed-Choice Experiment and the Bohr–Einstein Dialog." Paper presented at the *American Philosophical Society*, London, June 5, 1980, (Preparation for publication assisted by the *University of Texas Center for Theoretical Physics,* and by *National Science Foundation* Grant PHY78 – 26592).
SUMMARY: Briefly, we can say that a material particle (photon) has no past until observation, or at least only a potential for existing until a measurement or measurements (<u>observations</u>) has been made."

(14) – "... if you can get someone's attention and you can convince them that Well-being is the order of the day--there is no illness that will not leave them in the moment that they finally get that. "--- Abraham Excerpted from the workshop in North Los Angeles, CA on Saturday, March 2nd, 2002.

(15) Most working scientists hold fast to the concept of 'realism'--a viewpoint according to which an external reality exists independent of observation. But quantum physics has shattered some of our cornerstone beliefs. According to Bell's theorem, any theory that is based on the joint assumption of realism and locality (meaning that local events cannot be affected by actions in space-like separated regions) is at variance with certain quantum

predictions. Experiments with entangled pairs of particles have amply confirmed these quantum predictions, thus rendering local realistic theories untenable. Maintaining realism as a fundamental concept would therefore necessitate the introduction of 'spooky' actions that defy locality. Here we show by both theory and experiment that a broad and rather reasonable class of such non-local realistic theories is incompatible with experimentally observable quantum correlations. In the experiment, we measure previously untested correlations between two entangled photons, and show that these correlations violate an inequality proposed by Leggett for non-local realistic theories. <u>Our result suggests that giving up the concept of locality is not sufficient to be consistent with quantum experiments, unless certain intuitive features of realism are abandoned.</u>

An experimental test of non-local realism. Nature, 2—7: <u>Gröblacher S</u>, <u>Paterek T</u>, <u>Kaltenbaek R</u>, <u>Brukner C</u>, <u>Zukowski M</u>, <u>Aspelmeyer M</u>, <u>Zeilinger A</u>. Faculty of Physics, University of Vienna, Boltzmanngasse 5, A-1090 Vienna, Austria.

APPENDIX A

WORD DEFINITIONS

A few definitions of key words are given below in order for me to convey ideas based on a metaphysical or spiritual perspective. In addition, I make, in some cases, additional comments about the usage of the word.

WORD
Chaos
Evil
Healing (Faith healing; Spiritual healing)
Idea (Material; Spiritual)
Man
Matter
Metaphysics
Mind (mortal or material **m**ind; God, divine **M**ind)
Miracle
Prayer
Sin
Spiritual
Spiritual sense
Reality

CHAOS:

A state of things in which chance is supreme; nature that is subject to no law, or that is not necessarily uniform; a state of utter confusion completely wanting in order, sequence, organization, or predictable operation. [1]

EVIL:

Sometimes referred to as the Devil, evil would parade itself before human consciousness as a power and presence equal to God. As darkness (having no substance) is the absence of light, evil would be the absence of good; but God, being omnipresent, there can be no absence of good. Therefore, evil is the *supposed* absence of God, or good; *[2]

---

* A philosophical argument for the reality of good, and the unreality of evil is supplied by the following analogy: the principle of mathematics allows for no false law such as 2+2= 5. 2+2=5 is therefore a myth or unreality as seen from the perspective of mathematical principles. 2+2=5 is not positive; that is, obedience to this false law results in failure on the part of the user; and continual use of similar laws would result in

319

** Evil – Additional comments

To the materialist, one who believes in the absolute and independent reality of the evidence of the five senses, evil is a solid reality, sometimes even more real than good. To some physicists, because of the indeterminacy (*Uncertainty Principle*) of physical law at the fundamental level of reality, there will always be a finite probability that certain diseases will occur, certain people will be born as "pure evil", etc., no matter what human efforts are made to bring order and harmony in the world. Evil in some form will be seen as a hard reality and influence in the world, until at such time that humanity gives up this rock-hard conviction, and begin to discern the great truth that man – as a spiritual idea of God - *can never be separated from Love*, and that this universal Law of Love could never create the opposite of itself. Evil is the product of mankind's acceptance of physical laws as foundational; from these laws arise *probabilities* for the appearance of both good and evil in our human experiences.

In speaking of God and man, and of good and evil, Mary Baker Eddy [V] said: "God is Love. Can we ask Him to be more?" [3] And: "Does evil proceed from good? Does divine Love commit a fraud on humanity by making man inclined to sin, and then punishing him for doing it? Would any one call it wise and good to create the primitive, and then punish its derivative? Does subsequent follow its antecedent? It does. Was there original self-creative sin? [**] Then there must be more than one creator, more than one God. In common justice, we must admit that God will not punish man for what He created man capable of doing, and knew from the outset that man would do. God is 'of purer eyes than to behold evil.'" [4]

HEALING

** Faith Healing:

What has been called faith healing is a belief, usually accompanied by great sincerity and emotional love of God, in the ability of God to perform miracles.

--- Faith Healing – Additional comments

Faith healing is seldom accompanied by any real understanding of the nature of God or Reality as wholly good, because it first attributes disease and all disorders either directly to God, a devil or to the laws of physics, and then asks God to set aside His laws and perform miracles. "Blind" faith can sometimes result in remarkable physical transformations of the body, and aids mankind in discerning the mental nature of the

---

chaos. In like manner, the denial of the law or Principle of Good - that law which establishes order and certainty - and the acceptance of evil results in nothing positive and eventually leads to the opposite of Good: fear, indeterminacy, finiteness, disorder, disease, death and chaos.

[V] Mary Baker Eddy: a spiritual thinker and healer, the *Founder* of the *Christian Science* religion, and the author of *Science and Health, with Key to the Scriptures*.

[**] The *Doctrine of Original Sin*, which flies in the face of an omnipotent and good God.

universe, but it is the result of one *belief* - the belief of disease in matter (for the human mind and not physical law, is the actual cause of disease), being replaced by another belief - the belief of health in matter. The result is that the human mind still believes in the power of matter and physical laws to cause even greater disasters and diseases at some future time.

** Spiritual Healing:

In contrast with faith healing, which can be based somewhat on ignorance of the true nature of God and man, spiritual healing involves an understanding of the *science* of healing whereby the healer and the patient begin to understand the spiritual laws of changeless harmony, order and perfection governing man and the universe; and to recognize the nothingness of evil and the *allness* of God, good. If the healer and the patient can gain some appreciation of these great truths, he or she (and *anyone*) can demonstrate healing on a *consistent,* rather than on a random basis. Two of the clearest descriptions of spiritual healing are:
- "For the weapons of our warfare are not carnal, but mighty though God to the pulling down of strong holds; casting down imaginations, and every high thing that exalteth itself against the knowledge of God, and bringing into captivity every thought to the obedience of Christ." [5]
- "Jesus beheld in Science [V] the perfect man, who appeared to him where sinning mortal man appears to mortals. In this perfect man the Saviour saw God's own likeness, and this correct view of man healed the sick. Thus Jesus taught that the kingdom of God is intact, universal, and that man is pure and holy." [6]

--- Spiritual Healing – Additional comments

In the first paragraph (first bullet) the reader is urged to reject the imaginations of the carnal mind which projects ugly images upon the body, based upon fearful and sinful thoughts, and instead be obedient to the thoughts of God, these thoughts[Σ] being described as the Christ (Truth). In the second paragraph (second bullet), the reader is shown how Jesus' view of spiritual reality included man as sinless and whole, and that this view restored a lost sense of harmony.

Spiritual healing, as discussed and illustrated further along in this book, is not God reaching down and deciding to perform a miracle. It is not a process. And spiritual healing does not include the human mind as a healing agent. *Spiritual healing does not involve changing "sick" matter into "well" matter.* It is man reaching up in thought - in holy communion with divine Mind - to see himself as God sees him: *at this very moment*, an image of Love. "'He that believeth on me, the works that I do shall he do,' is a radical and unmistakable declaration of the right and power of Christianity to heal: for this is Christlike, and includes the understanding of man's capabilities and spiritual power." [7] Christ Jesus said that it is the *truth* that makes us free, but that this truth must be *known.*

[V] "Science," refers to everything relating to Mind, God and His Laws of the universe.
[Σ] Or more accurately: Mortals think, but God knows. Spiritual man knows ideas through Mind.

(8) This involves – through prayer - a change in the state of consciousness [V] of the individual seeking healing, whereby humbly he or she denies the false testimony of the physical senses and affirms the presence of God (Truth). Then he or she will begin to feel the presence of God (Love) and yield to harmony and the ever-present peace that flows from God (Mind). As important as healings are, we should not substitute healing for the *demonstration* of the divine Principle of man and the universe. That is, healings should lead us out of the belief in the pleasure of sinful ways. They should be signposts that begin - if ever so slightly - to lead mankind to the discernment of the allness of God, good, the nothingness of evil, and the totally spiritual nature of man and the universe. A man or woman healed of a bodily ailment, but still having sinful ways, has made no progress spiritward. Faith alone can sometimes heal, but faith alone will not accomplish the above transformation from matter to Spirit.

Dean Ornish, M.D., a prominent researcher in the origin of heart disease and of methods for reversing heart ailments and symptoms, has written best-selling books on the subject. (9) Ornish believes in loving broadly and bringing in the love of God as well as family and friends. He has remarked that our perception of the lack of love and intimacy in our lives is the prime factor that causes heart ailments, but when we feel loved, and have a loving relationship with others, we are less likely to become ill. He has said, "I am not aware of any other factor in medicine, not diet, not smoking, not exercise, not stress, not genetics, not drugs, not surgery - that has a greater impact on our quality of life, incidence of illness, and premature death from all causes." (10) Ornish has advocated exercise, a low-fat diet, and the exercise of the positive aspects of an emotional well being, called "love," believing, among other things, that this approach will lead to stronger immune and cardiovascular systems. Although this is certainly a giant step in recognizing the effect of consciousness on the physical body, hopefully it will lead to a greater recognition of the power of something besides a human sense of love, and a limited concept of God, to *Love* (God), itself, and to the recognition of the mental and wholly spiritual nature of man and the universe.

IDEA:

A mental image or concept. *Not all ideas that we entertain are spiritual*.

** Material:

Beliefs [⊕] or concepts originating in mortal mind(s); limited thoughts, ideas, or concepts manifested as hate, fear, lust, greed, revenge, finiteness, uncertainty - none of

---

[V] Although there is a direct relation between the human mind and the physical body (the so-called mind-body connection), spiritual healing is actually the result of communion with Mind, God; it is the result of prayer that changes our thinking from a material basis to a spiritual basis The mind-body connection is always there, since the body is the outward manifestation of thought. And it is always human thought that must be set straight.

[⊕] Throughout the book I generally refer to concepts of mind (lower case) as" ideas," rather than using the term "belief."

which are spiritual or divine (of God, Mind), and which lead to destruction, disease, chaos, death.

** Spiritual:

The spiritual creation or thoughts of the divine Mind; Ideas, concepts, manifested as love, honesty, purity, peace, joy, goodness, and which lead to life, harmony.

MAN:

"The compound idea of infinite Spirit; the spiritual image and likeness of God; the full representation of Mind." [11] Spiritual man [⊗] is not defined by material structure. Man, whose true nature is wholly spiritual, has a unity or oneness with God. If billions of individuals say they have a oneness with God, this does not mean God is many minds combined as one, or as divided into many small minds. Rather, God is ONE, expressing Himself as ALL.

MATTER:
"The Conceptual scheme of physical objects is a myth."
W.V. Quine [12]

The fundamental or foundational particles upon which all objects in the material universe are said to be constructed; equivalent to energy, $E = mc^2$; Physical theories, backed up by experimental results define matter as being in the form of subatomic and dimensionless particles, or by structures, such as, strings, bubbles or sheets in higher dimensions of space-time; From a quantum physics viewpoint the wave function of an individual sub-atomic particle, such as an electron, represents a superposition of many potential quantum states. Through a measurement or observation by a macroscopic recording device, [∇] the wave function collapses to a single value (called an *eigenstate*), and the material electron is found at a unique region in space. That is, the probability becomes unity that the electron will pop into existence near a specific region of space; It is thought by some physicists that an electron can be represented by a small-amplitude excitation of an electron field – a statement that has a remarkable similarity to Eddy's statement that "Electricity [a collection of electrons] is the sharp surplus of materiality…[13] *

** Matter – Additional comments

Mary Baker Eddy believed that a material particle such as an atom, " is an outlined falsity [or subjective state] of consciousness, which can gather additional evidence of consciousness and life only as it adds lie to lie." [15] That is, matter is known

---

[⊗] man: meaning men and women
[∇] The "macroscopic recording device" that "collapses" the wave function, is considered by some physicists to be consciousness. This concept is discussed at length in this part (Part II) of the book.
* Charles Steinmetz (1865-1923), one of America's greatest scholars and electricians, during the late 1800s, commented that Eddy's statement as to the nature of electricity was the best he had ever heard. [(1

to exist by its boundaries or limits. [16] An atom or molecule is seen or observed first by consciousness. (The reader should know that throughout this book I will sometimes compare physical theories and models of reality with spiritual models, and sometimes indicate a similarity between the two. But while physical theories come and go, the spiritual models are eternal.)

Eddy, before Einstein, must have recognized the equivalency of energy and matter, because she saw this most ethereal form of matter (energy) as *material intelligence*, matter thereby being a subjective state of mortal minds.

METAPHYSICS:

A science above physics, and one that does not include matter. "Divine metaphysics is that which treats of the existence of God, His essence, relations, and attributes. A sneer at metaphysics is a scoff at Deity; at His goodness, mercy, and might." [17]

MIND: The source of consciousness, intelligence and awareness.

** Mortal mind or minds (lower case):

The universal belief, delusion, or dream that consciousness, intelligence, awareness and willpower originate, evolve in, and depend on a matter-brain; that infinite **Mind** (upper case), God, can be subdivided into many minds. [18] Filled with erroneous concepts, mortal minds – the suppositious opposites of infinite Mind - have no real existence.

** Divine Mind (upper case):

The *I am, the one Ego;* God, Spirit, Principle, Life, Truth, Love, Soul, good, Reality; the *only* law, intelligence and consciousness, in whom spiritual man and the spiritual universe are ideas or images.[∇] [19]

--- Divine Mind – Additional comments

Physical theories cannot explain consciousness, but any description of reality must begin with Mind. There is only one Mind, one Consciousness. Man is not merely the *recipient* of Mind's thoughts (ideas); he is the individualized manifestation or expression (idea) of Mind, the *I AM*. [20] Any Truth, any good and right idea that is revealed in consciousness, is the actual presence of God. It is *not* a good, spiritually-minded person "thinking *about* God," "It is the divine Mind whose own knowing constitutes our consciousness." [21] In actuality there is no human mind (no brain-centered consciousness: an illusion of mind in matter). The so-called mind/ body connection,

---

[∇] As mentioned in Part I, Chapter 1, I have structured Part II of this book in such a way that ideas and concepts concerning God and man are frequently repeated and explained in different ways. This has been done in order to reinforce on the reader's thought the vast differences between orthodox views of God and man, and the views expressed in this book.

admittedly a step upward from the belief that consciousness is dependent on matter for its existence, cannot be a true agent in spiritual healing.

Consciousness is fundamental. In accordance with *Christian Science*, I believe strongly in the following statements:

- **The first and only cause is Mind.**
- **If God is not as described above (Divine Mind), then there is no God, only chaos.**

Now, thoughtful reader consider this: *St. John's* vision included the revelation *that* "God shall wipe away all tears from their eyes; and there shall be no more death, neither sorrow, nor crying, neither shall there be any more pain: for the former things are passed away…Behold, I make all things new." [22] I believe that St. John is saying that the belief of life, pain and sorrow in matter, which ends in the belief that all must die, will eventually yield to the understanding that if God, Mind, is truly eternal All, then all that He has created must be like Him - must be the expressions of Mind. That is, each of us, as individual manifestations of eternal Mind, has a consciousness and *unique identity*, which are maintained by God, the Creator, and which can never be lost through a belief of death! All things will become new - old beliefs will be given up for the new ideas of Mind. Can we then assert that diseases, disorders, accidents and other disruptive occurrences are the result of a law of probability or uncertainty? No, not if the first and primal cause is Mind.

MIRACLE :

A natural demonstration of a spiritual law.

PRAYER:

Mary Baker Eddy has said, "The prayer that reforms the sinner and heals the sick is an absolute faith that all things are possible to God – a spiritual understanding of Him, an unselfed love." "Prayer cannot change the Science of being, but it tends to bring us into harmony with it." [23] Abraham Heschel has given an interesting description of prayer. He has said, "The focus of prayer is not the self. A man may spend hours meditating about himself, or be stirred by the deepest sympathy for his fellow man, and no prayer will come to pass. Prayer comes to pass in a complete turning of the heart toward God, toward His goodness and power. It is the momentary disregard of our personal concerns, the absence of self-centered thoughts, which constitute the art of prayer. Feeling becomes prayer the moment in which we forget ourselves and become aware of God." [24]

SIN:

Ways that will not work; [*] the result of the belief that man, made in the image of a perfect God, Spirit, could fall out of the kingdom of heaven, be separated from God (in matter, space-time), and commit acts contrary to the divine Will.

SPIRITUAL:

Divine (of God, infinite Spirit); having nothing to do with matter or space-time; that which *spiritual sense* recognizes as substance and reality.

SPIRITUAL SENSE:

"Spiritual sense is a conscious, constant capacity to understand God…Spiritual sense, contradicting the material senses, involves intuition, hope, faith, understanding, fruition, reality." [25] It is discernment beyond the physical senses. The so-called physical senses discern man as finite, sinful, material. Our spiritual senses see spiritual man, created by God.

REALITY:

One Creator and one creation. The reader should know that I hold with the declaration of *Christian Science* that "There is but one creator and one creation. This creation consists of the unfolding of spiritual ideas and their identities, which are embraced in the infinite Mind and forever reflected. These ideas range from the infinitesimal to infinity, and the highest ideas are the sons and daughters of God."[26] But mortal thought entertains the belief that creation is material and probably did not require a creator to bring it about. More recently, some physicists are saying that mortal consciousness is prime, and that the physical universe that we perceive is the outcome of collective, unitive and non-local consciousness. To the *Christian Scientist* matter is the subjective state of this so-called consciousness, with an atom being defined as "…an outlined falsity of consciousness." [27] And matter "…being a frail conception of mortal mind; and mortal mind is a poorer representative of the beauty, grandeur, and glory of the immortal Mind." [28] It would appear that collective mortal consciousness has created the physical universe, but this universe ""exists" only in the realm of ignorant, finite belief about the nature of reality. This universe exists only in the realm of dreams or suggestions. In truth there are not two creations: one material and the other spiritual; one created by mortal consciousness and the other created by the divine Consciousness (God). What appears as material law in some way only imperfectly hints at spiritual law.[29] Substance no longer will appear as temporal, finite and limited objects of matter, but as *spiritual ideas,* manifesting spiritual qualities, such as, beauty, form, harmony, order, usefulness, love, purity, eternality. ***The universe of Spirit (Reality) is changeless, and is not affected by mortal beliefs or observations***. In summary, mankind have not

---

[*] I believe this phrase can be first attributed to Gordon R. Clarke, A *Christian Science Teacher* and *Practitioner.*

fallen out of the grace of God. And mankind are not dreaming that they are mortals, and have fallen out of the grace of God. But it is the ***belief*** that mankind are dreaming they are mortal, living in matter, space-time, and that they have fallen out of the grace of God![30]

If the reader finds the above statements difficult to accept, he or she should keep in mind that these ideas are certainly easier to digest than the conclusions arising out of the *Many-Worlds Interpretation* of reality, where individual quantum events (such as single photons passing through a *Double-Slit* apparatus) split the universe in two (See Part I, Chapter 17). The result being that over a period of time quantum events in our universe create an almost infinite number of universes, with "you", the observer, associated with each individual event, existing in each universe!

APPENDIX B

POSSIBLE MEANS FOR THE CREATION OF WHAT IS CALLED THE PHYSICAL UNIVERSE [*]

Could human beings in some distant future create in a laboratory a new universe[∇] that would eventually evolve intelligent, conscious beings? And would this achievement rule out the need of a Supreme Being as the creator of this new universe, or even our own universe? Would the being or beings who created this universe have the right to be called a god or gods?

At the very early stages of the universe (less than 1×10^{-43} sec, called the *Planck time*), the universe was infinitesimally small, less than 1×10^{-33} cm in diameter. According to the *Uncertainty Principle*, a *quantum fluctuation* of what has been called a pre-existing space-time foam could produce a small bubble of this "false vacuum"-[⊕] out of essentially nothing. According to Alan Guth, this infant universe, emerged from this false vacuum with a mass of about 10 kg and a diameter of about 10^{-24} cm. Then, if conditions were right the early universe then participated in the so-called *inflationary expansion era, which* lasted until 10^{-35} sec.[α] [(2)] According to some inflationary models the universe increased to a size of $10^{10^{12}}$ cm, although the *observable* universe today is only 10^{28} cm in size! [Σ] [(3)]

Although the creation of another universe in the laboratory seems ridiculously absurd, the authors of the *Nulcear Physics Journal* article believe that it is *theoretically* possible considering the small size of mass required (10 kg), but the hang-up at present is providing the initial conditions of high mass density, a mind-boggling number of 10^{76} grams per cubic centimeter! A new universe theoretically could be created in the laboratory from initial conditions, by the production of a "spherically symmetric bubble of 'false vacuum'."

---

[*] Note to reader: Certain quotations and observations that have been cited in the main part of this book are again cited in this APPENDIX, so that this APPENDIX is complete and stands alone.

[∇] New universe: a region of space effectively disconnected from the universe in which we live.

[⊕] A "false vacuum" is an excited vacuum state, which, although devoid of particles possesses enormous energy and what has been termed "negative pressure." This negative pressure- having the opposite effect of gravity - caused the rapid expansion. The authors mention briefly (*Nuclear Physics Journal*) that the false vacuum bubble (the result of quantum vacuum fluctuation) might possibly be created in the laboratory by at least two possible mechanisms: super-cooling, or by the compression of fermions (particles with half-integral spins, such as electrons, protons or neutrons). [(1)]

[α] The period of time for the period of inflationary expansion, and the size of the universe after the inflationary period, differ according to the inflationary model chosen.

[Σ] Note: Many physicists are generally able to accept the fantastic conclusions derived from admittedly hypothetical mathematical models of the universe, such as the incomprehensibly rapid expansion of the early universe from 10^{-24} cm in diameter to $10^{10^{12}}$ cm, but are unwilling to consider the primacy of consciousness and the possibility of true spiritual healing because they do not fit into their models of overall physical reality.

So, back to the original questions posed at the beginning of this APPENDIX. If the creation of another physical universe in a laboratory environment by a mere mortal is theoretically possible, is there any need for God? Is the universe governed by godless, mindless laws, whereby a knowledgeable being, through applying them can create a new universe containing life and intelligent awareness?

From our previous discussions on quantum theory and reality we may somewhat boldly consider the following possibilities as to how creation came about:

- The physical universe as we know it was created by some kind of inflationary process, possibly as described by Andrei Linde.[4] But Linde admits that explaining the initial conditions - where, and when reality began - "still remains the most intractable problem of modern cosmology." * Linde concludes his article by stating that if certain physical models of creation are correct, then physical laws by themselves cannot explain all the properties of the universe which we appear to inhabit. He asks the question, that if we are to acquire a complete knowledge of our universe, should we not also investigate deeply, "our own nature, perhaps even including the nature of our consciousness?" He ends by saying that this conclusion would be one of the most unexpected that might come out of the theory of inflationary cosmology.

- In accordance with some interpretations of quantum mechanical laws and the *Uncertainty Principle*, some sort of observation of quantum phenomena caused the creation of the universe. But what caused the quantum fluctuation to occur? As with the *Double-Slit* experiment, the quantum wave function (a quantum wave function for the early universe?) can only collapse to reveal a particle (the quantum universe?) when measurement or observation is made. Who or what made the observation? When did it occur? And was the observer a part of the universe or out of it? Recall what Wheeler (Part I, Chapter 15) has to say about *observation*: "By deciding which questions our quantum registering equipment shall put in the present we have an undeniable choice in what we have the right to say about the past... We do not simply observe the laws of nature, there is also a sense in which we create them." The conclusions, taken to extreme would seem to say that the existence of the universe, itself, is the "cumulative consequence of billions upon billions of elementary acts of observer - participancy reaching back into the past." [6]

- By utilizing timeless laws of physics arising out of chaos, finite mind or minds in the distant past may have created our universe (Guth, et al). There was no need for a Supreme Being to create our universe; as finite beings were sufficient to accomplish the task. However, this begs the question as to how the first minds were created.

- Finite mind or minds existing "before" the material universe came into being, actually created the material universe, either by (1) - mentally observing and collapsing the quantum wave function of the nascent universe; or (2) - first, believing in the paradigm that mortals could exist separate from God; and then believing in and

---

* Some physicists are busy calculating the possibility that the first inflating region could come into existence through quantum mechanical tunneling (the passage from one state to another of a microscopic system by a path that is classically forbidden), from absolutely nothing.[5] Some other physicists, however, say that going back to time, $t = 0$ (no existence of space-time), and asking, "What came before?" is meaningless.

"discovering" (*actually creating!*) physical laws that enabled creation to evolve essentially out of nothing. In (2), the material universe itself, is the subjective (mental) state of mortal minds. Wheeler has said, "I do take 100 percent seriously the idea that the world is a figment of the imagination." [7] (John Horgan, New York Times, 16 July, 1996) *

- *God never created a material universe.* Christ Jesus explained the apparent existence of a mixture of good and evil, of spirit-based and matter-based realities, when he presented to the people of that time the parable of the tares and the wheat.[8][9] Jesus spoke of the kingdom of heaven, or the kingdom of God (reality), *as* "likened unto a man which sowed good seed in his field: But while men slept, his enemy came and sowed tares among the wheat, and went his way." The "enemy" is the serpent, or devil (the serpent described in a parallel allegory given in Genesis 2 and 3 as an entity arising out of the mist or false claim of life in matter). [10] Jesus said that the tares (materiality, material sense of life, or *error*) and the wheat (spirituality, spiritual sense of life, or Truth) would appear to exist together (notice, the wheat is not touched or harmed by the tares), until the harvest, i.e., the revelation of Truth to human consciousness, at which time the tares would be gathered and burned, or destroyed.

    Notice also that Jesus said that the serpent, or devil, was a"... murderer from the beginning, and abode not in the truth, because there is no truth in him. When he speaketh a lie, he speaketh of his own: for he is a liar, and the father of it." [11] Christ Jesus also implied that the kingdom of God is within us: "The kingdom of God cometh not with observation: Neither shall they say, lo here! Or, lo there! For, behold, the kingdom of God is within you." [12] "Within you" - not inside a physical body - but in *consciousness.* Yes, there are observables or signs of the presence of the kingdom of God (reality), and these are manifested by spiritual healing and demonstrated by lives lived, but close scrutiny and observation of the material universe and its physical laws will not reveal reality. Nathan Talbot gives an example of how birth into matte, and death out of matter seem to be the reality of things. He asks the question of whether or not you would have existence if your parents had decided not to have children. The answer is "Yes", because mortal existence is no more than a dream of life in matter separate from God, Spirit. In a way we consent to being "born" into the material universe, to live there for a few years, and then we consent to "die" out of matter. Dreaming, and believing or consenting that you are a bear in a dream you are having at night does not make you a bear. When you awake from the dream you realize that you never had an existence as a bear. So it is with the dream of birth, life, and death in a material universe. When we learn of, and begin to comprehend our timeless, eternal being in Spirit, the dream begins to dissolve even if only for a moment, and lo: spiritual healing occurs! [13] The occurrence of a large number of high fidelity spiritual healings in this age is currently somewhat limited by mankind's resistance to, and fear of, radical new ideas about the nature of God, man and the universe.

---

* John Horgan believes that Wheeler did not mean to be taken seriously.

So the answer is, the author believes, that there is no beginning to reality, and that reality is wholly spiritual, and of God. In one of her writings Eddy says: "The fading forms of matter, the mortal body and material earth, are the fleeting concepts of the human mind. They have their day before the permanent facts and their perfection in Spirit appear. The crude creations of mortal thought must finally give place to the glorious forms which we sometimes behold in the camera of divine Mind, when the mental picture is spiritual and eternal. Mortals must look beyond fading, finite forms, if they would gain the true sense of things. Where shall the gaze rest but in the unsearchable realm of Mind?" [14]

If these "crude creations" - the physical universe, associated physical laws, and the beginnings of mortal life - are nothing more than the result of collective, mistaken mortal thought, then it would be well for each of us to consider our true, timeless, spiritual nature and origin. Eddy concludes the following about the origin of man and the universe: "The compounded minerals or aggregated substances composing the earth, the relations which constituent masses hold to each other, the magnitudes, distances, and revolutions of the celestial bodies, are of no real importance, when we remember that they all must give place to the spiritual fact by the translation of man and the universe back into Spirit. In proportion as this is done, man and the universe will be found harmonious and eternal." [15]

APPENDIX C

THE PARADIGM OF PHYSICS: WHY DOES WHAT IS CALLED THE PHYSICAL UNIVERSE[v] APPEAR AND ACT THE WAY IT DOES?

"Virtually every prevailing objective parameter of contemporary science can be traced, conceptually, epistemologically, and linguistically to some prior form of subjective human impression."
Robert G. Jahn
"The Challenge of Consciousness" [2]

"Matter is but the subjective state of mortal mind."
Mary Baker Eddy
"The First Church of Christ Scientist and Miscellany"[3]

Eugene Wigner has commented that consciousness plays a different role in quantum mechanics than inanimate recording devices. He has said that his comment, "…is entirely cogent so long as one accepts the tenets of orthodox quantum mechanics in all their consequences. Its weakness for providing a specific effect of the consciousness on matter lies in its *total reliance on these tenets* – a reliance which would be, on the basis of our experiences within the ephemeral nature of physical theories, difficult to justify fully" [4] (emphasis added).

The fundamental laws of physics governing the state and motion of material objects cause physical phenomena to exhibit the properties of *complementarity* or *duplicity, uncertainty* or *randomness,* and *inertia.*[*] But why are these specific properties manifested; that is, why does the physical universe appear and act the way it does? For example, why is it impossible to predict where an individual photon will strike a target in the *Double-Slit* experiment, or when an individual alpha particle will be emitted from Uranium –238 as it decays into Thorium-234? And how can a particle be said to occupy two different atomic states until an observation is made?

I do not presume to have the final answer, but the following discussion should be considered as a beginning attempt to shed some light on why I believe that the state of consciousness of collective, unitive and non-local minds plays a predominant role in defining what we call physical reality.[π]

Fred Alan Wolf, in his book, *Taking the Quantum Leap*, says the following about what Eugene Wigner, a Nobel prize winner in physics, believes about reality: "[Wigner]…believes that our consciousness alters the world itself because it alters how

---

[v] The physical universe is a poor counterfeit of the real universe: the spiritual universe of Mind. "The physical universe expresses the conscious and unconscious thoughts of mortals" (Eddy).[1]

[*] Inertia: the property of matter (mass) by which it remains at rest or in uniform motion until acted upon by an external force; indisposition to change.

[π] I have been helped greatly by a talk given by Rushworth Kidder, *Founder* and *President of the Institute for Global Ethics.*

we appraise the future. That is, we experience the world the way we do because we choose to experience it that way." [5]

COMPLEMENTARITY OR DUALITY

We have come to realize in the realm of the very small (the quantum) that through the act of observation this sub-atomic world is seen as a world of duality or of two-foldness. This phenomenon in quantum mechanics is known as the *Principle of Complementary* (see Part I, Chapter 9). But in the macroscopic realm we also experience a world of duality where a specific phenomenon will be manifested at a given time, but its complementary phenomenon will not be manifested. That is, we cannot experience both complementary components at the same time, although it is generally concluded that both concepts are necessary in order to provide a complete description of physical reality. This is the *yin-yang* [v] of the physical world. For example look at Table #1 below, which includes a few sub-atomic complementary examples and a few examples that are a part of subjective human experience.

---

[v] yin-yang: According to traditional Chinese cosmology, yin (the negative principle in nature, such as depth, passivity, darkness, cold) and yang (the positive principle in nature such as height, activity, light, heat) combine to produce all that comes to be.

TABLE 1

positive charge	negative charge
Precise measurement of the energy of an excited state of an atom	Precise measurement of the lifetime of an excited state of an atom
Precise measurement of quantum object position	Precise measurement of quantum object momentum
Knowledge of which path the quantum object took in the double-slit experiment	Possibility of observing an interference pattern in the double-slit experiment
red	green
wave	particle
income	outflow
sadness	happiness
hate	Love
sickness	health
impurity	purity
darkness	light
death	Life $^{\oplus}$
evil	good
discord, accident	harmony
finity	infinity
anger	forgiveness
matter	Spirit
material man (in accordance with physical law; Adam and Eve)	spiritual man$^{\nabla}$ (In accordance with Bible, Genesis: Chapter One)
Unreality, error	Reality, Truth
winning the lottery	losing the lottery
fear	assurance
chaos	order$^{\leftrightarrow}$
uncertainty	certainty

For example, we cannot simultaneously feel both sadness and happiness, although thought may move rapidly from one feeling to the other. When we see the redness of an object its complementary color of green is invisible. If the object would be red and green

---

$^{\oplus}$ The *Bible* declares God to *be* Life, and not just a loving anthropomorphic being. Then, since God is Life, there is no place in Reality for death.

$^{\nabla}$ I hasten to add that I believe that spiritual man is the permanent and only reality – a reality that cannot be brought into existence (or removed) by physical observation. Spiritual reality is not determined by a quantum wave function.

$^{\leftrightarrow}$ "The chaos of mortal mind is made the stepping-stone to the cosmos of immortal Mind"(Eddy).[6] Humanity, by recognizing the eternal order of Mind's creation will reverse evidence to the contrary, even to denying the theory that the universe is material and created out of chaos.

at the same time it would actually be gray. The precise measurement of position of a sub-atomic particle means that we have absolutely no knowledge of its momentum. In our subjective experience we cannot simultaneously experience winning the lottery and losing the lottery, nor can we simultaneously be alive and dead at the same time. *

Neils Bohr, one of principal discoverers and proponents of quantum theory maintained that waves and particles are "mutually exclusive concepts." [7] Both classical models are necessary for a complete description of a quantum object, but they can never be elucidated simultaneously. But how can a quantum object be sometimes a particle and other times a wave? The only way out of this contradiction in logic (if one does not accept the *Many Worlds* view of the universe) is to conclude quantum objects are mental concepts. They appear in the form that they do because of our methods of choosing how to observe them (see Wheeler's game of *Twenty Questions*) [8], based on prior beliefs of collective mortal consciousness.

RANDOMNESS OR CHANCE (UNCERTAINTY)

In APPENDIX I-15a, under the sub-heading "*Double-Slit* Experiment with Single Photon or Electron Pulses", the location of each new single particle impact on a downstream photographic screen appears to be random in nature. But over a period of time the cumulative recording is similar to that of a beam of particles passing through both slits, and causing an interference pattern to be registered on the screen. But these apparently random impacts are actually seen to be governed in some way by an unseen quantum law. This is the new paradigm of physics: at the sub-atomic level the prediction of the state and activity of individual quantum particles is uncertain, chancy or probabilistic.

The Sierpinski Triangle is an example of an orderly pattern developing out of seeming chaos or randomness. In a computer program to demonstrate how the triangle is constructed, an "operator" is asked to move his mouse and randomly place a dot anywhere inside the triangle. The computer program then randomly selects one of the triangle vertices and places a dot midway between the first dot and the selected vertex. The operator then pushes a button and the computer randomly selects another vertex and randomly places another dot midway between the second dot and the selected vertex. This procedure can be carried out indefinitely. At first the distribution of the dots inside the triangle appear to be entirely random, like in the single particle impacts on the photographic screen in the *Double-Slit* experiment. But eventually a pattern appears, an evolving pattern that reveals itself as an endless subdivision of repeatable, but ever smaller triangles, according to a simple, and initially unrecognized, law.

In our subjective human experiences events happen that we cannot predict; and it would seem that our lives sometimes change in fortune and in direction like a bouncing football. Look at Table #2 below, which includes a few sub-atomic examples of

---

* A few physicists have questioned whether the proper interpretation of quantum theory allows for macroscopic beings (humans and cats) to be described by a wave function which contains equal probability states of conscious life and death until some kind of observation is made by other beings, which then collapses the wave function to reveal either a live being or a dead one! In other words, they believe conscious beings can be described by a wave function..

randomness or uncertainty and a few examples that are a part of subjective human experience.

If matter is the subjective state of collective, unitive consciousness, then it may be possible to explain the apparent randomness of sub-atomic particle action. *Einstein's statement, "God does not play dice." may be true after all.*[∇] Consider a jar made of some thin material. The jar contains tiny solid pellets. As the jar is shaken vigorously, one pellet, through a complex exchange of energy between pellets, may suddenly and unpredictably acquire enough momentum to puncture the jar and escape. This is not unlike the decay of radioactive nuclei, where individual sub-atomic particles are randomly ejected, although physics can predict accurately the decay rate of the entire mass. As with the tossing of a die (see Part I, Chapter 10), although we cannot predict *when* the number "three" will appear, we can predict with great certainty the probability of "three" appearing for a great number of tosses.

Could we not say (or at least conjecture!) that the apparent randomness of sub-atomic events is caused by random, collective, universal (non-local) and unitive consciousness, a consciousness that either directly or indirectly accepts certain laws of physics (such as the laws governing wave interference) as fundamental? In a manner similar to the construction of the Sierpinski Triangle, the basic laws governing the overall distribution of cumulative single particle distribution through the *Double-Slit* experiment are the quantum laws formulated, accepted and described by yesterday's and today's physicists. But the randomness or quantum uncertainty of the state of individual particles is the result of collective, unconscious or unfocused thoughts of billions (or more!) of conscious beings in the universe, that appear as an apparent random mental action or "force." These unfocused, largely uncertain, non-local thoughts keep the photon in a state (superposition of states) described by a wave of probability, rather than as a particle, and enables it to pass simultaneously through both slits. Unless an observer is present to bring the particle into existence, the photon manifests its wavelike probability aspects, until observation of the screen reveals the impact of a particle ↔

Collective mental forces also cause the movement of sub-atomic particles, and for one sub-atomic particle to spontaneously decay in a radioactive mass. If this collective thought were focused * in an attempt to change the probability of decay of a radioactive mass, the effect might be seen in a different decay rate, or in perhaps *no decay rate at all*! [∇] Collective thought, based on the belief that life originated in matter, is basically fearful and *uncertain,* and this state of consciousness is manifested in the world around us, including the sub-atomic world of the quantum.

[∇] God certainly does not play dice, but the uncertainty and ignorance of collective mortal thought has lead in some intricate and complex way to the interpretation of law as embodying uncertainty, chance and mystery, thereby masking the real nature of law which is wholly spiritual and changeless. Man cannot create the spiritual laws of nature, but he has grossly misinterpreted them.

↔ See a roughly similar interpretation by Amit Goswami (Part II, Chapter 1): Unless we observe, the "undisturbed wave sustains the quantum dichotomy" [division into two mutually exclusive parts], as a sort of formless potential or possibility, and we observe a gradual build-up of an interference pattern on the screen.

* (See Robert Jahn experiments in Part II, Chapter 3, Experiments in Consciousness).[9]

[∇] (The reader is referred to the Internet for the article "The Quantum Zeno Effect" by Andrew Hamilton, pp. 2-3.) [10]: The measurement of a sub-atomic particle influences the particle's history. "Constantly measuring the particle could prevent it from decaying from a high energy to a lower energy…"

Someone may ask how could consciousness affect the early conditions of what is called the infant physical universe when consciousness supposedly evolved billions of years later. And although millions of people once believed the earth was flat, this collective belief apparently had no effect on the spherical properties of the earth. Recall Wheeler's comments: " The laws of physics themselves may come about as a result of the interaction between the universe and its participant-observer. We do not simply observe the laws of nature, there is also a sense in which we create them." Again, Wheeler: "It is wrong to think of the past as 'already existing' in all detail. The 'past' is theory…the past has no existence except as it is recorded in the present." [11] He asks the question as to whether the term "*Big Bang*" is merely a shorthand way of describing the "cumulative consequences of billions of billions of elementary acts of *observer-participancy* reaching back into the past." And the results of *observer-participancy* depend on the "agreed" fundamental beliefs of collective thought. Even so, consciousness, itself, being non-local and existing independent of matter, has always existed, even before what has been called the "Big Bang." The answer *may* be that only a few thousands of somewhat ignorant and non-scientific beings on the earth believed the world (a gigantic object) was flat, while the random thoughts of *universal* mortal thought believed in the so-called universal laws of physics which would prevent flat earths from existing.

Having said this, upon further reflection, the following may be closer to the truth! Suppose you have an ugly and painful lump or growth on your hand. The lump represents discord and inharmony. We know from experience that spiritual prayer can make the lump disappear, sometimes almost instantaneously; [∅] as Mary Baker Eddy has said that matter is the subjective state of mortal consciousness. In this kind of healing the laws of physics appear to be violated. But the hand, although appearing to the limited physical senses as material, does not disappear through prayer (prayer: a change in the state of thought whereby a person comes into communion with universal Mind or God and yields to His will). What disappears, in the words of Ralph Wagers (A *Christian Science Practitioner* and *Teacher* of the mid-Twentieth Century [13]), "…is that which would limit or restrict or pervert or distort or destroy [the hand]." The hand - *in the highest sense* - is a spiritual idea of "Primary Consciousness" (God). The hand manifests or reflects attributes of God such as: dexterity, usefulness, love and compassion (holding the hand of a loved one), creativity (painting, playing the piano, etc.).

Perhaps in like manner, the earth – *in the highest sense* – is a multifaceted spiritual idea of God, expressing God-like qualities, not the least of which is, as being a place of safety and the manifestation of life and activity. It is a haven for mankind. It would be impossible for a flat earth to be a haven for mankind, because in that form it could not sustain life and could not exist under the constraints of what we currently accept as physical law. A flat earth in its highest sense would not be a spiritual idea, and therefore could not exist. The earth as spherical gives (through God) life meaning and purpose. Π

∅ "almost instantaneously," showing that healing is not a process. (a process of restoring a damaged matter-body), but an awakening to spiritual reality. When Peter and John healed the lame man, he arose immediately, "walking, and leaping, and praising God." [12]

Π **Human thinking does not create the universe, but creates a *belief* in a *material universe*.**

ONE UNIVERSE (and misinterpretations thereof)

Wheeler's statement (See three paragraphs back) that there is a sense in which we create the universe and the laws governing it, is profound. We have already discussed how existence of sub-atomic and near-macroscopic assemblage of particles can be influenced by observation. But there is actually only one universe, the changeless universe of Spirit, Mind. A universe of ideas, both simple and complex. Mortal consciousness, out of ignorance, has misinterpreted the nature of the universe, and has - in belief –"created" the *Big Bang*, out of which evolved a finite universe of matter particles and objects. But this erroneous belief of creation is no more than a *mask* hiding the reality of Spirit and its multitudinous objects of expression of Mind and Life. $^{\Sigma}$

It is not that collective mortal consciousness has *created* material planets, stars, galaxies and human bodies with hands and feet. Rather, collective consciousness has, over a period of time, changed or modified its poor perception and interpretation of the spiritual universe and the laws governing it – sometimes for the better, and sometimes for the worse. Nevertheless, the *integrity* of all objects in the universe – the very large and the very small - are complex, changeless *spiritual ideas* in Mind, no matter how much mortals believe them to be finite objects made of material atoms. What form does a hand have in the realm of Spirit? The material senses cannot comprehend spiritual reality, cannot observe objects in their true forms, and cannot comprehend their natural functions. But we can understand that a hand manifests such attributes as dexterity, strength, the ability to grasp.

St. John is recorded in the *Bible* as saying, "Beloved, now are we the sons of God, and it doth not yet appear what we shall be: but we know that, when he [the Christ, or Truth, exemplified so magnificently by Jesus] shall appear, we shall be like him; for we shall see him as he is."[14] In like manner, Mary Baker Eddy said, "Every material belief hints the existence of spiritual reality; and if mortals are instructed in spiritual things, it will be seen that material belief, in all its manifestations , reversed, will be found the type and representative of virtues priceless, eternal, and just at hand." [15]

$^{\Sigma}$ It is appropriate here to again remind the reader that the theology of Christian Science reveals that the mortal or material sense of life as bound by space and time (space-time) is a "misapprehension of existence." Eddy called this experience the "waking dream."[14] Suppose you are dreaming you have been in a dark coal mine, for a very long time. You might ask yourself when you were outside in a field with bright sunlight. But the question has no meaning, because all the time you were in your bed dreaming! As Daniel Scott said, "temporal reasoning leads to paradoxes and limitation." Truly we live in the "now" of spiritual reality.[15]

TABLE 2

Determination of decay time of individual alpha particle from a radioisotope atom
Being involved in a car accident
Finding the right employment
Winning the lottery
Catching a serious contagious disease
Rise and fall of the stock market (almost random!)
Being born to rich parents
Finding the right person to marry
Trusting in physical law alone (no God), or in a God who (in belief) is both good and evil, and who has created a universe of both spirit and matter
Experiencing finite or non-continuous (quantized) good
Having the wrong kind of DNA

INERTIA OR RESISTANCE

Inertia is a property of matter. It is the resistance to movement or change until acted upon by some external force. An asteroid on a path to strike the earth would be an example of the effect of gravitational forces on large masses. Nothing can stop this large mass from impacting with the earth and causing death and destruction. For us humans this property of matter (inertia: resistance to change in velocity) would seem to be inevitable. In our subjective human experiences physical and mental forces happen that we apparently cannot prevent, at least not without great difficulty, and it would seem that our lives sometimes follow a path that once begun cannot be changed. Look at Table #3 below, which includes a few examples in the physical world of the effects of inertia and a few examples or inertia that are a part of subjective human experience.

TABLE 3

Trying to divert a falling asteroid
Moving very heavy matter objects
Difficulty in waking up in the morning
Resistance to changing careers
Difficulty in getting to work on time
Difficulty in safely eliminating a fever – "It must run its course"
Resistance in overcoming laziness
Difficulty in giving up smoking
Overcoming an "incurable disease"
Resistance in trying new foods
Resistance in overcoming the thought that "Everything is going bad, and it will continue that way."
Resistance in giving up immoral habits

In the macroscopic, subjective world of human consciousness we believe in duality and chance governing our lives, and we also believe that resistance to doing the proper action in some of life's experiences is inevitable. Because reality is *mental*, these beliefs cause mortals to collectively shape what we perceive as reality based on these beliefs. The result is the appearance to the five senses of the present paradigm of physics (see Figure (9-1), Part II, Chapter 9).

The laws of physics appear the way they do because of the way mankind has first perceived and formulated – with the aid of the evidence of the five senses – certain ideas about reality. Because we believe in *duality*, such as the presence of good *and* evil; in *chance*, such as the possibility of the occurrence of various types of evil and disasters; and *inertia*, such as resistance to change for the better; *is there any wonder that the laws governing ponderous matter - and which appear to govern our lives - are based on uncertainty, chance, and that they can cause disease, chaos, lack and death?* Since the manifestation of physical reality is a function of collective consciousness, it would follow that at the very fundamental level of things, matter itself would be indeterminate or illusory, a subjective state of mortal consciousness.

THE SOLUTION

COMPLEMENTARITY OR DUALITY

Many people try to ascribe to God the attributes of good and evil, but this is impossible. In the realm of Spirit there is no duality. Eddy speaks of the apparent duality of spiritual man (made in the image of God), and mortal man: "Delusion, sin, disease, and death arise from the false testimony of material sense, which, from a supposed standpoint outside the focal distance of infinite Spirit, presents an inverted image of Mind and substance with everything turned upside down." [16] This apparent duality of man is shown below in Table #4.

TABLE 4

Mind (Reality)	mind in matter (unreality)
⇓	⇓
spiritual man	mortal man
↓	↓
knowledge, certainty	Delusion, misconception, uncertainty
purity	sin
health	disease
life	death

RANDOMNESS OR CHANCE

Many people believe that it is by chance that we have inherited a strong, healthy body, or a sick body. "It's only because we believe in randomness that we think we can't know what's going to happen, that chance will dictate events," says Rushworth Kidder, *Founder* and *President* of the *Institute for Global Ethics*. [17] In the realm of Truth, God is changeless good. In the realm of Infinite Mind there is no law of chance that results in disease, poverty, accident, death.

INERTIA OR RESISTANCE

Many people believe that sin is inevitable. People will resist kindness, and the universe and everything in it will not be able to resist the inevitable "heat death;" but in the realm of Spirit, Mind, life, intelligence, and consciousness are eternal. God puts no roadblock between us and our ability to think, act and live in accordance with His laws governing reality.

INTRODUCTION TO THE ADDENDUM

Spirit or matter?
Mind or mind?
Soul or souls?

In recent years there has been a veritable explosion of studies, reports and articles and books on the effect of individual and collective consciousness on matter, physical law and on the broad definition of "prayer.' Larry Dossey, Depak Chopra, Bill Sweet, Donald Hoffman, Bruce Lipton, Dick Bierman, Edward Close, Amit Goswami, Markus Aspelmeyer, Nick Herbart, Anthony Zeilinger, Bruce Rosenblum, Fred Kuttner and others - in various ways - have either by experiment, rational thinking, or observation acknowledged the effect of consciousness in the world.

The world is ever slowly (but now increasingly) beginning to recognize the primacy of consciousness, but in large part they still believe that mind or matter-brain is the seat of consciousness and the cause of healing through prayer, while God (Mind, Soul) alone is Consciousness.

Some people have even gone so far as to attribute to human consciousness a weight or mass, such that when someone dies the consciousness – the identity or soul of the individual leaves the physical body and continues on. And if the weight of the dying individual can be measured just prior to, and after death, and be shown to decrease by some small amount, that this would indicate that man indeed has eternal life.

All of this is a gratifying expression of enlightenment that reality is more than mindless matter. **But the danger here is that as people begin to recognize the mental nature of reality, they will attribute all effects to the human mind (matter-brain) and not to the divine Mind or God.**

Mary Baker, the Discoverer of Christian Science, had much to say about the nature of man and his/her relation to God, and on genuine, scientific prayer that went beyond mental concentration or human will: "Soul, or Spirit, is God, unchangeable and eternal; and man coexists with and **reflects** Soul, God, for man is God's image." [1] [emphasis added] "Spirit is God, **Soul**; therefore **Soul** is not in **matter**. If Spirit were in matter, God would have no representative, and matter would be identical with God." [2] [emphasis added] Man does not have an individual soul that has mass which can be weighed.

For healing to be on a solid, scientific foundation, and to be accomplished on a consistent basis, it must rest on a Principle or *Law*: *Mind* - and not on a brain-centered mind, or mind-body basis; or else it will be sporadic and often ineffectual. Eddy early in her life concluded that reality was mental,[*] and that "... mind does the healing..." but she desired to "... learn which mind, whether the human or the mind of Christ." [3] "It may seem a tremendous leap from recognizing the effect of the human mind on the body to a realization that 'Mind is All'" (Nathan A. Talbot "The mind, the body, and God's allness," *Christian Science Journal*, Jan., 1997). [4]

ADDENDUM

PART I – THE QUANTUM UNIVERSE

Macroscopic Entanglement in Disordered Solids

Recall that entanglement is a property of quantum mechanics that allows two or more quantum systems with distinct quantum states to exhibit a close relationship with each other. (See Chapter 15, p. 50, The *EPR* Paradox)

Thomas Rosenbaum (University of Chicago) and colleagues (University of Wisconsin) have conducted an experiment on a single, macroscopic and visible crystal of a magnetic salt.[1] The salt is made up of holmium, lithium, yttrium and fluorine. [$L_i(H_oY)F_{4^1}$] The magnetic moments $^\nabla$ of the holmium atoms in the absence of a magnetic field point in random directions until a field is applied. Then the moments point in the field direction. The magnetic moments aligned easily with the magnetic field at different temperatures. But while the *magnetic susceptibility* (the degree of magnetization of a material in response to the magnetic field) increases in a uniform way as the material is cooled, the *heat absorption* "varies in a more irregular way," as reported by *Physics Web*. According to the experimenters, this is in contrast to ordinary materials, and the explanation is that there is a quantum mixing or "entanglement of the different magnetic states of the system." They said that quantum entanglement has greater effect on magnetic susceptibility than on heat absorption. Computer simulations verified the results. The results, say the experimenters, is that entanglement can occur in a far from perfect disordered solid.

Coming Closer to Quantum Effects in Macroscopic Objects

In April, 2004, Keith Schwab and colleagues from the National Security Agency (NSA) working at the University of Maryland have performed experiments aimed at the detection of quantum effects in macroscopic objects.[2] They wanted to find out if the Uncertainty Principle extends up to the macroscopic world. This quantum principle states that it is impossible to know with complete certainty the simultaneous values of a particle's position and momentum or velocity. The experiment is designed to study the motion of a vibrating mechanical arm made of silicon nitride. (See Physics Web, 2 April 2004) The arm length is only eight microns ($8x10^{-6}$ microns), and its mass is equal to 10^{12} hydrogen atoms. Next to the arm is an aluminum strip called a "Cooper pair box" $^\pm$ attached by insulating contacts to a loop of superconducting aluminum. The arm (beam)

$^\nabla$ The magnetic moment is the measure of the strength or flux of a magnetic source. The vector points along the axis of the magnet from S to N.

$^\pm$ A Cooper pair box is a superconducting version of a single electron box made of a normal metallic island connected to a normal reservoir through a tunnel junction, and capacitively coupled to a gate voltage source.

is situated about 600×10^{-9} meters from a single electron transistor.[∞] The transistor acts as a motion detector. A voltage pulse allows electrons to "tunnel" [⊕]between the aluminum loop and the Cooper pair box. Because tunneling is a quantum mechanical phenomenon, the electrons can simultaneously be in the loop and the box. The Cooper box is now in a superposition state because it contains two different numbers of electrons at the same time; that is two different charge states at once. The positively-charged beam should bend toward the box if the box has excess electrons. But, since the box has two different charges simultaneously, **the beam should be forced into two different places at the same instant.**

The beam is cooled to near absolute zero in temperature, with the objective of reducing thermal vibrations to the point where only "zero-point" quantum fluctuations remained. This zero-point motion is predicted by the *Uncertainty Principle*, which in effect says that the arm cannot be completely at rest if we know its position to some degree of precision. As the beam moves toward or away from the detector, the amount of current flowing through it changes. By measuring this current with the transistor, the beam displacement can be determined with a sensitivity that is only about a factor of 4.3 larger than the amplitude of zero-point fluctuations.

The physicists are working to increase detector sensitivity and reduce further thermal arm vibrations.[Σ] Test results should be available in the fall of 2006.

Quantum Preferred States

A Philip Ball article in *Nature* magazine (23 December, 2004) [(3)] says that "observing the world tends to change it," [⊕] [but]…how is it that we can agree on anything at all?" That is, why is it that we all see the same house, the same butterfly, and so on? The macroscopic or classical world appears to have a single objective state which comes about through "de-coherence:" a phenomenon that occurs to a system that initially possessed many possible states, but by its interaction with the environment, collapses to one stable state.

The article says that certain special states, called "pointer states" are promoted above all else by a quantum form of natural selection (called "quantum Darwinism"). Pointer states, says Ball, are states that can "withstand the scrutiny of the environment without getting perturbed." These robust and stable states seem to occupy a definite position rather than being "smeared out" in space.

Also, sensitivity to observation at the quantum level appears to decrease when macroscopic objects are observed. Information about these "preferred states" grow or increase in number, and these affect the local environment and get imprinted on it many times so that all observers tend to see the same world or preferred stable states called "pointer states." An example in the article pointed out when we look at a macroscopic

---

[∞] transistor: a solid-state electronic device consisting of a semiconductor with at least three electrodes that is used to control the flow of electricity in electronic equipment.

[⊕] Quantum tunneling is the quantum mechanical effect of transitioning through a classical forbidden energy state. (For example, see Part I, Chapter 12, Particles in Potential Wells.)

[Σ] Physicist Roger Penrose, at Oxford University, has proposed conducting similar experiments in space where environmental effects due to atmosphere and temperature can be drastically reduced.

[⊕] "The universe is quantum to the core." (Wojciech Zurek)

object such as a tree, we observe the effect of the tree's leaves and branches by way of the visible sunlight bouncing off them. As Ball points out, each individual observation is based on a very tiny part of the environmental imprint (for macroscopic objects), so that there are always more photons bouncing off the object for other people to observe and see the same object. It is not clear from the article how exactly these preferred states are selected. As Keith Schwab believes, there may be as yet an unknown mechanism that causes objects to collapse to a single state.

Recall for the moment Wheeler's game of *Twenty Questions*: It took the consensus of all of the members of the party to arrive at the same answer. Thus it would seem that what we see depends to some degree on what is collectively agreed upon as the *paradigm* of physical reality. What we see depends upon what our senses have "educated" us into accepting as certain physical rules and "facts". Fred Wolf takes a "quantum leap" in reasoning when he says that because of this collective agreement or observations, the past - or the record of the past - can be recreated or restructured provided, "...enough minds come to agreement." [40] (See p. 76)

Also, as discussed in this book, evidence from quantum experiments, and especially from spiritual healings, tend to support the claim that reality is non-local and that there is unity in consciousness. Therefore, we should at least consider that through collective, universal, non-local and ***unitive*** consciousness we create the "preferred states" (collective and intelligent consciousness may be the "unknown mechanism" that select states and cause objects to collapse to a single state), based on our acceptance of past paradigms of reality that have been largely influenced by fear, ignorance and finite thinking (See Appendix C). A collective state of consciousness – based on physical sense testimony and finite and fearful thought – forms the basis for what we perceive through the senses as the physical world and its actions.

Towards Quantum Superposition of a Mirror

In the fall of 2003 a Physical Review Letter, and a paper entitled "Entangled Light and Matter" (Dik Bouwmeester presented at the *Atomic, Molecular and Optical Science Seminar* discussed a proposed experiment for creating quantum superposition states comprising about 10^{14} atoms through the interaction of a photon with a very tiny micron-size moveable mirror that can be deflected if struck by a photon.[4] A single photon at a time is pulsed and directed toward a beam splitter: a mirror that is half-coated with silver so that on the average half of the incident photons will be transmitted through the beam splitter and head outward in one direction, while half will reflect off the beam splitter and head out in another direction. (In actuality, the incident single photon is put into a superposition of two quantum states: one transmitted and the other reflected.) The micron-size moveable mirror is placed in the path of, say, the photon in the reflected state, while a fixed mirror is placed in the path of the photon in the transmitted state. The moveable mirror is attached to a mechanical oscillator, which is part of a "high-finesse optical cavity" which forms one arm of a *Michelson* interferometer.[μ]

[μ] Michelson interferometer: a device that produces interference fringes by splitting a beam of monochromatic light, so that one beam strikes a fixed mirror and the other beam strikes a moveable mirror.

As stated in the paper, the experiment aims at "transferring the photon superposition of propagation in two directions after passing a beam splitter into a superposition of two center-of-mass motions of the tiny mirror that has been placed in one path downstream of the beam splitter." The photon and the mirror are said to be "entangled," and the tiny mirror can be said to be in two distinct locations at the same time – at rest when the photon is in the transmitted path (fixed mirror), and in a deflected state when the photon is in the reflected path (moveable mirror). After striking both mirrors the photon - which has taken both paths – then bounces back to interfere with itself causing interference. Bouwmeester says that observed photon interference will allow physicists to study the "creation of coherent superposition states periodic with the motion of the mirror; (See "Towards quantum superposition of a mirror, June 5, 2005") and he expects that quantum superposition about ten orders of magnitude more massive will be achieved compared to previous experiments.

Hot Entanglement

It has been almost universally believed that entanglement could only occur at extremely low temperatures, because above a certain temperature thermal effects cause decoherence $^\varnothing$ with the result that the system becomes classical instead of remaining quantum. But not so say a team of physicists from the UK, Austria and Portugal.[5] They say that laser light photons can be quantum mechanically entangled with the vibrations of the crystal lattice of a macroscopic mirror regardless of the mirror temperature. That is, the photons in the laser pulse and the *phonons* (quantized mode of vibrations occurring in a rigid crystal lattice) are entangled, and this entanglement can persist at high temperatures. The pressure on the mirror caused by the photons increases with the increase in the number of photons in the laser pulse, and the more the mirror vibrates. For five photons striking the mirror there would correspondingly be five phonons - five modes of vibration – in the mirror. This phenomenon also works for large systems of billions of mirror atoms; and one of the physicists (Viatko Vedral, the *University of Leeds*) has said that "If our analysis is confirmed in an experiment…then this would push the limits of the validity of quantum mechanics further."

Is it Consciousness that Collapses the Wave Function?

In the Schrodinger's Cat experiment, according to the Copenhagen Interpretation of quantum theory, the alpha particle source, the Geiger Counter and the cat are all in a state of quantum superposition – a state which includes both a dead and a live cat – until an observation or measurement has been made by a macroscopic system. The question is: is consciousness required to collapse the wave function to reveal a single state for the cat, either dead or alive?

When the two reflected beams are brought together, an interference pattern results. In the above experiments the interferometer is used to verify the existence of the superposition states of the tiny mirror.

$^\varnothing$ Decoherence (collapse of the wave function) arises through interaction of the quantum system being measured with the measurement apparatus itself, and the external environment. That is, the collapse of the wave function occurs naturally through the interaction of the particle with the environment.

Present and future experiments by Dick Bierman of the *Department of Psychology, University of Amsterdam, The Netherlands*, aim to verify whether or not a conscious being (the observer or measuring device) is needed in order to collapse the wave function to yield a single state for the cat. [6]

The experiment consists of two observers, #1 and #2. Observer #1 sat next to a computer screen, while observer #2 was situated in another room, and had EEG electrodes connected to his head. Quantum events were generated so that on the average about one particle per second was detected by the Geiger Counter. When an event occurred, the counter pulse was amplified and fed to the trigger channel of an EEG data-acquisition system. Software detects the trigger and transforms it into an audio-beep, but this audio-beep is delayed for one second. Before the audio-beep occurs observer #1 receives a visual stimulus of the Geiger Counter (a macroscopic device) reading via the computer screen. Therefore, observer #1 has a conscious experience of the quantum event *before* observer #2 receives the audio-beep. The decision to show observer #1 the visual stimulus (or not show it) before observer #2 receives the audio-beep is pseudo random or classical. Each subject was asked to count the number of observed quantum events.

See experiment outline below:

Pre-observation by observer #1..........................>	Observer #1 sees visual stimulus
	Observer #2 hears audio-beep
No pre-observation by observer #1......................>	Observer #1 does not see visual stimulus
	Observer #2 hears audio-beep

The average difference in evoked potential between pre-observation and non pre-observation was such that the probability of the differences being due to chance was about 0.0115. **The conclusion is that the results of experiments "support a solution of the measurement problem that assigns a special status for conscious observation in the measurement process --- Conscious observation is a condition to make a measurement complete." Significant differences between the brain responses of observer #2 are found to be dependent upon whether observer #1 is looking at, or not looking at a quantum event.** At this time the results should be treated cautiously because of the lack of statistical power in the later phases of the response (significant differences decreased after about 100 msec.) The results to date "are not enough to unequivocally accept the hypothesis that consciousness collapses the state vector. Strong claims need strong evidence."

In a second series of experiments, the source of the trigger that results in a beep was a radioactive decay in some cases, and in other cases a classical count down clock. In this series there was no effect of pre-observation, but there was a difference in EEG of observer #2 depending on the source of the trigger. As Bierman concludes, "The increase in complexity of the situation did apparently result in a decrease of the effect of pre-observation, possibly because the beep that was observed did not provide full information (i.e. of the source)." Further experiments will be performed to test this potential explanation. [7]

Bierman also suggests that these kinds of experiments might be able to determine if so-called "artificial intelligence" devices such as advanced computers can be considered "conscious." ↓

If future experiments prove conclusively that consciousness is a factor in the collapse of a quantum wave function, this will be a profound statement about the nature of what we term "physical reality." But it will not bring us closer to increasing the efficacy of healing by spiritual means alone; although we should now more clearly recognize that consciousness, and not matter is prime – that reality is more mental than physical. Healing by spiritual means alone, means recognizing that consciousness is prime, but that true Consciousness is the infinite, ever-present Mind, Spirit, and not human consciousness as manifested by evoked brain potentials.

Test of Non-local Realism

In APPENDIX I-15B (E- The EPR Paradox) it was stated that information accumulated in recent years from numerous experiments support the conclusion that quantum theory is complete and the doctrine of local reality is false. Reality **appears** to be "non-local realism." But maintaining reality (realism) as "a fundamental concept would therefore necessitate the introduction of "…spooky' actions that defy locality," ▫ [8]

But it was also mentioned in the APPENDIX that some physicists believe that particles have no objective existence until observed. That is, reality is not only non-local, but non-objective: particles have no objective reality until observed.

In experiments physicists have measured previously untested correlations between two entangled photons. The correlations violate an inequality proposed by Anthony Leggett (Professor of Physics at the University of Illinois at Urbana-Champaign) for non-local realistic theories. In the experiments, photon polarizations did not exist until measured. By experiment and theory the physics group of Markus Aspelmeyer, Anton Zeilinger and others (in Vienna, Austria, and Gdansk, Poland) have shown that "…a broad and rather reasonable class of such non-local realistic theories is incompatible with experimentally observable quantum correlations." In summary, they say "…giving up the concept of locality [reality must be at least non-local] is not sufficient to be consistent with quantum experiments, unless certain intuitive **features of realism are abandoned**." (emphasis added)

But some physicists are not convinced that realism (at least at the quantum level) has to be abandoned. They await a space test where there is sufficient distance between human "detectors" and a sufficiently small number of particles that might impede the

---

↓ See my comments about testing AI devices for "consciousness," p. 197.
▫ Locality: local events cannot be affected by actions in space-like separated regions; non-locality: local events **can** be affected by actions in space-like separated regions. Local realistic theories have been shown to be invalid.

entangled particles from reaching the detectors. Also each experimenter could decide independently which photon polarization to measure.

Hold a Living Creature (Virus) in a Superposition of Quantum States?

A group of physicists who are in Germany and Spain believe it is possible to put living macroscopic things, such as a virus into superposition of quantum states. The living organism would be confined inside an optical cavity by using a laser beam tightly-focused on a tiny region of space. A second laser's radiation pressure would slow down the motion of the organism's center of mass, so that it exists essentially in its motional ground state. Then the second laser would fire a single-photon pulse that would"...put the organism into a superposition of its ground state and an excited motional state." [9]

The physics group points out that for an organism to be placed in a superposition state, it should approximate a dielectric object,$^\Psi$ so that it is transparent but still refracts light. The size of the object must be smaller than the wavelength of the light used so it can it be "... confined between the peaks and troughs in the light wave." Lastly, the organism should be able to withstand extremely low pressures because if air molecules in sufficient quantity exist, the quantum state would rapidly evolve to de-coherence.

Maciej Lewstein of the institute of Photonic Sciences in Barcelona, is of the opinion that success in experiments similar to the above, will lead us to eventually gaining a better understanding of the relationship between quantum mechanics and consciousness.

Consciousness and the Double-slit Experiment

Dean Radin/Institute of Noetic Sciences, and his group are conducting experiments using a double-slit optical system.[10] Participants in the experiments are asked to focus their attention either toward or away from the system during this time the double-slit interference pattern is being recorded by a high resolution camera. What the experiments want to discover is the "... ratio between the spectral power of double-slit versus single-slit patterns. It is predicted that this ratio will decrease during observation by nonlocal consciousness, compared to times when no observation is being made.

At this time the experiments are under way, and no conclusion can be reached, but "...the results so far support the prediction that consciousness is a causal factor in shaping how some aspects of the physical world manifest."

Quantum Effect in Visible Object

Physicists in California have succeeded in demonstrating quantum effects in an object just large enough (macroscopic) to be visible to the human eye, meaning that the object – a mechanical resonator made of aluminum and aluminum nitride – existed in superposition of states by eliminating the object's thermal vibrations which would mask

---

$^\Psi$ dielectric: a nonconductor of direct electric current

or destroy quantum effects. The researchers were able to place the resonator *simultaneously* in two states: (1) an excitation state in the resonator, and (2) no excitation in the resonator. When a measurement is made, reports Belle Dume (a contributing editor to nanotechweb) the object – a forty micron, trillion atom device - "chooses" which state it is in. The research is published in *Nature*. (See Physicsworld.com, March 18, 2010)

PART II – THE UNIVERSE OF SPIRIT

"If God is at the mercy of matter, then matter is omnipotent…The three great verities of Spirit, omnipotence, omnipresence, omniscience, — Spirit possessing all power, filling all space, constituting all Science, — contradict forever the belief that matter can be actual. These eternal verities reveal primeval existence as the radiant reality of God's creation, in which all that He has made is pronounced by His wisdom good."

Mary Baker Eddy
Science and Health with Key to the Scriptures

Intercessory Prayer

Recently (April, 2006) I read in the paper about a study, financed by the *Templeton Foundation* that concluded that heart surgery patients showed no benefit when strangers prayed for their recovery; and patients who knew someone was praying for them actually had a higher rate of complications. The patients were prayed over by two Catholic and one Protestant group from one to four times each day for a period of about fourteen weeks. They prayed for successful surgery, quick recovery and no complications. Those who did the praying never came into contact with the patients, and knew only their first names and the first initial of their last names. (See www.harvard.edu.gazette/2006/04.06/05-prayer.html) The results fly in the face of many of the results of several past studies, which I believe were legitimate.

But I believe that this heart patient study may have had several flaws. Expecting significant and positive results from the Templeton Foundation-supported study, indicates– in my mind – a profound lack of understanding of the nature of God, and of practical, effectual prayer. The way I see it as a Christian Scientist is that much of what is called prayer to God is not effectual prayer because it is based on the belief that God is the author of both good and evil, and that man – as a poor, sinning mortal living in matter – is separate from God. Eddy has said, "Holding the right idea of man in my mind, I can improve my own, and other people's individuality, health, and morals; whereas, the opposite image of man, a sinner, kept constantly in mind, can no more improve health or morals, than holding in thought the form of a boa-constrictor can aid an artist in painting a landscape…Science ⊕ can heal the sick, who are absent from their healers, as well as those present, since space is no obstacle to Mind" [1]

And what were the prayer groups in the study praying *for*? Prayer that is ignorant of the nature of God as unconditional Love, and that is based on faith and often human will, says to God, "Please heal me of a disease that either you or the Devil created." ("But since you are the only Creator, you must have created the Devil.")

We know from EPR experiments and "prayer at a distance" that consciousness is non-local; but what were the states of the thought of the people praying? Were they persistent in prayer? Did they have "blind" faith, only? Did they have an expectancy that

---
⊕ Science: everything relating to God, Mind

their prayers would be effective? Did they have a joyful expectancy that their prayers would be effective? Did they pray with love for their patients? Was it their human minds that were attempting to heal, or were they actually entertaining the Christ or angel thoughts of God who is universal Mind? Faith has been known to change material conditions, but faith alone is not enough in many instances, changing one belief in matter ("I am sick") for another belief in matter ("I am well.") Strong and emotional thought can sometimes change the body for the better, but is this really "prayer?" And, what were the states of thought of the patients in the study? Were they *concerned* because strangers were praying for them?

If one prays with humbleness of mind and a sincere desire to *listen* for what God has to say, then the thoughts of Mind – which are pouring forth abundantly – will lift us up and guide us in some way to a better understanding of God, and of ourselves. Even the sincere, simple and humble prayer of faith can unite us with God to receive blessings, but something more is needed if we are to pray more consistently and effectively: a knowledge of the nature of God. Eddy has said, "If we pray to God as a corporeal person, this will prevent us from relinquishing the human doubts and fears which attend such a belief, and so we cannot grasp the wonders brought by infinite, incorporeal Love to whom all things are possible." [2]

Lastly, combining material means of medicine and surgery with metaphysical or spiritual means in order to heal a patient generally results in partial or no success, because Spirit/ Mind, and matter are opposites. Prayer is not simply asking God to do something, because God has already made His creation in His image, so prayer must be an awakening to the ever present reality of harmony, order, good.

"The demands of God appeal to thought only; but the claims of mortality, and what are termed laws of nature, appertain to matter. Which, then, are we to accept as legitimate and capable of producing the highest human good? We cannot obey both physiology and Spirit, for one absolutely destroys the other, and one or the other must be supreme in the affections. It is impossible to work from two standpoints. If we attempt it, we shall presently 'hold to the one, and despise the other.'…It is our ignorance of God, the divine Principle, which produces apparent discord, and the right understanding of Him restores harmony." (Eddy) [3]

■■
****

Although most of the spiritual healings accomplished solely by prayer and recounted in this book are in Part II, Chapter 8, I have added several more that seemed appropriate. Continue reading.

Quadruple Blessings

In 1992 a man was having a difficult time in working a full day as he would become very tired doing just light work.[4] He was examined by a doctor who then told him that two of the arteries of his heart were almost completely blocked, and that he should be immediately scheduled for bypass surgery. Through a series of events, he was given a copy of "Science and Health, with Key to the Scriptures." Over the next few months he studied this book and other similar literature, spending as many hours as he could each day. Meanwhile the surgeon kept calling him urging him to have the operation, or he would die.

He was finally put on disability, and decided to move to San Francisco. He spent the next three months going to a *Christian Science Reading Room* where he studied "Science and Health" and prayed. During this period, he said, "I achieved a level of peace and happiness that I didn't know existed." He felt by this time he was ready to have help through prayer from a *Christian Science Practitioner*. Before the meeting with the Practitioner, he had to walk up a small hill to reach his car, finally arriving there completely out of breath.

He related that he had a wonderful hour-long conversation with the Practitioner who discussed with him spiritual thoughts and ideas. When he was ready to leave, he asked when they would have the next meeting. The Practitioner answered, "What for? You're healed!"

When the man returned home he tested his blood sugar, and found it was normal for the first time in seven years since he had been diagnosed with diabetes.

Later in the day the man had to walk three blocks up the steepest hill in San Francisco. He prayed for a while and then walked quickly up the hill with no loss of breath. He was exhilarated!

Two and a half years later, after moving back to Carmel, he met his former doctor, who inquired if he had had his surgery while in San Francisco. The man said that *Christian Science* (prayer) had healed him. The doctor was taken aback by this statement and insisted the man have a treadmill test. The man did so, and passed with flying colors. The doctor said that his arteries were clear, and called the man his "miracle patient."

It could be asked what caused the nearly instantaneous healings of the two physical diseases. It would seem to me first that the dedicated study and prayer by the man *before* meeting with the Practitioner ("I achieved a level of peace and happiness that I didn't know existed,") opened his thought to accept a blessing. Secondly, the Practitioner's certainty of the presence of the Divine contributed to the quick healings.

It should also be mentioned that the man was also healed of serious depression episodes; and later – after a month of intense study and prayer – was healed of the need of wearing glasses for reading.

All Things are Possible

In 1999, a woman fell and broke her shoulder. During surgery a metal implant about six inches long was put into her shoulder, but during later therapy, it was evident that something was wrong.[5] The doctor wanted to re-do the operation, but the woman decided she wanted to put her whole trust in God. She began to study the Bible and "Science and Health" with the prayerful purpose of learning more about God and her relationship to Him.

But the difficulty remained over a period of several years: she continued to feel pain in her shoulder, and the incision continued to drain. She wrestled with discouragement, and with resentment toward the doctor who had performed the surgery. Then one day she read an article in a *Christian Science Journal* about a man who was healed of anger and resentment toward a person who had shot him. Doctors had been unable to remove that bullet which had lodged near his heart. But when he finally overcame resentment, the bullet "came out of his chest naturally."

After reading about this experience the woman had such a "strong feeling that 'with God all things are possible.'" (Mark 10:27) All resentment toward the doctor left her. About two months later she awoke in the morning with a feeling that something with some weight was lying on her chest. The metal implant had come out of her shoulder during the night. The incision stopped draining and closed up.

Recently I was in the company of a woman who had just had an operation to repair dislocated bones in her foot. Post-operation was painful, and recovery took many weeks. This experience reminded me of Jesus' healing of the man with the withered hand, and of a healing that was recounted in a *Christian Science Journal* of a man with an incorrectly grown foot.[6] The foot was painful, and the problem had existed for so many years that the man felt that it would never be possible for it to be healed through prayer alone. He said that after hearing about other people's healings by prayer, and by praying himself, he would, upon observation of his foot, discover that nothing had changed. Very discouraged, he felt that he just did not have the spiritual inspiration and understanding to effect a healing.

One evening while in church listening intently to the service, he silently asked God "what *He* knew about this condition instead of 'leaning on my own understanding'" He had asked God this same question many times before, but this time, he said, he was not so wrapped up in himself and was actually ready to hear. While the answer did not come in any audibly discernable manner, the man said he could feel that it was genuine; in essence: "You have always been...my cherished, perfect child...You are my exact reflection, so *I* would have to have this problem in order for you to reflect it. But my allness is absolutely good, and I forbid it."

What the man called, "this revelation," could not be detected by any sensing device, but it was extremely substantial and real to him. A few days later while getting dressed he noticed his foot was normal and perfectly formed, and it has stayed that way for well over nineteen years. (No recuperative time needed.)

This experience brings to mind a healing in the mid-eighteen hundreds of a seven-year boy who had been born with what is called club-feet, both feet being turned backward. The child had never walked. One day the mother and son visited a near-by beach, the woman leaving her child lying on the beach while she hitched her horse and went for water. Shortly on her return, she finally found him down by the water and holding the hand of a strange woman. As Yvonne Cache von Fettweis and Robert Townsend Warneck relate in their book, *Mary Baker Eddy – Christian Healer* [7], the woman – Mary Baker Eddy – released the child's hand, and he stood alone. "Later he took a few steps and from that time on was able to walk. The boy later told his mother that the lady had asked him why he was not playing with the other children, and after she saw why (lifted the shawl that covered his feet), she put her hands under his arms and asked him to stand. Despite his protests she lifted him into an upright position, and guided his feet with her own, until he could walk on his own.

Mind, not Brain: Two Experiences

(1) – One night, around the year 2001, a man awoke in great distress, unable to move his left arm or leg.[8] At a hospital emergency room, he was told by physicians that he had suffered a massive stroke. After undergoing intensive rehabilitation therapy, he was told that he had suffered permanent damage to his brain: the left side of his body was completely paralyzed.

After about two years of going to the hospital three times a week for physical, occupational and speech therapy, with little progress being made, he was told that they had done all that was humanly possible for him. He was certified totally and permanently disabled. One afternoon he came across the book, *Science and Health, with Key to the Scriptures* by Mary Baker Eddy, which had remained on his book shelf for twenty-five years, having never been opened. When the following words were read to him from the first page: "To those leaning on the sustaining infinite, to-day is big with blessings," he was suddenly filled with an "overwhelming sense of hope." Several days later he read a passage from the book, and realized he was reading for the first time in two years, and *understanding* the spiritual message. He began studying *Science and Health* along with the *Bible*.

One morning after some study, he later related that "A sense of peace and joy like I'd never known before flooded over me." That same afternoon, the telephone rang and he lifted the receiver with the *left arm*, the one that was paralyzed. But late one evening his body began to tremble as if he were going to have a seizure. He immediately prayed with the Biblical statement, "Be still and know that I am God." He was healed of seizures in that moment, permanently. Over the next several months his depression began to turn into joy. He no longer felt he was subject to so-called laws of heredity. He read, "Citizens of the world, accept the 'glorious liberty of the children of God,' and be free! This is your divine right. The illusion of material sense, not divine law, has bound you, entangled your free limbs, crippled your capacities, enfeebled your body, and defaced the tablet of your being." He began to weep with joy. He rose unaided from his chair and took his first steps alone. Today – more than five years later since he read from *Science and Health*- he remains completely healed and free from any limitations.

(2) – A woman received a call that she was needed at her parents' home immediately. She called a *Christian Science Practitioner* to pray with her, and went to the home where she discovered that her father was paralyzed. [9] She asked if she could pray for him (He was not a Christian Scientist.) He agreed. As she prayed silently and deeply, she later related she began to feel at peace, and the fear dissipated. They called a doctor who came and examined her father, and who then told them that her father had had a paralytic stroke. He added that the man would have to live out the rest of his life in that condition. An ambulance was called to take her father to the hospital. The physician went on ahead and said he would meet them there. The woman made another call to the Practitioner, and in less than a minute her father was able to again move freely. Out of respect for the physician, they went to the hospital where the physician again saw her father. He said, "I have been a physician for over forty years and have never seen anything like this."

Her father had no recurrence of stroke and lived about seven more years. The woman had her thought so opened to the "greatness and goodness of God" that she eventually became a *Christian Science Practitioner* so she could help others in prayer.

Severe Internal Pain Eliminated by Prayer

A number of years ago a man was struck by severe pain in the upper abdomen. Although the man and a Christian Science *Practitioner* prayed for over a week, his condition continued to deteriorate rapidly.[10] At the end of that time – with no improvement whatsoever - he thought about admitting himself to a hospital; but he remembered his parent's plight which had not been helped by the best medical treatment. He decided to pray by himself. One night later, he was literally doubled up in pain, and he called another *Practitioner* in the middle of the night, whispering his request for help because he was so weak. As he later related, "Within *five minutes*, I felt more relief and comfort then I had at any time during the past two weeks, and what a feeling of joy came over me as I enjoyed a few hours' rest."

However, two nights later he again was in great pain and discomfort, and again called long distance, whispering his great need for prayerful help. *Immediately* after hanging up the telephone he felt as if a "hot poker had been thrust into my midsection," He thought he was going to die. Then the pain stopped, and he knew he was entirely healed – all this occurring within minutes of the telephone call. All the discomforts and attending hallucinations disappeared. He felt he had caught a recognition of the fact that God has created man in His image and likeness: spiritual, perfect and eternal. [∇]

All of God's Creation is Blessed

(1) –A woman I know related that her Labrador puppy struggled with a severe vision problem. Upon realizing this she expressed an "active stillness," ("Be still and know that I am God," (*Bible* [11]) praying and letting Truth come alive in her in "fresh, inspiring ways." (Testifier's comments) In her prayer for the dog, she came upon this statement in *Science and Health with Key to the Scriptures*: "The decaying flower, the blighted bud, the gnarled oak, the ferocious beast, - like the discords of disease, sin and death, - are unnatural. They are the falsities of sense, the changing deflections of mortal mind; they are not the eternal realities of Mind." [12] Blindness, then was not a part of the realm of Mind. Every time the woman looked at the dog or even thought about her, she would refuse to accept the idea that blindness could be part of her.

For a number of weeks the Labrador could not see movement even as close as ten feet, but after persistent prayer over a month she could suddenly see the woman's daughter coming around the corner from the bus stop one block distant. The healing has been permanent. [13]

(2) – A woman had a Great Dane named, "Regis" who was taken regularly for a number of years to the veterinarian to get his required shots. [14] After a few years the dog began to have pain through his midsection. The vet asked the woman and her husband to leave

---

[∇] I am personally acquainted with the testifier.

the dog at the clinic so tests could be made. The clinic discovered that the dog had cancer that had spread throughout his body; they recommended the dog be put to sleep. The woman told the vet she was a Christian Scientist (her husband was not) and that she wanted to deal with the cancer through prayer. She prayed every day, reasoning "that since God is all [good] there is no room for cancer."

She later related that taking care of the dog was not easy, and she agreed with the vet that if the dog began to suffer greatly they would put the dog to sleep. The next eight months were hard and sometimes discouraging, but conditions did not warrant ending the dog's life. The couple noticed that Regis had more pain when the husband was near the dog, even though he loved the dog very much. It was suggested to the husband by a *Christian Science Practitioner* who was praying with them that every time the man thought about the dog he could pray the *Lord's Prayer* that Christ Jesus gave to humanity.

One day the husband asked the wife why she was continually feeding the dog by hand because he appeared to be healthy. And the dog was: the weight was returned to normalcy and his coat was healthy.

The vet said later that initially he had serious doubts about the dog being treated through prayer, but he also did not want to put the dog down. He acknowledged that Regis made a complete recovery; and since then he says he has had "several other experiences of the power of prayer and healing with wonderful results.' He added that with several cases that he had seen, that it does depend on whether patients have the will to live and feel that they have a purpose to live life, and not die.

Listening…and Being Obedient

The experiences of two young people who had been taught to daily listen for Mind's thoughts and to act upon them, to be obedient to them, are illustrated below: [15]

One young man went to a used car lot searching for parts for his car. As he walked into the area, he suddenly "heard" in thought the command to "run!" This did not make sense to him, but he was obedient and ran. Seconds later the truck he had been passing blew up, the pieces scattering everywhere, but none touching him.

A fellow Sunday School student, also having learned about the need to listen and be obedient to Mind's unceasing outpouring of ideas was led to pull his motorized bike off the side of the road, get off, and look down into a ravine. He saw a car with a woman inside it, who had been trapped for over two hours, He was able to call for help to rescue her.

Metaphysics over Physics

The experience of the man falling with a partially-opened parachute, but was unharmed comes to mind (Part II, Chapter 2, "Conscious Union with Mind"). A woman had taken her child to a park with some friends. After a while she looks around and notices some distance away that her little boy has climbed to the top of a very high slide.[16] As described in a Christian Science Sentinel, "He falters, then falls off the slide." After a "frozen" moment, she and a friend run to the slide. "She witnesses something truly awesome. It's as though her child is floating downward like a feather."

They reach the base of the slide just as the child reaches the ground, "completely unharmed."

The mother of the young boy was beginning to learn about and love the liberating truths relative to God and His/Her creation. Until recently the human mind would categorically reject such an experience as a possibility outside of physical law. But as mentioned in Introduction to the ADDENDUM, the emerging awareness of consciousness, and of a universal Consciousness, should give people pause in considering such experiences as related here.

The author of the above-mentioned Sentinel article also told me of his personal experience of falling backward onto a concrete floor as he began to climb down from a twelve foot high stack of wood. He said, "It felt as though I landed in a pile of those styrofoam peanuts, totally unaffected. I spent days pondering the implications of that experience."[17] ⊕

God Governs the Weather – and Animals

A friend in England related to me her experience: Back in the 1980's she was a purser (flight attendant) for British Airways. Her flight was scheduled for Cork in Ireland. But the First Officer told her they, instead, would be flying to Shannon because Cork was fog-bound and below limits. The Captain then told her the same story. But the woman had been praying to realize that God is infinite good, and in control of the weather, and that the passengers had a legitimate right to get to their destination on time to meet their loved ones. She then asked the Captain, "Captain, can you please TRY to get in?" He - rather startled – said that he would only make one attempt. To which she replied, "We'll get in the first time."

The plane headed for Cork and did land successfully. The only flight in the entire day. But almost immediately thick clouds of fog started to roll in and the terminal faded from view. The Captain was furious. "Look at this. This is all your fault. I should never have listened to you. We're going to be stuck here all day!"

"No we're not! She retorted. "We got in and we're going to get out!" The passengers boarded, and as they did so the fog parted (like Moses and the Red Sea). To her knowledge her flight was the only one in or out that day.

****

More recently, the same friend related that her dog was attacked by a Jack Russell Terrier. The tooth of the Russel caused a deep hole in her dog, with blood and matted fur all around the wound. She could not clean the wound because it caused her dog distress. She and a friend who was staying with her prayed, knowing that all of God's creatures come under the Law of divine protection.

⊕ I had a similar but very minor experience of falling off the third rung of a ladder. I appeared to fall slowly and gently to the ground.

When she arrived home the next day there was no sign of the injury – "…no hole, no missing fur, no blood, no matted hair. The flesh had filled in, the hair was all grown back." [18]

Quick Healing of Diagnosed H1N1 Flu

A woman in New York State was diagnosed with H1N1 influenza, or "swine flu." That evening and throughout most of the night she struggled with the flu symptoms. In the morning, still suffering and afraid she called a Christian Science Practitioner to pray with her. As a result of prayer she began to realize that "… sin, sickness and death are not of God [A God who is good, only]. She thought of Psalms 23 (verse 4): "Yea, though I walk through the valley of the shadow of death, I will fear no evil: for thou art with me." She realized, among other ideas, that God would lead her in paths of goodness, righteousness, peace and joy. She continued in prayer, and eventually felt the sickness begin to lose its hold on her. This was replaced by an "overwhelming sense of joy." She climbed out of bed, put on her running shoes and went for a four mile run, completely healed. [19]

Pancreas and Liver Cancers Healed by Scientific, Spiritual Prayer

In the late 1980's a man owned a small construction company. It was a very time-consuming and stressful job. He had been recently married and was trying to maintain a home and family life. This, too, was somewhat stressful. [20]

One day the man began to manifest the symptoms of what he thought was a stomach or intestinal virus. A few weeks later in the middle of a very large and demanding job, his marriage fell apart, and a key employee left the company. About that time he was invited to relocate his business in Guam. This effort proved draining and put additional demands on him in regard to moving, finding supplies for his business and in setting up new schedules. Also, the island was hit by typhoons which battered the region in which he was relocating.

By this time the man had lost over 70 pounds, and was in great pain. He decided now to visit a doctor who examined him, took many tests including a CAT scan. The resulting conclusion? The doctor said the man was seriously ill with cancer of the pancreas and liver, and had – at best – three months to live. There was no hope, he said, unless medical treatment was begun immediately; but even then the chances of survival were slim. [∉]

The man was stunned! He decided now to call a Christian Science Practitioner to pray with him. Gradually, he began to replace hateful thoughts with thoughts of gratitude, and he began to realize that God, and not fleshly body, was "the source of my life." Fear began to disappear as he found himself gaining mentally and spiritually. But he still was losing ground physically.

One night he could not sleep because of severe pain. He was exhausted and felt that he could not go on. But then he remembered a passage from *Science and Health*,

---

[∉] Obviously, because of the man's delay in visiting the doctor, there was no early detection of the cancers. They were well-developed.

with Key to the Scriptures, "Become conscious for a single moment that Life and intelligence are purely spiritual, - neither in nor of matter, - and the body will then utter no complaints." The answer that came as a result of this "angel" thought was: just "let go of it," – let go of hatred, resentment, and the idea he was a victim, and that he could be separated from God or divine Love.

As he later related, "I felt a great sense of peace, and I willingly agreed with 'Not my will, but thine be done.' " (Luke 22:42) He slept that night for the first time in a long time. The pain was gone – never to return.

In 2000, the man was examined be a doctor in order to get a Scuba instructor's certificate, No cancer.

The man is grateful for the healing, but even more for learning to humbly trust in God who is Life itself! ♥

Placebo Effect Increasing

"Why are inert pills [placebos] suddenly overwhelming promising new drugs and established medicines alike?" This statement or question appeared in *Wired,* September, 2009. [21] It has also been demonstrated that volunteers who received real medication were also subject to placebo effects: the very act of taking a pill *boosted the curative power of the medicine.* Only by subtracting the improvement in a placebo control group could the actual value of the drug be calculated. (*Wired*)

But why the sudden increase in the effectiveness of placebos? One reason could be that the public has less trust in the benefits of medicine. In "Placebos Aren't a Mystery," (*Christian Science Sentinel*) [22] the writer says," ... it seems possible that news reports, individual experiences, published exposes by medical doctors, revelations of collusions between drug manufactures and even the most respected doctors and academic research laboratories have combined to lessen public trust in traditional chemical-based drugs, and to increase the public intrinsic trust in drugless cures."

The Pure Simplicity and Effectiveness of Divine Love

A two year old boy asked his daddy about an ugly looking wound his father had on his nose. [23] The man was fearful that a small wound that had been troubling him had been compounded because of his many years of surfing in the strong Florida sun. He told his son that the nose wound had happened when the child had accidently scratched him a few days ago when they were playing together. The little boy said, "Oh, I'm sorry Papa." He then placed his hand over his father's nose and sang the only song he knew: "Jingle Bells." The father had often sung hymns to his son at bedtime, and so the little boy was doing the same thing for him. The father later recounted, "It was bedtime, it was dark, and as my son sang to me my eyes filled with tears, and my heart filled with Love [another name for God]. How could I ever believe that a scratch from this dear child

---

♥ Sometimes we hear the comment that if so- and- so had gone to a doctor instead of seeking prayer he/she would be alive today. In this experience above, the man would have surely died if he had sought medical treatment.

could grow into an ugly, inflamed wound?" When the father awoke the next morning, there was no trace of the wound. The man realized that just as he loved his son, so does our Father, God love us, and would never do anything to consciously cause us pain. (Matt.7:9, "… what man is there of you whom if his son ask bread, will he give him a stone?")

Light of Truth Dispels Darkness of Atheism and Heredity

A man had been an atheist [Π] since getting out of college, and had believed for more than thirty years that he had no connection with God. [24] Also, since the age of fourteen when he legally received a driver's license, he had been required to wear glasses.

For some years the man had suffered from a tremor in his right hand, a condition that his mother, her two sisters and her father, had also suffered along with severe tremors. Eventually, the tremors became so severe that he consulted a orthopedist who diagnosed the condition as "focal action dystonia." The prescribed medication did not help at all. The tremors worsened. Finally, at the insistence of his wife who was a Christian Scientist, he visited a Christian Science practitioner "just to get her off my back." The man believed that Christian Science was "goofy," and – from his perspective as an atheist – was "nuts."

The practitioner spoke to the man for about twenty minutes, but the man later related that at that time none of what she said made any sense to him – it made no sense at all. The practitioner then handed the man a piece of paper and pen and asked him to write something on the paper with his right hand (the hand that suffered tremors). And for the first time in many, many years he wrote freely, without pain and without shaking. He was completely healed. He said that at that moment, "I was as certain of the existence of God after my healing, as I was of the nonexistence of God before my healing." He said it was as if a light had been turned on in a pitch-black room! It was not "faith" that healed him because at that time he had not faith.

His explanation for the immediate healing was "The practitioner's knowledge of what was true was more powerful than something that I believed to be true" [no God, and a diseased hand]. The magnificent power of divine Truth held firmly in consciousness can dissolve human resistance (the "patient's") to new and healing ideas.

Later, the man also was healed of the need of wearing glasses. The only "specific" prayer (after looking more deeply into the nature of God and of man's inseparable relation to Him,) was to daily thank God for his perfect vision. He eventually put aside his glasses, and soon passed his driver's eye test with perfect vision.

[Π] atheist: one who believes there is no God; or, *one who does not believe in what he thinks God is.*

FINAL, FINAL THOUGHTS
And
BOOK CONCLUSIONS

****

FINAL, FINAL THOUGHTS

"Christianity...is all about unconditional Love. And Science is all about unconditional Truth. ..." One of the greatest scientific achievements will be the "... unification of Love and Truth..." which will show that they were one and the same thing. "...this is the Grand Unification [Theory] that physicists and cosmologists are seeking today. [All is infinite Mind]"[1]

"We lose the high signification of omnipotence, when after admitting that God, or good, is omnipresent and has all-power, we still believe there is another power, named *evil.*"[2]

"The kingdom of God is within you."[3]

"Time" is an interval between material events.
"Space" is the distance between material objects.

- If matter does not exist, there is no time; there is no space; there is no space-time (relativity)[4]
- The *Delayed-Choice Double-Slit* experiments (and other similar experiments) indicate that a sub-atomic particle has no definite path from source to target, and no objective existence until measured or observed.
- Sub-atomic particles have been shown to have equal potential of existing in two different places (quantum superposition of states) until a measurement has been made.
- *EPR* experiments have shown that there is instantaneous correlation between two sub-atomic particles jointly emitted in opposite directions from some event, and now separated from each other (quantum entanglement), even by great distances. The conclusion from the experiments is that reality is non-local and non-objective, since observer or experimentalist A, by his measurement of the characteristics of particle A, determines instantaneously the characteristics of particle B. The individual particles have no objective characteristics until measured. Instantaneous correlation indicates No SPACE, NO TIME, and consequently, NO MATTER, and an interconnectedness or ONENESS with all that exists. All substance is consciousness.
- Therefore, all that exists is CONSCIOUSNESS, and IDEAS of CONSCIOUSNESS. Consciousness is the primary measurement.[5] If the ideas are limited, fearful, hateful, etc., they give wrong and illusory results (chaos, destruction, material objects in space-time), and are unreal. If the ideas are unlimited, good, loving, and give

blessings, they come from God, the one and only Mind or Consciousness, and they are real and spiritual.
- The final observer of the so-called physical universe is collective, unitive, non-local and aware consciousness. As Nick Herbert points out in his book "Quantum Reality" that it is difficult to understand how a random, irreversible process can exchange uncertainty or ignorance at the quantum level (a quantum wave function containing a multiplicity of potential quantum states) for information at the macroscopic level (wave function collapses to a single state; and a record made by an inanimate or non-conscious recording device, *with this information still hidden from a conscious observer.* That is, how can any material object collapse a wave function; how could a material structure gain information or knowledge unless it possessed or shared in some conscious awareness? How can a wave function (a "probability wave") collapse into a particle if the wave function is no more than a mathematical formulation?
- The first (and only) Cause is Mind, the only true Consciousness.
- "Time" is the sense that we have to wait for some event to happen, when the idea of the event already exists, and only needs to be apprehended in consciousness. A physical difficulty may seem to exist over a long period of time, or good may seem to be years away. But both the difficulty and the good are ideas; the former "exists" only as a false belief, and can be dispensed with now, and the latter is a divine, unlimited idea and ever-present.
- "Space" is the sense that we can be separated from ideas or objects. Galaxies are too far away in space and time (space-time) that if there were intelligent beings living there on a planet orbiting a star, we would never be able to touch them or give them a hug. (We should not have to travel through a black hole in order to reach so-called distant objects! Consider Jesus' instantaneous transfer across the Sea of Galilee). But a galaxy is a compound idea of Spirit, and never separated from other spiritual ideas. A physical difficulty may seem to prevent someone from walking to the local grocery store, when in reality the divine ideas of true substance are already present (including the idea of limitless being.)

Has Mankind Descended from Monkeys?

Mary Baker Eddy said, "May not Darwin be right in thinking that apehood preceded mortal manhood? Did man, whom God created with a word, originate in an egg? When Spirit made all, did it leave aught for matter to create? Ideas of Truth alone are reflected in the myriad manifestations of Life, and thus it is seen that man springs solely from Mind. The belief that matter supports life would make Life, or God, mortal, and also make man mortal."[6] This book has defended the statement that the real nature of man is wholly spiritual, and the claim that man has descended from monkeys is based on the illusion of the senses, which see what collective human thought believes. But how do we know this? How can we say that man is spiritual, and "…not made up of material history, evolution or otherwise…that disease is unreal?"[7]

The answer is that spiritual healings, especially the so-called instantaneous ones, "…are what show an individual that he/she is spiritually made and good – entirely derived from Spirit [God], not matter or [evolving over time] from monkeys."[8] Physics and medical experiments and data are strongly indicating that at the very ground of reality consciousness is prime and universal, and not evolved from matter or constrained by a matter-brain. And the source of all true consciousness and right ideas is Mind, God.

BOOK CONCLUSIONS – What of the Future ?

Quantum entanglement (quantum non-locality), quantum superposition at the macroscopic level with the future possibility of superposition of living organisms, the suggested claim for the falsity of the doctrine of local reality (realism) - all of these – challenge the material senses' concept of reality. $^{\Psi}$

Spiritual healings – especially the very quick or "instantaneous" ones that appear to defy the laws of physics as we know them, strongly point to a different kind of realty beyond matter and space-time – a reality of Spirit/Mind. Much has been said in this book about the mental nature of the so-called physical reality and in the primacy of consciousness. An overnight healing of a large cancerous growth on the face, the disappearance of cataracts in a matter of hours, or the slow fall of a child from the top of a high slide point to a change in the state of consciousness, a consciousness now imbued with the thoughts or truths of God who is infinite Love! Not of a capricious God who mysteriously decided to set aside laws of physics and perform a "miracle".

We could say (for example in the case of the cancer) that the individual's original state of thought was more like being in a dream-state, or an hypnotic state, because upon gaining some beginning awakening to Truth (the love of Love; the absolute unreality of life and substance in matter), the cancer disappeared from conscious thought and from the body – as if it never existed. Could we not say that the appearance of the cancer was like the first layer of skin on an onion, the removal of which by an increase in the spiritualization of thought brought a somewhat higher or awakened sense of the reality of Spirit which appeared to be hidden by multiple layers (like onion skins) of false, fearful thoughts and conclusions? In her book, "Science and Health with Key to the Scriptures", Mary Baker Eddy says "… the heavens and earth to one human consciousness, that consciousness which God bestows, are spiritual, while to another, the unillumined human mind, the vision is material. This shows unmistakably that what the human mind terms matter and spirit indicates states and stages of consciousness." [9]

Speaking of his close friend, Lazarus who had died, Christ Jesus said, "Our friend Lazarus sleepeth; but I go, that I may awake him out of sleep." (John 11). [10] And in Romans 13, Paul said, "Love worketh no ill to his neighbour: therefore love is the fulfilling of the law. And that, knowing the time, that now it is high time to awake out of sleep: for now is our salvation nearer than when we believed." [11] Jesus must have known that the so-called mortal existence is a dream, with a smattering of signs of a spiritual reality, of harmony, of good largely hidden from the material senses, and with mostly

---

$^{\Psi}$ Non-locality: a direct or instantaneous influence or relationship of one object on another, as if there is no physical separation between them; i.e., between God(Mind), and Mind's ideas (mankind).

Quantum entanglement (example) : Two particles are created from some kind of atomic reaction, the particles travel outward from the reaction in opposite directions. The quantum wave function describes the state of the two-particle system. The spin of both particles of the entangled pair are indeterminate until the spin of one particle (say, #1) is observed or measured. Upon observation of particle (#2) it is discovered that there is a direct correlation of the particle (#2) spin with that of particle (#1). This phenomenon occurs instantaneously over vast distances.

Quantum superposition of states : A particle or particles can exist simultaneously in two different quantum states, until a measurement or observation is made, at which time the quantum wave function collapses to a single state.

Objective reality or realism : the assumption that objects possess a reality that is independent of observation

dream-like states of so-called material life with its pains, hatred, suffering, violent weather, and eventual death. Thus, through the prayers of Jesus, Lazarus was "awakened" from a belief of death.

Christ Jesus knew so well his relationship with God, (a non-local relationship, or a relationship independent of space and time) that in his Ascension he rose in thought above all sense of material limitations: he entirely peeled off all the onion layers!

May we not also reason that Life, Soul, and Mind or consciousness ⊕ are non-local, not found in, or dependent on, the creation of billions of finite, physical bodies for expression? Man individually reflects God, who is Mind (divine consciousness), Life and Soul. Since Soul is now seen to be God, and man individually has no soul or life in a matter body, but reflects Soul/Spirit, the experience called "death" would not snuff out our life and identity since they have their source in eternal God, Spirit. "The educated belief that Soul is in the body causes mortals to regard death as a friend, as a stepping stone out of mortality into immortality and bliss. The Bible call death and enemy, and Jesus overcame death and the grave instead of yielding to them." [12]

At this period humanity has an opportunity to drop outmoded and worn-out concepts of God as either non-existent, indifferent to the sufferings of mankind, incapable of helping the world, or being the creator of evil, itself. We have the opportunity, and choice now to embrace a higher concept of God!

What is your choice, and what will the future bring for you?

⊕ If thought can result in changes in the body, then consciousness, not matter is prime and real. And what kind of thoughts? Not finite, limited and fearful matter brain- centered thoughts, but higher and real spiritual thoughts of divine Spirit.

Bibliography

Part I: References listed under each Chapter include references for the Chapter APPENDIX, if that chapter has an APPENDIX.

Introduction and Historical Perspective

1. Mary Baker Eddy, *Christian Healing*, (The First Church of Christ, Scientist, Boston, Massachusetts, U.S.A.), p. 23.
2. Tom Alexander, "The Shimmery New Image of Matter," *Fortune,* (June1, 1968), p.11.
3. Lucretius, (First Century BC).
4. John Archibald Wheeler, *Gravity and Space-time*(Scientific American Library: A division of HPHLP, 1990), p. 230.
5. Encyclopedia Americana.
6. *Bible*: Acts 7:48.
7. Stephan Hawking, *Black Holes and Baby Universes*. (Bantom Books, New York, 1993).
8. Mary Baker Eddy, *Science and Health with Key to the Scriptures* (The First Church of Christ, Scientist, Boston, Massachusetts, U.S.A), p. 124.
9. *Bible:* John 1:1.
10. Robert Park, quoted by Constance Holden in "Subjecting Belief to the Scientific Method", *Science,* (May 21, 1999).
11. P. C. W. Davies, *God and the New Physics* (Simon and Schuster, Inc., 1983), pp. 102, 103.

Part I
The Quantum Universe

1. Sir Arthur Eddington, "The Domain of Physical Science," in *Essay in Science and Reality*
2. John Archibald Wheeler, "Hermann Weyl and the Unity of Knowledge," *American Scientist*, (July-August, 1986), vol.74, p. 374,

Chapter One
Quantum Physics : What is it?

1. Pierre de Laplace, (1749-1827).

Chapter Two
Newtonian Universe vs. Quantum Universe

1. Hugh Elliot, (1881-1930).

Chapter Three
Wave – Particle Duality of Nature

1. D. Halliday, R. Resnick, *Fundamentals of Physics*, 2nd Edition, Chapter 40, (John Wiley and Sons).

Chapter Four
Black Body Radiation

1. Asimov, *The History of Physics,* Chapter 23, (Walker and Company, New York,1966).

Chapter Five
Quantum World Beginnings – The Photoelectric Effect

1. W. E. Lamb, M. O. Scully, *Polarization, Matiere et Rayonnment* (Presses University de France, 1969).
2. P. Granglier, G. Roger and A. Aspect, "Experimental for a photon anti-correlation effect on a beam splitter," *Europhys. Lett*, vol. 1, pp 173-179, 1986.
3. George Greenstein and Arthur G. Zajonc, *The Quantum Challenge* (Jones and Bartlett Publishers, Sudbury, Massachusetts, 1997).

Chapter Seven
Quantized Electron Energy States

1. D. Bohm, *Wholeness and the Implicate Order,* (Routledge and Kegan Paul, London, Boston and Henley), p-ix.
2. *Bible*: II Peter 3:8.
3. R. T. Weidner, R. L. Sells, *Elementary Modern Physics,* Chapter 5 (Allyn and Bacon, Inc, Boston, 1960).

Chapter Nine
The Principle of Complementarity

1. Ibid., *Elementary Modern Physics*, Chapter I.
2. Ibid., *Elementary Modern Physics*, Chapter 4.

Chapter Ten
Probability

1. R. P. Feynman, R. B. Leighton, M. Sands, *The Feynman Lectures on Physics,* vol. 1, Chapter 6 (Addison-Wesley Publishing Company, New York, 1963).
2. A. Goswami, M. Goswami, *The Cosmic Dancers,* Chapter 15 (Harper and Row Publishers, New York, 1983).
3. Nick Herbert, *Quantum Reality* (Anchor Press/Doubleday, Garden City, New York, 1985), pp. 190-191.

Chapter Eleven
The Wave Equation

1. W, Heisenberg, Physics and Beyond (Harper and Row, New York, 1971)
2. D. C. Giancoli, *Physics for Scientists and Engineers,* 2nd Edition (Prentice Hall, Englewood Cliffs, New Jersey, 1989).
3. "Gravity Leaps into Quantum World," *Nature* Science Update, January 14, 2002

Chapter Twelve
Electron in a Potential Well

1. D. C. Giancoli, *Physics for Scientists and Engineers,* 2nd Edition (Prentice Hall, Englewood Cliffs, New Jersey, 1989), Chapter 42.
2. D. C. Giancoli, *Physics for Scientists and Engineers,* 2nd Edition (Prentice Hall, Englewood Cliffs, New Jersey, 1989), Chapter 43.
3. "Gravity Leaps into Quantum World," *Nature* Science Update, January 14, 2002

Chapter Thirteen
Electron in a Hydrogen Atom

1. D.C. Giancoli, *Physics for Scientists and Engineers,* 2nd Edition (Prentice Hall, Englewood Cliffs, New Jersey, 1989), Chapter 43.
2. F. A. Wolf, *Star Wave* (Collier Books, Macmillan Publishing Company, New York, N.Y), p. 77-79.
3. F. A. Wolf, *Star Wave* (Collier Books, Macmillan Publishing Company, New York, N.Y), p. x.
4. D. C. Giancoli, *Physics for Scientists and Engineers,* 2nd Edition (Prentice Hall, Englewood Cliffs, New Jersey, 1989), Chapter 15.
5. R. L. Sproull, *Modern Physics* (John Wiley and Sons, Inc, New York, N.Y., 1956),

Chapter Fourteen
The Heisenberg Uncertainty Principle

1. F. A. Jenkins, H. E. White, *Fundamentals of Optics*, 3rd Edition (Mc Graw-Hill Book Company, 1957), Chapter 13.
2. F. A. Jenkins, H. E. White, *Fundamentals of Optics*, 3rd Edition (Mc Graw-Hill Book Company, 1957), Chapter 15.

Chapter Fifteen
Physical and Thought Experiments in Quantum Physics

A - Double and Single Slit Experiments

1. D. C. Giancoli, *Physics for Scientists and Engineers,* 2nd Edition (Prentice Hall, Englewood Cliffs, New Jersey,1989), Chapter 38.
2. R. P. Feynman, R .B. Leighton, M. Sands, *The Feynman Lectures on Physics,* vol 1, Chapter 37 (Addison-Wesley Publishing Company, New York, 1963), pp. 37-3.
3. R. P. Feynman, R. B. Leighton, M. Sands, *The Feynman Lectures on Physics,* vol 1, Chapter 37 (Addison-Wesley Publishing Company, New York, 1963), pp. 37-7.
4. R. P. Feynman, R. B. Leighton, M. Sands, *The Feynman Lectures on Physics,* vol 1, Chapter 37 (Addison-Wesley Publishing Company, New York, 1963), pp. 37-11.
5. Amir D. Aczel, *Entanglement* (Four Walls Eight Windows, New York, 2002), pp. 25-27.

B - The Delayed – Choice Experiment

1. J. A. Wheeler, "Delayed-Choice Experiment and the Boh –Einstein Dialog," Paper presented at the *American Philosophical Society*, London, June 5, 1980, (Preparation for publication assisted by the *University of Texas Center for Theoretical Physics,* and by *National Science Foundation* Grant PHY78 – 26592).
2. Ibid.
3. Ibid.
4. Ibid.
5. Ibid.
6. Ibid.

C – The Non-Interfering Delayed-Choice Double-Slit Experiment

1. John Horgan, *"Quantum Philosophy", Scientific American,* July, 1992
2. Correspondence with Leonard Mandel, Lee DuBridge *Professor of Physics and Optics, Department of Physics and Astronomy, University of Rochester,* February, 1994.
3. John Horgan, *"Quantum Philosophy", Scientific American,* July, 1992. .

4. George Greenstein and Arthur G. Zajonc, *The Quantum Challenge* (Jones and Bartlett Publishers, Sudbury, Massachusetts, 1997), p. 90.
5. D. M. Greenberger, M. A. Horne, A. Zeilinger, "Multiparticle Interferometry and the Superposition Principle," *Physics Today*, August, 1993, p. 25.
6. D. M. Greenberger, M. A. Horne, A. Zeilinger, "Multiparticle Interferometry and the Superposition Principle," *Physics Today*, August, 1993, p. 27.

D – Wheeler's Game of Twenty Questions

1. John Archibald Wheeler, "Time Today", Physics Dept., *University of Texas*, (1993), to appear in proceedings of workshop: *Physical Origins of Time Symmetry* (Cambridge University Press) p. 24.
2. J. A. Wheeler, "Beyond the Black Hole, Some Strangeness in the Proportion: A Centennial to Celebrate the Achievements of Albert Einstein," H. Woolf, Ed (Preparation for publication assisted by *University of Texas Center for Theoretical Physics* and by NSF grant PHY 78-26592).
3. Heisenberg, *Physics and Beyond*, (New York, Harper and Row, 1971)
4. John Archibald Wheeler, "Hermann Weyl and the Unity of Knowledge," *American Scientist*, vol. 74, July-August, 1986, p. 374.
5. J. A. Wheeler, *"Delayed- Choice Experiment and the Bohr-Einstein Dialog,"* Paper presented at the *American Philosophical Society*, London, June 5, 1980, Preparation for publication assisted by the *University of Texas Center for Theoretical Physics, and by National Science Foundation* Grant PHY78 – 26592).

E – The EPR Paradox

1. A. Einstein, B. Podolsky, N. Rosen, "Can Quantum – Mechanical Description of Physical Reality Be Considered Complete?," *The Physical Review,* 47 (1935) : 777.
2. B. d' Espagnat, "The Quantum Theory and Reality," *Scientific American*, Nov.,1979.
3. H. R. Pagels, *The Cosmic Code*, Chapter 12 (Bantam Books, New York,1983, p. 138.
4. George Greenstein and Arthur G. Zajonc, *The Quantum Challenge* (Jones and Bartlett Publishers, Sudbury, Massachusetts, 1997), p. 110.
5. P. C. W. Davies and J. R. Brown, Eds, *The Ghost in the Atom*, Chapter 1(Cambridge University Press, New York, 1986), p. 14.
6. J. Gribbon, *In Search of Schrodinger's Cat,* Chapter 9 (Bantam Books, New York, 1984), p. 182.
7. John Horgan, "Quantum Philosophy,*" Scientific American,* July, 1992.
8. B. d' Espagnat, "The Quantum Theory and Reality," *Scientific American*, Nov., 1979.
9. B. d' Espagnat, "The Quantum Theory and Reality," *Scientific American*, Nov., 1979.
10. B. d' Espagnat, "The Quantum Theory and Reality," *Scientific American*, Nov., 1979.
11. J. Bell, "On the Einstein-Podolsky-Rosen Paradox", *Physics*, vol.1, 1964, pp.195-200.
12. J. Bell, "On the Problem of Hidden Variables in Quantum Mechanics", *Rev. Mod. Phys.*, vol. 38, 1966, pp. 442-447.
13. F. David Peat, *Einstein's Moon,* Chapter 5 (Contemporary Books, Inc, Chicago, 1990), p. 105.

14. D. M. Greenberger, M.A. Horne, A. Zeilinger, "Multi-particle Interferometry and the Superposition Principle," *Physics Today.*
15. David Peat, *Einstein's Moon,* Chapter 5 (Contemporary Books, Inc, Chicago, 1990), p. 108.
16. David Peat, *Einstein's Moon,* Chapter 5 (Contemporary Books, Inc, Chicago, 1990), p. 108.
17. B. d' Espagnat, "The Quantum Theory and Reality," *Scientific American*, Nov. 1979.
18. David Peat, *Einstein's Moon* (Contemporary Books, Inc, Chicago, 1990), p. 109.
19. Ibid., p. 112.
20. Ibid., p. 112.
21. A, Aspect, J. Dalibard, G. Roger, "Experimental Test of Bell's Inequalities," *Physical Review Letters*, vol. 49, p. 91.
22. A, Aspect, J. Dalibard, G. Roger, "Experimental Test of Bell's Inequalities," *Physical Review Letters*, vol. 49, p. 91.
23. "Quantum Spookiness Wins, Einstein Loses in Photon Contest", *Science,* vol. 277, (25 July, 1997).
24. "Atom Tangle," *Nature*, 413, 27 September 2001, pp. 400-403; and "Trillion–atom Triumph", *Nature Science Update,* (October 1, 2001).
25. Tony Leggett, "Quantum Theory: Weird and Wonderful"*, Physics World*, (December, 1999).
26. George Greenstein and Arthur G. Zajonc, *The Quantum Challenge* (Jones and Bartlett Publishers, Sudbury, Massachusetts, 997), p. 144.
27. J. S. Bell, "The Moral Aspect of Quantum Mechanics" in *Preludes in Theoretical Physics* (North-Holland Publishing, Amsterdam, 1966, p. 284.
28. George Greenstein and Arthur G. Zajonc, *The Quantum Challenge* (Jones and Bartlett Publishers, Sudbury, Massachusetts, 1997), p. 144-145.
29. Ibid.
30. Ibid.
31. "Exorcising Einstein's Spooks,*" Nature Science Update,* 29 November, 2001

F. <u>Experiments in Quantum Teleportation</u>

1. Dik Bouwmeester, et al, "Experimental Quantum Teleportation," *Nature*, vol. 390, 11 Dec., 1997.
2. King James Bible, John 6:21

Chapter Sixteen
Virtual Particles

1. C. Sutton, *The Particle Connection*, Chapter 4 (Simon and Schuster, New York, 1984).
2. C. Sutton, *The Particle Connection*, Chapter 4 (Simon and Schuster, New York, 1984).
3. "Space-Time: The Final Frontier," *Sky and Telescope*, Feb. 1996.

4. Private communication with J. Hubbell, Palo Alto, California, quoted in a public talk: "Divine Truth Frees You From Limitation,"1990.
5. J. Gribbon, *In Search of Schrodinger's Cat* (Bantam Books, New York,1984), p. 271-272.
6. "Universe Expansion is Accelerating, UK and Australian Researchers Say, " *Monthly Notice of the Royal Astronomical* Society, March 20, 2002.
7. J. A. Wheeler, "Delayed-Choice Experiment and the Boh –Einstein Dialog," Paper Presented at the *American Philosophical Society*, London, June 5, 1980, (Preparation for publication assisted by the *University of Texas Center for Theoretical Physics,* and by *National Science Foundation* Grant PHY78 – 26592), pp. 37-39.
8. Sir A. Eddington, *"The Domain of Physical Science",* in *Essay in Science, Religion and Reality*, and referenced in public talk: "Exploring the Realm of Divine Spirit," by J. Hubbell.
9. J .Hubbell, public talk: "Exploring the Realm of Divine Spirit."
10. *Science*, Feb 9, 1996.

Chapter Seventeen
Possible Interpretations of Quantum Phenomena

1. B. De Witt, "Quantum Mechanics and Reality," *Physics Today,* September, 1970.
2. N. Herbert, *Quantum Reality-Beyond the New Physics* (Anchor Press / Doubleday, Garden City, New Jersey,1985), p. 157-197.
3. J. A. Wheeler, "Mercer Street and Other Memories," 1979 (P. C. Aichelburg and R. Sexl, eds), in *Albert Einstein : His Influence on Physics, Philosophy and Politics,* (Braunschweig: Vieweg), p. 201-211.
4. D. Bohm, *Wholeness and the Implicate Order,* (Routledge and Kegan Paul, London, Boston and Henley).
5. M. Talbot, *Beyond the Quantum*, Chapter 2, (Bantam Books, New York, 1988), pp. 41-42.
6. Ibid., p. 43.
7. Ibid., p. 43.
8. Ibid., Chapter 2.
9. F. A. Wolf, *Parallel Universes* (Simon and Schuster, New York, 1988), p. 110.
10. M. Talbot, *Beyond the Quantum*, Chapter 2, (Bantam Books, New York, 1988).
11. M. Talbot, *The Holographic Universe* (Harper Collins Publishers, 1991), pp. 33, 47.
12. E. Harrison, *Masks of the Universe* (Macmillan Publishing Company, New york / Collier Macmillan Publishers, London, 1985).
13. B. Josephon, *"The Reach of the Mind"* : *Nobel Prize Conversations* (Dallas, Texas, Saybrook Publishing Company, 1985).
14. E. A. Abbott, "Flatland"*, The World of Mathematics,* vol 4 (Simon and Schuster, New York, 1956) p. 2385.
15. *Bible*: II Cor. 13:12.
16. N. Herbert, N. Herbert, *Quantum Reality-Beyond the New Physics* (Anchor Press / Doubleday, Garden City, New Jersey, 1985), p. 162.

17. Ibid., p. 167.
18. Ibid., p. 192.
19. George Greenstein and Arthur G. Zajonc, *The Quantum Challenge* (Jones and Bartlett Publishers, Sudbury, Massachusetts, 1997), p. 159.
20. F. David Peat, *Einstein's Moon,* Chapter 5 (Contemporary Books, Inc, Chicago, 1990), (As quoted in Chapter 6), p. 123.
21. H. R. Pagels, *The Cosmic Code* (Bantam Books, New York, 1983), p. 129.
22. Ibid., p. 106.
23. Ibid., pp. 107-108.
24. J. A. Wheeler, "Bits, Quanta, Meaning" (Publication assisted by *Center for Theoretical Physics* and by NSF Grant PHY 8205717, 1984)
25. N. Herbert, *Quantum Reality-Beyond the New Physics* (Anchor Press / Doubleday, Garden City, New Jersey,1985), p. 189.
26. H. R. Pagels, *The Cosmic Code* (Bantam Books, New York, 1983), Chapter 10.
27. N. Herbert, *Quantum Reality-Beyond the New Physics* (Anchor Press / Doubleday, Garden City, New Jersey, 1985), p. 191.
28. Eugene P. Wigner, *Symmetry and Reflections* (Bloomington, Indiana University Press, 1967).
29. F. A. Wolf, *Parallel Universes* (Simon and Schuster, New York, 1988).
30. Richard Morris, *The Nature of Reality* (McGraw-Hill Book Company, 1987).
31. Richard Morris, *The Nature of Reality* (McGraw-Hill Book Company, 1987), p. 181.
32. Richard Morris, *The Nature of Reality* (McGraw-Hill Book Company, 1987), p. 184
33. F. A. Wolf, *Parallel Universes* (Simon and Schuster, New York, 1988), p. 39.
34. F. A. Wolf, *Parallel Universes* (Simon and Schuster, New York, 1988), p. 39.
35. F. A. Wolf, *Parallel Universes* (Simon and Schuster, New York, 1988), Chapter 3.
36. D. Z. Albert, "How to Take a Photograph of Another Everett World", in *New Techniques and Ideas in Quantum Measurement Theory* (*Annals of the New York Academy of Sciences,* vol. 480, Ed., D. M. Greenberger, December 30, 1986).
37. E. Harris Walker, "Consciousness as a Hidden Variable", *Physics Today,* (April, 1971).
38. F. A. Wolf, *Parallel Universes* (Simon and Schuster, New York, 1988), p. 285
39. D. Z. Albert, "How to Take a Photograph of Another Everett World", in *New Techniques and Ideas in Quantum Measurement* Theory: *Annals of the New York Academy of Sciences,* vol. 480, Ed., D. M. Greenberger, (December 30, 1986).
40. F. A. Wolf, *Parallel Universes* (Simon and Schuster, New York, 1988), p. 293.

Chapter Eighteen
Macroscopic Phenomena, Experiments, an Another Interpretation

1. J. Gribbin, *In Search of Schrodinger's Cat* (Bantam Books, New York, 1984).
2. A. Shimony, "The Reality of the Quantum World", *Scientific American,* (January, 1988).
3. W. H. Zurek, *"De-coherence and the Transition from Quantum to Classical," Physics Today*, (April, 1993).

4. "Schrodinger's Squid," *Scientific American Magazine, Physics and Quantum Mechanics*, (Oct, 2000).
5. Jeffrey Winters, "Quantum Cat Tricks", *Physics Watch, Discover*, (Oct., 1996).
6. Personal correspondence with David Windland, (February 17, 2002).
7. Philip Yam, "Bringing Schrodinger's Cat Back to Life", *Scientific American*, (June, 1997).
8. *Physics World*, (March, 2000), and J. W. Pan in Nature, (2000).
9. Siyuan Han, R. Rouse, J. E. Lukens, "Generation of a Population Inversion Between Quantum States of a Macroscopic Variable," *Dept. of Physics, University at Stony Brook*, New York, 1794, *Physical Review Letters, The American Physical Society*, (29 April, 1996).
10. W. H. Zurek, "De-coherence and the Transition from Quantum to Classical," *Physics Today*, (April, 1993).
11. George Greenstein, Authur G. Zajonc, *The Quantum Challenge* (Jones and Bartlett Pub, Sudbury, Mass., 1997).
12. Philip Yam, "Bringing Schrodinger's Cat Back to Life", *Scientific American*, (June, 1997).
13. Philip Yam, "Bringing Schrodinger's Cat Back to Life", *Scientific American*, (June, 1997).
14. Siyuan Han, R. Rouse, J. E. Lukens, "Generation of a Population Inversion Between Quantum States of a Macroscopic Variable," *Dept. of Physics, University at Stony Brook*, New York, 11794, *Physical Review Letters, The American Physical Society*, (29, April, 1996).
15. J. L. Anderson, "Response to W. H. Zurek letter", *Physics Today*, (April, 1993).
16. A. J. Leggett, *Dept. of Physics, University of Illinois* at Urbana-Champaign; Anupam Garg, *University of Illinois* at Urbana-Champaign, "Quantum Mechanics versus Realism: Is the Flux There When Nobody Looks?" *Physics Review Letters, The American Physical* Society, (4 March, 1985).
17. R. Rouse, Siyuan Han, J. E. Lukens, "Observation of Resonant Tunneling Between Macroscopically Distinct Quantum Levels" *Physics Review Letters* (75, 1614-1617, 1995).
18. Philip Yam, "Bringing Schrodinger's Cat Back to Life," *Scientific American*,(June, 1997).
19. Roger Penrose, *The Large, The Small and the Human Mind*, p-183-184, (Cambridge University Press, 1997).
20. Serge Haroche, "Entanglement, De-coherence and the Quantum / Classical Boundary," *Physics Today*, 1998 *American Institute of Physics.*(July, 1998),
21. Philip Yam, "Bringing Schrodinger's Cat Back to Life," *Scientific American*,(June, 1997).
22. L. Dossey, *Space,Time and Medicine* (New Science Library, Shambala, Boston, 1982).
23. J. Gribbon, *In Search of Schrodinger's Cat,* Chapter 10 (Bantam Books, New York, 1984).
24. J. Gribbon, *In Search of Schrodinger's Cat,* Chapter 10 (Bantam Books, New York,1984).
25. "Wave particle duality" *Nature,* (Oct 14, 1999).

26. "Waves, Particles and Fullernes," *Nature*, (Oct 14, 1999).
27. "Experimental Metaphysics," *Quantum Mechanical Studies for Albert Shimony* (Kluwer Academic Publishing, Dordvecht, vol. 1, May, 1007. p. 11.
28. Tony Leggett, "Quantum Theory: Weird and Wonderful," *Physics World*, December, 1999, p. 75.
29. "Atom Tangle," *Nature* 413, 400-403, 27 September, 2001
30. I. Chiorescu, et al, " Coherent Quantum Dynamics of Superconducting Flux Qubit", *Science*, 21 March, 2003
31. Ibid.
32. John Clarke, "Flux Qubit Completes the Hat Trick," Science, 21 March, 2003
33. Mike Disney, *University of Wales* at Cardiff, "Standard Cosmology Might Be Turned On Its Ear," *Science*, vol. 271, Feb. 9, 1996.

Part II
The Universe of Spirit

1. Sir Arthur Eddington, *The Domain of Physical Science.*
2. Robert M. Augros and George N. Stanciu, *The New Story of Science* (Gateway Editions, Chicago, Illinois, 1984), pp. 63-64.
3. H. P. Stapp, *S-Matrix Interpretation of Quantum Theory Physics Review* (D3, 1303 (1071).
4. Eugene P. Wigner, *Symmetry and Reflections* (Bloomington, Indiana University Press, 1967).
5. Brian Josephson, "The Reach of the Mind", in *Nobel Prize Conversations* (Dallas, Texas, Saybrook Publishing Company, 1985).
6. Mary Baker Eddy, *Science and Health with Key to the Scriptures* (The First Church of Christ, Scientist, Boston, Massachusetts, U.S.A.), p. 35.
7. Ibid, p. 171.
8. Albert Einstein, *"Space and Spirit: Theories of the Universe and the Arguments for the Existence of God,"* (Also listed in http://www.brainyquote.com).
9. *Bible*: Luke 17:21.
10. *Bible*: John 14:12.
11. *Quantum Questions*, edited by Ken Wilbur (New Science Library, Shambhala,1984).
12. George Gilder, "The Soul of Silicon," *Forbes* ASAP, (June 1, 1998).
13. Charles Leighton, "A Change of Heart"*, American Journal of Nursing*, (October, 1998).

Chapter One
The Quantum and Consciousness

1. J. Gribbon, *In Search of Schrodinger's Cat,* Chapter 10 (Bantam Books, New York,1984), p.208.
2. *Bible*: Acts 7: 57-60 / Acts 8: 12.
3. *Bible*: Acts 14; 19, 20.
4. N. Herbert, *Quantum Reality –Beyond the New Physics* (Anchor Press/Doubleday, Garden City, New Jersey,1985), p. 171.
5. P. Davies, *God and the New Physics*, Chapter 6 (Simon and Schuster, Inc., New York, 1983), p.79.
6. David Pratt, "John Eccles on Mind and Brain," Sunrise Magazine, June/July, 1995 (Theosophical University Press).
7. C. Honorton, "The Role of Consciousness in the Physical World", quotation of Sir J. Eccles, in *Psychophysical Interaction, AAAS Symposium*, (after 1977).
8. R. G. Jahn and B. T. Dunne, *Margins of Reality* (Harcourt Brace Jovanovich, Publishers, New York, 1987).
9. J. A. Wheeler, "The Universe as a Home for Man", *American Scientist*, vol.62, Nov-Dec., 1974).
10. J. A. Wheeler, "Include the Observer in the Wave Function?," in *Quantum Mechanics, a Half Century Later* (D. Reidel Publishing Company, J. Lopes, M. Paty, Eds., 1977), pp. 1-8.
11. P. C. W. Davies and J. R. Brown, Eds., *The Ghost in the Atom*, Interview with J. Wheeler (Cambridge University Press, New York, 1986), p. 63.
12. J. A. Wheeler, "Bits, Quanta, Meaning," in *Problems in Theoretical Physics* (Publication assisted by *Center for Theoretical Physics*, and by *NSF* Grant PHY 8205717, 1984), p. 129.
13. Ibid., p.129, Figure 9.
14. Ibid., p.132.
15. Tim Folger, "Does the Universe Exist if We're Not Looking?" Discover vol. 23, no 6, June, 2002)
16. Ibid.
17. F. A. Wolf, *Star Wave* (MacMillan, New York, 1984), p. 75.
18. Ibid., p. 63-67.
19. Ibid., p. 12.
20. E. P. Wigner, *Einstein and the Unity of Theoretical Physics/Thirty Years of Knowing Einstein*, (original notes of E. P. Wigner, for address made in honor of Einstein), p. 14.
21. Ibid., p. 15.
22. Amit Goswami, "The Idealistic Interpretation of Quantum Mechanics," *Physics Essays*, vol.2, #4, (1989), p. 387.
23. Ibid., p. 389.
24. Amir D. Aczel, *Entanglement* (Four Walls Eight Windows pub, New York, 2001), pp. 252-253.

25. Amit Goswami, "The Idealistic Interpretation of Quantum Mechanics," *Physics Essays*, vol.2, #4, (1989).
26. Henry Stapp, "Mind, Matter and Quantum Mechanics", reviewed by Piero Scaruffi (http://www.thymos.com/mind/stapp.html).
27. Mary Baker Eddy, *Science and Health with Key to the Scriptures,* (The First Church of Christ, Scientist, Boston, Massachusetts, U.S.A), pp. 502-503.
28. *Bible*: Mark 11: 23.
29. Mary Baker Eddy, *Science and Health with Key to the Scriptures* (The First Church of Christ, Scientist, Boston, Massachusetts, U.S.A), pp. 217.
30. Mary Baker Eddy, *Miscellaneous Writings* (The First Church of Christ, Scientist, Boston, Massachusetts, U.S.A), p. 60.
31. Henry Swift, "Is SWC a Superior Science?," *Science Within Conscious,* vol. 2, no 1, (Spring, 1997).
32. Edward R. Close, *Transcendental Physics* (to Excel pub, New York, 1997), p. 234.
33. Ibid., p. 132.
34. Ibid., p. 155.
35. Mary Baker Eddy, *Science and Health with Key to the Scriptures* (The First Church of Christ, Scientist, Boston, Massachusetts, U.S.A), p. 264.
36. Edward R. Close, *Transcendental Physics* (to Excel pub, New York, 1997), p. 156.
37. Amir D. Aczel, *Entanglement* (Four Walls Eight Windows pub., New York, 2001), p. 252.
38. Edward R. Close, *Transendental Physics* (to Excel pub, New York, 1997), p. 48.
39. Amir D. Aczel, *Entanglement* (Four Walls Eight Windows pub, New York, 2001), p. 214.
40. Edward R. Close, *Transendental Physics* (to Excel pub, New York, 1997), pp. 154-155.
41. Review of Andre Kukla's book, *Social Constructivism and the Philosophy of Science,* by Seminary Co-op Bookstore (www.semcoop.com/0415234190).

Chapter Two
Is Consciousness Found in the Brain, and in Computers?

1. Lewis Carroll, *Through the Looking Glass*, Chapter 5 (New York, Random House, 1946).
2. R. Sperry, "The Reach of the Mind": *Nobel Prize Conversations,* Dallas, Texas, (Saybrook Publishing Company, 1985).
3. Ibid., pp. 51-56.
4. Ibid., p. 54.
5. Roger Penrose, *The Emperor's New Mind* (Oxford University Press, New York, 1989), pp. 439-449.

6. Deeke, I, et al, "Voluntary Finger Movements in Man: Cerebral Potentials and Theory", *Biological Cybernetics*, pp. 23, 99.
7. Ibid., p. 59.
8. Ibid., p. 60.

9. Ibid., p. 72.
10. Ibid., p. 94.
11. Ibid., p. 98.
12. D. R. Hofstadter, *Godel, Escher, Bach : An Eternal Golden Braid*, Chapter 15 (Basic Books, Inc, published in the United States by Random House, New York,1980), p. 473.
13. E. Harrison, *Masks of the Universe* (Macmillan Publishing Company, New York / Collier Macmillan Publishers, London, 1985), pp. 232-234.
14. D. R. Hofstadter, *Godel, Escher, Bach: An Eternal Golden Braid,* Chapter 15 (Basic Books, Inc, published in the United States by Random House, New York,1980).
15. J. D. Barrow, *The World Within the World* (Oxford University Press, New York, 1990), p. 259.
16. F. Scheid, *Introduction to Computer Science, Schaum's Outline Series*, chapter 1, (Mc Graw-Hill Book Company, New York, 1970.)
17. J. R. Seales Chinese Room (http://www.helsinki.fi/hum/kognitiotiede/searle.html).
18. P. C .W. Davies, *The Mind of God* (Simon and Schuster, New York, 1992), pp. 110-139.
19. William Poundstone, *Recursive Universe* (Oxford University Press, Oxford, 1985).
20. Stephen Wolfram, "Undecidability and Intractability in Theoretical Physics", *Physical Review Letters,* 5 (1985), p. 735.
21. Stephen Wolfram, *Computer Software*, (as quoted in P. C. W. Davies, *The Mind of God* (Simon and Schuster, New York,1992), p. 119.
22. P. C. W. Davies, *The Mind of God* (Simon and Schuster, New York, 1992), p. 123.
23. William Shakespeare, *The Merchant of Venice*.
24 Ella Wheeler Wilcox: (source unknown).
25. P. Davies, *God and the New Physics*, Chapter 6 (Simon and Schuster, Inc., New York, 1983), p. 61.
26. D. Chopra, *Quantum Healing: Exploring the Frontiers of Mind / Body Medicine* (Bantam Books, New York,1990).
27. Larry Dossey, *Healing Words/the Power of Prayer and the Practice of Medicine* (Harper, San Francisco, 1993).
28. Mary Baker Eddy, *Science and Health with Key to the Scriptures* (The First Church of Christ, Scientist, Boston, Massachusetts, U.S.A), p. 108.
29. *Bible*: Ezekiel 18: 2, 3.
30. Mary Baker Eddy, *Science and Health with Key to the Scriptures* (The First Church of Christ, Scientist, Boston, Massachusetts, U.S.A.), p. 125.
31. Antonio R. Damascio "How the Brain Creates the Mind," *Scientific American*, (December, 1999)
32. "A Genetic Basis for Intelligence?" *Christian Science Sentinel* (The First Church of Christ, Scientist, Boston, Massachusetts, U.S.A., January 3, 2000).
33. Ibid., p. 28.
34. *The Christian Science Journal*, (The Christian Science Publishing Society, Boston, MA, U.S.A., September, 1990), (Testimonial section).
35. Mary Baker Eddy, *Science and Health with Key to the Scriptures* (The First Church of Christ, Scientist, Boston, Massachusetts, U.S.A.), p. 236.

36. J. A. Wheeler, "Delayed-Choice Experiment and the Boh –Einstein Dialog," paper presented at the *American Philosophical Society*, London, (preparation for publication assisted by the *University of Texas Center for Theoretical Physics*, and by *National Science Foundation* Grant PHY78-26592, June 5,1980).
37. Mary Baker Eddy, *Science and Health with Key to the Scriptures* (The First Church of Christ, Scientist, Boston, Massachusetts, U.S.A.), p. 553.
38. Bart Kosko, *Fuzzy Thinking/ The New Science of Fuzzy Logic* (Hyperonj, New York, 1993).
39. http://www.imagination-engines.com
40. Bob Holmes, "The Creativity Machine", *New Scientist*, 20 January, 1996).
41. http://www.imagination-engines.com
42. http://www.imagination-engines.com/cmexescu.htm
43. Bob Holmes, "The Creativity Machine", *New Scientist*, 20 January, 1996.
44. http://www.imagination-engines.com/daguc.htm
45. http://www.imagination-engines.com/daguc.com
46. Mary Baker Eddy, *Science and Health with Key to the Scriptures* (The First Church of Christ, Scientist, Boston, Massachusetts, U.S.A.), p. 462.
47. Ibid., p. 128.
48. *Bible*: John 14:12.
49. *"Artificial Intelligence, Christian Science Monitor*, (The First Church of Christ, Scientist, Boston, Massachusetts, U.S.A., April 1, 1999), p. 14.
50. Personal correspondence with Bringsjord, February 5, 2001.
51. Betty Whitfill, "Recovering the Soul": Interview with Larry Dossey, *Share Archives International*.
52. "Jumpers Safe After Parachute Accident," *Christian Science Sentinel* (The First Church of Christ, Scientist, Boston, Massachusetts, U.S.A., July 6, 1998).
53. *Bible*: Psalms 91: 11, 12.
54. "Jumpers Safe After Parachute Accident," *Christian Science Sentinel* (The First Church of Christ, Scientist, Boston, Massachusetts, U.S.A., July 6, 1998).
55. J. A. Wheeler, "Delayed-Choice Experiment and the Boh –Einstein Dialog," paper presented at the *American Philosophical Society*, London, (preparation for publication assisted by the *University of Texas Center for Theoretical Physics*, and by *National Science Foundation* Grant PHY78-26592, June 5, 1980).
56. Ibid.
57. R. Penrose, *The Emperor's New Mind* (Oxford University Press, New York, 1989), p. 429.
58. Ibid., p. 415.
59. "Here's the Future: Your Move.", Interview appearing in the *Christian Science Monitor*, (The First Church of Christ, Scientist, Boston, Massachusetts, U.S.A., April I, 1999), (quotation from Selmer Bringsjord).
60. http://www.well.com/user/jaron/aichapter.html
61. David Chalmers, "The Puzzle of Conscious Experience", *Scientific American*, (December, 1995).
62. *Bible*: John 8:51.
63. "Letter by Mrs. Eddy on Vision," from a collection of articles entitled, "My Grace is Sufficient for Thee." (author unknown).

64. P. C. W. Davies, *The Mind of God,* quotation of Kurt Godel (Simon and Schuster, New York,1992), pp. 100-101.
65. Renee Weber, "The Physicist and the Mystic - Is a Dialogue Between Them Possible?", *The Holographic Paradigm,* p. 190.
66. D. Hofstadter, *Godel, Escher, Bach: An Eternal Golden Braid* (Vintage Books, A division of Random House, New York, 1980), p. 477.
67. R. M. Augros and G. Stanciu, *The New Story of Science* (Gateway Editions, Chicago, Illinois, 1984), pp.11-12.
68. D. Chopra, *Quantum Healing: Exploring the Frontiers of Mind / Body Medicine,* (Bantam Books, New York,1990), p. 21.
69. Mary Baker Eddy, *Science and Health with Key to the Scriptures* (The First Church of Christ, Scientist, Boston, Massachusetts, U.S.A.), p. 530.
70. Camille Bains, "Perceptions, thoughts, beliefs more important than genes," (Canadian Press Newswire, November 10, 2002).
71. "Consciousness – and the Expanding Universe," *Christian Science Sentinel* (The First Church of Christ, Scientist, Boston, Massachusetts, U.S.A., July 1, 2002).
72. Ibid.

Chapter Three
Experiments in Consciousness

1. R. G. Jahn and B. T. Dunne, *Margins of Reality* (Harcourt Brace Jovanovich, Publishers, New York, 1987).
2. Ibid., p. 93.
3. Ibid., p. 95.
4. Ibid., p. 144.
5. Ibid., p. 147.
6. Ibid., p. 199.
7. L. Dossey, *Space, Time and Medicine* (New Science Library, Shambala, Boston, 1982), p. 206).
8. May, E. C. Utts, J. M. and Spottiswoode, S. J. P. (1995), "Design Augmentation Theory", *Journal of Scientific Exploration*, 9(4), pp. 453-488.
9. "Experimental Test for the Exploration of Psychokinesis", *Newsletter*, *The Center for Unified Science Within Consciousness*, vol. I, no.1, (Spring, 1996).
10. "Physicists Probe the Paranormal," *Physics Web, v*ol.13, issue 5, (May, 2000).
11. L. Dossey, *Space, Time and Medicine* (New Science Library, Shambala, Boston, 1982).
12. L. Dossey, *Healing Words/ the Power of Prayer and the Practice of Medicine*, quotation of Daniel J. Benor (Harper, San Francisco, 1993).
13. Ibid.
14. Ibid., p. 247.
15. D. L. Radin and R. D. Nelson, "Evidence for Consciousness-related Anomalies in Random Physical Systems," *Foundation of Physics (*1989), p. 10.
16. *Bible*: Jer. 29:11.

17. *Bible*: Isa. 55:8.
18. *Bible*: I Cor 2:16.
19. Larry Dossey, "Lessons From Twins: of Nature, Nurture, and Consciousness", *Alternative Therapies*, vol. 3, no. 3, (May, 1997).
20. Ibid.
21. Ibid.
22. Ibid.
23. D. Chalmers, "The Puzzle of Consciousness Experience", *Scientific American*, (1995), 273(6): 80-86.

Chapter Four
Paradigm Shifts

1. T. Kuhn, *The Structure of Scientific Revelations* (University of Chicago Press, Chicago, 1984).
2. P. Davies and J. Gribbin, *The Matter Myth*, Preface, (Simon and Schuster, New York, 1992).
3. J. A. Wheeler, "On Recognizing 'Law Without Law,'" Oersted Medal Response at the joint *APS-AAPT* Meeting, New York, (25 January, 1983).
4. T. Kuhn, *The Structure of Scientific Revelations* (University of Chicago Press, Chicago, 1984), pp.130-135.
5. J. P. Briggs, Ph.D., F. David Peat, Ph.D., *Looking Glass Universe*, Chapter 1, quotation of T.
Kuhn (Simon and Schuster, Inc, New York, 1984).

Chapter Five
The Scientific Method

1. Alfred North Whitehead, *Science and the Modern World* (Macmillan, N.Y., 1926), p. 66.
2. Fritjof Capra, *The Turning Point* (Bantam Books, 1983), P. 375.
3. *A Century of Christian Science Healing* (The Christian Science Publishing Society, Boston, Massachusetts,1966), pp. 168-172.
4. *Bible*: Matthew 6:24.
5. *The Amplified Bible*, Expanded Edition (Zondervan Bible Publishers, Grand Rapids, Michigan, 1987).
   Sandra Blakeslee, "Placebos Prove So Powerful Even Experts are Surprised," *New York Times*, (October 13,1998), p. F1.
7. Mary Baker Eddy, *Science and Health with Key to the Scriptures*, (The First Church of Christ, Scientist, Boston, Massachusetts, U.S.A.), p. 116.

Chapter Six

A MINDLESS, PURPOSELESS UNIVERSE, OR AN ETERNAL, PURPOSEFUL UNIVERSE OF SPIRIT?

1. *Bible*: Ps.14:1.
2. B. Russell, "A Free Man's Worship", in *Why I Am Not a Christian* (Simon and Schuster, New York, 1975), p. 107.
3. M. Kafaatos and R. Nadeau, *The Conscious Universe* (Springer-Verlog, New York, 1990), p. 144.
4. D. A Cowan, *Mind Underlies Spacetime* (Joseph Publishing Company, San Mateo, California, 1975), p. 85.
5. Private communication with J. Hubbell, Palo Alto, California.
6. A. Linde, quoted in the *International Harold Tribune*, (May 19, 1989).
7. Richard Dawkins, "God's Utility Function," *Scientific American*, (November, 1995).
8. Private communication with the author, Bob Mc Free.
9. *Bible*: Matt.13:13, 5.
10. Reported in "On Einstein's interest in the metaphysics of Mary Baker Eddy," School of Information, University of California, Berkeley, CA, 2008), W. S. Cooper is Professor Emeritus, School of Information, University of California, Berkeley, CA, 94720; interviewed by Cooper, June 11, 2001.
11. "On Einstein's interest in the metaphysics of Mary Baker Eddy," (School of Information, University of California, Berkeley, CA, 2008), W.S. Cooper is Professor Emeritus, School of Information, University of California, Berkeley, CA, 94720.
12. David L. Keyston, "The Healer: The Healing Work of Mary Baker Eddy, 2nd Edition (Seattle, Washington: Healing Unlimited, 1996, p. 189; also seen by Frederick Stoessal in 1934; letter to Hough and interviewed by W. Cooper, August 18, 2001.
13. Bailey letter to Robert Hough, March 12, 2001.
14. Robert Peel ("Spiritual Healing in a Scientific Age" (San Francisco: Harper and Row, 1987, pp. 28, 201 n.16; also witnessed by George Millar, 34 Esmond Rd., London, England; interviewed by William Cooper, July 9, 2001.
15. "On Einstein's interest in the metaphysics of Mary Baker Eddy," (School of Information, University of California, Berkeley, CA, 2008), W.S. Cooper is Professor Emeritus, School of Information, University of California, Berkeley, CA, 94720
16. (Mentioned during his lecture, "Spiritual Forces Bring Mankind's Liberation," public lecture printed in the Christian Science Monitor, October, 20, 1965; also noted in Cooper paper).
17. "On Einstein's interest in the metaphysics of Mary Baker Eddy," (School of Information, University of California, Berkeley, CA, 2008), W.S. Cooper is Professor Emeritus, School of Information, University of California, Berkeley, CA, 94720
18. Pat Archer of Boynton Beach, Florida in a letter to Robert Hough, April 15, 2002,
19. *Bible*: II Peter 3:8.

20. B. Hoffman, *Albert Einstein, Creator and Rebel* : quotation of Albert Einstein (New York, Plume, 1973); and related by L. Dossey in *Space, Time and Medicine* (New Science Library, Shambala, Boston, 1982).
21. L. Dosscy in *Space, Time and Medicine* (New Science Library, Shambala, Boston, 1982), p. 158.
22. "A remark on the relationship between relativity theory and idealistic philosophy", in *Albert Einstein: Philosopher and Scientist*, vol. II (Harper and Row, 1959), pp. 557-562.
23. Mary Baker Eddy, *Science and Health with Key to the Scriptures* (The First Church of Christ, Scientist, Boston, Massachusetts, U.S.A.), p. 598.
24. Ibid., p. 468.
25. John Archibald Wheeler, "Time Today", Physics Dept., *University of Texas*, (1993), to appear in proceedings of workshop: *Physical Origins of Time Symmetry* (Cambridge University Press).

Chapter Seven
Evidence for the Existence of God

1. W. Shakespeare, *The Merchant of Venice*.
2. Charles A. Whitney, *The Discovery of Our Galaxy* , quotation of Johannes Kepler (Alfred A. Knopf, Inc., Publisher, New York), p. 40.
3. E. Schrodinger, *Mind and Matter,* Contained within *What is Life? With Mind and Matter and Autobiographic Sketches* (Cambridge University Press,
4. J. A. Wheeler, "Genesis and Observership," *Foundational Problems in the Special Sciences,* (Butts and Hintikka, Eds, D. Eidel Publishing Company, Dordrecht, Holland, 1977), p. 18.
5. F. A. Wolf, *Parallel Universes* (Simon and Schuster, New York, 1988), p. 60.
6. R. Penrose, *The Emperor's New Mind* (Oxford University Press, New York, 1989), p. 221.
7. R. G. Jahn and B.T. Dunne, *Margins of Reality*, quotation of Erwin Schrodinger (Harcourt Brace Jovanovich, Publishers, New York, 1987), p. 258.
8. *Bible*: Mark 8:18.
9. *Bible*: John 8:4.
10. *Webster Third International Dictionary*.
11. *Bible*: Isaiah 29:16.
12. *Bible*: Phil 2:5.
13. Robert Peel, *Mary Baker Eddy, The Years of Trial* (Holt, Rinehart and Winston, 1971), p. 233.
14. Mary Baker Eddy, *Science and Health with Key to the Scriptures* (The First Church of Christ, Scientist, Boston, Massachusetts, U.S.A.), p. 468.
15. *We Knew Mary Baker Eddy,* First Series (The Christian Science Publishing Society, Boston, Massachusetts, USA, 1943), p. 22.
16. Mary Baker Eddy, *Miscellaneous Writings* (The First Church of Christ, Scientist, Boston, Massachusetts, U.S.A.), p. 72.

17. Ibid., p. 185.
18. *Bible*: I John 1:5.
19. Steven L. Fair (staff editor), "Keeping a spiritual perspective on the new physics," *Christian Science Jour*nal (The First Church of Christ, Scientist, Boston, Massachusetts, U.S.A., July, 1988).
20. Mary Baker Eddy, *Science and Health with Key to the Scriptures* (The First Church of Christ, Scientist, Boston, Massachusetts, U.S.A.), p. 264.
21. Lauran Neegaard, *Associated Press, The Cincinnati Enquirer*, November 13, 1996), p. A7.
22. Robert and Michele Root-Berstein, "Honey, Mud, Maggots and Other Medical Marvels", http://www.ralphmag.org/maggots.html.
23. *Bible*: James 3:17 (the), 18.
24. Mary Baker Eddy, *Science and Health with Key to the Scriptures* (The First Church of Christ, Scientist, Boston, Massachusetts, U.S.A.), p. 390:7
25. James G. Mc Murtry, "My Own Interpretation of the Twenty-Third

Chapter Eight
Meaningful Coincidences, Spiritual Prayer and Healing

1. C. G. Jung and Wolfgang Pauli, "The Interpretation of Nature and the Psyche," in *Synchronocity: An Acausal Connecting Principle* (Pantheon Books, 1955), pp. 20, 21.
2. Ibid.
3. Ibid.
4. Information on file with the author.
5. John Randell Dunn, as quoted in *Miscellaneous Writings* by Mary Baker Eddy (The First Church of Christ, Scientist, Boston, Massachusetts, U.S.A.), p. 51.
6. Mary Baker Eddy, *Science and Health with Key to the Scriptures* (The First Church of Christ, Scientist, Boston, Massachusetts, U.S.A.), p.474.
7. L. Miller, "The Healing Power of Prayer," *USA Today,* (December 21, 1993).
8. *Healing Spiritually* (The Christian Science Publishing Society, Boston, Mass., 1996).
9. L. Dossey, *Space, Time and Medicine (*New Science Library, Shambala, Boston, 1982).
10. M. Talbot, *The Holographic Universe* (Harper Collins Publishers, 1991).
11. R. Peel, *Spiritual Healing in a Scientific Age* (Harper and Row Publishers, San Francisco, 1987).
12. D. Chopra, *Quantum Healing : Exploring the Frontiers of Mind / Body Medicine* (Bantam Books, New York, 1990).
13. "The True Story of Today's Miracles", reprinted from *Guideposts* (Guidepost Associates, Carmel, New York, 1985).
14. K. O' Toole, "Researcher Says Prayer is Good for Your Health"*, San Francisco Examiner,* (January 24,), 989: A-2.
15. "Religion in Healing", *Southern Medical Journal*, (July 7, 1988), 81:819 – 820.

16. "Spirituality and Healing in Medicine," Harvard Symposium, sponsored by *the Harvard Medical School and the Mind/Body Medical Institute*, Deaconess Hospital, Boston, Massachusetts, (December 3-5, 995).
17. *Christian Science Sentinel,* (15 January, 1996), and *Christian Science Journal*, February, (1996) (The First Church of Christ, Scientist, Boston, Massachusetts, U.S.A.).
18. Mary Baker Eddy, *Science and Health with Key to the Scriptures* (The First Church of Christ, Scientist, Boston, Massachusetts, U.S.A.), p. 153.
19. Christian Science Church History Document: A11021.
20. Nathan A. Talbot, "The Mind, the Body, and God's Allness," *Christian Science Journal* (The First Church of Christ, Scientist, Boston, Massachusetts, U.S.A.), Jan., 1997).
21. *Freedom and Responsibility* (The First Church of Christ, Scientist, Boston, Massachusetts, U.S.A.), p. 118.
22. *Bible*: Genesis, Chapter I.
23. Robert Peel, *Spiritual Healing in a Scientific Age* (Harper and Row Pub., San Francisco, 1987).
24. Mary Baker Eddy, *Science and Health with Key to the Scriptures* (The First Church of Christ, Scientist, Boston, Massachusetts, U.S.A), p. 12.
25. Ibid., p.303.
26. Robert Peel, *Spiritual Healing in a Scientific Age* (Harper and Row Pub., San Francisco, 1987), p. 196.
27. Larry Dossey, "The Reach of the Mind", *The Sun*, (Dec., 1994).
28. *Bible*: John 9:1-41.
29. *Bible*: Luke 8:49-56.
30. *Bible*: Luke 8:52, 53.
31. Mary Baker Eddy, *Science and Health with Key to the Scriptures* (The First Church of Christ, Scientist, Boston, Massachusetts, U.S.A.), p. 330.
32. B. Josephson, "The Reach of the Mind", *Nobel Prize Conversations* (Dallas, Texas, Saybrook Publishing Company, 1985), p. 170.
33. *Bible*: Matt.7:13,14; and *The Amplified Bible*: Lamentations 3:22, 23 (to ;).
34. R. Peel, *Mary Baker Eddy: The Years of Authority* (Holt, Rinehart and Winston, 1971).
35. *Christian Science Journal*, Quotation of John Templeton in "Christian Science, Spirituality and the Sciences: Discovery and Progress," (The First Church of Christ, Scientist, Boston, Massachusetts, U.S.A., August, 1999).
36. Mary Baker Eddy, *Unity of Good* (The First Church of Christ, Scientist, Boston, Massachusetts, U.S.A.), p. 7, also…Yvonne Cache von Fettweis and Robert Townsend Warneck, *Mary Baker Eddy/Christian Healer*, p. 253, (Christian Science Publishing Society, Boston, Mass., 1998).
37. Mary Baker Eddy, *The First Church of Christ Scientist* (The First Church of Christ, Scientist, Boston, Massachusetts, U.S.A.), p. 105.
38. Yvonne Cache von Fettweis and Robert Townsend Warneck, *Mary Baker Eddy/Christian Healer*, Part II , Christian Science Publishing Society, Boston, Mass.,1998).
39. Ibid., p. 115

40. Irving C. Tomlinson, *Twelve Years with Mary Baker Eddy* (The Christian Science Publishing Society, 1945), p. 91.
41. Yvonne Cache von Fettweis and Robert Townsend Warneck, *Mary Baker Eddy/Christian Healer* (Christian Science Publishing Society, Boston, Mass, 1998).
42. *Bible:* John 5: 30.
43. *A Century of Christian Science Healing* (The Christian Science Publishing Society, Boston, Massachusetts,1966), p. 8.
44. Graham Ikin, *New Concepts of Healing* (New York: Association Press, 1956), pp. 104-108).
45. R. Peel, *Spiritual Healing in a Scientific Age* (Harper and Row Publishers, San Francisco, 1987), pp.17-18.
46. Ibid., p. 36.
47. Information on file with the author.
48. *Bible*: Matt. 15:13.
49. Private communication with S. Ekkens, Dayton, Ohio.
50. Private communication with J. Hubbell, Palo Alto, California.
51. Private communication with Bob Mc Fall, Roanoke, Virginia.
52. Private communication with J. Hubbell, Palo Alto, California.
53. Mary Baker Eddy, *Science and Health with Key to the Scriptures* (The First Church of Christ, Scientist, Boston, Massachusetts, U.S.A.), p. 502.
54. Private communication with Thomas Gross, Dayton, Ohio.
55. Private communication with J. Hubbell, Palo Alto, California.
56 Ibid.
57. Ibid.
58. Daniel Goleman, "New Focus on Multiple Personalities" (*New York Times*, May 21, 1985), p.c-1.
59. Mary Baker Eddy, *Science and Health with Key to the Scriptures* (The First Church of Christ, Scientist, Boston, Massachusetts, U.S.A), p. 297.
60. Jack Hubbell, *The Science of Christian Healing,* public lecture.
61. Mary Baker Eddy, *Science and Health with Key to the Scriptures* (The First Church of Christ, Scientist, Boston, Massachusetts, U.S.A.), p. 155.
62. Ibid., p.113.
63. *Bible*: II Kings 5:7-15.
64. *Christian Science Sentinel* (The First Church of Christ, Scientist, Boston, Massachusetts, U.S.A., November 11, 1991).
65. R. Peel, *Spiritual Healing in a Scientific Age* (Harper and Row Publishers, San Francisco, 1987).
66. *Bible*: Micah 6:8.
67. "The Truth That Heals," Radio Program #48 (The Christian Science Publishing Society, Boston, Massachusetts, November 28, 1971).
68. *Christian Science Sentinel,* vol. 92, no.18 (The First Church of Christ, Scientist, Boston, Massachusetts, U.S.A., April 30, 1990).
69. *Christian Science Journal* (The First Church of Christ, Scientist, Boston, Massachusetts, U.S.A., September, 1981), 99: 543-544.
70. *Bible*: Matt. 6: 6.

71. "The Truth That Heals", Radio Program # 76R, (The Christian Science Publishing Society, Boston, Massachusetts, U.S.A., 1972).
72. *Christian Science Journal* (The First Church of Christ, Scientist, Boston, Massachusetts, U.S.A., Feb. 1998), pp.17-18.
73. *Christian Science Sentinel* (The Christian Science Publishing Society, Boston, MA, U.S.A., May 21,1984), 86: 895 – 897.
74. *Bible*: Isaiah 41:10.
75. Mary Baker Eddy, *Science and Health with Key to the Scriptures* (The First Church of Christ, Scientist, Boston, Massachusetts, U.S.A.), p. 423.
76. *Christian Science Journal* (The First Church of Christ, Scientist, Boston, Massachusetts, U.S.A., April, 1964), 82: 223-224.
77. *Christian Science Sentinel* (The First Church of Christ, Scientist, Boston, Massachusetts, U.S.A., May 25, 1987) 89: 33-34.
78. Private communication between young girl and the author.
79. *Christian Science Journal* (The First Church of Christ, Scientist, Boston, Massachusetts, U.S.A.), July, 1996, p. 61.
80. *Christian Science Journal* (The First Church of Christ, Scientist, Boston, Massachusetts, U.S.A., May, 1996), pp.17-19.
81. *Bible*: John 18:37.
82. Daniel Jensen, speech at *Principle Foundation*, 1990 Annual Meeting.
83. *Christian Science Journal* (The First Church of Christ, Scientist, Boston, Massachusetts, U.S.A, March, 1987), 105:48-50.
84. Mary Baker Eddy, *Science and Health with Key to the Scriptures* (The First Church of Christ, Scientist, Boston, MA, U.S.A.), p. 313.
85. *Christian Sentinel* (The First Church of Christ, Scientist, Boston, Massachusetts, U.S.A., February 26, 1996).
86. *Bible*: Ps. 46:1.
87. *Bible:* Luke 17:21.
88. Daniel Jensen, "Beginning Rightly," a public talk.
89. Ibid.
90. *The Truth That Heals,* Program # 62, (Christian Science Board of Directors, Boston, Mass., March 5, 1972).
91. *Christian Science Sentinel* (The First Church of Christ, Scientist, Boston, Massachusetts, U.S.A, Oct. 13, 1956), pp.1799-1800.
92. "The Evidence of Things Not Seen", *Radical Reliance in Healing* (The First Church of Christ, Scientist, Boston, Massachusetts, U.S.A., 1956).
93. "Everything That I've Been Given by God", *Christian Science Journal*, Special Issue (The First Church of Christ, Scientist, Boston, Massachusetts, U.S.A., 1991), pp. 32-43.
94. *Bible*: Psalms 46:1.
95. *Bible*: Luke 5:18-26.
96. *Bible*: Luke 6:6-11.
97. *Surgery of the Soul: Healing the Whole Person – Spirit, Mind and Body*, (publisher unknown).
98. *Christian Science Sentinel* (The First Church of Christ, Scientist, Boston, Massachusetts, U.S.A., June 24, 1996).

99. *Christian Science Journal* (The First Church of Christ, Scientist, Boston, Massachusetts, U.S.A., April, 1997.
100. Daniel Goleman, "Forget Money, Nothing Can Buy Happiness" (*New York Times,* July 16, 1996).
101. *New York Times*, (Feb. 4, 1994).
102. David T. Lykken, *Physchological Science*, (May, 1996).
103. *Bible:* Psalms 16:11.
104. *Christian Science Sentinel* (The First Church of Christ, Scientist, Boston, Massachusetts, U.S.A., 15 July, 1996), pp.36-38.
105. *Bible*: I John 4:16.
106. *Bible*: Luke 17:20, 21.
107. Mary Baker Eddy, *Science and Health with Key to the Scriptures* (The First Church of Christ, Scientist, Boston, MA, U.S.A.), pp. 603, 604.
108. Private communication with Jack Hubbell.
109. "How Christian Science Heals," Radio Program # 183, *Christian Science Sentinel*, vol. 59, no.12 (The First Church of Christ, Scientist, Boston, Massachusetts, U.S.A., March 23, 1957.
110. *Bible*: John 9:39
111. Information on file with the author.
112. *Christian Science Sentinel* (The First Church of Christ, Scientist, Boston, Massachusetts, U.S.A., December 17, 1990), pp. 16-19.
113. "The Truth that Heals," Program #48 (The First Church of Christ, Scientist, Boston, Massachusetts, U.S.A., Nov. 28, 1971).
114. *Christian Science Journal* (The First Church of Christ, Scientist, Boston, Massachusetts, U.S.A., October 1986), pp. 628-629.
115. *Christian Science Sentinel* (The First Church of Christ, Scientist, Boston, Massachusetts, U.S.A., May 31, 1999), p. 23.
116. *Bible*: Matt. 10:8.
117. Jack Hubbell, a public talk.
118. *Christian Science Sentinel* , NEWS OF HEALING: "Father and Daughter freed from HIV" (The First Church of Christ, Scientist, Boston, Massachusetts, U.S.A, July 22, 2002).
119. *Christian Science Sentinel*, "Responding to AIDS with unconditional Love" (The First Church of Christ, Scientist, Boston, Massachusetts, U.S.A, February 17, 2003).
120. Ibid.
121. *Christian Science Sentinel*, "My journey forward to complete health," (The First Church of Christ, Scientist, Boston, Massachusetts, U.S.A, July 22, 2002).
122. Mary Baker Eddy, *Science and Health with Key to the Scriptures* (The First Church of Christ, Scientist, Boston, MA, U.S.A.), pp. 365
123. *Christian Science Sentinel*, "My journey forward to complete health," (The First Church of Christ, Scientist, Boston, Massachusetts, U.S.A, July 22, 2002).
124. Bible: I Cor.15: 26.
125. Bible: John 11: 1-45.

126. Yvonne Cache von Fettweis and Robert Townsend Warneck, *Mary Baker Eddy/Christian Healer* (The Christian Science Publishing Society, 1998), pp. 200-201).
127. John and Jerry Vines, *Phillips*: "The Exploring Series" (Neptune, New Jersey: Loizeaux Bros, 1988).

Chapter Nine
The Nature of Reality

1. Richard Feynman, *Surely You're Joking Mr. Feynman!* (W.W. Norton and Co., 1985), pp. 50-51.
2. Mary Baker Eddy, *Science and Health with Key to the Scriptures* (The First Church of Christ, Scientist, Boston, MA, U.S.A.), p.479.
3. Edward R. Close, "Can Matter be Explained in Terms of Consciousness?" in *Science Within Consciousness* (Henry Swift, Editor, Fall,1998).
4. Ibid.
5. Mary Baker Eddy, *Science and Health with Key to the Scriptures* (The First Church of Christ, Scientist, Boston, MA, U.S.A.),p.188.
6. *Christian Science Sentinel*, "Perception Beyond the Retina" (The First Church of Christ, Scientist, Boston, Massachusetts, U.S.A, April 16, 1966).
7. Mary Baker Eddy, *Science and Health with Key to the Scriptures* (The First Church of Christ, Scientist, Boston, MA, U.S.A.),p.399.
8. Fred Wolf, *Parallel Universes* (Simon and Schuster,1988), p.284.
9. Mary Baker Eddy, *Science and Health with Key to the Scriptures* (The First Church of Christ, Scientist, Boston, MA, U.S.A.), p. 209.
10. Ibid., p. 269.
11. Noel D. Bryan Jones, "I See," *Christian Science Journal* (The First Church of Christ, Scientist, Boston, Massachusetts, U.S.A,, Dec. 1946also, the author has on file a letter from The Mary Baker Library for the Betterment of Humanity, November 1, 2002).
12. Bible: Mark 8:18.
13. "Healing of a blind girl is one of St. Padre Pio's miracles," http://www.inq7.net/lif/2002/jun/23/lif_9-1.htm.
14. Mary Baker Eddy, *Science and Health with Key to the Scriptures* (The First Church of Christ, Scientist, Boston, MA, U.S.A.), p. 479.
15. Bible: Mark 8:18.
16. Mary Baker Eddy, *Science and Health with Key to the Scriptures* (The First Church of Christ, Scientist, Boston, MA, U.S.A., p. 95.
17. Daniel Jensen, public talk.
18. Williams James, *Principles of Psychology*, p. 615.
19. Sandra Blakeslee, *"Placebos Prove So Powerful Even Experts are Surprised"* (New York Times, Oct. 13, 1998). p. F1.
20. Larry Dossey, "Healing and Modern Physics, Alternative Therapies in Health and Medicine", [Editorial], 1999, 5(4):12-17, 102-108.
21. M. Talbot, *The Holographic Universe* (Harper Collins Publishers, 1991), pp. 93-94.
22. *Christian Science Sentinel* (The First Church of Christ, Scientist, Boston, Massachusetts, U.S.A., May 26, 1997), pp. 37, 38.

23. Mary Baker Eddy, *Science and Health with Key to the Scriptures* (The First Church of Christ, Scientist, Boston, MA, U.S.A.), p. 115-116.
24. Sandra Blakeslee, *"Placebos Prove So Powerful Even Experts are Surprised,"* New York Times, Oct.13, 1998), p. F1.
25. Larry Dossey, *Healing Words/ the Power of Prayer and the Practice of Medicine*, (Harper, San Francisco, 1993), pp. 84, 85.
26. Bible: John 6: 20, 21.
27. *Bible*: Luke 8: 51-55.
28. Bible: Exodus 16: 4.
29. Arthur Eddington, *The Nature of the Physical World*, (Macmillan, New York,1929).
30. *Quantum Questions,* edited by Ken Wilbur (New Science Library, Shambhala, 1984).
31. J. A. Wheeler, "Delayed-Choice Experiment and the Bohr – Einstein Dialog," paper presented at the *American Philosophical Society*, London, (June 5, 1980), preparation for publication assisted by the *University of Texas Center for Theoretical Physics*, and by *National Science Foundation* Grant PHY78 – 26592.
32. John Horgan, *New York Times*, (16 July, 1996).
33. Mary Baker Eddy, *Science and Health with Key to the Scriptures* (The First Church of Christ, Scientist, Boston, MA, U.S.A.), p. 323.
34. *Christian Science Journal*, (The First Church of Christ, Scientist, Boston, MA, U.S.A.), (May, 2000).
35. *Bible*: Matt.12: 29.
36. *Bible*: John 14:10.
37. "The Original Medicine – Mind," *Christian Science Sentinel* (The First Church of Christ, Scientist, Boston, MA, U.S.A., Aug 7, 2000),
38. "The Rebirth of Medicine," *Christian Science Journal* (The First Church of Christ, Scientist, Boston, MA, U.S.A., June, 2000,
39. Mary Baker Eddy, *Science and Health with Key to the Scriptures* (The First Church of Christ, Scientist, Boston, MA, U.S.A.), p. 176.

Chapter Ten
A New Paradigm

1. Freeman Dyson, 2000 Winner of the *Templeton Prize for Physics*.
2. P. C. W. Davies and J. R. Brown, Eds., *The Ghost in the Atom*, Chapter 9, Interview with Basil Hiley, Reader in physics *at Birkbeck College, University of London* (Cambridge University Press, New York, 1986).
3. G. Berkeley*, Treatise Concerning the Principle of Human Knowledge*, Part I.
4. *Miscellaneous Writings* (The First Church of Christ, Scientist, Boston, Massachusetts, U.S.A.), p. 87.
5. *The New Encyclopedia Britannica,* vol. II, p. 133.
6. Ibid.

Chapter Eleven
Summary

1. Ilya Prigogone and Isabelle Stengers, *Order Out of Chaos* (Bantom Books, 1984).
2. *Bible*: John 11:11.
3. *Bible*: II Corinthians 4:18.
4. Mary Baker Eddy, *Science and Health with Key to the Scriptures* (The First Church of Christ, Scientist, Boston, MA, U.S.A.), pp. 129, 207.
5. J. A. Wheeler "How come the quantum?, in *Time Today*, 1993).
6. J.A. Wheeler "Hermann Weyl and the Unity of Knowledge, American Scientist, vol. 74, July-August,1986.
7. Arthur Eddington, *The Philosophy of Physical Sciences* (University of Michigan Press, 1958).
8. J. Gribbon, *In Search of Schrodinger's Cat,* quotation of Arthur Eddington ((Bantam Books, New York, 1984). p. 162.
9. Ibid.
10. David Darling, *Equations of Eternity* (Hyperion Publishers, 1993).
11. *Bible*: John 5:30.
12. Mary Baker Eddy, *Science and Health with Key to the Scriptures* (The First Church of Christ, Scientist, Boston, MA, U.S.A.), p. 13.
13. *Bible*: John 8:5.
14. *Bible*: John 8:32.
15. Bible: Matt 5:8.
16. Mary Baker Eddy, *Miscellaneous Writings* (The First Church of Christ, Scientist, Boston, Massachusetts, U.S.A.), p. 355.
17. Bible: I Kings 19:12.
18. *Babe*, the movie.
19. Bible: John 5:30.
20. Bible: John 10:30.
21. Mary Baker Eddy, *Science and Health with Key to the Scriptures* (The First Church of Christ, Scientist, Boston, MA, U.S.A.), p. 247
22. Bible: Romans 13:10.
23. R. Browning.
24. Bible: I Cor. 13:12, (From the New Testament in Modern English).

Appendix A

1. *Webster's Third International Dictionary.*
2. Mary Baker Eddy, *Science and Health with Key to the Scriptures* (The First Church of Christ, Scientist, Boston, MA, U.S.A.), p. 186.
3. Ibid., p. 2.
4. Ibid., pp. 356-357.
5. Bible: II Cor. 10:4, 5.
6. Mary Baker Eddy, *Science and Health with Key to the Scriptures* (The First Church of Christ, Scientist, Boston, Massachusetts, U.S.A.), p. 476.

7. Mary Baker Eddy, *Miscellaneous Writings* (The First Church of Christ, Scientist, Boston, Massachusetts, U.S.A.), p. 193.
8. Bible: John 8:32.
9. Dean Ornish, *Love and Survival: the Scientific Basis for the Healing Power of Itimacy,* (Harper Collins Publishers, 1998).
10. Dean Ornish, quoted in "A Change of Heart", *American Journal of Nursing*, Oct., 1998.
11. Mary Baker Eddy, *Science and Health with Key to the Scriptures* (The First Church of Christ, Scientist, Boston, Massachusetts, U.S.A.), p. 591.
12. W. V. Quine, quoted in *A Logical Point of View* (Harvard University Press, Dec., 1980).
13. Mary Baker Eddy, *Science and Health with Key to the Scriptures* (The First Church of Christ, Scientist, Boston, Massachusetts, U.S.A.), p. 293.
14. Statement of Charles Steinmetz.
15. Mary Baker Eddy, *Unity of Good* (The First Church of Christ, Scientist, Boston, Massachusetts, U.S.A.), p. 35.
16 "Are You Your Genes?" *Christian Science Sentinel* (The First Church of Christ, Scientist, Boston, Massachusetts, U.S.A., January 3, 2000).
17. Mary Baker Eddy, *Miscellaneous Writings* (The First Church of Christ, Scientist, Boston, Massachusetts, U.S.A.), p. 69.
18. Mary Baker Eddy, *Science and Health with Key to the Scriptures* (The First Church of Christ, Scientist, Boston, Massachusetts, U.S.A.), pp. 591-592.
19. Ibid., p. 591.
20. Private communication with Jack Hubbell.
21. Ralph Richter, "What are you accepting?, Number 122, *Messenger*, Overlook House, Cleveland, Ohio, (Spring, 2002).
22. Bible: Rev 21:4.
23. Mary Baker Eddy, *Science and Health with Key to the Scriptures* (The First Church of Christ, Scientist, Boston, Massachusetts, U.S.A.), pp. 1-2.
24. Abraham Heschel, "Focus Over Fifty" Eastern North Dakota Synod, Evangelical Lutheran Church in American, May, 2001.
25. Mary Baker Eddy, *Science and Health with Key to the Scriptures* (The First Church of Christ, Scientist, Boston, Massachusetts, U.S.A.), p. 209, and p. 298.
26. Ibid., p. 502.
27. Mary Baker Eddy, *Unity of Good*, (The First Church of Christ, Scientist, Boston, Massachusetts, U.S.A.), p. 35.
28. Mary Baker Eddy, *Miscellaneous Writings* (The First Church of Christ, Scientist, Boston, Massachusetts, U.S.A.), p. 87.
29. Private communication with J. Hubbell.
30. Ibid.

Appendix B

1. Edward Farhi, Alan Guth and Jemal Guven, "Is it possible to create a universe in the laboratory by quantum tunneling?" *Nuclear Physics*, (1990B), pp. 417-490.

2. Ibid.
3. Andrei Linde "The Self-Reproducing Universe," *Scientific American*, (November, 1994), and "Particle Physics and Inflationary Cosmology," *Physics Today*,(September, 1987).
4. Andrei Linde "The Self-Reproducing Universe," *Scientific American*, (November, 1994).
5. "Which way to the Big Bang?", *Science*, (May, 1999).
6. J. A. Wheeler, "Delayed-Choice Experiment and the Boh –Einstein Dialog," Paper presented at the *American Philosophical Society*, London, June 5, 1980, (Preparation for publication assisted by the *University of Texas Center for Theoretical Physics,* and by *National Science Foundation* Grant PHY78 – 26592).
7. John Horgan, quotation of John Archibald Wheeler, *New York Times*, (16 July, 1996).
8. Bible: Matt. 13:24-30.
9. Mary Baker Eddy, *Science and Health with Key to the Scriptures* (The First Church of Christ, Scientist, Boston, Massachusetts, U.S.A.), pp. 72, 300.
10. *Bible*: Genesis 2 and 3.
11. *Bible*: John 8:44.
12. *Bible*: Luke 17:20, 21.
13. Nathan Talbot, "Withdraw your consent", *Herald of Christian Science* (The First Church of Christ, Scientist, Boston, Massachusetts, U.S.A, July, 1983).
14. Mary Baker Eddy, *Science and Health with Key to the Scriptures* (The First Church of Christ, Scientist, Boston, Massachusetts, U.S.A.), p. 263.
15. Ibid., p. 209.

Appendix C

1. Mary Baker Eddy, *Science and Health with Key to the Scriptures* (The First Church of Christ, Scientist, Boston, Massachusetts, U.S.A.), p. 484.
2. Robert G. Jahn, "The Challenge of Consciousness," *Journal of Scientific Exploration*, vol.15, no. 4, (2001), p. 445.
3. Mary Baker Eddy, *First Church of Christ, Scientist and Miscellany* (The First Church of Christ, Scientist, Boston, Massachusetts, U.S.A.), p. 109.
4. Eugene Wigner, "Remarks on the Mind-Body Question," in *The Scientist Speculates* (Basic Books, Inc, Publishers, New York, 1962), p. 284.
5. Fred Alan Wolf, *Taking the Quantum Leap*, (Harper and Row, New York, 1989)
6. Mary Baker Eddy, *Unity of Good* (The First Church of Christ, Scientist, Boston, Massachusetts, U.S.A.), p. 56.
7. George Greenstein and Arthur G. Zajonc, *The Quantum Challenge* (Jones and Bartlett Publishers, Sudbury, Massachusetts, 1997), p. 85.
8. Wheeler's game of *Twenty Questions*, see *Physics, Metaphysics and God, Part I*, Chapter 15-D.
9. Robert Jahn, see *Physics, Metaphysics and God*, Part II, Chapter 3.
10. Andrew Hamilton, "The Quantum Zeno Effect," see News Article: "Quantum physics experiment proves two counterintuitive and contradictory quantum effects," erstringtheory.com/forum/messages4/28.html.

11. J. A. Wheeler, "Delayed-choice Experiment and the Bohr-Einstein Dialog," (Paper presented at the Joint Meeting of the American Philosophical Society and the Royal Society, London, June 5, 1980. Preparation for publication assisted by the *University of Texas Center for Theoretical Physics* and by *National Science Foundation* Grant PHY 7826592), pp. 37-39 (Note to Reader: The statement attributed to Wheeler in APPENDIX C of my book, that there is a sense in which we create the laws of physics, is implied in the above reference. I have been unable to locate the reference that contains the exact quote.)
12. *Bible*: Acts 3: 8.
13. Ralph Wagers, Address to Superintendents of Nursing, at *Tenacre*, Princeton, NJ, (around 1970, exact date unknown).
14. Baker Eddy, *Science and Health with Key to the Scriptures* (The First Church of Christ, Scientist, Boston, Massachusetts, U.S.A.), p. 250.
15. *Christian Science Journal*, (The First Church of Christ, Scientist, Boston, MA, U.S.A.), (August 2008, p-8May, 2000).
16. Bible: I John 3:2.
17. Mary Baker Eddy, *Miscellaneous Writings* (The First Church of Christ, Scientist, Boston, Massachusetts, U.S.A.), p. 60.
18. Mary Baker Eddy, *Science and Health with Key to the Scriptures* (The First Church of Christ, Scientist, Boston, Massachusetts, U.S.A.), p. 301.
19. Rushworth Kidder, quoted from a talk given by at the *Glenmont Christian Science Sanatorium*, (1999).

Introduction to the ADDENDUM

1. Mary Baker Eddy, *Science and Health with Key to the Scriptures* (The First Church of Christ, Scientist, Boston, Massachusetts, U.S.A.), p. 120
2. Mary Baker Eddy, *Science and Health with Key to the Scriptures* (The First Church of Christ, Scientist, Boston, Massachusetts, U.S.A.), p. 300
3. (p-209 CS History Document a11021
4. *Christian Science Journal* (The First Church of Christ, Scientist, Boston, Massachusetts, U.S.A., January, 1997,
(Nathan A. Talbot "The mind, the body, and God's allness,")

ADDENDUM

Part I; The Quantum Universe

1. Belle Dume, Science Writer, *Physics Web*), 3 September, 2003
2. *Physics Web*, 2 April, 2004 and M.D. LaHaye *et al*, 2004, *Science* 304 74
3. Phillip Ball, *News @ Nature.com*, 23 December 2004
4. Dik Bouwmeester, Department of Physics, Center for Spintronics and Quantum Computation, *University of California*, Santa Barbara, Physical Review Letters,

"Entangled Light and Matter," October 8, 2003, and Dik Bouwmeester, *et al*, "Towards Quantum Superposition of a Mirror," June 5, 2005

5. Belle Dume, Science Writer, *Physics Web*, 23 February, 2006
6. Dick J. Bierman, "Does Consciousness Collapse the Wave-Packet?" Dick J. Bierman, "Does Consciousness Collapse the Wave-Packet?" Mind and Matter, Vol. (1), pp. 45-47.
7. Correspondence with Dick Bierman
8. Nature, 19 April, 2007, and article……by Joshua Roebke, 4 June, 2008
9. "Creating 'Schrodinger's virus in the lab", Physics World.com, Sept 12, 2009, by Edwin Cartlidge, freelance journalist based in Rome
10. Dean Radin, Institute of Noetic Sciences, article by Brian Clegg, science writer, July, 2009

Part II: The Universe of Spirit

1. Mary Baker Eddy, *Miscellaneous Writings* (The First Church of Christ, Scientist, Boston, Massachusetts, U.S.A.), p. 62; *and Science and Health with Key to the Scriptures*, p. 179
2. Mary Baker Eddy, *Science and Health with Key to the Scriptures* (The First Church of Christ, Scientist, Boston, Massachusetts, U.S.A.), p. 13
3. Mary Baker Eddy, *Science and Health with Key to the Scriptures* (The First Church of Christ, Scientist, Boston, Massachusetts, U.S.A.), p. 182
4. *Christian Science Journal*, (The First Church of Christ, Scientist, Boston, MA, U.S.A.), (June, 2002).
5. *Christian Science Journal*, (The First Church of Christ, Scientist, Boston, MA, U.S.A.), (February, 2006).
6. *Christian Science Journal*, (The First Church of Christ, Scientist, Boston, MA, U.S.A.), (Special Issue, 1991, p. 8).
7. Yvonne Cache von Fettweis and Robert Townsend Warneck, *Mary Baker Eddy/Christian Healer*, pp. 43-44, (Christian Science Publishing Society, Boston, Mass., 1998).
8. *Christian Science Journal*, (The First Church of Christ, Scientist, Boston, MA, U.S.A.), (April, 2005).
9. *Christian Science Sentinel*, (The First Church of Christ, Scientist, Boston, Massachusetts, U.S.A, August 22, 2005, p. 25).
10. *Christian Science Sentinel*, (The First Church of Christ, Scientist, Boston, Massachusetts, U.S.A, August 17, 1998, p. 23).
11. Bible, Psalms 46:10
12. Mary Baker Eddy, *Science and Health with Key to the Scriptures* (The First Church of Christ, Scientist, Boston, Massachusetts, U.S.A.), p. 78.
13. *Christian Science Journal* (The First Church of Christ, Scientist, Boston, Massachusetts, U.S.A, February, 2000), pp. 10-11
14. *Christian Science Journal* (The First Church of Christ, Scientist, Boston, Massachusetts, U.S.A, October, 2001), p. 31

15. Experiences related to author
16. *Christian Science Sentinel*, (The First Church of Christ, Scientist, Boston, Massachusetts, U.S.A, August, 2009, "Traveling from Earth to Heaven."
17. Experience related to author
18. Experience related to author
19. *Christian Science Sentinel*, (The First Church of Christ, Scientist, Boston, Massachusetts, U.S.A, October 26, 2009
20. *Christian Science Sentinel*, (The First Church of Christ, Scientist, Boston, Massachusetts, U.S.A, Jun4, 2007
21. Steve Silberman, "The Placebo Problem," *Wired*, September, 2009, and in the Christian Science Sentinel, October 5, 2009
22. *Christian Science Sentinel*, (The First Church of Christ, Scientist, Boston, Massachusetts, U.S.A, October 5, 2009
23. Metaphysical Application ideas for the Christian Science Bible Lesson for November 16-22, 2009; subject: Soul and Body; by Rick Stewart, C.S., Dresden, Germany
24. *Christian Science Sentinel*, (The First Church of Christ, Scientist, Boston, Massachusetts, U.S.A, March 15, 2010, "To See and Know God"

FINAL, FINAL THOUGHTS and CONCLUSIONS

1. Laurance Doyle, "The Universe in Life," given at Twelve Acres, Sept 13, 2003
2. Mary Baker Eddy, *Science and Health with Key to the Scriptures* (The First Church of Christ, Scientist, Boston, Massachusetts, U.S.A.), p.469:25
3. Christ Jesus, Luke 17:21
4. Private communication with Jack Hubbell/CSB
5. *Christian Sentinal* (The First Church of Christ, Scientist, Boston, Massachusetts, U.S.A.), December 30, 2002, p-7.
6. Mary Baker Eddy, *Science and Health with Key to the Scriptures* (The First Church of Christ, Scientist, Boston, Massachusetts, U.S.A.), p.543:20
7. Tad Blake-Weber, Community.ChristianScience.com, Dec. 2009
8. Ibid
9. Mary Baker Eddy, *Science and Health with Key to the Scriptures* (The First Church of Christ, Scientist, Boston, Massachusetts, U.S.A.), p.573:6
10. Bible, John 11:11
11. Romans 13:10
12. Mary Baker Eddy, *Science and Health with Key to the Scriptures* (The First Church of Christ, Scientist, Boston, Massachusetts, U.S.A.), p.39:13

About the Author

Jack William Geis was formerly employed at *Wright Patterson Air Force Base* (near Dayton, Ohio) as an *Aerospace* Engineer, where he worked in the areas of electric propulsion engines and space power devices for spacecraft, and magnetic bearings for jet aircraft engines. He has an A.E. degree in *Aeronautical Engineering* from the *University of Cincinnati*, and a *Masters of Science* degree (M.S.) in *Physics* from the *Ohio State University*. An amateur astronomer, Jack has been interested since childhood in the universe about him, and of man's efforts to explore the moon and the planets. As a class-taught student of the *Christian Science* religion, Jack has had an abiding faith in the practical power of prayer to heal the ills of mankind through gaining a greater understanding of the nature of God as Love or Mind. Encouraged by his two sons to write a book that would discus both physics and metaphysics, he began as far back as 1968 to research and gather his thoughts on these apparently diametric areas.

Jack currently in engaged part-time on the *Astronomy Staff* at the Dayton *Boonshoft Museum of Discovery*, and lives with his wife Marian near Tipp City, Ohio. He and his wife (a *Master Gardner*) spend quality time whenever they can with their five grandchildren, and find as much time as they can to enjoy life.